The 1951 Los Angeles Rams

GREAT TEAMS IN PRO FOOTBALL HISTORY

*The 1966 Green Bay Packers:
Profiles of Vince Lombardi's Super Bowl I Champions*
(George Bozeka, editor, 2016)

*The 1958 Baltimore Colts:
Profiles of the NFL's First Sudden Death Champions*
(George Bozeka, editor, 2018)

The 1951 Los Angeles Rams: Profiles of the NFL's First West Coast Champions (George Bozeka, editor, 2022)

The 1951 Los Angeles Rams

Profiles of the NFL's First West Coast Champions

EDITED BY GEORGE BOZEKA

Associate Editors
*Derek M. Ciapala, Denis M. Crawford,
Ron Fitch, and John Maxymuk*

GREAT TEAMS IN PRO FOOTBALL HISTORY

McFarland & Company, Inc., Publishers
Jefferson, North Carolina

All photos (and the 1951 Player Questionnaire)
courtesy of The Los Angeles Rams, LLC, unless otherwise noted.

ISBN (print) 978-1-4766-7842-9
ISBN (ebook) 978-1-4766-4413-4

LIBRARY OF CONGRESS AND BRITISH LIBRARY
CATALOGUING DATA ARE AVAILABLE

Library of Congress Control Number 2022010018

© 2022 George Bozeka. All rights reserved

*No part of this book may be reproduced or transmitted in any form
or by any means, electronic or mechanical, including photocopying
or recording, or by any information storage and retrieval system,
without permission in writing from the publisher.*

Front cover: Rams fullback Paul "Tank" Younger (13) runs
the ball behind blockers Bill Lange (26), Dick Daugherty (67)
and Lester "Dick" Hoerner (31) against the San Francisco 49ers
on November 4, 1951 in Los Angeles Memorial Coliseum
(Photograph courtesy of The Los Angeles Rams)

Printed in the United States of America

*McFarland & Company, Inc., Publishers
Box 611, Jefferson, North Carolina 28640
www.mcfarlandpub.com*

Acknowledgments

George Bozeka

This book on the 1951 Los Angeles Rams represents the third entry in the Professional Football Researchers Association's (PFRA) series Great Teams in Pro Football History. The first two books in the series, which covered the 1966 Green Bay Packers and the 1958 Baltimore Colts, were published in 2016 and 2018. Special thanks to Mark Durr and the PFRA Board of Directors for their helpful guidance and support throughout the development and completion of this project.

This book project has been a collaborative effort of the PFRA. Thanks to all our contributors for their commitment to the project and for the many hours they spent researching, writing, and rewriting the biographies and features included in this book.

I would like to thank Jon Kendle, Vice President of Archives, Education Football Information at the Pro Football Hall of Fame's Ralph Wilson, Jr. Pro Football Research and Preservation Center, for his help in providing archived files to our contributors and archived photos for the book. I would also like to thank Artis Twyman, Vice President of Communications for the Los Angeles Rams, for his help in securing permission from the Rams' organization to use photos from various Rams publications and the Rams' 1951 player questionnaire in the book.

Special thanks to Joshua Milton Anderson for conducting an interview of former 1951 Rams player Joe Reid before his death, and thanks to Joe's wife Kim for providing photos of Joe from the Reid family collection for the book. Additional thanks to Tina Salvatore, the daughter of the late Andy Robustelli, another former 1951 Rams player, for providing family history and photos to John Vorperian while John was conducting research for his chapter on her father.

Thanks to Rick Schabowski for researching and compiling a newspaper article database on the 1951 Rams and to Nick Ritzmann for researching and compiling book excerpts on the 1951 Rams for use by our contributors.

Finally, special thanks to associate editors Derek M. Ciapala, Denis M. Crawford, Ron Fitch, and John Maxymuk for their help during the editing process.

Table of Contents

Acknowledgments (George Bozeka) — v
Preface (George Bozeka) — 1

Part 1: The City and the Organization

The City of Angels *(George Bozeka)* — 5
History of Pro Football in Los Angeles *(Joshua Milton Anderson)* — 10
Owner Daniel Reeves *(George Bozeka)* — 20
Head Coach Joe Stydahar *(Lee Elder)* — 27
Assistant Coaches *(Ryan C. Christiansen, Bert Gambini, Bryan Lutes and Joe Ziemba)* — 34
Building the 1951 Rams *(Matthew Keddie)* — 59
The 1951 Draft *(Bert Gambini)* — 65

Part 2: The 1951 Season

1951 Training Camp and Preseason *(Mark L. Ford)* — 77
1951 Rams Offense—The Xs and Os *(Lee Elder)* — 89
1951 Regular Season Game Summaries *(Rupert Patrick, Rich Shmelter and Neal Golden)* — 98
Rams/Browns Rivalry *(Ed Gruver)* — 136
1951 NFL Championship Game *(Rupert Patrick)* — 140
1951 Rams Statistics *(Rupert Patrick)* — 147
1951 Rams Superlatives *(Rupert Patrick)* — 150

Part 3: The Team

Bob Boyd *(Bill Lambert)* — 155
Larry Brink *(Patrick Gallivan)* — 159
Bobby Collier *(Greg Selber)* — 162
Tom Dahms *(Nicholas Ritzmann)* — 164

Dick Daugherty *(Mark L. Ford)* — 169
Glenn Davis *(Randy Snow)* — 173
Tom Fears *(Rick Schabowski)* — 178
Jack Finlay *(John Maxymuk)* — 184
Jack Halliday *(Joshua Milton Anderson)* — 187
Norb Hecker *(Greg D. Tranter)* — 192
Elroy Hirsch *(Rick Schabowski)* — 195
Dick Hoerner *(Greg D. Tranter)* — 202
Marvin Johnson *(John Maxymuk)* — 206
Tommy Kalmanir *(John Grasso)* — 209
Tom Keane *(John Grasso)* — 215
Bill Lange *(Richard C. Flowers II)* — 219
Woodley Lewis *(Mark Fellin)* — 221
Leon McLaughlin *(John Maxymuk)* — 224
Don Paul *(Patrick Gallivan)* — 227
Joe Reid *(Joshua Milton Anderson)* — 231
Herb Rich *(Mark Fellin)* — 235
Andy Robustelli *(John M. Vorperian)* — 238
Don Simensen *(Mark L. Ford)* — 246
Vitamin Smith *(Randy Snow)* — 252
Harry Thompson *(Nicholas Ritzmann)* — 256
Charlie Toogood *(Bill Lambert)* — 260
Deacon Dan Towler *(Richard C. Flowers II)* — 264
Norm Van Brocklin *(Bryan Lutes)* — 268
Bob Waterfield *(George Bozeka)* — 276
Stan West *(Jay Zahn)* — 284
Jerry Williams *(Gary A. Sarnoff)* — 290
Jim Winkler *(Greg Selber)* — 295
Tank Younger *(Rich Shmelter)* — 298
Jack Zilly *(Joe Ziemba)* — 303
Racial Integration and the Rams *(Ryan C. Christiansen)* — 309
The NFL's Fashion Pioneers *(John M. Vorperian)* — 326

Part 4: The Stadium

Memorial Coliseum *(Massimo Foglio)* — 331

Part 5: The Press

Bob Kelley *(Joe Marren)*	339
Bud Furillo and Sid Ziff *(Joe Marren)*	343
Bob Oates and Melvin Durslag *(Joe Marren)*	349
Paul B. Zimmerman, Dick Hyland and Frank Finch *(Joe Marren)*	355
About the Contributors	363
Index	367

Preface

George Bozeka

In 1946, the Rams became the first team in a major professional sports league to relocate to the West Coast, making the NFL a truly "national" league. Pioneer owner Daniel Reeves had dreamed of such a move, understanding the vast, untapped potential that existed for the National Football League to thrive and prosper in Southern California. Reeves also realized that the Rams needed star power and a healthy dose of glamour to succeed in the larger-than-life entertainment mecca of Los Angeles.

Once Reeves settled into his new home, he continued to innovate. The Rams were the first team to put a logo on their helmet. Reeves created the foundation for the NFL's modern-day television policies, and Reeves and his scouting guru Eddie Kotal were the architects of a sophisticated scouting system that became the model for the rest of the league. In addition, the Rams were the first team to reintegrate the NFL, ending an unwritten ban on African American players that had existed since the end of the 1933 season. The scouting system and reintegration allowed Reeves to assemble a stable of contract players that would be the envy of the professional football world. MGM once boasted that it had more stars than there are in heaven. With all due respect, Louis B. Mayer had nothing on Dan Reeves and the 1951 Rams.

The Rams had not one but two Hall of Fame quarterbacks—Bob Waterfield and Norm Van Brocklin—and they successfully coexisted, breaking the age-old football axiom that a team with two starting quarterbacks has no quarterback. Waterfield's wife was none other than Hollywood sex symbol Jane Russell. Add to the mix two Hall of Fame receivers in Elroy "Crazylegs" Hirsch and Tom Fears, a cadre of talented running backs including Dick Hoerner, Tank Younger, Deacon Dan Towler, Vitamin Smith, and Glenn Davis (who dated Elizabeth Taylor and was married to actress Terry Moore), and a solid supporting cast and defense led by Don Paul and Hall of Famer Andy Robustelli, and you had the celebrity laden nucleus of a Rams team that won the NFL's first West Coast championship in 1951.

Reeves' 1951 Rams were the original "Showtime" in Los Angeles. Years before Pat Riley, Magic Johnson and the Lakers made the term famous, the 1951 Rams were an exciting juggernaut that took the NFL by storm. Reeves successfully married the NFL and Hollywood. To borrow a motion picture industry term, Reeves and the 1951 Los Angeles Rams brought technicolor to the staid, monochromatic world of the National Football League.

The Professional Football Researchers Association (PFRA) is a nonprofit corporation that was founded and organized in 1979 in Canton, Ohio, at the Pro Football Hall of

Fame. The purposes of the organization are to foster the study of professional football as a significant cultural and athletic institution; to establish an accurate historical account of professional football; and to disseminate research information. In 2016, the PFRA began a book series titled Great Teams in Pro Football History.

Following in the footsteps of our initial entries in the series on the 1966 Green Bay Packers and the 1958 Baltimore Colts, the life stories of the 1951 Rams' players and coaches are inspiring, enlightening, insightful and amusing.

This book offers a detailed history of the Rams' 1951 season, including coach and player biographies, game summaries and statistics, photographs, and feature essays about the City of Angels, the Rams' visionary owner Daniel Reeves, the 1951 Rams' training camp and preseason, the 1951 draft, how the team was built, Los Angeles Memorial Stadium, racial integration and the Rams, the Rams' uniform and helmet history, and the Rams-Browns rivalry. Biographies of key media personalities who covered the team complete the book.

Contributors to the project thoroughly researched the 1951 Rams by consulting newspaper articles, magazines, media guides, yearbooks, programs, internet sites and books written by and about the team and its members. Some contributors also visited the research center at the Pro Football Hall of Fame to review materials about the team and others conducted interviews.

The 1951 Rams are a deserving choice as the third entry in PFRA's Great Teams in Pro Football History book series, as we celebrate the 70th anniversary of their landmark championship game victory over the Cleveland Browns.

Part 1

The City and the Organization

The City of Angels

George Bozeka

Los Angeles was originally founded as a small Spanish farming settlement or pueblo of 44 people on September 4, 1781. The first name given to the settlement is a source of debate, known as either "El Pueblo de la Reina de los Angeles" ("The Town of the Queen of the Angels") or "El Pueblo de Nuestra Señora de los Angeles de Porciuncula" ("The Town of Our Lady of the Angels of Porciuncula").

In 1877, William Mulholland arrived in Los Angeles, which had grown to a population of 9,000 people, and worked his way up through the ranks of the private Los Angeles Water Company, starting as a deputy zanjero (water distributor) and eventually becoming the chief engineer of Los Angeles' publicly owned water works. Public works projects overseen by Mulholland contributed to the expansion of the area, and by 1910, Los Angeles had grown to a city of nearly 320,000 people. Mulholland realized that the continued growth of the city was dependent on a reliable water supply. Controversially dramatized in *Chinatown*, the 1974 Roman Polanski film starring Jack Nicholson, Mulholland oversaw the construction of the Los Angeles Aqueduct from 1907 to 1913, and "delivered to the city from 233 miles away its first abundant water supply," famously stating, "There it is. Take it."[1]

On March 12, 1928, hours after Mulholland had inspected it, the Saint Francis Dam collapsed. Over 400 lives were lost. Mulholland took responsibility for the disaster, effectively ending his career.[2]

Buoyed by the vision of Mulholland, who was both loved and reviled, and coupled with the California Dream, Los Angeles grew rapidly, reaching a population of 1,238,048 in 1930.[3]

In his series on the history of California, author Kevin Starr outlined that "California was perceived as a place of new beginnings, where great wealth could reward hard work and good luck. The notion inspired the idea of an American Dream. California was seen as a lucky place, a land of opportunity and good fortune. It was a powerful belief, underlying many of the accomplishments of the state, and equally potent when threatened."[4] The proximity of the glamour factory of Hollywood, which merged with Los Angeles in 1910, also played a major roll in the allure of the area and the perpetuation of the dream.

During the depths of the Great Depression in 1932, Los Angeles heroically hosted the Summer Olympics. As recounted on the Memorial Coliseum website, "During the 1920s there were no other cities that were financially able to bid for hosting the 1932 Games due to the long and overwhelming economic downturn of the Great Depression.

Many nations and athletes were unable to pay for the trip to the remote location of Los Angeles. But it was indeed Los Angeles that successfully hosted the Games and originated many successful firsts of influential endeavors. Los Angeles handled its finances successfully and inspired an encouraging awe that reassured the world of future Olympic Games to come."[5]

By 1940, Los Angeles had swelled to 1.5 million inhabitants. As the country entered the Second World War, Los Angeles became a center for war production and military training and deployment. According to the California State Military Museum, "During World War II Los Angeles was the boom town of boom towns. The Los Angeles metropolitan area grew faster than any other major metropolitan area in the U.S. and experienced more of the traumas of war while doing so. By 1943 the population of metropolitan L.A. was larger than 37 states, and was home to one in every 40 U.S. citizens. By the end of the war, the L.A. area had produced 17% of all of America's war production."[6]

Steve Bisheff described Los Angeles of 1940s as

> a much kinder, gentler, easier-to-breathe place.... There were no freeways crisscrossing the landscape, no bumper-to-bumper traffic clogging even the surface streets and none of the thick, choking smog the city would become famous for enduring in later years.
>
> Los Angeles was centered downtown, where you could see a first-run movie at the swanky Loews State for a quarter, eat lunch at the sumptuous Clifton Cafeteria for under a buck and, if you were more the adventurous type, you could pay a few pennies for a ride on the legendary incline railway known as Angel's Flight.
>
> Los Angeles was your basic minor league sports town just starting to spread its celebrated wings.
>
> The gentleman wise enough to grab hold of them and fly in first was Reeves.[7]

For Daniel Reeves, Los Angeles was a glitzy football promised land.[8] Having worked and played in his hometown of New York City, the urbane Reeves was like a fish out of water in the industrial environs of Cleveland. Add to that the fact that he was losing money, and one understands why he could not wait to move his club to the West Coast and experience the California Dream. Even the satisfaction and excitement of winning the NFL championship in 1945 came with a catch—the game was played on the frozen turf of Cleveland Municipal Stadium with heavy wind gusts and patches of snow and ice. The morning temperature was eight below zero.[9]

Reeves quickly took to the Los Angeles lifestyle. Author James Sulecki described that Reeves moved into a "sprawling French Chateau in the Bel Air hills, just above the leafy neighborhood's famed country club and UCLA. There he often hosted many of his players as his wife raised roses and orchids, and he commuted to the Beverly Hills office of his Daniel Reeves & Co. investment firm.... Reeves loved the sun and sported a deep tan, ditching his New York suits for golf shirts, khakis, and cardigan sweaters and happily played golf at Bel Air Country Club with celebrities including Dean Martin."[10]

The social scene in post-war Los Angeles was exciting and varied. Restaurants and nightclubs such as Chasen's, Formosa's, the Brown Derby, Romanoff's, Ciro's, Mocambo, and the Cocoanut Grove were frequented by a who's who of the entertainment community including Humphrey Bogart, Clark Gable, Frank Sinatra, Groucho Marx, Cary Grant, Jimmy Stewart, Lana Turner, Judy Garland, Ava Gardner, and Lauren Bacall.

Hollywood was going through a transitory period. After supporting the war effort, the movie industry started dealing with serious adult themes. In 1946, *The Best Years of Our Lives* dealt with the difficult adjustments of three World War II veterans returning to civilian life. In 1947, *Gentlemen's Agreement* and *Crossfire* tackled anti–Semitism, and in 1948, *The Snake Pit* told the harrowing story of a mentally ill woman in an insane asylum. The late forties and early fifties also saw the introduction of the first method actors in Hollywood as Montgomery Clift and Marlon Brando stormed onto the scene. Clift and Brando seared the screen with ultra realistic performances in films such as *Red River* (1948), *The Search* (1948), *A Place in the Sun* (1951), *The Men* (1950), and *A Streetcar Named Desire* (1951).

The post-war years also saw the movie industry under attack by the House Un-American Activities Committee (HUAC). In 1947, the Committee subpoenaed a number of people working in the film industry as it investigated whether Communists or Communist sympathizers had infiltrated Hollywood. As a result the Hollywood blacklist was born, ending or suspending the careers of hundreds of actors and actresses, writers, directors, producers, musicians and composers, and technicians who refused to testify, or were Communist party members, alleged members, or party sympathizers.

The HUAC investigations helped foster the political career of one future president—Richard Nixon. Born in Yorba Linda, a conservative suburb of Los Angeles, Nixon rose to prominence in 1946 when he was elected to the House of Representatives from California's 12th District, the district currently represented by House Speaker Nancy Pelosi. By early 1947, Nixon had become a member of HUAC, and quickly became one of the leading anti–Communists in Congress as a result of his dogged pursuit of Alger Hiss. Hiss was a State Department employee accused of espionage, who was eventually indicted and found guilty of perjury after Nixon dramatically testified before the grand jury with the so-called Pumpkin Papers (State Department documents and microfilm hidden in a pumpkin that implicated Hiss) in tow. Author Roger Morris stated that "everywhere the symbol of the Committee's vigilance and success was Congressmen Nixon. For most of December 1948, his photograph and name were rarely missing from front pages throughout the country. He had become a national hero and a favorite of the media."[11]

Nixon won reelection to the House in 1948. In 1950, he handily defeated fellow House member Helen Gahagan Douglas to represent California in the U.S. Senate after branding the liberal Douglas as sympathetic to communism with the dissemination of the infamous "Pink Sheet" which outlined her alleged pro–Communist voting record.[12]

During the post-war years, Los Angeles had one mayor—Fletcher Bowron. Bowron was elected to his first term in 1938 as a non-partisan candidate during a recall election that ended the scandal-ridden term of Mayor Frank L. Shaw. Bowron pledged to reform city government and end graft and corruption.[13]

Bowron served from 1938 to 1953. The *New York Times* stated in his obituary that, Bowron oversaw a boom in the City's population ... and "the inauguration of its freeway and airport systems."[14] By 1950, L.A.'s population had reached nearly two million.

Despite his initial crusade, Bowron continued to deal with issues involving the treatment of minorities and crime and corruption throughout his term.

Los Angeles had a very diverse population with a variety of ethnic groups and races represented in their own distinct neighborhoods such as Boyle Heights (Mexican) Chinatown, Little Tokyo, and South Central and Watts (black). However, until the Supreme Court banned racially motivated restrictive covenants in 1948 in the case of *Shelley v. Kraemer*, non-whites were not welcome in many neighborhoods.[15] In addition, beginning in 1942, Bowron supported the internment of Japanese-Americans during World War II.

This fostered a highly charged racial atmosphere in Los Angeles. In early June 1943, the Zoot Suit Riots broke out. As the History Channel website explains, the riots "were a series of violent clashes during which mobs of U.S. servicemen, off-duty police officers and civilians brawled with young Latinos and other minorities in Los Angeles. The June 1943 riots took their name from the baggy suits worn by many minority youths during that era, but the violence was more about racial tension than fashion ... wartime patriotism didn't help matters: After the bombing of Pearl Harbor and the U.S. entry into World War II, wool and other textiles were subject to strict rationing. The U.S. War Production Board regulated the production of civilian clothing containing silk, wool and other essential fabrics ... despite these wartime restrictions, many bootleg tailors in Los Angeles, New York and elsewhere continued to make the popular zoot suits, which used profligate amounts of fabric. Servicemen and many other people, however, saw the oversized suits a flagrant and unpatriotic waste of resources."[16]

The racial strain continued into the post-war years. The minority press in Los Angeles took Bowron and his administration to task for paying lip service to police brutality against minorities.[17]

Two highly publicized events further shook the city in 1947, the "Black Dahlia" murder and the Mafia execution of Benjamin "Bugsy" Siegel.

On January 15, 1947, the badly mutilated body of Elizabeth Short, severed at the waist, was discovered in a vacant lot in the Leimert Park neighborhood of Los Angeles. The grisly crime, which became known as the "Black Dahlia" murder, was the subject of an intense investigation by the Los Angeles Police Department and much like the O.J. Simpson case captivated the whole country. To contribute to the lore, the case was never solved.

On June 20, Bugsy Siegel was found shot to death in the living room of his mistress Virginia Hill's Beverly Hills mansion. Siegel was a charming hitman and crime syndicate founder who "hobnobbed with Hollywood celebrities, including Jean Harlow, George Raft, Clark Gable, Gary Cooper, and Cary Grant."[18] Siegel was allegedly murdered by the Mafia as payback for cost overruns and skimming of mob finances during his construction of the Flamingo Hotel in Las Vegas.

Further, Bowron's attempts to curb corruption in the police force were ineffective. In 1948, a scandal surrounding Brenda Allen, a madam who was allegedly receiving police protection as a result of a relationship with a vice squad member, led to the eventual appointment in 1950 of William Parker as police chief.

Though Parker curbed corruption, charges of brutality against the minority community still dogged the department and came to a head days after the Rams won the 1951 NFL championship. In his *Pacific Historical Review* article author Edward J. Escobar described the event that notoriously became known as "Bloody Christmas." "Early on the morning of December 25, 1951, officers of the Los Angeles Police Department (LAPD) severely beat seven young men, five of whom were of Mexican descent. All the beatings took place after officers had the victims in custody. Much of the violence occurred at the central city jail where over 100 had gathered for a Christmas party. Responding to false rumors that a fellow officer had lost an eye in a brawl with the young men, drunken policemen fought with each other and slipped on the victims' blood to beat, batter, knee, and kick the prisoners."[19]

Initially denying charges of brutality, Parker started an internal investigation that according to the *Los Angeles Times* resulted in the transfer of 54 officers, the suspension of 39 officers, the indictment of eight officers, and the conviction of five.[20]

It was into this complicated tapestry that the Rams arrived and existed in the late 1940s and early 1950s. It's rather ironic, given Los Angeles' less than sterling racial past, that the Rams would be the first team to reintegrate the NFL and end the unofficial league ban on African American players that had existed since 1933. In the end, it was in part a pragmatic business decision for Reeves—a way for him to fulfill his California Dream.

The initial success his team experienced during its early seasons on the West Coast enamored the team to a Los Angeles community that valued and loved star quality and glamour. Meanwhile, the team he left behind in Cleveland—the Browns—was quickly embraced by the blue-collar community they so aptly embodied.

Bisheff could have easily been describing the City of Angels when he characterized the Rams, stating that "except for the all-winning years of 1949–1955, this was an organization beset by controversy and change,"[21] because, despite its dazzling exterior and image, Los Angeles has always been an enigmatic city.

Notes

1. Catherine Mulholland, *William Mulholland and The Rise of Los Angeles* (Berkeley: University of California Press, 2000), 4.
2. Mulholland, *William Mulholland*, 325–331.
3. "Los Angeles, California Population History 1890–2018," *Biggestuscities.com*, https://www.biggestuscities.com/city/los-angeles-california.
4. "California Dream," *Wikipedia.org*, https://en.wikipedia.org/wiki/California_Dream.
5. "The 1932 Olympic Games-83 Years Later," *Lacoliseum.com*, July 30, 2015, https://www.lacoliseum.com/the-1932-olympics-83-years-later/.
6. "California in World War II: Los Angeles Metropolitan Area During World War II," *Militarymuseum.org*, http://www.militarymuseum.org/LAWWII.html.
7. Steve Bisheff, "NFL 2016: Rams' Roots in L.A. Started With Pioneer Team Owner Dan Reeves," *Orange County Register*, https://www.ocregister.com/2016/09/07/nfl-2016-rams-roots-in-la-started-with-pioneer-team-owner-dan-reeves/.
8. Bob Oates, "The New Hall of Famer," *Los Angeles Herald-Examiner*, February 9, 1967, RC.
9. Joseph S. Page, *Pro Football Championships Before the Super Bowl* (Jefferson, NC: McFarland, 2011), 75.
10. James C. Sulecki, *The Cleveland Rams* (Jefferson, NC: McFarland, 2016), 192.
11. Roger Morris, *Richard Milhous Nixon: The Rise of an American Politician* (New York: Henry Holt, 1990), 480.
12. Morris, *Richard Milhous Nixon*, 566–621.
13. "Fletcher Bowron Is Dead at 81; Mayor of Los Angeles,'38-'53," *New York Times*, September 12, 1968, 47; "Fletcher Bowron, Former L.A. Mayor and Judge, Dies at 81," *Los Angeles Times*, September 12, 1968, 1, 32–33.
14. "Fletcher Bowron Is Dead at 81," 47.
15. Hadley Meares, "Crenshaw Boulevard Rising," *La.curbed.com*, May 17, 2019, https://la.curbed.com/2019/5/17/18563304/crenshaw-blvd-los-angeles-nipsey-hussle-history.
16. "Zoot Suit Riots," *History.com*, September 15, 2020, https://www.history.com/topics/world-war-ii/zoot-suit-riots.
17. John Buntin, *L.A. Noir* (New York: Harmony Books, 2009), 258.
18. Carl Sifakis, *The Mafia Encyclopedia* (New York: Checkmark Books, 1999), 339–340.
19. Edward J. Escobar, "Bloody Christmas and the Irony of Police Professionalism," *Pacific Historical Review*, May 2003, 171–193.
20. Cecilia Rasmussen, The 'Bloody Christmas' of 1951," *Los Angeles Times*, December 21, 1997, https://www.latimes.com/archives/la-xpm-1997-dec-21-me-1006-story.html.
21. Steve Bisheff, *Great Teams' Great Years: Los Angeles Rams* (New York: Macmillan, 1973), 150.

History of Pro Football in Los Angeles

Joshua Milton Anderson

Pro football has existed in many formats besides the National Football League (NFL). The Los Angeles area lacked an NFL or major league team that was actually based in California during the early decades of the league. As a result, SoCal had an amazingly wide variety of minor league and independent pro football teams. Some played for years, others for weeks, but all helped to build interest in professional football on the West Coast.

As pro football developed in the East and Midwest, Los Angeles was just developing as a city. In 1900, the city had barely over 100,000 residents and there did not seem to be much interest in pro ball on the West Coast.[1] Over the next few decades a number of pro football teams and leagues were formed around the country. Of course, the most significant of these was the National Football League (NFL), first called the American Professional Football Association (APFA), founded in Canton, Ohio, in 1920. In 1925, the NFL had "barnstorming" tours featuring Red Grange and the Chicago Bears.[2]

In the winter of 1925–1926, Grange and the Bears traveled to the South and the West Coast for a nine-game swing. Grange was a national phenomenon. Nearly 75,000 people came to the Los Angeles Memorial Coliseum to see Grange and the Bears play the Los Angeles Tigers, an All-Star team, on January 16, 1926.[3] The Tigers were led by Washington Huskies All-American George Wilson, who rushed for 118 yards in a 17–7 loss to the Bears.[4] The huge Coliseum crowd not only led to significant press coverage but also caused many to start thinking about how professional football might work on the West Coast.

Grange's business manager, C.C. Pyle, had a lease at Yankee Stadium, but Tim Mara, the owner of the New York Giants, resisted Pyle's attempt to put an additional NFL team in New York City.[5] Pyle responded by creating the first American Football League (AFL) in 1926—with Grange as its top star.[6] Grange could not play everywhere at once, so the league needed to attract a few other big-name stars that fans would support at the ticket window. Wilson was believed to be such a star. He played against Grange and the Bears several times during their barnstorming tours and even outperformed him in the Bears' sole loss during the Southern/West Coast tour.[7] Pyle thought Wilson would be able to bring out spectators and offered him the AFL's traveling Los Angeles team, the Wildcats.

The Wildcats were based out of the Chicago area though most of their players were from the West Coast. The team finished with a 6–6–2 record even though they routinely would play one game Saturday, ride several hours in a train after the game and then play another game the following day. They never played west of the Chicago area during the regular season, so the Wildcats "wouldn't see the Pacific Ocean until long after the football season ended"[8] when they played a couple of games on the West Coast.

Not wanting to be outdone, the NFL tried to put a team in Los Angeles as well, the Buccaneers. It was originally hoped that the Buccaneers would play home games in the Memorial Coliseum, but the Coliseum's governance, made up largely of UCLA and USC graduates, was motivated to make sure collegiate football remained supreme, so they unofficially banned pro teams from playing in the Coliseum. Denied permission to play in the Coliseum, the Buccaneers also became a traveling team out of Chicago.[9] The Buccaneers would not play a single game in Los Angeles or on the West Coast until they played several exhibition games on the West Coast after their NFL regular season ended, including two games at L.A.'s Wrigley Stadium against the AFL's New York Yankees. Even a postseason exhibition game against the Wildcats was not played in Los Angeles. The two teams met in San Francisco with the Wildcats winning 17–0. Interestingly, the papers referred to the Buccaneers not as a team from Los Angeles but as "Brick" Muller's Buccaneers. Muller was a former University of California star who was a player/coach with the Buccaneers.[10] Though the team had gone 6–3–1, the NFL did not need a competing team in Los Angeles when the AFL dissolved after one season, especially one with such an expensive traveling situation, so the Buccaneers also folded.[11]

Meanwhile, Californians desired more than just having traveling teams in major pro leagues; they wanted their own league. The Pacific Coast Football League (PCFL) was created in 1926.

This PCFL had four teams with two teams (the Los Angeles Angels and the Hollywood Generals) centered around Los Angeles.[12] The woeful Angels were outscored 90 to 9, going 0–4 for the season. The Generals were the cream of the league, posting a 5–0 record and outscoring opponents 63 to 3. They even beat the NFL's Duluth Eskimos 6–3 on Christmas Day.[13] Attendance numbers are very incomplete, but no interleague game drew even 5,000 fans, save the Generals' 28–7 loss to the AFL Wildcats, which might have drawn 10,000.[14]

The PCFL lasted only one season, but it was nearly a decade before there was another attempt made to play professional football on the West Coast. Why so long? The attendance numbers assuredly concerned others who might have been interested in fielding a team the following year or two but do not explain the eight-year break. Also, some journalists argued that the attendance for the Grange tour was more about the experience of watching Grange than it was about professional football.[15]

The primary reason, however, was events outside of football. The "Great Crash" in late October 1929 affected many. It was hard for entrepreneurs to imagine people shelling out money for a game when they didn't have money to feed their families.

With the election of Franklin Delano Roosevelt in 1933 and the passing of New Deal legislation, the economic status for many began to improve. This led to numerous attempts for various teams to be formed on the West Coast and for them to try to either join established leagues, such as the NFL, or, more commonly, to form their own regional leagues. The longest lasting of these teams was the Los Angeles Bulldogs, created in 1936 and lasting over a decade, but there were many other teams from the Los Angeles area as well.

In 1934, the Pacific Coast Pro Football League (PCPFL) was created with six teams—the Berkeley Giants, Southern Cal Maroons, Westwood Cubs, Stanford Braves, Del Rey Shamrocks, and Moraga Wolves. The league schedule originally called for ten games, but no team played more than five. The Maroons, who played out of the newly built Gilmore Stadium in Los Angeles, finished second with a 3–1–1 record and the Cubs and Braves tied for third with 2–2–1 records.[16] Since the league "championship" was based on winning percentage, had the Maroons beaten the undefeated and untied Berkeley Giants near the end of the season they would have won the league, but the Maroons lost 17–14 and the Giants finished 3–0 and won the championship.[17]

The PCPFL had several strong players, such as backs Don Moses of the Maroons and Joe Keeble and Joe Lillard of the Cubs.[18] Moses was the Maroons' leading scorer. He played fullback and quarterback on offense and played defense as well.[19] Keeble played some quarterback for the Cubs, throwing for several touchdowns, but usually he started at fullback.[20] Lillard led the PCPFL in touchdown passes and finished second in rushing touchdowns. He had played in the NFL in 1932 and 1933 for the Chicago Cardinals, but 1934 was the first year of the NFL's unofficial ban on African Americans, so he was forced to play elsewhere.[21] During an exhibition game at Gilmore Stadium in December 1934, Lillard got to face his old Cardinals team while playing on the Stanford Braves' roster, but it did not help the Braves as the Cardinals won 37–2.[22]

The PCPFL returned in 1935, renamed the American Legion Pro Football League (ALPFL). The Cubs and Maroons (now called the Los Angeles Maroons) remained. The Stanford Braves and Del Rey Shamrocks became the Hollywood Braves and California Shamrocks.[23] The Westwood Cubs (5–2–1) had lost Lillard to the New York Brown Bombers, an all-African American team led by Fritz Pollard, but were still good enough to win the league by half a game when they beat the Los Angeles Maroons (4–2–1) in the final game of the season.[24] The Cubs may have been good enough to defeat the Maroons, but they were annihilated by the NFL Champion Detroit Lions, 67–14, on January 12, 1936. A team of ALPFL All-Stars faired only slightly better the next week, losing 42–7 to the Lions.[25]

By 1936, the ALPFL had folded, and when no league could be formed, the Los Angeles area had numerous independent teams. The Hollywood Stars and Los Angeles Bulldogs were the two most successful of these teams.

Backed by actor Victor McLaglen, the Stars, made up of many former ALPFL players, started off nicely with home and road wins over the San Diego Dons and a road victory over the Salinas Iceberg Packers.[26] The second half of the season did not go as well as they lost badly on the road to the crosstown Bulldogs 36–0 and the Packers 33–0 to finish 3–2.

The Bulldogs played all their games at Gilmore Stadium, and they opened with the 36–0 win over the Stars followed by a 40–7 victory over Antioch American Legion. The following week the NFL sent the Philadelphia Eagles to play against the Bulldogs. With the NFL looking to expand to ten teams, the Bulldogs had been given probationary status as a league member, and the NFL sent some teams to the West Coast to "test the waters." In the first contest of this type, the Bulldogs beat the Eagles 10–7 on a late Gordon Gore 44-yard field goal.[27] The following week the NFL's Pittsburgh Pirates, now called the Steelers, suffered similarly, losing 27–7 to the Bulldogs. Then a non–NFL team, the Salinas Iceberg Packers, came to town and handed the Bulldogs their first loss 21 to 17. Though many Bulldogs were undoubtedly disappointed to lose to Salinas, this loss led to a rivalry that had several good paydays over the next few years.[28]

A win against the Rock Island Tigers was followed by two more games against NFL opponents. The Bulldogs beat the Chicago Cardinals 13–10, then the Brooklyn Dodgers tied the Bulldogs 13–13.[29] After a game with Salinas was cancelled, the Bulldogs closed out their season with home games against two more NFL opponents- the Chicago Bears and the Green Bay Packers. They lost a tight game to the Bears 7–0 and then were crushed by the Packers 49–0. Though the Bulldogs had done well against the NFL teams and finished 6-3-1, the NFL decided to accept the Cleveland Rams as their 10th team, a team that was certainly closer geographically to the other NFL franchises at that time.

In 1937, the Hollywood Stars played just two games, losing twice to Salinas. The Bulldogs, on the other hand, had an incredible season. The Bulldogs took the Rams' spot in the second American Football League (AFL). The NFL considered the new AFL an "outlaw league," meaning they wouldn't let their teams schedule exhibition games with its members.[30]

The Bulldogs started the AFL season barnstorming through the East, playing not only the other AFL teams, but also the Providence Steam Roller and the Bristol West Ends, two independent New England teams. The Bulldogs' style of play featured "reverses, laterals, double laterals, forward passes combined with laterals—all run from an exaggerated spread formation that befuddled the AFL's other teams."[31] They used this style to beat everyone they played.[32]

Late in the season and sporting a 14–0 record, the Bulldogs agreed to play the Coast All-Stars, a team made up of AFL and NFL players. The game was almost washed out, but the Bulldogs won 7–3 in front of an estimated crowd of 500 at Gilmore Stadium.[33] With six minutes left, the Bulldogs trailed 3–0 and the All-Stars were punting. Bulldogs' end Bill Moore blocked the punt and it was scooped up by fellow Bulldogs' end Ike Frankian and returned for the winning touchdown.[34] Though the "management collected a fat rain insurance check and more than broke even," if players only got a portion of the gate, it was not much of a payday for them.[35] The All-Stars argued the results were a "fluke" and a second game was arranged.[36] In front of 14,000 at Gilmore Stadium the All-Stars lost the rematch 13–10 in a game that was close only because of a late All-Star touchdown. The All-Stars did not argue for a third game, though tempers ran high as All-Star Joe Keeble "hurled a blanket challenge to the entire Bulldog eleven" for a "knuckle dusting session."[37]

In 1938, the Hollywood Stars were resurrected by Paul Schissler, the former head coach of the NFL's Cardinals and Dodgers, and joined the new California Football League (CFL) with teams in Stockton, Fresno, Salinas and Oakland.[38] The Stars went 4–1 (with two additional losses to the crosstown rival Bulldogs), while the Stockton Shippers went 4–0.[39] Interestingly, rather than have Hollywood and Stockton play for the championship, in what presumably would have been a decent payday, the two teams never met on the field.

The Bulldogs were unaffiliated in 1938 as the AFL folded, and the Bulldogs chose not to join the newly formed CFL. This probably doomed the CFL as it meant the league did not include the best team in California.[40] As an independent, the Bulldogs could once again play NFL teams. They opened their 1938 season with an easy win over Salinas before traveling to Charlestown, West Virginia, for games against the NFL's Chicago teams. They lost to the Bears 14–12 and tied the Cardinals 14–14. The Bulldogs then suffered a 3–0 loss to the Cincinnati Bengals (not related to the current NFL Bengals), who had beaten the NFL's Bears and Pirates.[41] In response to this loss the Bulldogs quickly arranged to play an "All-Star" team from the Tulsa area (Bulldogs head coach Gloomy Gus Henderson had coached at the University of Tulsa) in a game the Bulldogs won easily, 33–0.[42] Just two weeks after the shocking loss to the Bengals, the Bulldogs hosted the Bengals and beat them soundly 48–17. The Bulldogs then beat their crosstown rivals, the Hollywood Stars, and beat and then tied the NFL's Pittsburgh Pirates.

14   Part 1: The City and the Organization

Their next opponent was the team the NFL chose to become a league member over the Bulldogs in 1937. The Cleveland Rams made their first, but certainly not their last, visit to Los Angeles. The Bulldogs took care of the Rams easily, winning 28–7. Three more games, and three more wins—Salinas, Salinas again, and Hollywood—and the Bulldogs had gone 8-0-1 over their last nine games. This led to a final game against the Louisville Tanks, a three-time champion of Midwest leagues, who were 10–4 in league and non-league games throughout the Midwest.[43] The Bulldogs won 16–0 and finished 10-2-2 for the season, having gone 2-1-2 against NFL competition.

The CFL folded before the 1939 season.[44] This left the Stars without a league, so the Stars did not play during the 1939 season. The Bulldogs, however, were accepted by the newly reborn AFL. In 1939, the Bulldogs also had a new head coach, Ike Frankian, as Henderson became the Detroit Lions' head man.

The Bulldogs' 1939 AFL season opened on September 4 with a loss to the NFL's Washington Redskins, 21–6. Nearly a month later on October 1, the Bulldogs began a Midwestern jaunt. Stops in Iowa and Ohio led to victories over the Des Moines Comets, 36–6, and Cincinnati Bengals, 16–12, sandwiching a 7–0 loss to the Columbus Bullies. Then they traveled home where they had several strong wins over the St. Louis Gunners, the Oakland All-Stars, the Columbus Bullies, and the Dayton Bombers. This was all before traveling to Portland to beat the Bullies and then returning to Los Angeles to beat the Bullies again. The Bulldogs then annihilated the Gunners and a Hollywood All-Star team put together just for that game. Despite finishing the league season with a 7–1 record, including multiple victories over the 9–4 Columbus Bullies, the Bulldogs were not named league champions. By the end of November, a number of AFL teams had ceased playing because of financial difficulties. As a result, the league invalidated all games played after November 30, paving the way for the Columbus Bullies to be declared champions.

The Bulldogs' last game of 1939 calendar year was against a team sometimes referred to as the Washington All-Stars. In this case, the Washington referred to was Kenny Washington, a UCLA All-American who could easily have been making a name for himself in the NFL, except the NFL was still in the middle of their "unofficial" policy of not letting African Americans play.[45] Washington was the most dynamic player on the West Coast.[46] Washington's All-Stars also featured Washington's UCLA teammate Woody Strode.[47] The Washington All-Stars lost to the Bulldogs 22–6 in front of a crowd of 15,000, but Washington scored the All-Stars' only touchdown.[48]

This large number of spectators inspired Jerry Corcoran, the Bulldogs' owner, and Paul Schissler, who had coached the Washington All-Stars, to find a way to keep this rivalry going.[49] The Bulldogs left the AFL, and Corcoran and Schissler created the 1940 version of the Pacific Coast Professional Football League (PCPFL), which would operate through 1948.

Unlike the mass chaos of the 1930s, pro football was relatively stable in 1940s California, especially during the first half of the decade. This is not to say that there were never surprises and changes, but there were not as many leagues and fewer teams that lasted only part of a season.

Three other teams joined Corcoran's Bulldogs and Schissler's Hollywood team, now called the Bears, in the new PCPFL: the Oakland Giants, Phoenix Panthers, and San Diego Bombers. The Bulldogs and the Bears were the largest draws in the league and the closest geographic rivals. The Bulldogs had been dominant since their inception going 43-8-4 (38-3-1 excluding games against NFL competition). The Bears had Washington, the PCPFL's biggest individual star.

Though there were five teams in the PCPFL, only two games during the entire 1940 season didn't involve either the Bears or Bulldogs. The Bears led the league standings for most of the season, based on two early season victories over the Bulldogs. However, late in the season, the Bears and Bulldogs faced each other twice, with the Bulldogs winning both games by a total of three points: 14–13 and 16–14. Those victories were enough for the Bulldogs to claim the league championship with a 7–2–1 record over the 6–2 Bears.

In 1941, the two Los Angeles area teams dominated the now four-team PCPFL. The Bears led the league going 8–0, with the Bulldogs second best at 4–4. Three of those losses were to the Bears. The most noteworthy games occurred late in the season. On November 30, the Bulldogs beat the visiting Columbus Bullies, champions of the American Football League, 7–0. The Bears did even better the following week, beating the Bullies 21–9 on December 7, with news of the game being largely overshadowed by the Japanese attack on Pearl Harbor.[50]

The following week, the Bulldogs were looking for a way to improve on the field and attract larger crowds, so they signed UCLA back Jackie Robinson. Robinson's debuted on December 14, 1941 against the San Francisco Packers, which had joined the PCPFL in 1941.[51] The Bulldogs, eager to avenge an early season loss to the Packers, dominated the game and won 36–0. Robinson did not get to play until 10 seconds were left in the first half, but he had a 41-yard touchdown run for the Bulldogs' last score of the game.[52] In the final game of the season on December 21 against the rival Bears, Robinson led the Bulldogs to a 10–3 lead in the 4th quarter, but two touchdown passes by Washington gave the Bears a 17–10 victory.[53]

By the time the 1942 season rolled around, the United States was embroiled in the Second World War. Many NFL players and some PCPFL players had joined the military. Due to the fear of a Japanese attack there were many troops stationed on the West Coast, and a number of military service teams were formed.

Both Los Angeles teams had a rough 1942 season with the Bulldogs going 2–2 and the Bears 0–4 in league play, as the San Diego Bombers led the PCPFL with a 4–1 record. Both teams also played games against local military service teams that did not count in the league standings.

In 1943, the PCPFL discontinued games against service teams. Bill Freelove began raiding the roster of the Los Angeles Bulldogs, signing most of the Bulldogs' best players to play for his Los Angeles Mustangs, a new league member. Bulldogs' owner Jerry Corcoran was furious. However, with the Bears granted a leave of absence by the league because owner Paul Schissler was busy serving in the war, the Bulldogs were able to add a number of former Bears to their roster, including player-coach Kink Richards.[54] The Bulldogs started 0–3, but won three of their last four to finish 3–4, while the Mustangs went 4–4. Neither of these Los Angeles area teams were able to challenge the San Diego Bombers, who easily won the league with a 7–1 record, however, the Bulldogs won three exhibition games against the Bombers in the two weeks after Christmas.[55]

Because of his behavior the other PCPFL owners had no interest in allowing Freelove to return for the 1944 season. Freelove responded by quickly putting together his own league. The new league, yet another American Football League, had eight teams, with three in the Los Angeles area: the Hollywood Rangers, Los Angeles Wildcats, and Los Angeles Mustangs. The Rangers were excellent, going 11–0 and easily winning the league. The Mustangs and Wildcats combined for a 5–11–2 record, and both finished in the bottom half of the league standings with the Wildcats failing to finish their season schedule.

Meanwhile, the San Diego Bombers dominated the PCPFL, going undefeated and untied in nine games. The Bulldogs and a new Hollywood franchise- the Wolves- were in the league basement, going a combined 2–11. The sole bright spot for the Bulldogs was the return of Jackie Robinson to the team, but even with him the Bulldogs still lost two of its last three games to finish 2-5. Both victories were over the woeful 0-6 Wolves.[56] At the end of the season the two competing leagues merged and the respective league champions, the Rangers and the Bombers, played twice with the Rangers winning both games.[57]

In 1945, two Los Angeles area teams would not survive the season. The Hollywood Rangers, who had refused to merge, played as an independent team for six games, including one against the Los Angeles Mustangs, also playing as an independent, and both folded.[58] However, the Hollywood Bears returned to the PCPFL in 1945, and finished first in the final standings with an 8-2-1 record. The Bulldogs fashioned a very average 5-5-1 record to finish third in the PCPFL.

With the war over, the return to normalcy would bring two new teams to the Los Angeles area in 1946: the NFL's Cleveland Rams, last seen losing to the Bulldogs before the war, relocated to Los Angeles and the Los Angeles Dons were granted a franchise in the upstart All-America Football Conference (AAFC).

On the field, the two remaining Los Angeles area PCPFL teams were still very active in 1946. The 9-2-1 Los Angeles Bulldogs won the PCPFL Southern Division crown over the new Hawaiian Warriors franchise and then easily beat the Northern Division champion Tacoma Indians 38–7 on January 19, 1947 for the league championship.[59] Tacoma had disbanded and had to recall all of their players for the championship game after the apparent Northern Division Champion San Francisco Clippers used an ineligible player and had to forfeit a win. The championship did not help the Bulldogs at the gate as they routinely drew less than 10,000 spectators and a win over the San Diego Bombers at Gilmore Stadium drew only 507.[60] The Hollywood Bears finished behind the Bulldogs and Warriors in the Southern Division with a mediocre 5–5–1 record.

To counter the AAFC, the NFL had a working agreement with the PCPFL. The PCPFL would not use any AAFC players, not play in the same city as the NFL on the same day, and would schedule games to compete with the AAFC when the NFL was not playing on the West Coast.

The AAFC Dons trained in Ventura, well outside of Los Angeles proper. Ventura was happy to have the Dons and covered them regularly in the daily paper.[61] This was especially true when they began to play intersquad games and exhibition games that drew good crowds.[62] The Dons played their first regular season game in Los Angeles sixteen days before the Rams. While gate receipts were important and they certainly hoped to fill the 100,000-plus-seat Coliseum for home games, having a connection to film industry notables Don Ameche, Louis B. Mayer, Bob Hope and Bing Crosby was a great "source of publicity" for the Dons.[63] Ameche, Mayer, Hope and Crosby were part of the Dons' ownership group headed by Ben Lindheimer, a "well-to-do Chicago racetrack owner."[64]

As a product the Dons were a solid football team finishing 7–5–2 in their first season, third in the AAFC Western Division behind the Cleveland Browns and San Francisco 49ers. On November 3, 1946, the Dons were even able to upset the eventual AAFC champion Browns, 17–16, at the Memorial Coliseum in front of a crowd of approximately 24,800, their largest home crowd of the season to that point.

In 1947, the Bears left the PCPFL, and the Bulldogs, at 5–3, finished second to the 7-2 Hawaiian Warriors. The Bulldogs could only play two "home" games, which were played at Ramsaur Stadium in Compton, a suburb, and drew less than 10,000 total spectators for the two "home" dates. The Bulldogs only drew large numbers in Hawaii where the Warriors played all their games against visiting teams on back-to-back weeks to make travel more cost effective. The Warriors, who made use of their home advantage by doing such things as having a luau or pretty girls with leis to distract the visiting team, lost to the Bulldogs, 35–34 on November 30, and beat them, 7–6, the following week.[65]

Meanwhile, in 1947 the Dons again were stuck in the same division as the dominant Browns and the strong San Francisco 49ers. This kept them from leading their division, but attendance was high. In just one game on Friday, September 12, 1947, 82,675 fans turned out to see the 1–1 Dons lose to the New York Yankees at the Memorial Coliseum by a score of 30–14. The attendance from that single game far exceeded all the games played by the Bulldogs that season.

In 1948, the PCPFL, the Bulldogs, and the Bears were back for another season, but the league was in its death throes and it would not survive into the 1949 season. The Bulldogs had lost so many fans to the other Los Angeles teams that they played home games in Long Beach. The Bears, now managed by Jerry Corcoran who had sold his interest in the debt-ridden Bulldogs, were a traveling team playing home games in San Bernardino.[66] The Warriors, who had survived a gambling scandal, led the league with a 5-1 record. The Bulldogs lost their first game but won their next three games including victories over the champion Warriors in Honolulu and the Bears in the only game played in Long Beach. The Bulldogs had two more games to play, but never completed their schedule.[67] Hollywood fared even worse, finishing a dismal 1–3–1.[68]

The Dons had owners and a league with much more money, and the problems they faced were not as severe as those faced by the Bulldogs and Bears. Still, the Dons experienced numerous difficulties. The Dons were never able to win a divisional title or play in an AAFC championship game, but they played well enough to average slightly over 20,000 spectators for every 1949 home date in a city that now had nearly two million people.[69] Unfortunately for the Dons, after finishing with a 7-7 record in both 1947 and 1948, they suffered their first losing season, going 4-8 in 1949. Worse, their owner suffered from a serious heart problem, so hopes of combining their team with the Rams, an idea bandied about as it became clear the AAFC would not survive, ended when Lindheimer dismissed trying to merge the two teams.[70] For the first time in decades Los Angeles would only have one pro football team in 1950 and it was the Rams.

In the quarter century between the 1926 traveling teams that simply said they were from Los Angeles until the 1951 NFL champion Rams, professional football had seen tremendous growth on the West Coast. This was reflected in the numerous minor league and independent football teams that tried their hand at professional football in the Los Angeles area. Not all the leagues or teams were successful, but all kept fans interested enough to attract the NFL and give the Rams a strong foundation once they had arrived.

NOTES

1. "General Population by City, Los Angeles County," *Laalmanac.com*, http://www.laalmanac.com/population/po25.php.

2. Bob Gill with Tod Maher, "California Dreamin,'" *The Coffin Corner* 6, Nos. 7 & 8 (1984), 1; John M. Carroll, *Red Grange and the Rise of Modern Football* (Urbana: University of Illinois Press, 1999), 107–139, passim.

3. John M. Carroll, "The Impact of Red Grange on Pro Football in 1925," *The Coffin Corner* 20, No. 2 (1998), 1.

4. Carroll, *Red Grange and the Rise of Modern Football*, 124.

Part 1: The City and the Organization

5. "The Grange League," *The Coffin Corner* 19, No. 1 (1997), 1.
6. "The Grange League," 3.
7. Carroll, *Red Grange and the Rise of Modern Football*, 124–125.
8. "The Grange League," 8.
9. Michael MacCambridge, *America's Game: The Epic Story of How Pro Football Captured a Nation* (New York: Random House, 2005), 16–17.
10. "Wilson's Wildcats Win Over Muller's Gridders by Easy 17 to 0 Victory," *Stockton Independent*, January 24, 1927, 5.
11. "Los Angeles Buccaneers," *Sportsercyclopedia.com*, http://sportsecyclopedia.com/nfl/lab/labucs.html.
12. "1926 Hollywood Generals," *Profootballarchives.com*, http://www.profootballarchives.com/1926pcflhol.html.
13. "Hawkins' Generals Defeats Nevers' Team 6 to 3," *Los Angeles Times*, December 26, 1926, 1a-1.
14. "1926 Hollywood Generals"; "1926 Los Angeles Angels," *Profootballarchives.com*, https://www.profootballarchives.com/1926pcflla.html.
15. Carroll, "Impact," 1.
16. Gill, "California Dreamin,'" 1; "1926 Los Angeles Angels"; "Gibbs Is Named Starting Guard on Pro Eleven," *The Whittier News*, September 22, 1934, 5.
17. Gill, "California Dreamin,'" 1.
18. Bob Gill with Tod Maher, *Outsiders: Minor League and Independent Football, 1923-1950* (Haworth, NJ: St. Johann Press, 2006), 48.
19. "Maroons Win Pro Loop Opener, 21–0," *Santa Ana Register*, September 24, 1934, 6; "Giants Defeat Maroons 17–14," *Petaluma Argus-Courier*, October 15, 1934, 4.
20. "Braves Defeat Cubs in Pro Game by 7–0 Score," *Los Angeles Times*, October 1, 1934, I-11; "Cubs Beat Pro Rivals," *Los Angeles Times*, December 3, 1934, I-11.
21. Bob Gill and Tod Maher, "Not Only the Ball Was Brown: Black Players in Minor League Football, 1933–46," *The Coffin Corner* 11, No. 5 (1989), 1.
22. "Chicago Cardinals Tackle Braves in East—West Pro Game Today at Gilmore," *Los Angeles Times*, December 9, 1934, I-26.
23. Gill, "California Dreamin,'" 2.
24. Gill, "California Dreamin,'" 1; John M. Carroll, "Fritz Pollard and the Brown Bombers," *The Coffin Corner* 12, No. 1 (1990), 3.
25. Gill, "California Dreamin,'" 1.
26. Gill with Maher, *Outsiders*, 49; "1936 Hollywood Stars," *Profootballarchives.com*, https://www.profootballarchives.com/1936hol.html.
27. Gill, *Outsiders*, 72.
28. Bob Gill, "The Bulldogs: L. A. Hits the Big Time," *PFRA Annual* 5 (1984), 2.
29. Gill, "The Bulldogs," 2.
30. Gill, "The Bulldogs," 3.
31. Gill, *Outsiders*, 74.
32. "1937 Los Angeles Bulldogs," *Profootballarchives.com*, https://www.profootballarchives.com/1937aflla.html.
33. Gill, *Outsiders*, 75.
34. Gill, *Outsiders*, 75; Frank Finch, "Bulldogs Triumph, 7–3: Local Pros Defeat All-Stars on Rain-Soaked Field," *Los Angeles Times*, December 27, 1937, II-13. *Outsiders* gives credit for blocking the punt to Frankian, but the article gives credit to "gallant southern gentleman, Squire Bill Moore."
35. Finch, "Bulldogs Triumph," II-13.
36. Gill, *Outsiders*, 75.
37. Gill, "The Bulldogs," 4; Frank Finch, "Bulldogs Beat Foes, 13–10: Passing Attack in Second Period Defeats All-Stars," *Los Angeles Times*, January 3, 1938, II-13.
38. Gill, "California Dreamin,'" 3.
39. "1938 Season," *Profootballarchives.com*, https://www.profootballarchives.com/1938.html.
40. Gill, "The Bulldogs," 4; Gill, *Outsiders*, 49.
41. Gill, *Outsiders*, 76.
42. Gill, "The Bulldogs," 5.
43. Gill, *Outsiders*, 78; "1938 Louisville Tanks," *Profootballarchives.com*, https://www.profootballarchives.com/1938afllou.html.
44. Gill, *Outsiders*, 49.
45. Gill, "California Dreamin,'" 3.
46. Gill, *Outsiders*, 84.
47. Gill, "The Bulldogs," 10.
48. Gill, "The Bulldogs," 10; "Washington Scores but His Team Loses," *The Sacramento Bee*, January 1, 1940, 12; "1939 Los Angeles Bulldogs," *Profootballarchives.com*, https://www.profootballarchives.com/1939aflla.html.

49. Gill, "California Dreamin,'" 3.
50. Bob Gill, "PCPFL: 1940–45," *The Coffin Corner* 4, No. 7 (1982), 2.
51. Bob Gill, "Jackie Robinson: Pro Football Prelude," *The Coffin Corner* 9, No. 3 (1987), 1.
52. Bob Smyser, "Bulldogs Run Over Hapless Packers, 36–0," *Los Angeles Times*, December 15, 1941, II-9.
53. Gill, "Jackie Robinson," 1–2.
54. Gill, "PCPFL," 3.
55. Gill, *Outsiders*, 168; "1943 Los Angeles Bulldogs," *Profootballarchives.com*, https://www.profootballarchives.com/1943pcfllab.html.
56. Gill, "Jackie Robinson," 1–2.
57. Gill, "PCPFL," 4; "1944 San Diego Bombers," *Profootballarchives.com*, https://www.profootballarchives.com/1944pcflsd.html.
58. "Rangers Win, 26–7, in League Debut," *Oakland Tribune*, October 1, 1945, 13.
59. Bob Gill, "The End of the PCPFL," *The Coffin Corner* 5, No .4 (1983), 1; Bob Braunwart, "All Those A.F.L.'s: N.F.L. Competitors, 1935–41," *The Coffin Corner* 1, No. 2 (1979), 7.
60. 1946 Los Angeles Bulldogs," *Profootballarchives.com*, https://www.profootballarchives.com/1946pcfllab.html.
61. Ray Schmidt, "Welcome to L.A.," *The Coffin Corner* 25, No. 6 (2003), 5–8.
62. Schmidt, "Welcome to L.A.," 5–8.
63. Schmidt, "Welcome to L.A.," 5–8.
64. Jerry Crowe, "The Dons of L.A. Pro Sports," *Los Angeles Times*, September 13, 2006, D7.
65. Bart Ripp, "The Tacoma Story," *The Coffin Corner* 24, No. 3 (2002), 18; "1947 Los Angeles Bulldogs," *Profootballarchives.com*, https://www.profootballarchives.com/1947pcfllab.html.
66. Gill, "The End of the PCPFL," 1–2.
67. "1948 Hollywood Bears," *Profootballarchives.com*, https://www.profootballarchives.com/1948pcflhol.html; Gill, "The End," 2.
68. "1948 Hollywood Bears."
69. "Historic General Population City & County of Los Angeles, 1850–2010, " *Laalmanc.com*, http://www.laalmanac.com/population/po02.php.
70. Crowe, "The Dons," D[7].

Owner Daniel Reeves

George Bozeka

Upon the death of pioneer Rams owner Dan Reeves in 1971, Steelers owner Art Rooney said of him, "He was a reserved man, a man who never sought the headlines, but behind the scenes, in league meetings, his voice, his ideas were listened to by his fellow owners.... Moreover, Dan must be rated as one the most honest, honorable and thoughtful men among my acquaintances."

Daniel Farrell Reeves was born on June 30, 1912, in New York City, the son of Irish immigrant parents, James Reeves and Rose Farrell. His father and uncle Daniel started peddling fruit on the streets of New York. By 1911, they had grown their fruit business into a chain of 35 grocery stores. Daniel died suddenly, and to honor him James incorporated the chain of stores and named it Daniel Reeves Inc.[1]

Reeves attended the Newman Prep School in Lakewood, New Jersey. He was captain of the football team at Newman playing quarterback and the man in motion. Reeves was awarded the Semple Award as the best athlete at the school.[2]

Too light to play sports at the collegiate level, Reeves attended Georgetown University, and began scouting for his brother Edward, who was a minority owner of the then Boston Redskins.[3]

On October 24, 1935, Reeves married Mary Carroon at the Carroon Estate on Long Island. More than 1200 people attended the reception including former New York governor Al Smith, New York Supreme Court Justice John H. McCooey, and former New York mayor John P. O'Brien. All had ties to Tammany Hall.[4]

Reeves had caught the football bug. As Michael MacCambridge stated, "like many men before him, and millions more to follow, Daniel Reeves loved the game of football for reasons he could neither articulate nor fully understand. With the wealth to do whatever he wanted, Dan Reeves wanted to buy a football team." Reeves once stated, "doesn't every boy dream of owning a football team?"[5] He bid

Rams pioneer owner Daniel Reeves helped reintegrate the NFL in 1946.

unsuccessfully to purchase the Pittsburgh Steelers and the Philadelphia Eagles.[6] By 1940, the Reeves grocery chain had grown to 600 stores, and Dan was working in the company's investment office. The chain was sold to Safeway for $11 million in 1941.[7]

On June 11, 1941, the Cleveland Rams were sold to a group headed by Reeves and Fred Levy, Jr., for approximately $125,000 to $140,000, depending on the source, with Reeves maintaining 60 percent controlling interest.[8]

The Rams were a team that had been struggling both on the field and at the turnstiles. When asked why he purchased a team in Cleveland, Reeves simply stated, "Because it was the only one for sale."[9] Per MacCambridge, the visionary Reeves confided privately to "fellow owners that he hoped to move the team to Los Angeles at the earliest opportunity. That, Reeves emphasized, was a place where the sport could grow and prosper." Since visiting Los Angeles and attending a USC game at the Los Angeles Memorial Coliseum in 1935, "he was captivated by Los Angeles and the glamour of football" there. He "was one of the first … to envision the pro game as a rival, potentially, of baseball as the national pastime."[10]

In his book *The Cleveland Rams*, author James Sulecki described the look and zeitgeist of the Rams' new owner circa 1941. "Reeves' face was sharp and handsome with a high forehead, later likened to Frank Sinatra. He dressed in tweeds and button-down-collar shirts, had a glib sense of humor, and always enjoyed a good time and a drink, frequently holding court at P.J. Clarke's bar on Third Avenue in midtown Manhattan. He favored daiquiris—rum in particular, like many men of his generation; in imitation of Ernest Hemingway and his hard-living ways—and he especially loved hanging out with sportswriters. He was a consummate New York cosmopolitan of the prewar era and likely held some indifference to the nation's interior."[11]

During Reeves first season of ownership in 1941, the Rams finished a dismal 2–9, but before the season was over, Reeves' "hopes and plans, like that of most other Americans, would have to be put on hold."[12] On December 7, 1941, the last day of the NFL regular season, the Japanese attacked Pearl Harbor and the United States was at war.

The NFL and the Rams played on. For the duration of the war, the NFL "fought manpower trouble, declining gates, and travel restrictions … and it operated in the shadow of baseball," a sport President Franklin Delano Roosevelt felt was essential to the well-being of the country.[13]

In 1942, the Rams experienced a mediocre 5–6 season. Before the 1943 season, the Rams' roster heavily depleted by the war effort, Reeves and Levy petitioned NFL commissioner Elmer Layden and the league office for permission to suspend operations of the Rams. The league owners approved the request.[14]

Reeves joined the U.S. Army Air Corps and served stateside as a second lieutenant and later captain at the Rome Air Station in Rome, New York. He bought out the interests of the other owners of the Rams, and after league approval on December 8, 1943, became the sole owner of the team.[15]

The Rams resumed operations in 1944, with new head coach Aldo "Buff" Donelli. Despite a promising 3–0 start, the Rams limped home, losing six of their last seven games to finish 4–6 with Reeves able to attend most of the Rams' games.

The 1945 season brought an apparent savior to the Rams, quarterback Bob Waterfield, and a new head coach, Adam Walsh, as Donelli was inducted into the Navy. As the war came to a close in August 1945, Reeves completed his three-year tour of duty and returned home just as the NFL regular season began in September.

22   Part 1: The City and the Organization

Washington Redskins owner George Preston Marshall (left) and Rams owner Daniel Reeves. Washington and the then–Cleveland Rams played in the 1945 NFL Championship Game with the Rams winning 15–14.

As Waterfield led the Rams to a 9–1 regular season record and a 15-14 NFL championship game victory over the Washington Redskins, things were to get complicated for Reeves, the Rams, and their future in Cleveland.

Despite the championship season, strong rumors surfaced and persisted that the Rams were looking to leave Cleveland for sunny California. The Rams were still a losing proposition at the box office for Reeves, plus in 1946, the Rams would have a football competitor on the shores of Lake Erie—the new AAFC franchise Cleveland Browns owned by Mickey McBride and coached by Paul Brown.

When Reeves initially purchased the Rams, the NFL had plans to move the club to Boston after one season in Cleveland. Surprisingly, Reeves and the Rams' administration decided to stay.[16] This time, "Reeves had decided, win or lose, that when the NFL held its annual meeting in January [1946] he would insist on fulfilling his goal, stated for years in private sessions with the owners, to move the franchise to Los Angeles.... Dan Reeves was heading west, or else Dan Reeves was leaving football."[17]

Reeves also considered Dallas, but he still realized that Los Angeles was the ideal destination for his franchise. As Bob St. John stated in *Tex!*, his biography of Tex Schramm, who was an assistant to Reeves from 1947 until 1956, Reeves was well aware of the advantages presented by Los Angeles—a booming population, a stadium (the Memorial Coliseum) that seated 100,000 for football, and a supportive fan base for football collegiately and professionally through the minor league Los Angeles Bulldogs and Hollywood Bears.[18]

The annual meetings began on January 11, 1946, in New York at the Commodore Hotel. On January 12, after the owners named Bert Bell as their new commissioner, Rams general manager Chile Walsh presented the Rams' request to move to Los Angeles as Reeves quietly listened. A unanimous vote was necessary. Several teams, including the Bears, Redskins, Cardinals, and Giants, opposed the move.

Things got contentious. Reeves was incensed, stating, "You call yourself a NATIONAL league? I suppose Texas doesn't interest you, either." George Halas explained that the opposition was concerned about traveling expenses. Reeves stormed out of the meeting threatening to leave the league. Bell recessed the meeting. The opposing owners met with Reeves in his hotel room to resolve the travel issues. The meetings went back into session, and the owners finally approved the move after Reeves agreed to offer teams an additional road guarantee to cover travel to Los Angeles.[19]

Reeves now needed a place to play. He set his sites on the aforementioned Memorial Coliseum. At the time, college football was king in SoCal, and there was an unofficial ban on pro teams at the Coliseum, plus Los Angeles was also to be home to a new AAFC franchise beginning play in 1946—the Los Angeles Dons—who also wanted to make the Coliseum their home field. The Dons ownership group was headed by Ben Lindheimer, a wealthy Chicago racetrack owner, and included a who's who of Hollywood—Don Ameche, Louis B. Mayer, Bing Crosby, and Bob Hope.[20]

The Rams and the Dons made applications to the Coliseum commission on January 15, 1946. During his presentation Chile Walsh stated, "From here on it is the 'Los Angeles Rams.' We have a feeling that in the league Los Angeles is one of the greatest, if not the greatest football cities in the country."[21]

Halley Harding, of the *Los Angeles Tribune*, an esteemed member of the black press, then spoke to the commission. Since 1933, the NFL had been a segregated league. Harding spoke eloquently about the injustices of such a practice. In response, Chile Walsh committed on behalf of the Rams that Kenny Washington would be invited to try out for the Rams, and Buddy Young would be signed upon his graduation from Illinois if he was made available to the Rams. On January 23, the commission approved five Sunday home games for the Rams at the Coliseum.[22]

The realization of Reeves's dream was a seismic moment in the history of professional football and professional sports in America. Wellington Mara, the late president of the New York Giants, put Reeves' move to the West Coast in perspective. "He broke the barrier. It was Dan who took the first small step that became the giant leap for organized sports."[23]

Before Reeves and the Rams, the furthest west any major league pro sports team called home was St. Louis, Missouri. The Rams paved the way for the move west by Major League Baseball's Brooklyn Dodgers and New York Giants, the National Basketball Association's Minneapolis Lakers, and the creation of the National Hockey League's Los Angeles Kings and California Seals.

Perhaps more significantly from a cultural standpoint, Reeves helped to reintegrate the NFL by signing Kenny Washington and Woody Strode to player contracts a full year before Branch Rickey broke the color barrier in Major League Baseball by calling Jackie Robinson up to the Dodgers' major league roster in 1947.

Reeves continued to innovate and revolutionize the game. In his book *Los Angeles Rams*, Steve Bisheff states, "It was Reeves who organized the first full-time scouting staff, an ingenious system of evaluating and drafting players that soon spread throughout the sport."[24]

Schramm explained that "Dan's scouting system was so much more sophisticated than the other teams' at the time and it had a definite bearing on the draft…. By the early 1950s, every team was copying the Rams' scouting form."[25]

Reeves also realized the power that the new medium of television could mean to the growth of the NFL. In 1950, he experimented with the medium, televising some Rams home games, but suffered a loss in attendance. He later became the first owner to establish policies for and televise away games.[26] Reeves explained, "This convinced us that home TV would be disastrous to the economics of the game. So we hit on a plan of road television which gave our fans half of the schedule free and at the same time exposed pro football to millions of new fans.... A local blackout is essential to stay in business, but road television is the most important thing pro football has done to build up the sport."[27]

He also started a "Free Football for Kids" program so children in Los Angeles could attend Rams games free of charge. After all, if the kids get in for free, the parents follow.[28]

Reeves was now in an area where entertainment was king, and he wanted a winning, colorful team that Los Angeles and Hollywood could embrace. Reeves wanted his team to have an exciting personality. He already had the ideal quarterback in Waterfield with a glamorous movie star wife—Jane Russell. In 1948, the Rams, with Reeves' support, became the first NFL team to don helmets with a logo.

Despite drawing over 95,000 for their first preseason game against the Redskins at the Coliseum, things started slowly for Reeves and the Rams in their new West Coast home. Billed as "America's Most Colorful Football Team" the Dons actually outdrew the Rams in two of their four seasons of existence.[29]

From 1946 to 1948, the Rams' combined record was a mediocre 18–15–2, and Reeves' checkbook was hemorrhaging. To stem the tide, Reeves sold shares in the team for $1 each to four investors. In turn, the investors agreed to share in the losses. Reeves maintained 33.33 percent of the ownership with his new partners holding the following percentages: Ed Pauley, Sr., 30.56, Hal Seley 13.89, Fred Levy, Jr., 11.121, and comedian Bob Hope 11.11.[30]

The franchise then embarked on a golden era from 1949 to 1955, appearing in four NFL championship games (1949, 1950, 1951, 1955), narrowly missing in 1952, and winning the first West Coast championship in any major league sport in 1951. More importantly for Reeves and his investors the team was now turning a profit. MacCambridge stated that after the championship game victory, "Reeves wryly noted that the second title was so sweet, it was probably worth the fortune he'd lost getting it. And that he was pleased, this time, to be staying put in a city that had embraced his team."[31]

Reeves was a brilliant administrator, but he also had demons that would affect the rationality of his decisions, often drinking to excess and saddled with a less-than-satisfactory marriage. During his ownership of the Rams from 1941 until his death in 1971, the Rams went through 12 different head coaches.

The relationship between the owners was disintegrating. Pauley, Levy and Seley were at odds with Reeves. Reeves' drinking was taking its toll and he was spending less and less time handling the day-to-day operation of the club. The other owners wanted Reeves out. Amid the turmoil, Schramm left the club in 1957 after the owners agreed that Commissioner Bert Bell would arbitrate decisions when the owners were at an impasse. At Bell's urging, Pete Rozelle, who previously had worked for the Rams as a publicity assistant while attending community college and again from 1952 to 1955 as publicity director, returned to the club as general manager. Rozelle was able to stabilize the tenuous situation in the front office, and he later became the NFL commissioner in 1960.[32]

Though the Rams continued to excel at the box office, the friction in the front office affected the product on the field. In 1957, the Rams became the first NFL team to draw over one million fans in a single season, drawing a single game league record 102,368 for a November 10 game against the 49ers at the Coliseum.[33] Ever the showman, Reeves honored the one-millionth fan with a special promotion. From 1956 to 1962, the Rams had only one winning season (1958), hitting rock bottom with a 1–12–1 record in 1962 under head coaches Bob Waterfield and Harland Svare.[34]

Reeves had curtailed his drinking, and in 1962, in an attempt to resolve the ongoing issues in the Rams front office, Rozelle refereed a closed auction of the club. On December 27 it was announced that Reeves was the winning bidder at $7.1 million. Reeves now owned 51 percent of the club and was president and general manager. Asked how the deal would affect the Rams, Reeves stated, "Probably all that will happen is that we will make the same mistakes a little more efficiently."[35]

Reeves was prophetic. Svare continued as head coach through the 1965 season, finishing with a 14–26–2 mark over his last three seasons. Svare was fired and Reeves lured George Allen away from the Chicago Bears' coaching staff. George Halas was livid, filing suit against Allen for breach of contract. Halas relented, and the Rams had a new head coach.

Hiring Allen was a stroke of genius. He quickly turned the Rams around going 29–10–3 in his first three seasons. A power struggle ensued between Reeves and Allen, and Reeves fired Allen without consulting with the other owners. As *Herald Examiner* editor Bud Furillo reported at the time, "the firing of Allen by Reeves packed all the subtlety of Deacon Jones cutting down a quarterback."[36]

Rumors abounded that Reeves wanted to bring Vince Lombardi to Los Angeles to be his next coach. Rams players and fans supported Allen. Reeves resolved his differences with Allen and rehired him but claimed that the player support had little to do with his decision. "I recognize that many of our players did support George. They felt that a change of head coach might disrupt their newly found winning formula. At the time, I decided to rehire George, I cannot stress enough that it was this support that was actually a hindrance to my decision because I didn't want the players to get the idea they could hire the coach. If they figure they can do that, they also can figure they can fire the coach."[37]

The forced honeymoon didn't last long. Allen coached for two more seasons fashioning a 20–7–1 record, but Reeves and Allen barely spoke. After the 1970 season, Reeves announced that Allen's contract would not be renewed.[38]

Reeves last major decision would be to hire UCLA coach Tommy Prothro as the Rams' new head coach on January 2, 1971.

On April 15, 1971, Reeves died at the age of 58 after a five-year battle with Hodgkin's disease.[39]

In 1967, Reeves was inducted into the Pro Football Hall of Fame. Upon his induction, he summarized his football life, stating, "Enjoyment isn't the word for it. Every minute has been fascinating. My enthusiasm never has flagged."[40]

Pete Rozelle paid tribute to his former boss and mentor. "Dan Reeves was a man of great integrity who placed strong emphasis on loyalty. He, himself, generated great loyalty. I think his biggest impact was in making football a year-round operation. Scouting was a focal point, but it extended into other areas, too. He was convinced that to be a success, you had to work all year at it…. Of course he truly did open the West to major professional sports. All you have to do is add up the teams operating west of Missouri to realize that. And I'm talking about all sports, not just football. He was the first major league owner to gamble. All the rest came later. Around the National Football League, I think his greatest contribution of all was that he helped generate more of a commitment to excellence on everyone's part. He was, needless to say, quite a man."[41]

Notes

1. James C. Sulecki, *The Cleveland Rams* (Jefferson, NC: McFarland, 2016), 92–94.
2. Steve Bisheff, *Great Teams' Great Years: Los Angeles Rams* (New York: Macmillan, 1973), 14.
3. Sulecki, *The Cleveland Rams*, 95.
4. "Mary Carroon Married to Daniel Reeves as Notables Among 800 Guests Look On," *New York Times*, October 25, 1935, 18.
5. Michael MacCambridge, *America's Game: The Epic Story of How Pro Football Captured a Nation* (New York: Random House, 2004), 10.
6. Bisheff, *Los Angeles Rams*, 14.
7. Bob Oates, *The Los Angeles Rams* (Los Angeles: Murray & Gee, 1955), 22.
8. Sulecki, *The Cleveland Rams*, 97–98.
9. Todd Anton and Bill Nowlin, *When Football Went to War* (Chicago: Triumph Books, 2013), 162.
10. Bob Oates, "The New Hall of Famer," *Los Angeles Herald-Examiner*, February 9, 1967, RC.
11. Sulecki, *The Cleveland Rams*, 96.
12. MacCambridge, *America's Game*, 10.
13. MacCambridge, *America's Game*, 10–12.
14. Anton and Nowlin, *When Football Went to War*, 162.
15. Anton and Nowlin, *When Football Went to War*, 162; "Reeves Gets Grid Team," *The Troy* (NY) *Record*, December 9, 1943, 18.
16. Sulecki, *The Cleveland Rams*, 98.
17. MacCambridge, *America's Game*, 7.
18. Bob St. John, *Tex!* (Englewood Cliffs, NJ: Prentice Hall, 1988), 164.
19. MacCambridge, *America's Game*, 15–16.
20. Jerry Crowe, "The Dons of L.A. Pro Sports," *Los Angeles Times*, September 13, 2006, D7.
21. Paul Zimmerman, "Rams Ask Five 1946 Dates in Coliseum," *Los Angeles Times*, II-8.
22. MacCambridge, *America's Game*, 19; "L.A. Rams to Use Coliseum Sunday," *The Hanford* (CA) *Sentinel*, January 24, 1946, 7.
23. Bisheff, *Los Angeles Rams*, 12.
24. Bisheff, *Los Angeles Rams*, 13.
25. Bisheff, *Los Angeles Rams*, 14.
26. Bisheff, *Los Angeles Rams*, 13.
27. Oates, "The New Hall of Famer," RC.
28. Bisheff, *Los Angeles Rams*, 13.
29. *Pro-Football-Reference.com*
30. Oates, *The Los Angeles Rams*, 24–25.
31. MacCambridge, *America's Game*, 73.
32. MacCambridge, *America's Game*, 144; Bisheff, *Los Angeles Rams*, 153–159; St. John, *Tex!*, 206–210.
33. Joseph Hession, *Rams: Five Decades of Football* (San Francisco: Foghorn Press, 1987), 69.
34. Bisheff, *Los Angeles Rams*, 161.
35. Edwin Shrake, "A Private Eye on the Rams," *Sports Illustrated*, October 3, 1966, 36; Bisheff, *Los Angeles Rams*, 161–162.
36. Bud Furillo, "Reeves Didn't Consult Partners Before Blitzkrieg," *Los Angeles Herald-Examiner*, December 27, 1968, D-1.
37. Bud Furillo, "Reeves Wants Allen Back," *Los Angeles Herald-Examiner*, January 2, 1969, C-1; Mal Florence, "Reeves Led Stampede to West Coast," *The Sporting News*, April 17, 1971, 45–46.
38. Mal Florence, "Allen Sacked Again—Grounds: Incompatibility," *Los Angeles Times*, December 31, 1970, III-1.
39. William N. Wallace, "Dan Reeves Dies; Owner of Rams," *New York Times*, April 16, 1971, 40.
40. Florence, "Reeves Led Stampede to West Coast," 45–46.
41. Bisheff, *Los Angeles Rams*, 180.

Head Coach Joe Stydahar

Lee Elder

On October 7, 1950, The Los Angeles Rams suffered a 56–20 beating at the hands of the Philadelphia Eagles. The defeat was as ugly as the score indicates. Rams quarterbacks Norm Van Brocklin and Bob Waterfield combined to toss five interceptions, and the Eagles gashed the Rams defense for 298 rushing yards and 473 total yards.[1]

According to legend, first-year Rams head coach Joe Stydahar was so furious with his players that he shouted at them following the game, "No wonder you guys got kicked around. Every guy on the team still has all his teeth."

Dentistry records aside, Stydahar was a tough man in a rough business. The first man ever drafted by the Chicago Bears, Stydahar was an all-league offensive tackle four times and played on three NFL championship teams, all with the Bears. Playing in an era when few players used facemasks, Stydahar spent part of his NFL tenure playing without a helmet. But Stydahar was a study in contrasts because he had brains to go along with the brawn. He earned a Bachelor of Science degree in agriculture and somehow successfully managed the tricky business of switching Van Brocklin and Waterfield in and out of the lineup.

During their first stay in Los Angeles, the Rams were coached by the likes of Hall of Famers Sid Gillman and George Allen. But Stydahar was the only man to coach the city to an NFL championship in the 20th century.

Pat Summerall, a member of the Chicago Cardinals' teams Stydahar coached after his time with the Rams, wrote in his autobiography of Stydahar, "He was the only guy I've ever known to drink whiskey, smoke a cigar and chew tobacco—all at the same time. He was an intense, driven man, and losing a game was like lighting a fuse for him."[2]

Joseph Lee Stydahar was born March 17, 1912[3] in Kaylor, Pennsylvania, the son of Peter P. Stydahar and Lucille Naglic Stydahar. Joe was one of seven Stydahar children. Peter Stydahar was a Croatian immigrant and supported the family by working in coal mines.[4]

An outstanding high school athlete at Shinnston (West Virginia) High School, Joe earned all-state

Rams head coach Joe Stydahar won three NFL championships as a player with the Chicago Bears.

honors twice in football (once as a tackle, once as a fullback) and three times as a center on the basketball team. He also played third base on the school's baseball team.[5] Stydahar started his college football career at the University of Pittsburgh in 1932 but he left campus for home after a month and later enrolled at West Virginia University. There are several stories about how Stydahar ended up at West Virginia. The version repeated most frequently is that the freshman became homesick and, during a break in summer practice at Pittsburgh, he went home and enrolled at West Virginia instead. Stydahar completed his studies, having played well enough at West Virginia to be selected to play in the East-West Shrine Game and in the College All-Star Game. He was elected to the College Football Hall of Fame in 1972.[6]

The National Football League was still relatively young in 1936, having been born just 16 years earlier. The league was adapting as the times changed and it introduced the first-ever draft of college players before the 1936 season. The University of Chicago's Heisman Trophy winner, Jay Berwanger, was selected first overall by the Philadelphia Eagles. Stydahar was the first player selected by the Chicago Bears and the sixth player selected overall after Carl Brumbaugh and West Virginia alum Bill Karr recommended Stydahar to Bears owner George Halas.[7]

"That was the turning point of my life," Stydahar said. "[George] Halas has been like a second father to me. I didn't know anything about football until I had a chance to play for him."[8]

Once he had his chance to play for Halas, Stydahar made the draft pick pay off. The coal miner's son earned all-league recognition five straight seasons, 1936–1940, and Stydahar later said his biggest thrill in football came at the end of the 1940 season, the day the Bears destroyed the Washington Redskins 73–0 in the NFL championship game in Washington, D.C.

Total Football II, the authoritative encyclopedia of the professional game, ranked Stydahar among the 300 greatest players the game has seen. It said, in part, "By 1940, when the Bears earned their 'Monsters of the Midway' reputation, Stydahar was firmly entrenched as the league's premier left tackle. He was the anchor of an exceptional line that included Hall of Fame inductees Dan Fortmann, Clyde 'Bulldog' Turner and George Musso. Fearless and huge by 1940 standards, 'Jumbo Joe' possessed incredible power and remarkable speed. Flaunting his disdain for superstition by wearing jersey number 13, he was a near 60-minute performer who preferred not to wear a helmet until NFL rules forced him to comply."[9]

He wasn't just a lineman. During his career, Stydahar is credited with converting 28 of 31 conversion kick attempts with the Bears, although he missed on both of his field goal attempts, and he had one pass interception that he returned 55 yards without scoring.[10]

The chance to play the game for a living meant a great deal to Stydahar. He had seen the inside of a coal mine where his father worked and did not want that for himself. Football injuries were less concerning than what he'd seen in a coal mining community. He was quoted by the *Washington Star* as saying, "One little kneecap isn't too much to pay for a kid who might be shoveling coal."[11]

And the Bears were winners. During Stydahar's playing tenure, Chicago earned division championships in 1937, '40, '41 '42 and '46. The Bears won the world title in 1940, '41 and '46.

Joe Stydahar registered for a draft of a different sort on October 16, 1940, when he added his name to the list of men eligible to serve in the United States military. Stydahar served aboard the USS *Monterey* as a gunnery officer in 1943 and '44.[12] The *Monterey* was active in the Pacific theater of the war. Stydahar may have come to know another former college football player who was a future United States president, Gerald R. Ford, while serving on the *Monterey*.

In 1944, Stydahar played tackle for the Fleet City Bluejackets armed services football team earning a spot on the 1944 AP Service All-America Team, although Stydahar, who was huge by NFL standards of the day at six feet, four inches and about 230 pounds, later claimed that he did not participate in service football on what he said were humanitarian grounds.

"I just didn't have the heart to play against some of those kids," he said. "They were just too damned small."[13]

Stydahar returned to the Bears in 1945, playing two more seasons before stepping away from his playing career to become an assistant coach for the Los Angeles Rams in 1947.

Before moving to Los Angeles, Stydahar married Yolanda Monet Margowski on February 24, 1947, in Harrison, West Virginia. The union eventually produced four children: David, Joseph, Stephanie and George.[14]

For his first coaching assignment, he joined a club that had won the 1945 title as the Cleveland Rams. The Rams had the parts and pieces in place to keep winning, but somehow, they did not. Head coaches didn't last very long for the Rams during that era. Team president Dan Reeves went through coaches like the stock market used to spin out ticker tape. Adam Walsh, who had coached the championship team in 1945, was fired after the 1946 season. Former Bear Bob Snyder was the head coach in 1947 and then Clark Shaughnessy took over for two seasons. The Rams lost the 1949 title game to the Eagles, but their four-year regular season record between championship game appearances was 26–17–4.

Shaughnessy offered a no-nonsense opinion of Stydahar when told that Stydahar would succeed him as the Rams' new head coach for the 1950 season. "Stydahar—coach of the Rams," Shaughnessy asked. "Why, I could take a high school team and beat him."[15]

Stydahar, with his false teeth, hulking frame and championship pedigree, was the next man up. He coached the Rams to two championship game appearances and won one of them. All he did was win, but Joe Stydahar lasted only two seasons as the Rams' coach, plus one game.

Shaughnessy would have needed a pretty good high school team to beat Stydahar and the Rams in 1950 and '51. Flying high with the Fly T offense designed by assistant coach Hamp Pool, the 1950 Rams set an NFL record by scoring 466 points in 12 games and the Rams scored a more pedestrian 392 the following year. The Rams scored 60 or more points twice in 1950, a record, and set a record for scoring in three consecutive games, with 165 points to rout the Lions, Colts and Lions again in 1950. The 1951 championship team led the league in points scored, total yards and passing yards. The Rams were third in rushing yards. The Rams and Browns split their two meetings in the title games, with the 1950 finale decided by a field goal by the Browns' Lou Groza in the final minute of the game. Stydahar's head coaching record in post-season play was 2–1, including a 1950 conference championship playoff victory over the Bears.

And Stydahar had to balance a tricky situation with his quarterbacks, Bob Waterfield and Norm Van Brocklin. There was only one football and the Rams had two future Hall of Famers to throw it. While the quarterback controversy later became a Los Angeles tradition, no Rams head coach handled those situations so well as Stydahar.

Stydahar was 39 when his Rams won the '51 championship and was seemingly on top of the world. He'd branded the organization with the same toughness he learned while playing for Halas. When he wasn't shaking his teeth at the Rams, Stydahar was plucking cash from their wallets. In September of the championship season, the Rams defeated the Eagles in Little Rock, Arkansas. The celebration, apparently, went deep into the night. After a bed check that discovered missing players, Stydahar sat in the hotel lobby and caught 28 players coming in after curfew. All 28 were fined (though he would later rescind the fines with Frank Finch reporting that "beneath that rough exterior there beats a heart softer than an over ripe tomato").[16]

Stydahar's Rams went 17–8 in his two regular seasons plus one game at the helm, but things came to a head with Reeves in 1952. Despite a new, three-year contract extended by the Rams after the championship, Stydahar and the owner had a disagreement over assistant coach Pool.

The Rams opened the 1952 season with a 37–7 loss to the Browns in Cleveland, and Stydahar was unhappy with his team's performance. Before returning home to Los Angeles, Stydahar talked to Reeves. "I told Dan that for the good of the club there ought to be a change made.... I didn't offer to resign. I can't afford to resign. Dan told me to go back home and sleep on it and we would talk it over, probably Tuesday," Stydahar told the *News-Press*. Later, in the same article, Stydahar was quoted as saying, "Yes, there has been dissension between Pool and myself. I believe a coaching staff should work hand in hand." Stydahar, the report said, was irritated at what he said was a lack of help from Pool during the Cleveland game. Reeves, reportedly, sat next to Pool during the game in question.[17]

"What it amounted to," Stydahar was quoted as saying, "was that I had the big head and I thought I couldn't be replaced. I didn't know how wrong I was."[18]

In his October 13, 1963, *Los Angeles Herald-Examiner* column, "Bud Furillo's Steam Room," the long-time Southern California reporter stated that after the 1951 title game, Rams fans did not even know how to boo.

They soon learned, Furillo wrote. "A rift developed between the coach and his president, Dan Reeves. Both might agree today it could have and should have been healed. But they were both headstrong individuals at the time. The town was shocked when they parted ways after the first game of 1952."[19]

Stydahar was replaced by Pool, whose Rams finished second, third and then fourth in their conference the next three seasons. In 1955, with Sid Gillman at the helm, the Rams again reached the NFL title game, losing to their old rival, the Browns, 38–14. The Rams would not win in the postseason again until they lost a playoff game to the Packers in December of 1967 and then played a meaningless game called the Playoff Bowl after the same season beating, of all teams, the Browns. After Stydahar was fired and before George Allen took over in 1966, the Rams went through four head coaches and compiled a record of 74–96–7.

Late in the 1952 season, Stydahar was hired as an assistant coach by the Green Bay Packers. Packers head coach Gene Ronzani needed an administrative assistant to help the Packers prepare for the upcoming draft. Jack Vainisi, who handled that responsibility for the Packers, had been hospitalized with a serious illness. Stydahar's hire in '52 was never meant to be permanent, but Ronzani and Stydahar had a history together. Ronzani had wanted to hire Stydahar as his line coach when Ronzani became the Packers' head coach in 1950. Before the Packers could lure Stydahar away from the Rams, the former Bears star was promoted to be the Rams' head coach.

In the 1953 NFL draft, the Packers' first seven selections included first choice Southern California halfback Al Carmichael, who played eight years in the league; SMU linebacker Bill Forester, the Packers' third pick who played 11 professional seasons; and Syracuse center Jim Ringo, the Packers' seventh pick, who played 15 seasons and was later inducted into the Pro Football Hall of Fame.

The Packers released Stydahar when Vainisi regained enough of his health to return to work, but Stydahar did not stay unemployed very long. He returned to Chicago to be head coach of the Chicago Cardinals. The Cardinals had suffered through seven wins and 17 losses the previous two seasons and things did not get better after Stydahar's arrival. The club suffered through a pair of bad seasons in 1953 and 1954, posting an overall record of 3–20–1. Stydahar discovered it was one thing to have Van Brocklin and Waterfield passing to Tom Fears and Elroy Hirsch, but that it was another to have the likes of Jim Root, Steve Romanik and Ray Nagel playing quarterback.

Stydahar's Cards went 1–10–1 in 1953. Their only victory came on the last week of the season when the Cardinals beat their cross-town rivals, the Bears, 24–17.

Pat Summerall, who later became America's favorite play-by-play announcer, played on the 1953 Cardinals' team and related that Stydahar had not mellowed since the day he bemoaned the fact that so many Rams players retained their own teeth.

"Joe came in after a loss the week before the Bear game carrying all our paychecks with a rubber band wrapped around them," Summerall said. "He threw the packet across the room at Comiskey Park and said, 'All right, you gutless sons of bitches, if you don't beat the Bears, you don't get paid.' That's about as severe a fine as you can get.... Some players wanted to go to the owners to complain, but nothing ever happened. We beat the Bears anyway. So, we got paid."[20]

The Cardinals improved only marginally in 1954 to go 2–10.

Stydahar had done nothing but win since the Bears drafted him. Losing was something he seldom experienced since leaving West Virginia. Summerall said Stydahar did not respond supportively after the Cardinals lost their first five games in '54. "Our coach responded by losing his cool, if not his mind. Stydahar issued a decree prohibiting sex before games. You can imagine how that went over," Summerall wrote.[21]

Stydahar was dismissed by the Cardinals on June 2, 1955, after the Cards bought out the final year of his three-year contract.

Stydahar was never a head coach again, but he was not done with football.

Before the 1963 season, the former Bears star was re-hired by Halas to coach the defensive line, replacing Shaughnessy, who resigned three weeks before the end of the 1962 season. At the same time another former Rams assistant coach, named George Allen, was promoted to become what would be called the Defensive Coordinator in later years. Stydahar would work with Allen, primarily coaching the defensive linemen.

Stydahar said at the time, "Since I left the Cardinals, I turned down a lot of offers. The Bears were the only team I was interested in. It has been my ambition for years to be back with them. I'd like to help Halas win a championship." He added, "I approached Halas about a month ago [in January of 1963] and said I'd like to be on his staff. Yesterday he told me I had the job." It was a part-time job for Stydahar. He also was the vice president of the Starr Container Corporation at the time.[22]

Allen, who eventually joined Stydahar in the Pro Football Hall of Fame in Canton, was given a game ball after the Bears won the 1963 championship game, beating the New York Giants, 14–10. The Bears allowed just 10.3 points per game and allowed a league-lowest 3.5 yards per rushing play. The Bears allowed just seven rushing touchdowns over the 14-game schedule and were the only team to surrender less than 10 scores on the ground. The 1964 Bears did not fare so well, finishing at 5–9. Stydahar finally left football for good after the 1964 season, but he left with another championship to his credit.

"I have been trying to make the two jobs go," said Stydahar. "But I don't feel it's really fair to either organization. Moreover, two years ago when I got permission to join the Bear staff, it was understood that it was not to be a permanent arrangement." He added, "I regret very much leaving the Bear organization, particularly after a losing season. I will always have a deep affection for Coach George Halas and the Bears."[23]

Halas said at the time that Stydahar's decision to leave the club was not a big surprise. Halas said, "We did discuss this last spring when the president of his company wanted Joe to give up coaching at that time."

There may have been more to Stydahar's decision to leave football than just the business opportunity he had. In an August 9, 1967, story in the *Pittsburgh Press*, roughly a week after he was inducted into the Pro Football Hall of Fame, Stydahar revealed that he had decided to stop drinking alcohol 13 years earlier. The story, written by sports editor Lester J. Biederman, called the decision "Stydahar's greatest victory. Over himself."[24]

Stydahar told Biederman, "People in sports expect you to be a social drinker and then it becomes more than that. But liquor always made me ill. One day I emptied all the liquor in my home down the sink. But that didn't stop me. Next day I bought another bottle. But I beat the habit by keeping the liquor out in the open and using will power. I haven't touched a drop to this day."

A newspaper article from 1952 describes Stydahar as smoking evil-smelling cigars and using chewing tobacco. Several news reports from the time mention that Stydahar drank on occasion. He seemed a jovial sort, except when he wanted to motivate his players.

"I was never classified as an alcoholic," Stydahar told the *Chicago American*'s Bill Gleason. "But I think I was."[25]

With football firmly behind him, Stydahar eventually became the assistant eastern regional manager for the container division of Southwest Forest Industries. He lived near Chicago in Highland Park but was in Beckley, West Virginia, on a business trip when he suddenly passed away on March 23, 1977, at age 65.

"Joe was something special for me," Halas said. "Football fans know him as the first lineman drafted in the first round in 1936 and as a true All-Pro, as a great player, as one of the Bears' all-time greats and as a Hall of Famer. But more important to any of these football accomplishments, Joe Stydahar was a man of outstanding character and loyalty. We had a warm personal relationship all these years."[26]

NOTES

1. "Los Angeles Rams at Philadelphia Eagles—October 7, 1950," *Pro-football-reference.com*, https://www.pro-football-reference.com/boxscores/195010070phi.htm.
2. Pat Summerall; *Summerall: On and Off the Air* (Nashville: Thomas Nelson, 2006), 40.
3. Social Security Death Index, www.ssd.gov. The 1952 Rams press book lists Stydahar's birthdate as March 3, 1912, but most sources agree that he was born on March 17 in Kaylor and that the family moved to Shinnston, West Virginia, when Stydahar was four years old.
4. Frank Finch, "Jumbo Joe Stydahar Sits on Top of World," *The All-Sports News*, January 16, 1952. See Stydahar file at the Pro Football Hall of Fame.
5. Finch, "Jumbo Joe." See Stydahar file at the Pro Football Hall of Fame.

6. "Joe Stydahar," *Cfbhall.com*, https://www.cfbhall.com/about/inductees/. While he was at West Virginia, Stydahar played on some very average Mountaineers teams. Under head coach Greasy Neale, the school went 3–5–3 in 1933. Trusty Tallman replaced Neale and coached the team to records of 6–4 in 1934 and 3–4–2 in 1935. The Mountaineers' record with Stydahar on the roster was 12–13–5.

7. Jeff Davis, *Papa Bear: The Life and Legacy of George Halas* (New York: McGraw-Hill, 2005), 131.

8. Finch, "Jumbo Joe." See Stydahar file at the Pro Football Hall of Fame.

9. Bob Carroll, et al., *Total Football II* (New York: HarperCollins, 1999), 353–354.

10. Carroll, *Total Football II*, 1318.

11. "Joe Stydahar Burial Is Slated Tomorrow," *Washington Star*, March 25, 1977. See Stydahar file at Pro Football Hall of Fame.

12. "Joe Stydahar Burial"; "Joe Stydahar Dead at 65," *Chicago Sun-Times*, March 25, 1977. See Stydahar file at the Pro Football Hall of Fame.

13. Finch, "Jumbo Joe." See Stydahar file at the Pro Football Hall of Fame.

14. Bob Duvall, "What Ever Became Of," *Football Digest*, November 1971. See Stydahar file at the Pro Football Hall of Fame.

15. Finch, "Jumbo Joe." See Stydahar file at the Pro Football Hall of Fame.

16. Finch, "Jumbo Joe." See Stydahar file at the Pro Football Hall of Fame.

17. "Trouble Between Coaches Bared," *News-Press*, September 30, 1952, 5.

18. See newspaper account headlined "Obituaries—Joe Stydahar" in the Stydahar file at the Pro Football Hall of Fame. The notice is dated 4–77 (April of 1977).

19. Bud Furillo, "Bud Furillo's Steam Room," *Los Angeles Herald-Examiner*, October 13, 1963, E-4.

20. Davis, *Papa Bear*, 283–284.

21. Summerall, *On and Off the Air*, 44.

22. Ed Stone, "Stydahar Gets Wish, Rejoins Bears as Aid," *Chicago's American*, February 15, 1963. See Stydahar file at the Pro Football Hall of Fame.

23. Cooper Rollow, "Joe Stydahar Quits Bears," *Chicago Tribune*, December 16, 1964, 3-1.

24. Lester J. Biederman, "Stydahar's Greatest Victory—Over Himself," *Pittsburgh Press*, August 9, 1967, 67.

25. Bill Gleason, "They'll Uncork Hurrahs Tonight For Lovable Joe," *Chicago's American*, April 21, 1967. See Stydahar file at the Pro Football Hall of Fame.

26. "Joe Stydahar Dead."

Assistant Coaches

Ryan C. Christiansen, Bert Gambini,
Bryan Lutes *and* Joe Ziemba

Red Hickey
—Bert Gambini

Was it Dusty Rhodes? Or maybe Muddy Waters? Neither name was the correct response to the question, but those were Art Donovan's two best guesses when the former Baltimore Colts defensive tackle tried to recall the San Francisco quarterback who 16 years earlier helped introduce one of football's greatest offensive innovations.[1]

Though Bob Waters' name wasn't top of mind, Donovan clearly remembered the day professional football first saw the modern shotgun formation, brainchild of Red Hickey, head coach of the 49ers who had previously served as a Rams assistant from 1949 to 1954.

"Remember it!" said Donovan, a Hall of Famer known as much for his storytelling gifts as his football prowess. "How could I forget it? That was one of the longest days I've ever put in on a football field."[2]

Donovan's long day had its origins in Hickey's desperation. Leading up to the Baltimore game, Hickey asked his players in a team meeting who among them felt their lackluster standard offense could move the ball against Baltimore's strong defense.

No one, it turned out, including the coach.

The shotgun's debut on November 27, 1960, was as much adaptation as revolution. Its jarring appearance with the quarterback five yards behind the center broke from the T-formation which had dominated the game for 20 years, but the shotgun's genetics had traces of Pop Warner's double-wing and a whiff of the short-punt formation.[3]

San Francisco quarterback John Brodie dabbled with the formation in the first half but filling in when Brodie was hurt gave Waters the spotlight when his pass to Dee Mackey in the game's final two minutes became a game-winning improvisational lateral from Mackey to R.C. Owens, who completed the scoring play and secured the 49ers 30–22 victory over the heavily favored Colts.

The upset and continued use of the shotgun carried the 49ers to three wins in their last four games and energized an otherwise tepid 1960 campaign at the same time that some questioned if its aftershock derailed the remainder of the season for the two-time defending world champion Colts, who went winless in their final three games after the San Francisco loss.

Surprisingly, Donovan says the Colts thought they were ready for Hickey's unorthodox approach. Their head coach Weeb Ewbank couldn't ignore the 49ers' proximity when he learned the team would prepare that week on the campus of nearby Georgetown University.

"Weeb was a pretty good detective, you know, and he found out that the 49ers were fooling around with the shotgun in practice," said Donovan.[4]

But Ewbank dismissed the advanced knowledge because he didn't think Hickey had the guts to run it, according to Mike Hickey, Red Hickey's eldest son and a former scout for the New England Patriots and New York Jets in the 1970s and '80s.[5]

Despite the bang implied by its name, most everyone outside of San Francisco seemed unimpressed with the shotgun and to understand the frequency of its use is to imagine the arrival of some breakthrough creating a short-lived fanfare before slipping into obscurity, only to pervasively re-emerge nearly a generation later.

Even in defeat, Ewbank called the formation "rinky-dink."[6]

Red Hickey, meantime, didn't know what to call it. He first blandly said that it was "spread right and spread left," but quickly amended that, to the delight of headline writers across the country.

"Well, I'm an old country boy, and I used to go hunting with a shotgun," he said. "How about we call it the shotgun?"[7]

The name stuck; the method did not. Other teams failed to embrace any committed use of the shotgun, and even Hickey scuttled the formation prior to the 1963 season, calling it a "gone goslin [sic]."[8]

Aside from Dallas Cowboys head coach Tom Landry's infrequent use of the formation in 1963, and a more developed attempt in 1966 under Hickey's guidance when the former 49ers coach became a Dallas assistant, the shotgun remained a sentimental relic until 1975, when Landry began using it again in Dallas, this time regularly when his offense faced an obvious passing situation.

That 1970s permutation of the shotgun, which deviated from the original conception by keeping a running back in the pocket as an additional pass blocker, developed without Hickey's input, despite him still being a Dallas staff member.[9]

"I don't have anything to do with [the shotgun] this time," Hickey told the *Los Angeles Times* in 1975. "But I did help Tom with it when he used it in the 1960s."[10]

Today, nearly every team playing at every level uses the shotgun, giving every game of football Red Hickey's indelible stamp of influence.

Hickey's influence on another development tied to his legacy is less clear.

In the late 1950s, the 49ers' offense included as part of its arsenal, a high arching pass from quarterback Y.A. Tittle to the aforementioned R.C. Owens. The idea was to float a throw in Owens' direction at the end of a pass pattern, but unlike most pass plays drawn on a grid connecting two points, the alley-oop was an air-ball lobbed in three-dimensional space. The 6'3" Owens relied on his basketball rebounding skills to outleap defenders for the ball, pulling down what looked more like an errant satellite than a precision pass. It was effective at times, but hardly infallible.

Though Hickey, the 49ers' ends coach at the time, gets credit for creating the play, his thumbprint doesn't appear on the evidence. Later histories include the alley-oop on Hickey's resume, but the day's contemporary news reports do not.

Many stories point to the alley-oop originating during a 49ers practice in 1957.

Depending on the source, Tittle was either instructed to mimic the high-altitude passing style of Rams quarterback Norm Van Brocklin to help prepare the team for that week's game against Los Angeles or, growing so frustrated with his receivers' inability to make a catch in practice, aimed for the clouds out of exasperation, come what may.

When Owens however made the catch, Red Hickey yelled from the sidelines, "Hey! That's our alley-oop play," according to Dan McGuire, the 49ers' director of publicity at the time.[11]

Or maybe not.

Tittle couldn't confirm that story. Although someone apparently shouted "alley-oop," Tittle was never certain who said it.[12] Nevertheless, following that game against the Rams, Owens' teammates were calling him their "'Alley-Oop' man because he goes way oop [sic] for the ball."[13]

Another historical thread pulls the first "alley-oop" to a point earlier that year in a preseason game against the Chicago Cardinals, when a ball that slipped from Tittle's hand floated high in Owens' direction where he ultimately made a scoring reception.[14]

Yet another alley-oop origin tale points to two touchdown catches Owens made in 1954 while playing for the College of Idaho in a comeback win over Linfield College of Oregon.

"I thought the quarterback had put up a duck, but Owens jumped high, reached down over the defender, and took the ball away for a touchdown," said Dennis Anderson, a Linfield player that day and a future journalist. "I hadn't ever seen that done before, and I didn't see it done again until he played for the 49ers."[15]

Owens should know. Right?

In 2007, he said the alley-oop came out of that '57 practice.[16] But he also attributed the play's beginnings to that preseason game against the Cardinals.[17]

Whatever the case, Owens said it was Tittle[18] who suggested to Hickey that the pass enter the 49ers' playbook. Which it did, but even that fact is fuzzy, with some sources identifying the call as "West Four Right"[19] or "Fifty-One … Y Right … RIP … Alley-Oop."[20]

As the elements of the story swirl, keep in mind that Hickey was not the 49ers head coach when the alley-oop debuted and developed through '57. That was Frankie Albert, who also held the position in 1958 when a curious press during training camp wanted to know how the team planned to use the play in the coming season.

But Albert wasn't at the camp's opening. He was home with a case of the mumps,[21] so the press turned to Hickey, who without saying so seems to have unwittingly created the impression that the alley-oop was a product of his imagination.

Regardless of the play's mythology, its history points more to a happy accident, born of slippery circumstances or desperation, but not design.

"It was the mistake of a lifetime," said Tittle's daughter, in her book about her father.[22]

Howard (Red) Hickey was born in Hickeytown, Arkansas, a community named for his paternal grandfather. He played football and basketball in college for the Arkansas Razorbacks from 1938 to 1941 and was inducted into the Arkansas Sports Hall of Fame in 1968 and the University of Arkansas Sports Hall of Honor in 2000.

A sixth-round draft choice of the Philadelphia Eagles in 1941, Hickey was sent to Pittsburgh before the start of the season. He played in the Steelers' 1941 opener but was then sold to the Cleveland Rams the following week.[23] After nine games with the Rams, military service interrupted Hickey's NFL career. A lieutenant (j.g.) in the U.S. Navy, Hickey served as a gunnery officer on a Liberty ship and played for two service teams, Great Lakes in 1942 and Bainbridge in 1943 and 1944.[24]

He rejoined the Rams in 1945 and had his best season in his final year as a pro when he caught 30 passes for 509 yards and seven touchdowns in 1948. When Rams head coach Clark Shaughnessy released Hickey from the team prior to the 1949 season, he immediately hired him as an assistant. "We're going to build up our coaching staff through our own personnel wherever possible," said Shaughnessy.[25]

After six years as a Rams assistant, a tenure that included the team's 1951 championship season, Hickey left for a similar position in San Francisco. He eventually replaced Frankie Albert as the 49ers' head coach, compiling a 27–27–1 record from 1959 to 1963.

"Since I was a little boy, I've always dreamed of becoming a head football coach," said Hickey when the team announced his three-year contract in December 1958.[26]

Hickey resigned his head coaching job three games into the 1963 season and finished his career with a long tenure in Dallas, first as a Cowboys assistant from 1964 to 1965, and then as the team's chief national scout from 1966 to 1982.

Hickey died on March 30, 2006. He was 89 years old.

Eddie Kotal
—RYAN C. CHRISTIANSEN

It's natural to conclude that a professional football team is a manifestation of its principal leader, perhaps the head coach or the quarterback, or in the case of the earliest pro teams, of the region and of the men who showed up to play. But the 1951 Los Angeles Rams were the first of a new breed of teams that bore witness to the efforts of ownership and management and more primarily, its player scout, Eddie Kotal.

After the Cleveland Rams won the NFL championship in 1945,[27] the team moved to Los Angeles for the 1946 season,[28] and while making that move, Rams owner Dan Reeves hired Kotal to be his head player scout and de facto general manager.[29]

Born in 1902[30] in Chicago Heights, Illinois,[31] Kotal had been a star college football[32] and basketball[33] player at Lawrence College, now Lawrence University, in Appleton, Wisconsin, so much so the *Green Bay Press-Gazette* dubbed Kotal "the Lawrence Flash."[34] He was a star professional football player[35] who played on the Green Bay Packers' 1929 championship team,[36] a standout semi-professional basketball[37] and baseball player[38] in the state of Wisconsin, and a title-winning college football[39] and basketball[40] coach at Central State Teachers College, now the University of Wisconsin–Stevens Point.

While at Stevens Point in 1938, Kotal, with his eye for talent, recruited Ted Fritsch,[41] who later played in the NFL for Green Bay[42] and who is a member of the Packer Hall of Fame,[43] out of Spencer, Wisconsin. Fritsch had never played football before.[44]

After he left Stevens Point, Kotal returned to the Packers in January 1942[45] and joined Curly Lambeau's staff.[46] He was named the offensive backfield coach,[47] but he was a true first assistant for Lambeau as he was put in charge of a split squad in August 1942 when the Packers traveled to play exhibition games against the Brooklyn Dodgers[48] and the Washington Redskins.[49] By 1944, Kotal began moonlighting as an advance scout and on at least one occasion he scouted the University of Wisconsin for Purdue University.[50] Lambeau, too, began using Kotal to scout upcoming NFL opponents in 1944[51] when the Packers won the NFL championship.[52] By 1945, Kotal had become a celebrity of sorts as the press started asking for (or Lambeau started offering up) tidbits from Kotal's advance scouting.[53]

In the middle of the 1946 season, on October 11, 1946, the Rams announced they had hired Kotal to be the Rams' head player scout.[54] By the end of the 1946 season, after

38   Part 1: The City and the Organization

1951 Rams Coaching Staff (left to right): Head Coach Joe Stydahar and assistant coaches Hampton Pool, Eddie Kotal, Ray Richards, and Howard (Red) Hickey.

Adam Walsh was fired, there were rumors that the Rams might make Kotal the team's head coach.[55]

Kotal was the first full-time scout in the NFL,[56] which was unheard of at a time when the NFL draft was only a decade old and when many teams still used *Street & Smith's* college football yearbook and other magazines[57] like *College Football Illustrated*[58] and *Stanley Woodward's Football*[59] as well as college press releases[60] and All-America teams in newspapers[61] as resources for decision-making. At the time, the most-prepared teams scouted colleges within their own region[62] and only occasionally a team might send an assistant to watch a college football game, and so teams largely relied upon what they'd heard about players through word-of-mouth, and teams with longevity relied on former players for advice. Some teams offered finder's fees for discovering talent.[63]

Reeves, however, had a simple mantra for success for the Rams: Find the best players and then find the coach who can get the most out of their talents. And because his franchise would be new to Los Angeles, he recognized how he needed superstars to entice spectators to the games.[64] In Kotal, Reeves found a driven individual who shared an obsession with uncovering talent, and both men enjoyed jokes and parties,[65] and so the bushy-browed, neatly dressed and groomed card player[66] was a perfect fit for the job. For Reeves, the thrill of seeing young talent shine on the football field was the big payoff for his investment in Kotal and in scouting.[67]

In 1946, Kotal set about becoming the prototype of the modern scout while other teams continued to rely on college football magazines for information well into the 1950s and 1960s, sometimes marking up the pages with additional notes.[68] He slept little[69] and he was rarely seen in the Rams' front offices while he drove all over the country, as much as 40,000 miles to evaluate as many as 4,000 college students each year,[70] and at least one year he was only home two days out of nine months of travel.[71] He set out in the spring with the goal of documenting every senior in college football,[72] as well as standout freshmen and sophomores,[73] at major universities[74] and he spent 200 days a year visiting college campuses to watch players perform.[75] He'd observe training camps, and then on weekdays during the regular season he would visit with coaches, watch game film, and gather data, and on Saturdays, he'd watch the games.[76]

Kotal got along with everyone, and he set out to build relationships with coaches.[77] He would fish, golf, and go to church with them when he visited, and he'd spend time with their families in their homes and play with their kids. He'd remember what the coaches liked to eat and smoke.[78] And unlike the salesmen they occasionally met with, the coaches actually looked forward to having lunch with Kotal as he made his rounds.[79] The coaches Kotal befriended were more than willing to provide him with information.[80]

As he made his rounds, Kotal befriended sportswriters, too, and he would use his visits as opportunities to promote the Rams, but instead of talking up the Los Angeles team, Kotal would give a nod to the local talent where he visited, and sportswriters took the bait. After visiting with sportswriter Don Bryant of the *Lincoln Star*, Bryant noted in his column how, at the local diner, Kotal smiled at the cute waitress while she refilled his coffee cup and, in the same breath, he praised University of Nebraska football talent. "And Eddie Kotal—a fellow who sees a great deal of football—should know what he's talking about," wrote Bryant.[81] In Des Moines, sportswriter Tony Cordaro covered how Kotal had been looking at players on the semi-professional teams there, including former Iowa State Teachers College running back Paul DeVan and how Kotal had attended the Minnesota-Iowa college game while he was in Iowa.[82] DeVan later signed with the Rams.[83]

But Kotal didn't only scout football players while promoting the Rams. Somehow, he found time in his schedule to be the technical director for a film[84] titled *Easy Living*,[85] which involved spending hours coaching actor Victor Mature[86] how to pose as a quarterback throwing the ball from a leap.[87] Kotal scouted Notre Dame's Jerry Cowhig to be the body double for Mature for action shots.[88] Kotal also played the role of Curly in the film.[89]

While traveling, Kotal sent his data back to the Rams' organization, and they kept his documentation in black notebooks that hung on all four walls of a room in the Rams' front office.[90] Kotal's office, too, looked like a library.[91] To supplement Kotal's empirical research, the Rams paid college coaches, too, over 100 of them, to mail in reports twice a year, and the Rams sent out questionnaires to schools and players, and they built a library of dossiers.[92] In short order, the Rams divided the country into six sections on a map, and hired a head scout in each section to oversee the reconnaissance of the dozens of men they dubbed "bird dogs."[93] It's possible the Rams had more people working on finding talent in 1950 and in 1951 than all other NFL franchises put together.[94]

At the Rams' front office, the staff would pore through Kotal's reports looking for players and ranking them on "size, speed, ability, and desire"[95] to find the few hundred best players available, but they wouldn't just make a list. Instead, when team executives arrived at the designated hotel for the annual draft, they would hire bellhops to help haul in their trunks full of notes.[96] Soon, other teams purchased trunks, too, if only to appear as organized.[97] But Reeves was always one step ahead of the competition in terms of finding new ways to improve scouting,[98] and the Rams were the first franchise to have telephones at their draft table so they could obtain last-minute information and so they could speak to players directly to confirm their availability.[99] Reeves and his chief of staff, Tex Schramm,[100] also started the "take the best player available" philosophy at a time when other teams continued to draft for needs at positions.[101] In fact, they would draft the best athlete no matter whether that player would be available to play the following season due to conflicts with college eligibility or military duties.[102] For example, the Rams drafted Norm Van Brocklin even though they already had Bob Waterfield.[103] Their strategy for drafting Van Brocklin began in December 1947, when Kotal opened an envelope with a questionnaire returned by Van Brocklin when he was a sophomore at the University of Oregon. Kotal discovered in the form that the talented young quarterback hoped to graduate in 1949, ahead of schedule, so Kotal kept the information close to his vest until November 15, 1948, when the Rams drafted Van Brocklin in the fourth and final round of the NFL's secret early draft for the 1949 season.[104]

Impressed by Reeves' operation, other teams eventually tried to copy the Rams, and the Rams' system became the forerunner to the computerized systems that followed.[105] Some coaches wondered if their jobs might have been easier if things had never changed, because before Kotal and Reeves had started pushing things forward, coaches had been fairly successful at finding talent, anyway, and didn't care much if talent lay hidden in places they didn't care to look.[106]

But Kotal cared. The fact he signed the first black player from a black college to the NFL[107] is an example of his drive. In most cases, NFL coaches and scouts were simply ignorant of players in black colleges, mainly because newspapers didn't even mention them, except for perhaps a score.[108] But in 1947,[109] when Kenny Washington (who in 1946 was the first black player to be signed by the Rams[110] and by the NFL since 1933[111]) brought to Kotal a clipping from a black press newspaper about a fullback who had scored 25 touchdowns in one season for Grambling, Kotal pounced. At the time, he had never heard of Grambling, "but I could multiply, and 25 times six is still 150 points, and I don't care if a guy scores them against The Little Sisters of the Poor. I got me a plane ticket and a road map and I went down to see that boy play." Kotal went to see Paul "Tank" Younger, an athlete who resembled the legendary Bronko Nagurski in ability and utility,[112] play in the black-college Vulcan Bowl in Birmingham, Alabama, on New Year's Day in 1948. After that visit, Kotal started scouting black colleges, too. "It was apparent to me then that Negro college teams were coming up," Kotal told *Ebony* in 1970.[113] He defied conventions by befriending black college coaches and scouting their athletes, and he came to understand that despite having fewer resources and support than the mostly-white colleges—and despite the fact sportswriters largely ignored the black schools—colleges like Grambling played "good schedules" and their coaches were scholars of the game.[114]

Kotal met with Younger after the game, sent him a questionnaire, and kept his eye on him through his senior season. The Rams didn't bother to draft Younger, but Kotal's interest and persistence paid off, and in 1949, Younger became the first black college athlete to sign an NFL contract.[115] He became part of the Rams' "Bull Elephant" backfield along with another black player, "Deacon" Dan Towler,[116] with Kotal as backfield coach—a responsibility Kotal held from 1950 to 1953.[117]

In truth, Kotal must have been apprehensive about signing an athlete from a black college, because legendary Grambling head coach Eddie Robinson told Kotal, "Just give him the ball in practice. You make sure they get to see him run and then stop worrying because nobody is going to cut that boy off your squad."[118] Years later, *Ebony* magazine noted Kotal as a powerful influence in making football a racially integrated sport,[119] and by 1970, all-black or predominantly black colleges had become regular stops for NFL scouts.[120]

Ever-driven, Kotal continued to expand his footprint. As Roger Treat stated in *The Official National Football League Football Encyclopedia* in 1952, "No lazy big league scout can safely park himself in any one particular stadium, nor section of the country, and hope to bite his initials on the stars of the future."[121] Kotal searched for the stars, and within Reeves' system—which placed less emphasis on level of competition—he was able to find players in the smaller schools that other teams overlooked.[122] The Rams drafted Towler, for example, out of Washington & Jefferson in the 25th round in 1950. Towler went on to lead the Rams in rushing from 1951 to 1953.[123] In 1951 the Rams used a 19th round draft pick on a defensive end named Andy Robustelli from Arnold College. Robustelli went on to earn a bust in the Pro Football Hall of Fame.[124]

Because Kotal also helped to promote the Rams wherever he went, sportswriters like Paul Zimmerman at the *Los Angeles Times* took notice of his work as a scout. Zimmerman wrote, "Eddie Kotal, the Rams chief bush beater, can take a bow over the success of the rookies.... Look where some of them came from.... Norb Hecker, defensive back, hails from Baldwin-Wallace.... That's hard by Cleveland, but the Browns missed him.... Andy Robustelli, another end, came from Arnold College ... wherever that is. Don Simensen, tackle, played at St. Joseph's.... That's a tiny school in Minnesota.... And Tom Dahms, another tackle, hails from San Diego State.... Not exactly a big school in football ways."[125] Kotal also found Larry Brink at Northern Illinois State,[126] Eddie Meador at Arkansas Tech, Deacon Jones at South Carolina State,[127] and Bill Smyth at Cincinnati.[128]

But Kotal didn't only look at college athletes. In the 1950s, the Rams signed players who had served in the U.S. military[129] and who played service ball, including defensive tackle Gene "Big Daddy" Lipscomb, defensive back Dick "Night Train" Lane, and running back "Touchdown Tommy" Wilson.[130]

And Kotal didn't only look at football players, either. For the 1950 season, the Rams signed track star Bob Boyd from Loyola of Los Angeles who went on to play seven years as a receiver.[131] In 1955, they drafted K.C. Jones, a basketball player at the University of San Francisco who chose to play in the NBA, instead.[132] And they took Olympic gold medal-winning decathlete Rafer Johnson,[133] who did not play.[134]

And as if he hadn't already looked under every rock under the sun for talent, Kotal kept his eye on local Los Angeles area high school football players, too. In fact, 11 of the 35 players on the 1951 Rams' squad were from the Los Angeles area, including Bob Waterfield, Tom Fears, Woodley Lewis, Don Paul, Harry Thompson, Jack Finlay, Glenn Davis, Bob Boyd, Tom Dahms, Leon McLaughlin, and Vitamin T. Smith.[135]

Kotal's work paid off quickly,[136] and after half a decade of scouting and drafting, the Rams had assembled a powerhouse. Years before other teams had even begun to get organized in discovering new talent, the 1951 Rams had two great quarterbacks, the two best receivers in the NFL, and a fast and hard-charging backfield, all on one team.[137] And much of the credit for that team belonged to Kotal.[138] He brought in the talent that helped the Rams to compete in three consecutive NFL championship games, in 1949, 1950, and 1951,[139] and again in 1955.[140] During that span the Rams were 56–23–5.[141] The 1950 Rams' team set a list of all-time, single-season franchise and individual records, and the 1951 Rams' championship team had an offensive line made up entirely of rookies,[142] including Dick Simensen (left tackle), Dick Daugherty (left guard), Leon McLaughlin (center), Bill Lange (right guard), and Tom Dahms (right tackle). The Rams' defensive tackle corps in Jim Winkler, Jack Halliday, Bobby Collier, and Charlie Toogood were also rookies that year.[143] At one point, the Rams' backups were likely the second-best team in the league,[144] which allowed the Rams to trade away talent to acquire additional high draft picks, at a high rate.[145] The Rams were so deep in talent in 1952 they could afford to trade eleven players to Dallas for rookie lineman Les Richter, also a Hall of Famer.[146] When the Rams reached the championship game again in 1955, Lambeau gave Kotal and Reeves credit for the Rams' success.[147] And former Chicago Cardinals personnel director Ray Geraci said the Rams had made the rest of the league "look like we came from the boonies."[148] According to Schramm, some years the Rams would put together a list of the top 20 players in the country and would draft 10,[149] and he felt the Rams should have won every championship game they participated in.[150]

The Los Angeles Rams were no fairy tale. The front office was the stage of a power struggle between team owners, and the Rams went through five head coaches from 1950 through 1965. Hamp Pool,[151] head coach from 1952 to 1954,[152] and Sid Gillman, head coach from 1955 to 1959,[153] said the team had a dearth of good coaches in a sea of great talent. The Rams became a de facto personnel procurement service for the rest of the league.[154] The list of players who went on to play elsewhere is significant: Robustelli and Harland Svare went on to play for the Giants, Lipscomb and Billy Ray Smith for the Colts, Don Burroughs and Van Brocklin[155] for the Eagles,[156] Joe Marconi, Larry Morris, and Billy Wade[157] for the Bears,[158] and Frank Ryan[159] for the Browns.[160] In the Rams' organization, existing players were always fearful up-and-coming talent would replace them. The Rams tended to cut players when they were just entering their prime.[161]

It's not only in hindsight that we see how well Kotal did as a scout—and how the Rams' success in scouting would come back to haunt them. In 1951, *Los Angeles Times* sports editor Braven Dyer was prescient when he wrote, "Some of the nation's top grid coaches will be tearing their hair out faster than ever this fall…. Why?… Because of The Los Angeles Rams…. They probably won't win 'em all but they'll ruin a lot of good teams, sure as sin…. Give Eddie Kotal, chief talent scout, a boost…. The task of cutting that big squad is one which Joe Stydahar does not relish…. The tragedy of it is that he'll send away guys who'll be stars on other teams and may turn and beat him within a few weeks."[162]

By 1957, Kotal grumbled that the rest of the league had caught on to scouting.[163] By 1958, he was driving 25,000 miles per year by automobile and putting on 50,000 miles by plane, and he racked up "enormous" telephone bills as he catalogued 8,000 players a year.[164] And in 1960,[165] Schramm took what he learned from Reeves and Kotal to Dallas.[166] By 1961, the Rams were spending $100,000 annually on scouting operations.[167]

Kotal retired to live in North Hollywood, California. He loved golfing and playing cards,[168] and on January 27, 1973,[169] he died of a heart attack while playing gin rummy after a round of golf at a country club near his home.[170]

In 2011, Kotal was nominated for the Pro Football Hall of Fame.[171]

Hamp Pool
—BRYAN LUTES

> "As professional football evolves … the elements that make the game sparkle today can be traced to Los Angeles, California … where the modern pro offense was born. Offensively, The Los Angeles Rams were decades ahead of their time."—John Facenda, Best Ever Teams (NFL Films, 1981)

The Los Angeles Rams had won the 1951 NFL title, and the postgame gathering was underway. Hampton Pool was in his element, greeting people, backslapping old friends, making his way around the room. "When out of sight of his players," wrote Bob Oates of the *Los Angeles Examiner*, "he was invariably courteous, a gracious, friendly companion. Socially, he was the life of the party. An invitation to Hamp Pool, in fact, insured the success of any party."[172]

Compare this scene to the following season: Hamp Pool's first year as head coach of the Rams saw the defending champions overcome a slow start by winning the final eight games on the schedule to force a playoff with the Detroit Lions. A dramatic 4th quarter punt return score by Verda "Vitamin" Smith had brought the Rams to within three points of the Lions, but a time-consuming drive by Detroit culminated with Bob "Hunchy" Hoernschemeyer's nine-yard touchdown run and dashed the Rams' hopes for a second straight world championship. On the long plane ride back to Los Angeles, Pool was seen sitting on the floor of the airplane. "What are you thinking about, Hamp?" a sportswriter asked. The coach replied matter of factly: "Wouldn't it be wonderful if we ran into a mountain?"[173]

If anything, Hamp Pool was a complicated man. As Rams linebacker Don Paul said, "He is the greatest guy in the world on a social occasion; witty, gentle, vivid conversationalist. But when the football season is on he doesn't want to be bothered by anybody or anything until he's won the title."[174]

Pool's football experience was as diverse as his own personality. He played six different positions (end, guard, center, halfback, fullback and quarterback) at three different colleges (Stanford, California, and West Point). He was a reserve end for the great Chicago Bears teams of the early 1940s for four seasons, participating in the title game every year. Perhaps Pool's first brush with genius was the 1940 title game against the Washington Redskins, with Bears head coach George Halas utilizing Stanford coach Clark Shaughnessy as an "offensive consultant" prior to the game. Shaughnessy's modifications to the Bears' T-formation offense worked beautifully against the Redskins, as the 73–0 final tally attests. Pool and Shaughnessy would cross paths in the future, albeit indirectly.

Pool's NFL playing career ended after the 1943 season. The next two years saw Pool serving as a player-coach for the Fort Pierce Naval Amphibious Base during the end of World War II. The start-up of a new football league in 1946, the All-America Football Conference (AAFC), allowed Pool to resume his professional playing career with the Miami Seahawks. Disorganized and underfunded, the Seahawks were the weakest team in the fledgling league, and Pool found himself as the head coach of this ragtag operation in week seven after a dismal 1–5 start. The Seahawks allowed the most points in the AAFC, scored the fewest, but Pool got his first taste of coaching in the professional ranks leading the Seahawks to a 2–6 record over their last eight games. The next stop on Hamp's itinerary was Chicago, to be an assistant coach on Jim Crowley's staff with the AAFC Rockets. Unfortunately, the 1947 Rockets were even worse than the 1946 Seahawks, posting a 1–13 record. Pool moved to the West Coast, with the years of 1948 and 1949 being spent as an assistant coach at San Jose State University and later San Bernardino Valley College, setting the stage for Pool's return to the NFL.

A phone call to Los Angeles Rams head coach Clark Shaughnessy in the aftermath of the Rams' 1949 NFL title game loss to the Philadelphia Eagles put the wheels in motion for Hamp Pool's arrival. The 1949 Rams represented the future of the NFL. Shaughnessy's innovative schemes and some impressive newcomers (Elroy Hirsch, Tank Younger, Norm Van Brocklin, to name a few) took the league by storm. After six weeks, the Rams were in first place in the Western Division with a 6–0 record, including two wins over the hated Chicago Bears. Opposing defenses started adjusting to Shaughnessy's multiple formation offense, breaks started going the other way, and a 1–2–2 mark over the next five games put the dream season in jeopardy. The Rams had to win their final game of the regular season against Sammy Baugh's Washington Redskins to earn the right to play the Philadelphia Eagles for the league title. Clark Shaughnessy's maniacal approach and countless hours of practice paid off, as the Redskins' defense was ambushed. Quarterbacks Bob Waterfield and Norm Van Brocklin combined for six touchdown passes and the Rams tallied 584 yards of total offense in a 53–27 romp.

The high-flying Rams fell back to muddy earth in the league title game and were drowned by a quagmire and the power running of Eagles star Steve Van Buren, losing 14–0. Clark Shaughnessy was still getting phone calls of congratulations for capturing the 1949 divisional crown when another call came ... the one telling him that assistant Joe Stydahar was replacing him as head coach. Foreshadowing Hamp Pool's future hiring as the Rams' top man, Shaughnessy's response to this news was to claim that Stydahar had stolen his job.[175]

Although the firing of Shaughnessy was surprising to those outside the organization, player discontent had been constant throughout the season. There were new additions to the Rams' playbook on a weekly basis, leading Bob Waterfield to comment, "If he can sit down and write out 50 per cent of the plays he has given us this year, I'll learn the new stuff. Otherwise, nuts."[176] Shaughnessy was not a "people person," and viewed his players more like X's and O's on a chalkboard than individuals. Excessively long practices, a lack of connection with his players, and a general inability to relate to human beings is what sealed Shaughnessy's fate. These same charges would be brought against a future Rams head coach named Hampton Pool a few years later.

Many times an NFL team will replace a head coach with a person who is the opposite of his predecessor, and the Rams' hiring of Joe Stydahar was one of these instances. Whereas Shaughnessy was a strategist, the gruff Stydahar was a CEO and organizer. Shaughnessy was seen as the enemy to the players; Stydahar was a player's best friend. Shaughnessy was aloof; Stydahar wore his emotions on his sleeve. Yet for all of Stydahar's morale boosting and collegiate rah-rah style, an underrated aspect of his success was his ability to put together a top-notch coaching staff. His most important and perhaps most inspired hiring was Hampton Pool. As linebacker Don Paul put it, "Joe was a big happy guy, the nice guy, good with the press. Pool was the guy who worked his butt off and handled the offense and defense."[177]

Pool and Stydahar were teammates on the legendary Monsters of the Midway 1940s Chicago Bears clubs, and furthermore were close friends. Stydahar made Pool his top assistant heading into the 1950 season. Pool immediately got to work, paring down the old Clark Shaughnessy playbook to a more reasonable number of alignments and plays. A key trade prior to the season gave the Rams a new look on offense. Starting right offensive end Bob Shaw was sent to the Chicago Cardinals in exchange for the rights to tackle Bob Reinhard. The Rams finally had two quality tackles in Reinhard and Dick Huffman. In addition, Elroy Hirsch was moved from halfback to right end. Better pass protection and a deep receiving threat transformed the Rams' offense from being very good in 1949 to being one for the ages in 1950.

Pool retained Shaughnessy's approach of using multiple formations with and without motion. "We had all kinds of formations," Pool said. "We used quite a lot of the slot formation—with the halfback just outside the linemen and off the line of scrimmage. Then we'd put the other halfback in motion the other way. This would leave us with only one setback, the fullback, to block on pass protection. But we would get four men into deep patterns in a hurry and we would just eat them up. The defenses we were facing were exclusively man-to-man, and no one person could stay with Hirsch or Fears. One game [against the Colts], we scored seventy points."[178] Hamp also added some of his own wrinkles to the existing offense. For instance, the 1950 Rams successfully employed a tackle-eligible play. "We had a backwards offense," Pool once remarked. "We reversed the usual procedure so that instead of our running setting up the passing, our passing set up the runs, such as draws and the Statue of Liberty. Even against Browns we ran the Statue several times. Our quarterback would fake a pass and hand off to one of our quick little halfbacks on a reverse."[179]

Perhaps Pool's greatest singular achievement of that season occurred in the NFL title game against the Cleveland Browns. During the week of practice leading up to the game, he had installed a new play. "The Browns used a 5-3-3 alignment and we set out to take advantage of it as quickly as possible," Pool recalled. "We sent a man-in-motion to the right and had Fears, our left end, break inside. We knew they'd be watching Tom very closely, perhaps be a little over conscious. We kept Glenn Davis, our other halfback, in the backfield for a moment as if he was going to block. We'd hoped the Browns' linebacker responsible for his coverage would see that and then be more concerned with Fears right off the bat."[180] On the Rams' first play of the title game, Davis paused for a moment, then veered out of the backfield and raced down the sideline. The Browns defense was fooled, Waterfield lofted a perfect pass downfield, and Davis wasn't touched on the 82-yard scoring effort. The clock read 14:33. In 27 seconds, Hamp Pool's offense accomplished something which the New York Giants couldn't in 60 minutes of action during their conference playoff against the Cleveland Browns the previous week: score a touchdown.

While the 1950 Rams fell tantalizingly short of their ultimate goal, losing to the Browns 30–28, confidence abounded heading into the 1951 season. As Pool himself said, "When you start talking about Van Brocklin and Waterfield at quarterback, running backs like Dick Hoerner, Tank Younger, Deacon Dan Towler, Vitamin T. Smith, Glenn Davis, and receivers like Tom Fears, Elroy Hirsch, Bob Boyd—why, it sounds like you're listing an all-star team."[181] While the cast of characters remained virtually the same from 1950, the Rams' offense in 1951 would continue to evolve, much to the dismay of opposing defenses. Fears had been terrorizing the league over the past two seasons with his intricate short routes (and occasional utilization of another Hamp Pool wrinkle—the shovel pass), hauling in 77 and 84 receptions. Defenses began countering Fears' effectiveness with double coverage, which facilitated Elroy Hirsch's historic 1951 season.

Rams quarterbacks were given time to throw deep from their offensive line, which uniquely had rookie players manning all five starting positions. This might have seemed like a recipe for disaster on a lesser team, but the Rams had great offensive line mentors in Stydahar and positional coach Ray Richards. The Rams' pass protection scheme had the linemen maintain a wide base to wall off opposing pass rushers, and pulling offensive guards were used to block defensive ends, while the offensive tackles countered the defensive tackles. The result was the Rams having the fewest sacks allowed in the NFL in 1951.

Despite a roster that had more stars than the Western Sky, the driving force behind the Rams offense was Hampton Pool. His adeptness at game planning and strategy did not go unnoticed by Rams players. "He was a fine technician, a designer and architect of excellent plays," according to Fears. "He prepared us for our games very well. If a team didn't change some things against us, we'd hit 'em in their weak spot and run up a big score."[182] Comparing Pool to Shaughnessy, Hirsch remarked that Shaughnessy "tried to teach too many plays and formations. It was difficult to absorb them all. Pool liked to play wide open like Shaughnessy, but Hamp had more of a game plan. More of a ready list, you might say, on offense."[183] Added Stydahar, "I hate to think of the long hours Hamp Pool spent in designing plays for Bob Waterfield and Norm Van Brocklin. To my way of thinking, Pool is the best young coach in football."[184]

Pool often worked late into the night devising new offensive schemes, as alluded to by Stydahar's comment. Perhaps we can credit Hamp Pool with another innovation; while "situation substitution" on seemingly every down has become commonplace in both the pro and college games, Pool utilized this concept in a key 1951 rematch against the rival San Francisco 49ers. Elroy Hirsch sets the scene: "The 49ers had just clobbered us, 44–17, at Kezar Stadium, and by a quirk in the schedule we had to face them again the following Sunday at the Coliseum. Buck Shaw inserted two fleet halfbacks as his outside linebackers and they matched our halfbacks pound for pound and speed for speed. Coach Stydahar and his staff knew that every team in the league could come up with the same kind of answer and stop us. But at Tuesday's practice, a countermove jelled. The Rams had not one, not two, but three of the biggest, strongest, fastest and most devastating fullbacks at the time. So Younger was playing defense and Towler was alternating at fullback with Hoerner. Then came the idea. Why not use them all at once?"[185]

In the rematch with San Francisco, Pool had his alternate backfield at the ready. When San Francisco went with small, quick outside linebackers Jim Powers and Verl Lillywhite, Coach Pool countered this San Francisco defensive alignment with his situation substitution of Younger, Hoerner and Towler, who became known as the "Bull Elephant" backfield. The outcome was a vital 23–16 revenge victory. Tank Younger remembers, "Frank Finch of the *Los Angeles Times* gave us the name. And, to be honest, I rather enjoyed it. Dick Hoerner, Dan Towler and myself were all about the same size, between 225 and 230 pounds. We were about similar in speed, too, although Dan was probably a bit faster. He could run about a 9.8 100. We could all go inside or outside, and we could catch a forward pass. When we were in there, our offense was not in the least restricted."[186]

Though Coach Pool would alternate his substitutions, the "Bull Elephants" reached their peak against the Bears in Wrigley Field for an important late-season matchup. The Bears had none other than Clark Shaughnessy coaching their defense. Stydahar wanted this win very badly, as Shaughnessy's parting words in 1949 still rung in his ears. The Rams trailed early 14–0, but a beautifully-executed play action pass from Bob Waterfield to Elroy Hirsch covered 91 yards and had Los Angeles back in the game. It was then that the "Bull Elephants" took over. Two hundred and three rushing yards, 133 receiving yards and 3 touchdowns later, the backfield trio of Younger, Hoerner and Towler left the field triumphantly, basking in a 42–17 demolition of the hated Bears (and Clark Shaughnessy).

"There's never been a backfield like it," said Hirsch. "Imagine, three sprinters, weighing a total of 666 pounds, bulling their way downfield together. Two of them, shoulder to shoulder, blocking for a third, and all of them capable of matching speed with most of the league's top halfbacks."[187]

The 1951 championship would be the apex for this group of Rams players, as 1952 would bring about radical change to both Hampton Pool and the Rams organization.

Stydahar leaned heavily on Hamp Pool, placing Pool in charge of both the offense and the defense. As the Rams had success, it was Pool's name that dominated the newspaper stories. He was the one regarded as the young genius, not Stydahar. Furthermore, after the title-winning 1951 season, Stydahar became convinced that Hamp Pool was after his job. In training camp prior to the 1952 season, Don Paul recalls that Stydahar told him "I've got to fire Pool." When Paul asked Stydahar why he was being told this, the response was "Well, I have got to get the defenses; you're the only one who has 'em."[188] Instead of dismissing Pool, Stydahar reclaimed the responsibility for the offense and the defense for the 1952 season. In the opening game, the Rams were trounced by the Browns, 37–7. Afterwards, Stydahar allegedly issued an ultimatum to team owner Dan Reeves: either I go, or Pool goes. Reeves promptly elevated Hampton Pool to head coach, which led Stydahar to tell Sid Ziff of the *Los Angeles Mirror,* "I'll hate Hamp Pool until the day I die."[189]

For his part, Pool had this to say: "I couldn't convince Joe, haven't to this day, that I didn't want the job. I had everything just the way I wanted it. I could involve myself in the technical side of football, which I loved, and never had to talk to the press or fool with any other administrative duties."[190]

Reeves' decision seemed to pay off. After a slow start of going 1–3 in their first four games, the Rams caught fire and won eight straight, forcing a playoff with the Detroit Lions. As usual, Pool's offensive brilliance had the Rams leading the league in points, but perhaps the catalyst for the 1952 Ram resurgence was their defense. Amazingly, the Rams scored defensive touchdowns in seven games during their eight-game win streak. An unknown rookie named Dick "Night Train" Lane set the all-time record with 14 pass interceptions.

The Rams under Hamp Pool were hitting on all cylinders by the end of the year. In a game that Pool would call the toughest defeat he ever had to suffer, the Rams faced the Lions in Detroit to determine who would battle the Cleveland Browns in the 1952 NFL championship and lost 31–21. Detroit would go on to defeat the Browns the following week. Perhaps history would have been kinder to both Hamp Pool and the Rams had they been able to win this game.

As it stood, the Rams were still a force to be reckoned with in 1953. Pool was back as head coach. The defense had Hall of Fame caliber players in Andy Robustelli and Night Train Lane. Bob Waterfield had retired, but Norm Van Brocklin was more than capable of assuming the full-time quarterbacking responsibilities.

It can be argued that Hamp Pool's 1953 Rams were the best 3rd place team in NFL history. Be that as it may, it was ultimately a failure of a season. The Rams exacted a measure of pay back from the Lions for their 1952 playoff loss, winning both regular season matchups in 1953 by scores of 31–19 and 37–24. Unfortunately, the inconsistent Rams also lost games to weaker teams and finished out of the postseason with an 8–3–1 mark. Some of the blame for the disappointing season could be laid on Pool, as he stretched himself too thin by maintaining responsibility for both the offense and the defense.

If 1953 could be characterized as disappointing, then 1954 would have to be characterized as disastrous. Joe Stydahar had moved Night Train Lane from offensive end to defensive back during the 1952 training camp, and since then Lane had spearheaded an aggressive Rams defense. But Lane wasn't happy in Los Angeles. Comparing Stydahar to Pool, Lane said Stydahar "was great with the players. He understood them. But the Rams had other problems. Anyway, Hamp Pool eventually replaced Stydahar as head coach, and, well, I didn't do so well for him. He was different than Stydahar. I don't think he cared for the players."[191] Lane wasn't a big fan of Hamp Pool, and apparently the feeling was mutual as before the 1954 season, Pool shipped Lane to the Chicago Cardinals (coached by Joe Stydahar). Lane went on to lead the NFL with 10 interceptions that year, while the Rams struggled all season with their pass coverages. Another questionable move by Pool had him relieving Tank Younger of his linebacking duties and using him full-time on offense. The result of these changes was a 6–5–1 record, a fourth-place finish, and a defense that ranked 10th out of 12 teams in points allowed.

The year of 1954 would be Hampton Pool's last season as Rams head coach. The failure to rekindle the championship fires of 1951 was complete, as encapsulated by the pair of games the Rams played against a poor Baltimore Colts squad in 1954. The Rams had no trouble with the Colts in the season opener, winning 48–0 while totaling 563 yards to Baltimore's 196 yards. The rematch was a trickier proposition, as the Colts and their pedestrian quarterbacks of Cotton Davidson and Gary Kerkorian riddled the Rams defense with short passes. Pool never adjusted to this tactic, and the mighty Rams fell to the meek Colts, 22–21, in an embarrassing loss. Perhaps this was the reason why owner Dan Reeves did not hesitate to accept Hampton Pool's resignation after the regular season had concluded.

Pool was keenly aware of the emotional aspect of the sport. He worked with Stanford University's Center for Advanced Study in the Behavioral Sciences and created personality tests for his players, which again is an accepted practice nowadays but at the time was thought to be a waste of resources. "I felt it gave a coach a better understanding of an individual on his team," Pool said. "It made it easier for a coach to treat him as an individual and understand him better."[192] Unfortunately, these personality tests had the opposite effect, driving a wedge between the coach and his players. "That man is two men," said Tank Younger. "Maybe more. From January to July you couldn't meet a sweeter guy. But after football starts, I don't know what happens to him. He hardens up like this here ground."[193] Pool also recalled that the player reaction to his weekly posted performance chart was problematic: "It was my personal opinion that we could eliminate errors by pinpointing the breakdown of plays to individual responsibility. This way, we had the breakdown of each play signaled out in rating form. Naturally, this created quite a furor among our players and then it was brought out in the press which was my undoing and eventually cost me my job."[194]

For a man who had a short shelf life as an NFL head coach, Hampton Pool would seemingly fit right in with the modern NFL. He popularized the flankerback position. He was an early proponent of offensive personnel groupings at the dawn of the free-substitution era. He believed in sending multiple receivers into pass routes, looking for favorable matchups. Don Paul said of Pool, "He was the best technical coach I ever ran across. He had charts broken down in those days that some teams are just starting to use today. Everyone likes to talk about how hard head coaches work today. Let me tell you, no one ever worked any harder than Hamp."[195]

Despite his contributions to professional football, Pool's NFL head coaching career lasted only 35 games. Looking back on his time with the Rams, "I realize now there are a lot of things I should have done differently," Pool recollected. "I should have spent less time on the field, held fewer meetings, kept everything simpler. I would change the offense every week to fit the opponent. I was a stickler for detail. Football should be a simple game, really, more the way Lombardi had it at Green Bay. My way, there was too much to learn and not enough time to learn any of it."[196]

A maverick to the end, Hamp never had a formal contract with the Rams. When he sent his resignation to owner Dan Reeves after the 1954 season, he asked for no compensation. Reeves offered six months' salary as a settlement. Pool took it and departed. Later, Elroy Hirsch gave a succinct yet appropriate summation of Hampton Pool's tenure, "I can honestly say I didn't realize how good a coach Pool was until I got out of football."[197]

Pool later coached the Toronto Argonauts in Canada to a 10–25 record from 1957 to 1959, before returning to the NFL as an assistant under new Rams head coach Bob Waterfield in 1960. Another players' revolt in 1962 ousted him from coaching for good. He went on to form the Quadra Scouting Agency in 1964, and that combine provided the Rams, Cowboys, 49ers and Chargers data for 20 years.

Ray Richards
—JOE ZIEMBA

Just prior to the start of the 1951 NFL championship game at the Los Angeles Coliseum, Ray Richards settled into the worst seat in the house.

Or maybe it was the best....

Perched high above the playing field, Richards, the highly regarded line coach for the Rams, was about to take advantage of one of the newer technologies available at that time in the NFL: the telephone. With four coaches scattered in the upper echelons of the Los Angeles Coliseum, head coach Joe Stydahar was able to access strategic information immediately from his spotters, including Richards. Reporter Jack Geyer bravely accompanied Richards (along with fellow assistant coach Hampton Pool) and was quickly impressed: "Richards and Pool, who watched the game through rose-colored binoculars, poured advice into the phone, pointing out [Cleveland] Brown weaknesses and Ram mistakes. The plays the coaches called were like old cigarette lighters—sometimes they worked and sometimes they didn't."[198]

On December 23, 1951, most of what Richards recommended (or observed) did work for the Rams as the club slipped past the Browns 24–17 to grab the title, although some of their efforts failed to initially produce results on the field: "When the Rams couldn't score in eight plays from within the five-yard line, Pool and Richards were as frustrated as a sailor trying to button his pants with boxing gloves on," noted Geyer.[199]

No one doubted the key role that Richards played in developing the 1951 Rams' line, but just the fact that he was with the team in the first place was the result of a very odd occurrence. In January of 1951, Richards was quietly preparing his Pepperdine College football team for the upcoming season. After taking over as the Pepperdine head coach in 1949, Richards had compiled an 8–10 record, but was anxious to push his improving squad into a higher level of collegiate competition. As a former assistant coach at UCLA for a decade, Richards was admired for his skills in developing players and identifying flexible means to utilize the talent of his linemen. In fact, Richards was invited to be a guest speaker at the annual football awards dinner sponsored by the Scholastic Sports Association in Los Angeles on January 20, 1951.[200] Yet before Richards could unveil his carefully prepared remarks, he learned that his job had been terminated by Pepperdine athletic director A.O. Duer due to the "national emergency." With the escalation of the Korean conflict around this time, Duer called for a "temporary adjustment" of the football program and handed the reins of the team over to basketball coach Robert Dowell. Little of this made much sense to the average football fan, although Duer attempted to provide somewhat of an explanation: "Richards is a fine coach and we are well satisfied with the job he and his staff have done. This change is due to the necessity of cutting our athletic budget in line with prospects of decreased enrollment during the national emergency."[201]

In reality, the surprise "adjustment" initiated by Pepperdine may have been one of the biggest breaks of Richards' lengthy coaching career. Less than two months later, the Rams announced on March 8 that Richards had inked a one-year contract to serve as line coach for the team. By the time the club convened for its training camp on July 16 at the University of Redlands, it was clear that the Rams were loaded with potential—except for their inexperienced line. Yet Richards tinkered with the parts, mixed largely inexperienced veterans with newcomers, and fashioned a group that would prove effective on both sides of the ball throughout the championship campaign. But prospects were few and far between for Richards when camp opened: "The Rams undoubtedly will set a new track record for the National Football League by going into camp without a single experienced tackle. Since the close of the '50 campaign Gil Bouley, Bob Reinhard and Bill Smyth retired while Canada beckoned to Dick Huffman and Ed Champagne.... The Rams' line coach, Ray Richards, has less than a month to build up this vital department," reported the *Los Angeles Times*.[202]

Faced with the challenge of developing at least five adequate tackles (and other linemen) during the training sessions, Richards focused on team drills and individual skills in an effort to personally sculpt a front line capable of protecting the Rams' vaunted backfield. His efforts did impress assistant coach Pool who praised Richards during a community luncheon held near the end of training camp.[203]

The first big preseason test for the Rams' line was on August 15 against Washington when Richards sent out rookie tackles such as Howard Ruetz, Tom Dahms, Bobby Collier, Jim Winkler, Jack Halliday and Charlie Toogood to face the Redskins. With Winkler, Halliday, and guard Stan West leading the way, the green Los Angeles line performed admirably in helping the Rams to a surprisingly easy 58–14 conquest for which the local press indicated that Richards "can take a bow."[204] Eventually, Richards settled on a squadron of rookie offensive linemen to open the season after the Rams completed a lengthy exhibition slate. "They've done an outstanding job, considering their inexperience," Richards told the media prior to the first game.[205]

The performance of the first-year linemen was essential to the success of Los Angeles in 1951, especially when considering the critical responsibility of protecting the Rams' talented quarterbacks Bob Waterfield and Norm Van Brocklin. As the season progressed in an extremely tight National Conference race, the Rams snared the conference title with an overall 8–4 record. Despite the inexperience in the line with a bevy of rookie starters, the yearlings, under the guidance of Coach Richards, did more than enough to push the Rams to the top of the conference according to *Los Angeles Times* sports editor Paul Zimmerman: "Because of so many rookies, Los Angeles has been rather inconsistent in its play. However, the Rams never have come up with two bad games in a row. On occasion [Coach Joe] Stydahar's line—and a deep bow to Ray Richards, too—outplayed the most powerful forward walls in the league—Cleveland, Detroit, Philadelphia, New York Giants and Chicago Bears."[206]

The joy of the resulting NFL championship was short-lived, however, as head coach Joe Stydahar was ousted after just one game into the 1952 season. Stydahar was succeeded by assistant Hamp Pool, but Richards' days with the Rams were numbered. Despite a solid 9–3 record in 1952, Richards was not rehired as the Rams' line coach at the conclusion of the season. "Pool simply told me that he preferred to choose his own assistants," explained Richards. "It's something you've got to expect in this business."[207] The move to dismiss Richards was surprising considering the success of the team in recent years, but Richards was hired by Stydahar and suffered the consequences of the deteriorating relationship between Stydahar and Pool that evolved into the ouster of the former. Still, the media was kind to Richards and the work ethic that he brought to the Rams: "Richards, a former All–American at Nebraska and later a top professional tackle, did an outstanding job for the Rams, particularly in 1951 when the team won the world's championship. He faced the monumental task of rebuilding the line from tackle to tackle … the sensational play of two of Richards' rookie tackles, Tom Dahms and Don Simensen, marked the Rams' drive to the NFL title."[208]

With Richards now unemployed, albeit briefly, his long career as both a player and coach prompted possible suitors in the NFL to quickly consider adding the talented Richards to their roster of coaches. When Stydahar was named as the new head coach of the Chicago Cardinals in January 1953, he promptly sought to add Richards to his staff. However, Richards had previously verbally agreed to coach the line for the newly minted Baltimore Colts, forcing NFL commissioner Bert Bell to intercede on behalf of the Colts when Stydahar attempted to bring Richards to Chicago.[209] Following a gloomy 3–9 initial season in Baltimore, there was speculation that Richards would be named as the next head coach for the Colts, according to the *Baltimore Sun*: "Ray Richards, line coach, is a prime candidate to move into [Keith] Molesworth's job. The players love the old Chicago Bear pro for his knowledge of football and football players."[210] Instead, Richards answered the call of Stydahar and joined his former colleague from the Rams on the Cardinals' staff on January 28, 1954. It is likely that Richards might have remained in Baltimore if he had secured the head coaching position that ultimately went to Weeb Ewbank. "I liked Baltimore very much. I have made many friends there and I think it has a great future as a big-league town," said Richards upon accepting the Cardinals' position. "I'm glad to be back with Joe [Stydahar]. He is a wonderful guy. There is no one I would rather coach under."[211]

In Chicago, Stydahar and Richards were faced with salvaging a franchise that was spiraling quickly downward after back-to-back NFL championship game appearances in 1947 and 1948. The current squad in 1954 bore little resemblance to those powerful teams and, moreover, was a gutted version of the unsuccessful two-year reign (1950–51) of Curly Lambeau as head coach. Stydahar's initial effort in 1953 was a disaster (1–10–1) and even with the capable aid of Richards, the Cards stumbled to a woeful 2–10 mark in 1954, prompting his dismissal. This opened the door for Richards to finally accept his first NFL head coaching assignment with the 1955 Chicago Cardinals.

For Richards (born July 16, 1906, in Liberty, Nebraska), it was perhaps the pinnacle of a lengthy personal football experience that stretched back to his high school days at Pawnee City, Nebraska, where he was both a football and track star.[212] After high school, he moved on to the University of Nebraska where he immediately grabbed a starting spot at left tackle at the beginning of his sophomore year in 1927.[213] By 1929, he was selected as a First-Team All-America selection, played in the East-West Shrine game, and then decided to continue his football career in the NFL.[214] After getting married in the off-season (and undergoing surgery for a broken nose suffered at Nebraska), Richards joined the Frankford Yellow Jackets as the starting left tackle. However, after the season concluded, Richards embarked on a new athletic career as a professional wrestler and opted to stay out of football until 1933. Meanwhile, he earned a living traveling around the country (mostly in the Midwest) as the star attraction in wrestling events. Perhaps his most famous (or infamous) appearance took place on March 6, 1933, in Omaha, Nebraska. Richards was paired against one Jack Vincent of Oklahoma City. The match was refereed by none other than former heavyweight boxing champion Jack Dempsey and the bout was a close one with Vincent claiming the first fall and then Richards securing the second via what appeared to be a "right uppercut." Dempsey cautioned Richards against using such a tactic (punch) in a wrestling match. For the next nine minutes all was well as the grapplers pursued normal attacks in the ring. Then according to news sources, "Richards forgot all about Dempsey's admonitions and let loose another uppercut. His aim was good and Vincent promptly lost interest in the proceedings."[215]

Dempsey quickly disqualified the former Nebraska tackle and Richards lost his composure and charged after the startled referee, swinging freely at the former champ. Although Dempsey endured a few harmless punches, he managed to escort Richards into his corner and "spoke soothingly in his ears and started across the ring. Richards, apparently mollified, stood still for a few seconds, then plunged across the ring in a wild charge. He struck Dempsey amidships, others in the ring restored order."[216]

Perhaps it was time to return to football....

Although Richards continued to wrestle in the off-season, he signed with the Chicago Bears in time for the 1933 season and was rewarded with a berth on the NFL championship team of that year. He scored the only points of his NFL career when he tackled Chicago Cardinals punter Mike Koken for a safety in a 22–6 Bears win on November 30.[217] Following the conclusion of the 1933 campaign, Richards joined the Bears on a post-season tour through Texas and California. He then returned to the wrestling ring in early 1934 and crisscrossed the country taking on all comers. One of the more intriguing matches pitted Richards against his Bears teammate Bronko Nagurski. The pair met in both "tag" team and individual matches during their "vacation" time from pro football. In a prime-time matchup on March 20, 1934, the *Star Tribune* failed to make the connection between the two Chicago Bears but focused on the gridiron athletic abilities of the two grapplers: "Nagurski faces his toughest competition since embarking upon a wrestling career. The Gopher All-American has been tossing his antagonists with comparative ease, but in Ray Richards, former All-American lineman at Nebraska, he will be up against an outstanding grappler. Richards has been meeting the best of them for a number of years and will have a decided advantage in experience over the Bronko."[218]

In 1934, Richards drifted over to the Lions, appearing in just six games before bouncing back to the hazy world of professional wrestling once the NFL schedule was completed. He later offered a glimpse into both his reason for wrestling as well as for his future football plans: "Richards feels that maybe professional wrestling is more lucrative over a long period and may call the 1934 season his last on the gridiron to concentrate on wrestling more."[219] Instead of retiring, Richards decided to rejoin the fold of the Chicago Bears in 1935, reclaiming his starting slot (this time as a guard) as the Bears stumbled to a 6–4–2 record and fell out of championship contention. At the age of 29, Richards was now listed as 6'1", 230 pounds and was still a solid force in the middle of the line. However, after just one game in the 1936 season, the Bears released Richards, although he quickly found employment as a guard/line coach with the Los Angeles Bulldogs. In April of 1937, it was reported that Richards had been hired as the line coach for UCLA on the collegiate level, but that report apparently was erroneous as Richards remained with the Bulldogs in 1937.[220]

Meanwhile, Richards continued his wrestling career with several appearances around the west coast and debated whether to continue his playing career on the gridiron. A rash of stubborn injuries had nagged Richards during his brief sojourn in Los Angeles so on March 8, 1938, Richards signed a one-year contract to serve as the line coach for UCLA under veteran head coach Bill Spaulding. For Richards, it was his first experience coaching on the collegiate level except for a brief taste as an assistant coach during spring practice at the University of Wyoming in 1930.[221] The response to the appointment of Richards was immediately embraced by both the players at UCLA and the local media: "Ray Richards is making good at U.C.L.A. For little more than a week now he's been coaching those Bruin linemen for Bill Spaulding and he likes every boy on the squad. But what is more important, they like him. Without their respect and confidence, he wouldn't get to first base."[222] As part of his subtle career change, Richards vowed to retire from both playing pro football and wrestling.

For Richards, the transformation from the grizzled individuals in the pro ranks to the fresh-faced collegians was refreshing: "It's more interesting to coach college boys," Richards said. "Most of the pros figure that they know it all…. With the college players, it's different. They've played the same type of ball as freshmen as they will on the varsity, and the job is that much easier. By that I mean it's easier to coach them."[223] Richards remained at UCLA for 10 years, and enjoyed a couple of Rose Bowl appearances, until resigning in December of 1947. Stints at Pepperdine (1948–1950) and with the Los Angeles Rams (1951–1952) followed before he left the warmth of California for his new responsibilities with the Chicago Cardinals where he eventually became the head coach on June 2, 1955.

The situation in Chicago was not favorable for Richards. He favored the inconsistent Lamar McHan as his quarterback and then still maintained some backfield fireworks in speedy Ollie Matson and veteran Charley Trippi. In Richards' first season, the Cardinals improved to 4–7–1 despite dropping four of their last five contests. In 1956, the Cards showed flashes of brilliance in securing a 7–5 mark, the team's first winning season since 1949. After a 2–2 start in 1957, highlighted by a 44–14 win over the Redskins, the Cardinals dropped seven of their final eight games to finish 3–9 prompting Richards to resign as head coach on January 4, 1958.

Richards added one final season to his football resume when he joined the Green Bay Packers as the defensive coach on February 6, 1958. Packers head coach Scooter McLean was pleased to add the experienced Richards to his staff: "I've known Ray a good many years as player and coach and I know he's a good, sound football man. He knows the systems and the personnel and what to expect of opponents."[224]

During the 1958 season, it was the offense, not the defense that held back the Packers as the team finished with a 1–10–1 record, the worst in Green Bay history. Immediately after the final game, Richards announced his resignation from the club—and from football: "Football has been wonderful to me. I've had the pleasure of working with many fine men and not the least of them being Scooter [McLean]."[225] The departure of McLean soon followed, and the Packers secured their ticket to a successful future by hiring Vince Lombardi as their new coach.

Richards would never again return to coaching but was anxious to begin a new life with a new bride and an enticing job outside of football. The long days of endless hours,

Part 1: The City and the Organization

incessant travel, and the stressful pursuit of victories were over. For Ray Richards—the All-American lineman, an NFL champion as a player and coach, and a successful pro wrestler—an enviable career in sports was about to blossom into a new endeavor: general manager and vice-president of Pemaco, Inc. in Los Angeles, a firm specializing in chemical products, metal working fluids, and solvents.[226] The veteran coach passed away on September 19, 1974, in La Habra, California. He was 68 years old.

Notes

1. Bob Maisel, "The Morning After," *Baltimore Sun*, January 10, 1976, B5.
2. Maisel, "The Morning After," B5.
3. Arthur Daley, "Sports of the Times: Spiking the Shotgun," *New York Times*, October 26, 1961, 44.
4. Daley, "Sports of the Times," 44.
5. Kevin Lynch, "'Red' Hickey 1917–2006: Pioneering Head Coach," *San Francisco Chronicle*, March 31, 2006, https://www.sfgate.com/sports/article/RED-HICKEY-1917-2006-Pioneering-head-coach-2538278.php.
6. Bob Maisel, "Morning After," *Baltimore Sun*, November 28, 1960, S17.
7. Richard Goldstein, "Red Hickey, 89, Coach of 49ers; Introduced Shotgun to the N.F.L.," *New York Times*, April 3, 2006, B6.
8. Hal Wood, "Red Hickey Says Shotgun Formation, 'Now Gone Goslin,'" *Atlanta Daily World*, August 7, 1963, 5.
9. John Jeansonne, "Dallas Cowboys at New York Giants," *Newsday*, October 12, 1975, D22.
10. Dwight Chapin, "A Texas Spread: The Shotgun Formation is Back; Cowboys May Show It to the Rams," *Los Angeles Times*, August 4, 1975, III-1.
11. Dan McGuire, *San Francisco 49ers* (New York: Coward-McCann, 1960), 102–103.
12. Y.A. Tittle and Kristine Setting Clark, *Nothing Comes Easy: My Life in Football* (Chicago: Triumph Books, 2009), 135–137.
13. Art Rosenbaum, "Dejected Gillman Says Early Setbacks Hurt, Praises 49ers," *Los Angeles Times*, October 7, 1957, IV-4.
14. Sam Farmer, "49ers Receiver Who Originated the 'Alley Oop,'" *Los Angeles Times*, June 24, 2012, A33.
15. Dave Newhouse, *Founding 49ers: The Dark Days Before The Dynasty* (Kent, OH: Black Squirrel Books, 2015), 93–95.
16. Daniel Brown, "Former San Francisco 49ers Star R.C. Owens, Known for 'Alley-Oop' Catches, Dies at 77," *The Mercury News*, June 18, 2012, https://www.mercurynews.com/2012/06/18/former-san-francisco-49ers-star-r-c-owens-known-for-alley-oop-catches-dies-at-77/.
17. Farmer, "49ers Receiver," A33.
18. Jerome Crowe, "R.C. Owens' 'Alley-Oop' Catches for 49ers Were a High Right from the Jump," *Los Angeles Times*, December 12, 2010, C2.
19. Farmer, "49ers Receiver," A33.
20. Martin S. Jacobs, *San Francisco Legends: The Golden Age of Pro Football* (Scotts Valley, CA: CreateSpace, 2016), 205–206.
21. "Albert Ailing with Mumps," *Los Angeles Times*, July 27, 1958, III-3.
22. Dianne De Laet Tittle, *Giants & Heroes: A Daughter's Memories of Y.A. Tittle* (South Royalton, VT: Steerforth Press, 1995), 101, 118.
23. "Steeler End Sold to Rams," *Pittsburgh-Post Gazette*, September 9, 1941, 22.
24. "Know Your Ram and Redskin Pro Gridders," *Los Angeles Times*, August 30, 1946, I-9; John Daye, *Encyclopedia of Armed Services Football* (Haworth, NJ: St. Johann Press, 2014), 254.
25. Frank Finch, "Red Hickey Signs One-Year Pact to Coach Ram Ends," *Los Angeles Times*, April 21, 1949, IV-2.
26. "Red Hickey New Coach of 49ers," *Hartford Courant*, December 17, 1958. 17.
27. "NFL Champions 1920–2018," *Profootballhof.com*, https://www.profootballhof.com/nfl-champions/.
28. Tiffany White and Doug Kelly, "The Rams Story," *Therams.com*, November 22, 2018, https://www.therams.com/news/the-rams-story.
29. Pete Dougherty, "Packers Back, Rams 'Hound Dog' Kotal Laid Groundwork for NFL Scouting," *Green Bay Press-Gazette*, October 15, 2011, E1.
30. John Maxymuk, "Eddie Kotal," *Packers Past Perfect: History, Opinions, Imaginings*, September 1, 2016, https://packerspastperfect.wordpress.com/2016/09/01/eddie-kotal/.
31. Dougherty, "Packer Back," E1.
32. "Lawrence Football Lettermen Choose Eddie Kotal Chief," *Appleton Post-Crescent*, December 3, 1924, 15.

33. "Kotal and Briese Picked on Midwest Squad by Coaches," *Appleton Post-Crescent*, March 24, 1925, 13.

34. "Eddie Kotal Signs Football Contract with Bay Packers," *Green Bay Press-Gazette*, July 30, 1926, 24.

35. "Eddie Kotal Named on Second All-Pro Grid '11,'" *Appleton Post-Crescent*, December 17, 1928, 14.

36. David S. Neft and Richard M. Cohen, *The Football Encyclopedia: The Complete History of Professional NFL Football from 1892 to the Present* (New York: St. Martin's Press, 1991), 78–79.

37. "Eddie Kotal Signs with Star Pro Five," *Appleton Post-Crescent*, February 16, 1927, 15.

38. "Eddie Kotal Turns Down Diamond Job," *Appleton Post-Crescent*, June 1, 1928, 16.

39. John Anderson, "UW-SP To Enshrine Kotal: 'Builder of Champions' Back After 3 Decades on Sept. 30," *Stevens Point Daily Journal*, August 31, 1972, 11.

40. "Eddie Kotal, Former CSC Coach, in 13th Year as Scout for Rams," *Stevens Point Daily Journal*, March 3, 1958, 6.

41. Bill Berry, "Coach's Lasting Contribution to Football Was Colorblindness," *Wausau Daily Herald*, January 17, 1999, 4A.

42. John Maxymuk, *Packers by the Numbers: Jersey Numbers and the Players Who Wore Them* (Black Earth, WI: Prairie Oak Press, 2003), 45.

43. Cliff Christl, "Notable Undrafted Rookie Free Agents," Milwaukee Journal Sentinel, August 15, 1998, 3.

44. Berry, "Coach's Lasting Contribution," 4A.

45. "Eddie Kotal Is Named Assistant Coach of Packers," *Green Bay Press-Gazette*, January 17, 1942, 13.

46. Christl, "Notable Undrafted Rookie Free Agents," 3.

47. Dale R. Schallert, *A History of Intercollegiate Football at Wisconsin State University*, Stevens Point 1894–1964 (Winona, MN: Winona State College, August 1966), 59.

48. "Hutson to Get Award," *Daily Tribune* (Wisconsin Rapids, WI), August 28, 1942, 5.

49. "Packers Here for Big Game," *Baltimore Sun*, September 1, 1942, 17.

50. Don Unferth, "Looking 'Em Over with Don Unferth," *Daily Tribune* (Wisconsin Rapids, WI), October 17, 1944, 5.

51. Edward Prell, "Lambeau Cracks Information Line in Bears-Packers Quiz," *Chicago Tribune*, November 1, 1944, 29.

52. "Eddie Kotal, Former CSC Coach," 6.

53. "Underestimate Bear? Not Us, Asserts Coach of Packers," *Chicago Tribune*, October 31, 1945, 31.

54. "Eddie Kotal Named as Head Player Scout for Los Angeles Rams," *Oshkosh Northwestern* (Oshkosh, WI), October 11, 1946, 4.

55. "Scout Eddie Kotal Mum About L.A. Coaching Rumors," *Green Bay Press-Gazette*, December 27, 1946, 11.

56. Maxymuk, "Eddie Kotal."

57. Orlando D. Ledbetter, "The List: Five Key Influences," *Atlanta Journal-Constitution*, April 21, 2013, 2C.

58. Conor Orr, "The History of Scouting," *NFL.com*, March 18, 2015, http://www.nfl.com/historyofscouting.

59. Cliff Christl and Don Langenkamp, *Sleepers, Busts & Franchise-Makers: The Behind-the-Scenes Story of the Pro Football Draft* (1936–Present) (Seattle: Preview Publishing, 1983), 45.

60. Dougherty, "Packers Back," E1.

61. Orr, "The History of Scouting."

62. Dougherty, "Packers Back," E1.

63. Christl and Langenkamp, *Sleepers, Busts & Franchise-Makers*, 45.

64. Steve Bisheff, *Great Teams' Great Years: Los Angeles Rams* (New York: Macmillan, 1973), 19.

65. Christl and Langenkamp, *Sleepers, Busts & Franchise-Makers*, 47.

66. Jim Hock, *Hollywood's Team: Grit, Glamour, and the 1950s Los Angeles Rams* (Los Angeles: Rare Bird Books, 2016), 213.

67. Christl and Langenkamp, *Sleepers, Busts & Franchise-Makers*, 46.

68. Orr, "The History of Scouting."

69. Christl and Langenkamp, *Sleepers, Busts & Franchise-Makers*, 47.

70. Christl and Langenkamp, *Sleepers, Busts & Franchise-Makers*, 48.

71. Clark Judge, "State Your Case: Why It's Time Hall Wakes Up to Eddie Kotal," *Talkoffamenetwork.com*, October 16, 2018, http://www.talkoffamenetwork.com/state-your-case-why-its-time-hall-wakes-up-to-eddie-kotal/.

72. Michael MacCambridge, *America's Game: The Epic Story of How Pro Football Captured a Nation* (New York: Random House, 2004), 57–58.

73. "Eddie Kotal, *Former CSC Coach*," 6.

74. MacCambridge, *America's Game*, 58.

75. MacCambridge, *America's Game*, 56.

76. MacCambridge, *America's Game*, 58.

77. MacCambridge, *America's Game*, 57.

78. "Eddie Kotal, *Former CSC Coach*," 6.

79. Christl and Langenkamp, *Sleepers, Busts & Franchise-Makers*, 52.

80. Christl and Langenkamp, *Sleepers, Busts & Franchise-Makers*, 48.
81. Don Bryant, "LA Rams Scout Praises Toogood, Ray Richards," *Lincoln Star*, November 14, 1951, 16.
82. Tony Cordaro, "Pro Grid Scout Inspects D.M. Talent," *Des Moines Tribune*, November 8, 1951, 40.
83. "Paul DeVan," *Unipanthers.com*, https://unipanthers.com/hof.aspx?hof=51.
84. Arch Ward, "In the Wake of the News," *Chicago Tribune*, September 27, 1948, 37.
85. Easy Living (1949) *Full Cast & Crew*, IMDB.com, https://www.imdb.com/title/tt0041328/fullcredits.
86. Ward, "In the Wake of the News," 37.
87. "Pro Gridders Turn to Movies for Some Pay," *Pottstown Mercury*, July 10, 1948, 10.
88. Bob Myers, "Several Members of Los Angeles Grid Rams Aid to Make Movie Film," *Bradford Era*, July 10, 1948, 11.
89. Easy Living (1949) *Full Cast & Crew*.
90. Christl and Langenkamp, *Sleepers, Busts & Franchise-Makers*, 48.
91. Dougherty, "Packers Back," E1.
92. MacCambridge, *America's Game*, 58.
93. Bisheff, *Los Angeles Rams*, 14.
94. Cliff Christl, "Kotal, Vainisi Found Talent to Build Powerhouse Teams," *Packers.com*, April 28, 2016, https://www.packers.com/news/kotal-vainisi-found-talent-to-build-powerhouse-teams-17073993.
95. "Eddie Kotal, Former CSC Coach," 6.
96. Christl and Langenkamp, *Sleepers, Busts & Franchise-Makers*, 48.
97. Christl and Langenkamp, *Sleepers, Busts & Franchise-Makers*, 49.
98. Christl and Langenkamp, *Sleepers, Busts & Franchise-Makers*, 46.
99. Christl and Langenkamp, *Sleepers, Busts & Franchise-Makers*, 49.
100. Bob Oates, *The Los Angeles Rams* (Culver City: Murray & Gee, 1955), 21.
101. Judge, "State Your Case."
102. Oates, *The Los Angeles Rams*, 21.
103. Dougherty, "Packers Back," E1.
104. Bisheff, *Los Angeles Rams*, 68.
105. Bisheff, *Los Angeles Rams*, 14.
106. Orr, "The History of Scouting."
107. Christl, "Kotal, Vainisi Found Talent."
108. Alan H. Levy, *Tackling Jim Crow: Racial Segregation in Professional Football* (Jefferson, NC: McFarland, 2003), 101.
109. Christl and Langenkamp, *Sleepers, Busts & Franchise-Makers*, 50.
110. A.S. "Doc Young," "The Black Athlete in the Golden Age of Sports: Part VIII Pro Football Discovers the Black College," *Ebony*, September 1970, 117.
111. Hock, Hollywood's Team, 102–103.
112. Young, "The Black Athlete," 117.
113. Maxymuk, "Eddie Kotal."
114. Young, "The Black Athlete," 117.
115. Young, "The Black Athlete," 117.
116. Judge, "State Your Case."
117. Maxymuk, "Eddie Kotal."
118. Jerry Izenberg, "A Whistle-Stop School with Big-Time Talent," in *Football: Great Writing About the National Sport*, edited by John Schulian, 119–134 (New York: Library of America, 2014).
119. "UWSP Hall of Famer Eddie Kotal Considered for Pro Football Hall of Fame," *Athletics.uwsp.edu*, October 28, 2011, https://athletics.uwsp.edu/news/2011/9/29/GEN_0929114428.aspx.
120. Young, "The Black Athlete," 117.
121. Roger Treat, *The Official National Football League Football Encyclopedia* (New York: A.S. Barnes, 1952), 347.
122. Pete Williams, *The Draft: A Year Inside the NFL's Search for Talent* (New York: St. Martin's Griffin, 2007), 44.
123. Dougherty, "Packers Back," E1.
124. Williams, *The Draft*, 44.
125. Paul Zimmerman, "Sportscripts," *Los Angeles Times*, September 28, 1951, IV-1.
126. Maxymuk, "Eddie Kotal."
127. Judge, "State Your Case."
128. John Anderson, "UW-SP To Enshrine Kotal: 'Builder of Champions' Back After 3 Decades on Sept. 30," *Stevens Point Daily Journal*, August 31, 1972, 11.
129. Dougherty, "Packers Back," E1.
130. Judge, "State Your Case."
131. Williams, *The Draft*, 44–45.
132. Judge, "State Your Case."
133. Christl, "Kotal, Vainisi Found Talent."

134. Sports Reference LLC, *1959 NFL Draft*.
135. Shav Glick, "On Prayer and a Pass, a Title Came to Town," *Los Angeles Times*, August 30, 1991, C1.
136. Treat, *The Official National Football League Football Encyclopedia*, 232.
137. Bisheff, *Los Angeles Rams*, 28.
138. Glick, "On Prayer and a Pass," C1.
139. MacCambridge, *America's Game*, 57.
140. Dougherty, "Packers Back," E1.
141. "Cleveland/St. Louis/LA Rams Franchise Encyclopedia," *Pro-football-reference.com*, https://www.pro-football-reference.com/teams/ram/.
142. Judge, "State Your Case."
143. Christl and Langenkamp, *Sleepers, Busts & Franchise-Makers*, 51.
144. Orr, "The History of Scouting."
145. Christl and Langenkamp, *Sleepers, Busts & Franchise-Makers*, 51.
146. Judge, "State Your Case."
147. Hock, *Hollywood's Team*, 214.
148. Judge, "State Your Case."
149. Mickey Herskowitz, *The Golden Age of Pro Football: NFL Football in the 1950s* (Dallas: Taylor, 1990), 54.
150. Christl, "Kotal, Vainisi Found Talent."
151. Christl and Langenkamp, *Sleepers, Busts & Franchise-Makers*, 53–54, 56.
152. "Rams Coaches through the Years," *Losangeles.cbs.local.com*, September 8, 2016, https://losangeles.cbslocal.com/photo-galleries/2016/09/08/rams-coaches-through-the-years/
153. "Sid Gillman," *Profootballhof.com*, https://www.profootballhof.com/players/sid-gillman/.
154. Judge, "State Your Case."
155. Judge, "State Your Case."
156. "Norm Van Brocklin," *Pro-football-reference.com*, https://www.pro-football-reference.com/players/V/VanBNo00.htm.
157. Judge, "State Your Case."
158. "Billy Wade," *Pro-football-reference.com*, https://www.pro-football-reference.com/players/W/WadeBi00.htm.
159. Judge, "State Your Case."
160. "Frank Ryan," *Pro-football-reference.com*, https://www.pro-football-reference.com/players/R/RyanFr00.htm.
161. Christl and Langenkamp, *Sleepers, Busts & Franchise-Makers*, 53–54, 56.
162. Braven Dyer, "Sports Parade," *Los Angeles Times*, August 28, 1951, IV-1.
163. Maxymuk, "Eddie Kotal."
164. "Eddie Kotal, Former CSC Coach," 6.
165. Pro Football Hall of Fame, Tex Schramm.
166. Judge, "State Your Case."
167. Judge, "State Your Case."
168. Christl and Langenkamp, *Sleepers, Busts & Franchise-Makers*, 47.
169. Maxymuk, "Eddie Kotal."
170. Christl and Langenkamp, *Sleepers, Busts & Franchise-Makers*, 47.
171. "UWSP Hall of Famer Eddie Kotal."
172. Steve Bisheff, *Great Teams' Great Years: Los Angeles Rams* (New York: Macmillan, 1973), 37.
173. Bisheff, *Los Angeles Rams*, 37.
174. Mickey Herskowitz, *The Golden Age of Pro Football* (New York: Macmillan, 1974), 61.
175. Bisheff, *Los Angeles Rams*, 32.
176. Bisheff, *Los Angeles Rams*, 18.
177. Herskowitz, *The Golden Age of Pro Football*, 59.
178. Herskowitz, *The Golden Age of Pro Football*, 59.
179. Jack Clary, *Great Teams' Great Years: Cleveland Browns* (New York: Macmillan, 1973), 65.
180. Clary, *Cleveland Browns*, 67.
181. Herskowitz, *The Golden Age of Pro Football*, 58.
182. Bisheff, *Los Angeles Rams*, 106.
183. Bisheff, *Los Angeles Rams*, 110.
184. Bisheff, *Los Angeles Rams*, 35.
185. Bisheff, *Los Angeles Rams*, 144.
186. Bisheff, *Los Angeles Rams* 32.
187. Herskowitz, *The Golden Age of Pro Football*, 60.
188. Herskowitz, *The Golden Age of Pro Football*, 60.
189. Bisheff, *Los Angeles Rams*, 36.
190. Herskowitz, *The Golden Age of Football*, 60.

58   Part 1: The City and the Organization

191. Bisheff, *Los Angeles Rams*, 37.
192. Bisheff, *Los Angeles Rams*, 126.
193. Bisheff, *Los Angeles Rams*, 36.
194. Bisheff, *Los Angeles Rams*, 126.
195. Bisheff, *Los Angeles Rams*, 122.
196. Herskowitz, *The Golden Age of Pro Football*, 61.
197. Bisheff, *Los Angeles Rams*, 110.
198. Jack Geyer, "Party Line Aids Rams in Finding Weak Spots," *Los Angeles Times*, December 24, 1951, IV-2.
199. Geyer, "Party Line," IV-2.
200. "More Honors for Charley Black," *Desert Sun*, January 19, 1951, 8.
201. "Richards Out, Name Dowell Wave Coach," *Los Angeles Times*, January 20, 1951, III-3.
202. Frank Finch, "Sixty Players Go After Thirty-Three Ram Jobs," *Los Angeles Times*, July 16, 1951, IV-3.
203. "Pool Praises UR Training," *San Bernardino County Sun*, August 2, 1951, 34.
204. Frank Finch, "Rams Rest After Romp Over 'Skins," *Los Angeles Times*, August 17, 1951, IV-1.
205. Frank Finch, "Rams Rookie Tackles Make Coach Look Good," *Los Angeles Times*, September 25, 1951, IV-3.
206. Paul Zimmerman, "Sportscripts," *Los Angeles Times*, December 6, 1951, IV-1.
207. Frank Finch, "Pool Lops Off Richards as Rams' Line Coach," *Los Angeles Times*, December 31, 1952, IV-1.
208. Finch, "Pool Lops Off," IV-1.
209. "Cards Select Joe Stydahar," *Baltimore Sun*, January 30, 1953, 17.
210. Cameron C. Snyder, "Colts Head West Today," *Baltimore Sun*, December 3, 1953, 27.
211. Cameron C. Snyder, "Ray Richards Named Cards Line Mentor," *Baltimore Sun*, January 28, 1954, 15.
212. "Record List for State Hi Meet," *Lincoln Sun*, May 2, 1925, 8.
213. Floyd Olds, "Huskers Impress in Yearling Battle," *Nebraska State Journal*, September 25, 1927, 5.
214. "Football Lettermen," *University of Nebraska, Official Athletics Website*, https://huskers.com.
215. "Dempsey Learns About Wrestling," *The Dispatch*, March 7, 1933, 12.
216. "Dempsey Learns," 12.
217. "Bears Close to Pro Title," *Decatur Daily Review*, December 1, 1933, 17.
218. "Famous Matmen on Card Here Tonight," *Star Tribune*, March 20, 1934, 15.
219. "Ray Richards Back to Mat Wars Tuesday," *Minneapolis Star*, December 7, 1934, 27.
220. "Ray Richards Will Be Line Coach at U.C.L.A.," *Fresno Bee*, April 5, 1937, 10.
221. "Richards to Assist Rhodes at Wyoming," *Lincoln Journal Star*, March 1, 1930, 8.
222. Frank Finch, "Ray Richards Scores Hit Coaching Bruin Front Wall," *Los Angeles Times*, March 16, 1938, II-11.
223. Finch, "Ray Richards Scores," II-11.
224. "Packers Name Ray Richards Defense Coach," *Rhinelander Daily News*, February 6, 1958, 8
225. Art Daley, "Richards, Packer Aide, Quits Grid," *Green Bay Press-Gazette*, December 15, 1958, 37.
226. Al Wolf, "Richards Raves About Matson," *Los Angeles Times*, August 17, 1959, IV-1.

Building the 1951 Rams

Matthew Keddie

As Otto Graham took the snap on the game's final play, Rams head coach Joe Stydahar was intensely focused on the field, as the Rams held a seven-point advantage over the Browns. This back-and-forth contest with the defending champion Browns had been like a heavyweight title bout from start to finish.

Suddenly, moving to his right, Graham lateraled the ball to Ken Carpenter on the near side of the field.[1] Carpenter gripped the football tightly and heaved it with everything he had, launching the ball downfield to Dante Lavelli. The ball sailed wide of Lavelli, falling incomplete. The game was over. The Rams' bench emptied, as players and coaches embraced one another, jumping up and down in celebration. Stydahar could finally relax as he was engulfed in handshakes, fighting his way through the crowd to midfield.[2]

The 1951 Los Angeles Rams were champions of the football world. The 24–17 defeat of the Cleveland Browns went beyond the final score. The Rams not only ended the Browns' reign atop the pro football world, but the title was the first pro sports championship for the city of Los Angeles and the Rams first triumph in three consecutive tries in the league championship game.[3]

Were these Rams among the greatest teams of all-time? They had the talent and the leadership and demonstrated their worthiness by dethroning the defending NFL champions, exacting revenge on the Browns after Cleveland had beaten them, 30–28, in the 1950 championship game, with the outcome hinging on a late field goal victory for Cleveland. Cleveland had won four consecutive AAFC titles (1946–1949) prior to joining the NFL.[4]

Cleveland coach Paul Brown was a good sport about the loss. "Paul Brown walked into the L.A. locker room and shook Tom Fears' hand. 'Here's the guy who did it, right here.'" Cleveland was bound for a loss, according to Brown. "We lost a football game, that's all. We played as hard as we could.… It was a strange day. But that's part of the business. We've had a strange day coming for some time."[5]

How did this Rams franchise, just six years removed from Cleveland, reach the top? The Rams were constructed primarily by discovering talent through the draft. They also made several key undrafted free agent signings that proved successful. Team owner Dan Reeves, an innovative entrepreneur, was mostly responsible for building the team. Twenty-three members of the 1951 championship team were drafted by the Rams, three were obtained via player transactions and eight were signed by the Rams as undrafted free agents. (See tables below.)

Reeves developed an interest in football during his early years, starring as the team captain at the Newman School in New Jersey. The daily grind instilled a strong work ethic in him, molding his ruthless and driven personality. Reeves worked in his father's grocery store chain and joined the ownership ranks of pro football in 1941 when he acquired a stake in the Cleveland Rams. With his fiery nature and bold actions, Reeves always sought to improve his club.[6]

The mercurial Reeves tended to have rocky relationships with his coaches and routinely cut players if he felt the need. No player or coach was safe, but his demanding personality led to innovation. He was the first to employ scouts full-time, in order to obtain insight on college players. Reeves stated, "There were four teams—New York, Green Bay, Chicago and Washington—that had been very successful and were getting a lot of information from their alumni." Reeves decision rapidly paid off. Quarterback Bob Waterfield was drafted in 1945 and won the NFL championship as a rookie, just eight years after the Rams joined the league.[7]

Reeves' choice for coach was Joe Stydahar. Stydahar grew up in a blue-collar family in Shinnston, West Virginia, where coal mining was the means of a living.[8] He had outstanding athletic ability that led him from collegiate ball at West Virginia University to the NFL. Joe earned respect from his peers and had a reputation as a "vicious tackler and a bruising blocker."[9] As a result, he developed into a Hall of Fame left tackle for the Chicago Bears.

Due to his extensive NFL experience, Stydahar was brought in to coach the Rams' offensive line in 1947 under Bob Snyder.[10] Snyder was replaced by Clark Shaughnessy in 1948, but by 1950, Dan Reeves was upset with Shaughnessy for causing "internal friction" inside the organization. Thus, Stydahar was promoted to lead the team. Stydahar was successful in simplifying the playbook. "The primary principle of Halas' offense is that the running attack must go. I'm not going to give the boys more plays than they can understand or remember."[11]

The Rams' rush offense kept it simple in 1951, improving its average by a full yard per carry from 4.2 to 5.2, and from ranking eighth in total rushing yards to third overall. The "Bull Elephant" backfield of Dick Hoerner, Paul "Tank" Younger, and Dan "Deacon" Towler benefited greatly from Stydahar's improvements to the offensive line. The trio totaled 1,646 rushing yards and 13 rushing touchdowns in 1951.[12]

Towler was drafted by the Rams late in the 1950 draft, 324th overall out of a small Western Pennsylvania college, Washington & Jefferson. Towler was a steal for Los Angeles, as he was a dominant back early in the 1950s, finishing in the top four in rushing from 1951 through 1954. Towler would lead the Rams in prayer in his six seasons, attending the University of Southern California's School of Religion while he played in Los Angeles.[13]

Younger attended Grambling State University in Louisiana, where he played linebacker, tackle, and running back and was coached by the legendary Eddie Robinson. Collie Nicholson, Grambling's sports information director, recalled Younger's play at the time. "It was just after World War II, I was watching him run over everybody he couldn't run around. I'd been a marine in the South Pacific, and it reminded me of what I saw those tanks doing down there."[14] Younger went undrafted because historically black schools such as Grambling were ignored by NFL scouts. However, the Rams signed Younger as a free agent in 1949, making him the NFL's first player from a historically black school. This took place about a year after Rams super scout Eddie Kotal watched Younger play in the Vulcan Bowl.[15]

The third running back in the trio, Dick Hoerner, played collegiately for the Iowa Hawkeyes and was drafted by the Rams in the 1945 draft with the 169th overall pick. He was the fourth ranked rusher in the NFL in 1951 based on yards per carry.[16]

Then there were the two starting halfbacks. Vitamin Smith signed with the Rams as a free agent from Abilene Christian in 1949, while Jerry Williams was a seventh-round selection, 63rd overall, from Washington State by the Rams in 1949.

Los Angeles featured two highly skilled quarterbacks: Bob Waterfield and Norm Van Brocklin. Waterfield was not highly touted or recruited coming out high school but was a very hard worker and earned his stripes. He walked on at UCLA and set six school records in football, leading to the Rams selecting him in the 5th round of the 1944 draft. In his first season, he won the league MVP and led the Rams to the 1945 championship over the Washington Redskins.

Waterfield was a versatile athlete for the Rams in 1951. Not only did he star at quarterback, but also was the team's placekicker, while ceding his regular punting duties to Van Brocklin that year after being the Rams' regular punter from 1945 to 1950.

Teaming with Waterfield was Norm Van Brocklin. Akin to Waterfield, the Dutchman was a versatile athlete as well. Van Brocklin was a skilled quarterback in college at the University of Oregon, foregoing his senior year after being drafted 37th overall by the Rams during the 1949 draft because he had enough credits to graduate. He impressed at Oregon, earning All-America status during his junior year, and finishing sixth in voting for the Heisman Trophy.[17]

Waterfield and Van Brocklin enjoyed the services of two talented and gifted receivers. Elroy "Crazylegs" Hirsch was the fifth overall selection in the 1945 draft from the University of Michigan, by the Rams. However, he initially signed with the Chicago Rockets of the All-America Football Conference and spent three seasons in the Windy City before jumping to the Rams in 1949. Tom Fears was also taken in the 1945 draft by the Rams, 103rd overall, as a local product from UCLA.

Los Angeles' starting offensive line was composed of all rookies. Left tackle Don Simensen was signed by Los Angeles in 1951 as a free agent. He played college ball at St. Thomas College. Left guard Dick Daugherty was an 18th round draft selection in 1951, 217th overall, from Oregon. Center Leon McLaughlin was also drafted by the Rams. The local UCLA product was chosen in the 1947 draft in the 21st round, 193rd overall. However, by the time he was ready to try the pros, Washington had obtained his rights, so the Rams needed to reacquire those rights in 1951. Right guard Bill Lange from Dayton was a late round pick by the Rams in the 1950 draft, 389th overall. Tom Dahms, the right tackle, was signed in 1951 as a free agent out of San Diego State College.

Likewise on defense, the Rams acquired most of their talent via the draft, with 10 of 11 starters taken that way. All but two-way linebacker/running back Tank Younger were drafted between 1947 and 1951.

The Rams slowly built their 1951 defense, beginning with linebacker Don Paul selected in the 1947 draft, 21st overall in the third round from UCLA. Los Angeles selected defensive end Larry Brink in the 1948 draft with the 150th overall choice from Northern Illinois University. Defensive tackle Jim Winkler and defensive halfback Jerry Williams both were drafted in 1949; Winkler was chosen 27th overall, in the third round from Texas A&M, but his road to Los Angeles was winding. He had also been drafted by San Francisco of the AAFC, so when the leagues merged, his rights were in dispute. In a convoluted pair of deals involving Glenn Davis described below, he became a Ram.

The 1950 draft saw Los Angeles select two starters: middle guard Stan West, twelfth overall; and Oklahoma and defensive halfback Woodley Lewis, taken at 103rd from Oregon. Defensive tackle Jack Halliday was taken 54th from SMU by the Colts and was obtained by the Rams later.

The 1951 draft rounded out the Rams' starters with end Andy Robustelli, 228th, from tiny Arnold College in Connecticut and defensive backs Norb Hecker at 72 and Herb Rich at 24. Hecker played ball at Baldwin-Wallace College in Ohio. Rich played collegiately at Vanderbilt and was originally drafted in the sixth round by Baltimore in 1950. After the Colts folded, Los Angeles nabbed him in the second round in 1951.

The Rams reserves were signed between the 1947 and 1951 seasons. Defensive end Jack Zilly was chosen 32nd in the 1945 draft and joined the team in 1947. Guard/defensive tackle Jack Finlay was signed as a free agent from UCLA in 1947. In 1948, end/defensive back Tom Keane was taken at 18 overall. In 1949, the Rams acquired running back and kick returner Tommy Kalmanir from the Pittsburgh Steelers for Don Samuel.[18] End/defensive back Bob Boyd signed with the club in 1950 as an undrafted free agent out of Loyola Marymount, as did guard Harry Thompson of UCLA. Defensive tackle Bobby Collier was selected at 233 in the 1950 draft from SMU. Charlie Toogood from Nebraska was selected with the 35th pick in the 1951 draft, and linebacker/guard Joe Reid from LSU came with the 156th pick. Marvin Johnson was also a free agent signee in 1951 from San Jose State.

Lastly, Heisman Trophy winner Glenn Davis, celebrated halfback known as "Mr. Outside" at West Point, was acquired in a trade with the San Francisco 49ers, alluded to above. Both the Niners and Rams held the rights to several players. Davis was originally drafted by the Lions with the second overall pick in 1947, while the 49ers took him with a bonus pick that same year. In September 1947, Reeves sent Detroit the Rams' first round pick in the 1948 draft for the rights to Davis. Then, on January 21, 1950, Los Angeles gave San Francisco Jim Winkler and Emil Sitko for their rights to Davis. On February 25, 1950, the Rams reobtained Winkler by ceding the rights to Hillary Chollet and Clay Matthews, Sr., to San Francisco.[19]

The 1951 Rams benefited greatly from drafting and developing young talent. Tom Keane gave much of the credit to chief scout Eddie Kotal. "There was no such thing as draft combines in those days. Kotal was the guy who found players like Andy Robustelli at Arnold, Tank Younger at Grambling—he was the first player ever signed from Grambling—and Larry Brink from North Illinois State. He was always finding great players in out-of-the-way places."[20]

Key decisions made by management, such as intensive scouting of collegiate athletes and utilizing a two-quarterback system paid off for the club, culminating in an impressive championship run. The Rams also were buoyed by starting an all-rookie offensive line, which was another testament to the efficacy of Dan Reeves' scouting program. When mentioning the greatest teams in league history, this Rams' squad has to be in the conversation.

Table 1. 1951 Rams Drafted by Los Angeles

Name	Position	Year	Round
Bob Waterfield	QB	1944	1
Elroy Hirsch	E/HB	1945	1
Jack Zilly	DE	1945	4
Tom Fears	E	1945	11
Dick Hoerner	FB	1945	17
Don Paul	LB	1947	3
Leon McLaughlin	C	1947	21
Tom Keane	E/DB	1948	3

Name	Position	Year	Round
Larry Brink	DE	1948	17
Jim Winkler	DT	1949	3
Dan Towler	FB	1949	4
Norm Van Brocklin	QB	1949	4
Jerry Williams	HB/DB	1949	7
Stan West	MG	1950	1
Woodley Lewis	DB	1950	8
Bobby Collier	DT	1950	18
Bill Lange	G	1950	30
Herb Rich	DB	1951	2
Charlie Toogood	T/DT	1951	3
Norb Hecker	DB	1951	6
Joe Reid	G/LB	1951	13
Dick Daugherty	G	1951	18
Andy Robustelli	DE	1951	19

Table 2. 1951 Rams Signed by Los Angeles as Undrafted Free Agents

Name	Position	Year
Jack Finlay	G/DT	1947
Vitamin Smith	HB	1949
Tank Younger	FB/LB	1949
Bob Boyd	E/DB	1950
Harry Thompson	G/DT	1950
Tom Dahms	T	1951
Marvin Johnson	DB	1951
Don Simensen	T	1951

Table 3. 1951 Rams Whose Rights Were Acquired from Other Teams

Name	Position	Original Team
Tommy Kalmanir	HB	Steelers
Glenn Davis	HB	Lions
Jack Halliday	DT	Colts

Notes

1. "1951 NFL Championship Game," *Youtube.com*, https://www.youtube.com/watch?v=mafG3kFJ56U.
2. Michael MacCambridge, *America's Game* (New York: Anchor Books, 2005), 82.

3. Scott Harrison, "From the Archives: The L.A. Rams Beat the Cleveland Browns for 1951 Championship," *Los Angeles Times*, January 5, 2018, https://www.latimes.com/visuals/photography/la-me-fw-archives-la-rams-beat-cleveland-browns-for-1951-championship-20171107-story.html.

4. "Cleveland Browns Franchise Encyclopedia," *Pro-Football-Reference.com*, https://www.pro-football-reference.com/teams/cle/index.htm.

5. "NFL Championship Games 1951: Cleveland Browns @ Los Angeles Rams," *Golden Football Magazine*, http://goldenrankings.com/nflchampionshipgame1951.html.

6. "Dan Reeves Biography—Brought First Major Team to West Coast, Hired George Allen, Chronology, Awards And Accomplishments," *Sports.jrank.org*, http://sports.jrank.org/pages/3826/Reeves-Dan.html.

7. Edwin Shrake, "A Private Eye on the New Rams," *Sports Illustrated*, October 3, 1966, https://www.si.com/vault/1966/10/03/610637/a-private-eye-on-the-new-rams.

8. Robert White, "Football Great Stydahar Dies, Had Planned to Live in Beckley," *Beckley Post-Herald*, March 25, 1977, 17.

9. Harry Grayson, "Joe Stydahar," *Muncie Evening Press*, November 12, 1935, 10.

10. "Joe Stydahar to Help Tutor L.A. Rams' Line," *Green Bay Press-Gazette*, February 7, 1947, 13.

11. "Stydahar to Be Coach of Rams," *The News*, February 20, 1950, 10.

12. "1951 Los Angeles Rams Statistics & Players," *Pro-Football-Reference.com*, https://www.pro-football-reference.com/teams/ram/1951.htm.

13. Dick Strite, "Highclimber," *The Eugene Guard*, August 7, 1957, 37.

14. Richard Goldstein, "Tank Younger, 73, First Star from Black College to Play in N.F.L., Dies," *New York Times*, September 19, 2001, 15.

15. Christopher Dabe, "Tank Younger, Grambling's Iconic First NFL Player, is No. 22 Among the Top 51 Louisiana Athletes," *New Orleans and Louisiana Sports*, July 31, 2014, http//www.nola.com/sports/index.ssf/2014/07/tank_younger_top_51.html.

16. "Dick Hoerner," *Pro-Football-Reference.com*, https://www.pro-football-reference.com/players/H/HoerDi00.htm.

17. "Van Brocklin Pitches L.A. Rams to Victory," *Spokane Daily Chronicle*, December 24, 1951, 10.

18. Shay Glick, "Tommy Kalmanir, 78, Halfback on L.A. Rams' '51 Championship Team," *Los Angeles Times*, October 15, 2004, http://articles.latimes.com/2004/oct/15/local/me-kalmanir15.

19. "Pro Sports Transactions," *Pro Sports Transactions*, http://www.prosportstransactions.com/football/Search/SearchResults.php?Player=&Team=rams&BeginDate=1944-01-01&EndDate=1952-01-01&PlayerMovementChkBx=yes&submit=Search&start=225.

20. Shay Glick, "On Prayer and a Pass, a Title Came to Town: History: Forty Years Ago, the Rams Won Los Angeles' First NFL Championship," *Los Angeles Times*, August 30, 1991, retrieved from http://articles.latimes.com/1991-08-30/sports/sp-1385_1_los-angeles-rams.

The 1951 Draft

Bert Gambini

By the late 1950s, The Los Angeles Rams had developed a college scouting network that included 115 assistants keeping tabs on pro prospects throughout most of the country.[1] Led by Eddie Kotal, the Rams' head scout since 1946, the team's system was a model far more robust than any of its counterparts in the National Football League. The Rams' advancements were so far reaching that the Brooklyn Dodgers, when preparing for their 1958 move to the west coast, asked Rams owner Dan Reeves how they might create something similar for a Major League Baseball team.[2]

But earlier in the decade, that scouting system was still in its infancy and even a forward-thinking innovator like Kotal needed to ask his own recruits for help identifying talent (see Player Questionnaire). The 1951 player draft was further complicated by a concurrent military draft that in many cases had its eyes on the same men who were of interest to NFL teams.

When it was over, Cleveland Browns head coach Paul Brown declared the draft among the "skimpiest" in pro football history[3]; Frank Finch, the *Los Angeles Times*' Rams beat writer, lamented, albeit inaccurately, how the team failed to "pluck a single star"[4]; and Joe Stydahar, the Rams' head coach, acknowledged that apparently solid choices remained questionable given lingering doubts over how many of those selections, in light of the military draft, would still be available by training camp.[5]

Despite all the inherent challenges, Brown's disgust and Stydahar's concerns, the class of 1951 included many collegians who had distinguished professional careers as players and coaches including Kyle Rote and Walt Michaels and future Hall of Famers Jack Christiansen, Dick Stanfel, Bill George, Mike McCormack, and Don Shula. Future enshrinees Art Donovan and Y.A. Tittle were also technically part of the class of '51, but they were among those players drafted for the second time in their football careers because of a franchise collapse on the day the draft was to begin. There was also, contrary to Finch's analysis, a Canton-bound Rams selection among that group of immortals from a little-known school in coastal Connecticut that was so small, its total enrollment consisted of fewer students than the number of players taken by all 12 NFL teams in the 1951 draft.

For scouts, coaches and general managers, the simultaneous drafts demanded casting an eye toward those players who were not good candidates for military service. With that mindset, fatherhood and a player's marital status, factors which made men less likely to be inducted into the armed forces, were as relevant as that player's size and strength. Teams therefore looked to "family men," those with previous military service, and 4-Fs

1951 PLAYER QUESTIONNAIRE

1. Kindly fill in this questionnaire and **return as soon as possible** so that our office records will be complete.
2. Answering this questionnaire will in no way affect your college eligibility.

LOS ANGELES RAMS FOOTBALL CLUB
7813 Beverly Boulevard, Los Angeles 36, California

Date _____

NAME (Please print) _____
LAST _____ FIRST _____ MIDDLE

Height ____ ft. ____ in.   Weight _____   Race _____

Age ____ Date of birth _____   Single ____ Married ____ Children ____

Your College address _____

Your College Telephone Number _____

Position you play (Offense) _____ Are you considered first string Offense? _____

Position you play (Defense) _____ Are you considered first string Defense? _____

Average minutes played per game last season _____ Years Varsity Letter earned _____

High School you graduated from _____ Year _____

Name of College or Junior College you **first** attended _____

Month and year you **first** registered at a Junior College or University _____
(Regardless of how long you attended)

Name of University you are **now** attending _____

Month and year you **first** entered University now attending _____

When will you actually graduate (Month and Year)? _____

In which Fall season will your College football eligibility end? _____

Have you college eligibility remaining? _____ How many years? _____

Best Playing Weight _____ College Jersey Number _____ 100 Yard Dash time _____

Statistics listed below cover _____
(INDICATE WHAT YEAR AND NUMBER OF GAMES)

Number of times carried ball _____ Yardage gained _____ Average per try _____

Number of Passes caught _____ Yardage gained _____ T.D. Passes caught _____

Are you a Passer? _____ State number thrown _____ Completed _____ Intercepted _____

Do you Punt? _____ Net average _____ Kick Off _____ Net Average _____

Do you Placekick? _____ Distance you are effective _____ Point after T.D.? _____

Do you consider yourself strong on Offense? _____ Defense? _____ Pass Defense? _____

Basic type of Pass Defense played: Zone _____ Man for man _____

Number Pass Interceptions made _____ Yards returned after Interceptions _____

Name of your Head Coach _____ Offensive system he uses _____

(OVER—CONTINUED ON OTHER SIDE)

1951 Los Angeles Rams Player Questionnaire.

(the military classification for those physically unfit to serve) as they once looked to the annual All-America teams.[6]

The situation was not as bleak as the World War II years when thin player ranks forced some teams to temporarily merge with one another as a means of survival, but the numbers were still worrisome from a football perspective.[7]

Parent's name .... Telephone Number ....

Parent's address ....

Your home address if different than parents ....

.... Telephone Number ....

What is your college major? ....

What are your future plans? ....

....

Would you be interested in playing football with the Los Angeles Rams? ....

List other Sports in which you participate. If in track, list events and best performances ....

....

....

Have you suffered any serious injuries in college sports? .... If so, please list ....

....

....

Have you had any previous Military Service? .... What branch? ....

How long? .... What is your present Draft Classification? ....
(INDICATE DATES)

Are you in any type of Military program such as, an active or inactive Reserve Unit, National Guard, R.O.T.C. or the like? If so, name program: ....

What is your present deferment based upon? ....

Please explain fully ....

....

Please list names and college addresses of any football players whom you feel would make good professional prospects:

   (1) Name .... Position ....

        Address or University ....

   (2) Name .... Position ....

        Address or University ....

   (3) Name .... Position ....

        Address or University ....

Please use the following space for any further comments you might have.

                                                                                                Thank you
                                                                                               LOS ANGELES RAMS

1951 Los Angeles Rams Player Questionnaire.

In 1950 and 1951, the Selective Service System conscripted more than 771,000 men, with more taken in 1951 (551,806) than in any other year from the conclusion of World War II to 1973, when the military draft was stopped.[8] Five colleges by the end of January 1951 announced they could not field teams that fall.[9] So desperate were NFL clubs to get a return on their investments that the Washington Redskins spent two of its late round picks in the 1951 draft to select assistant coaches from the college ranks in hopes that they'd consider returning to the game as professional players.[10]

* * *

Though the manpower shortage inspired at least Washington to take an unorthodox approach to drafting talent, the expected player shortfall had little effect on the pace of integration in professional football.

Teams were scouting and in rare cases selecting African American players. They also started to at least glance at the country's historically black colleges and universities, but in the end, only six African Americans were part of the NFL's 1951 draft class, including the Rams' Odie Posey and Alvin Hanley—and only those teams with African Americans already on their roster made those picks.

In addition to the Rams, they included the Cleveland Browns (Bernie Custis), New York Yanks (Jesse Thomas), and Green Bay Packers (George Rooks and Ed Withers). The San Francisco 49ers, Detroit Lions and New York Giants had all integrated their rosters by 1951, but none of them chose an African American player in that year's draft.

The Chicago Bears, Chicago Cardinals, Pittsburgh Steelers, Philadelphia Eagles and Washington Redskins had still not integrated their clubs by the end of January 1951.[11]

Though professional football, in its modern era, began to integrate its game the year before Jackie Robinson broke the color line in Major League Baseball, the league was hardly a civil rights leader. The number of African Americans taken in the annual player draft inched only slightly upward through the 1950s. By the decade's end, the 1959 draft class still consisted of only 30 African American selections.[12]

The military draft also created the looming reality that teams would lose some of their current players to the service, as the Rams did toward the end of the 1950 regular season when one of their starting defensive backs, George "Gabby" Sims received his induction notice.

Sims, in his second year with the Rams, played in the team's final regular season game against the Packers and was inducted into the military three days later as Los Angeles prepared for a playoff game with the Chicago Bears.[13]

The loss of Sims immediately shifted the Rams' priorities, not only for the postseason, but for the coming draft, which would begin on January 18, 1951, in Chicago's Blackstone Hotel, as part of the league's annual meeting, less than a month after the NFL championship game was played.

The Selective Service made picking college players in 1951 a "draft against [the] draft," as one major paper put it. Teams made choices hoping that half of their selections might be available by the time training camp opened six months later.[14]

That projection held mostly to form for the Rams, as the team signed 14 of their 30 draft choices in 1951. At the start of the regular season, seven of those signees were still on the roster, including Andy Robustelli, the future Hall of Famer from that tiny New England college.

Robustelli was the Rams' 19th round pick from Arnold College of Hygiene and Physical Education. Located on Point Beach in Milford, Connecticut, Arnold began its existence in 1886 as the Brooklyn Normal School of Gymnastics. The tiny, but progressive institution was the first co-educational physical education college in the country, and it also built solid athletic programs despite a student body of only 300 undergraduates.[15]

An obscure, but not entirely unknown quantity, Robustelli would likely have gone undrafted, or entirely unnoticed, if not for Kotal's confidence in his nascent scouting system and its ability to uncover great talent in unlikely places.

A dual sport athlete at Arnold, Robustelli briefly went to Canada to play minor league baseball before signing with the Rams in July 1951. That venture north led to erroneous reports that he had signed a contract with the Montreal Alouettes of the Canadian Football League. Robustelli squelched the unconfirmed report of the CFL signing in a *Los Angeles Times* story that mentioned the "Montreal Eleven," evidently written by a headline editor unaware that the Canadian game was played with 12 men a side.[16]

Robustelli spent five years on the Rams' defensive line. The team traded him to the Giants in 1956 and he played in New York through the end of his professional career in 1964.

Another late round selection, offensive lineman Dick Daugherty, taken in the 18th round just before Robustelli, became—along with third round choice Charlie Toogood—the longest tenured Rams from the 1951 draft, each playing six seasons with the team.

Though Daugherty was with the Rams in 1951, a two-year service commitment interrupted his six-year NFL career.

The Rams' first pick in 1951, Bud McFadin was a solid performer who joined the team following his military discharge in 1952. He entered the team's starting lineup in 1953 and played five years in Los Angeles as part of a 11-year career in the NFL and the American Football League.

Norb Hecker, the Rams' sixth-round selection, was a two-way player for the team in 1951. He spent three years in Los Angeles, played a year in Canada after that, returned to the NFL for three seasons in Washington, and concluded his career in the CFL after the 1958 season. Following his playing days, Hecker became an assistant in 1959 under head coach Vince Lombardi in Green Bay. In 1966, Rankin Smith, Sr., owner of the expansion Atlanta Falcons hired Hecker as his team's first head coach.

Looking at the Rams' entire draft class from 1951 is to see nine selections whose military commitments delayed, interrupted or prevented them from playing with the team. In addition to McFadin and Daugherty, they include George Kinek, who didn't play in the NFL until his 1954 season with the Chicago Cardinals, and six others: Alan Egler, Roland Kirkby, Earl Stelle, and Al Brosky, none of whom played in the NFL, along with the aforementioned Odie Posey and Alvin Hanley.

Hugo Primiani, Nolan Lang, John Natyshak, Bill Robertson, and Earl Jackson all signed contracts with the Rams following the 1951 draft but were released before the team announced its final 33-player roster for the season.[17] Tony Momsen and Howie Ruetz, meantime, were traded during the preseason.

The team's relationships with Don Hardy, Rob McCoy, Hal Riley, Jim Nutter, Dean Thomas, Harry Abeltin, Jackie Calvert, and Sterling Wingo went no further than their selections in the 1951 draft. None of them played professionally.

Two other Los Angeles picks, Joe Reid and Billy Baggett, were among the 11 Rams traded to the Dallas Texans in 1952 for linebacker Les Richter. But the military draft unexpectedly delayed Richter's arrival in Los Angeles and he wouldn't join the team until mid-way through the 1954 season.

* * *

The uncertainty which hung over the 1951 draft was further clouded by the Baltimore Colts, a sad-sack club that was barely breathing one year after being absorbed into the NFL along with the Cleveland Browns and San Francisco 49ers of the defunct All-America Football Conference (AAFC).[18]

The Colts' owner, Abe Watner, headed to Chicago for the NFL's 1951 annual meeting intending to join the league's 12 other teams in the player draft.

Although Baltimore's future was tenuous, the plan was to have the team take part in the draft before Watner announced its fate. Watner said he needed assistance from the other owners to keep the Colts in business. That assistance was not forthcoming. Commissioner Bert Bell had made that clear, despite Watner's plea for teams to surrender veteran players to the Colts, in a manner similar to an expansion draft. But teams were already facing labor shortages because of the military draft and uncertainty regarding how many college draft picks would actually be available to play in the fall.

Watner asked Bell to call the other owners together for one final request for help that was denied. That was the end of the Baltimore Colts. Watner folded the franchise.[19]

To help defray losses of $106,000, Watner asked the league to purchase the Colts' 28 active and 37 reserve players for $50,000.[20]

When the other owners agreed, that unexpectedly placed 65 additional candidates in the draft pool who weren't available a day earlier as teams finalized their preferences and considered the potentialities.

The Colts' collapse immediately rippled through the draft as four of their former players went as first round picks in 1951: Y.A. Tittle to the 49ers (a first round choice of the Lions in 1948), Chet Mutryn to the Philadelphia Eagles (a 20th round pick in 1943 of the merger between the Pittsburgh Steelers and Eagles), Jim Spavital to the Giants (a first round choice of the Cardinals in 1948) and Billy Stone (a 12th round pick of the Cardinals in 1949), who the Bears took with the second of their three first round picks.

The Rams grabbed a former Colts player in round two with their selection of Herb Rich, who Baltimore selected in round six the year before. Four rounds later, the Redskins tabbed Adrian Burk, an assistant at Florida State, who was one of the two coaches it hoped to convert. Although Burk played in Baltimore the year before, he had officially retired, and was not considered among the Colts' players purchased by the league. Though Burk never played for Washington, he did spend six seasons with the Philadelphia Eagles. He later became an attorney and NFL official and was the back judge in the 1972 playoff game between the Oakland Raiders and Pittsburgh Steelers remembered for its game winning "immaculate reception."

The identity of the other coach drafted by the Redskins is a mystery. A *Washington Post* story named Burk as one of the two coaches drafted but said only that the other selection was a tackle, working as an assistant line coach at a Southern Conference school.[21]

The *Chicago Daily Tribune* reported the second coach as Ted Hazelwood, an assistant at North Carolina.[22]

Hazelwood played for the Chicago Hornets of the AAFC and was on Washington's roster in 1953, but he does not appear on the Redskins 1951 draft list.

The Hazelwood story appeared in the *Tribune's* long-running Arch Ward column, "In the Wake of the News." Ward was on vacation when the story ran in the paper, so *Tribune* staff assembled it contents, perhaps hastily, in his absence.

When it was over, teams had picked 27 wayward Colts, including the 362nd (in round 30) and last player chosen, Sisto Averno, a defensive lineman chosen by Cleveland who played with a variety of teams through the 1954 season.

* * *

If the Colts' end was a minor surprise that served as the draft's prelude, there was no accompanying shock when the curtain finally opened with the Giants choosing Kyle Rote with that year's bonus selection.

The bonus pick is an artifact of NFL drafts from the 1940s and 1950s. At the time, there was a belief that the inverse draft order, which gave preference to the previous year's weakest teams, vaguely punished the success of stronger teams by forcing them to choose deeper in the draft order.

The bonus pick, an out-of-the-hat draw, gave teams an opportunity to make the draft's first choice, a selection that preceded the first pick of the first round.

Once a team received a bonus selection, they'd be out of the following seasons' drawings until all teams had won the pick.

The process began in 1947 and continued until the last eligible team made its selection in 1958.[23]

In 1951 Los Angeles, the Chicago Cardinals, Pittsburgh, Green Bay, the New York Giants, the New York Yanks, and Cleveland were in the running for the bonus pick. Baltimore would have also been eligible.

To see which team received the bonus pick, numbered slips of paper went into a hat based on the number of teams making the draw—seven in 1951. Each owner picked from the hat. The drawn number represented the next round's selection order where seven new slips of paper went into a hat—six blanks and one marked with an "X." The team drawing the "X" made that year's bonus pick and was dropped from subsequent bonus opportunities.

"It was the prettiest 'X' I ever did see," said Bears owner George Halas after winning the first bonus pick that allowed him to select Bob Fenimore of Oklahoma A&M.

In addition to determining 1951's bonus pick winner, the league also had to determine draft order. Tie-breaking procedures for teams with identical records did not exist at the time.

Green Bay, San Francisco and Washington all finished 1950 at 3–9; Pittsburgh, Philadelphia and Detroit at 6–6; and Cleveland and the New York Giants at 10–2.

Eight coin flips established the initial draft order which would rotate through the rounds for three-way ties and alternate for two-way ties.

By the time it was over, teams selected 362 players over the course of 30 rounds in a marathon 24-hour session that ended on January 19, 1951, at 2 o'clock in the afternoon CST.

The crop proved slightly more fruitful than anticipated, as roughly 62 percent of the entire draft class played at least one season in the NFL, including nearly 90 percent of the players selected in the draft's first five rounds.

1951 Los Angeles Rams Draft Choices[24]

1. (11) Bud McFadin (DT) Texas
2. (24) Herb Rich (B) Vanderbilt
3. (35) Charlie Toogood (DT) Nebraska
4. (48) George Kinek (E) Tulane
5. (59) Tony Momsen (C) Michigan
6. (72) Norb Hecker (DB) Baldwin-Wallace
7. (83) Alan Egler (B) Colgate

Part 1: The City and the Organization

8. (96) Hugo Primiani (T) Boston University
9. (107) Nolan Lang (B) Oklahoma
10. (121) Roland Kirkby (B) Washington
11. (132) John Natyshak (B) Tampa
12. (145) Don Hardey (B) Pacific
13. (156) Joe Reid (LB) LSU
14. (169) Rob McCoy (B) Georgia Tech
15. (180) Odie Posey (B) Southern
16. (193) Bill Robertson (E) Memphis
17. (204) Hal Riley (E) Baylor
18. (217) Dick Daugherty (G) Oregon
19. (228) Andy Robustelli (DE) Arnold
20. (241) Jim Nutter (B) Wichita State
21. (252) Earl Stelle (B) Oregon
22. (265) Billy Baggett (HB) LSU
23. (276) Dean Thomas (T) Michigan State
24. (289) Harry Abeltin (T) Colgate
25. (300) Jackie Calvert (T) Clemson
26. (313) Howie Ruetz (DT) Loras
27. (324) Al Brosky (DB) Illinois
28. (337) Sterling Wingo (B) Virginia Tech
29. (348) Earl Jackson (B) Texas Tech
30. (361) Alvin Hanley (B) Kentucky State

Notes

1. Jeane Hoffman, "Kotal's Scouting Job Frustrating but Vital," *Los Angeles Times*, August 13, 1959, IV-8.
2. Football Maven, "State Your Case: Why It's Time Hall Wakes Up to Eddie Kotal," *FOOTBALLMAVEN.io*, https://footballmaven.io/talkoffame/nfl/state-your-case-why-it-s-time-hall-wakes-up-to-eddie-kotal-Yc2uwCAk50CnVMsVhix7Zw/.
3. Frank Finch, "Rams Draft 30 Players for '51 Season; Browns Get 36," *Los Angeles Times*, January 20, 1951, III-2.
4. Frank Finch, "Scouting the Pros," *Los Angeles Times*, January 21, 1951, II-12.
5. Finch, "Rams Draft 30 Players," III-2.
6. "Pros Seek Vets, 4-Fs, Family Men," *Los Angeles Times*, January 18, 1951, IV-3.
7. For more on the player shortages during World War II, see Matthew Algeo, *Last Team Standing: How the Steelers and the Eagles—"The Steagles"—Saved Pro Football during World War II* (Boston: Da Capo Press, 2006).
8. Selective Service System, "Induction Statistics," *SSS.gov*, https://www.sss.gov/About/History-And-Records/Induction-Statistics.
9. "Duquesne Decides to Quit Football," *New York Times*, January 21, 1951, 141.
10. "Redskins Get Two Coaches in Pro Draft Who Are Expected to Turn Up as Players," *Washington Post*, January 21, 1951, C1.
11. "Pro Grid Teams Pick Six Negro Start in Draft," *Atlanta Daily World*, January 24, 1951, 5.
12. "Rams Draft 7 Tan Footballers," *Los Angeles Sentinel*, January 29, 1959. B7.
13. "Uncle Sam Delivers Draft Notice to Rams' Gabby Sims," *Los Angeles Times*, November 10, 1950, III-1.
14. National Football League Owners Draft Against Draft," *The Christian Science Monitor*, January 19, 1951, 16.
15. "Arnold College of Hygiene and Physical Education," *Lostcolleges.com*, https://www.lostcolleges.com/copy-of-arnold-college.
16. "Robustelli Denies Eyeing Job with Montreal Eleven," *Los Angeles Times*, July 13, 1951, IV-3.
17. It's possible that anyone in this group of four could have served in the military, but none of them received draft notices while still with the Rams. After their release from the team, information is difficult to obtain, since the press was no longer following their careers. The same is true for those players drafted, but who never signed with the Rams.

18. This Colts' franchise is in no way related to the Baltimore Colts (today's Indianapolis Colts) that entered the league in 1953.
19. Jesse A. Linthicum, "Professional Football Dies in City as Colts Disband; Players Sold," *Baltimore Sun*, January 19, 2019, 30.
20. Watner's losses adjusted for inflation in 2019 would total $1.05 million.
21. "Redskins Get Two Coaches in Pro Draft…"
22. "In the Wake of the News," *Chicago Daily Tribune*, January 22, 1951. B1
23. For more on the bonus pick see *The 1958 Baltimore Colts: Profiles of the NFL's First Sudden Death Champions* (Jefferson, NC: McFarland, 2018), 42.
24. Bob Carroll, et al., *Total Football II* (New York: HarperCollins, 1999), 1455–56.

PART 2

The 1951 Season

1951 Training Camp and Preseason

Mark L. Ford

"Imagine starting a campaign in the National Football League without a single, solitary veteran tackle on your squad," Frank Finch of the *Los Angeles Times* would write on the eve of the 1951 season's end. "Yet that was the pickle Jumbo Joe found himself in."[1] Though his Rams were the defending National Conference champions, Coach Joe Stydahar had a problem without precedent in the NFL[2]—no offensive tackles, no defensive tackles, and four vacancies at that position.

Indeed, all of the offensive line's front five spots (including the center and both guards) would have to be rookies. The 1951 Rams had two future Hall of Fame quarterbacks, Waterfield and Van Brocklin, but no experienced personnel to protect them.

Phase One (July 18 to July 23)

Training camp opened on Wednesday, July 18, at the University of Redlands[3] with 60 men (20 vets, 40 rookies) arriving on buses after making the 70-mile trip from Rams headquarters at 7813 Beverly Boulevard. Four other vets—Herb Rich, Jack Finlay, Stan West and Elroy Hirsch—would check in later, and veteran quarterback Bobby Thomason was traded to the Packers on the first day of camp.[4] In short form, the 63-man group competing for 33 spots looked like this[5]:

Center/Middle Linebacker:
Veterans—Don Paul (3 yrs)
Rookies—Jerry Greiner (University of Detroit), Leon McLaughlin (UCLA), Tony Momsen (5th Round/Michigan); Joe Reid (13th/LSU)

Guards/Linebackers:
Veterans—Jack Finlay (4 yrs), Dave Stephenson (1 yr), Harry Thompson (1 yr), Stan West (1 yr)
Rookies—Dick Daugherty (18th/Oregon); Bill Lange (Dayton); Dick Nanry (Loyola); Don Simensen (St. Thomas); Claude Zoch (Oshkosh Teachers)

Tackles:
Veterans—NONE
Rookies—Bobby Collier (SMU); Tom Dahms (San Diego State); Jack Halliday (SMU); John Natyshak (11th/Tampa); Sam Nevills (Oregon); Harry Neugold (Rensselaer

Poly); Hugo Primiani (8th/Boston University); Howard Ruetz (26th/Loras); Charles Toogood (3rd/Nebraska): Jerry Vanderhorst (Dayton); Jim Winkler (Texas A & M)

Ends:
Veterans—Larry Brink (4 yrs); Elroy Hirsch (4 yrs); Jack Zilly (4 yrs); Tom Fears (3 yrs); Bob Boyd (1 yr)
Rookies—Norb Hecker (6th/Baldwin-Wallace); Dick Moje (Loyola); Bill Robertson (16th/Memphis State); Andy Robustelli (19th/Arnold College)

Halfbacks:
Veterans—Tom Keane (3 yrs); Tom Kalmanir (2 yrs); Verda "Vitamin T." Smith (2 yrs); Jerry Williams (2 yrs); Glenn Davis (1 yr); Woodley Lewis (1 yr); Herb Rich (1 yr)
Rookies—Roy Barni (USF); Jack Finney (USF); John Freeman (Portland); Madill Gartiser (Missouri); Denver Grigsby (Tulsa); Alvin Hanley (30th/Kentucky State); Earl Jackson (Texas Tech); Marvin Johnson (San Jose State); George Kinek (4th/Tulane); Odie Posey (15th/Southern); Don Rogers (USC); Tom Williams (Los Angeles State)

Fullbacks:
Veterans—Dick Hoerner (4 yrs); Paul "Tank" Younger (2 yrs); Ralph Pasquariello (1 yr); "Deacon" Dan Towler (1 yr)
Rookies—Charles Hicks (Loyola); Nolan Lang (9th/Oklahoma); Mike Nolan (Loyola)

Quarterbacks:
Veterans—Bob Waterfield (6 yrs); Norm Van Brocklin (2 yrs)
Rookies—Joe Zaleski (Dayton)

Over the next 10 weeks, 30 of the 63 would have to be waived or traded in time to reach the NFL's 33-man roster limit. Once on campus, the players moved into their dormitory at Melrose Hall and began with a training camp feast at lunchtime, then started workouts the next day.[6]

In less than a week, six of the rookies requested a cut and were sent home on Monday the 23rd, catching buses from nearby San Bernardino. Alvin Hanley joined the armed services, Jerry Vanderhorst left after his wife was hospitalized, and John Natyshak was overweight. Hugo Primiani, Earl Jackson and Denver Grigsby departed on their own.[7] The next cuts would wait until after the 1951 team's first, and only, public scrimmage.

Phase Two (July 24 to August 1)

Now down to 57 players, the 1951 team's first public showing was the full dress scrimmage, held on July 28 on a muggy Saturday at 3:00 in the afternoon at the University of Redlands Stadium.[8] Admission was free, but donation boxes were at the entrance for the Redlands' athletic scholarship fund, and there were mimeographed lists of players handed out.[9] Veterans Don Paul and Jack Zilly, and rookies Bobby Collier and Marv Johnson, were sidelined from minor injuries sustained in the first week of practice.[10] Bob Waterfield and rookie Joe Zaleski took turns at quarterback. Norm Van Brocklin had been given leave to go back home to Oregon after his daughter had been born earlier than expected.[11] About 2,000 people turned out to get a view of the other 53 players, whose numbers and names were listed on the mimeographed sheets.[12]

The format was the scrimmage standard of offense-against-defense drills, albeit with the players in helmets, pads and their full uniforms. There was no kicking of field goals, no conversion attempts, and no punting on fourth down. Each drive was a separate 11-on-11 drill. One could say that the score was 30–0 for the offense for reaching the end zone five times.

The official stats were that Waterfield completed 16 of 25 for 219 yards and two touchdowns (one to Jerry Williams, who lateraled to Bob Boyd on a 15-yard play, the other a 32-yard pass to rookie Norb Hecker). Zaleski was seven of 11 for 133 yards, including a 49-yard pass to Boyd. Roy Barni, Johnny Freeman and Nolan Lang were the only rookies allowed to carry the football on a running play, and Freeman even got to score a touchdown on a two-yard run. None of the three, nor Zaleski, would make the team. The other touchdown came on Dan Towler's nine-yard run.[13] The real excitement, however, came from the defense. "The scrimmage produced at least one jewel," Finch wrote the next day, "in Andy Robustelli, 220-pound defensive end from Arnold College in Connecticut.... Time after time he crashed through to spill [Waterfield and Zaleski] for big losses on pass plays."[14] The coaches also praised Moje, Dahms, Toogood, Halliday and Winkler on defense, and Daugherty, Momsen and McLaughlin on the offensive line.

Monday brought the news of the next departures. Five more rookies—Mizzou track and field star Madill Gartiser, Harry Neugold, Mike Nolan, Don Rogers and Tom Williams—were all let go.[15] The next day, veteran fullback Ralph Paquariello was traded to the Chicago Cardinals "for a high round 1952 draft pick," and Hamp Pool noted that "There just wasn't room enough on our club for four fullbacks. We carried four last year and as a result were short a halfback, which we needed more."[16] Now down to 51 players, the Rams prepared for the first of seven preseason games (six within the league), against nine different teams (not a misprint) starting in San Diego.

Phase Three (August 2 to August 7)

Assistant coach J. Hampton Pool—who would succeed Stydahar as head coach—was effusive in his praise of the University of Redlands, calling it "the greatest place for a football team to train in the state of California" and joking that "the university has done everything for the Rams, but air condition the playing fields."[17] He was addressing a gathering of 300 members of San Bernardino's service clubs, and he followed up with even higher accolades for the rookie candidates for linemen, predicting that "this year we will have a line 100 times more potent than any previous Rams line."[18]

The line's first test would come in one of the most unusual formats ever for a preseason football game, never done before and never again. It wasn't unprecedented for NFL teams to play a non-league club, but the Rams played three of them on the same evening. Not all at once, of course, although the 1951 Rams could probably have won an 11 against 33 match-up, but the 11th U.S. Naval District in San Diego County had several armed forces football teams among its Navy and Marine bases. At a time when "service football" was very popular, the Camp Pendleton Marines, the San Diego Naval Training Center Bluejackets, and the San Diego Marine Corps Recruit Depot Devildogs all agreed (in that sequence) to play the NFL's defending National Conference champions.[19]

Since there were three different sets of players facing the Rams on behalf of the 11th District, the event also marked the only known time that a football game was played in three 20-minute periods rather than two halves or four quarters. It's the format for ice hockey games, but it had never been done on the gridiron before, nor has it since. There was no "halftime," but a 10-minute break between each period. The servicemen had enthusiasm and heart but were outmatched on first downs (24 vs. 8), passing yardage (373 vs. 98) and rushing (235 vs. 32).[20] Camp Pendleton got a safety when Hoerner fumbled an end zone handoff from Waterfield and had to fall on the ball.[21] There was one major injury; rookie end Ben Procter cracked three vertebrae in his spine, effectively ending his pro football career.[22]

Friday, August 3, 1951
Balboa Stadium, San Diego

Los Angeles Rams	21	21	13	55
11th U.S. Naval District	2	0	0	2

LA–Jerry Williams 36 run (Bob Waterfield kick)
LA–Bob Boyd 11 pass from Waterfield (Waterfield kick)
LA–Dan Towler 10 run (Waterfield kick)
NAV–Safety, Dick Hoerner tackled in end zone
LA–Tank Younger run (Waterfield kick)
LA–Tommy Kalmanir 9 run (Waterfield kick)
LA–Tom Keane 21 pass from Norm Van Brocklin (Elroy Hirsch kick)
LA–Tom Fears 67 pass from Waterfield (Waterfield kick)
LA–Boyd 40 pass from Waterfield (kick failed)
A–20,000

It was Coach Stydahar's first chance to test all of his new recruits in game conditions, and Finch commented the next day that the Rams "employed so many combinations of players, both on offense and defense, that inmates of the press box and visiting scouts were left a bit dazed trying to keep track of the talent."[23]

Throughout the preseason, the 12 rookies who would eventually make the team were assigned jersey numbers other than the ones they would wear in regular play. Bill Lange, #26, was the only exception. Thus, Andy Robustelli wore #39 in exhibitions, and #84 in his Rams career; Bobby Collier went from #27 to #72.[24] Stydahar did settle on the regular starters for his rookie front five (Dahms, Lange, McLaughlin, Daugherty and Toogood) and he was impressed on defense with rookies Robustelli, Winkler, Halliday and Dick Moje. Afterwards, Stydahar bragged to the press, "The gang rocked and socked, they kept the pressure on and they gang-tackled like no Ram team I've ever seen.... I want to repeat what I said before and that is that our rookie tackles as a group will be just as good as the tackles we had last year. Those were three fired-up teams we played last night and they only netted 32 yards rushing against us."[25] Three other rookies didn't impress during the game. On Tuesday, Charles Hicks, Nolan Lang and Dick Nanry were give their bus tickets, bringing the camp roster down to 48.[26]

Phase Four (August 8 to August 17)

Half a century before the league made "NFL Kickoff Weekend" a star-studded extravaganza, the *Los Angeles Times* hyped the Rams' preseason home opener a midsummer night's dream game. Hollywood celebrities and big bands entertained the crowds who came for the annual Rams vs. Redskins meeting, with all the profits going to charity.

Every day brought new reminders from the *Times* that there was something really, really big happening on the 15th, even if the game didn't actually count. "Anyone who does not know that The Los Angeles Rams and the Washington Redskins are tangling in the Coliseum tomorrow evening for the benefit of underprivileged boys of Los Angeles," columnist Dick Hyland commented, "simply does not read sports pages." If guilt wasn't enough to make you buy tickets, Hyland brought out the all-caps to let you know that "this IS a football game. This IS entertainment of the highest order, athletically."[27]

During the summertime, the Washington Redskins were Southern California's other pro football team, their training camp at L.A.'s Occidental College getting regular coverage from reporter Jack Geyer.[28] Redskins owner George Preston Marshall lived in Beverly Hills and had first approached the *Times* in 1945 with the idea for a Los Angeles match that would bring his team and the Cleveland Rams to the Coliseum for an evening. As fate would have it, Dan Reeves soon brought the Rams to L.A. for an extended stay.[29]

In the days leading up to the game, both teams brought NFL officials to their camps to explain the new rules for 1951 ("there'll be a minimum of penalties as a result of this foresight," Finch promised readers).[30] The biggest change was that there was now an ineligible receiver penalty. The center, the guards and tackles could no longer touch a forward pass, on pain of a 15-yard penalty and loss of down if they did so. Another was the rule that if the punting team touched the ball before an opposing player did, the line of scrimmage was where the contact occurred. One change no longer in use today was that the football could not be replaced until the next quarter.

Starting at 7:15 for the show, and 8:30 for the game, the event at the Coliseum did live up to its promise of "a scintillating pregame show and a thrilling halftime program,"[31] with three marching bands, a team of acrobats called the Gaskills, and singers before the kickoff, and Jack Benny entertained the crowd at halftime.[32] The game itself wasn't close. Stydahar used the opportunity to experiment with the 5–2 defense instead of the 5–3 from 1950 (in 1951 parlance, the "5-2-4" rather than the "5-3-3").[33] Between Harry Gilmer and Sammy Baugh, the Redskins were intercepted six times in 29 attempts. Stydahar said later, "I think the Redskins quit passing even when they were behind 37 points because they didn't want us to get the ball."[34]

When the offense had the ball, they scored six touchdowns in the first half and went into the locker room with a 41–14 lead. In the second half, the second string was put in, and although the Redskins didn't score again, *Times* reporter Finch complained that "after intermission the Rams could muster 'only' 17 points…. In this league you can't afford to coast. If we try that against the Bears, we'll be dead ducks for sure."[35]

Wednesday, August 15, 1951
Los Angeles Memorial Coliseum

Washington Redskins	7	7	0	0	14
Los Angeles Rams	13	28	10	7	58

    LA–Elroy Hirsch 48 pass from Bob Waterfield (Waterfield kick)
    WAS–Eddie Saenz 35 pass from Gilmer (Bill Dudley kick)
    LA–Tommy Kalmanir 46 run (kick failed)
    LA–Tom Fears 10 pass from Norm Van Brocklin (Waterfield kick)
    LA–Hirsch 48 pass from Van Brocklin (Waterfield kick)
    WAS–Hugh Taylor 51 pass from Harry Gilmer (Bill Dudley pass from Sammy Baugh)
    LA–Vitamin Smith 12 run (Waterfield kick)
    LA–Tank Younger 49 run (Waterfield kick)
    LA–Hirsch 54 pass from Waterfield (Waterfield kick)
    LA–Field Goal Waterfield 38
    LA–Odie Posey 36 pass from Joe Zaleski (Waterfield kick)
    A–91,985

82   Part 2: The 1951 Season

By Friday, three more rookie linemen were sent away. Center Jerry Greiner got traded to the Packers for their fourth-round draft choice, and tackles Tom Machtolf and Sam Nevills were waived.[36] The roster was now 45 and needed to be trimmed by 12 more.

Phase Five (August 18 to August 28)

Monday brought the release of three halfbacks, Marvin Johnson, George Kinek and John Freeman[37]; 42 were left, nine of whom would have to be cut. The rest of the team prepared for Thursday's game against the Chicago Bears. Although the Bears had played the Rams in Los Angeles five years in a row, the team had never made a trip by airplane (for the 1950 National Conference playoff, they made a 2,215-mile journey to Pasadena in 45 hours on the Atchison, Topeka & Santa Fe's Chief Streamliner, then chartered buses to L.A.).[38]

This time, the Bears chartered a United Airlines DC-6 on Tuesday morning, flying nonstop and arriving at 4:00 in the afternoon. Halas took them straight to their hotel and avoided the press. Finch commented that Halas "was harder to locate than a uranium deposit" and mentioned the Bears' coach and the Soviet Union's dictator in the same sentence ("placing a person-to-person call to Stalin is a breeze compared to nailing the wily Bohemian").[39] Still, his colleague Paul B. Zimmerman got to talk to Halas, who said that "the Rams have the greatest aerial game I've ever seen. There's nothing like it in football today.... Loss of veteran tackles apparently hasn't hurt the Rams. They've been fortunate in landing some new ones."[40]

It was the Rams' third game of the summer, the Bears' first.

The Rams came close to winning by five touchdowns and, as Finch wrote the next day, "The mighty Chicago Bears came within two minutes of suffering their worst defeat in history last night. A fluke touchdown saved them from this ignominy, but they took an unbearable pasting as it was."[41] Rookie halfback Roy Barni fumbled a handoff from Van Brocklin, and the Bears recovered on the Rams' six-yard line.

Thursday, August 23, 1951
Los Angeles Memorial Coliseum

Chicago Bears	0	0	7	7	14
Los Angeles Rams	7	7	14	14	42

LA–Dan Towler 2 run (Bob Waterfield kick)
LA–Vitamin Smith 71 punt return (Waterfield kick)
CHI–Billy Stone 10 pass from Johnny Lujack (Lujack kick)
LA–Dan Towler 7 run (Waterfield kick)
LA–Elroy Hirsch 46 pass from Norm Van Brocklin (Waterfield kick)
LA–Vitamin Smith 21 pass from Van Brocklin (Waterfield kick)
LA–Jerry Williams 61 run (Waterfield kick)
CHI–Curly Morrison 6 run (Lujack kick)
A–65,314

Barni's mistake might have cost him a job with the Rams, though not in the NFL. He was traded to the Cardinals and would play five seasons on defense for the Cards, Eagles and Redskins—before getting killed in a bar the week before training camp was to open in 1957.[42] Another rookie, defensive tackle Jim Winkler, took advantage of the next day's break by eloping to Las Vegas with a Redlands girl whom he had met during training camp.[43]

As for Halas and the Bears, their fear of flying was confirmed the day after the game, when another United Airlines Flight DC-6 flying from Chicago crashed during its approach to Oakland, killing all 50 people on aboard.[44] The Bears faced the Rams and 49ers only once in the 1952 regular season, in Chicago, and they didn't play another preseason game in California for 24 years.[45] For the 1952 regular season game in Los Angeles, they took the train.[46]

Phase Six (August 29 to September 11)

The Rams' remaining four exhibition games were on the road, starting with more than a week out of town playing in Arkansas and Utah. On August 30, the team traveled to Little Rock (on a United DC-6, no less).[47] They arrived to 102-degree heat on "the hottest August 29 in Little Rock's history."[48] By game day, it had cooled to 100 in the shade in muggy weather. The Rams led the entire way in a game filled with long yardage plays, but Tom Fears was injured.

The win marked the first time since 1942 that the Rams defeated the Eagles in any game, exhibition or regular.[49] In the previous 13 attempts, they'd had three ties and 10 losses; they went back to losing in 1952, and finally beat the Eagles in regular play in 1955.

Saturday, September 1, 1951
War Memorial Stadium, Little Rock, Arkansas

Los Angeles Rams	14	10	7	0	31
Philadelphia Eagles	3	7	14	2	26

LA–Jerry Williams 34 pass from Bob Waterfield (Waterfield kick)
PHI–Field Goal Steve Van Buren 15
LA–Williams 61 pass from Waterfield (Waterfield kick)
PHI–Bosh Pritchard 70 punt return
LA–Field Goal Waterfield 13
LA–Elroy Hirsch 58 run (Waterfield kick)
PHI–Adrian Burk 11 pass from Pete Pihos (Van Buren kick)
LA–Dan Towler 33 run (Waterfield kick)
PHI–Frank Ziegler 2 run (Van Buren kick)
PHI–Safety, Tommy Kalmanir tackled in end zone by Chuck Bednarik and Gerry Cowhig
A–20,000

Little Rock, however, was more memorable for the team's off-field drama than for the game itself. Coach Stydahar moved the curfew to 1:30 in the morning to allow the players to celebrate their Saturday night win. Only 14 of the 42 returned to their rooms by 1:30. Finch wrote that the rest of them "straggled into their hotel at all hours after the game."[50] Stydahar and his assistants waited in the lobby before finally retiring at five in the morning. Even then, there were a few Rams still out, "enjoying Southern hospitality" somewhere in the Arkansas capital.

Jumbo Joe announced the consequences later in the day to the men with hangovers—fines of $300 each,[51] to be deducted from their first Rams paycheck, comparable to about $2,900 in today's dollars,[52] and it was at a time when the average NFL player didn't make that much. Bob Waterfield was the only one to publicly admit that he had broken the rules, and told the press, "We missed curfew and got caught. It happens occasionally to every pro club."[53]

In all, $7,900 worth of sanctions were levied against the offenders (the first two guys to return to the hotel were fined "only" $100). The team, as a group, appealed to Stydahar to rescind the punishment—he had wiped the slate clean after the 1950 season—but, he said, "this is one time the fines will stick. I've been all too lenient … this time, it's going to be different," starting with the first week's paychecks.[54]

Rather than heading back to California, the unhappy Rams boarded a plane to go to Salt Lake City to play the Chicago Cardinals in the next preseason game. One L.A. sports columnist wrote that the players were angry enough to rebel against their coach,[55] and at the first workout, Waterfield gathered his teammates to a mass huddle on the field, coaches not invited. But, Finch reported later, though nobody revealed what was said in the team meeting, "the gang broke from the impromptu pow-wow yelling and jumping around," and had a great workout. Nowadays, one might say they were "psyched up." Seventy years ago, however, the Rams were said to have "zip and ginger" as they geared up to face the Cards.[56]

If they were hoping that a win would rescind the fines, they ended up making their coach even more determined. The Rams, favored by two touchdowns, lost 36 to 21, after what Stydahar called "the worst case of overconfidence I ever saw."[57] Even Cardinals coach Curly Lambeau took time to say that "The Rams were just a little too complacent."[58] The *Salt Lake Tribune*'s Jack Schroeder wrote the next day that "the Chicago forward wall smeared a lot of the pass attempts,"[59] while those downfield "covered every potential receiver" along the way to a 36–21 upset.

Saturday, September 8, 1951
Utah Stadium, Salt Lake City

Los Angeles Rams	0	14	0	7–21
Chicago Cardinals	6	10	6	14–36

ChiC–Emil Sitko 4 run (kick failed)
LA–Tommy Kalmanir 4 pass from Norm Van Brocklin (Waterfield kick)
ChiC–Field Goal Vinnie Yablonski 16
ChiC–Don Paul 10 pass from Frank Tripucka (Yablonski kick)
LA–Herb Rich 102 interception return after lateral from Woodley Lewis (Waterfield kick)
ChiC–Field Goal Yablonski 33
ChiC–Field Goal Yablonski 33
ChiC–Sitko 24 run (Yablonski kick)
LA–Glenn Davis 2 run (Waterfield kick)
ChiC–Billy Cross 42 run (Yablonski kick)
A–15,594

The real loss, however, was the injury of the Rams' other star receiver, right before Tom Fears was set to return. While all the players wore helmets in 1952, the face mask wasn't yet part of the package. In the third quarter, Elroy Hirsch took a hit below his left eye and sustained a zygomatic fracture—a broken cheekbone—serious enough to require hospitalization and surgery at Latter Day Saints Hospital in Salt Lake.[60] The rest of the team returned to Redlands and went back to work on Monday to prepare for the Browns. Only one player got waived, rookie end Ben Procter, who had broken three vertebrae in San Diego.[61] Camp at Redlands closed on Wednesday, when the Rams flew east for their last two preseason meetings.[62]

Phase Seven (September 12 to September 14)

"The word 'exhibition' could not be used to describe this contest," Finch noted after the Rams faced the Browns in Cleveland. "They hammered at each other as if it were a matter of life and death."[63] Their last meeting had been there on Christmas Eve, for the 1950 National Football League championship. Determined to preserve the honor of the NFL against the upstart newcomer from the All-America Football Conference, Stydahar's Rams had an eight-point lead going into the final quarter, only to lose to Paul Brown's men, 30–28, in the final half minute. The injury ($427 per player, the difference between the share for the winners and losers) was given a side dish of insult three weeks later.

For the revived Pro Bowl, Stydahar and Brown (and many of their star players) met again, this time in L.A., and Brown's Americans beat Stydahar's Nationals, 28–27. The preseason rematch was in much warmer weather, but, like the title game, the Browns won in the final minute, and the victory came with the inadvertent help of Jim Beiersdorfer. For the first 59 minutes of play, neither team could reach the end zone. Bob Waterfield scrambled across the goal line from the Browns six in the second quarter, but Dick Hoerner was called for holding.[64] Not only was an apparent score nullified, but in those days, offensive holding was a 15-yard penalty, so the ball was moved to the 21. On third down, Waterfield was sacked at the 30; so he kicked the first of two field goals.

Still, the Rams' defense had stopped one Cleveland drive after another, intercepting four of Otto Graham's passes. With 42 seconds left to play, they almost picked off five, right as Graham threw to Horace Gillom. Frank Finch of the *Times* told the story the next day: "Just as defending halfback Norb Hecker reached for the ball he collided with Umpire Jim Beiersdorfer and they fell in a heap at the goal line. 'I'm sure I would have intercepted the pass if I hadn't hit the umpire,' said Hecker." Finch added, "Maybe so, but those Browns just seem to win no matter what happens."[65] Lou Groza added the point after, and the Browns beat the Rams again, 7–6 instead of 30–28.

Friday, September 14, 1951
Cleveland Municipal Stadium

Los Angeles Rams	0	3	0	3	6
Cleveland Browns	0	0	0	7	7

LA–Field Goal Bob Waterfield 37
LA–Field Goal Waterfield 28
CLE–Horace Gillom 5 pass from Otto Graham (Lou Groza kick)
A–38,851

The exhibition took a toll on the losers as well, with four of the Rams' starters (Bob Waterfield, Vitamin Smith, Charlie Toogood and Dan Towler) leaving for injuries.[66] The loss notwithstanding, Stydahar was impressed with the effort, commenting afterward, "I am proud as a peacock about my team. I have no complaints. The breaks decided it."[67] Still, he wasn't proud enough of them to rescind the fines.

Final Phase (September 15 to September 26)

They may have been the losers in Cleveland, but the Rams were heroes in the small town of Newburgh, New York. A parade and a brass band greeted them[68] a few hours after they had left Cleveland to proceed further east for their final tune-up game, against the football Giants at the Polo Grounds in New York.

Four of the 41 players didn't make the trip. Quarterback Joe Zaleski, who had the bad luck to be the understudy on a team that had both Bob Waterfield and Norm Van

Brocklin, was waived, along with end Bill Robertson.[69] Center Tony Momsen was traded to the Steelers for their sixth round draft choice (they would use it to select Duane Putnam) and Howard Ruetz's contract was sold to the Packers.[70] Of the 37 left before the Giants' game, four would have to be cut. They could only hope that they could impress Coach Stydahar at the Polo Grounds.

Newburgh was where the Rams chose to practice, located upstate, 50 miles further up the Hudson River than New York City. On the eve of the game, the Rams booked rooms at the Plaza Hotel, across the Harlem River from the stadium.[71] The next day, the Rams and Giants faced off for the *New York Herald Tribune*'s charity event for the Fresh Air Fund (which, then as now, gave children from the inner city a few weeks at summer camp).

The Rams took an early lead, with two touchdowns within less than a minute of each other in the first quarter. Hoerner plunged for one score with 5:45 left in the period, and Lewis picked off Travis Tidwell's pass and ran it back for a score at the 4:58 mark.[72] The Giants took a 21–17 lead with 19 minutes to play, but the Rams went back ahead after Tidwell fumbled on the Giants' 17.

With 4:48 in the game, Van Brocklin (who came in after Waterfield injured his knee) found Tom Fears in the end zone. Fears and New York's Otto Schnellenbacher both leapt high for the ball, and Fears managed to grab it and keep it for the score. The pulled knee ligament also meant that Waterfield couldn't kick, so rookie halfback Odie Posey made his first, and only, try for an NFL score.[73] The kick was blocked, so the Giants only needed a field goal to win; in the final minute, Tidwell's passing got the Big Blue into the red zone. With 0:15 to go, Ray Poole prepared to kick the game winner from 23 yards out, but rookie Jack Halliday saved the day, breaking through the line to block Poole's kick.[74]

Thursday, September 20, 1951
Polo Grounds, New York

Los Angeles Rams	14	3	0	6	23
New York Giants	7	7	7	0	21

NYG–Joe Scott 2 run (Ray Poole kick)
LA–Dick Hoerner 1 run (Waterfield kick)
LA–Woodley Lewis 22 interception return (Waterfield kick)
LA–Field Goal Waterfield 29
NYG–Bob Wilkinson 4 pass from Travis Tidwell (Poole kick)
NYG–Forrest Griffith 1 run (Poole kick)
LA–Tom Fears 13 pass from Norm Van Brocklin (kick failed)
A–27,912

The final exhibition took its toll, as 14 of the Rams ended up needing medical treatment in advance of the September 28 regular season opener against the New York Yanks. Elroy Hirsch had watched from the bench, but his fractured cheek bone had healed enough for him to start the Yanks game with Tom Fears (as Finch described it, "The pass-snatching firm of Fears & Hirsch will be in business again come Friday night").[75] On its way from New York back to Los Angeles, the chartered flight stopped at Chicago so that Hirsch could get a final fitting for his protective mask (described in the press as "an elegant bird cage").[76]

To reach the 33-man roster limit, the Rams sold the contracts of Dave Stephenson and Dick Moje to the Green Bay Packers (that had already acquired L.A. castoffs Jerry Greiner and Howard Ruetz).[77] Odie Posey, who had already been notified by his draft board that he would get a deferment as long as he was playing pro football, went ahead and joined the United States Navy. Roy Barni was placed on waivers. Training camp and the preseason were over. The team began regular practices at L.A.'s Gilmore Field on Monday and was ready to open the 1951 season with nine rookie starters.

By the way, if you've read this far, remember those $300 penalties from the Little Rock hotel incident, the ones that Jumbo Joe Stydahar vowed that he would never cancel? He canceled them. Three days before the season opener, the coach told a press conference that he would put an end to rumors about the 28 men's night on the town … and that in order to "completely erase any questions surrounding the good character of our players—which is beyond reproach—I have rescinded the fines."[78]

Notes

1. Frank Finch, "Rams Rookie Tackles Make Coach Look Good," *Los Angeles Times*, September 25, 1951, IV-3.
2. Frank Finch, "Rams Must Depend on Rookie Tackles," *Los Angeles Times*, July 26, 1951, IV-1.
3. Frank Finch, "Ram and Redskin Football Teams Open Practice Sessions This Week," *Los Angeles Times*, July 15, 1951, II-9.
4. "Three Ram Veterans Expected Soon at U. of R. Pro Camp," *San Bernardino County Sun*, July 26, 1951, 34; "Packers Get Quarterback Bobby Thomason from Rams," *Racine Journal-Times*, July 19, 1951, 26.
5. "Rams Roster," *Los Angeles Times*, July 18, 1951, IV-2.
6. Claude Anderson, "'Dress' Scrum Set by Stydahar for Saturday," *San Bernardino County Sun*, July 24, 1951, 18
7. Anderson, "'Dress' Scrum," 18.
8. "L.A. Rams Hold Scrimmage at U. of R. This Afternoon," *San Bernardino County Sun*, July 28, 1951, 6.
9. "Vets, Rookies Clash Today in Ram Scrimmage," *Los Angeles Times*, July 28, 1951, III-2.
10. "Vets, Rookies," III-2.
11. "Vets, Rookies," III-2.
12. Frank Finch, "Robustelli, Rookie Ram, Steals Show," *Los Angeles Times*, July 29, 1951, II-9.
13. Finch, "Robustelli," II-9.
14. Finch, "Robustelli," II-9.
15. "L.A. Rams to Scrimmage at U. R. Tuesday; Play at Navy," *San Bernardino County Sun*, July 31, 1951, 16.
16. Frank Finch, "Rams Trade Pasquariello to Cardinals," *Los Angeles Times*, August 1, 1951, IV-3.
17. "Pool Praises U.R. Training," *San Bernardino County Sun*, August 2, 1951, 34.
18. "Pool Praises," 34.
19. Frank Finch, "Rams Face Navy, Marine Elevens," *Los Angeles Times*, August 3, 1951, IV-1.
20. Frank Finch, "Rams Trample Service Foes," *Los Angeles Times*, August 4, 1951, III-1.
21. Finch, "Rams Trample," III-1.
22. Frank Finch, "Stydahar Happy Over Line Punch," *Los Angeles Times*, August 5, 1951, II-10.
23. Finch, "Rams Trample," III-1.
24. "Rams, Redskins Mix," *San Bernardino County Sun*, August 15, 1951, 21.
25. Finch, "Stydahar Happy," II-10.
26. Frank Finch, "Guard Stan West Joins Ram Squad," *Los Angeles Times*, August 8, 1951, IV-1.
27. Dick Hyland, "The Hyland Fling," *Los Angeles Times*, August 14, 1951, IV-2.
28. Jack Geyer, "Huge Throng Thrilled by Football Spectacle," *Los Angeles Times*, August 16, 1951, IV-1.
29. Paul Zimmerman, "Sportscripts," *Los Angeles Times*, August 15, 1951, IV-2.
30. "Curb on Penalties Planned for Ram-Redskin Game," *Los Angeles Times*, August 7, 1951, IV-1.
31. "Stars Galore to Entertain Grid Crowd," *Los Angeles Times*, August 15, 1951, IV-1.
32. Geyer, "Huge Throng," IV-1.
33. Frank Finch, "Rams' Line Better Than Last Year," *Los Angeles Times*, August 16, 1951, IV-1.
34. Finch, "Rams' Line," IV-1.
35. Frank Finch, "Rams Rest After Romp Over 'Skins," *Los Angeles Times*, August 17, 1951, IV-1.
36. Frank Finch, "Bears Due to Arrive Here Today," *Los Angeles Times*, August 21, 1951, IV-1.
37. Frank Finch, "Rams' Line Better Than Last Year," *Los Angeles Times*, August 16, 1951, IV-1.
38. Edward Prell, "Bears Depart for West and Rams Playoff," *Chicago Tribune*, December 14, 1950, 6-4.
39. Frank Finch, "Rams, Bears May Attract 70,000 Fans," *Los Angeles Times*, August 22, 1951, IV-1.
40. Paul Zimmerman, "Sportscripts," *Los Angeles Times*, August 22, 1951, IV-1.

88   Part 2: The 1951 Season

41. Frank Finch, "Savage Rams Win, 42–14," *Los Angeles Times*, August 24, 1951, IV-1.
42. "Roy Barni Shot in Street by Berserk Gunman," *San Francisco Examiner*, July 22, 1957, 1.
43. "Rams' Winkler Reveals Wedding," *Los Angeles Times*, September 7, 1951, IV-2.
44. "Airliner Crashes; 44 Feared Killed," *Los Angeles Times*, August 24, 1951, I-1.
45. Although the Bears played regular games on the west, it took until 1975 for them to visit in the preseason, when they came to San Diego, see *The Pro Football Archives*, www.profootballarchives.com.
46. "Bears in California," *Chicago Tribune*, October 25, 1952, 32.
47. Frank Finch, "Rams Leave Today for Exhibitions," *Los Angeles Times*, August 30, 1951, IV-2.
48. Frank Finch, "Rams Figured to Triumph by 10 Points," *Los Angeles Times*, September 1, 1951, III-1.
49. Frank Finch, "Rams Capture 31–26 Thriller from Eagles," *Los Angeles Times*, September 2, 1951, II-17. The Cleveland Rams had defeated the Eagles, 24–14, in Akron on September 20, 1942. Scores for later games are from www.profootballarchives.com.
50. Frank Finch, "Stydahar Fines Tardy Ram Gridders $7900—Coach Lowers Boom on Players Out Past 1:30," *Los Angeles Times*, September 3, 1951, IV-1.
51. "Rules Broken! 28 Rams Fined $7900 by Coach," *Oakland Tribune*, September 3, 1951, 32.
52. For an authoritative way to back up statements of what a price in the past "would be like today," the U.S. Department of Labor's Bureau of Labor Statistics has a comparison based on the monthly Consumer Price Index. The "CPI Inflation Calculator" is a useful tool on the Bureau's website at https://data.bls.gov/cgi-bin/cpicalc.pl.
53. "Rules Broken!" 32.
54. "Rules Broken!" 32.
55. Frank Finch, "Rams Show Zip in Drill After Secret Pep Talk," *Los Angeles Times*, September 6, 1951, IV-4.
56. Finch, "Rams Show Zip," IV-4.
57. Frank Finch, "Rams' Hirsch Will Play in Opener," *Los Angeles Times*, September 10, 1951, IV-3.
58. Finch, "Rams' Hirsch," IV-3.
59. Jack Schroeder, "Cards Register 36 to 21 Grid Upset Over Rams," *Salt Lake Tribune*, September 9, 1951, 27.
60. Frank Finch, "Joe Stydahar Checks Report on Browns," *Los Angeles Times*, September 11, 1951, IV-3.
61. Frank Finch, "Browns Favored over Rams," *Los Angeles Times*, September 12, 1951, IV-3.
62. Finch, "Joe Stydahar," IV-3.
63. Frank Finch, "Groza Again 'Kicks' Rams," *Los Angeles Times*, September 15, 1951, III-1.
64. Finch, "Groza Again," III-1.
65. Finch, "Groza Again," III-1.
66. Finch, "Groza Again," III-1.
67. Finch, "Groza Again," III-1.
68. Frank Finch, "Rams Get Big Welcome Despite Loss to Browns," *Los Angeles Times*, September 16, 1951, II-12.
69. Finch, "Rams Get Big Welcome," II-12.
70. Finch, "Rams Get Big Welcome," II-12.
71. "Stydahar Fears Giants May Use 'A' Formation," *Los Angeles Times*, September 19, 1951, I-31.
72. Frank Finch, "Rams Win Thriller from Giants, 23–21," *Los Angeles Times*, September 21, 1951, IV-1.
73. Finch, "Rams Win Thriller," IV-1.
74. Finch, "Rams Win Thriller," IV-1.
75. Frank Finch, "Waterfield, Four Other Rams Out of Loop Opener," *Los Angeles Times*, September 22, 1951, III-3.
76. Frank Finch, "Firm of Fears & Hirsch in Business Again Come Friday," *Los Angeles Times*, September 24, 1951, IV-2.
77. Frank Finch, "Hoerner to Start at Fullback Spot," *Los Angeles Times*, September 27, 1951, IV-3.
78. "Fines Rescinded by Rams' Coach," *Los Angeles Times*, September 16, 1951, IV-1.

1951 Rams Offense—
The Xs and Os

Lee Elder

The Rams' offenses of the 1950s are best known for their high-octane passing attack. Hall of Fame quarterbacks Bob Waterfield and Norm Van Brocklin threw passes to Hall of Fame receivers Elroy Hirsch and Tom Fears. The Rams wracked up points like a wet foot collects sand on a Southern California beach. They scored 32.7 points per game the year they won the title, down from an amazing 38.8 the year before.

Almost any offense might have worked with that personnel. The Rams employed assistant coach Hampton Pool's Fly T offense, an attack which had some ideas still in use today. Oddly, for all the glitz and glamour the Rams' passing attack generated, the Fly T was a running attack at its heart. A 1951 mid-game decision by Joe Stydahar took advantage of that fact and gave prominence to the other well-known piece of the Rams' attack: the Bull Elephant Backfield.

In his 1957 book, *Fly T Football*, Pool said, "The heart of the Fly offense was (a) the HB and FB Flys which include always the fake of one and the running of the other, (b) quick traps up the middle, (c) HB sweeps opposite the flanker (d) statues, particularly to the weak side and (e) a few passes off the running fakes…. To these basic maneuvers, the Rams added only those plays which were suggested by the observations made during game time or were picked up by in-person scouting or viewing movies of opponents." Pool added, "The philosophy of the Fly series is one of men who love daring offensive football…. We put great emphasis on deception by the whole team…. The basic strategy is…. The HB and FB Flys work together so as one is run, the other is always faked to hold the defense a moment … to give the runners a few steps advantage."[1]

The deceptions and the skill of the deceptors made for a maddening brew. Defend the pass and the Rams would run. "Deacon Dan" Towler, Paul "Tank" Younger and Dick Hoerner gave the Rams three running backs who all weighed 220 pounds and were the Bull Elephants. Younger was a starting linebacker for the Rams that season. The starting running backs were Hoerner, Jerry Williams (5–10, 175) and Verda Thomas "Vitamin T" Smith (5–8, 179).

NFL squads were limited to 33 players in 1951. It was much harder to match a defense with specialists against a given offensive alignment in that era. In fact, it was hard to make a change of personnel on offense to counter a defensive move, too. Remember that Younger, a bulwark of the Bull Elephants, was a defensive starter.

The Fly T was an outgrowth of the T Formation used by the Chicago Bears. Both

90 Part 2: The 1951 Season

Stydahar and Pool had been assistants for George Halas in Chicago and the Rams' head coach prior to Stydahar, Clark Shaughnessy, also coached for Halas. The Rams lined up with three runners behind the quarterback and both ends split a few yards from the tackle on each side.[2]

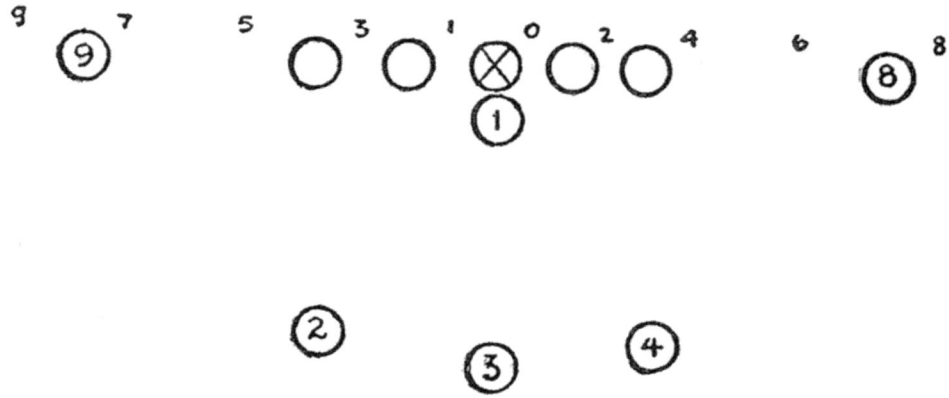

Basic Formation (from *Fly T Football*).

The basic formation for the 1950 and 1951 Rams. The Bull Elephant backfield (players 2, 3 and 4) frequently lined up this way. The ends (players 9 and 8) typically lined up within two to three yards of the tackles unless a back was deployed as a flanker. The small numbers indicate the numbering system for the holes ball carriers were to run through.

This fake-toss play came from the Rams' standard offensive formation for 1950 and much of the 1951 season. Notice the faking required of the quarterback for this play. The

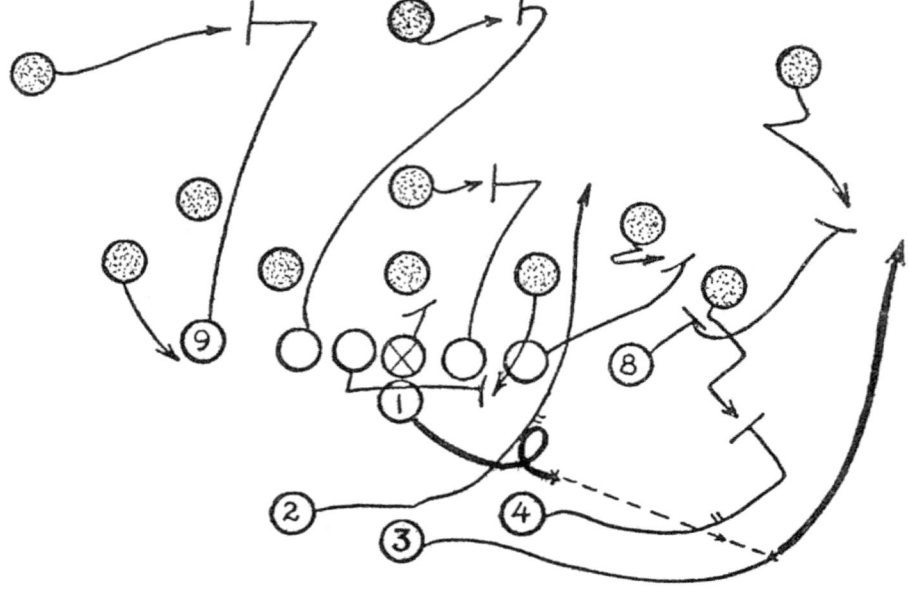

Fake Toss Series Play (from *Fly T Football*).

basic Fly T play required sophisticated ball handling by the quarterback and that the running backs carry out convincing fakes.

Late in the 1951 season, the Rams curtailed their use of a man in motion on passing plays in favor of using one running back as a flanker back.

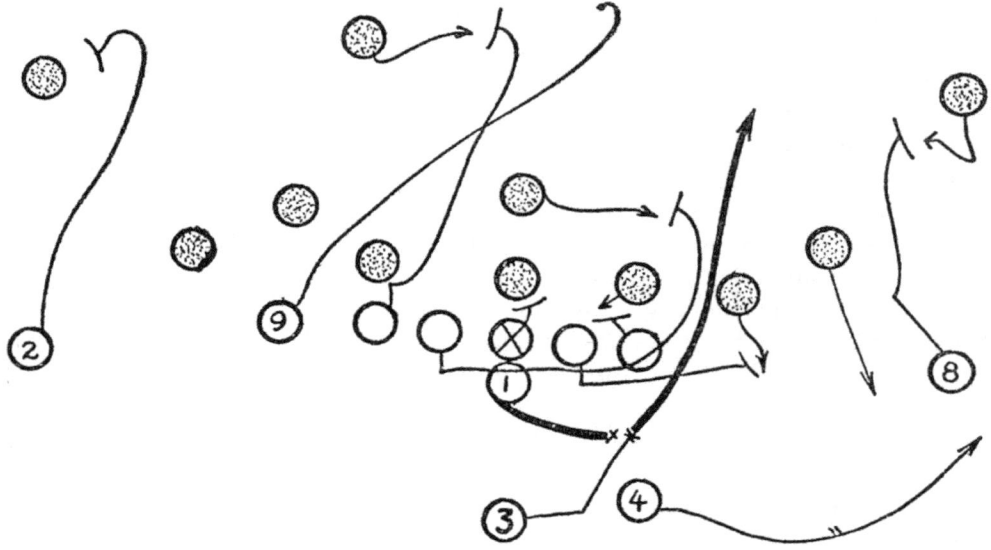

1951 FB Fly (from *Fly T Football*).

The Rams flanked a receiver outside the ends in this formation (to the left here). The ability to attack a defense across the width of the field was new. The Rams and the Cleveland Browns trailblazed the idea in the early 1950s. The play diagrammed here is the version of the Fullback Fly the Rams used most frequently during the 1951 campaign.

Defenses in the league were evolving as well. Pool wrote that defensive schemes from the college game came into pro ball through coaches in the then-defunct All-America Football Conference. AAFC teams used combinations of zone defenses, Pool wrote. Then the Eagles' defense, an alignment with five down linemen and two linebackers named after the Philadelphia Eagles whose coach Greasy Neal invented it, came into use. The linebackers, Pool wrote, "harass and delay the receivers and cover short passes, and the deep umbrella covers the long passes." Adherents of the 5–2 could use either zone or man-to-man defenses in the deep backfield, Pool said, but the teams who covered Fears and Hirsch with man-to-man schemes got punished.[3] As much as anything, the 5–2 was a solid format to use against the run.

Hirsch said most teams used, "mainly 6–1, 5–2 or 5–3 sets. There were no complicated zones, bump and run or any of those things. When I first got to the Rams, it was a daring move to rush a linebacker. If you did it, everyone made a big thing of it."[4] Hirsch added, "Mostly they'd [opposing defenses] work me over at the line. They'd either rotate their defensive backs or put one deep and one nose up on me at the line of scrimmage. That was okay, though, because when they did that it left a wide open situation on the other side. After a while, they started shifting linebackers over to bother me. But even that helped us. We ran a lot better with that linebacker out of there."

The Fly T put a premium on ball handling and fakes by the quarterback. Pool's book shows some of the intricate footwork required for the passer as he progresses through fakes in the running game. The Rams' first three offensive plays of the second half of the championship game serve as primary examples of the intricate dynamics of Fly T backfield play. All three plays were run out of a two-back set. On first down, Waterfield spun to his left around so far as to fake a pitch out for a fullback run around the *right* side. Waterfield completed spinning and handed off to Glenn Davis, the left halfback, on a drive up the middle. The second-down play was dazzling; Waterfield faked a pitch to Towler going right, spun around and faked again on a give to Davis up the middle and finally spun around far enough to pitch to Towler for a run around the right end. Waterfield spun about 540 degrees on the play. On third down, with both guards pulling, and perhaps to avoid getting dizzy, Waterfield executed a simpler fake pitch to his right before handing the ball to Towler on a drive off the right side for a first down.

The mind-numbing backfield fakes were designed to confuse the opposition's defenders. When the Rams began using sets with three receivers and two running backs, they challenged defenses to deal with the deceptions in the backfield and an extra wide out. This was really the birth of the modern-day offense. Still, with all of the fancy foot work and the quarterback's trickery with the football in his hands, the saying about football and most other sports still rang true for the 1951 Rams: It isn't the X's and O's, coaches say, it's the Billys and Joes.

The Rams had great players and Stydahar understood that great players make coaches look smart. For all of the futuristic ideas in Pool's offense, it was Stydahar's decision to use three human bulldozers in the backfield at the same time that gave the running attack its oomph. The Rams lost to the 49ers in San Francisco, 44–17, on October 28 that season and were scheduled to play the same team a week later in Los Angeles. The Rams rushed for 131 yards on 31 attempts, averaging 3.8 yards a run in the first 49ers game. Hoerner was the Rams leading ball carrier, gaining 45 yards on 10 carries.

Legend has it that Stydahar came up with the Bull Elephant idea between games and installed it during Tuesday's practice. It was enough to make defensive backs shudder. Stydahar unleashed the Elephants in the second half of the second game against San Francisco and things were different for Los Angeles. The Rams ran the ball 43 times in the rematch and plowed forward for 155 yards. Towler led the Rams with 54 yards on just 11 carries, including a 31-yarder. Ironically, Waterfield scored the only rushing touchdown for the Rams, but they avenged their loss with a 23–16 victory. Waterfield and Van Brocklin passed for an additional 202 yards. Los Angeles went into the game sputtering along with a 3–2 record. They finished the season with a 5–2 run before beating the Browns for the championship.[5]

It wasn't the only time an adjustment reaped good results that season. In the October 21 game against the Packers in Wisconsin, the teams struggled to a scoreless tie after two quarters. Then the Rams scored a touchdown in the third quarter and three more in the final stanza to win easily, 28–0. The Packers had invented a scheme to stop the Rams' running game and the Rams tweaked their most basic blocking assignment to blow a hole in the Green Bay defense.

"In 1951 the first Green Bay game ... the halfback pitchout was run into a split E side for the first time, and again it was noticed that the defensive end pursued to the outside and, in addition, the adjacent T pinched hard so he couldn't be trapped. This left the off T hole on the spread side wide open, and at half-time, the answer was devised in the form of a fake HB pitch and feed to the FB, as in the Yank game" of 1950. The Rams finished with 323 rushing yards that day. In the rematch the Rams averaged 5.8 yards per carry, passed for 256 additional yards and beat the Packers 42–14.

The 1951 Rams might have been the first NFL team to win a championship game with five rookies starting along the offensive line. Given the complexity of Pool's offense, for its time, it was amazing to see what was accomplished by the group.

The typical offensive line calls for its guards to be quicker afoot than the tackles. Guards do the pulling on sweeps and other wide plays. But Pool's preference was for his tackles to be the fastest linemen. Pool wrote, "In our system the T's [sic][6] are faster than the G's; in fact fast G's and big blocking E's who have poor pass receiving and ball-carrying ability are converted into T's. Speed is essential because the HB Fly plays require the T to pull and lead the Fly man.... The T's will also have to become adept at pp blocking."[7]

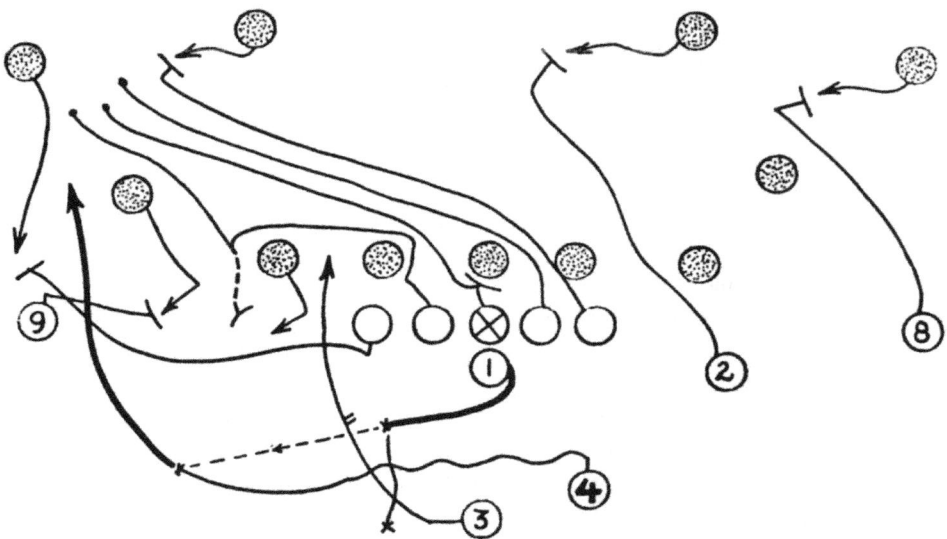

49 Halfback Fly (from *Fly T Football*).

Note that in this play, the 49 Fly or Halfback Fly, the left halfback starts in pre-snap motion and the left tackle leads the halfback around end and upfield. In Pool's offense, the tackles were the quickest linemen rather than the guards. Pool wrote that this specific version of the play is the one used by the Rams. The Rams stopped using motion plays late in the season after they started using three-wide receiver sets, but this diagram shows both elements.

In the play diagrammed below on page 74, the 35 Fly (Fullback Fly), the fullback runs off left tackle. The left tackle blocks the defensive tackle to his front and the right tackle is responsible for blocking upfield. Pool wrote that "the FB off T Fly was the only one the Rams used—the other FB plays over the interior of the line were traps, draws, etc."

Pool's Fly T theory called for a revolutionary type of pass protection. "Our pass protection strategy will sometimes vary with the methods used by the opposition to rush the QB, but in general the best plan is to have the T's block toward the middle with the G's

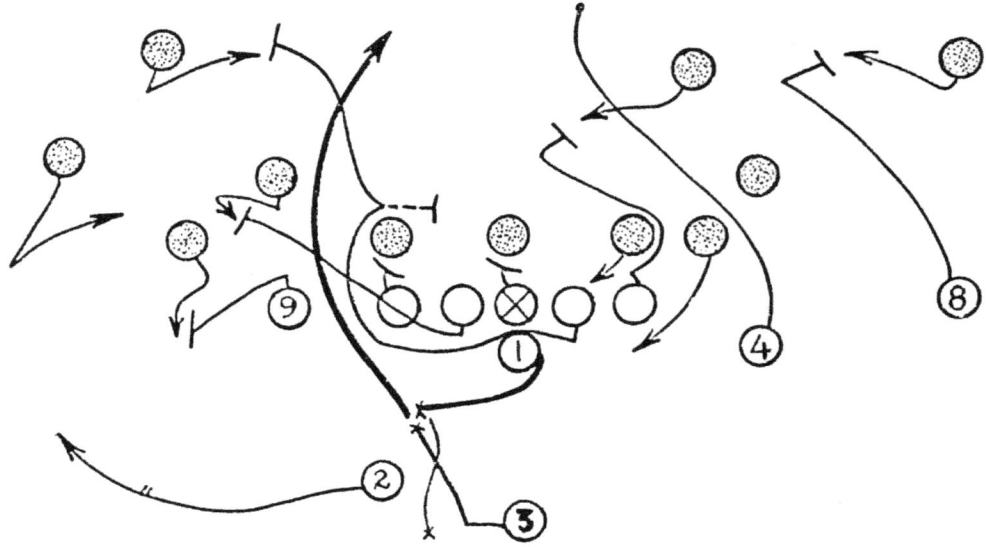

35 Fullback Fly (from *Fly T Football*).

bump and retreat slightly. Their movements set up plays like the statues in which they fake pp, then pull out," Pool wrote.[8]

In the championship game the Rams proceeded as called for, sweeping left guard (Dick Daugherty) to the outside of left tackle (Don Simensen) on some pass protection plays. The Browns put seven men on the line of scrimmage most of the game but shifted the down linemen so that they were offset to the left. The Browns' linebacker and defensive end on the offensive left side were on the line of scrimmage and were in upright positions. The Rams used Simensen to block down on a Cleveland interior lineman. Daugherty was assigned to block Cleveland's great defensive end Len Ford.[9] In some sets Daugherty got help from a back. In other situations, if Ford did not rush the passer, Daugherty acted more like a personal protector for the Rams' passer, floating back toward the quarterback and looking for leaks in the protective pocket. On Van Brocklin's fourth-quarter 73-yard bomb to Fears, the play that broke the 17–17 tie and provided the Rams with the winning points, the Rams lined up in their three-back set. Both Hirsch and Fears lined up within two or three yards of a tackle, Fears left and Hirsch right. At the snap the Rams' left guard drifted back and picked up the rushing Ford, with help from fullback Dan Towler. The left tackle blocked down on the play and Fears, the Rams' left end, had to fight through a defender on the line of scrimmage in order to get downfield. The Rams right halfback stayed in for pass protection and left halfback, Glenn Davis, drifted into the left flat. Van Brocklin had enough time to throw a strike to Fears, who had run a sideline pattern on the play and caught the pass between two defensive backs. The Cleveland defenders bumped into each other, and the play went the distance.

The single biggest problem Stydahar and Pool had in coaching the Rams' offense in 1950 and 1951 was that there was only one football used on a given play. As noted above, the Rams had four future members of the Pro Football Hall of Fame between its quarterbacks and primary wideouts. When the team started flanking halfbacks out as receivers in 1951, the formation allowed the Rams to attack the defense across the width of the field through the air but the backs the Rams employed then were all potential receivers whether sent out as flankers or lined up as running backs. Even the Bull Elephants were potential pass catchers. Further, Pool's offense was still developing. The Rams stopped using the man-in-motion procedure late in the season when they started flanking their backs. The Rams' formation thus gradually loosened up by comparison with its standard T predecessor in order to help the already strong passing game.

Pool told Steve Bisheff, "Clark Shaughnessy was the first coach to split his receivers out in the late 40s. What I did really was make a running back into a flanker. Before that, they often would send him in motion and utilize him as a receiver. But we put him out there from the beginning. I guess what made me do it was our personnel. It seemed made for it. We had a bunch of guys who were equally adept catching the ball as they were running with it. People like Glenn Davis, Tommy Kalmanir and Vitamin T. Smith."[10]

Pool wrote, "The spread of the Fly formation puts three receivers out fast and a fourth if we can spare him from blocking. ... One also has the further offensive option of spreading the defense (a) lengthwise, with a wave of receivers simultaneously springing off the line, and (b) sideways, with the delayed swing man who shows after the decoys have gone deep. Many of our patterns are four men out."[11]

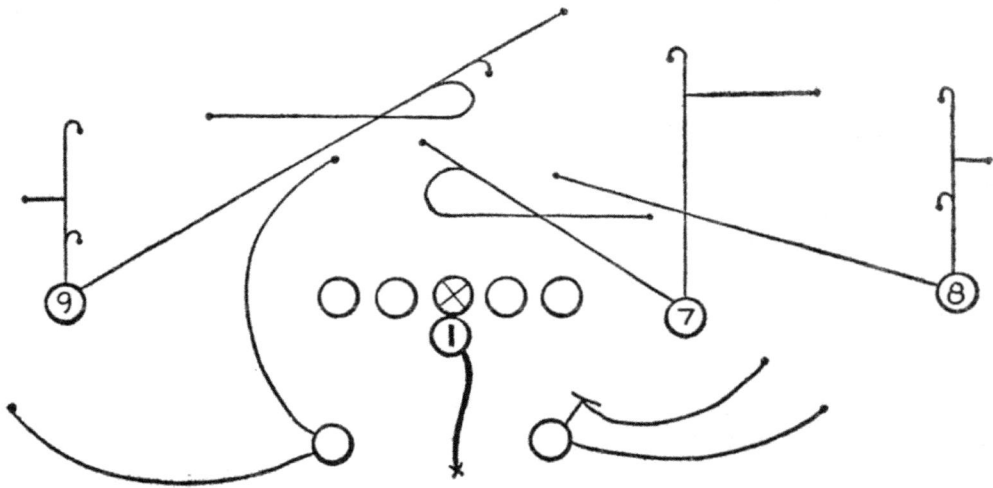

Fly Formation (from *Fly T Football*).

With three wide receivers and two running backs, the Rams did not employ a tight end. Players 8 and 9 in the illustration above are the ends. Player 7 is the flanker. Most of the patterns in this diagram result in the receiver facing the quarterback, which Pool felt helped guard against interceptions.

The fullback screen (on page 96) run out of what Pool termed an "abnormal" backfield. Note that both guards initially pull out of the line for pass protection before the left guard bumps a rusher and then leads the fullback downfield. The fullback fakes pass protection before drifting out to catch the pass. This play initially looks like a pass to the left halfback.

The Rams passed to their backs frequently in 1951. The Bull Elephants, Towler, Hoerner and Younger, caught 29 throws for 431 yards and a touchdown. Towler and Smith led the running backs in receptions with 16 each. Smith gained 278 yards and

96   Part 2: The 1951 Season

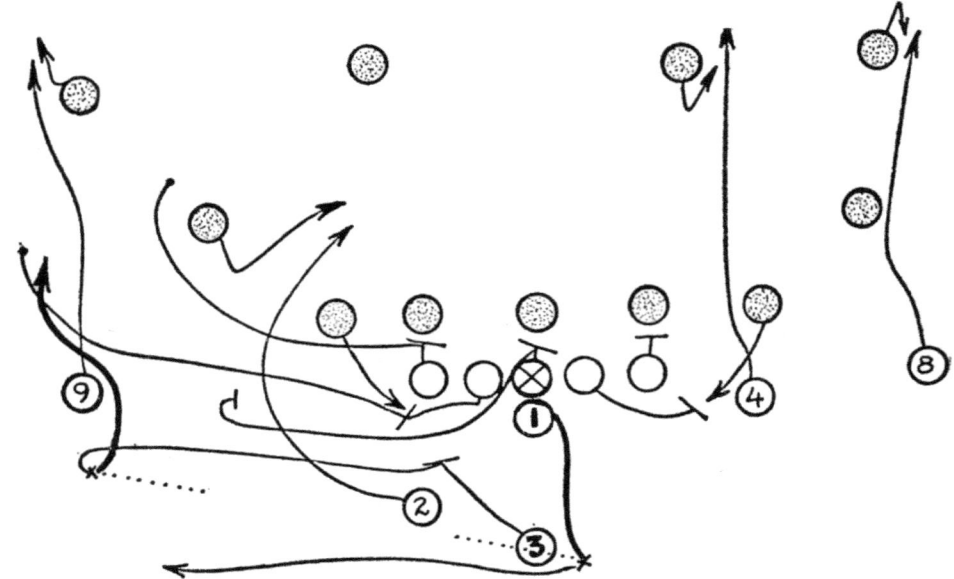

FB Screen Left (from *Fly T Football*).

scored a touchdown. Towler gained 257 yards on aerial plays. The shifty, quick backs like Smith and Glenn Davis gave opposing defenses a witch's brew of receivers coming out of the backfield to worry about.

With all of the above explained, the Rams' offense leaned heaviest upon the passing chemistry between Van Brocklin and Waterfield throwing to Fears and Hirsch.

Waterfield explained to Bisheff that while he and Van Brocklin played together, "I started almost all games. I'd come out at the end of the first quarter and go back at the start of the third. Norm would play the second and fourth periods. Unless one of us was off. Then the procedure would be altered."[12]

Fears said being teamed with Hirsch made his job easier. "It was helpful, no question about it. Not only that, we had a lot of backs who were all very mobile and fast. And all of them were good receivers, too…. Hirsch was the deep threat and I was the short yardage specialist. But that can be exaggerated a bit. You know there's only four yards difference in our career averages. His is 18 something and mine was 14 something."[13]

Hirsch's lifetime average was 18.2 yards per catch. He averaged a bit more as a Ram, 18.4 yards. Fears averaged 13.5 through his career but his playoff game average was significantly better at 19.6 yards per reception. Hirsch averaged 13.1 yards per reception in playoff games.[14]

The Rams developed Hirsch as a deep threat by having Waterfield and Van Brocklin throw long passes in practice. The idea was that Hirsch would catch the ball as it came directly over his head, something many wide outs couldn't do then or now.

"Then we had Tom Fears playing the other end," Hirsch said. "There was no finer end in football when it came to running the buttonhook and sideline patterns. And he had deceiving speed. I think we all kind of complimented each other."[15]

"Hirsch had that great quickness and tremendous moves," Waterfield said. "He could go deep very well. Fears was big and strong. Both were excellent runners after they caught the ball. When it was third and three, you'd go to Fears. When it was first and 40, you might go to Hirsch."[16]

And, just to shake everything up a little, Pool devised a system of quarterback drills in which there would be no huddle. The Rams could run more plays this way and one is left with the imaginative potential of the 1951 Rams running a no-huddle offense. They did not play without huddling often. The Rams were explosive enough without rushing up to the line between plays.

Pool's instructions were finely detailed for the offensive backfield. The quarterback's steps and fakes were carefully choreographed. The fullbacks and halfbacks also had very precise instructions for each play. But it was different for the passing game. The receivers were assigned a location where they were to arrive in time to catch a pass. How they reached the correct position was mostly up to the receiver.

Hirsch said, "I never ran any patterns, as such, until Sid Gillman became our coach. Before Sid, it was all mostly individual stuff. They'd just call wide post and they knew where I'd end up. The moves were up to me. Under Sid, I had more trouble. He wanted the patterns precise and he wanted them called by number. So all of a sudden, they'd call the blocking formation and then say 92. It was really a tough thing for me to adjust to."[17]

The freedom Hirsch, Fears and the other Rams receivers enjoyed in Pool's offense may have allowed for more creativity, as Hirsch said. That alone gave the opposition problems. Considering the deceptive ball handling the Fly T demanded, the quick backs and ground pounders the Rams' running game had, and the Hall of Fame passing attack and field-stretching formations the Rams employed at will, it's a wonder that the Rams didn't score more points than they did.

Notes

1. Hamp Pool, *Fly T Football* (Englewood Cliffs, NJ: Prentice-Hall, 1957), 18–19.
2. Pool, *Fly T Football*, 9–10.
3. Pool, *Fly T Football*, 10.
4. Steve Bisheff, *Great Teams' Great Years: Los Angeles Rams* (New York: Macmillan, 1973), 109.
5. The statistics for the two 49ers game came from *Pro-Football-Reference.com*.
6. Pool's text uses letter abbreviations for positions: T-tackle, G-guard, E-end, HB-halfback, FB-fullback, QB-quarterback, pp-pass protect.
7. Pool, *Fly T Football*, 30.
8. Pool, *Fly T Football*, 91.
9. Ford is a member of the Pro Football Hall of Fame. Ironically, he started his pro career as a member of the AAFC's Los Angeles Dons. Ford played for the Browns from 1950 through 1957 and finished his career with a season in Green Bay.
10. Bisheff, *Los Angeles Rams*, 125.
11. Pool, *Fly T Football*, 95.
12. Bisheff, *Los Angeles Rams*, 135.
13. Bisheff, *Los Angeles Rams*, 104.
14. *Pro-Football-Reference.com*.
15. Bisheff, *Los Angeles Rams*, 111.
16. Bisheff, *Los Angeles Rams*, 134.
17. Bisheff, *Los Angeles Rams*, 113. Gillman became the Rams head coach in 1955.

All illustrations are from Fly T Football.

1951 Regular Season Game Summaries

RUPERT PATRICK, RICH SHMELTER
and NEAL GOLDEN

September 28, 1951—Week 1: New York Yanks at Los Angeles Rams

Los Angeles Memorial Coliseum

NY Yanks	0	7	0	7	14
Los Angeles	21	13	7	13	54

Los Angeles—Hirsch 41 pass from Van Brocklin (Fears kick)
Los Angeles—Hoerner 22 run (Fears kick)
Los Angeles—V Smith 67 pass from Van Brocklin (Fears kick)
Los Angeles—Van Brocklin 1 run (Fears kick)
Los Angeles—Hirsch 47 pass from Van Brocklin (kick failed)
New York—Young 79 punt return (Johnson kick)
Los Angeles—Hirsch 26 pass from Van Brocklin (Fears kick)
New York—Tait 30 fumble return (Johnson kick)
Los Angeles—Hirsch 1 pass from Van Brocklin (Fears kick)
Los Angeles—Towler 1 run (kick failed)
A—30,310

	NYY	LA
First Downs	13	34
Rushing A-Y	34-103	29-181
Passing C-A-I	10-35-0	27-42-3
Passing Yards	63	554
Sacked N-Y	6-55	1-13
Total Plays, Yards	69-166	71-735
Punts-Yards	14-484	4-160
Field Goals M-A	0-0	0-1
Fumbles-Lost	1-0	2-2
Penalties-Yards	7-91	11-80

Rushing
(Attempts, Yards)

New York—Toth 15-57; Howard 11-34; Young 3-16; Celeri 2-7; Pollard 1-(-1); Taliaferro 1-(-2); Wallace 1-(-8).
Los Angeles—Hoerner 8-81; Williams 8-29; Kalmanir 4-38; V Smith 3-27; Towler 3-6; Van Brocklin 2-(-3); Hirsch 1-3

Passing
(Attempts, Completions, Interceptions, Yards)
New York—Rauch 17-7-0-38; Celeri 10-2-0-16; Wallace 8-1-0-9
Los Angeles—Van Brocklin 41-27-2-554; Keane 1-0-1-0

Receptions
(Catches, Yards)
New York—Edwards 3-25; Young 3-17; Toth 2-19; Howard 2-2
Los Angeles—Hirsch 9-173; Fears 7-162; V Smith 2-103; Kalmanir 2-40; Towler 2-30; Williams 2-22; Keane 2-10; Boyd 1-14

Interceptions
New York—Crowe; Griffen; Aldrich
Los Angeles—None

Fumbles Recovered
New York—Nagel; Tait
Los Angeles—None

Missed Field Goals
New York—None
Los Angeles—Hecker 34

The 1951 NFL season began under the lights, with the defending National Conference champion Los Angeles Rams hosting the New York Yanks at the Los Angeles Coliseum on a clear Friday night. The game was originally scheduled to be held at Yankee Stadium on Monday, October 1, but with the New York Yankees in the World Series, the game had to be shifted to the West Coast to keep Yankee Stadium open,[1] and the game was also moved up three days, with an 8:30 p.m. PST kickoff.

The Rams came into the contest without their starting quarterback, Bob Waterfield, who injured his knee in the final preseason game against the Giants.[2] Fortunately for Los Angeles, they had a backup named Norm Van Brocklin who along with Waterfield and Otto Graham of Cleveland were the three best quarterbacks in the NFL. "Mr. Outside" would be on the outside looking in on this game for Los Angeles, as halfback Glenn Davis was out with a hip pointer.[3] Herb Rich and Charlie Toogood would also be sitting this game out due to injuries, but Elroy "Crazylegs" Hirsch would be back after breaking a cheekbone in an exhibition contest.[4]

Dick Hoerner, who had a big game in the Rams' 43–35 victory over the Yanks in Week 10 of the 1950 season (14 rushes for 129 yards and three touchdowns), would be starting at fullback.[5] Coach Joe Stydahar would also be starting five rookies on his offensive line; tackles Don Simensen and Tom Dahms, guards Dick Daugherty and Bill Lange, and Center Leon McLaughlin.[6]

The Yanks were coached by Jimmy Phelan, who was hired when Coach Red Strader parted ways with the team early in training camp,[7] and the team struggled in the preseason, dropping all six exhibition contests. Phelan was no stranger to the Southland, as he coached the Los Angeles Dons of the AAFC during the 1948 and 1949 seasons. The Yanks' offense would be controlled by quarterback John Rauch, who took the reins when George Ratterman left to play for the Montreal Alouettes of the CFL.[8] Zollie (Tugboat) Toth, Buddy Young and Sherman Howard looked to be the main ballcarriers, and Dan Garza and Bruce Alford were penciled in to be the starting ends for the game against the Rams.[9]

The Rams came into the game a three-touchdown favorite,[10] but Coach Stydahar was worried the Rams would not take the Yanks seriously, and said, "The Yanks are in a perfect spot to pull an upset. They didn't win an exhibition game and we won four out of six,"

He added, "And our guys are looking forward to next week's game with the Browns. Some of them feel we can take the Yanks in stride."[11]

The Rams' first drive petered out and Norb Hecker (who took over the kicking duties for the injured Waterfield), attempted a field goal that came up short.[12] After the Yanks failed to respond, the first of Van Brocklin's salvos on the day went to "Crazylegs" Hirsch, who beat Bob Celeri on a scoring pass that went for 41 yards. Tom Fears added the extra point to make it 7–0 Los Angeles four minutes into the game.[13]

Los Angeles got the ball back at their 32, and it took three plays before Hoerner burst through the middle for 22 yards, carrying a couple Yanks into the end zone with him, with the ensuing extra point making it 14–0 Rams.

Once again, the Rams got their hands on the ball, and it didn't take long to put points on the board, as Vitamin T. Smith took a pass from the Dutchman 67 yards to make it 21–0 Rams after one period.

The Rams got the ball back at their two-yard line and took the ball the length of the field. Van Brocklin snuck it in from a yard out to give the Rams a 28–0 lead, and the rout was on.

After another unsuccessful New York drive, Van Brocklin and Hirsch hooked up again, this time from 47 yards away. The extra point attempt failed, and the Rams led by 34.

The Yanks finally held the Rams on downs, and Van Brocklin punted, with Young taking the punt at his 21 and weaving his way through the Los Angeles defenders before breaking free near midfield and taking it to the end zone. The extra point from Harvey Johnson cut the Los Angeles lead to 34–7.

Shortly before halftime, Rauch was ejected from the game for throwing a punch.[14] The Yanks' passing duties were shared between Celeri and Bev Wallace for the remainder of the game.

In the third frame, Hirsch pulled in another touchdown pass from Van Brocklin, this time from 26 yards out, making the score 41–7.

On the first play of the fourth quarter, the Yanks got on the board again when Art Tait snatched a lateral from Van Brocklin to Hoerner and ran it 30 yards to the end zone, trimming the Rams lead to 41–14.

Later in the fourth, the Rams faced a third-and-goal at their one-yard line, and Van Brocklin faked a handoff to Towler, who ran into the line. Hirsch started moving into the left flat unguarded, where he caught Van Brocklin's toss and stepped across the goal line for the score. This pass tied the record for most passing yards in a game of 468 held by Johnny Lujack of the Chicago Bears in a game against the Chicago Cardinals in 1949.[15] Fears added the conversion, making the score 48–14.

Deacon Dan Towler burst over from one yard out to end the scoring for the day. The extra point failed, and the final score was Rams 54, Yanks 14.

As you can guess, a lot of people were talking about what they had just seen. "They don't need me anymore,"[16] Bob Waterfield joked. "It was the finest exhibition of passing I've ever seen,"[17] Yanks coach Phelan admitted. "Our defensive team played a great game," Coach Stydahar said sarcastically, but when asked about the offense, he added, "That was good, too"[18] and added that Van Brocklin's performance was "as good as any I have ever seen anywhere, anytime."[19]

Numerous records were set in this game, including the Rams' record of 735 total yards of offense, which broke the mark of 682 the Bears accumulated against the Giants in 1943. Norm Van Brocklin's record of 554 passing yards has never been broken, and the

Rams' single-game offensive yards mark of 735 also stands to this day. The 34 total first downs by Los Angeles broke the previous single game record of 32 held by the Rams in 1950 and the Cardinals in 1949, and the record stood until the Steelers picked up 36 first downs against the Cardinals in 1958. George Taliaferro's 14 punts for New York tied a single game record that lasted until 1987.[20] Elroy Hirsch's four touchdown catches was a personal career high, and his nine receptions set a personal record that he tied twice later in his career; this was arguably the greatest game of his Hall of Fame career.

October 7, 1951—Game 2: Cleveland Browns at Los Angeles Rams

Los Angeles Memorial Coliseum

Cleveland	7	0	21	10	38
Los Angeles	10	0	7	6	23

Los Angeles—Hirsch 34 pass from Van Brocklin (Waterfield kick)
Los Angeles—Field Goal Waterfield 47
Cleveland—Carpenter 45 pass from Graham (Groza kick)
Cleveland—Carpenter 2 run (Groza kick)
Cleveland—Carpenter 7 run (Groza kick)
Cleveland—Lahr 23 interception return (Groza kick)
Los Angeles—Davis 1 run (Waterfield kick)
Cleveland—Field Goal Groza 44
Los Angeles—Davis 14 pass from Van Brocklin (kick failed)
Cleveland—D Jones 1 run (Groza kick)
A—67,186

	CLE	LA
First Downs	26	18
Rushing A-Y	49-293	28-88
Passing C-A-I	10-19-2	12-33-3
Passing Yards	219	235
Sacked N-Y	7-62	1-11
Total Plays, Yards	68-512	61-323
Punts-Yards	4-180	5-230
Field Goals M-A	1-2	1-2
Fumbles-Lost	2-1	1-1
Penalties-Yards	18-145	6-40

Rushing
(Attempts, Yards)
Cleveland—D Jones 15-110; Motley 13-106; Carpenter 8-39; Bumgardner 6-16; Phelps 3-20; Graham 3-2; Cole 1-0
Los Angeles—Towler 8-33; Davis 8-27; V Smith 5-12; Kalmanir 3-9; Williams 2-(-3); Hoerner 1-6; Van Brocklin 1-4

Passing
(Attempts, Completions, Interceptions, Yards)
Cleveland—Graham 19-10-2-219
Los Angeles—Van Brocklin 17-6-2-129; Waterfield 16-6-1-106

Receptions
(Catches, Yards)
Cleveland—D Jones 3-57; Lavelli 3-39; Carpenter 1-45; Speedie 1-41; Gillom 1-20; Cole 1-17

Los Angeles—Fears 5–45; Hirsch 4–69; V Smith 1–61; Towler 1–46; Davis 1–14

Interceptions
Cleveland—Adamle; Lahr; Lavelli
Los Angeles—Younger; Keane

Fumbles Recovered
Cleveland—Thompson
Los Angeles—W Lewis

Missed Field Goals
Cleveland—Groza 44
Los Angeles—Waterfield 31 blocked

The defending NFL champion Cleveland Browns came to Los Angeles to face the Rams in a rematch of the 1950 title game. Paul Brown's crew lost their season opener in San Francisco 24–10 but were still a formidable team. Despite injuries to Hal Herring and Chubby Grigg that would force them to miss the Rams' game,[21] the Browns still had numerous weapons such as quarterback Otto Graham, running back Marion Motley, a great pair of receivers in Mac Speedie and Dante Lavelli, along with kicker Lou Groza, whose toe produced a last-minute defeat for the Rams in the previous championship game.

The Rams came into the game relatively healthy, as Bob Waterfield, Glenn Davis and Jack Finlay would be available against Cleveland after having missed the opener against the Yanks. Norm Van Brocklin would again get the start at quarterback.[22]

This would be the first time the Browns ever came into a game as an underdog,[23] as the betting public made the Rams seven-point favorites. Browns coach Paul Brown commented, "We have a 33-man squad and exactly one-third of it is in no condition to play."[24] The crowd of over 67,000 spectators would also have to contend with the heat as it was the hottest day of the year in Los Angeles. With the temperature in the mid–90s,[25] about 50 fans were treated for heat prostration during the game.[26] The conditions would be even worse for the players as the temperature on the field reached 114 degrees during the game.[27]

The game began at 2:15 p.m. PST, with the Browns starting out on offense. The drive petered out after Graham was sacked on third down, with the short punt by Horace Gillom going out of bounds at the Rams' 34-yard line.

An interference penalty against the Browns (one of 18 Cleveland penalties on the afternoon) put the ball at midfield. After a pass to Davis for 14 yards, Van Brocklin dropped back and aimed it for Crazylegs Hirsch on a deep pattern. Hirsch had a step on Warren Lahr and Cliff Lewis, and made a fingertip catch in the middle of the end zone. The extra point from Waterfield made it 7–0 Rams as just over four minutes were elapsed.

One play after the ensuing kickoff, Graham threw to Gillom in the left flat, but the ball went off his hands and was intercepted by Tank Younger at the Cleveland 36. The Rams' offense was unable to move the ball, and Waterfield booted a 47-yard field goal to make it 10–0 in favor of the home team.

Graham got the Browns' offense moving, with passes to Dub Jones for 12 yards, and Speedie for 41 more to the Rams' 39. Lavelli pulled in a pass for 15, and then Dub ran left, getting to the 12-yard line where he coughed it up, with Woodley Lewis recovering for the Rams at their seven-yard line.

After an exchange of punts, Vitamin T. Smith fumbled, and Tommy Thompson recovered for Cleveland at their 42. Motley took a handoff through right tackle for 13 yards, and then, Otto threw a screen to Ken Carpenter who zipped down the left side and just got by Woodley Lewis to slip into the end zone. The successful point after touchdown from Groza cut the Rams' lead to 10–7 after the first quarter.

Graham went deep to Jones in the middle left, gaining 36 yards to the Rams' 35. The drive stalled after a couple penalties and a sack by Younger, and Groza failed on a 44-yard field goal attempt midway through the second frame.

The Rams lost a golden opportunity when Tommy Kalmanir caught a pass at midfield and took it to the Browns' 25, but a penalty wiped out the 40-yard pass play. Waterfield connected with Hirsch in the middle for 14 and nine yards, and Kalmanir carried left for five yards to the Cleveland 24 where the Browns' defense stiffened. Waterfield attempted a 31-yard field goal, but it was blocked by John Sandusky, who took the kick directly in the face, with the Rams taking over at their 41. The Browns got to the Rams' 32 when time ran out on the first half with Los Angeles holding onto a 10–7 advantage.

The Rams started the second half on offense, but a sack on third down (when Bill Willis got to Van Brocklin) brought out the punt team. Cleveland started from their 42-yard line, and over the course of 15 plays put the ball in the end zone. Jones caught a pass on the right sideline for nine yards, and after a penalty against the Browns, a screen to Dub was good for 14 yards to the Los Angeles 40. Otto snuck it on fourth-and-inches, picking up four yards, and Emerson Cole made his only touch of the day a good one, when he took a pass from Graham 17 yards before going out of bounds at the Rams' five-yard line. Jones ran it to the two, and after Carpenter was stuffed on second down, he got the call again on third down and ran at right tackle and went over for the score. Groza added the extra point, and the Browns had a 14–10 lead with six and a half minutes to play in the third.

On the first play after the kickoff, a pass from Van Brocklin was batted at the line by John Kissell and went up in the air like a volleyball before coming down in the hands of Tony Adamle at the Rams' 19. Dub ran around the left side of the line for 12 yards, and Carpenter took a pitch and went through left tackle for the remaining seven yards. Groza nailed the extra point, giving Cleveland a 21–10 lead with four and a half minutes left to play in the third stanza.

Jerry Williams took the kickoff from Groza just inside the end zone and returned it to the Rams' 16-yard line. After two running plays went nowhere, Waterfield went to the air on third down, but Lahr stepped in front of Hirsch and intercepted the ball at the 23, dashing down the left sideline untouched for the pick six. After scoring three touchdowns in three minutes, Cleveland built up a commanding 28–10 lead with a couple minutes to play in the period.

A penalty on the kickoff return set the Rams back to their 11, and a pass from Waterfield to Fears was good for six yards. Waterfield fired to Vitamin T. at the Los Angeles 30, and Smith zipped down the right sideline before he was knocked out of bounds at the Cleveland 22 after a 61-yard gain. Runs by Towler for six, six and nine yards put the ball three feet short of the goal line, where Davis ran it across to cut the Cleveland lead to 28–17 after three quarters.

Following an exchange of punts, Otto nailed Lavelli on the right sideline for 18 yards to the Los Angeles 45. Two runs gained nine yards, and after an offside penalty against the Browns, Motley ran the ball up the gut on third-and-six but came up two yards short. Groza split the uprights from 44 yards out to extend the Cleveland lead to 31–17 with just under 10 minutes to play.

The kickoff went for a touchback, and two runs by Towler were enough for a first down. The drive stalled after that, until Van Brocklin faked a punt on fourth down, throwing to Towler at midfield and the Deacon broke several tackles before going down at the Cleveland 13 after the play gained 46 yards. After a pass to Davis in the left flat failed on first down, Van Brocklin called the same play again and this time Davis reeled in the pass at the seven-yard line and took it the remainder of the way. The extra point was no good, and Cleveland led 31–23 midway through the fourth quarter.

Rex Bumgardner took the ensuing kickoff and weaved his way to the Cleveland 37-yard line. Runs by Jones and Bumgardner put the ball at the 50-yard line, and Motley blew through the middle for 16 more. Two plays later, Motley carried inside for 13 yards, and then ran it inside again, putting the ball at the 12-yard line. Dub ran the ball for two yards, and a penalty against the Rams gave the Browns five more yards. Bumgardner took a handoff but came up a yard short of the goal line, but Jones got the call on second down and crossed over. The conversion from Groza made it 38–23 Cleveland with about a minute to go.

Starting from his 27, Van Brocklin went deep on first down, but Lavelli intercepted at the Cleveland 42, returning it 14 yards. Two runs by Carpenter moved the ball to the Los Angeles 30, and the gun sounded before Van Brocklin could get another play off.

Jolly Joe Stydahar felt the Rams might have underestimated the Browns, and said, "We must have figured 'em too lightly following their defeat last week by the 49ers. We couldn't do a thing right; on the other hand, the Browns played as well as they've ever played against us."[28] Paul Brown commented, "The Rams still have a potent team, but we were up for them and they were obviously off."[29]

October 14, 1951—Week 3: Los Angeles Rams at Detroit Lions

Briggs Stadium

Los Angeles	10	7	10	0	27
Detroit	0	14	0	7	21

Los Angeles—Field Goal Waterfield 37
Los Angeles—Hirsch 70 pass from Waterfield (Waterfield kick)
Detroit—Dibble 36 pass from Layne (Walker kick)
Detroit—Christiansen 69 punt return (Walker kick)
Los Angeles—Fears 43 pass from Van Brocklin (Waterfield kick)
Los Angeles—Hecker 20 pass from Waterfield (Waterfield kick)
Detroit—Christiansen 47 punt return (Walker kick)
A—50,567

	LA	DET
First Downs	20	14
Rushing A-Y	32–150	39–127
Passing C-A-I	16–32–1	6–20–4
Passing Yards	272	70
Sacked Y	25	17
Total Plays, Yards	64–422	59–197
Punts-Yards	7–301	7–329
Field Goals M-A	2–2	0–0
Fumbles-Lost	3–2	0–0
Penalties-Yards	13–110	10–107

Rushing
(Attempts, Yards)

Los Angeles—Davis 11–41; Towler 7–58; Hoerner 6–32; V Smith 3–9; Williams 3–4; Kalmanir 1–4; Younger 1–2

Detroit—Hoernschemeyer 15–52; Harder 10–28; Walker 9–39; Layne 4–10; Doran 1–(–2)

Passing
(Attempts, Completions, Interceptions, Yards)
Los Angeles—Waterfield 23–12–0–198; Van Brocklin 9–4–1–74
Detroit—Layne 19–5–4–63; Walker

Receptions
(Catches, Yards)
Los Angeles—Hirsch 7–147; Fears 4–77; V Smith 2–22; Hecker 1–20; Davis 1–4; Towler 1–2
Detroit—Dibble 2–49; Doran 2–14; Hoernschemeyer 1–7, Hart 1–0

Interceptions
Los Angeles—Lewis; Hecker (2); Boyd; Keane
Detroit—Flanagan

Fumbles Recovered
Los Angeles—None
Detroit—Smith; Martin

Sacks
Los Angeles—Unknown
Detroit—Unknown

Missed Field Goals
Los Angeles—None
Detroit—None

Briggs Stadium (which would be renamed Tiger Stadium in 1961) was the site of the Rams' first road contest of the season, where they took on the 2–0 Detroit Lions. The Detroit Lions had never beaten the Los Angeles Rams in a regular season game, with their last victory against the Rams' franchise coming in 1944 when the team was still in Cleveland.[30] Even though the Lions had lost 11 straight games to the Rams, the bettors had the conference-leading Lions as 2.5-point favorites.[31] Temperatures would be in the upper 60s, and a then-record crowd of over 50,000 would attend the 2 p.m. EST kickoff.

The Lions were a good team in 1950, with quarterback Bobby Layne, versatile and talented back Doak Walker, Heisman Trophy winner Leon Hart, who anchored right end, and lineman Les Bingaman. The 1951 draft produced arguably the finest bumper crop in franchise history, delivering most of the missing pieces for their 1950s dynasty—ends Jim Doran and Dorne Dibble, linebacker LaVern Torgeson, defensive back Jim Hill, and future Hall of Fame defensive back Jack Christiansen, who twice led the NFL in interceptions. Their first draft pick, Dick Stanfel, would also make it to Canton, but sat out his rookie season due to a knee injury he suffered during a practice at the Chicago All-Star Game.[32] Trades would bring in Pat Harder, a fullback who would share the kicking duties with Layne, and flanker Jim Martin, who would take over the kicking job later in the decade.

On the Rams' second drive of the afternoon, Deacon Dan Towler took a pitch and got loose around the right side for 42 yards to the Detroit 24. After a delay of game penalty nullified a Waterfield field goal and set the Rams back five yards, he booted another from 37 yards away and this one counted, putting the Rams on the board 3–0 with five minutes to play in the first period. The Lions were unable to respond, and the Rams got the ball back. From the Detroit 30, Waterfield faked twice, and hit Crazylegs at the

Detroit 42, with Hirsch taking it the rest of the way. The extra point from Number 7 gave the Rams a 10–0 lead with two and a half minutes to play in the first.

Christiansen broke off a 48-yard return on the ensuing kickoff, putting the Lions just across midfield, but on second down, Layne was picked by Norb Hecker, who returned it 25 yards to the Detroit 39-yard line. Waterfield pitched it to Hoerner, who took the ball to the nine, but on the final play of the first quarter, Hoerner fumbled, with Martin recovering at the Lions' 18. With 15 minutes in the books, the Rams had a 10–0 lead.

At this point, Detroit put together their only successful offensive drive of the game, which began when Walker passed to Bob Hoernschemeyer for seven yards, followed by Hoernschemeyer cutting through the left side of the line for 12 more to the Detroit 37. A key interference penalty on third down gave Detroit new life at midfield, and Hoernschemeyer crashed through the middle for seven yards on a third-and-two, putting the ball at the Rams' 36. Two plays later, Layne fired to Dibble at the goal line, and the Lions were on the board. Walker's conversion trimmed the Rams' lead to 10–7 about four minutes into the second frame.

Walker kicked off to Los Angeles, who went three-and-out, and Norm Van Brocklin punted to Christiansen at the Detroit 31-yard line. Christiansen weaved his way through the horned helmets to his left sideline and his blockers cleared the way from there to the end zone. The last guy who had a chance at him was Towler at the Los Angeles 20, but Hart took him out.[33] With six minutes played in the second period, the Lions held a 14–10 lead.

The Rams took over at their 40 following an exchange of punts, and on first down, an interference flag against Don Doll on a pass to Tom Fears put the ball at the Detroit 43. From there, Van Brocklin went back to Fears again, who pulled it in at the three-yard line and scooted across the goal line, with the Rams regaining the lead at 17–14 five minutes before halftime.

In the remaining time, the Lions got a first down and the drive petered out and they punted, the Rams got as far as the Detroit 40 before Dick Flanagan intercepted Van Brocklin, and as the half ended, Bob Boyd made his first career interception, picking off Layne at the Rams 27-yard line. At the midway point, the Rams led by three points.

Once the teams returned to the field, the Lions made a couple first downs and made it as far as midfield before the punt from Bob Smith went into the end zone for a touchback. Vitamin T. swept left for eight yards, then, caught a pass at the Detroit 42. Waterfield fired to Fears for 11 yards, but a holding penalty on the following play set the Rams back five yards. Davis slipped through the left side for 16 yards and a first down at the Lions' 26, and Fears hauled in a pass that was good for 11 more. Another penalty against the Rams, this time for motion, cost them another five yards, and Bob Momsen hit Waterfield jarring the ball loose, with Crazylegs recovering at the Detroit 39. From there, Waterfield salvaged three points from the drive with a 47-yard field goal. With six and a half minutes elapsed in the third period, Los Angles increased their lead to 20–14.

On the third play after the kickoff, Layne was picked again, this time by Woodley Lewis at the Detroit 48. The Lions were assessed a penalty for roughing the passer, followed by a leaping catch by Crazylegs that put the Rams at the outer edge of the red zone. Waterfield tossed to Hecker, who wrestled loose from Dibble and Jack Lininger at the 15 and sailed into the end zone, widening the Rams lead to 27–14 with six minutes to play in the third.

Detroit got a first down due to a roughing penalty, then failed to do anything on the next series of downs and punted. The Rams failed to make a first down and punted back with Detroit taking over at the Los Angeles 48 with a minute to go in the third quarter trailing 27 to 14.

Runs by Hoernschemeyer and Harder for four and nine yards moved the chains as the fourth quarter began. At that point, the drive lost steam, as Harder lost a couple yards, a pass to Hart gained nothing, and Layne was thrown for a nine-yard loss, putting the Lions out of field goal range. Lewis returned Walker's punt 10 yards to the Detroit 17.

Smith ran left but was caught for a three-yard loss, and after an incompletion on second down, Davis took a handoff, but Doran read the play and took Davis down at the Rams' four-yard line. Van Brocklin punted out of his end zone and the ball went to Christiansen, who fielded the punt at the Los Angeles 47. Displaying the fancy footwork once again, he wormed his way through the wall of oncoming Rams on the way to the end zone, making it a one-possession game at 27–21 with less than 12 minutes to play.

Starting from his 25 following the kickoff, Van Brocklin failed on three passes, and punted to Christiansen, who returned the ball five yards to the Detroit 40-yard line. Runs by Hoernschemeyer and Walker came up two yards short of the marker, and from punt formation, Walker took the snap and ran around right end, gaining 16 yards to the Los Angeles 36. Three more runs followed, leaving the Lions facing a fourth-and-two at the Rams' 28. Layne handed off to Harder, who swept right, but Tank Younger and Jim Winkler were all over him, taking him down for a six-yard loss.

Van Brocklin hit Hirsch for 10 yards on a third-and-eight, putting the Rams at their 46, and on the next play, The Dutchman went back to Crazylegs again, this time for 15 more, to move the ball into Detroit territory. After a delay penalty against the Horns, runs by Kalmanir and Towler were enough for another first down at the Detroit 29. Towler lost six yards on a run and drew a personal foul penalty that cost the Rams 15 yards and put the ball at midfield. Things went downhill from there, as Van Brocklin handed off to Towler, but "Deacon Dan" couldn't hold on, and Bob Smith of Detroit recovered with less than three minutes to play.

Layne was a master of the clock and handed off to Hoernschemeyer to fool the defense but the play only gained two yards. Doran caught a pass for eight yards and a first down at the Rams' 38. Three incompletions followed, and the Lions were down to their last chance. Layne put it up for Walker at the Los Angeles 25, but Hecker was there to make the interception.

Trying to run out the remaining time on the clock, Van Brocklin handed off three times for a total of four yards, which killed most of the clock. A delay of game penalty followed which moved the ball back five yards. Only eight seconds remained,[34] and in order to win the game, the Rams would have to figure out a way to do something they failed to do twice already in the game—stop Jack Christiansen. Van Brocklin punted to Christiansen at the Lions 32, but Christiansen tried to get out of bounds immediately to leave some time on the clock as the Rams' cover team was all over him. However, he got out of bounds just as the clock struck zero and the game ended. The Rams had hung on for a 27–21 victory.

The Rams' win and the Lions' loss put the National Conference into a five-team tie, where everybody was knotted at 2–1 with the exception of the 0–3 New York Yanks. It turned out to be a bad game for Tom Fears, who suffered a knee injury in the third period and would wind up being out of the lineup for several weeks.

October 21, 1951—Week 4: Los Angeles Rams at Green Bay Packers

Wisconsin State Fair Park

Los Angeles	0	0	7	21	28
Green Bay	0	0	0	0	0

Los Angeles—Towler 79 run (Waterfield kick)
Los Angeles—Kalmanir 38 pass from Waterfield (Waterfield kick)
Los Angeles—Hirsch 81 pass from Van Brocklin (Waterfield kick)
Los Angeles—Williams 5 run (Waterfield kick)
A—21,393

	LA	*GB*
First Downs	21	15
Rushing A–Y	50–323	20–77
Passing C–A–I	10–25–1	22–50–1
Passing Yards	179	243
Sacked N–Y	1–6	2–18
Total Plays, Yards	75–502	70–320
Punts–Yards	2–101	7–280
Field Goals M–A	0–3	0–0
Fumbles–Lost	2–1	2–0
Penalties–Yards	5–55	7–77

Rushing
(Attempts, Yards)

Los Angeles—Towler 11–144; Hoerner 11–97; V Smith 11–21; Davis 10–20; Williams 3–36; Kalmanir 3–5; Younger 1–0

Green Bay—Cone 8–29; Canadeo 4–6; Grimes 4–(-2); Girard 1–32; Rote 1–13; Mann 1–0; Cloud 1–(-1)

Passing
(Attempts, Completions, Interceptions, Yards)

Los Angeles—Waterfield 12–5–1–85; Van Brocklin 12–4–0–89; Davis 1–1–0–5

Green Bay—Thomason—38–19–0–207; Rote 12–3–1–36

Receptions
(Catches, Yards)

Los Angeles—Hirsch 3–111; Kalmanir 2–36; Hecker 2–14; Boyd 2–8; V Smith 1–10

Green Bay—Mann 6–90; Pelfrey 6–35; Grimes 3–47; Cone 3–37; Reid 2–19; Canadeo 1–11; Elliott 1–4

Interceptions

Los Angeles—Boyd
Green Bay—Davis

Fumbles Recovered

Los Angeles—None
Green Bay—Summerhays

Sacks

Los Angeles—Paul; Brink
Green Bay—Unknown

Missed Field Goals

Los Angeles—Waterfield 21, 40, 21 blocked
Green Bay—None

The 2–1 Rams traveled to the outskirts of Milwaukee to take on the 2–1 Packers at the Wisconsin State Fair Park, which is where the Packers played their Milwaukee games until County Stadium was opened in 1953. The Packers had retooled their lineup during the off-season, and among those who were wearing the Green would be starting quarterback Bobby Thomason (who was the Rams' third-string backup in 1949) along with former Rams linemen Dave Stephenson and Howie Reutz.[35] Packers coach Gene Ronzani turned over about half the roster following a 3–9 finish in 1950, and a quarter of the way through the 1951 season, it seemed like the Packers were on the path back to respectability.

Tom Fears would be out with a knee sprain, missing the first game of his pro career, and rookie Norb Hecker would replace him in the lineup.[36] Hecker had some huge shoes to fill as Fears led the NFL in pass receptions and receiving yards the previous season. The Rams would also be missing Tom Keane, who separated a shoulder when he slipped and fell during a rainy mid-week workout.[37] Even without the two starters, the visiting Rams went into the game as nine- to 12-point favorites over the Pack.[38] This contest would also feature the two leading scorers in the NFL through the first three weeks of the season, as ends Bob Mann from Green Bay and Elroy Hirsch came into the game tied for the league lead in points scored with 36 each.[39]

It rained heavily in the morning, but somebody forgot to put a tarp over the field,[40] and the field was a mess. The temps were in the mid–60s at game time, but the rainy conditions (it drizzled in the fourth quarter) kept the attendance down about 30 percent from what was expected. When the opening whistle blew at 2:30 p.m. EST, 21,000 fans were there to see the contest.

On the opening drive of the game, Harper Davis picked off Bob Waterfield at the Rams' 45, returning it 12 yards. After a Tony Canadeo run barely converted a fourth-and-one to the 23, a nine-yard pass from Thomason to Billy Grimes moved the ball to the Los Angeles 11-yard line, giving the Packers another fresh set of downs. A pass to rookie Fred Cone left the ball three yards short of the end zone. Don Paul shut down Grimes on third down, costing the Packers a yard. On fourth down, Green Bay went for it, but Paul came through again with a sack of Thomason.

Following an exchange of punts, Vitamin T. Smith returned a Jug Girard punt 37 yards, giving the Horns good field position at the Green Bay 41. Dick Hoerner took a handoff 31 yards up the middle to the Green Bay five-yard line, but that would be as close as the Rams would get to the Promised Land. Smith was stopped on runs on first and second downs, and Glenn Davis lost eight yards on third down when he started running left and tried to change direction and the Packers were all over him. Waterfield tried to salvage three points from the drive, but his 21-yard field goal try didn't stand a chance, as the kick was low.

Girard faked a punt from his 20-yard line, gaining 32 yards to put Green Bay just past the midfield stripe. However, the Packers could not capitalize when a bomb from Tobin Rote to an open Ray Pelfrey inside the Rams' 10-yard line barely missed, leading to a Girard punt on the first play of the second quarter with both teams scoreless.

Girard's aforementioned punt went to Smith, who broke off another great return, this one for 35 yards, to put the Rams at their 39-yard line. Van Brocklin came in to replace Waterfield at quarterback, as they usually alternated quarters. Runs by Hoerner, Smith and Glenn Davis moved the pigskin to the Green Bay 38. From there, Dan Towler broke off a touchdown run, but the powers that be decided that the Deacon had actually gone down at the Rams' 20. The Packers held the Rams from moving the ball any further, and Waterfield came in to try another field goal, this one from 26 yards out. Glenn Davis, his holder, bobbled the snap and unsuccessfully tried to run with the ball, and Green Bay got the ball back at their 34-yard line.

Green Bay moved the ball to midfield again, and on a second-and-one, Rote went deep for an open Mann at the Los Angeles 20, but the sure touchdown pass was wet and went off his hands. Rote gambled a second time the following play, going for a short pass instead of a quarterback sneak to pick up the needed three feet, but again the pass fell incomplete, and the punting team came out.

After the Rams failed to do anything and punted, Bob Boyd intercepted a Rote pass at midfield. Waterfield got the Rams close enough for a 40-yard try, but it was low again. At the half, there was no score.

Early in the third stanza, a punt by Girard pinned the Rams at their six-yard line. Five straight runs by Hoerner netted 37 yards, and Vitamin T. carried the ball to midfield. Two runs by Towler were good for 14 yards, and a pass to Hecker and another run by Towler gave Los Angeles another first down at the Packers' 27. Waterfield, who was back in at QB for the third period, connected with Vitamin T. for 10 yards on third-and-seven. The drive petered out at this point, and Waterfield came in for another try at three points. This time, his 21-yard attempt was blocked by Dan Orlich.

After the block, Thomason completed eight straight passes, putting the Pack two yards short of the goal line as it started to rain again. The Rams' defense held, and on fourth-and-goal, Thomason went for broke, but Jerry Williams knocked down his pass that was intended for Breezy Reid, and Los Angeles took over at their 20.

Two plays later, Towler swept left and broke loose, with Harper Davis the only one who had a chance at the Deacon at the Packers' 30, but it was not to be. After the 79-yard touchdown run, Waterfield nailed the extra point. The Rams finally got on the scoreboard 7–0 with about a minute to go in the third quarter.

After three Thomason passes failed to find their mark, Los Angeles had the ball back following Girard's punt. Two runs by Hoerner netted eleven yards, and then, Waterfield finally got the big play passing game going, when he connected with Crazylegs for 25 yards to the Green Bay 38. Captain Bob put it up for Tommy Kalmanir at the three-yard line, with Kalmanir waltzing across the goal line to give the Rams a 14–0 lead two minutes into the final period.

Thomason fired to Canadeo for 11 yards, but the Packers were forced to punt following three straight incompletions. Starting from their 12-yard line, two runs by Towler were good for 17 yards for the Rams, but Girard caught Glenn Davis for an eight-yard loss. From the Los Angeles 19, Van Brocklin threw for Hirsch (who had beaten Harper Davis on the coverage) on a post pattern at the Green Bay 45, and Elroy's crazy legs did the rest of the work, running the ball into the end zone. Waterfield attached the extra point, making the score 21–0 with nine and a half minutes to play.

With the game already decided, the Packers did not give up. Midway through the fourth, Billy Grimes took a screen from Thomason 37 yards to the Rams' 38-yard line. A penalty for being offside set the ball back five yards, and then, a touchdown pass from Rote to Mann was whistled back due to an offensive pass interference call on Mann. The Packers turned the ball over on downs after three straight incomplete passes.

After a bomb from Van Brocklin to Andy Robustelli that would have put the Rams inside the Green Bay five-yard line was called back due to holding, a reverse to Jerry Williams gained 34 yards to the Packers' 30. The drive bogged down, and Glenn Davis ran for 17 yards on a fake field goal attempt, setting the stage for Williams to take a handoff through right tackle for five yards to conclude the scoring at 28–0.

A fracas broke out with less than two minutes to go, which began with Younger kneeing Rote while Rote was on the ground, and ended with Larry Brink getting ejected.

It was the first time the Los Angeles Rams ever shut out an opponent.

October 28, 1951—Game 5: Los Angeles Rams vs. San Francisco 49ers

Kezar Stadium

Los Angeles	3	7	7	0	17
San Francisco	10	28	0	6	44

San Francisco—Field Goal Soltau 23
Los Angeles—Field Goal Waterfield 26
San Francisco—Arenas 2 run (Soltau kick)
San Francisco—Soltau 10 pass from Albert (Soltau kick)
Los Angeles—Hirsch 79 pass from Van Brocklin (Waterfield kick)
San Francisco—Strzykalski 1 run (Soltau kick)
San Francisco—Nomellini 20 blocked punt return (Soltau kick)
San Francisco—Soltau 13 pass from Tittle (Soltau kick)
Los Angeles—Hoerner 12 run (Waterfield kick)
San Francisco—Soltau 48 pass from Tittle (kick failed)
A—49,538

	Los Angeles	*San Francisco*
First Downs	23	19
Rushing A–Y	34–131	43–194
Passing C–A–I	20–46–6	8–12–0
Passing Yards	240	160
Sacked N–Y	0–0	4–33
Total Plays, Yards	80–371	55–354
Punts–Yards	4–183	6–260
Fields Goals M–A	1–1	1–2
Fumbles–Lost	2–0	1–0
Penalties–Yards	9–42	8–60

Rushing
(Attempts, Yards)
Los Angeles—Hoerner 10–45; Davis 8–25; Towler 7–43; Kalmanir 5–5; V Smith 3–12; Williams 1–1.
San Francisco—Perry 13–45; Strzykalski 12–43; Schabarum 7–70; Arenas 5–17; Monachino 2–8; Lillywhite 2–3; Albert 1–8; Tittle 1–0

Passing
(Attempts, Completions, Interceptions, Yards)
Los Angeles—Van Brocklin 30–13–5–167; Waterfield 16–7–1–73
San Francisco—Albert 8–6–0–99; Tittle 4–2–0–61

Receiving
(Catches, Yards)
Los Angeles—Hirsch 7–163; V Smith 4–(-2); Williams 2–19; Kalmanir 2–15; Boyd 1–16; Davis 1–11; Hoerner 1–9; Towler 1–8; Hecker 1–1
San Francisco—Soltau 6–132; Wilson 1–16; Berry 1–12

Interceptions
Los Angeles—None
San Francisco—Berry; Powers (2); Cason (2); Lillywhite

Fumbles Recovered
Los Angeles—None
San Francisco—None

Missed Field Goals
Los Angeles—None
San Francisco—Soltau 22

With one quarter of the season complete, the Rams were in a first-place tie atop the National Conference with the Chicago Bears, both with 3–1 records. The Bears gained a share of the Conference lead with a 13–7 win over San Francisco.

After two weeks on the road, the Rams were on their way back to the West Coast by way of a United Airlines flight after their overwhelming victory in Milwaukee. They landed in Los Angeles to prepare for a trip to San Francisco on Sunday, October 28, against a 49ers team they beat twice during the previous season.

The San Francisco 49ers came into the fifth week of the season with a record of 2–2. It was felt that this meeting with the Rams was a "must win" for San Francisco under head coach Lawrence "Buck" Shaw. The former Notre Dame tackle and placekicker was a long-time coach with nearly three decades of experience guiding teams on the collegiate and professional level. His stay in San Francisco dated back to the AAFC's first season in 1946.

In the AAFC's four-season existence, Shaw's 49ers posted a 38–14 record. If it were not for the Cleveland Browns' total dominance of the AAFC, the 49ers would have been the talk of the league instead of the second-best franchise. In 1950, Shaw suffered his first losing season in the pros, as San Francisco finished with a 3–9 record.

That lone blemish on his record in professional football might have sparked a bit of resentment for the success of his interstate rivals. In an interview with the *San Francisco Call-Bulletin*, Shaw disagreed with the opinion felt by many in professional football circles that the Rams were the best team in the National Football League. Shaw claimed in the interview that he doubted the Rams were the best in over-all speed and passing and felt the Cleveland Browns were better equipped on both sides of the ball over Los Angeles. He went on by claiming that Bob Waterfield and Norm Van Brocklin were good quarterbacks, but their talents did not make the passing game as good as Cleveland's. San Francisco tackle Ray Collins added more fuel by singling out Jim Winkler as not being very good. He had played against Winkler in college and felt the Los Angeles star rookie tackle was not that talented.[41] In conclusion, the word from San Francisco was that the Rams were just a hollow collection of players that deserved little respect as one of the NFL's top teams.

With those harsh words circling their way through the ranks of Rams players and Joe Stydahar, tempers flared, and the team was ready to tear through the 49ers.

The Rams were favored by seven points when they took the field at Kezar Stadium with sunny skies and 70-degree temperatures serving as the backdrop in the San Francisco Bay area. The weather was not the only thing that was perfect on that final weekend in October. Unfortunately, it was not the gridiron delegation from SoCal.

Even though Shaw's comments in the press fired them up, the Rams went cold in San Francisco, while the 49ers were all up for the game and wanted to take the Rams apart, and that is what happened, as Los Angeles took a tremendous 44–17 beating. This proved to be their second worst defeat since moving to Los Angeles. The worst was recorded the previous year when the Philadelphia Eagles beat them, 56–20.

The 49ers' pass defense was the tightest Los Angeles had seen up to this point of the season. It accounted for six interceptions that were returned for 136 yards and led to two touchdowns. The men up front also mauled the Rams' linemen at will, and San Francisco never trailed in the game. The closest Los Angeles got to making the game interesting was when Bob Waterfield's 26-yard field goal tied the game at 3–3 in the first quarter. The 49ers blew the game wide open in the second quarter by scoring four touchdowns to take a 38–10 advantage at the end of the first half. The lone bright spot for the Rams was the performance of Elroy Hirsch. Crazylegs caught seven passes for 163 yards, including a 79-yard touchdown from Van Brocklin in the second quarter. Dick Hoerner, who led the Rams with 45 yards on the ground, scored the other Los Angeles touchdown on a 12-yard run in the fourth quarter. With the loss the 3–2 Rams dropped into a three-way tie for second place in the National Conference with the 49ers and the Packers. As the season moved into November, the Chicago Bears stood alone at the top of the conference with a 4–1 record after defeating the Lions 28–23.

A complete team effort earned the 49ers this lopsided victory, but several key performances stood out. On the defensive side of the ball, Jim Powers and Jim Cason each had two interceptions, and Leo Nomellini returned a blocked punt 20 yards for a touchdown. Buck Shaw and his staff also came up with a successful way to stop the Rams' powerful passing attack. The plan was to insert two fast halfbacks at the outside linebacker positions. This allowed the 49ers to keep up with the swift receiving corps that the Rams possessed. Stydahar was concerned that other teams throughout the league would decide to try the same strategy, making it extremely difficult for Los Angeles to make another run at a championship.

In addition to those yeoman efforts, the 49ers also possessed one of the roughest linebackers in the NFL in Hardy Brown. For his era, Hardy was excellent size for a linebacker, and hit like a freight train. At age four, the Texas native witnessed his father's murder. His mother then sent her four youngest children, including Hardy, to an orphanage in Fort Worth. Following that experience, he served in the Marine Corps during World War II.[42]

He lived to make hard hits on the football field and had the look of a wild animal in his eyes prior to every snap. His signature move was to level an opponent with his shoulder, and he delivered enough punishment to rank as the fifth most feared tackler of all-time by the NFL Network. In 1951 alone, it was claimed that he knocked out 21 opponents. In this big win over the Rams, he applied his vicious "shoulder push" to Glenn Davis and Dick Hoerner, with the results being two of most lethal hits ever witnessed by the press corps covering the game.[43]

On the offensive side, a raw-boned Swede from Minnesota named Gordon Soltau helped out in a major way. The 6'2", 195-pound receiver, in his second NFL season, was on his way to the first of three Pro Bowl and All-Pro selections when he had the game of his life. He caught six passes for 132 yards and three touchdowns. He added a field goal and five conversion kicks for a total of 26 points. That point total stood as the team record until Jerry Rice surpassed it 39 years later.

After the mauling, Stydahar was snorting fire. He saw his team outfought and outplayed until it was too late to put together a rally. Possibly what steamed Stydahar in addition to the defeat was that the words of Buck Shaw held true, at least for the time being. However, the chance at redemption against the 49ers would not take long, as the 49ers were set to visit the Los Angeles Memorial Coliseum one week later.

Over in the American Conference, the Cleveland Browns remained in first place with a 14–13 victory over their top conference rivals, the New York Giants. Otto Graham's first quarter touchdown passes to Dub Jones and Dante Lavelli were all Cleveland needed, and the win allowed the Browns to share the league's best record with the Bears at 4–1.[44]

November 4, 1951—Game 6: San Francisco 49ers vs. Los Angeles Rams

Los Angeles Memorial Coliseum

San Francisco	0	7	6	3	16
Los Angeles	10	3	0	10	23

Los Angeles—Field Goal Waterfield 39
Los Angeles—Waterfield 1 run (Waterfield kick)
San Francisco—Perry 58 run (Soltau kick)
Los Angeles—Field Goal Waterfield 20
San Francisco—Albert 7 run (kick failed)
San Francisco—Field Goal Soltau 11
Los Angeles—Hirsch 76 pass from Waterfield (Waterfield kick)
Los Angeles—Field Goal Waterfield 38
A—59,346

	Los Angeles	*San Francisco*
First Downs	16	15
Rushing A–Y	43–155	49–234
Passing C–A–I	12–25–2	5–16–2
Passing Yards	202	33
Sacked N–Y	0–0	2–14
Total Plays, Yards	68–357	65–267
Punts–Yards	6–244	5–221
Fields Goals M–A	3–3	1–1
Fumbles—Lost	2–1	3–3
Penalties–Yards	7–69	3–25

Rushing
(Attempts, Yards)

Los Angeles—Hoerner 13–39; Towler 11–54; V Smith 9–24; Davis 4–24; Waterfield 3–6; Younger 2–4; Van Brocklin 1–4
San Francisco—Perry 12–115; White 6–22; Albert 5–27; Strickland 5–6; Schabarum 4–20; Strzykalski 4–13; Lillywhite 4–12

Passing
(Attempts, Completions, Interceptions, Yards)

Los Angeles—Waterfield 22–11–2–188; Van Brocklin 2–1–0–14; Davis 1–0–0–0
San Francisco—Albert 11–4–0–32; Tittle 5–1–2–1

Receiving
(Catches, Yards)

Los Angeles—Hirsch 4–103; Keane 4–42; Towler 2–38; V Smith 1–14; Davis 1–5
San Francisco—Soltau 1–9; Strzykalski 1–9; White 1–8; Monachino 1–6; Perry 1–1

Interceptions
Los Angeles—Paul; Rich
San Francisco—Cason; Wagner

Fumbles Recovered
Los Angeles—Winkler; Rich; Robustelli
San Francisco—Cason

Missed Field Goals
Los Angeles—None
San Francisco–None

The world of professional sports runs the gamut between hot and cold. One week a team can look like no opponent in the world can defeat it. The following time out, an opponent walks all over them to prove that even athletes are human with good days and bad. The obvious goal is to be world-beaters in every outing, but unfortunately, that occurrence is rare.

Such was the case of the Rams after the San Francisco massacre on the final weekend of October. The wounds of defeat might have still been fresh, but the schedule makers did not allow them time to heal. Of course, that might have been a good thing for the Rams on this occasion. The 49ers were set to complete a back-to-back meeting with the Rams at the Coliseum, and revenge was on the minds of everyone in the Los Angeles locker room.

On Tuesday's practice at Gilmore Field, Stydahar and his staff set out to counterbalance the alignment San Francisco used with a pair of halfbacks at outside linebacker. What Stydahar and his staff came up with was brilliant, and just might have saved the team's fortunes over the remaining weeks of the regular season. On the Rams' roster were three of the biggest running backs in the NFL. "Deacon" Dan Towler, Paul "Tank" Younger, and Dick Hoerner, were all big, powerful, possessed speed, and were capable of catching passes. This trio was dubbed "the Bull Elephant Backfield," and when added into the Rams' already devastating offensive scheme, the results proved highly successful.[45]

The approach was quite simple, with Stydahar incorporating two separate backfields into the game plan. When the 49ers had their two smaller, quicker players, Jim Powers and Verl Lillywhite, at outside linebacker, Stydahar used his bull elephant backs to pound away. All three bull elephants were over 220 pounds, so when one of them was carrying the ball, all 450-pounds of the other two were leading the way out of the backfield. This allowed for the Rams to punish a defense and wear it down. When the 49ers went with heavy linebackers, then Stydahar used either Hoerner or Towler at fullback, and inserted speed burners like Glenn Davis or Vitamin T. Smith, who could simply outrun the bulky outside linebackers. With the defense either being pounded by brute force or winded from keeping up with sprinters coming out of the backfield, then Bob Waterfield and Norm Van Brocklin would attack the worn-out defense with the team's deadly passing attack.[46]

A crowd of 59,346 came out to see the rematch between the Rams and 49ers on Sunday, November 4. Since dismissing local television broadcasts of home games, which was the Rams' policy during the previous season, attendance at the Coliseum had nearly doubled. Herb Rich was ready to return to action and help tighten up the defensive backfield. Tom Fears was still unable to play, and defensive right end Jack Zilly suffered a season ending broken arm the week before against the 49ers and be lost for the remainder of the season.[47]

Mother Nature did her part by bringing perfect weather conditions to the Southland for the two o'clock kickoff. Clear skies graced the area with the temperature in the low 80s at kickoff.

For the third time in their first six games, the Rams got out to a 10–0 lead in the opening quarter. With two of the bull elephants eating up a large portion of Coliseum real estate, the Rams got close enough for a field goal to start the scoring. Deacon Towler busted off a 31-yard run, and Dick Hoerner moved the chains another 12 on the ground before Bob Waterfield kicked a 39-yard field goal to give Los Angeles an early 3–0 advantage. Rich recovered a fumble on the San Francisco 43. Waterfield connected with Crazylegs Hirsch on a pair of passes that got the Rams to the 28. Waterfield mixed things up by taking the ball himself up the middle for a gain of seven. After Towler was knocked back for a loss of two yards, Hoerner made up the lost ground by running to the 14-yard line. Vitamin Smith sprinted to the one, and from there, Waterfield scored on a quarterback sneak before adding the conversion to give the Rams a 10–0 lead at the end of the first quarter.

Joe "the Jet" Perry was one of the top running backs in the NFL during the 1950s. A straight-ahead runner who combined speed, power, and elusive moves, Perry grew up in Los Angeles. At Jordan High School he was a four-sport star who dreamed of following Kenny Washington and Jackie Robinson's legacies at UCLA. Unfortunately, UCLA rejected Perry. Still looking to be an athlete at the next level, he enrolled at Compton Junior College and scored 22 touchdowns during the 1944 season. That display allowed UCLA to take notice of the "Compton Comet," but this time, it was Perry that declined. With World War II raging on, he enlisted in the Navy. During his military service, Perry played for Naval Air Station Alameda. It was while at Alameda that the Rams scouted Perry. Instead of playing for his hometown team, Perry ventured up the coast and signed with the San Francisco 49ers (then in the AAFC) in 1948.[48]

Midway through the second quarter, Perry took a handoff from quarterback Y.A. Tittle on the San Francisco 42-yard line. Using all the assets in his arsenal, Perry wiggled free from the first wall of defense and got to the outside. He then shook off Tank Younger along the sideline near midfield, weaved his way past Woodley Lewis and Norb Hecker, and made it into the end zone standing up to complete a magnificent 58-yard scoring trek. Perry led all ball carriers with 115 rushing yards on only 12 carries before being taken off the field on a stretcher later in the game due to a strained ligament in his right knee. The star of the previous clash with the Rams, Gordie Soltau, added the conversion to make the score 10–7.

With the first half only 30 seconds away from completion, Don Paul intercepted a Tittle pass and returned it 16 yards to the San Francisco 28. After Waterfield threw a pair of short passes to Glenn Davis and Hirsch, he successfully split the uprights from 20 yards out for a field goal that gave the Rams a 13–7 halftime advantage.

Early in the third quarter, Perry proved he was human. Rookie lineman Andy Robustelli, destined for the Hall of Fame years later, blasted Perry so hard that he fumbled the ball. Robustelli then recovered the loose ball on the Los Angeles 49. Tom Keane and Towler churned out yardage to get the ball to the Niners' 26. It was then that the magic vanished, as Lowell Wagner intercepted Waterfield on the goal line and ran it back 15 yards.

In a testament to using all his assets, quarterback Frankie Albert employed the services of seven different ball carriers, including himself, to drive 85 yards in 14 plays. On the final play of the drive, Albert called his own number, sweeping the left end to score from seven yards out. Soltau's conversion kick hit the goalpost and bounced back onto the field. Instead of a one-point lead, the 49ers had to settle for a 13–13 deadlock at the end of three quarters.

On the fourth play of the final quarter, following a Jim Cason interception, Soltau made up for his miss on the conversion attempt when he hit on an 11-yard field goal to put the 49ers up 16–13 for their first lead of the game.

Things began to get a little tense for the Rams a short time later when Frankie Albert ran instead of punting on fourth down. He picked up a first down at the Los Angeles

41, and a pair of Bob White runs moved the chains to the 22-yard line. An illegal use of hands penalty knocked the 49ers back and the drive stalled. On fourth down, Albert punted instead of hoofing it, and his kick sailed into the end zone with 8:30 remaining on the game clock and the Rams in possession on their own 20.

Vitamin Smith and Towler picked up a combined four yards on the first two downs. Facing a third-and-six from the 24, Waterfield dropped back nine yards as Hirsch bolted downfield. Waterfield unleashed a rocket shot that connected with Hirsch's fingertips on an over-the-shoulders catch. That was close enough for the talented receiver. He hauled the ball into his body and went the distance to complete a 76-yard go-ahead touchdown. The incredible catch was routine for Hirsch, but Joe Stydahar felt it one of the greatest he ever saw. It also came at a time in the game when the Rams needed a lift. Waterfield's extra point gave the lead back to the Rams at 20–16.[49]

Following the ensuing kickoff, Jim Winkler recovered a fumble at the San Francisco 29. Three running plays lost two yards, but Waterfield salvaged Winkler's efforts by kicking a 38-yard field goal, which was his seventh three-pointer in six games. It made the score 23–16, and that was how the game concluded.

Waterfield scored 17 of Los Angeles' points and threw for the team's other six points on the day. He completed 11 of 22 pass attempts for 188 yards. Hirsch turned in another spectacular performance with four receptions for 103 yards. Don Paul was knocked a bit woozy due to a slight concussion. The tough two-way performer was able to shake off the effects of the collision within a short time and was awarded the game ball by Waterfield for his efforts.[50]

Coach Stydahar was obviously pleased with the outcome and thrilled that his matchups with San Francisco were over for the year. After witnessing his team's suffering through bad breaks in a humiliating loss the previous week, Stydahar felt the breaks more than evened out this time.

With the victory the Rams improved to 4–2 while the 49ers slipped to 3–3. The win allowed Los Angeles to stay in second place in the National Conference behind the Chicago Bears, who improved to 5–1 with an easy 27–0 victory over Washington in the nation's capital. The Lions then held off a late Green Bay rally for a 24–17 victory to improve to 3–2–1 for third place in the National Conference. Over in the American Conference, the Cleveland Browns remained dominant, improving to 5–1 with a 34–17 win over the last place Chicago Cardinals. The Giants faced the Yanks in an all–New York battle, and the Yanks, still looking for their first win, put up a great fight at the Polo Grounds. However, in the end, the Giants improved to 4–1–1 with a 37–31 win to stay in second place behind the Browns.[51]

November 11, 1951—Game 7: Chicago Cardinals vs. Los Angeles Rams

Los Angeles Memorial Coliseum

Chicago	7	0	0	14	21
Los Angeles	0	7	28	10	45

Chicago—Cross 80 pass from Hardy (Patton kick)
Los Angeles—Hoerner 11 run (Waterfield kick)
Los Angeles—Waterfield 1 run (Waterfield kick)
Los Angeles—Kalmanir 67 punt return (Waterfield kick)
Los Angeles—Hoerner 3 run (Waterfield kick)
Los Angeles—Hirsch 53 pass from Waterfield (Waterfield kick)

Chicago—Trippi 3 run (Patton kick)
Los Angeles—Hirsch 54 pass from Van Brocklin (Waterfield kick)
Los Angeles—Field Goal Waterfield 26
Chicago—Polsfoot 80 pass from Trippi (Trippi kick)
A—29,995

	Los Angeles	*Chicago*
First Downs	23	16
Rushing A–Y	38–237	39–128
Passing C–A–I	13–25–1	9–24–3
Passing Yards	281	239
Sacked N–Y	0–0	3–25
Total Plays, Yards	63–518	63–367
Punts–Yards	4–166	8–352
Fields Goals M–A	1–3	0–0
Fumbles–Lost	2–1	3–1
Penalties–Yards	6–60	6–62

Rushing
(Attempts, Yards)
Los Angeles—Towler 11-109; Hoerner 9-47; V Smith 7-(-19); Waterfield 3-35; Williams 3-33; Younger 3-11; Davis 1-23; Van Brocklin 1-(-2)
Chicago—Cross 11-43; Trippi 8-29; Angsman 6-36; Sitko 6-19; Pasquariello 4-6; Paul 2-4; Panelli 1-3; Hardy 1-(-12)

Passing
(Attempts, Completions, Interceptions, Yards)
Los Angeles—Van Brocklin 16-8-1-165; Waterfield 9-5-0-116
Chicago—Trippi 17-6-3-135; Hardy 7-3-0-104

Receiving
(Catches, Yards)
Los Angeles—Hirsch 6-195; V Smith 2-24; Johnson 1-28; Boyd 1-14; Keane 1-7; Towler 1-7; Hoerner 1-6
Chicago—Polsfoot 2-94; Cross 2-90; Paul 2-12; Ramsey 1-35; Stonesifer 1-12; Svoboda 1-(-4)

Interceptions
Los Angeles—Lewis; Hecker; Williams
Chicago—Wallner

Fumbles Recovered
Los Angeles—Brink
Chicago—McDermott

Missed Field Goals
Los Angeles—Waterfield 31, 46
Chicago-None

Under Curly Lambeau, in his second season at the helm, the Cardinals were in the midst of a four-game losing streak, and at the bottom of the American Conference, with a 1–5 record. Despite the bleak circumstances surrounding the Cardinals in the first half of the season, they were still a team that made Stydahar nervous. The Rams' mentor felt his woes were justified after reviewing the Cardinals' exhibition victory over Los Angeles in September. Stydahar focused on the Rams' problem in stopping Chicago's running game, and with quarterback Jim Hardy ready to go, the passing game came into play.

Stydahar was stumped that the Cardinals had such a poor record. He felt they possessed some excellent talent, especially tackle Bill Fischer, whom Stydahar regarded as one of the best blockers he had ever seen.[52] In that exhibition game loss, Fischer controlled the Los Angeles linemen with ease. The Cardinals also had other linemen that were huge, a solid receiver in Fran Polsfoot, a good group of linebackers, and two of the best offensive halfbacks in veteran Elmer Angsman and rookie Bill Cross. Stydahar felt the Cardinals were due to win again soon, but the Rams' faithful hoped their losing streak would reach five at the Coliseum on Sunday, November 11.

Good news for the Rams came when it was released that Tom Fears was ready to return to action against the Cardinals, but he was obviously still not in top physical shape just yet. Tom Keane was set to start at left end, but the coaching staff expected to insert Fears throughout the game to ease the star receiver back into action slowly.

The oddsmakers were confident that the vaunted Los Angeles offense would come through and made them 10-point favorites.

With cloudy skies, a threat of rain, and temperatures in the high 60s, a crowd of 29,995 turned out at the Coliseum.

The Cardinals drew first blood. On the first scrimmage play of the game from the Chicago 20-yard line, Hardy connected on a pass with fleet-footed rookie Bill Cross at midfield. Cross got behind Woodley Lewis to catch the arching pass. Lewis managed to get a brief grasp of Cross, but the 155-pound speedster from West Texas State shook free at the Los Angeles 35 and completed his 80-yard catch and run with only 29 seconds removed from the game clock. Cliff Patton added the conversion kick, and the Cardinals were quickly up, 7–0.

Near the end of the first quarter, the Rams were threatening until Dan Towler fumbled on the Chicago 13 and Lloyd McDermott recovered for the visitors. The Cardinals failed to capitalize on the turnover and returned possession back over to the Rams with a punt on fourth down on the third play of the second quarter.

From the Chicago 43, the Rams' backfield got into the end zone in three plays. Dick Hoerner started the swift drive with a gain of 15 yards up the middle. Towler swept to the right side of the field for 17 more. From the Chicago 11-yard line, Norm Van Brocklin pitched the ball to Hoerner on the left side of the line. With key blocks coming from Charlie Toogood and Bill Lange, Hoerner made it across the goal line. Bob Waterfield then knotted the game at 7–7 with his conversion kick, and that was the way the first half ended.

Even though the teams were locked in a close, low scoring affair, the Rams appeared to have the advantage going into the second half. Their defense held firm by not allowing the Cardinals to advance any farther than the Los Angeles 37-yard line following their early touchdown, and Jim Hardy had been knocked out of the game. With the score tied at 7–7 in the second quarter, Hardy faded back to pass as a fierce rush was converging on him. Hardy was knocked to the ground and needed assistance to get off the field. Hardy was later taken to the locker room on a stretcher and then transported to the hospital for examination. It was concluded that Hardy had no fracture, but just a strained ligament that caused severe discomfort.

Stydahar opened the second half with his Bull Elephant backfield. The decision proved to be an excellent choice. Starting from the Los Angeles 26, the Rams charged down the field in eight plays to take a lead they never relinquished. The big gains were a 30-yard run by Towler and a pickup of 25 yards by Waterfield on a bootleg. Waterfield then capped the drive off with a 1-yard run and added the conversion to make it 14–7.

That go-ahead touchdown was just the beginning of the Rams' third quarter exploits. A minute after Waterfield gave the Rams the advantage, Tommy Kalmanir received a punt on the Los Angeles 33, and within seconds, raced to the end zone untouched to compete a 67-yard return to blow the game wide open. Waterfield's extra point made the score 21–7. Woodley Lewis intercepted a Charley Trippi pass to quickly return possession back over to the Rams. As a thank you for the great defensive effort, the Los Angeles offense swiftly got back into the end zone. Hirsch caught a 34-yard pass from Waterfield that ate up the bulk of real estate on this drive, placing the Rams on the Chicago 6-yard line. Two plays later, Hoerner plowed across the goal line standing up from three yards out for his second touchdown of the afternoon. Waterfield's conversion virtually put the game out of reach at 28–7.

The Rams might have had the game totally under control, but they still added points on the board. Norb Hecker intercepted Trippi on the Los Angeles 20 and raced 26 yards with his theft to return possession back to the Rams near midfield. On third down, Waterfield connected with Hirsch on a 53-yard scoring strike. Hirsch leaped high in the air at the Chicago 18 to secure the ball, and then shook off three defenders on his way to the end zone. Waterfield added his fifth extra point kick, and at the end of three quarters, the Rams led 35–7.

The Cardinals finally got back on the board shortly after the fourth quarter got underway. Trippi, whose two interceptions in the third quarter led to Los Angeles touchdowns, scored on a 3-yard run. Cliff Patton's conversion made the score 35–14.

With Norm Van Brocklin now at the controls of the offense, the Rams struck for 10 more points before the game was complete. With the ball on the Los Angeles 46, Van Brocklin hit Hirsch with a pass, and the elite receiver outran the defenders to the end zone for his second six-pointer of the game, with this one coming from 54 yards out. Waterfield added his sixth conversion kick, and the Rams were up 42–14. Van Brocklin then guided the Rams to their final points of the day. A pass on fourth down to rookie Marv Johnson gained 28 yards and set up a 26-yard field goal by Waterfield. On the first play following the ensuing kickoff, Fran Polsfoot caught an 80-yard pass from Trippi for the game's final touchdown. Patton's extra point brought an end to the scoring, and the Rams were easy winners by a final score of 45–21.[53]

Crazylegs had another great performance, catching six passes for 195 yards and two touchdowns. The Bull Elephants chipped in with a bruising display of ground-pounding achievement. "Deacon" Dan Towler easily led all ball carriers with 109 rushing yards on 11 attempts, and Dick Hoerner added 47 yards on nine carries and a pair of touchdowns.

The win took the Rams to a 5–2 record. The Detroit Lions were on the verge of becoming the elite team of the Conference, but that success was still one year away. However, before taking over that alpha dog status, they gave the Rams a present by defeating the Chicago Bears, 41–28, which allowed Los Angeles the chance to gain a share of the National Conference lead.

Over in the American Conference, the Browns prevailed for their sixth win of the season with a 20–17 victory over the Eagles. The Browns rallied from a 10–0 halftime deficit, and Lou Groza provided Cleveland with what turned out to be the game-winning points on a 13-yard field goal with nine-and-a-half minutes left in the game. The New York Giants stayed close to Cleveland in the conference standings with a 28–14 win over the Washington Redskins at the Polo Grounds. The New York defense intercepted six passes and recovered three fumbles to pace the Giants rise to 5–1–1 on the season.[54]

November 18, 1951—Game 8: New York Yanks vs. Los Angeles Rams

Los Angeles Memorial Coliseum

New York	0	21	0	0	21
Los Angeles	20	14	0	14	48

Los Angeles—Hoerner 1 run (kick failed)
Los Angeles—Hoerner 43 run (Waterfield kick)
Los Angeles—Smith 31 run (Waterfield kick)
New York—Taliaferro 16 run (Johnson kick)
Los Angeles—Towler 69 run (Waterfield kick)
New York—Celeri 20 pass from Taliaferro (Johnson kick)
Los Angeles—Williams 4 run (Waterfield kick)
New York—Taliaferro 65 run (Johnson kick)
Los Angeles—Waterfield 13 run (Waterfield kick)
Los Angeles—Hirsch 33 pass from Van Brocklin (Waterfield kick)
A—34,717

	Los Angeles	New York
First Downs	24	24
Rushing A–Y	44–371	24–224
Passing C–A–I	12–23–1	19–43–2
Passing Yards	212	291
Sacked N–Y	1–9	4–36
Total Plays, Yards	67–583	67–515
Punts–Yards	8–317	9–383
Fields Goals M–A	0–0	0–0
Fumbles–Lost	0–0	2–1
Penalties–Yards	6–70	10–80

Rushing
(Attempts, Yards)

Los Angeles—Towler 13–155; V Smith 9–59; Davis 9–30; Hoerner 7–78; Younger 3–34; Waterfield 1–13; Williams 1–4; Van Brocklin 1–(-2)

New York—Taliaferro 12–166; Howard 7–44; Ratterman 2–5; Young 2–0; Celeri 1–9

Passing
(Attempts, Completions, Interceptions, Yards)

Los Angeles—Van Brocklin 12–7–0–129; Waterfield 11–5–1–74

New York—Celeri 22–7–1–61; Ratterman 16–9–1–111; Taliaferro 5–3–0–83

Receiving
(Catches, Yards)

Los Angeles—Hirsch 4–97; V Smith 3–46; Boyd 2–21; Towler 1–26; Williams 1–8; Davis 1–5

New York—Garza 5–68; O'Connor 4–60; Edwards 3–55; Crowe 3–20; Young 1–30; Celeri 1–20; Taliaferro 1–4; Howard 1–(-2)

Interceptions
Los Angeles—Lewis; Rich
New York—Crowe

Fumbles Recovered
Los Angeles—Reid
New York—None

Missed Field Goals

Los Angeles—None
New York—None

The Rams were home for their eighth game of the season against the conference bottom-feeders, the New York Yanks. Since getting rocked on the floor of the Coliseum on opening day, the Yanks' fortunes stayed dismal at best. The only bright spot came in their fourth game when they managed a tie with Detroit. They then lost three straight to be at 0–6–1 as they headed back to the Coliseum for a rematch. However, in defense of the Yanks' horrific record, the three games they lost prior to coming into Los Angeles were by a combined 13 points.

New York head coach Jimmy Phelan brought his sad sack collection of players to Los Angeles with solid respect from the Southland scribes. The observation of Phelan was that he was doing a good job with what he had to work with considering he was only appointed head coach just minutes before the start of training camp. He also lost out to the Canadian Football League for the services of some of his top players, and still managed to have his team play tough in the majority of their games.[55]

Even though the Yanks were the league's only winless team, Stydahar did not consider them pushovers. The Yanks had three backfield performers that had Stydahar's focus during practice sessions at Gilmore Field. Quarterback George Ratterman had a pair of good games against the Rams in 1950, and was capable of executing well in both the T-formation or double wing. Ratterman left the Yanks to play in Canada, but rejoined New York at the beginning of November. Halfbacks George Taliaferro and Buddy Young also caused Stydahar concern. Taliaferro was considered New York's best all-around back, and Young was a slippery runner that had the ability to score whenever he got his hands on the ball.[56]

In the later stages of November throughout much the United States, the weather had turned cloudy, cold, rainy, and sometimes snow hampered the masses. Southern California on November 18, 1951, had none of those things, as the skies above the Coliseum were mostly sunny with the temperature near 80 degrees by the two o'clock kickoff.

Concerned about a possible upset, Stydahar decided to start his Bull Elephants of Dan Towler, Dick Hoerner and Paul Younger in an attempt to pound the feistiness out of Jimmy Phelan's charges early. The Elephants were gaining momentum with the public's affections, and for good reason. This behemoth trio gained 264 yards in close to three quarters of work together, averaging 5.4 yards per carry.

Stydahar's decision turned out to be a brilliant one in a 48–21 Los Angeles victory in front of 34,717 sun-drenched spectators. His Elephants hammered away at the New York defense, pounding their massive frames at it 23 times for 267 yards, and set the game's tempo early. Towler led the way with 155 yards on 13 carries for an incredible 11.9 yards per carry. Hoerner came in second with 78 yards on seven carries and scored the Rams' first two touchdowns. Younger added 34 yards on just three carries. In all, the backfield of the Elephants and the speed merchants of Vitamin Smith and Glenn Davis helped account for 356 of the team's total offensive production of 583 yards. Smith ran for 59 yards and one score on nine attempts, and Davis ran for 30 yards on nine carries.

The Rams got out to an early lead and never gave it up. Their first points came on a one-yard run by Hoerner that capped a 67-yard drive in the opening quarter. Hoerner recorded another touchdown on a 43-yard run after a Woodley Lewis interception. On the final play of the first quarter, Vitamin Smith ran off tackle for a 31-yard touchdown gallop. Bob Waterfield added two extra point tries, and the Rams were comfortably up by a 20–0 margin heading into the second quarter.

George Taliaferro lived up to his reputation as the Yanks' best all-around backfield star by running for a 16-yard touchdown in the second quarter, in which 35 combined points were scored. Taliaferro led all rushers for the game with 166 yards on 12 carries and two touchdowns. He also completed three of five pass attempts for 83 yards and a touchdown. Los Angeles came right back with a six-point tally of their own. Behind great blocks from Bill Lange and Dick Daugherty, Towler ate up 69 yards of Coliseum real estate crossing the goal line with the Rams' fourth touchdown of the afternoon. Waterfield's extra point upped the Los Angeles advantage to 27–7.

An exchange of punts temporarily slowed the scoring fest down, but then the scoreboard began lighting up once again. Taliaferro ran for a gain of 30, and then he threw a 30-yard pass to Buddy Young. Taliaferro capped the drive off by finding Bob Celeri from 20 yards out, and following Harvey Johnson's conversion kick, the Yanks cut their deficit to 27–14.

On the Rams' next offensive series, Norm Van Brocklin completed a long pass covering 44 yards to Crazylegs Hirsch. That huge chunk of turf was the key play in a drive that was finished off with Jerry Williams running the final four yards to make it 34–14 after Waterfield's extra point kick. Taliaferro had one more act of brilliance in his arsenal on this day. The ensuing kickoff had the ball on the New York 35, and it was from there that Taliaferro swept the right end and outran the entire Los Angeles defense to complete a 65-yard jaunt. Harvey Johnson added his 125th straight conversion kick, and the game stood at 34–21 heading into the second half. Don Paul's services were lost to the Rams when officials ejected him from the game for an infraction during Taliaferro's run. Paul was blocked, and after jumping up he threw a shoulder block and an elbow at New York's Dan Edwards. Both teams agreed that Paul's actions did not deserve an ejection, but the officials thought differently.

The third quarter belonged to New York, as they dominated play, but they failed to produce any points for the effort. Their best opportunity came when they marched 72 yards down to the Los Angeles one only to lose possession when Ratterman fumbled and Joe Reid recovered for the Rams.

By the end of the third quarter, the Los Angeles offense appeared to be getting into a groove. Towler ran for 27 yards to set the tempo for the final 15 minutes after a scoreless third quarter. At the beginning of the fourth quarter, Waterfield passed to Smith and Hirsch on back-to-back plays, and both were good for first downs. Waterfield called his own number to cap the drive off successfully with a 13-yard run behind solid blocking from Bill Lange and Harry Thompson on the third play of the fourth quarter. Waterfield's conversion extended the lead to 41–21.

For most the final quarter, the teams exchanged punts until the clock ran down to 1:25 remaining. It was then that Hirsch caught a 33-yard scoring strike from Van Brocklin, and Waterfield rang up the final point of the game with a conversion kick. Hirsch's scoring grab allowed him to extend his streak of catching at least one touchdown pass in every game up to this point of the season. It was his 12th of the year, and he finished the game with four receptions for 97 yards.[57]

The Rams' victory did not come without loss, however. Hoerner and Lange suffered slight concussions, Tank Younger had a hip pointer, and Jack Finlay injured a foot. Also added to the list of wounded were rookie standout Andy Robustelli (bruised knees), Marv Johnson (headaches from a concussion), Stan West (sprains in back, left knee and ankle), Leon McLaughlin (right knee sprain), Jerry Williams (pulled muscle in right leg and one loose front tooth) and Norb Hecker (cracked cheekbone).[58]

This win improved the Rams' record to 6–2 and they remained in a first-place tie with the Chicago Bears in the National Conference. The Bears defeated the Packers, 24–13, at a frigid Wrigley Field. What was heralded as the "game of the year" in the American Conference, turned out to be a 10–0 victory by the Cleveland Browns over the New York Giants. With both teams coming into the game with one loss apiece, this battle of NFL elite was played in front of 52,215 fans at the Polo Grounds. The attendance was the largest at the Polo Grounds since 1946. The Browns disappointed the large throng with an incredible defensive effort. Cleveland improved to a league-best 7–1 record, while the Giants fell to 5–2–1. In inter-conference action, Detroit beat Philadelphia, 28–10, to improve to 5–2–1 on the year, a half-game behind the Rams and the Bears.[59]

November 25, 1951—Week 9: Los Angeles Rams vs. Washington Redskins

Griffith Stadium

Los Angeles	7	0	0	14	21
Washington	7	14	10	0	31

Los Angeles—Williams 7 interception return (Waterfield kick)
Washington—Goode 1 run (Dudley kick)
Washington—Goode 3 run (Dudley kick)
Washington—Taylor 24 pass from Baugh (Dudley kick)
Washington—Field Goal Dudley 23
Washington—Dudley 9 pass from Baugh (Dudley kick)
Los Angeles—Hirsch 3 pass from Waterfield (Waterfield kick)
Los Angeles—Boyd 28 pass from Waterfield (Waterfield kick)
A—50,286

	Los Angeles	*Washington*
First Downs	23	26
Rushing A-Y	28–61	65–352
Passing C-A-I	22–43–2	7–12–1
Passing Yards	315	117
Sacked N-Y	0–0	0–0
Total Plays, Yards	71–376	77–467
Field Goals M-A	0–1	1–2
Punts- Yards	2–65	2–73
Fumbles-Lost	3–3	4–2
Penalties-Yards	4–40	9–101

Rushing
(Attempts, Yards)
Los Angeles—Hoerner 11–29; Towler 11–14; Younger 4–14; V Smith 1–4; Davis 1–0
Washington—Goode 23–148; Papit 14–41; Heath 13–54; Dudley 6–58; Dowda 4–44; Thomas 4–7

Passing
(Attempts, Completions, Interceptions, Yards)
Los Angeles—Waterfield 30–16–2–236; Van Brocklin 13–6–0–84
Washington—Baugh 12–7–1–117

Receptions
(Catches, Yards)
Los Angeles—Hirsch 7–104; Keane 5–74; Towler 5–56; Boyd 2–55; Hoerner 2–21; Johnson 1–10
Washington—Taylor 4–57; Thomas 1–34; Brito 1–15; Dudley 1–9

Interceptions
Los Angeles—Williams
Washington—Gilmer; DeMao

Fumbles Recovered
Los Angeles—Daugherty; Collier
Washington—Buskar; Ricca; Yowarsky

Missed Field Goals
Los Angeles—Waterfield 26
Washington—Dudley 39

The Rams embarked on a two-game road trip starting in Washington and ending in Chicago. You couldn't blame Joe Stydahar's club for looking past the 3–5 Redskins to the Bears. The Rams had clobbered the Skins 58–14 in the *Los Angeles Times* Charity Football Game back in August during the preseason. Furthermore, the Rams brought the league's best offense to attack the NFL's worst defense.[60]

File this one under Don't Count Your Chickens before They Hatch. Los Angeles scored the game's first touchdown and the last two on the 37-degree day. In between, the Redskins tallied four touchdowns and a field goal to get some revenge 31–21. With the Bears losing to the Browns, the Lions took over first place after clobbering the woeful Packers in the annual Thanksgiving game.

One way to slow down a high-powered offense is to control the clock. Led by fullback Bob Goode, the Redskins pounded the Rams for 352 yards rushing. That took the burden off 37-year-old Sammy Baugh, who threw only 12 passes, completing seven for 117 yards. Goode personally gained more yards on the ground, 148, than the Rams' vaunted Bull Elephant backfield of Younger, Towler, and Hoerner could muster on the mushy turf: 57.

One bright spot for the visitors was the performance of Elroy Hirsch. The league's top receiver caught seven passes for 104 yards, including his 13th touchdown catch to continue his string of snagging a six-pointer in every game of the season.

The fans had barely settled into their seats when Jerry Williams swiped Baugh's first pass and returned it seven yards to pay dirt. But the Old Pro came right back to engineer a 68-yard drive to tie the score. In the waning moments of the opening period, Harry Gilmer picked off Rob Waterfield's aerial to set up a 39-yard field goal attempt by Bullet Bill Dudley. The kick was no good. Waterfield had entered the game after Norm Van Brocklin had been flattened by Walt Yowarsky. To show how the day went for the Rams, Bob threw a fourth down pass to Tom Keane, who was in the clear at the 10. But the receiver slipped, and the ball bounced off the top of his helmet.[61]

The Redskins added two touchdowns in the second quarter. The first score came on a nine-play, 74-yard drive with Rob Goode going over from the three-yard line. The second came on a 10-play, 80-yard drive with a Baugh to Hugh Taylor pass covering the final 24 yards to pay dirt.

Trailing 21–7, the Rams came out fired-up after halftime. They followed Washington's script by running Hoerner seven times in 10 plays to move into enemy territory. But the big fullback's seventh carry resulted in a fumble that Yowarsky recovered at the 23. On the next play, Goode steamed off tackle for 36 yards to help set up a successful Dudley field goal. A few minutes later, an interception led to another Skins touchdown to make it 31–7.

The Rams made the final score more respectable with two fourth quarter touchdowns. After Bobby Collier recovered Leon Heath's fumble on the Rams' 14, Waterfield directed an eight-play drive that was aided by two roughing penalties. Hirsch snared a three-yard pitch in the corner of the end zone to keep his record of a touchdown reception in every game intact. In the closing minutes, Waterfield led another march that ended with a 28-yard touchdown pass to Bob Boyd.

Stydahar said afterward, "We didn't know the Redskins had such a strong defense against a running attack. They didn't have it the first time we played them, but this time they were as good and sharp as any line we've played against this season."[62]

The Rams flew straight to Chicago on Monday to spend the next week preparing for the must-win game against the Bears.[63]

December 2, 1951—Week 10: Los Angeles Rams vs. Chicago Bears

Wrigley Field

Los Angeles	7	14	7	14	42
Chicago	17	0	0	0	17

Chicago—Lujack 1 run (Blanda kick)
Chicago—Lujack 1 run (Blanda kick)
Los Angeles—Hirsch 91 pass from Waterfield (Waterfield kick)
Chicago—Field Goal Blanda 27
Los Angeles—Fears 11 pass from Van Brocklin (Waterfield kick)
Los Angeles—Van Brocklin 1 run (Waterfield kick)
Los Angeles—Towler 3 run (Waterfield kick)
Los Angeles—Towler 16 run (Waterfield kick)
Los Angeles—Younger 20 run (Waterfield kick)
A—50,286

	Los Angeles	*Chicago*
First Downs	25	24
Rushing A-Y	27–206	56–266
Passing C-A-I	13–19–0	10–26–0
Passing Yards	307	123
Sacked N-Y	2–17	4–38
Total Plays, Yards	46–513	82–389
Field Goals M-A	0–0	1–2
Punts-Yards	3–121	5–162
Fumbles Lost	3–3	2–0
Penalties- Yards	11–89	11–111

Rushing
(Attempts, Yards)

Los Angeles—Towler 14–76; Younger 7–71; Hoerner 5–56; Van Brocklin 1–1; Williams 0–2
Chicago—Dottley 16–54; Hunsinger 13–95; Gulvanics 11–31; Lujack 6–8; Stone 4–11; Rykovich 3–57; White 1–10; Morrison 1–0

Passing
(Attempts, Completions, Interceptions, Yards)
Los Angeles—Van Brocklin 12-8-0-120; Waterfield 7-5-0-187
Chicago—Lujack 20-7-0-95; Williams 5-3-0-28; Rykovich 1-0-0-0

Receptions
(Catches, Yards)
Los Angeles—Fears 5-68; Hirsch 3-106; Younger 2-75; Towler 2-44; Hoerner 1-14
Chicago—Stone 5-69; Gulvanics 2-21; Keane 1-14; Schroeder 1-13; Hunsinger 1-6

Interceptions
Los Angeles—None
Chicago—None

Fumbles Recovered
Los Angeles—None
Chicago—Hansen; Cowan; Bray

Missed Field Goals
Los Angeles—None
Chicago—Blanda 40

If the Rams were to win their third straight conference title, they would have to win their next two games—at Chicago, then the Lions at home. Since those were the other two contenders for first place, a loss to either would drop Los Angeles into a hole too big to climb out of with only one more game, albeit against the Packers, left to play. But captain Bob Waterfield promised Coach Stydahar on Monday that "the Rams won't lose another game this year."[64]

Determined to avoid falling behind early as they did in Washington, the Rams did just that in standing-room-only Wrigley Field.[65] The Bears took the opening kickoff and drove 80 yards for the first points. Tank Younger had a chance to end the march, but he muffed an interception of Johnny Lujack's pass in the flat that would surely have resulted in six points the other way. Given a reprieve, the Bears smashed to the one, from where Lujack sneaked over.

On the Rams' first possession, Dick Hoerner, who had a crucial fumble that changed the momentum against the Redskins, coughed up the ball to put the Bears right back in business on the Los Angeles 35. Power running by John "Kayo" Dottley, Julie Rykovich, and George Gulyanics set up another Lujack one-yard sneak. Just like that, the Rams trailed 14–0.

Soon afterward, the visitors found themselves on their own nine after a clipping penalty on a punt return. But that's when two future Hall of Famers teamed up to start the comeback. Waterfield faded back into the end zone and heaved the ball far downfield to Crazylegs Hirsch, who took the ball over his shoulder on the 44 and outran two Bears defenders to the end zone. The longest play of the season pushed Hirsch's total receiving yardage for the 1951 season past the record of 1,211 set by Green Bay great Don Hutson in 1942.[66] Bob's extra point cut the Bears' lead in half.

Once again, though, the Rams' defense could not stop Lujack & Company from penetrating deep into their territory. But Larry Brink and Stan West sacked the Heisman Trophy winner from Notre Dame at the 19 to bring on George Blanda, who booted a 27-yard field goal to make it 17–7. No one could have guessed that the Bears would not register another point the rest of the game.

Norm Van Brocklin led an 89-yard march in the second period that featured Hoerner roaring through right tackle for gains of 21 and 18 yards. That set up the Dutchman's passes—one to Dan Towler and three to Tom Fears, the last over Lujack in the end zone for 11 yards and a touchdown.

It wasn't long before the Rams were knocking on the door again. Playing both ways, Younger rambled for 21 yards, and Towler caught a 35-yard aerial to give Van a chance to sneak over from the one-foot line.

The Bears stormed back, but the Rams' defense drew a line in the sand again. This time Blanda missed a field goal from the 40.

In the final minute of the half, Van tossed a short pass to Younger who streaked 76 yards to pay dirt. But a holding penalty cancelled the effort. As they often did under George Halas, the Bears turned to roughhousing to intimidate the opponent. They drew unnecessary roughness penalties on two plays. The teams left the field with Los Angeles ahead 21–17.

The Rams wasted no time in increasing their lead in the third quarter. Younger caught a short pass and sped 52 yards, this time with no flags. Towler did the honors from the three.

Later in the period, Deacon Dan fumbled, and Les Cowan recovered for Chicago. The Rams' defense stifled the threat, but they had to come back out to the field after Hoerner was bitten by fumbleitis and Ray Bray recovered at the 32. The Bears moved to the six, but Lujack twice failed to hit Jim Keane in the end zone to turn the ball over on downs as boos cascaded from the stands.

The Rams made the Bears' fans even more disgruntled by driving the length of the field to extend the lead to 18 points. The Tank again led the way, busting loose for 23 yards on the ground and catching a Waterfield floater for 21 more. Towler scored his second touchdown of the day, "spilling Bears all over the turf"[67] from the 16 on the first play of the final period.

Then the Bears once again gave the Rams an opportunity to demonstrate their bend-but-don't-break defense. Roaring to first-and-goal from the five, the Halas Men ran the ball four times and ended up on the six.

Los Angeles' last scoring opportunity came when Andy Robustelli blocked Curly Morrison's punt and the ball rolled out of bounds at the Chicago 28. After Van Brocklin connected with Fears for eight, Younger showed why he, Hoerner, and Towler were called the Bull Elephant backfield by bulling his way over the goal from the 20 to give the Rams a 42–17 victory.

Late in the game, veteran Bears guard Ray Bray added a touch of hilarity to the afternoon. He rushed onto the field from the sidelines to grab Jerry Williams, who was threatening to break into the clear after intercepting rookie quarterback Bob Williams' pass on his own seven. But a Rams penalty saved the officials from having to figure out how to handle the situation.[68]

Coach Stydahar proclaimed that he "was mighty proud of the way the Rams bounced back after that awful drubbing by the Redskins last week."[69]

Further North, in Detroit, the pesky 49ers upset the Lions 20–10 to put the Rams back in first place by a half game. Los Angeles now controlled their own destiny. Win the final two games and earn the National crown.

December 9, 1951—Week 11: Los Angeles Rams vs. Detroit Lions

Los Angeles Memorial Coliseum

Detroit	0	10	7	7	24
Los Angeles	3	6	7	6	22

Los Angeles—Field Goal Waterfield 17
Detroit—Field Goal Harder 33
Los Angeles—Field Goal Waterfield 40
Detroit—Harder 3 run (Walker kick)
Los Angeles—Field Goal Waterfield 25
Los Angeles—Towler 2 run (Waterfield kick)
Detroit—Walker 11 run (Walker kick)
Los Angeles—Field Goal Waterfield 20
Los Angeles—Field Goal Waterfield 39
Detroit—Hart 22 pass from Walker (Walker kick)
A—67,892

	Los Angeles	Detroit
First Downs	27	19
Rushing A-Y	47–156	39–163
Passing C-A-I	17–33–0	7–16–2
Passing Yards	247	91
Sacked N-Y	0–0	0–0
Total Plays, Yards	80–403	55–254
Field Goals M-A	5–7	1–1
Punts-Yards	1–28	4–164
Fumbles -Lost	1–0	3–0
Penalties-Yards	9–99	9–95

Rushing
(Attempts, Yards)

Detroit—Layne 13-67; Walker 10-44; Harder 8-31; Hoernschemeyer 8-21
Los Angeles—Towler 17-60; Younger 11-75; Davis 10-14; Hoerner 6-18; Waterfield 2-(-5); V. Smith 1-(-6)

Passing
(Attempts, Completions, Interceptions, Yards)

Detroit—Layne 15-6-2-69; Walker 1-1-0-22
Los Angeles—Van Brocklin 21-11-0-148; Waterfield 12-6-0-99

Receptions
(Catches, Yards)

Detroit—Hoernschemeyer 3-28; Hart 1-22; Walker 1-20; Harder 1-11; Swiacki 1-10
Los Angeles—Hirsch 6-81; Fears 5-93; Hoerner 2-37; Davis 2-34; Younger 2-2

Interceptions
Detroit—None
Los Angeles—Toogood; Williams

Fumbles Recovered
Los Angeles—None
Detroit—Hansen; Cowan; Bray

Missed Field Goals
Detroit—None
Los Angeles—Waterfield 49, 23 blocked

A fundamental rule of football is that one touchdown equals two field goals. So settling for three-pointers in the red zone instead of touchdowns can cost you the game. That maxim was never illustrated better than in the Rams' loss to the Lions on the second-to-last weekend of the 1951 NFL season.

Los Angeles had 27 first downs to 19 for Detroit, ran 80 plays to the opponents' 55, and had the advantage in total yardage, 403–254. The Rams even had a turnover margin of +2. But they lost the game 24–22 because the Lions scored three touchdowns to their one. As a result, the Motor City crew moved back into first place with a 7-3-1 record while the Rams fell into a second-place tie with Chicago at 7-4. Buddy Parker's Lions could now clinch the conference by winning their final game at San Francisco.

The key play that ended the Rams' 12-game winning streak against the Lions came with Los Angeles on top 22–17 with only 2:18 left to play. Triple-threat halfback Doak Walker took a handoff from quarterback Bobby Layne and, running to his right, fired a touchdown pass to Leon Hart—one Heisman Trophy winner to another. The only reception of the afternoon for the 255-pound end from Notre Dame produced the sixth and final lead change of the afternoon.

Desperately trying to get into field goal range, the Rams reached the Lions' 48 thanks to a roughing the passer penalty and Norm Van Brocklin's pass to Crazylegs Hirsch. Then confusion reigned as quarterback and receivers didn't seem to be on the same page. Three incompletions sandwiched around a six-yard loss by Vitamin Smith sealed the Rams' fate as they lost the ball on downs.

The Rams started the game strong, marching from their 11 to the six-inch line. But a Waterfield fumble and an offside penalty forced them to settle for Bob's 17-yard field goal.

In the second quarter, the Lions drove from their 12 to the Rams' 24. When the defense stiffened, Pat Harder banged through a 33-yard field goal to tie the score at 3. With coach Joe Stydahar continuing his plan of alternating signal-callers, Van Brocklin hit Tom Fears for 18 and 19 yards to set up Waterfield's second three-pointer. Rams 6, Lions 3.

The Lions responded with the first touchdown drive of the game. Sparked by quarterback Bobby Layne's running, Detroit marched 53 yards, the final three covered by Harder around right end. Lions 10, Rams 6.

Two personal foul penalties and runs by Dan Towler and Tank Younger made possible Waterfield's 25-yard field goal on the last play of the half. Lions 10, Rams 9.

The Rams took the second half kickoff and traveled 79 yards in 13 plays to retake the lead. Waterfield connected with Hirsch, Fears, and Glenn Davis, who was in the game because Dick Hoerner was injured while blocking earlier in the possession. Towler punched over from the two. Rams 16, Lions 10.

The lead held until the last play of the period when Walker scored on a double reverse from the 11 "after fumbling the handoff and dribbling the ball like Hank Luisetti for [a] few steps."[70] Lions 17, Rams 16.

Van Brocklin unleashed a flurry of passes to Hirsch and Fears to move to the Detroit six. But once again, the Rams had to content themselves with a Waterfield three-pointer from 20 yards out. Rams 19, Lions 17.

Later in the period, Davis caught a 13-yard pass from Norm and added seven more yards on a handoff. But on third-and-two at the 31, the Heisman Trophy winner from

West Point hit a brick wall. So Waterfield booted his fifth field goal, a 39-yarder. Instead of being two scores behind, the Lions could win with a touchdown. Rams 22, Lions 17.

With the clock under four minutes, Layne got hot. After throwing only a dozen passes to that point, he hit Bill Swiacki for 10, then 20 more to Walker, his high school teammate.[71] Back to pass again, the Texas gunslinger tucked the ball under his arm and hot-footed 25 yards to the Rams' 22. From that spot, the Doaker threw the winning pass to Hart. Lions 24, Rams 22.

Cal Whorton wrote in the *Los Angeles Times*: "Gloom-thick smog that sometimes engulfs our fair City of the Angels would have looked like a clear day compared to the atmosphere inside the Rams' dressing quarters after yesterday's heartbreaking 24–22 loss to the Detroit Lions. A library would have sounded like a foundry alongside the silence one could almost feel."[72] Whorton added, "To a man the Rams knew they had all but kicked themselves out of the championship. What made the feeling so painful was the knowledge that they should have won-but didn't."[73]

Stydahar blamed poor tackling for the defeat but didn't single out any individuals. He thought his men were too keyed up to start the game. Line coach Ray Richards pointed to the fumble inside the one during the first drive as the turning point of the game. "If we'd have made a touchdown then, I believe we'd have won going away. We never did fully recover from that one bobble."[74] Hirsch, who failed to catch a touchdown pass for the first time all season, gave his take on the loss. "We were our own worst enemy. Maybe we were too tight."[75] The Lions' celebration in their locker room next door could be heard through the wall. "Let 'em stay that way, and maybe the 49ers will beat 'em again next week," said one Rams player.[76]

First-year Lions coach Buddy Parker said his men were more inspired for this game than any they had played thus far. He had special praise for Hart, who played both offense and defense, and for Layne and Harder. When asked if he thought his team got some gifts from the Rams, he insisted his club was responsible for forcing the mistakes.[77]

December 16, 1951—Week 12: Los Angeles Rams vs. Green Bay Packers

Los Angeles Memorial Coliseum

Green Bay	7	7	0	0	14
Los Angeles	14	0	14	14	42

Los Angeles—Hoerner 15 pass from Waterfield (Waterfield kick)
Green Bay—Grimes 33 pass from Rote (Cone kick)
Los Angeles—Hirsch 72 pass from Waterfield (Waterfield kick)
Green Bay—Elliott 14 pass from Rote (Cone kick)
Los Angeles—Fears 39 pass from Waterfield (Waterfield kick)
Los Angeles—Williams 99 field goal return (Waterfield kick)
Los Angeles—Hirsch 37 pass from Waterfield (Waterfield kick)
Los Angeles—Hirsch 19 pass from Waterfield (Waterfield kick)
A—23,698

	Los Angeles	*Green Bay*
First Downs	18	20
Rushing A-Y	26–151	21–45
Passing C-A-I	15–27–2	27–56–2
Passing Yards	256	379
Sacked N-Y	1–11	2–21

	Los Angeles	*Green Bay*
Total Plays, Yards	53–407	77–424
Punts-Yards	6–266	4–174
Field Goals M-A	0–1	0–2
Fumbles-Lost	1–1	3–2
Penalties-Yards	7–59	9–74

Rushing
(Attempts, Yards)

Green Bay—Rote 8-24; Canadeo 6-21; Reid 2-6; Cone 1-4; Grimes 1-3; Moselle 1-1; Pelfrey 1-1; Thomason 1-(-15)

Los Angeles—Towler 13-102; Hoerner 8-41; Younger 3-12; Davis 2-(-4)

Passing
(Attempts, Completions, Interceptions, Yards)

Green Bay—Rote 40-20-3-335; Thomason 16-7-0-44

Los Angeles—Waterfield 18-10-2-204; Van Brocklin 9-5-0-52

Receptions
(Catches, Yards)

Green Bay—Mann 11-123; Elliott 5-58; Cone 4-28; Grimes 3-66; Canadeo 1-46; Pelfrey 1-24; Girard 1-21; Reid 1-13

Los Angeles—Hirsch 6-146; Fears 6-83; Davis 1-17; Hoerner 1-15; Younger 1-(-5)

Interceptions
Green Bay—Davis, Collins
Los Angeles—Rich, Keane

Fumbles Recovered
Green Bay—Moselle
Los Angeles—Daugherty, Johnson

Missed Field Goals
Green Bay—Cone 50; Michaels 34
Los Angeles—Waterfield 43

The Rams entered their final game with the 3–8 Packers knowing they had to win, and the Lions and Bears had to lose for Los Angeles to host the NFL championship game the following Sunday. By the time the West Coast games started, the Bears had already lost to the crosstown Cardinals 24–14. Joe Stydahar's club took care of their end of the bargain before only 23,698, about a third as many as saw the Lions' game the previous Sunday.

The 49ers-Lions game was underway when the Rams and Packers kicked off, and telegraph reports to the press box kept Los Angeles fans up to date with what was happening at Kezar Stadium. Coliseum P.A. announcer Frank Bull was so excited by the San Francisco game that he once referred to the Packers as the 49ers.[78]

After a lackluster first half that ended in a 14–14 tie, the Rams caught fire in the second 30 minutes to win going away 42–14. The game featured an NFL record-setting performance by Elroy Hirsch and a league-record longest run by Jittery Jerry Williams. The Rams also tied a league record by totaling 278 first downs for the season.[79]

The Packers stopped the Rams on their first two possessions but could not generate any offense themselves. Glenn Davis's 31-yard punt return gave the Rams great field position at the Green Bay 33, and they took advantage of it. Bob Waterfield dropped a short pass into fullback Dick Hoerner's hands that resulted in a 15-yard touchdown.

Sparked by a 37-yard return of the kickoff to the Packers' 47 by Don Moselle, the

Packers answered with a touchdown drive of their own. Despite a fierce pass rush, quarterback Tobin Rote sailed a throw from the 33 to Billy Grimes streaking toward the goal line. Defensive back Marvin Johnson deflected the ball, but it landed in Grimes' arms as he fell into the end zone.

The Rams wasted no time in regaining the lead. On the first play after the kickoff, Waterfield connected with Hirsch on a 72-yard touchdown. "Crazylegs made a great stab at the Packer 46 and started down the sidelines. Soon he was pinned in by defender Ray Pelfrey. Hirsch slowed his gait and so did Pelfry, whereupon the Ram racer stepped on the gas and roared right by the bewildered Packer."[80]

Another Rote-Grimes hookup, this time for 38 yards, gave the visitors an excellent chance to tie the score again. But the Rams forced a field goal try that missed.

With their defense finally stopping the L.A. Express, the Packers succeeded in tying the score late in the second quarter as Carl Elliott outfought two defenders in the end zone for the 14-yard touchdown.[81]

Early in the third period, Tom Fears did his best Elliott imitation by winning a scramble with two defensive backs for Waterfield's 39-yard aerial to give the Rams a seven-point lead for the third time.[82]

Obviously, the Rams couldn't just trade touchdowns with the Packers and win. So the turning point came when the Packers bogged down at midfield. Coach Gene Ronzani decided to let Fred Cone try a field goal from that spot. But it fell short, and Williams fielded it at the one. The "shifty, speedy runner from Washington State"[83] raced 99 yards to extend the Rams' lead to 28–14.

But the Packers' offense, which would outgain the Rams 424–407, kept pushing the issue. Rote found 10-year veteran Tony Canadeo for a 46-yard gain during a march that reached the 12. After three runs gained eight yards, the Pack went for it, but Canadeo was stopped, and the Rams took over.

Los Angeles salted the game away in quarter four on two more Waterfield strikes to Hirsch for 37 and 19 yards. With the two touchdown catches, Hirsch equaled Don Hutson's 1942 record of 17 touchdown receptions in one season. Elroy's 18 points also gave him 102 for the season, tops in the league.[84]

During the final period, fans were given play-by-play reports from San Francisco. The 49ers trailed 17–14 but had first-and-goal on the two with less than four minutes to play. The crowd let out "a mighty shout," players on the Rams' bench leaped to their feet, and the Rams on the field drew a five-yard penalty for delay of game as they joined in the excitement.[85] The crowd knew when San Francisco scored before it was announced because the reporters in the press section went wild.[86] The 49ers' 21–17 lead held up, giving the Rams the National Conference title.

Comedian Bob Hope, a part owner of the Rams, greeted the champs when they arrived in their locker room. "If Warner Bros. tried to make a [motion] picture like this, no one would believe it. This is the first game I ever attended where I watched the press box more than the playing field."[87]

Rams president Dan Reeves said about the 49ers, "We'll invite the whole bunch of them to a whopping dinner." Bob Waterfield admitted, "I don't know how to thank 'em. Guess we should whip off a big 'thank you' telegram."[88]

Stydahar, "who only a week ago was the picture of dejection after losing to the Lions,"[89] couldn't find the words to describe the confluence of events that propelled his team into the championship game. Being a coach through and through, his only comment when asked about meeting the Browns the next Sunday was "We have to improve our tackling more than anything else if we're going to whip those guys."[90]

Notes

1. "Pro Yanks Shift Contest," *New York Times*, September 26, 1951, L-51.
2. "Yanks Take on Injury Riddled Rams Tonight," *Riverside (CA) Independent Enterprise*, September 28, 1951, 10.
3. "Yanks Take," 10.
4. "Rams Meet Yanks Tonight," *San Bernardino (CA) County Sun*, September 28, 1951, 27.
5. Frank Finch, "Hoerner to Start at Fullback Spot," *Los Angeles Times*, September 28, 1951, IV-3.
6. Finch, "Hoerner to Start," IV-3.
7. "Strader is Out as Coach of the Football Yanks," *New York Times*, August 6, 1951, 27.
8. "Ratterman Signs with Montreal," *New York Daily News*, July 3, 1951, 36.
9. "How They Line Up," *Los Angeles Times*, September 28, 1951, IV-1.
10. Frank Finch, "Rams Choice over Yanks in Opener," *Los Angeles Times*, September 28, 1951, IV-1.
11. Finch, "Rams Choice," IV-1.
12. "Rams Wallop Yanks, 54–14," *Portland Oregonian*, September 29, 1951, 3-1, 2.
13. Henry Reiger, "Van Brocklin Sets NFL Aerial Mark," *Riverside Independent Enterprise*, September 29, 1951, 8.
14. Fred Delano, "Rams Grid Machine Blasts Yanks, 54–14," *Long Beach Press-Telegram*, September 29, 1951, B-2.
15. Reiger, "Van Brocklin Sets NFL Aerial Mark," 8.
16. Paul Zimmerman, "Rams Passing Best Ever Seen by Either Coach," *Los Angeles Times*, September 29, 1951, III-3.
17. Zimmerman, "Rams Passing," III-3.
18. Zimmerman, "Rams Passing," III-3.
19. "Van Brocklin Shatters NFL Passing Mark as Rams Win," *Oakland Tribune*, September 29, 1951, D-9.
20. National Football League, *2018 NFL Record and Fact Book*, 555.
21. Harold Sauerbrei, "Browns Get Lift Drilling for Rams," *Cleveland Plain Dealer*, October 3, 1951, 29–30.
22. Frank Finch, "Van Brocklin to Start Against Browns Sunday," *Los Angeles Times*, October 5, 1951, IV-4.
23. Frank Finch, "Rams Favored by Touchdown Over Rams in Clash Today," *Los Angeles Times*, October 7, 1951, II-7.
24. "Los Angeles Rams Picked Over Browns," Chillicothe (OH) *Gazette and News-Advertiser*, October 5, 1951, 15.
25. "The Weather," *Los Angeles Times*, October 7, 1951, 1.
26. "Blazing Sun Flattens Fans at Coliseum," *Los Angeles Times*, October 8, 1951, IV-1.
27. Frank Finch, "Late Rally by Browns Ruins Rams, 38 to 23," *Los Angeles Times*, October 8, 1951, IV-1, 3.
28. Cal Whorton, "We Were Up; They Were Off, Says Brown," *Los Angeles Times*, October 8, 1951, IV-1, 3.
29. Whorton, "We Were Up," IV-1, 3.
30. Bob McClellan, "42,000 to Watch Lions Battle Rams," *Detroit Times*, October 14, 1951, 3–3.
31. Frank Finch, "Detroit Lions Choice Over Rams Today," *Los Angeles Times*, October 14, 1951, II-14.
32. "Injury Costs Lions Services of Stanfel," *Detroit Free Press*, September 9, 1951, C-3.
33. Bob Latshaw, "52,907 See Rams Gain 27–21 Edge," *Detroit Free Press*, October 15, 1951, 26, 28.
34. Frank Finch, "Rams Capture 27–21 Thriller," *Los Angeles Times*, October 15, 1951, IV-1, 2.
35. Frank Finch, "Scouting the Pros," *Los Angeles Times*, October 17, 1951, IV-2.
36. Frank Finch, "Knee Sprain Sidelines Fears for Important Packer Contest," *Los Angeles Times*, October 16, 1951, IV-1.
37. Frank Finch, "Keane Injured, Out Two Weeks," *Los Angeles Times*, October 18, 1951, IV-3.
38. "Packers and Rams to Play Before 25,000 Here Today," *Milwaukee Journal-Sentinel*, October 21, 1951, 3–5.
39. "Mann, Hirsch Tied for Point Lead in NFL," *Green Bay Press-Gazette*, October 17, 1951, 21.
40. Frank Finch, "Rams Batter Packers 28–0," *Los Angeles Times*, October 22, 1951, IV-1, 2.
41. Frank Finch, "Shaw's Statement on Sunday Clash Generates Steam Under Ram Collars," *Los Angeles Times*, October 26, 1951, IV-2.
42. "Hardy Brown," *The Fabulous 50s Volume 1*, NFL Films, 1987.
43. Frank Finch, "Rams Buried Under 44–17 Avalanche by 49ers," *Los Angeles Times*, October 29, 1951, IV-1.
44. "NFL Game Results," *Los Angeles Times*, October 29, 1951, IV-1.
45. Steve Bisheff, *Great Teams' Great Years: Los Angeles Rams* (New York: Macmillan, 1973), 29–32.

46. Bisheff, *Los Angeles Rams*, 29–32.
47. Frank Finch, "Rams Remain in Running for Crown," *Los Angeles Times*, November 6, 1951, IV-1.
48. George Sullivan, *The Great Running Backs* (New York: G.P. Putman's Sons, 1972), 63–64.
49. Cal Whorton, "Climax Catch Just Routine, says Elroy," *Los Angeles Times*, November 5, 1951, IV-1.
50. Frank Finch, "Waterfield & Co. Deal 23–16 Loss to 49ers," *Los Angeles Times*, November 5, 1951, IV-1.
51. "NFL Game Results," *Los Angeles Times*, November 5, 1951, IV-1.
52. Frank Finch, "Card Cellar Berth Puzzles Stydahar," *Los Angeles Times*, November 8, 1951, IV-1.
53. Frank Finch, "Rams Thump Cards, 45–21, to Tie for Lead," *Los Angeles Times*, November 12, 1951, IV-1.
54. "NFL Game Results," *Los Angeles Times*, November 12, 1951, IV-1.
55. Frank Finch, "Yanks Start Drills Today at Brookside," *Los Angeles Times*, November 14, 1951, IV-1.
56. Frank Finch, "Flashy Yank Quintet Worries Ram Coach," *Los Angeles Times*, November 17, 1951, III-2.
57. Frank Finch, "Rams Conquer Yanks, 48–21," *Los Angeles Times*, November 19, 1951, IV-1.
58. Frank Finch, "Towler Takes Pro League Running Lead," *Los Angeles Times*, November 20, 1951, IV-3.
59. "NFL Game Results," *Los Angeles Times*, November 19, 1951, IV-1.
60. Frank Finch, "Redskins Blast Rams by 31–21," *Los Angeles Times*, November 26, 1951, IV-1.
61. Finch, "Redskins Blast," IV-1.
62. Finch, "Redskins Blast," IV-1.
63. Finch, "Redskins Blast," IV-1.
64. Frank Finch, "Rams Take Loop Lead, Batter Bears, 42–17," *Los Angeles Times*, December 3, 1951, IV-1.
65. Charles Chamberlain, "Rams Overpower Bears, 42–17, to Take Lead in N. L.'s National Division," *Cleveland Plain Dealer*, December 3, 1951, 29.
66. Edward Prell, "Lions Lose Lead; Rams Jar Bears, 42–17," *Chicago Daily Tribune*, December 3, 1951, 6–1.
67. Prell, "Lions Lose Lead," 6–1.
68. Prell, "Lions Lose Lead," 6–1.
69. Finch, Rams Take Loop Lead," IV-1.
70. Frank Finch, "Lions Defeat Rams, 24–22," *Los Angeles Times*, December 10, 1951, IV-1, 4.
71. Jan Reid, "The Immortals," *Alcalde.texasexes.org*, December 30, 2013, https://alcalde.texasexes.org/2013/12/the-immortals/.
72. Cal Whorton, "Stydahar Blames Poor Tackling for Ram Loss," *Los Angeles Times*, December 10, 1951, IV-1, 4.
73. Whorton, "Stydahar Blames," IV-1.
74. Whorton, Stydahar Blames," IV-4.
75. Whorton, Stydahar Blames," IV-4.
76. Whorton, Stydahar Blames," IV-4.
77. Whorton, Stydahar Blames," IV-4.
78. Cal Whorton, "Rams Celebrate Two Victories After Game," *Los Angeles Times*, December 17, 1951, IV-1, 4.
79. Frank Finch, "Rams Win Crown with 42–14 Victory," *Los Angeles Times*, December 17, 1951, IV-1, 4.
80. Finch, "Rams Win," IV-1.
81. Bob Myers, "Packers Scare Rams, 14–14, Then Lose 42–14 Game," *Green Bay Press-Gazette*, December 17, 1951, 17.
82. Myers, "Packers Scare," 17.
83. Myers, "Packers Scare," 17.
84. Finch, "Rams Win," IV-4.
85. "Rams Win Third National Conference Title," *The San Bernardino County Sun*, December 17, 1951, 12.
86. Whorton, "Rams Celebrate," IV-4.
87. Whorton, "Rams Celebrate," IV-4.
88. Whorton, "Rams Celebrate," IV-1.
89. Whorton, "Rams Celebrate," IV-4.
90. Whorton, "Rams Celebrate," IV-4.

Rams/Browns Rivalry

Ed Gruver

Cleveland's Tommy James kneeled at the Los Angeles Rams' 16-yard line on the frozen field inside the Browns' cavernous Municipal Stadium.

Christmas Eve 1950 was a cloud-covered, wind-whipped winter's day in the northeast. The daytime temperature for the NFL championship game featuring the gritty Browns, in their first year of NFL football after dominating the renegade All-America Football Conference for the four years of its existence, and the glossy Hollywood Rams dipped to 27 degrees.[1]

Howling winds off Lake Erie made the temps feel even colder, turning the gray air brittle and whipping players and patrons alike like a razor on a barber's strop.

Struggling to stay warm, some fans in the crowd of 29,751 built a bonfire in a wastebasket in the centerfield bleachers. Ushers ultimately extinguished the blaze, but not before city firefighters had arrived after an alarm had sounded.[2]

Color and dash ruled the day. The Rams were outfitted in California gold jerseys, trimmed in dark blue. Their iconic helmets featured a golden rams horn in profile against a bright blue background. Cleveland wore white uniforms trimmed in burnt orange and brown. The crowd was equally colorful, many wearing red winter gear along with the bright colors of the Christmas season.

The Browns trailed the Rams 28–27 with just 28 seconds remaining in the game. Cleveland quarterback Otto Graham's sneak into the line on the previous play had netted a hard yard but more importantly, placed the ball directly in front of the goal posts. James took center Hal Herring's snap and placed the ball cleanly on the icy turf.

In the pressure-packed moment, placekicker Lou Groza sought to stay calm by thinking only of his fundamentals, going over in his mind what he needed to do.[3]

Nicknamed "The Toe" for his proficiency in placekicking, Groza took three short steps toward the ball and, with a gusting gale at his back, swung his strong right leg. A sepia photo snapped from behind the goal posts captured the players' frozen faces forever frozen in time as the ball split the uprights.[4]

Browns broadcaster Bob Neal called the decisive play: "Less than 30 seconds remaining, Tommy James kneeling on the 16-yard line. The wind is blowing; it's cold! Here's the pass from center, James putting it down. Groza boots it! It's up in the air, heading toward the goal post…. It is good! The Browns lead 30–28!"[5]

Groza's game-winning kick, disputed by the Rams, closed the book on arguably the greatest game in pro football history to that point. In the Cleveland locker room, Browns head coach Paul Brown, seemingly stunned by the titanic struggle that had just taken place, kept repeating, "Never a game like this one."[6]

Brown was right, and yet this game, great as it was, would serve as just one chapter in one of the more compelling and largely unforgotten stories in NFL annals—a Browns-Rams rivalry that extended far beyond the football field.

Nearly a decade before Browns head coach Paul Brown introduced his juggernaut to the fledgling AAFC in 1946, the Cleveland Rams had been introduced to the NFL as the league's newest franchise in 1937. The Rams, refugees of the financially challenged second American Football League, joined the NFL and filled the vacancy created in the Western Division by the failure of the St. Louis Gunners/Cincinnati Reds in 1934. The Rams had known success the season before in the AFL, reaching the title game against the Boston Shamrocks. The game was never played; money was scarce in the depths of the Great Depression and the Shamrocks refused to take the field unless they were paid first.[7]

When the Rams took up residence in the NFL, only three players from their AFL title contenders remained on the roster. Predictably, the Rams struggled, finishing 1–10 in their inaugural season and 4–7 in 1938. Following another less than stellar season in 1940, Rams owner Homer Marshman, a Cleveland lawyer, sold the team to Dan Reeves and Fred Levy, Jr., for approximately $140,000.[8]

The Rams started the 1941 season strong, but World War II came to America that December and Clevelanders turned their attention from beating the Giants of New York to beating the giants overseas—Hitler, Mussolini and Tojo. In 1945, Clevelanders celebrated not only V-E (Victory in Europe) and V-J (Victory in Japan) Day, but also the signing of a new star—UCLA quarterback Bob Waterfield.

Waterfield was a star in every sense of the word. Hollywood handsome, Waterfield married his high school sweetheart, starlet Jane Russell. But Waterfield was more than just a California celebrity. His rocket right arm terrorized defenses, and he teamed with wide receiver Jim Benton to rewrite the NFL record books. In the traditional Thanksgiving Day game against the Lions in Detroit's Briggs Stadium, Waterfield found Benton 10 times for 303 yards in a stirring 28–21 win.[9]

Waterfield led the Rams to a 9–1 season, earned the league's Most Valuable Player honors and then outdueled Washington quarterback "Slingin'" Sammy Baugh 15–14 in a thrilling NFL championship game played in minus-8 degrees cold in Municipal Stadium. It marked the first title game ever played in Cleveland's lakefront stadium.

Feeling threatened by the arrival of a new pro football team in Cleveland, Reeves took Horace Greeley's advice and went west, moving his flashy NFL champions to, fittingly enough, Los Angeles. Replacing the Rams in the pro football void in Cleveland were the Browns, who promptly dominated *their* league, the AAFC.

Loaded with future Hall of Famers and All-Pros, the Browns picked up where the Rams left off, delivering a second straight league championship to Cleveland's football fans. Where the Rams had Waterfield, the Browns boasted Graham. The Rams were led by the NFL's Coach of the Year in Adam Walsh; the Browns were headed by Paul Brown. The latter was a legend who had previously worked his magic at nearby Massillon High School and Ohio State.

Calling the Rams' former residence—Municipal Stadium—home, the Browns battled the ghosts of the departed NFL champs to win the hearts and loyalties of Cleveland's passionate fan base. The Browns helped soothe Cleveland's hurt feelings following the abandonment by the Rams, winning four straight AAFC championships. Following the

1949 season, the Browns followed in the footsteps of the 1936 Rams and left their league to join the NFL.

On Christmas Eve 1950, the Rams-Browns rivalry came full circle. No longer competing for the loyalties of Cleveland fans, the Rams and Browns battled in Municipal Stadium for the championship of the NFL. Waterfield and his fellow golden boy, Graham, met in a much-anticipated matchup of signal callers, but they weren't the only high-gloss talents to take the frozen field that day. In truth, a galaxy of stars was on hand as Cleveland's past and present collided for supremacy in the NFL.

Graham, Groza, power back Marion Motley, wide receivers Mac Speedie and Dante Lavelli and defensive studs Len Ford and Bill Willis were among the Browns' greats.

The Rams answered with Glenn Davis, "Mr. Outside" from Army's glory years, Dick Hoerner, receivers Elroy "Crazylegs" Hirsch and Tom Fears and quarterbacks Waterfield and Norm Van Brocklin, the fiery "Dutchman." They combined to make the Rams one of the most prolific point-scoring machines of all time, a team that produced 41 points in one quarter in the Coliseum against Detroit.

The star-studded squads had enormous respect for one another. Graham called the Rams "pretty tough" and most of his teammates and his head coach considered Los Angeles the finest team they had ever faced. The Rams returned the compliments; head coach Joe Stydahar calling Cleveland a "helluva good club."[10]

The late game-winning field goal by Groza gave the Browns the victory in the first ever meeting between Cleveland's champions of the past and present. But the war was not over, far from it, in fact.

On October 7 of the following season, the Browns made it two straight for the new guard when they came from behind to gain a wild, 38–23 win in the Los Angeles Coliseum. The Rams finally exacted revenge on December 23, beating the Browns almost a year to the day following their 1950 classic, this time in another championship thriller that saw Los Angeles earn a 24–17 win in the Coliseum.

The following September in Cleveland, the Browns routed the Rams 37–7, and the two teams didn't meet again until the championship game in December 1955. Played on the day after Christmas in a cloud-shrouded Coliseum, Cleveland cruised past L.A. 38–14 in Graham's last game.

Life in the NFL had become a tale of two cities for the Rams, who turned a title trifecta in 1999 when they won the Super Bowl as representatives of the city of St. Louis, ironically the gateway to the golden west where they won a title in 1951.

One more twist in the Rams-Browns rivalry is that Marshman, the Rams' original owner, sought to amend his mistake of selling the team to Reeves in 1946 and becoming part of an ownership group that bought the Browns from Mickey McBride in 1953. Eight years later, Marshman and the other owners sold the Browns to young Art Modell.

In 1995 Modell moved the Browns out of Cleveland and to Baltimore. Ironically, Baltimore had been the former home to Colts owner Carroll Rosenbloom. Following Reeves' passing in 1971, Rosenbloom swapped teams with new Rams owner Robert Irsay in 1972.

It was Irsay who took the Colts to Indianapolis under the cover of darkness, leaving jilted Baltimore free to welcome with open arms Modell and his displaced Browns, who were renamed the Ravens.

In 1999 and 2000, the former Los Angeles and Cleveland franchises claimed consecutive Super Bowl victories. Like their high-profile Hollywood predecessors, the Rams boasted one of the great offenses in NFL history, the famed "Greatest Show on Turf."

In the tradition of the great Cleveland defenses featuring Ford and Willis, the Ravens' record-setting unit included future Hall of Famers Ray Lewis and Rod Woodson.

The ex–Los Angeles and Cleveland champions were back on top of the pro football world, just as they had been half a century before.

Notes

1. Steve Bisheff, *Great Teams' Great Years: Los Angeles Rams* (New York: Macmillan, 1973), 60.
2. Harry Jones, "Groza's Field Goal Is Signal for Celebration," *Cleveland Plain Dealer*, December 25, 1950, https://www.cleveland.com/datacentral/2009/12/this_day_in_browns_history_lou.html.
3. Jones, "Groza's."
4. Andrew Clayman, "The Cleveland Rams: Remembering the Original L.A. Move and a Rivalry Born," *Waitingfornextyear.com*, January 13, 2016, https://waitingfornextyear.com/2016/01/cleveland-rams-browns-nfl-history/.
5. "The 1950 NFL Championship: Cleveland Browns vs. Los Angeles Rams," *The Way It Was*, PBS, 1974.
6. Jones, "Groza's."
7. Clayman, "The Cleveland Rams."
8. James C. Sulecki, "The Cleveland Rams: The City's Pre-Browns NFL Champions," *Clevelandhistorical.org*, February 6, 2017, https://clevelandhistorical.org/items/show/781.
9. Clayman, "The Cleveland Rams."
10. Jones, "Groza's."

1951 NFL Championship Game

RUPERT PATRICK

December 23, 1951—NFL Championship Game: Cleveland Browns at Los Angeles Rams

Los Angeles Memorial Coliseum

Cleveland	0	10	0	7	17
Los Angeles	0	7	7	10	24

Los Angeles—Hoerner 1 run (Waterfield kick)
Cleveland—Field Goal Groza 52
Cleveland—D Jones 17 pass from Graham (Groza kick)
Los Angeles—Towler 1 run (Waterfield kick)
Los Angeles—Field Goal Waterfield 17
Cleveland—Carpenter 2 run (Groza kick)
Los Angeles—Fears 73 pass from Van Brocklin (Waterfield kick)
A—59,475

	CLE	LA
First Downs	22	20
Rushing A–Y	23–92	43–81
Passing C–A–I	19–41–3	13–30–2
Passing Yards	280	253
Sacked N–Y	5–47	0–0
Total Plays, Yards	64–372	73–334
Punts–Yards	4–148	5–217
Field Goals M–A	1–2	1–2
Fumbles–Lost	4–1	2–1
Penalties–Yards	6–41	5–25

Rushing
(Attempts, Yards)

Cleveland—D Jones 9–12; Graham 5–43; Motley 5–23; Carpenter 4–14

Los Angeles—Towler 16–36; V Smith 9–15; G Davis 6–(-6); Hoerner 5–5; Younger 4–20; Waterfield 2–8; Van Brocklin 1–3

Passing
(Attempts, Completions, Interceptions, Yards)
Cleveland—Graham 40-19-3-280; Carpenter 1-0-0-0
Los Angeles—Waterfield 24-9-2-125; Van Brocklin 6-4-0-128

Receptions
(Catches, Yards)
Cleveland—Speedie 7-81; Lavelli 4-65; D Jones 4-62; Carpenter 3-49; Motley 1-23
Los Angeles—Fears 4-146; Hirsch 4-66; G Davis 3-10; V Smith 1-18; Hoerner 1-13

Interceptions
Cleveland—T James; Lahr
Los Angeles—M Johnson; Paul; Williams

Fumbles Recovered
Cleveland—Herring
Los Angeles—Robustelli

Sacks
Cleveland—None
Los Angeles—Brink (2); Robustelli (3)

Missed Field Goals
Cleveland—Groza 23
Los Angeles—Waterfield 23 Blocked

Joe Stydahar's Rams teams of the early 1950s had the most explosive offense the NFL had ever seen to that point, leading the NFL in points scored from 1950 to 1952. In 1951, their average of 32.67 points per game is still one of the 25 best single season totals ever. The Rams' quarterback tandem of Bob Waterfield and Norm Van Brocklin finished 1-2 in NFL passing[1]; any other NFL team besides the Browns and maybe the Lions would kill to acquire either of them.

Elroy Hirsch had a season for the ages, leading the NFL in receptions (66), receiving yards (1495), yards per reception (22.7) and touchdown catches (17). Their Bull Elephant rushing trio of Deacon Dan Towler, Tank Younger and Dick Hoerner[2] each rushed for over six yards per carry. Despite missing the middle half of the season with knee problems, end Tom Fears still managed to snag 32 passes for 528 yards and three touchdowns.

The Browns lost to the 49ers on opening day and were riding an eleven-game winning streak, which included a 38-23 win over the Rams in week two in which Ken Carpenter scored three touchdowns and the Browns rushed for nearly 300 yards on the afternoon. Paul Brown's club was a team seemingly without a weakness, and since their debut in 1946, they'd won their respective league championship every season. The Browns would have an edge in experience, as they had two rookies on their roster (one was a defensive back named Don Shula) compared to 13 newbies for Los Angeles.[3] Eleven members of the Browns' squad had 66 combined years of experience while the entire Rams squad (all 33 players) had 81 years of pro experience.

Otto Graham won the United Press MVP award based on his 55.5 pass completion percentage and 17 touchdown passes, and the Browns threw fewer interceptions than any other team in the league. His backfield included halfbacks Dub Jones (father of Bert) and Ken Carpenter, and fullback Marion Motley, who was slowing down at the age of 31 due to his knees,[4] but was still nearly impossible to haul down once he built up steam. Ends

Dante Lavelli and Mac Speedie were a dangerous duo, combining for 77 catches for nearly 1,200 yards and nine touchdown receptions. The Browns' offensive line was anchored by two future Hall of Famers, center Frank Gatski and tackle Lou Groza, with Groza also taking care of the placekicking duties. Three other members of the Browns' offensive line, Lin Houston, Abe Gibron and Lou Rymkus, would also appear on various postseason All-Pro teams.

The Browns defense was impenetrable, leading the NFL in 1951 in fewest points allowed, fewest pass TDs allowed, and fewest rushing touchdowns allowed. The key defensive linemen were future Hall of Famers Bill Willis and Len Ford, and defensive tackle John Kissell would make the *New York Daily News* All-Pro second team in 1951. Linebacker Tony Adamle made a couple All-Pro teams in 1951, and middle linebacker Tommy Thompson picked a couple passes and recovered four fumbles. Cornerback Warren Lahr and safety Cliff Lewis each intercepted five passes.

The weather would be perfect, with temps in the high 60s and clear. The bad weather in the Midwest the previous weekend would hamper the Browns, as the team had to split up in order to fly to the West Coast, and their equipment was late in arriving to the West Coast, forcing the team to cancel their first day of practice in Los Angeles.[5] The Browns were favored to win by seven points over the Rams,[6] who were winless in three previous contests against Cleveland.

Stydahar gave the defending champs their due coming into the contest, commenting that, "The Browns are the best-coached, best-conditioned, and best-balanced team in football. It's going to be a real good game."[7] Coach Brown knew the Rams wanted blood, quipping, "They haven't forgotten the game we played against them in Los Angeles in October and will really be after us in this one. They'll want revenge."[8]

It was a rematch of the classic title game from the previous season and this one promised to be another masterpiece. In attendance were 59,745 when the game commenced at 1 p.m. PST. Dumont Network paid $95,000 for TV rights to the first coast-to-coast championship telecast—a five-year contract totaling $475,000 to telecast the title games from 1951 to 1955, however the game was blacked out in the Southern California television market.

Cleveland won the toss and elected to receive, with Carpenter returning Woodley Lewis' kickoff from the goal line to the Browns' 23. Graham fired left to an open Mac Speedie in the middle for 12 yards, then, went to Dante Lavelli in the middle again for 15 yards to midfield. Motley burrowed through the line for four yards, and then, Graham bootlegged right and ran for 10 yards to the Los Angeles 35, moving the chains again. Two plays later, Otto went back to Lavelli on the right side for 16 more to put the Browns in the red zone. The drive stalled after Cleveland moved the ball three yards on three plays, and Lou Groza attempted a 23-yard field goal, but it was wide left as about five minutes were elapsed.

Towler ran for a first down on the Rams' opening drive, but the Rams were forced to punt, with the Browns starting from their 34. Otto hooked up with Dante Lavelli for 17 yards, putting the ball just into Rams territory. Three incompletions followed (the pass on third down would have been a touchdown to Lavelli but it was just beyond his reach), and the punt from Horace Gillom was fair caught at the Los Angeles 12-yard line.

Deacon Dan picked up a first down for the Rams after runs of four and seven yards, and Tank Younger ran off left tackle for 14 yards to the 37-yard line. On second down, Waterfield connected with Hirsch (despite tight coverage from Cliff Lewis) for 19 yards to the Browns' 43. A flag against Los Angeles for holding cost them five yards, and the drive lost momentum. The punt from Waterfield landed in the end zone for a touchback.

An illegal motion flag against the Browns and an Andy Robustelli sack of Graham doomed the next Cleveland drive, with Gillom punting to the Rams' 45 on the final play of the first quarter with no score.

The second quarter began with a handoff to Younger, who fumbled, and Tom Keane fell on the ball at midfield. Towler was stopped for no gain on a run to the right, Younger suffered an injury and would not return.[9] Waterfield converted the first down on a pass to Vitamin T. Smith (who replaced Younger) to the Cleveland 33. Smith tried to sweep left on first down but could not turn the corner and was pulled down by Tommy James for a five-yard loss. A 13-yard screen to Dick Hoerner set up a third-and-two, and Vitamin T. burst through the middle for eight yards and another first down at the Browns' 17. Smith crashed through left tackle for three more yards, but Waterfield overthrew Fears in the end zone. An interference penalty was called on Tommy Thompson during a pass to Smith, giving the Horns an automatic first down at the 12-yard line. From there, Smith and the two remaining Bull Elephants moved the ball to the one-yard line, where Hoerner's second effort put him into the end zone to conclude the 13-play drive. Waterfield tacked on the extra point to put the Rams ahead 7–0 with 9:16 left in the first half.

Cleveland started from their 14 after the kickoff return by Carpenter, and on first down, Graham fired to Speedie for 17 yards and Otto went back to Speedie for nine more. Carpenter slid off left tackle for three yards to convert the first down at the 43. Carpenter took a screen 17 yards along the right side to the Rams' 40, and on first down, Graham went deep for Jones, but Marv Johnson broke up the pass play at the five-yard line. Sacks on second and third downs (by Andy Robustelli and Larry Brink, respectively) brought on the punting team, which set the Rams back to their 18-yard line.

On third-and-seven, Waterfield aired it out, but Warren Lahr stepped in front of Hirsch and intercepted at the Cleveland 45-yard line. Graham and Speedie connected on a 10-yard pass, but three incomplete passes (two of them dropped by Carpenter) followed and Groza kicked a then-postseason record field goal from 52 yards out to cut the Rams' lead to 7–3 with 3:52 remaining in the half. Groza's 52-yard record postseason boot was later tied by Curt Knight and Matt Bahr, and it remained in the record books until Eddie Murray of the Detroit Lions kicked a 54-yard field goal in the 1983 NFL playoffs.

The ensuing kickoff went for a touchback, but the Rams went three-and-out, leading to a Waterfield punt that put the Browns at their 46-yard line. It only took three plays for Cleveland to take the lead—a pass to Speedie in the middle for 14 yards, then, a screen right to Marion Motley for 23, and finally, Graham rolling right and throwing to a wide-open Jones, who caught it at the three and ran untouched into the end zone. The Toe made it 10–7, advantage Cleveland, with 2:08 to play before intermission.

Starting from his 20, Waterfield failed on passes on first and second downs, then, he got hot. Jane Russell's husband hit on passes to Glenn Davis in the right flat for 11 yards and Crazylegs on the left sideline for 14 more. Hirsch caught a pass in the middle for 17 more yards, and then Fears collected a pass for 18 yards to the Browns' 21. Waterfield fired it toward the end zone, but a leaping James intercepted the ball that was intended for Fears at the Cleveland one-yard line to end the first half, with the Browns leading 10–7.

Jerry Williams took the second half kickoff from Groza at his five-yard line and returned it 21 yards. Runs by Davis and Towler produced a first down, but the Rams soon found themselves in a third-and-eight, when Waterfield hooked up with Hirsch for 15 yards over the middle to move the ball into Cleveland territory. Towler took a handoff on the following play. Thompson hammered the Deacon, and the ball came loose, with Herring recovering for Cleveland at the Browns' 41.

Two plays later, Otto dropped back, but Brink came around the right side, his right arm hooking Graham around the neck, causing a fumble. Robustelli recovered the loose ball and carried it to the Browns' two-yard line where Motley took him down. It took the Deacon three cracks at the goal line before he got the ball across, and after Waterfield kicked the extra point, the Rams regained the lead at 14–10 with 8:44 to play in the third frame.

Carpenter took the kickoff a couple yards deep in the end zone and returned it to the Cleveland 27-yard line. A pass to Jones gained 26 yards to the Rams' 43 but facing a third-and-nine after Carpenter dropped another pass, Graham went to the air. He threw deep for Lavelli in the right flat, but Herb Rich got a hand on the pass, and Williams stole it at the Los Angeles 18, returning it 15 yards.

The Rams were unable to capitalize on the turnover due to incompletions on second and third downs, and a clipping penalty against Emerson Cole on the punt return set the Browns back to their nine-yard line.

Graham fired to Jones on the right sideline for 14 yards, followed by a sure touchdown pass to Carpenter that was overthrown and a pass that Rich nearly intercepted. Otto put it up again, with Speedie making a diving catch for 10 yards to the Browns' 40. Motley shot through right tackle for 12 yards to put the ball across midfield, but in what might have been the play that turned the game around, a touchdown pass to a wide-open Speedie was nullified by a holding penalty against Rex Bumgardner, costing the Browns 27 yards, back to their 25-yard line. Things went from bad to worse when Robustelli sacked Graham on first down, setting up a second-and-49 predicament. The drive petered out, and Tommy Kalmanir made a fair catch of Gillom's punt at the Cleveland 49-yard line.

Van Brocklin entered the game at quarterback for the Rams and came out firing. Crazylegs was wide-open but failed to hold onto a pass in the right flat at the 20-yard line, and the Dutchman went deep again. This time, he connected with Fears in the left flat at the Cleveland 25, with Fears falling at the eight-yard line, getting up again, and finally being stopped a yard short of the end zone. Two runs by Towler set the Rams back to the four, and Hoerner was stopped at the line on a third down run. On the first play of the final period, Waterfield set up for an 11-yard field goal attempt, but Davis (the holder) took the snap and ran left, but Darrell Palmer took him down at the 18-yard line for a loss of 14 yards.

With just under 15 minutes to play in the 1951 NFL season, the Browns trailed, 14 to 10.

On third-and-five, Graham put it up for Carpenter at the Browns' 36, but Johnson got to it first, taking the pick down the left sideline before he was stopped by Graham at the one-yard line. Hoerner took a handoff on first and second down but both times was stopped for no gain. A penalty against the Rams for illegal motion moved the ball back to the six, and again, the Browns' defense bent but did not break when Van Brocklin's pass for Davis fell incomplete. This time, when presented with a chip-shot field goal try, Coach Stydahar wisely went for the three points and Waterfield's kick was good from 17 yards out. With 11:50 left in regulation, the Rams increased their lead to 17–10.

Carpenter returned the deep kickoff to the Cleveland 30-yard line, and on the first play from scrimmage, Graham went to Speedie on the left side for 18 yards. After two passes intended for Jones failed to find their marks, Otto dropped back into the pocket, but the rush was on him, and he had to run for his life. Graham broke left and ran down the left sideline for 34 yards before he was knocked out of bounds at the Rams' 18-yard line. After runs by Carpenter and Graham set up a third-and-three, Jones took a handoff and cut through the left side of the line for six yards, giving Cleveland a first-and-goal at the Rams' five-yard line. On third down, Carpenter carried the ball the final two yards for the score. Groza kicked the extra point, and with 7:50 left on the clock, the game was tied at 17–17.

Starting from their 20 after a touchback on Groza's kickoff, Davis swept right for two yards, and an offside penalty against the Browns set up a second-and-three from the Los Angeles 27. From there, Van Brocklin dropped back and went deep to Fears, who got free from James[10] and Lewis and pulled it in near midfield and took it down the left sideline untouched. The 73-yard touchdown pass put the Rams up 24–17 after the extra point from Waterfield.

Cleveland began their next drive from their 28, and on first down, Graham's pass was picked off by Don Paul, who returned the pigskin 26 yards to the Cleveland 14-yard line. Another score by Los Angeles would have put the game away, but the Browns' defense held, forcing the Rams to attempt a 23-yard field goal try by Waterfield. The kick was blocked by Bill Willis, and the ball rolled out of bounds at the Cleveland 38-yard line, giving the Browns another chance to tie the game.

With about six minutes to play, Graham went deep but his pass was nearly intercepted. Carpenter reeled in a pass at midfield, but the Rams' defense did their job, setting up a third-and-12 for the Browns. Carpenter came through with a clutch catch in the middle but came up a yard short of the first down marker. On fourth down from the Los Angeles 42, Jones got the call, taking the handoff from Graham and sweeping left, but Norb Hecker was on him and stopped him for a two-yard loss. The Rams took over on downs at their 44-yard line with about three minutes to go.

Vitamin T. swept left for eight yards, and Van Brocklin picked up three more on a keeper, giving the Rams a fresh set of downs. Two runs by Davis lost a total of three yards, and Van Brocklin dumped it off to Fears for seven yards to the 41. On fourth down, Waterfield ran the clock down as far as he could, drawing a delay of game penalty, and then, his punt went into the end zone for a touchback. The Browns took over at their 20-yard line with 10 seconds remaining.

Graham passed the ball to Speedie at the 30, who lateraled to Carpenter, gaining eight more yards before he went out on the left sideline with six ticks left on the clock. On the final play of the game, Otto lateraled the ball to Carpenter on the right side, and Carpenter fired it deep for Lavelli at the Rams' 25. The pass went into double coverage and was knocked to the grass. The gun sounded, and for the first time in their six-year history, the Cleveland Browns were not the champions of their respective league at the end of the season. The Rams had a 24–17 victory.

In the locker room after the game, Rams quarterback and captain Bob Waterfield was presented with the game ball. When asked about his game-winning catch, Tom Fears said, "That was the best thrown pass I ever caught in my life.... [Van Brocklin] laid it right in there when I was going full stride."[11] Norm Van Brocklin admitted, "I wanted to win so badly I couldn't sleep last night."[12]

After the game, both Paul Brown and Otto Graham made their way to the Rams' locker room to congratulate the new NFL Champions. Brown told Rams coach Jumbo

Joe Stydahar, "You beat us all the way. I know how you feel."[13] Brown told the reporters in the Browns' dressing room, "It had to happen sometime.... My boys played well, just not quite well enough."[14] Otto Graham said, "We just made more mistakes than they did."[15]

Final 1951 NFL Standings*

American Conference	W	L	T	Pct	PF	PA	Home	Away
x–Cleveland Browns	11	1	0	.917	331	152	6–0–0	5–1–0
New York Giants	9	2	1	.818	254	161	5–1–0	4–1–1
Washington Redskins	5	7	0	.417	183	296	2–4–0	3–3–0
Pittsburgh Steelers	4	7	1	.364	183	235	1–4–1	3–3–0
Philadelphia Eagles	4	8	0	.333	234	264	1–5–0	3–3–0
Chicago Cardinals	3	9	0	.250	210	287	1–5–0	2–4–0

National Conference	W	L	T	Pct	PF	PA	Home	Away
x–Los Angeles Rams	8	4	0	.667	392	261	5–2–0	3–2–0
Detroit Lions	7	4	1	.636	336	259	3–3–1	4–1–0
San Francisco 49ers	7	4	1	.636	255	205	5–1–0	2–3–1
Chicago Bears	7	5	0	.583	286	282	3–3–0	4–2–0
Green Bay Packers	3	9	0	.250	254	375	2–4–0	1–5–0
New York Yanks	1	9	2	.100	241	382	0–3–1	1–6–1

*Standings from *The Football Database*.

Notes

1. "Waterfield Snares NFL Aerial Crown," *Los Angeles Times*, December 20, 1951, IV-1.
2. Frank Finch, "Backfield Key to Ram Hopes," *Los Angeles Times*, December 21, 1951, IV-1.
3. Frank Finch, "Browns Here for Sunday's Title Tussle," *Los Angeles Times*, December 18, 1951, IV-1, 2.
4. Harold Sauerbrei, "Motley Bids for Title Stardom Again in What May Be Final Game," *Cleveland Plain Dealer*, December 22, 1951, 22.
5. Frank Finch, "Polls Prove Browns Have Personnel Edge on Rams," *Los Angeles Times*, December 20, 1951, IV-1.
6. Frank Finch, "Rams, Browns Meet for Title," *Los Angeles Times*, December 23, 1951, II-6, 8.
7. Jack Guyer, "Even Santa Aided in Rams' Victory," *Los Angeles Times*, December 18, 1951, IV-1.
8. Harold Sauerbrei, "Groza Ready to Play for Browns in Title Game," *Cleveland Plain Dealer*, December 18, 1951, 23, 26.
9. Frank Finch, "Rams Whip Browns 24–17; Win Pro Title," *Los Angeles Times*, December 24, 1951, IV-1, 2.
10. Harold Sauerbrei, "Browns Lose Title to Rams, 24–17," *Cleveland Plain Dealer*, December 24, 1951, 1,15.
11. Paul Zimmerman, "Fears Calls Van Brocklin's Toss 'Best Thrown Pass I Ever Caught,'" *Los Angeles Times*, December 24, 1951, IV-1, 2.
12. "Rams 'Not Sure' Until Final Gun," *Cleveland Plain Dealer*, December 24, 1951, 15.
13. "'Rams Won All the Way,' Says Brown," *Cleveland Plain Dealer*, December 24, 1951, 16.
14. "Rams Won," 16.
15. "Rams Won,"16.

1951 Rams Statistics*

Rupert Patrick

Passing

	Att	Cmp	Pct	Yds	YPA	TD	TD%	Int	Int%	Lg	Rat
Norm Van Brocklin	194	100	51.5	1,725	8.9	13	6.7	11	5.7	81	80.8
Bob Waterfield	176	88	50.0	1,566	8.9	13	7.4	10	5.7	91	81.8
Glenn Davis	2	1	50.0	5	2.5	0	0.0	0	0.0	5	56.2
Tom Keane	1	0	0.0	0	0.0	0	0.0	1	100.0	0	0.0

Rushing

	Att	Yds	Avg	Lg	TD
Dan Towler	126	854	6.78	79	6
Dick Hoerner	94	569	6.05	43	6
Tank Younger	36	223	6.19	24	1
Glenn Davis	64	200	3.12	23	1
Vitamin Smith	52	143	2.75	31	1
Jerry Williams	21	106	5.05	32	2
Tommy Kalmanir	16	61	3.81	23	0
Bob Waterfield	9	49	5.44	25	3
Elroy Hirsch	1	3	3.00	3	0
Norm Van Brocklin	7	2	0.29	4	2

Receiving

	Rec	Yds	Avg	Lg	TD
Elroy Hirsch	66	1,495	22.65	91	17
Tom Fears	32	528	16.50	54	3
Vitamin Smith	16	278	17.38	67	1
Dan Towler	16	257	16.06	46	0

*Stats Tables from *The Football Database*.

	Rec	Yds	Avg	Lg	TD
Tom Keane	12	133	11.08	21	0
Bob Boyd	9	128	14.22	28	1
Glenn Davis	8	90	11.25	21	1
Dick Hoerner	8	102	12.75	21	1
Tommy Kalmanir	6	91	15.17	38	1
Jerry Williams	5	49	9.80	13	0
Tank Younger	5	72	14.40	52	0
Norb Hecker	4	35	8.75	20	1
Marvin Johnson	2	38	19.00	28	0

Kickoff Returns

	Num	Yds	Avg	TD
Vitamin Smith	15	274	18.27	0
Glenn Davis	9	179	19.89	0
Jerry Williams	6	133	22.17	0
Tommy Kalmanir	6	120	20.00	0
Woodley Lewis	4	67	16.75	0
Dick Hoerner	1	22	22.00	0
Don Simensen	1	13	13.00	0
Dan Towler	1	10	10.00	0
Bobby Collier	1	8	8.00	0

Punt Returns

	Num	Yds	Avg	TD
Vitamin Smith	12	139	11.58	0
Tommy Kalmanir	5	86	17.20	1
Glenn Davis	15	85	5.67	0
Jerry Williams	4	22	5.50	0
Woodley Lewis	1	12	12.00	0

Punting

	Punts	Yds	Avg	B
Norm Van Brocklin	48	1,992	41.5	1
Bob Waterfield	4	166	41.5	0

Kicking

	PAT	FG	Pts
Bob Waterfield	41/43	13/23	80

	PAT	FG	Pts
Tom Fears	6/7	0/0	6
Norb Hecker	0/0	0/1	0
Elroy Hirsch	0/1	0/0	0

Defense

Interceptions

	Int	Yds	Avg	TD
Bob Boyd	2	3	1.50	0
Norb Hecker	3	74	24.67	0
Tom Keane	2	2	1.00	0
Woodley Lewis	3	34	11.33	0
Don Paul	1	16	16.00	0
Herb Rich	3	11	3.67	0
Charlie Toogood	1	0	0.00	0
Jerry Williams	3	53	17.67	1
Tank Younger	1	0	0.00	0

Scoring

	Tot	R	P	KR	PR	IR	FR	BK	BP	FGR	PAT	FG	Conv	Saf	Pts
Elroy Hirsch	17	0	17	0	0	0	0	0	0	0	0/1	0/0	0	0	102
Bob Waterfield	3	3	0	0	0	0	0	0	0	0	41/43	13/23	0	0	98
Dick Hoerner	7	6	1	0	0	0	0	0	0	0	0/0	0/0	0	0	42
Dan Towler	6	6	0	0	0	0	0	0	0	0	0/0	0/0	0	0	36
Tom Fears	3	0	3	0	0	0	0	0	0	0	6/7	0/0	0	0	24
Jerry Williams	4	2	0	0	0	1	0	0	0	1	0/0	0/0	0	0	24
Glenn Davis	2	1	1	0	0	0	0	0	0	0	0/0	0/0	0	0	12
Tommy Kalmanir	2	0	1	0	1	0	0	0	0	0	0/0	0/0	0	0	12
Vitamin Smith	2	1	1	0	0	0	0	0	0	0	0/0	0/0	0	0	12
Norm Van Brocklin	2	2	0	0	0	0	0	0	0	0	0/0	0/0	0	0	12
Bob Boyd	1	0	1	0	0	0	0	0	0	0	0/0	0/0	0	0	6
Norb Hecker	1	0	1	0	0	0	0	0	0	0	0/0	0/1	0	0	6
Tank Younger	1	1	0	0	0	0	0	0	0	0	0/0	0/0	0	0	6

1951 Rams Superlatives

Rupert Patrick

Team

The Rams' offense led the NFL in numerous offensive categories—Points Scored (392), Yards per Play (6.7), First Downs (272), Yards Passing (3199), Passing Yards per Attempt (8.8), Passing Yards per Completion (17.4), Lowest Interception Percentage (5.9), Fewest Sacks (12), First Downs Passing (130), Yards per Rushing Attempt (5.2), Extra Points (47) and Field Goals (13).[1]

The Rams set a league record for Total Yards with 5506, and it stood until 1961 when the Houston Oilers of the rival AFL gained 6,288 yards, although it took the Oilers 14 games as opposed to 12 for the 1951 Rams.[2] The 1951 Rams' average of 458.83 offensive yards per game also set a record, which stood until 2011 when the New Orleans Saints broke it with an average of 467.12 offensive yards per game.[3]

Defensively, the Rams' defensive Completion Percentage of 42.6 was second best in the NFL, behind the Eagles, and their defensive Passing Yards per Attempt of 6.1 was just behind the Browns for tops in the league.[4] The Rams sacked the opposing quarterback 40 times, third best in the league behind the Browns and Bears.[5]

Individual

Bob Waterfield and Norm Van Brocklin tied for the league lead in Passing Yards per Attempt with 8.9,[6] and Waterfield led in Average Yards per Completion with 17.8, with Van Brocklin third at 17.3.[7] Waterfield and Van Brocklin were 1–2 in the NFL in Passer Rating (when applied retroactively) with ratings of 81.8 and 80.8, respectively.[8] The Dutchman and Captain Bob were fourth and fifth in Passing Yards, respectively, and also fourth and fifth in Pass Completion Percentage.[9] They also tied for fifth with 13 touchdown passes each.[10] Waterfield was second in the loop in points scored with 98, third in the league in Extra Points with 41, and his 13 field goals topped the circuit.[11]

Dan Towler was third in the NFL in Rushing Yards with 854 yards, and Dick Hoerner was seventh with 569.[12] Hoerner and Towler tied for fifth with six Rushing Touchdowns each.[13] Towler's 6.8 Yards per Rushing Attempt were second in the league, just behind Tobin Rote of Green Bay, and Hoerner was fourth with 6.1 yards per carry.[14] Deacon Dan was second in the league in Yards from Scrimmage with 1,111 yards.[15]

In 1951, Elroy Hirsch had the finest season of his Hall of Fame career, leading the

NFL in Receptions (66), Receiving Yards (1,495), Yards per Reception (22.7), and Touchdown Receptions with 17.[16] Don Hutson in 1936 is the only other player to lead the league in all four receiving categories in the same season.[17] Hirsch's 17 touchdown catches tied Hutson's 1942 single-season touchdown record,[18] and it stood until 1984 when Mark Clayton of Miami caught 18 touchdown tosses.[19] In addition, Elroy also set a record for most receiving yards in a season, breaking Hutson's 1942 record of 1,211,[20] and he held the professional record until 1961 when Charlie Hennigan of Houston from the rival AFL racked up 1,746 receiving yards.[21]

Crazylegs also led the league in Points Scored with 102,[22] Yards from Scrimmage with 1,498 yards,[23] and he also scored at least a touchdown in every game during the season except for the Week 11 game against the Lions.[24] Expanding Hirsch's 1951 stats to a 16-game season (the Rams played a 12-game schedule in 1951), his season works out to 99 catches for 1,993 yards, 22.7 yards per catch and 23 touchdown receptions. An argument could be made that Hirsch's 1951 season was the single greatest receiving season in pro football history.

As far as awards are concerned, eight Rams were awarded some sort of All-Pro recognition in 1951, lineman Larry Brink, end Elroy Hirsch, and running back/linebacker Tank Younger were all named first team All-Pro by the Associated Press.[25]

Brink, Hirsch, running back Dan Towler and lineman Stan West were named first team All-Pro, and end Tom Fears and quarterback Bob Waterfield were named to the second team by the New York Daily News.[26]

Hirsch and Towler were named first team All-Pro, while Brink, Waterfield and West were named to the second team by the UP.[27]

Brink, Fears, Hirsch, linebacker Don Paul, Towler, quarterback Norm Van Brocklin, Waterfield, West and Younger were all invited to play in the Pro Bowl.[28]

Notes

1. https://www.pro-football-reference.com/years/1951/.
2. https://www.pro-football-reference.com/years/1961_AFL/.
3. https://www.pro-football-reference.com/years/2011/.
4. https://www.pro-football-reference.com/years/1951/opp.htm.
5. https://www.pro-football-reference.com/years/1951/opp.htm.
6. Joseph T. Labrum, *National Football League 1952 Record and Rules Manual* (Philadelphia: National Football League, 1952), 40–41.
7. https://www.pro-football-reference.com/years/1951/leaders.htm.
8. https://www.pro-football-reference.com/years/1951/leaders.htm.
9. Labrum, *NFL 1952 Record*, 40–41.
10. Labrum, *NFL 1952 Record*, 40–41.
11. Labrum, *NFL 1952 Record*, 47–49.
12. Labrum, *NFL 1952 Record*, 37–38.
13. Labrum, *NFL 1952 Record*, 37–38.
14. https://www.pro-football-reference.com/years/1951/leaders.htm.
15. https://www.pro-football-reference.com/years/1951/leaders.htm.
16. Labrum, *NFL 1952 Record*, 42–43.
17. https://www.pro-football-reference.com/years/1936/leaders.htm.
18. Labrum, *NFL 1952 Record*, 11.
19. *2006 NFL Record and Fact Book* (New York: National Football League, 2018), 635.
20. Labrum, *NFL 1952 Record*, 11.
21. https://www.pro-football-reference.com/leaders/rec_yds_year_by_year.htm
22. Labrum, *NFL 1952 Record*, 47–49.
23. https://www.pro-football-reference.com/years/1951/leaders.htm.

Part 2: The 1951 Season

24. https://www.pro-football-reference.com/players/H/HirsEl00/gamelog/1951/.
25. "Bears' Connor, Barween Gain All-Pro Team," *Chicago Tribune*, January 9, 1952, C-4.
26. Hy Turkin, "9 Brownie Gridders on News All-Pro," *New York Daily News*, December 16, 1951, 22.
27. "Two Rams, Nine Browns Honored on United Press' All-Pro Teams," *Los Angeles Times*, December 20, 1951, IV-1.
28. Frank Finch, "Rams Dominate National Squad for Pro Bowl Tilt," *Los Angeles Times*, December 23, 1951, II-6, 8.

PART 3
The Team

Bob Boyd

Bill Lambert

Robert "Bob" Boyd was born on March 7, 1928, in Riverside, California. Boyd was considered the fastest receiver in the NFL during his seven-year playing career with the Rams, earning the nickname "Seabiscuit" after the famous thoroughbred racehorse. He was the oldest of three brothers. Boyd followed in his father Willis' footsteps, who was an outstanding athlete at Poly High School.[1]

Bob graduated from Poly in 1945 and lettered in football, basketball and track. Poly was the home of a number of world class athletes including Bobby Bonds and Reggie and Cheryl Miller.[2] Boyd was the first of five graduates of Poly to play in the NFL. He was the first and his career was the most prolific.[3]

From Poly High Boyd matriculated to Riverside Junior College (referred to also as Riverside City College), where he again excelled on the football field.[4]

Boyd was at Riverside JC for two years and then transferred to Loyola University of Los Angeles (now Loyola Marymount), where he had solid careers in football, track, and boxing for the Lions. The football teams were mediocre during Bob's two seasons (1947 and 1948) at Loyola fashioning a combined record of 6–12–1.

Boyd garnered a plaque in the LMU Hall of Fame in 1986 as one of the most versatile athletes in school history. He had two all-time school records in the 100-yard dash (9.6) and 220-yard dash (21.5). In 1950, he won the NCAA national championship in the 100 with a splendid time of 9.8 seconds.[5]

Boyd was not drafted by any NFL teams. In 1950, he signed with the Rams as a free agent. Boyd was one of the earliest African American players in the newly

One of the fastest men in the NFL, Rams receiver and defensive back Bob Boyd was nicknamed "Seabiscuit" after the famous racehorse.

reintegrated NFL. When he entered the NFL there were only a few teams that had integrated rosters. In a 1945 article, from his time at Riverside Junior College, Boyd was characterized as "Bob Boyd, Negro end."[6]

Bob Boyd played in 12 games during his 1950 rookie season with the Rams. He had a decent season on a record-setting Rams team that loss to the Browns in the championship game, catching nine passes for 220 yards and four touchdowns for the season, which tied for third on the team for receiving touchdowns (with Glenn Davis, and Vitamin Smith). He ran the ball once but lost two yards on the attempt. Boyd played defense as well that season and recorded one fumble recovery.[7]

The Rams' 1951 championship season was not as productive for Bob Boyd. Boyd again played in 12 games and started seven. He did not have any rushing attempts but caught nine balls. He gained 128 yards on those catches but scored only one touchdown. He continued to play both ways and had two interceptions during the season for three yards.[8]

Boyd was not a member of the 1952 Rams as he was in the Navy fulfilling military obligations. He was not idle during the season as he competed for the San Diego Naval Training Center Bluejackets, and also participated in the all-services track and field meet. The Bluejackets were an outstanding service football team winning the West Coast Service championship by defeating the San Diego MCRD in the Red Feather Bowl and finishing with a stellar 11–2 record. Bob was named to the All Service team and to the Navy All-Star team for his efforts.[9]

In an article from September 10, 1953, Bob was mentioned as he rejoined the L.A. Rams. "The Los Angeles Ram football squad was strengthened today with the return from the Navy of end Bob Boyd, former national collegiate 100-yard dash champion."[10]

The 1953 Rams were led by Hampton Pool, who took the reigns during the 1952 season. They finished a solid 8–3–1 for the season but ended up 3rd in the NFL Western Conference behind the Detroit Lions and San Francisco 49ers.[11]

Bob played in 12 games that season, starting seven. He caught 24 passes for 548 yards and four touchdowns for a league leading 22.8 yard per catch average. He notched one interception for a 35-yard return and recovered one fumble for eight yards. The Rams also utilized his speed as a returner. Bob returned five punts for 26 yards and three kickoffs for 42.[12]

Boyd experienced his best statistical season in 1954, as the Rams finished 4th in the NFL Western Conference with a 6–5–1 record. He played in all 12 games, while starting 11 of them. He led the team with 53 catches for a league leading 1212 yards. Boyd's six touchdowns also lead the Rams' receiving crew. Bob was no longer returning kicks or punts but was still playing defense. Boyd was named first team All-Pro by the AP and *New York Daily News* and second team All-Pro by the UP. He also made the Pro Bowl for the only time in his career.[13]

The Los Angeles Rams bounced back in 1955 under new head coach, Sid Gillman. They finished first in the NFL Western Conference and ended up once again playing the Cleveland Browns for the NFL championship, losing 38–14.[14]

Bob Boyd suffered a knee injury during the 1955 season and played in only seven games, starting six. He dropped to 22 receptions for 383 yards but did manage to score three touchdowns; two on Van Brocklin bombs, one for 74 yards and another for 67, He did not play defense or return kicks during the season and only played minimally in the championship game.[15]

The Toronto Argonauts made Bob an offer after the 1955 season that he found tempting. Boyd indicated that he received a "fabulous offer" from the Argonauts and was considering another one, also from Canada, he found less attractive. The Toronto offer was for two years. "I have reached no decision, but both Canadian offers are worth considering," said Boyd. "The Rams have been most generous to me, but the Toronto offer is one I certainly can't ignore."[16]

Boyd decided to remain with the Rams. In 1956, the Rams dropped to 4–8 and finished last in the NFL Western Conference. Boyd had seven receiving touchdowns, many again coming on long bombs from Van Brocklin. He caught 30 passes for 586 yards and ran the ball once but lost seven yards on that attempt. Bob played in 12 games during 1956, starting four. He was back playing defense and recovered two fumbles during the season.[17]

Boyd's last season in the league was 1957. The Rams, again under Gillman, finished a mediocre 6–6. Bob played in all 12 games, while starting nine. He caught 29 passes for 534 yards and added three touchdowns He played defense again and finished the season with one fumble recovery.[18]

Bob had four seasons in the NFL top 10 in yards per reception. He also had two seasons in the top 10 in receiving yards per game and led the NFL in 1954 with 101. He scored 28 touchdowns during his seven-year career and played in 79 regular season games. He caught 176 balls in the NFL and gained 3,611 yards with an average per catch of 20.5 yards.

A 2019 *Pro Football Journal* blog by John Turney listed the top 20 fastest receivers in NFL history. No surprise with Bob Hayes at the top. Boyd was listed at #5, which is impressive considering he played in the 1950s. The only other peers of Bob on the list were Harlan Hill and Del Shofner, both listed below him. Several Olympic athletes were also a part of the list, including Willie Gault (6), Ron Brown (2), and Lam Jones (8).[19]

Boyd ran a 9.5 100 in 1950, played with the Rams for two years, and ran another 9.5 after entering the Navy. At 27 years old in 1955, Bob felt that if he had trained specifically for the sprints, he could have run another 9.5. He opted instead to avoid the mistake of coming into camp too fine.[20]

A 1952 match race against Elroy Hirsch was a prime example of Boyd's speed. Both players ran on grass from goal line to goal line. Boyd ran in full uniform while carrying a football and stumbled at the start. He was clocked in 10.4 and easily beat Hirsch, who ran in shorts without a football.[21]

During Boyd's rookie season the deep threat scored touchdowns on the first four passes he caught for the Rams. Van Brocklin said that "it's almost impossible to overthrow Boyd when he runs all-out. However, he's hard to hit when he runs with a broken gait. Most ends have two speeds—slow and fast. After Boyd is in high gear he sometimes shifts into overdrive. You've got to sense when he's going to do it."[22]

Safety Will Sherman commented on Bob's speed as well: "It amazes me that Boyd, being so fast, can maintain his balance to carry out his fakes. He's aggressive and he will run right by you, but if you play him nice and loose, he'll kill you catching those hooks."[23]

Bob Boyd parlayed his success in the NFL and degree in economics from Loyola into his business life. He served as executive vice president of a national motel chain, vice president of Continental Bank in Philadelphia, and president of the Freedom National Bank, which was the first black owned and controlled financial institution in New York State history. He finally retired as head of Financial Services Organization, a firm that he formed.[24]

Boyd passed away in 2009 in California City. He was survived by three sons, a daughter and three grandchildren.

Notes

1. "Bob Boyd," *Riverside Sports Hall of Fame*, www.riversidesporthalloffame.com/bob-boyd/.
2. Nita Hiltner, "Poly Not the Oldest Riverside High School," *The Press-Enterprise*, January 22, 2011, https://www.pe.com/2011/01/22/poly-not-the-oldest-riverside-high-school/.
3. "Riverside Polytechnic Alumni Pro Stats," *Pro-Football-Reference.com*, www.pro-football-reference.com/schools/high_schools.cgi?id=93b9a72c.
4. "Riverside Junior College Defeats S.B. Indians 19–12," *San Bernardino County Sun*, November 3, 1945, 3.
5. "Bob Boyd," *Loyola Marymount Hall of Fame*, accessed July 25, 2020, lmulions.com/hof.aspx.
6. "Riverside Junior College Defeats S.B. Indians 19–12," 3.
7. "1950 Los Angeles Rams Statistics & Players," *Pro-Football-Reference.com*, www.pro-football-reference.com/teams/ram/1950.htm.
8. "1951 Los Angeles Rams Statistics & Players," *Pro-Football-Reference.com*, www.pro-football-reference.com/teams/ram/1951.htm.
9. "Lagorio Wins Most Valuable Service Honors," *Fresno Bee*, December 16, 1952, 29.
10. "Bob Boyd Rejoins Los Angeles Rams," *La Crosse Tribune*, September 10, 1953, 14.
11. "1953 Los Angeles Rams Statistics & Players," *Pro-Football-Reference.com*, www.pro-football-reference.com/teams/ram/1953.htm.
12. "1953 Los Angeles Rams Statistics & Players."
13. "1954 Los Angeles Rams Statistics & Players," *Pro-Football-Reference.com*, www.pro-football-reference.com/teams/ram/1954.htm.
14. "1955 Los Angeles Rams Statistics & Players," *Pro-Football-Reference.com*, www.pro-football-reference.com/teams/ram/1955.htm.
15. "1955 Los Angeles Rams Statistics & Players."
16. "Argonauts After Bob Boyd," *The Ottawa Citizen*, January 7, 1955, 24.
17. "1956 Los Angeles Rams Statistics & Players," *Pro-Football-Reference.com*, www.pro-football-reference.com/teams/ram/1956.htm.
18. "1957 Los Angeles Rams Statistics & Players," *Pro-Football-Reference.com*, www.pro-football-reference.com/teams/ram/1957.htm.
19. John Turney, "The Top Wide Receivers in NFL History," *Pro Football Journal*, June 3, 2019, nflfootballjournal.blogspot.com/2019/06/the-top-wide-receivers-in-nfl-history.html.
20. Frank Finch, "Ram's Bob Boyd Still Speed King on Grid," *Los Angeles Times*, August 11, 1955, IV-1, 4.
21. Finch, "Ram's Bob Boyd Still Speed King on Grid," IV-1, 4.
22. Finch, "Ram's Bob Boyd Still Speed King on Grid," IV-1, 4.
23. Finch, "Ram's Bob Boyd Still Speed King on Grid," IV-1, 4.
24. "Bob Boyd," Riverside Sports Hall of Fame.

Larry Brink

Patrick Gallivan

"When we got [Larry] Brink, it was like finding a fat wallet on the sidewalk," said then *Los Angeles Rams* head coach Clark Shaughnessy. "He [Brink] developed faster than any young end I've seen in a long time."[1]

It might have come as a surprise to some that the lanky end who grew up in Minnesota became a strong player for the Los Angeles Rams. It should not have come to a surprise to those in the Rams' organization. Los Angeles had a strong scouting group in the late forties and early fifties that could find small college prospects who developed into strong professional players.

"In 1951 the Los Angeles Rams had the most talent of any pro team and they won the NFL title," wrote Tex Maule in *Sports Illustrated*. "One reason for their success was their scouting system, which was ten years ahead of the competition."[2] Larry Brink was just one more in a long line of the Rams' successful scouting system.

It should not have been a surprise to anyone watching the Huskies play at Northern Illinois State Teachers College (now Northern Illinois University). "When he was here, there was no one like Brink," recalled Northern Illinois Hall of Fame athletics trainer Al Kranz. "Larry was tall, raw-boned, tough, and could move. At this level and that time, he was exceptional."[3] The Rams made Brink the first Huskie selected in the NFL draft when they selected Brink as the 150th player chosen overall in the 17th round of the 1948 draft.

Brink was born in Pease, Minnesota, on September 12, 1923, as one of twelve children raised on a family-owned 200-acre farm. He grew to six-feet-five inches by the end of this time at Foley High School. The University of Illinois offered a scholarship. World War II started, and Brink ended up in Italy with the Army Air Corps instead of on campus in Champaign, Illinois. After the war, he attended Northern Illinois State Teachers College.

Rams All-Pro lineman Larry Brink scored a touchdown in the Rams' 1950 NFL championship game loss to the Browns on a fumble return.

"I grew up in small communities named Pease and Oak Park," said Brink. "I attended Foley High School, competing in football and basketball."[4] Looking back, Brink recalled fond memories of his athletic career at Foley, both in football and basketball. "Back then, basketball was really more of my sport," he said. "In fact, I had a scholarship offer from Hamline, which at that time was an outstanding small college program. But the football coach at Foley at that time was a big Illinois booster. And he helped get a number of us to go down there."[5]

Brink never dreamed of a career as a professional athlete growing up. "I didn't have the slightest idea I was good enough [to play pro football]," Brink told a local reporter in 1998. "I didn't even play until my junior year in high school. Even in college [at Northern Illinois], I never thought about it. [Not until] I was drafted by the Rams, and then it entered my mind."[6]

Brink went on to a successful collegiate football career. He said the delay helped because it made him more mature so that he was ready for college football. It was during his time at Northern Illinois that he met his future wife, Leatha Hyland.

Brink had some interactions with other stars of the game during an era when facemasks were not widespread. "One hot day against the Rams, I think in 1954, I tossed aside the helmet that had a fitted mask for me for one without a mask," said Joe Perry of the 49ers. "Three plays later, I got elbowed by the Rams' Larry Brink who knocked out nine of my teeth, two from a bridge I had fitted, after a game against the Steelers. Still, I scored three touchdowns that day."[7]

There is no doubt that the game was much more physical in those days. Brink was able to play the rough game and save his biggest moments for the biggest games. Brink scored a touchdown in the 1950 title game. Marion Motley, who led the league in rushing in 1950, had limited success running the ball in the first half. Early in the second half, perhaps eager to make something happen, Motley reversed his field and waited for blockers. Before help arrived, Rams ends Brink and Jack Zilly hit him simultaneously. The ball squirted out and rolled back to the six-yard line. Brink picked it up and ran into the end zone to give the visiting team the lead.

During the 1951 NFL championship game against the Cleveland Browns, Brink's play helped seal the victory for the Rams. Early in the second half, with the Browns leading 10–7, Otto Graham attempted a pass. Rams defensive ends Brink and Andy Robustelli converged on the quarterback. Brink got there first and knocked the football from Graham's hand. Robustelli scooped up the ball at the thirty-yard line and started running towards the goal line.

"I never got a really good grip on the ball because I just grabbed it off-balance and began to run," recalled Robustelli. "I stumbled as soon as I started, and it seemed I kept stumbling all the way down the field, trying to keep the ball in my grasp."[8] Motley caught Robustelli at the two-yard line. Two plays went for one yard before Deacon Dan Towler powered the ball over on third down to put the Rams back in the lead, 14–10.

Cleveland writers said Otto Graham had not been hit as hard all season as he was when Brink caused that fumble before the Rams scored their second touchdown.[9] "Brink is one of the roughest players I have seen in the National Football League," said George Preston Marshall of Washington. "He also is one of the most underrated."[10]

When Brink joined the Rams in 1948, he started out on offense. The NFL record book credits Brink with four receptions for 36 yards during the 1948 season. It was not a pretty sight.

"Playing offense, he had all the grace of a giraffe on ice skates," Frank Finch wrote in the *Los Angeles Times*.[11] Red Hickey, his roommate at the time, suggested to coaches that Larry play defense. Opposing quarterbacks would learn to regret that suggestion. Brink made the most of his opportunity. "It was necessary to go all out with 120 percent effort on every play," he recalled later. "When the coach saw that, I was part of the team, I was given an opportunity to play defense. I knew I could make it in pro ball. That was my goal."[12]

Brink nearly did not play in the 1951 title game. During the summer, without a contract, Brink negotiated for a short time with a team in Canada. Fortunately for Rams fans, a small article in newspapers in June across southern California said he was going to negotiate with the Rams to continue his career with the NFL team.[13] The rest, as they say, is history.

Brink finished his career by playing the 1954 season with the Chicago Bears. He returned a fumble 84 yards for a touchdown against his former team, the Rams, in Wrigley Field. The score helped the Bears to a 24–13 victory. Brink ended his career with several first and second team All-Pro selections from 1951 through 1953. "Plus I played in the first two Pro Bowl games," said Brink.[14]

After his NFL career ended, Brink opened a Lincoln Mercury dealership in Mill Valley, California. After work, he coached Little League Baseball and Pop Warner football teams in the neighborhood. He played tennis at Mill Valley Tennis Club, where he met and later married his second wife, Betty Stephens. They moved to Hawaii for three years but returned to California. Brink opened and ran a tennis equipment business for more than two decades.

Larry Brink passed away in 2016 at age 92. Prior to his death, Brink appeared on the list of the oldest living former National Football League players.

Notes

1. Mike Korcek, "Viewpoint: Don't Forget About Larry Brink," *Daily Chronicle*, March 13, 2009, https://www.daily-chronicle.com/2009/03/13/viewpoint-dont-forget-about-larry-brink/aosp69u/.
2. Tex Maule, "Bigger and Better Than Ever," *Sports Illustrated*, September 20, 1971, https://www.daily-chronicle.com/2009/03/13/viewpoint-dont-forget-about-larry-brink/aosp69u/.
3. Korcek, "Viewpoint: Don't Forget About Larry Brink."
4. Dan Verdun, "On the Brink with First NIU Huskie NFL Draft Pick," *ChicagoNow.com*, June 28, 2016, http://www.chicagonow.com/prairie-state-pigskin/2016/06/on-the-brink-with-first-niu-draft-pick/.
5. Frank Rajkowski, "Foley's Brink had Falcons Flying High in 1940," *St. Cloud Times*, December 14, 2015, D-1.
6. Rajkowski, "Foley's Brink had Falcons Flying High in 1940."
7. Martin Jacobs, "Flashback Interview: Flying with 'The Jet,'" *SportscollectorsDigest.com*, September 12, 2001, www.sportscollectorsdigest.com/joe_perry-interview/.
8. Joseph S. Page, *Pro Football Championships Before the Super Bowl* (Jefferson, NC: McFarland, 2011), 120–121.
9. Paul Zimmerman, "Fears Calls Van Brocklin's Toss 'Best Thrown Pass I Ever Caught,'" *Los Angeles Times*, December 24, 1951, IV-1.
10. Frank Finch, "Brink and Zilly Give Rams Top Defensive Combination," *Los Angeles Times*, August 9, 1951, IV-3.
11. Finch, "Brink and Zilly Give Rams Top Defensive Combination," IV-3.
12. Verdun, "On the Brink with First NIU Huskie NFL Draft Pick."
13. "Larry Brink Decides to Stay in U.S.," *Colton Courier*, June 20, 1951, 6.
14. Verdun, "On the Brink with first NIU Huskie NFL Draft Pick."

Bobby Collier

Greg Selber

It is taken for granted these days that when a guy is a good enough football player to advance to the highest level, he'll scratch and claw to make the grade and enjoy the astronomical multi-million-dollar salaries in the high-profile NFL.

But back in the early 1950s, the professional football game was not quite the blockbuster it is today, and that explains why a star lineman from SMU won a championship with the 1951 Rams as a rookie but retired from the game thereafter.

Bobby Frank Collier was that rookie, and indeed he left the league after the title of 1951, returning to Longview, Texas, to coach at his high school alma mater for 13 years before going to work full-time in the family furniture business.

When Collier passed on in 2000, his obituary in the local Longview paper quoted several longtime friends who attested to his pleasant demeanor and devotion to his six children and explained his decision to quit the game after just one season.

"He spent a year in the big city," said John Harrison, a childhood chum from Longview. "And he was ready to come home. He'd had enough and was ready to teach and coach, and rejoin the family business."[1]

At 6-foot-3, 230 pounds, Collier was a key member of the Rams' offensive line. For that, he earned $5,500 plus the hefty winner's share bonus of $2,108.44 when L.A. defeated the Browns for the NFL title.

Collier was born in Arkansas but moved as an infant to Longview, where he eventually became an All-State football guard and lettered in three other sports, baseball, basketball, and track. He passed up a scholarship offer with the powerful SMU program but changed his mind a year later and went to Dallas to join the Mustangs.[2]

SMU had won a national title in 1935 and into the 1940s was one of the Southwest

Rams offensive lineman Bobby Collier played college football at SMU.

Conference elites, going 9–0–2 in 1947 and 9–1–1 in 1948 under Coach Matty Bell. The 1947 Mustangs ranked No. 3 in the final AP poll, tying Penn State in the Cotton Bowl, and in 1948 completed a fine 9–1–1 season with a victory over Oregon in the Cotton Bowl, coming in ranked No. 10 in the nation versus the No. 9 Webfoots.

The program averaged three to four draftees a season in the period from the 1940s through the 1950s, with six going in the NFL draft of 1945, and seven in 1949. Notable SMU alums from the '50s included Kyle Rote, Ray Berry, Jerry Norton, Bill Forester, Forrest Gregg, and Don McIlhenny.

All-Southwest Conference on the offensive line, blocking first for the great Doak Walker—Heisman Trophy winner of 1948—and later Rote, Collier lettered from 1948 to 1950 and was one of 13 offensive linemen selected by the Rams in their heavy-duty draft of 1950, going in the 18th round as the 233rd pick.

The 1951 Rams would make history as the only team to start five "rookies" on the offensive line in a title game, with Collier as a backup. Left tackle Don Simensen and right tackle Tom Dahms had gone undrafted while left guard Dick Daugherty (18th round, 1951) and center Leon McLaughlin (originally picked in the 1947 draft) joined right guard Bill Lange (30th round, 1950) in the starting lineup.

In making the pros, Collier was the first in a line of professionals who would come out of Longview to make the big time. Kicker Mike Clark and lineman Loyd Phillips were others, and later on, kicker Josh Scobee, defensive back Bobby Taylor, running back Chris Ivory, and OL Trent Williams continued the tradition of Lobos attaining the highest football honor.

By all accounts, Collier never looked back after saying goodbye to the game following the 1951 title season. At a 1995 ceremony in Longview honoring a number of graduates, Jerry Wayne Watson, Class of 1955 and by then a successful attorney, credited Collier—his coach—as one of the most important influences he'd had back in high school.[3]

Notes

1. "Obituary: Bobby Frank Collier," *Longview News Journal*, November 16, 2000, 1A.
2. "Obituary: Bobby Frank Collier," 1A.
3. Bridget Ortigo, "Foundation Honors Distinguished Longview Alumni," *Longview News Journal*, May 9. 2015, https://www.news-journal.com/news/local/foundation-honors-distinguished-longview-alumni/article_9bea80f7-b8cd-53ec-8525-46c38c64e631.html.

Tom Dahms

Nicholas Ritzmann

Just before Independence Day 1951, Tom Dahms traveled to the offices of the Rams at 7813 Beverly Boulevard in Los Angeles and signed a contract to play professional football. Having not played in a football game since his senior season at San Diego State College in 1949 and having not been selected with *any* of the nearly 400 picks in the 1950 NFL draft, he naturally chose to sign with a team that had played in the last two NFL championship games and was less than twenty days from beginning training camp. Tom Dahms would do much more than simply make the Rams in 1951, as he started every game as their rookie right tackle and began a playing and coaching career in professional football that would last for over a quarter century.

Thomas Gordon Dahms was born on April 19, 1927, in San Diego, California, to Gustav A. Dahms, a baker who had immigrated from Germany in 1907, and Lenna (Eathom) Dahms. He was one of seven children in an athletic family, as all five boys earned a varsity letter at San Diego High School.[1] San Diego High School had a celebrated football tradition before 1960 and from 1911 to 1935 never lost a game to another San Diego County team.[2] Dahms played right tackle in 1942, 1943, and 1944. During his senior season the 6-foot-3-inch, 220-pounder was named to the All-Southern California Interscholastic Federation first team.[3] Fifty years later he was named as a first team lineman for the "Modern Era" (post–1935) All-Time All-Star football team at San Diego High School,[4] and in 2013 he was named by the *San Diego Union-Tribune* as a member of their All-Time All County Football Team (third team offensive line).

As Dahms was finishing high school in the spring of 1945, the administration at San Diego State College was restoring the Aztec football program, which had shut down in 1943 and 1944 due to World War II. While Tom's older brother John lettered for the Aztecs in 1945, Tom also stayed in San Diego, spending a "a one-year session with the U.S. Naval Training Center,"[5] where he played football on a Bluejackets team that went 5–2 on the season. After following his brother to San Diego State, Tom started at offensive tackle in 1947 on the first Aztecs squad to play in a Bowl game. In 1948 he was named all-league (California Collegiate Athletic Association) by the United Press,[6] and was named to the United Press's Little All-Coast football team, which included schools from the State of Washington to Arizona.[7] In 1949 he was the only repeat member of the CCAA all-league team, a repeat member of the Little All-Coast team, where he was referred to as San Diego State's "60-minute player,"[8] and was named honorable mention on the Associated Press's All-Pacific Coast 11.

The 1950 NFL draft came and went in January, but Dahms was not selected by any of the 13 teams. He spent the season coaching high school football, while the Rams, behind their prolific scoring offense, were blasting their way to the NFL championship game.

In 1951 Dahms was one of 63 men (including forty rookies) in the Rams' training camp competing for a place on the 33-man active roster. Now standing six feet, five inches tall and weighing 240 pounds, and having "worked out for two hours a day for two months before reporting,"9 Dahms began scrimmaging with the Rams. Initial reports from training camp termed him "scrappy, hard to handle."10 Sportswriter Frank Finch of the *Los Angeles Times* wrote at the start of camp that Coach Stydahar "repeatedly has said that this 1951 club can be even more potent [than 1950] if the rookie tackles come through."11 The rookie wearing number 71 more than came through, going from a man who was not on the team in late June to starting at right tackle.

Tom Dahms was one of five rookie starters on the 1951 Rams' offensive line.

Frank Finch noted that "Dahms is the kind of blocker who goes downfield looking for people to knock down, the more the merrier. He doesn't listen for the referee's whistle. If he flattens a bloke after the whistle's been tootled, well, that's the other guy's hard luck."12 In a November 1952 home game against the Dallas Texans, Dahms missed blocking Hall of Famer Art Donovan, who remembered "Bill Lange, the right guard, picked me up. With that, Tom Dahms turned around and jumped on my leg and broke it."13 Coach Hamp Pool benched both starting offensive tackles for the following week's game, also against the Texans, but both Dahms and Don Simensen returned the following week to help the Rams score 40 points against the Chicago Bears.

In the spring of 1953, Pool put Dahms "on the spot" by pushing John Hock and Bud McFadin to compete for his tackle position.14 But when the Rams' regular season began with a 21–7 victory against the New York Giants on September 27, Dahms remained in the starting lineup and stayed there for the entire year, helping the Rams to finish with an 8–3–1 record. His play was recognized with an honorable mention selection to the Associated Press's All-Pro team.

On June 3, 1954, Dahms quit professional football to become an assistant football coach at San Diego High School. Rams head coach Hampton Pool said, "It would be a severe blow if we were to lose Dahms ... we knew he was considering the high school coaching offer, but we hoped-and still do-to keep him."15 Coach Pool even "tried to lure wrestler Wilbur Snyder back in the pro grid ranks to fill Dahms' tackle post. But Snyder said ... he would make far more of the folding stuff in the grunt-and-groan past-time."16 But on June 11 Dahms announced, "[The Rams] made such a good offer I couldn't afford to turn it down.... I still hope to go into coaching eventually, but I should have at least two or three years of football left so I've decided to stay with it."17 The Rams were no doubt motivated by the fact that "only two members of [their 1953] squad, Charley [*sic*]

Toogood and Tom Dahms help man the tackle positions—likely to be the Rams' most critical problems [in 1954]."[18] Dahms pulled a hamstring muscle in the preseason, then was moved to the defensive side of the ball before the Rams' fourth game of the year against the Green Bay Packers in Milwaukee. Coach Pool's idea was to "put three big tackles in the middle—Dahms, Gene Lipscomb, and Bud McFadin,"[19] but the move to defense from offense was done at "at his own request."[20]

After marrying Diane Ewing on June 25, Dahms began the 1955 season with the Rams, only at a different position. At the start of training camp, new head coach Sid Gillman moved Dahms from defensive tackle back to offensive tackle.[21] While Dahms was moving positions in California, the Green Bay Packers' offensive line was falling apart in Wisconsin. Tackle Art Hunter, guard Al Barry and end Max McGee had military service obligations, other players left training camp, and tackle Bob Lucky, newly acquired from the Cleveland Browns in a trade for Art Hunter needed an emergency appendectomy. So in what Packers coach Lisle Blackbourn called a "deal of necessity," the Packers acquired Dahms to play tackle in early August.[22] Wearing uniform number 78, Dahms played in all 12 games.

After signing a contract with the Packers in May 1956 for the upcoming season, Dahms was listed in a late July edition of the *Green Bay Press-Gazette* as standing 6 foot five inches tall and weighing 240 pounds.[23] In addition to playing on the offensive line, he also worked some on defense in an August 25 exhibition game against the New York Giants,[24] then played on defense for a September 8 exhibition game against the Redskins.[25] After the Packers traded with the Cleveland Browns for offensive tackle John Sandusky in August, and drafted offensive linemen Forrest Gregg and Bob Skoronski in November 1955 and January 1956, they found themselves with an abundance of quality offensive linemen. The Packers played the Chicago Cardinals in an exhibition game on September 15, and the following Wednesday Dahms was "plucked off the field of practice … and dispatched [in exchange for a 1957 draft choice] to the Chicago Cardinals."[26] Cardinals head coach Ray Richards was Dahms' offensive line coach in 1951 with the Rams.[27] Dahms switched his uniform number back to 71, and in mid–October was described as being "an integral force in [the Cardinals] rise to the leadership in the Eastern Division of the National Football League."[28] After a November victory over the Eagles, he was described as a "willing combatant … in a free for all in the final minute of play."[29]

Dahms began the 1957 season with the Cardinals but was waived at the end of the exhibition season in late September. However, after star San Francisco 49ers tackle Bob St. Clair suffered a separated shoulder on October 6 in a victory over the Rams in Kezar Stadium, the 49ers placed linebacker Stan Sheriff on waivers and signed Dahms to a contract.[30] He saw action in a victory over the Packers in Milwaukee on October 20[31] and "came in for some plaudits after taking over at right tackle for the first time"[32] the following week in a comeback victory in Kezar Stadium against the Bears where 49ers team owner Tony Morabito suffered a fatal heart attack during the game. In November the contributions of three former Los Angeles Rams were noted as "responsible for the [49ers'] tremendous success this season…. [Dahms] has taken over injured tackle Bob St. Clair's spot so successfully that the 49er ground attack is moving better now than at any time in five years."[33] St. Clair returned to the starting lineup at right tackle in December and the host 49ers beat the Green Bay Packers 27–20 in their final regular season game to finish with an 8–4 record, setting up a playoff game with the Detroit Lions to determine the championship of the Western Conference. Tom Dahms' last game as a player was a playoff thriller, as the 49ers held a 27–7 lead early in the third quarter, before the Lions came back to win 31–27.

Tom Dahms quit playing football in 1958 and worked as an athletic director at San Diego Junior High School.[34]

After assistant coach Don Shula left the University of Virginia in February 1959 to take a position under head coach Blanton Collier at the University of Kentucky, Tom Dahms became a college football coach, replacing Shula on head coach Dick Voris' staff. Voris, Dahms' line coach with the Rams in 1954, had an extraordinarily poor record at Virginia, winning his second game as the Cavaliers' coach in 1958, then losing 28 games in a row before being replaced at the end of the 1960 season. Dahms left the University of Virginia in April 1960 after one season, joining the professional coaching ranks when Tom Landry hired him to coach the defensive line for the expansion team Dallas Cowboys. He continued to coach the Cowboys' defensive line in 1961, then transitioned into a role as their Chief Scout in 1962. He resigned from the Cowboys in January 1963 and expressed an interest to "continue coaching, in the West, if possible."

In March 1963, Dahms was hired by 33-year-old Al Davis, the new head coach and general manager of the American Football League's Oakland Raiders, to coach their defensive line, largely because Davis admired the "precise notebooks Dahms kept for Landry, beautifully diagrammed."[35] He remained with the Raiders through the 1978 season, leaving after head coach John Madden resigned in January 1979. He worked some in the semi-professional California Football League, and in 1986 was the head coach at Mountain Empire High School in Pine Valley, California. He passed away on November 30, 1988, in Orange County, California. Three years later he was posthumously inducted into the San Diego State University Athletic Hall of Fame.

Notes

1. Donald R. King, *Caver Conquest: An Athletic History of San Diego High School* (San Diego: San Diego High School Alumni Association,1994), 320.
2. Dana Haddad, "Rebuilt Cavers Want to Add a Chapter to School's Lore," *Los Angeles Times*, October 10, 1991, https://www.latimes.com/archives/la-xpm-1991-10-10-sp-167-story.html.
3. "Helms Football Annual 1944," LA48 Foundation Digital Library, *Digital.la84.org*, https://digital.la84.org/digital/collection/p17103coll7/search/searchterm/football./field/subjec/mode/exact/conn/and/order/title/ad/asc.
4. King, *Caver Conquest*, 307–308.
5. "Rams Get Two Ball Carriers Plus a Tackle," *Los Angeles Times*, July 4, 1951, IV-3.
6. "Tigers, Spartans Top CCAA Team," *Oakland Tribune*, November 30, 1948, 30.
7. "Gauchos' S. Cathcart named on All-Little Coast Eleven," *Bakersfield Californian*, December 2, 1948, 28.
8. "Spartans' Russell Gains Star Team," *Oakland Tribune*, November 26, 1949, 12.
9. Frank Finch, "Rams Must Depend on Rookie Tackles," *Los Angeles Times*, July 26, 1951, IV-3.
10. Finch, "Rams Must Depend," IV-3.
11. Frank Finch, "Rams Launch Drills Today at Redlands U," *Los Angeles Times*, July 18, 1951, IV-1.
12. Frank Finch, "Rams' Clutch Kids in Fold for '52 Race," *Los Angeles Times*, July 10, 1952, IV-2.
13. Arthur J. Donovan, Jr., and Bob Drury, *Fatso: Football When Men Were Really Men* (New York: Avon Books, 1987), 165.
14. Frank Finch, "Scouting the Pros," *Los Angeles Times*, June 7, 1953, II-11.
15. Frank Finch, "Rams' Dahms Announces Retirement," *Los Angeles Times*, June 4, 1954, IV-2.
16. Claude Anderson, "Sport Slants," *San Bernardino County Sun*, June 9, 1954, 24.
17. "Dahms Reverses Field, to Play for Rams Again," *Los Angeles Times*, June 11, 1954. IV-3.
18. "Ram Vets Join Training Camp," *San Bernardino County Sun*, July 19, 1954, 11.
19. "See Rain for Rams-Packers," *Long Beach Independent*, October 15, 1954, 24.
20. "Rams Rule 13.5 Point Choice to Defeat Packers Tomorrow," *Los Angeles Times*, October 16, 1954, III-2.

21. Frank Finch, "Hirsch to Stay Retired—Maybe," *Los Angeles Times*, July 16, 1955, III-3.
22. Art Daley, "Pack Obtains Dahms From LA; Offensive Wall Taking Shape," *Green Bay Press-Gazette*, August 4, 1955, 21.
23. "Roster of Packer Veterans," *Green Bay Press-Gazette*, July 27, 1956, 13.
24. Art Daley, "Packers Top Giants for Second Straight Win 17–13," *Green Bay Press-Gazette*, August 27, 1956, 17.
25. "Packers Test Skins Tonight; Seek No. 4," *Green Bay Press-Gazette*, September 8, 1956, 15.
26. Art Daley, "Pack Deals Dahms to Cards for Draft Pick," *Green Bay Press-Gazette*, September 20, 1956, 45.
27. John Maxymuk, *NFL Head Coaches: A Biographical Dictionary, 1920–2011* (Jefferson, NC: McFarland, 2012), 250.
28. Walter Taylor, "Packers Producing Offensive Tackles," *The Evening Sun*, October 25, 1956, 33.
29. George Strickler, "Cardinals Defeat Eagles, 28 to 17," *Chicago Tribune*, November 5, 1956, 4–4.
30. Wally Willis, "49ers Sign Ex-Ram Star to Help Line," *Oakland Tribune*, October 8, 1957, 44.
31. Wally Willis, "Moegle Groomed for Offense as Flu Hits 49er Backs," *Oakland Tribune*, October 25, 1957, 49.
32. Wally Willis, "49ers Back to Work for Lions Game," *Oakland Tribune*, October 29, 1957, 41.
33. Hank Hollingworth, "Sports Merry-Go-Round," *Long Beach Independent*, November 8, 1957, C-2.
34. Dallas Cowboys 1960 Press Radio TV Guide
35. Murray Olderman, *Just Win, Baby: The Al Davis Story* (Chicago: Triumph Books, 2012), 69.

Dick Daugherty

Mark L. Ford

By 1958, Richard Lee Daugherty was the last man standing. "In 1951," Wally Willis of the *Oakland Tribune* wrote before the 49ers faced their California rival, "the Rams won the world championship and the only man left on the squad is Dick Daugherty, the right linebacker."[1] Historian Bob Oates would comment decades later, "The attrition of but eight years had wiped out all thirty-four of Daugherty's teammates."[2]

Daugherty himself had only played six of those eight years, his career interrupted by military service, and linebacker was the most recent of several starting jobs for the Rams. In '58, the front office noted that in its preseason feature for southern California newspapers. "Meet Your Rams" described Daugherty as "a versatile lineman ... claiming the unusual distinction of being a starter at three different positions with the Rams."[3] Unusual, indeed; from 1951 to 1953, he was the starting left guard. He came back in 1956 as starting center, then closed out in 1957 and 1958 as a linebacker.

Born in Moundsville, West Virginia, on March 31, 1929, he was adopted by his childless uncle and aunt and grew up in Toronto; not the one in Canada, but little Toronto, Ohio, outside of Steubenville. "While Dick's life would take him to far more cosmopolitan locations than rural Ohio," his children wrote in his obituary, "he was always grateful for the love and guidance provided by his adoptive parents and the sacrifices they made for him, their only child."[4]

Graduating from Jefferson Union High in 1947, he won a football scholarship to the University of Oregon to become the first person in his family to attend college. A multiple letterman for the Webfoots, he earned honorable mention on the coaches' 1950 All-Pacific Coast Conference Team.[5] His best days were yet to come.

In 1951, Daugherty was the 217th selection in the NFL draft, picked on the second day in Round 18. As an offensive lineman, it was his

Dick Daugherty started at offensive guard for the 1951 Rams.

good fortune to be chosen by the Rams, the NFL team most in need of linemen that year.

During training camp, Coach Joe Stydahar tested Daugherty at different spots on the line before settling on left guard. Cutting or trading players to reach the 33-man limit, Stydahar began the NFL season with an all-rookie front five. From left to right, Don Simensen, Dick Daugherty, Leon McLaughlin, Bill Lange and Tom Dahms had replaced the 1950 lineup of Dick Huffman, Jack Finlay, Fred Naumetz, Dave Stephenson and Bob Reinhard.[6]

Except for the center, offensive linemen are the least noticed of players. In front of every great rusher is a man who cleared the path with a key block; every successful pass is made during the seconds purchased by the quarterback's core of protectors. After four games, the press was taking notice. "The Rams couldn't run a lick last year," Frank Finch of the *Times* stated. But, Finch wrote as he named the five linemen, "thanks to the block-buster efforts of such rookies, the Ram runners now find a few holes to sneak through."[7] Usually, Daugherty weighed less than the players he faced, 205 by season's end.[8] In some instances, Stydahar would put him in at defense, as in the critical December 2 win over the Bears where he was helpful in "hurling back one Bear thrust after another." The rookie front five certainly yielded results, in that the Rams finished 1951 well out in front in the NFL in yards per attempt on both rushing (5.2) and passing (8.3).

After the championship season, Daugherty continued as the starting guard in 1952 and 1953. The 18th round draftee was preparing for his fourth pro season when he got selected by another draft in the summer of 1954. Despite being the sole support for his parents and his expectant wife, Daugherty was denied a deferment.[9] Came July, and he was in training camp with Tom Brookshier, Babe Parilli and Don Steinbrenner[10] at Sampson Air Force Base, where the four pros were commissioned as second lieutenants.

Like a lot of pro athletes drafted into peacetime military service, Daugherty played service ball during his two-year tour, and was fortunate to remain stateside—literally. His new team was the Hamilton Air Force Base Defenders, about 20 miles north of San Francisco. Besides playing guard for Hamilton, he was also placekicker on extra point tries, something he never had to do in the NFL.[11] In 1955, he was the Defenders' head coach. He guided them to a perfect 6–0 record before losing to the Fort Ord Warriors, 14–10, in a game referred to as a "Pacific Coast military championship contest."[12]

Reporting back to the Rams in the summer of 1956, he made the team again. This time, he was the starting center, and he had benefited from a relatively new training method. Weightlifting is now universal in the NFL but was still optional when Daugherty learned it from teammate Duane Putnam. Jack Geyer of the *Los Angeles Times* noted that, nearing the end of his tour of duty, "Dick started to worry about his heft. Or more accurately, his lack of same. Players in the NFL are getting larger every year and little guys, particularly offensive guards who tangle regularly with giant tackles and ends, are becoming increasingly rare."[13] The 205-pound guard of 1951 had added muscle and had passed the 100-kilo mark to reach 223 pounds. "It's 'good' weight," he said, adding, "It hasn't hurt my speed. In fact, if anything I'm faster than I ever was."[14]

Daugherty also found that the expectations for pro players had changed during his absence. The old school methods of head coaches Stydahar and Hamp Pool had been replaced by the more complex strategy of Sid Gillman. "It would have been amusing," Daugherty told historian Bob Oates at century's end, "to bring in the 1951 team for one week at the end of the '50s. They'd have thought somebody invented a new game."[15] In

1951, he recalled, players practiced two hours a day, read scouting reports rather than study game films of their opponents and called it a day by 6 o'clock. "A football practice was a lark," Daugherty said of 1951. "In my rookie year, it required practically no mental effort. We could have done that in our sleep. In fact, I often did."[16] By the time of his return, though, "preparing for a football game became a full-time thinking job," especially on defense. Daugherty remembered that Stydahar and Pool had two basic defenses: "We had more than two hundred defenses under Gillman."[17]

Dick Daugherty quickly adapted to life under the new regime, both physically and mentally. He spent 1956 as the Rams' starting center but was assigned also to "filling in for injured teammates."[18] Gillman shifted him to the defense in 1957 as the right linebacker. He appeared in the 1957 Pro Bowl and was named second team All-Pro by the New York Daily News. By 1958, however, Daugherty had had enough. The game that had once been "fun seven days a week" was now "only fun on Sunday afternoons."[19] The pay scale hadn't increased to meet the new skill level required, and Daugherty was among the players who realized that the labor would eventually have to organize to be on even terms with management (in 1956, he and four other players had been the first to negotiate additional benefits from an NFL team). With his abilities, he could make more money running a business than working for one. So, at the age of 29, Daugherty retired from professional football.[20]

For the rest of his life, Daugherty built his fortune, becoming a stockbroker and then a real estate developer in Glendale, California, then in Tucson, Arizona. In the mid–1970s, he opened David Copperfield's, a theme restaurant in Arcadia, before selling it and moving to Tucson. Despite his success, though, he never really left pro football, and helped found the NFL Alumni Association in 1967. An articulate spokesman, he organized fundraisers and lobbied for the pre–NFLPA players who weren't covered by a pension. He was among the first to call attention to the long-term effects of the battering sustained in the NFL.

By the time he turned 50, Daugherty's arm was already partially immobilized by pain. As the NFLAA's western branch chairman in 1981, he told a reporter, "Anybody playing professional football has athletic arthritis in either his shoulders, back, knees or neck."[21] He died of complications from Alzheimer's disease on March 10, 2009. His only regret, he said near life's end, "was that he had been too young to serve his country in World War II."[22] As for the consequences of his six years in the NFL, there was no second-guessing. He told a reporter, "You play because there is no other game like it…. A guy can do something safe like sit at a desk and push a pencil all his [life] and end up with ulcers and heart trouble. You take your chances no matter what you do. That's life."[23]

Notes

1. Wally Willis, "49ers Open Secret Workouts for Rams," *Oakland Tribune*, October 1, 1958, 52-E.
2. Bob Oates, *Football in America: Game of the Century* (Coal Valley, IL: Quality Sports Publications, 1999), 113.
3. "Meet Your Rams," *Redlands* (CA) *Daily Facts*, August 15, 1958, 7.
4. "Funeral Notices," *Arizona Daily Star* (Tucson), March 14, 2009, A22.
5. "Stelle Captures Defensive Spot," *Eugene* (OR) *Guard*, December 18, 1950, 13.
6. Frank Finch, "Stydahar Ready to Settle for 9-and-3 Mark," *Los Angeles Times*, October 23, 1951, IV-2.
7. Frank Finch, "Rams Setting Torrid Pace with Offense," *Los Angeles Times*, October 22, 1951, IV-1.
8. Paul Zimmerman, "Sportscripts," *Los Angeles Times*, December 6, 1951, IV-1.
9. Bob Kelley, "Parade of Sports," *Covina* (CA) *Argus-Citizen*, July 22, 1954, II-4.

10. "Four NFLers in Service," *Long Beach* (CA) *Independent*, July 17, 1954, 12.
11. "Hamilton Loses in Service Bowl," *San Francisco Examiner*, December 13, 1954, 39.
12. "Fort Ord Defeats Hamilton," *Santa Rosa* (CA) *Press Democrat*, November 6, 1955, 4C.
13. Jack Geyer, "Weight-Lifting Puts Eighteen Hard Pounds on Dick Daugherty of Rams," *Los Angeles Times*, July 16, 1956, II-6.
14. Geyer, "Weight-lLfting," II-6.
15. Oates, *Football in America*, 114.
16. Oates, *Football in America*, 114.
17. Oates, *Football in America*, 114.
18. "Daugherty, Houser Sign '57 Ram Pacts," *Oxnard* (CA) *Press-Courier*, July 8, 1957, 11.
19. "Daugherty, Houser," 11.
20. Cal Whorton, "Daugherty to Retire After Packer Game," *Los Angeles Times*, December 12, 1958, IV-1.
21. Katie Castator, "Residue of an NFL career—pain," *The Sun*, San Bernardino (CA), July 19, 1981, B-1.
22. "Funeral Notices," A22.
23. Castator, "Residue," B-1.

Glenn Davis

Randy Snow

One of the greatest backfield tandems in the history of college football is one that produced back-to-back Heisman Trophy winners and back-to-back national champions. The school was the United States Military Academy at West Point. The players were fullback Felix "Doc" Blanchard, a.k.a. Mr. Inside, and halfback Glenn Davis, a.k.a. Mr. Outside. Blanchard won the Heisman in 1945. Davis won in 1946 after finishing second in Heisman voting in 1944 and 1945. They shared the Army backfield for three seasons, 1944–1946, and never lost a game. Their record was 27–0–1. The only blemish came on November 9, 1946, when top-ranked Army played second-ranked Notre Dame to a 0–0 tie. Army won back-to-back Associated Press (AP) college football national championships in 1944 and 1945, but the AP decided to award the 1946 national championship to Notre Dame.

Davis grew up in California, along with his twin brother, Ralph. They attended Bonita High School in La Verne. In high school, Glenn was known as Junior because he was born moments after Ralph.[1]

Glenn was a superb all-around athlete in high school, earning 13 letters. His athletic prowess brought him to the attention of Army head football coach Earl "Red" Blaik by way of Warner Bentley, a Davis family friend who was coaching at West Point. Recruiting a young man from the other side of the country was not something Blaik usually did. Upon hearing about Davis, however, Blaik contacted Davis's parents and made a pitch for him to come play at West Point. Glenn was receptive to the idea, but he had one stipulation. He wanted his brother, Ralph, to attend West Point also. Blaik agreed and the two boys traveled to the East Coast in the spring of 1943.

Because World War II was going on, and many young men were off fighting overseas, colleges were allowing freshmen to compete at the varsity level in football. Prior

Rams running back Glenn Davis, famed "Mr. Outside" at West Point.

to that, schools had freshman football teams and players were allowed only three years of varsity eligibility. At five feet nine and weighing 170 pounds, Davis did well in his first season, scoring eight touchdowns and finishing seventh in the nation in total yardage.[2]

Even though Davis was in fine form on the football field, he was struggling in the classroom. In March of 1944, he failed a math test and was "found deficient" academically. He was dismissed from West Point and returned home to California. He enrolled at Cal Poly-Pomona, a college prep school, to help him in math. He returned to the academy in the fall for his sophomore year.

On the train heading back to West Point, the Davis brothers happened to meet Clark Shaughnessy who, at the time, was the head coach at the University of Pittsburgh. Shaughnessy told the boys about a player by the name of Felix "Doc" Blanchard who was going to be playing for Army that season. He told them that Blanchard was going to be a great player. Years earlier, Shaughnessy had coached Blanchard's father, who was a star fullback, while both were at Tulane University.

In his last three seasons at West Point, Davis ran for 2,309 yards on 266 carries, averaged 8.7 yards per carry and scored 36 touchdowns. He caught 38 passes for 790 yards, averaging 20.8 yards per reception and scored 12 receiving touchdowns. Davis also completed 36 of 78 passing attempts for 846 yards, a 10.8-yard average per attempt. He threw five touchdown passes and five interceptions.[3]

Davis was the number two overall pick in the 1947 NFL draft by the Detroit Lions. (In September of 1947, The Los Angeles Rams acquired his rights from the Lions.) He was also selected in a special draft by the San Francisco 49ers of the rival All-America Football Conference (AAFC).[4] The 49ers were planning to offer both Davis and Blanchard contracts worth $130,000 ($40,000 a year for three years plus a $10,000 signing bonus), which was an unheard-of sum at the time. The Army refused to allow them to play professional football because they still had a military obligation to serve. The Army did, however, allow Davis and Blanchard to go to Hollywood and play themselves in a movie called *The Spirit of West Point*. Blanchard and Davis each received $20,000 for appearing in the film.

While filming the movie, Davis was injured during a scene in which he was simulating play on the field, something that never happened to him while playing in college. He aggravated the injury while practicing for the College All-Star Game against the Chicago Bears in 1947 and missed the game. He also injured his knee playing in an All-Star charity game against the New York Giants later that year.[5]

On September 2, 1948, Davis played in the Los Angeles Rams annual preseason charity football game against the Washington Redskins in L.A. He carried the ball four times for only one yard and caught one pass for 13 yards. Washington won the game 21–10. This occurred while he was on leave from the service, prior to deploying to Korea.[6]

After serving in Korea, Davis returned to West Point in 1949 and became the freshman football coach. He officially signed with the Los Angeles Rams in 1950. In his rookie season, he led the team in rushing. He carried the ball 88 times for 416 yards and three touchdowns during the regular season. He also caught 42 passes for 592 yards and four touchdowns.[7] Not bad for a guy who had not played football for two years.

The Rams advanced to the 1950 NFL title game but lost to the Cleveland Browns 30–28. Davis scored the first touchdown in the title game on an 82-yard pass from Bob Waterfield. He was also selected to the 1950 Pro Bowl and was an honorable mention on the All-Pro team that year.

During the 1951 preseason, the Rams hosted the Washington Redskins in the

Seventh Annual *Los Angeles Times* Charity Football Game. The week before the game, both teams got together at the Southern California Football Writer's luncheon. During the luncheon, Davis was asked about the recent cheating scandal at West Point in which a total of ninety cadets, including thirty-seven football players, were dismissed from the academy. Among them was the son of Army football coach, Red Blaik.

"I doubt if there was any cheating at West Point when I was there. If there was, I didn't know anything about it," Davis said.[8]

After his successful rookie season, many fans were expecting even greater things from Davis on the gridiron in 1951. Even opposing players and coaches were expecting Davis to improve on his 1950 performance. Among them was Chicago Bears head coach George Halas. When the Bears traveled to Los Angeles for a pre-season game against the Rams in August, Halas was quoted in the *Los Angeles Times* as saying, "I expect Glenn Davis to have an even greater year than last season when he was terrific."[9]

Davis suffered a hip pointer in the final preseason game against the Giants and subsequently missed the regular season home opener again the New York Yanks.

In week two, the Cleveland Browns came to town for a rematch of the previous year's NFL title game. Davis returned to the field and scored on a one-yard run in the third quarter. He also caught a 14-yard touchdown pass from Norm Van Brocklin in the fourth quarter, but it was not enough as the Browns came out on top once again, 38–23.

Davis was injured again a few weeks later in a road game against the San Francisco 49ers. He was the victim of 49ers linebacker Hardy Brown, who was famous for his devastating shoulder tackle.[10] Davis suffered a cracked nose but did not miss any playing time because of it and continued to play.

Late in the season, a reporter for the *Los Angeles Times*, Dick Hyland, questioned the Rams' coaching staff's use of Davis in certain situations in his column, "The Hyland Fling." In college he was known as Mr. Outside, but Davis, weighing in at 170 pounds, was used many times to try and advance the ball up the middle where the linemen outweighed him by 50–75 pounds.[11]

Davis' regular season statistics were not nearly as good as they were during his rookie season with the Rams. In 1951, he carried the ball 64 times for just 200 yards and one touchdown. He also caught eight passes for 90 yards and one touchdown.[12]

Los Angeles finished the regular season with an 8–4 record, winning the National Conference. The Rams hosted the NFL championship game against the American Conference champs, the Cleveland Browns, at the Coliseum in Los Angeles on December 23, 1951.

In the title game against the Browns, Davis rushed only six times for minus six yards. He also caught three passes for 10 yards and scored no touchdowns. Davis' bad day did not stop his teammates. The Rams avenged their loss the previous year to the Browns by the score of 24–17.

Davis planned to play for the Rams again in 1952 but reinjured his knee during an exhibition game and decided to sit out the season. He tried to come back once more in 1953, but it was not to be. His last gridiron appearance was in a preseason game against the Philadelphia Eagles in Little Rock, Arkansas, on September 12, 1953. Davis was released by the Rams, and after no other teams showed an interest, he officially retired from professional football.[13]

Looking back on his brief pro career, Davis was once quoted as saying, "I was a mere image of what I had been. I was a better player my senior year in high school than I was with the Rams."[14]

Even before his professional football playing career began, Davis found the Hollywood lifestyle in Los Angeles to his liking. He met actress Elizabeth Taylor in 1948 when she was just 16 years old. The two began dating and gave the Hollywood newspapers and magazines the kind of story they crave. He escorted her to the Academy Awards ceremony in 1949. There were rumors that the two were engaged at one point, but Davis claims it never happened.

Davis also dated actress Ann Blyth, who was nominated for an Academy Award for Best Supporting Actress in 1945 for her performance in the movie *Mildred Pierce*, and starlet Susan Morrow.

In 1951, he married actress Terry Moore. She was nominated for an Oscar as Best Supporting Actress for her work in the 1952 film *Come Back, Little Sheba*. Unfortunately, the marriage only lasted 14 months.

Then, in 1953, Davis married Harriet Lancaster Slack, the widow of a World War II pilot who was killed when his plane was shot down over Europe. The two had a son together, who was named Ralph after Glenn's twin brother. Harriet passed away in 1995.

Davis went on to work for the *Los Angeles Times* in 1954 as an assistant director of special events. He later became the paper's director in charge of charity sports events until 1987 when he retired at the age of 62.

In 1996, Davis married Yvonne Ameche, the widow of another Heisman Trophy winner, Alan Ameche, who played college football at Wisconsin. Ameche won the Heisman in 1954 and went on to play in the NFL for the Baltimore Colts. He scored the winning touchdown in overtime of the 1958 NFL championship game between the Colts and the New York Giants. The picture of him crossing the goal line has become an iconic image in NFL history. Yvonne had been married to Alan from 1952 to 1988, when he passed away.

Davis was inducted into the College Football Hall of Fame in 1961. He donated his Heisman Trophy statue to his high school alma mater. In fact, he even had the name of Bonita High School added to the name plate on the trophy, along with the years he attended there. Since 1986, the Bonita Bearcats have played their home football games in Glenn Davis Stadium.[15]

Davis passed away on March 9, 2005, at the age of 80. He is buried in the West Point Cemetery near his former college football head coach, Earl "Red" Blaik.

Notes

1. "Glenn Davis," *Bonita High School Web Site*, https://bonitahigh.net/doc/history-of-glenn-davis/.
2. Jack Clary, *Field of Valor: Duty, Honor, Country, and Winning the Heisman* (Chicago: Triumph Books, 2002), 59–60.
3. "Glenn Davis," *Sports-Reference.com*, https://www.sports-reference.com/cfb/players/glenn-davis-1.html.
4. Professional Football Researchers Association, *The All-America Football Conference* (Jefferson, NC: McFarland, 2018), 148.
5. Jack Cavanaugh, *Mr. Inside and Mr. Outside: World War II, Army's Undefeated Teams, and College Football's Greatest Backfield Duo* (Chicago: Triumph Books, 2014), 92–94.
6. "Eagles Nose Out Lions; Redskins Defeat Rams," *The Milwaukee Journal*, September 3, 1948, Part 2-8.
7. "Glenn Davis," *Pro-Football-Reference.com*, https://www.pro-football-reference.com/players/D/DaviGl01.htm.
8. Frank Finch, "Rams, Redskins in Preview Meeting—Chow-Time Tie," *Los Angeles Times*, August 7, 1951, IV-2.
9. Paul Zimmerman, "Sportscripts," *Los Angeles Times*, August 22, 1951, IV-1.

10. Frank Finch, "Rams Buried Under 44–17 Avalanche by 49ers: Winners Score Four TD's in Second Quarter en Route to Victory," *Los Angeles Times*, October 29, 1951, IV-1.
11. Dick Hyland, "The Hyland Fling," *Los Angeles Times*, December 11, 1951, IV-2.
12. "Glenn Davis," *Pro-Football-Reference.com*, https://www.pro-football-reference.com/players/D/DaviGl01.htm.
13. Ron Fimrite, "Mr. Inside and Mr. Outside," *Sports Illustrated*, November 21, 1988, 76.
14. Fimrite, "Mr. Inside and Mr. Outside," 76.
15. "Glenn Davis," *Bonita High School Web Site*.

Tom Fears

Rick Schabowski

Thomas Jesse Fears played nine seasons in the National Football League as a receiver for the Los Angeles Rams. He also served as an assistant coach and head coach in the NFL. His accomplishments earned him election to the Pro Football Hall of Fame. He played collegiately at Santa Clara College (California) and UCLA and was inducted into the College Football Hall of Fame.

Fears was born in Guadalajara, Mexico, on December 3, 1922. His father, Charles William Fears, a native of Milford, Texas, was an American mining engineer working for Amparo Mining in Mexico. While there, Charles married a Mexican woman from Rosario, Sinaloa, named Carmen Valdes. When Fears turned six years old, the family moved to Los Angeles.

Fears exhibited a strong work ethic at a very young age. He had a job unloading flowers from trucks for 25 cents an hour, and also was paid big money, 50 cents an hour, working as an usher at football games at the Coliseum. He did great at both jobs, but he also developed another skill, playing football.

After being selected for the All-Southern California high school team while playing at Los Angeles' Manual Arts High School, Fears enrolled at Santa Clara. He attended Santa Clara for two years, 1941 and 1942, and played football his sophomore year. The Broncos posted a 7–2 record, and Fears was named to the All-Pacific Coast sophomore team. After the outbreak of World War II, Fears was drafted, ending his stay at Santa Clara.

Fears spent three years serving his country. His goal was to become a fighter pilot in the Pacific theater. Fears had a good reason for setting this goal. His father, while working as a civilian in the Philippine Islands, was captured and was

Tom Fears caught the game-winning touchdown pass in the 1951 championship game.

a Japanese prisoner of war. Fears earned his pilot's wings and was stationed in Colorado Springs serving as a flight instructor. He also played football for the Second Air Force Superbombers service team, serving as Captain of the team in 1944 and 1945. (Fears' father was released by the Japanese in August 1944.)

While Fears was serving in the military, the Cleveland Rams were so impressed with his performance at Santa Clara that they drafted him in the eleventh round (103rd overall player selected) of the 1945 NFL draft. He was the first Mexican-born player selected in an NFL draft.

After his discharge from the military, Fears passed up the opportunity to play for the Rams, who were now located in Los Angeles, and transferred to UCLA. Fears commented, "The Rams wanted me to sign when I got out of the Army, but I already made a commitment to UCLA."[1]

A big reason that Fears decided to attend UCLA was because his older brother Charles played for the Bruins, was a team captain, and was a part of their 1943 Rose Bowl team.

Things went pretty well at UCLA. Fears was named All-Pacific Coast both of his seasons at Westwood and was an All-American and team MVP his senior season. In the middle of his senior season in 1947, there was an issue that almost derailed his collegiate football career. UCLA supporters made sure that their student athletes had good jobs. They posed in advertisements for a local Los Angeles store, and they had opportunities to act in movies. Fears and some of his teammates appeared in the Humphrey Bogart film *Action in the North Atlantic*. Fears played a role with which he had prior experience, a fighter pilot. The segment in the movie in which he appeared lasted six seconds. After an investigation, all of the athletes were cleared of any wrongdoing.

On December 30, 1947, Fears signed with the Rams. The Rams were initially planning to use Fears as a defensive back, but once they saw his ability to run precise pass patterns, catch the ball in tight coverage, and use his six-foot-two, 215-pound size to gain yardage after the catch, that changed.

In his first regular season NFL game on September 22, 1948, against the Detroit Lions, Rams coach Clark Shaughnessy put Fears in, and he responded with a big game. He caught a four-yard touchdown pass from Jim Hardy and also scored on a 35-yard interception return in a 44–7 Rams victory. He had another multi-touchdown game at Comiskey Park in a 27–24 loss to the Chicago Cardinals on November 21, scoring on an 80-yard bomb from Bob Waterfield and a 16-yard toss from Jim Hardy. The Rams finished the season with a 6–5–1 record, and Fears led the NFL in pass receptions with 51.

Sophomore jinx? Not Fears. He and the Rams had better seasons in 1949. He continued his league-leading performance, setting a new league single season reception record with 77 catches for 1,013 yards and nine touchdowns while helping the Rams improve their record to 8–2–2.

On November 27, he had eight receptions netting 131 yards and scored three touchdowns in a 42–20 home victory over the New York Bulldogs at the Coliseum. In the final regular season game, a 53–27 rout over the Washington Redskins that clinched the Rams a spot in the NFL championship game against the Philadelphia Eagles, Fears had 10 catches for 159 yards, scoring two touchdowns, one of which was a 51-yard bomb from Norm Van Brocklin.

The Rams had a difficult time against the Philadelphia Eagles in the NFL title game. The Rams amassed only seven first downs and 119 total yards in a 14–0 loss. Fears had two catches for 15 yards.

Joe Stydahar was named as the Rams' head coach for the 1950 season, and Fears had a career year. He eclipsed his previous season's record performance with 84 receptions, a record that lasted 10 years, totaling a league leading 1,116 yards and scoring seven touchdowns.

Fears had two big games during the 1950 season. On October 29, in a 65–24 slaughter of the Lions, he had six catches for 85 yards, scoring two touchdowns. On November 12, in a 51–14 victory over the Packers, he caught 18 passes, a record that stood until Terrell Owens caught 20 while playing for the San Francisco 49ers in a game against the Bears on December 17, 2000.

Both the Rams and Bears had 9-3 regular season records, so they would face off in a National Conference playoff game at the Coliseum on December 17. Midway through the second quarter, with the Rams trailing 7–3, Fears and quarterback Bob Waterfield changed things quickly. They connected on two touchdown passes, one of 43 yards and one of 68, giving the Rams a 17–7 halftime lead. Fears and Waterfield hooked up again on a 27-yard touchdown pass in the third quarter, as the Rams ended up winning, 24–14. Fears caught seven passes for 198 yards.

On December 24, 1950, the Rams squared off against the Browns at Cleveland Municipal Stadium for the NFL championship. Lou Groza kicked a late field goal that gave the Browns a 30–28 win. Fears led the Rams with nine receptions for 136 yards.

For the third straight season, Fears was selected First Team All-Pro. Fears was also embroiled in a contract dispute with the Rams for the second consecutive season. In 1950, he threatened to retire and work for General Motors. On March 14, 1951, Fears announced his retirement to work for a liquor distributor. He was also mulling over a number of offers from the Canadian Football League. Negotiations worked out with the Rams though, and Fears agreed to a contract on May 31.

Rams assistant coach Red Hickey was pleased about Fears signing a contract, commenting, "I'm from Arkansas, but our Tom Fears is a greater offensive end than any of those Arkansas boys, Don Hutson, Jim Benton, or Ken Kavanaugh."[2]

Nineteen Fifty-one started out with a rash of injuries for Fears. During a 31–26 victory against the Eagles played in Little Rock, midway through the preseason on September 1, Fears strained his leg and was out of action. He was able to return to the starting lineup on September 14 during a 7–6 preseason loss to the Browns in Cleveland, and he played in the first three regular season games catching 16 passes for 284 yards and a touchdown. He injured his knee at Detroit on October 14 and was sidelined for several weeks. Fears was available for the game against the Cardinals on November 11, but he didn't catch another pass until the Rams' December 2 contest against the Bears.

Back at full strength, Fears caught 16 passes for 244 yards and two touchdowns over the last three games of the regular season. After leading the league in receptions for three consecutive years, Fears caught only 32 balls during his injury prone 1951 season.

On December 23, 1951, the Rams met the Browns for the NFL championship at the Coliseum. Fears had a huge game. He caught four passes for 146 yards, and with the game tied at 17 midway through the fourth quarter, Fears caught a 23-yard pass from Norm Van Brocklin, but he went the additional 50 yards needed to give the Rams a 24–17 lead and the NFL championship.

Dick Hyland of the *Los Angeles Times* wrote that it was an unforgettable moment. "The top thrill was the final score when Fears jumped high between two Browns defensive backs and came down with a Van Brocklin pass in his hands and a clear field in front of him. Mercury himself could not have caught Tom as he completed the final 50 yards of a play that gained 73 yards and the title."[3]

Melvin Durslag of the *Los Angeles Examiner* asked Fears what he was thinking about as he was running for what proved to be the winning touchdown. Fears responded, "I was thinking of the difference between the winner's and loser's share."[4] Each Rams player received a winner's share check of $2,108.44, while the Browns payout was $1,483.12.

Fears had a great first four seasons. He played in three championship games, winning one, and caught more than twice as many passes as any other end in the league in that four-year time period.

Avoiding the injuries that plagued him during the 1951 season, Fears caught 48 passes for 600 yards and six touchdowns in 1952.

Fears wasn't really a speed merchant, but he ran precise patterns. One of his favorites was the buttonhook route, and when he made a reception, he often broke it for additional yardage. A negative aspect of running this type of route is that it resulted in many blind-side hits, a factor which shortened his career.

Fears suffered a major injury in a game against the Detroit Lions on October 18, 1953. Fears fractured two vertebrae late in the game after catching a pass. He was on the ground, covered up by Jack Christiansen when linebacker Jim David dove in.

He completed the 1953 season with 23 catches for 278 yards and four touchdowns.

Despite nagging injuries in the following two seasons, he posted decent statistics. He had 36 catches with three touchdowns in 1954, and 44 receptions with two touchdowns in 1955.

On September 14, 1956, Fears suffered a knee injury in a preseason game against the 49ers. The injury didn't respond to treatment, so Fears retired on November 6. He stayed with the Rams for the remainder of the season, serving as an assistant coach.

Fears finished his career with 400 receptions for 5,397 yards and 38 receiving touchdowns. He was named to the NFL's All-Decade Team of the 1950s.

Looking back at Fears' career with the Rams, many acknowledged his clutch abilities. NFL receiver Billy Howton had high praise for Fears. "When I came to the pros, I got every film I could on the Rams and I studied every move Tom made. His finesse was tops! He was the all-time greatest for maneuvering and getting loose. Whatever success I've had I owe to Tom Fears."[5]

Norm Van Brocklin also spoke highly of Fears. "Fears was the greatest. He had size, speed, agility, and a tremendous desire to get the ball. In a pack jumping for a pass he was sure to come down with it. He was an infallible third-down end to get the first down. He had everything, and he was also a brilliant teacher. He trained me in timing, and the general technique of the co-operation between passer and receiver. I got a solid foundation as a pro thanks to Fears."[6]

Fears was out of the game for two years but returned as an assistant coach with Green Bay during the 1959 season, Vince Lombardi's first year with the Packers. After Fears retired, he opened a number of Taco Thoms restaurants in the Los Angeles area. Business concerns caused him to return home at midseason.

In 1960, Fears returned to coaching serving as an assistant with the Rams (1960–61), Packers (1962–65) and Falcons (1966).

On January 27, 1967, Fears got his first head coaching job when he was hired by the expansion New Orleans Saints. He signed a five-year contract for a reported $35,000 a year. He was the first Latino head coach in the NFL. John W. Mecom Jr., president of the

Saints, spoke highly of Fears. "Coach Fears is in keeping with our policy of youth. I feel he will be able to grow with the team and that he's a man with an eye on the future."[7]

Fears, obviously, was happy about his first head-coaching job. "Now the real work starts. At New Orleans, we'll strive for balance and that includes a good defense. Just because I was an offensive coach for all my career, I don't want people to think I am strictly an offense man."[8]

The Saints went 3–11 under Fears in 1967, improved to 4–9–1 in 1968, and compiled a 5–9 mark in 1969.

In 1970, Fears was elected to the Pro Football Hall of Fame. He was the first Mexican born player to receive the honor. On August 8, 1970, former Rams teammate Hal Dean gave a great presentation speech for Fears. "Tom has dedicated his whole life to professional football. His contributions to the technical aspects and his leadership will continue for years to come. No one could compare with Tom's statistics for catching passes on third-and-six situations, for most passes caught in the final five minutes to keep winning drives alive, and the most, long touchdown passes caught in championship games against the Chicago Bears and the Cleveland Browns."[9]

Fears said: "I am very happy and I'm extremely nervous. I believe I'm the first coach who has to field a team in an hour and a half. I'm proud to be here and I'm grateful for the people who brought me here."[10] The game Fears had to coach was the Hall of Fame exhibition game in which New Orleans defeated the Minnesota Vikings, 14–13.

The 1970 season started poorly for the Saints as they had a 1–5–1 record. Fears was dismissed as the Saints coach on November 3 after compiling an overall mark of 13–34–2.

Fears was back in coaching in 1971–1972, as an offensive coordinator for the Philadelphia Eagles, but was out of football again in 1973 when head coach Ed Khayat was fired.

Despite not being involved with football, Fears was very busy. He opened a bar/restaurant, Coach's Corner, in the South Coast Plaza Mall. At the time it was the largest shopping mall on the West Coast, located in Costa Mesa, California. Fears also invested in condominium rentals and avocado fields.

A new professional league, the World Football League, planned to start play in 1974, and on January 14, 1974, Fears was named head coach of the WFL's Southern California Sun. The new league drowned in a sea of red ink, and after Fears coached the Sun for less than two years, the league folded in October 1975.

He may have not been on the sidelines, but Fears made headlines in 1976 when he was named to the College Football Hall of Fame.

Fears also assisted as a technical adviser for movies with a football connection including *Two Minute Warning*, *North Dallas Forty*, and *The Best of Times*.

Staying involved with the game on the field, Fears started a scouting service and had three teams utilizing his knowledge and experience. After the movie *North Dallas Forty* was released, Fears' service was terminated by all three teams. The controversial film, based on former Dallas end Pete Gent's eponymous novel, was not popular with the sports establishment. Fears commented, "It filtered down to me. I took it with a grain of salt until it happened to me. I was working in an advisor situation with the Packers, Redskins and the Oilers. I had agreed to an agreement with Bum Phillips. Within a week, all three fell out on me. I'm very upset. I don't have anything concrete, but it makes you think there's something to it."[11]

UCLA inducted Fears into its Athletic Hall of Fame in 1989. Reflecting on his career, he said, "If I had it to do over again, I'd do it the same way."[12]

In 1994, he was informed that he had Alzheimer's disease. It was no surprise to Fears. "I know the last six months my memory has been slipping. Your neighbors, unless you see them regularly, you forget their names. It's embarrassing. That's the worst part. People think that you don't give a damn about them but that's not the way it is."[13]

Fears passed away in a convalescent home in Palm Springs, California, on January 4, 2000. He was survived by his wife of 48 years, Luella (Wintheiser), six children, and six grandchildren.

NOTES

1. Frank Litsky, "Tom Fears, N.F.L. End and Coach, Dies at 77," *New York Times*, January 8, 2000, C16.
2. Frank Finch, "Scouting the Pros," *Los Angeles Times*, September 13, 1951, IV-3.
3. "A Championship Pass," *The All-Sports News*, January 2, 1952, 2–9.
4. "It Was Hard to Believe," *The All-Sports News*, January 2, 1952, 2–7.
5. Don Smith, "Tom Fears," *The Coffin Corner* 6, Nos. 9 & 10 (1984): 1.
6. Joe King, "NFL Pass Pacers Feel Hot Breath of Van Brocklin," *The Sporting News*, October 9, 1960, 2–1.
7. Charles Young, "New Saints Go Marching into NFL with Tom Fears Leading the Band," *The Sporting News*, February 11, 1967, 9.
8. Young, "New Saints," 9.
9. Ralph Reeve, "The King Sheds Tears of Joy as Four Enter Pro Grid Shrine," *The Sporting News*, August 22, 1970, 49.
10. Reeve, "The King Sheds," 49.
11. Jonathan Gold, "NFL trailblazer Tom Fears came full circle with return to Mexican hometown," *ESPN.com*, November 19, 2018, https://www.espn.com/nfl/story/_/id/25288408/tom-fears-went-hall-famer-nfl-outcast-coming-full-circle-return-mexican-hometown-guadalajara.
12. "Significant Moments in Latino Bruin History," *Alumni.ucla.edu*, accessed August 1, 2020, http://alumni.ucla.edu/latino-bruin-history.
13. Litsky, "Tom Fears," C16.

Jack Finlay

John Maxymuk

A lifelong southern Californian, Jack Finlay was one of several UCLA Bruins to star for the Los Angeles Rams in the first decade after the team moved to the West Coast from Cleveland. Familiar local players like Finlay helped build a following for the team in its new locale at a time when pro football was still trailing the college game in popularity.

Jack Alexander Finlay was born in Los Angeles on September 8, 1921, to Dr. Alexander (Scotty) Finlay and his wife Maybelle Seitz Finlay. Scotty Finlay came to the U.S. from Scotland in 1909 at the age of 24. He became well-known in West Coast athletic circles by serving as the athletic trainer of two Pacific Coast League baseball teams in a time when major league baseball extended no further west than St. Louis.[1]

Scotty worked for the Los Angeles Angels from 1910 to 1920 and the Oakland Oaks in 1921 and 1922. In 1923, Hall of Fame baseballer Frank Chance was hired to manage the Boston Red Sox and hired Finlay as the team's trainer.[2] Scotty had some health issues that year, and Chance was replaced at year's end, so Finlay ended up back in Los Angeles as the trainer of the UCLA football and baseball teams.

In June 1929, though, tragedy struck when Scotty and another passenger were killed in a car crash in Los Angeles.[3] Son Jack was just seven years old. He grew up and excelled as a tackle for Fairfax High School in the city, where it was said of him in 1938 that he "was one of the hardest hitting linemen in the city."[4] Upon graduation, Jack enrolled at Oceanside Junior College. A year later, he and several teammates transferred to UCLA, where Jack would letter in football from 1940 to 1942.[5]

Finlay became a starter quickly as a sophomore at UCLA when tackle Del Lyman had his appendix removed two games into the season. Jack moved into the line and established himself as a solid

Jack Finlay became a successful film and television sound editor in Hollywood after his NFL playing career was over.

player, although the team would finish just 1–9 in 1940. A year later, Bob Waterfield, another local recruit, joined the Bruins and the team upgraded to a 5–5–1 record. Finlay missed several games in 1941 with an ankle injury and an illness but made a good impression.[6] By the season's end, Deke Houlgate, a nationally syndicated college football analyst, said that the 200-pound tackle was "a tough boy on defense who likes rough going."[7]

With the onset of World War II in 1942, Finlay got a job in the defense industry while attending school and then enrolled in the Navy's V-5 flight program.[8] Finlay continued at UCLA in the fall of 1942, focusing on the mathematics background he would need in the V-5 program. As such, he played for the Bruins as a senior, and the team upped their record to 7–3 and earned a trip to the Rose Bowl where they lost to Georgia 9–0.

Jack reported to Del Monte Pre-Flight in Monterey in 1943. Del Monte had a football team like many service bases at the time that included a mix of college and pro players. Del Monte's team featured Paul Christman at fullback and pro linemen Ray Bray and Charles Schultz. With that competition at his position, Finlay was moved to guard.[9] Del Monte defeated UCLA in November by a 26–7 margin. A few weeks later, they whipped California 47–8 in their season finale to finish with a 7–1 mark. In that finale, Coach Bill Kern presented the game ball to team captain Jack Finlay.[10]

Jack was assigned to Naval Air Station Moffett Field in Santa Clara as a lighter than air cadet in 1944.[11] He was discharged at the end of the war and played for the semipro Hollywood Wolves in 1944.[12] Finlay tried out for the newly relocated Rams' franchise in 1946, but he was cut that August.[13]

He got himself back in football shape in 1946 by joining the Los Angeles Bulldogs of the Pacific Coast Professional Football League, a gridiron minor league.[14] The Bulldogs finished 9–2–1 and won the league championship that year.

The Rams re-signed Jack in 1947, and he made the team. Finlay mostly played guard on both offense and defense throughout his five-year tenure with the Rams and generally on the left side. He also kicked off for the team. He was celebrated for being in excellent physical condition and was known as "The Trainer" in the locker room.[15] He was also recognized as the team's fastest lineman.[16]

Finlay was not a starter for the Rams' 1949 Western Division championship team, but he was a year later under new coach Joe Stydahar. Stydahar singled him out for praise early in the season after a victory over the New York Yanks: "Let's give a toot to Jack Finlay, Six out of seven of his kickoffs Friday night wound up in the end zone or farther."[17] He was considered the team's best all-around guard that year, despite missing a couple games with a knee ligament problem and started for the team in the title match in Cleveland.

For the 1951 championship season, the 30-year-old Finlay primarily played right defensive tackle sharing the position with rookie starter Jack Halliday, although he filled in at times at left guard on offense. By the title game with the Browns, Jack had ceded his slot on the defense to rookie Charlie Toogood as age took its inevitable toll. Finlay was invited back to training camp by the champion Rams in 1952, but in July, Jack decided to retire, citing lucrative outside interests. He had done graduate work at USC while his career wound down and would transition to the film industry.[18] Like many Rams of the time, Finlay had appeared as an extra in movies like *Battleground,* but his future was behind the scenes.

Although he had some interest in coaching, that never quite worked out. He was up for the head coaching slot at Bakersfield College in 1953, but that position went to Homer Beatty who led the Renegades to a national title in their division.[19] Finlay later coached the semipro Longshoremen's Athletic Club team in Long Beach where he ran a "semi-Clark Shaughnessy offense."[20] His 1957 squad faced the Rams in a preseason tune-up that the NFL squad won handily 56–0. Jack also headed up the Rams' Alumni group at that time.

In Hollywood, Finlay worked as a sound editor and sound effects editor for decades. He worked on such films as *Murphy's Romance*, *Rio Lobo* and *A Man Called Horse* and on many television shows and miniseries, such as *Laverne and Shirley* and *Shogun*. He was thrice nominated for a primetime Emmy, but never won one. Jack Finlay died at the age of 92 on March 6, 2014, in Rancho Mirage, California.

Notes

1. "Scotty Finlay, Noted Trainer, Buried in L.A.," *San Francisco Examiner*, June 26, 1929, 18.
2. "Trainer of Oaks Signs with Chance," *San Francisco Examiner*, November 29, 1922, 29.
3. "Auto Death Suits Lost by Widows," *Los Angeles Times*, February 12, 1931, II-3.
4. Carl Blume, "Fairfax Colonials Lighter and Slower This Year," *Los Angeles Times*, September 30, 1938, II-14.
5. "U.C.L.A. Tackle Undergoes Knife," *San Bernardino County Sun*, October 14, 1940, 9.
6. "Bruin Tackle Returns," *Oakland Tribune*, October 24, 1941, 36.
7. Frank Pericola, "Sports Slants," *Pensacola News Journal*, December 13, 1941, 2.
8. "Finlay Joins Naval Reserve," *Los Angeles Times*, August 20, 1942, I-19.
9. Al Wolf, "Sportraits," *Los Angeles Times*, November 5, 1943, 19.
10. Bob Blake, "'Pleasant Experience'—Stub," *Oakland Tribune*, November 28, 1943, 16.
11. Al Wolf, "Sportraits," *Los Angeles Times*, March 12, 1944, II-6.
12. "Wolves Tackle Packers, Rangers Meet Hornets," *Los Angeles Times*, October 8, 1944, II-6.
13. "Bruin Gridder Released," *San Francisco Examiner*, August 17, 1946, 15.
14. "Los Angeles Team Early Favorites to Win Coast League Grid Crown," *Honolulu Star-Bulletin*, September 14, 1946, 22.
15. Frank Finch, "Scouting the Pros," *Los Angeles Times*, November 24, 1948, IV-2.
16. Frank Finch, "Scouting the Pros," *Los Angeles Times*, December 4, 1949, IV-16.
17. Frank Finch, "'Rams Can Lick 'Em All'—Jumbo Joe," *Los Angeles Times*, September 26, 1950, IV-3.
18. Frank Finch, "Scouting the Pros," *Los Angeles Times*, February 12, 1950, II-14.
19. "Boise Coach Talks Over 'Gade Post," *Fresno Bee*, January 6, 1953, 15.
20. Bob Kelly, "Bob Kelly Says," *Long Beach Independent*, August 6, 1957, 19.

Jack Halliday

JOSHUA MILTON ANDERSON

"Faith, family, football," is a saying for many Americans. For Jack Halliday, it wasn't just a saying, it was a way of life.

Jack Parker Halliday was born on June 2, 1928, in Dallas, Texas, the fourth of five children.[1] His father, Thomas, came from a family of bankers, but he owned and ran a lumber company.[2] Jack's mother, Sidney, was a housewife and focused on raising her children.

Halliday went to Woodrow Wilson High School in Dallas, where he was a fine all-around athlete who lettered in football, baseball, and basketball, participated in track and won marksmanship medals.[3] After graduating high school in 1946, he continued working at the family lumberyard where he had been working since he was a young teenager.[4] His draft card referred to him as ruddy, green-eyed, blonde, 6'2½" and 215 pounds.[5]

Jack's brother Sid had played football for SMU during the 1942 season before joining the United States Marine Corps during the war. After returning from the service Sid resumed attending classes and playing end on the football team. In 1946 it was natural for Jack to choose SMU to further his education as he could join Sid on the football team.[6] At the beginning of Halliday's freshman season he was 10th on the list of tackles but was the only freshman to make the list "of serious candidates" for that position.[7] Early in his college career, he learned an important tactic for reading the opposing linemen. He would look at the linemen's fingers to see their coloration, which would vary depending on the amount of weight applied and type of stance the linemen were in. This helped Halliday predict how the play would unfold.[8]

The 1946 SMU team was average, finishing 4–5–1, but Jack did not play on the varsity his first year. Jack started at left

Jack Halliday played for SMU in its 1949 Cotton Bowl victory over Oregon.

tackle for the "B" team. This second-tier team would practice against other schools in the Southwest Conference and players could be moved up to the varsity if there were injuries.[9]

In 1947, SMU finished 3rd in the final AP Poll with a stellar 9–0–2 record. Sid was the team captain, but Jack spent most of the season playing behind tackles John Hamberger and Joe Ethridge.[10] Hamberger was All-Southwest Conference in 1947 and 1948 and was drafted by the Eagles in the 1947 NFL draft, then by the 49ers in the 1949 AAFC draft. Ethridge was also All-Southwest Conference in 1947 and 1948 and was drafted by the Packers during the 1949 NFL draft and the Dons during the 1949 AAFC draft on the same day—December 21, 1948.[11] In spite of not being a starter, Jack was still able to contribute to SMU's success. He had a fumble recovery in SMU's 21–14 victory over Texas A&M and received notice for his "rugged" play while earning a letter.[12]

SMU went 9–1–1 in 1948 and won the Cotton Bowl, finishing 10th in the country. Jack was moved from left tackle to right guard and started several games.[13] He didn't start SMU's week three game against Missouri, which was SMU's only loss of the season. In week four against Rice, he recovered the opening kickoff when the Owls Sonny Wyatt fumbled.[14] Jack had found his stride, and the following week against Santa Clara, his offensive blocking was being noticed. Jack Gallagher of the *Austin American-Statesman* was particularly impressed by "the way they [Halliday and teammate Neal Franklin] pulled out of the line to lead interference."[15] Halliday started at right guard in SMU's 21–13 Cotton Bowl victory over Oregon.[16]

After the Cotton Bowl win against Oregon at the end of the 1948 season, Halliday was expected to start at the guard position for the 1949 season. However, he also played some defense for the Mustangs. In the first game of the 1949 season, a 13–7 victory over Wake Forest, it was noted that he "stood out."[17] The following week against Missouri, Halliday had a number of defensive stops and blocked an extra point attempt, winning the game for SMU by holding the score at 28 to 27. Halliday's performance led SMU coach Matty Bell to declare, "I never saw a greater defensive game played." The Associated Press agreed and nominated him for Top Lineman of the Week.[18] By the end of the season Jack had earned the respect of the opposition, receiving honors from other teams and coaches in recognition of his outstanding performance. For example, when Arkansas ended its season, it elected Halliday as one of its toughest opponents and Texas did the same.[19]

At the end of the 1949 season, Halliday was invited to play as a starter in the Senior Bowl in Jacksonville, Florida. At the time players were paid to participate in the Senior Bowl using the justification that since the players had completed playing their final season in college, "paying [with] the gate receipts does not violate purity codes in collegiate athletics."[20] However, the Southwest Conference had passed a "rule that boys participating in the Senior Bowl would lose financial benefits at their schools."[21] Halliday received $343 for playing in the game but it cost him $300 for tuition in addition to $65 a month for his room, board, expenses, and laundry for the four months remaining until graduation. When commenting on why the athletes would continue to participate in the game despite the financial penalty, Dr. H.D. Mouson, Southern Methodist's conference faculty committee member, noted, "They all are figuring on signing professional contracts."[22] Despite this loss of funds, Halliday did not have to worry about how to pay to finish school since he was financially well off from his family's lumber business.[23]

Halliday was drafted by the Colts with the 54th pick in the fifth round of the 1950 NFL draft. He didn't play for the Colts. After the 1950 season, the Colts disbanded so

Halliday was free to sign with another team.[24] There were three teams that were interested in Halliday and he chose the Rams as they paid more and he could try out for the team with his SMU buddy, Bobby Collier.[25] A few days before training camp began Halliday signed with the Rams.[26]

Jack generally showed promise in training camp.[27] Rams beat writer Frank Finch described Halliday's performance as "has good use of hands and arms, knows how to play his position. Counted on for defensive duties."[28] He started preseason games at defensive tackle against the Redskins, Eagles, and Cardinals. Unfortunately he had a tough time defending the "NFL's best blocking tackle, Bill Fischer" in the preseason game against the Cardinals, and it cost him the starting position for the preseason game against the Browns.[29] With the Rams leading 23–21 in the final preseason game, Halliday and fellow rookie Joe Reid blocked a short New York Giants field goal attempt to clinch the win.[30] The team signed the ball and Halliday kept it as a prized memento.[31]

Throughout the season, he was listed as the starting defensive right tackle and mentored by head coach Joe Stydahar, whom Halliday loved playing for.[32] Halliday suffered a leg injury in a Week 9 loss to the Washington Redskins, but it was not substantial enough to keep him out of the next game against the Bears.[33] In the championship game he played right tackle along with Charlie Toogood and played well despite having his nose severely damaged.[34]

Halliday greatly enjoyed his 1951 season on the field and had a great time off the field as well, with lots of card playing, gambling, and keeping his playing weight up by "drinking a lot of beer"—or so he told his son, Jim, many years later.[35] In June 1952, however, Halliday was one of 11 players the Rams traded to the Dallas Texans for the rights to Les Richter.[36] Unfortunately, a few days before the beginning of the 1952 season, Halliday was part of a group of nine cut by the Texans.[37]

Halliday had grown up in the Dallas area and stayed in the region after being cut from the team. The girlfriend of Dick Hightower, a friend and former SMU teammate of Halliday's, set him up on a date with Cynthia Jane Bailey.[38] They married on April 2, 1954, and had their first child, James, in 1957 while still living in the Dallas area (a newborn daughter was tragically lost in 1959).[39] While in the Dallas area, Halliday worked in management of numerous Goodyear Service Stores but grew tired of that job after having to move four times in five years.[40]

Halliday and his family moved to Gulfport, Mississippi, in 1959, and for 30 years he worked for Mississippi Power Company, where he managed retail stores in the southern third of Mississippi.[41] Change in location did not change the importance that faith and family had in Halliday's life. At the beginning of their time in Mississippi, the Hallidays had two more children and this no doubt led to Jack's involvement with the Boy Scouts of America as a troop leader.[42] Halliday also remained active with his church, now the First Presbyterian Church of Gulfport, where he served as an elder and business manager.[43] Football was less of a focus for the aging Halliday, but in 1991, he made sure to attend the two-day festivities that celebrated the 40th anniversary of the 1951 Rams.[44]

During the second half of the 1990s, the Hallidays lived in a house overlooking the Gulf Coast, undoubtedly the perfect location for a couple active in the Gulfport Yacht Club; Halliday served as a commodore of the club, the perfect position for a friendly, outgoing retiree.[45] Halliday passed away from cancer on May 23, 2000, and rests in peace next to his beloved wife, Cynthia, in Floral Hills Memorial Gardens in Gulfport, Mississippi.[46]

Notes

1. 1930 United States Federal Census, *Ancestry.com*, https://www.ancestry.com/interactive/6224/4548203_00317/64697890?backurl=https://www.ancestry.com/family-tree/person/tree/72849830/person/122006139611/facts/citation/542008183552/edit/record; 1940 United States Federal Census, Ancestry.com, https://www.ancestry.com.

2. 1930 United States Federal Census; Thomas Wyatt Halliday, Jr., *Findagrave.com*, www.findagrave.com/memorial/38894949; "Tom Halliday's Rites in Dallas," *Longview News Journal,* February 17, 1963, 18.

3. Woodrow Wilson High School, Dallas, Texas, 1946 *Crusader* (yearbook), https://www.ancestry.com/interactive/1265/sid_2002_1946_0053/441229024?backurl=https://www.ancestry.com/family-tree/person/tree/72849830/person/122006139611/facts/citation/542008180553/edit/record.

4. Interview with John Halliday, May 28, 2020.

5. U.S. WWII Draft Cards Young Men, *Ancestry.com*, https://www.ancestry.com.

6. Interview with James Halliday, May 12, 2020; Interview with John Halliday, May 28, 2020. He went to a Presbyterian church later in life.

7. "1946 SMU Football Roster," *Austin American-Statesman*, September 15, 1946, 19.

8. Interview with James Halliday, May 12, 2020.

9. Jack Halliday, *Profootballarchives.com*, https://www.profootballarchives.com/playerh/hall06200.html; "SMU Squad Leaves for Fayetteville And Arkansas Tilt," Austin American-Statesman, November 15, 1946, 16.

10. Jinx Tucker, "Grid Chatter," *Waco News-Tribune*, September 17, 1947, 10, https://www.newspapers.com/image/48035647/?terms=Halliday%2BEthridge.

11. "All-Star Teams," *St. Louis Post-Dispatch*, November 29, 1947, 7A; John Hamberger, *Profootballarchives.com*, https://www.profootballarchives.com/playerh/hamb00250.html; Joe Ethridge, *Profootballarchives.com*, https://www.profootballarchives.com/playere/ethr00200.html.

12. Saul Feldman, "Early Scores Give SMU 21–14 Win Over Aggies," *Odessa American*, October 12, 1947, 6; "Brother Act (photo)," *Los Angeles Times*, October 24, 1947, II-7.

13. "Doak Walker in Eastern Grid Debut," *Pittsburgh Sun-Telegraph*, September 25, 1948, 10; "Raiders Ready for Clash with SMU Today—Techsans Will Face Smooth Working Passing Machine," *Lubbock Morning Avalanche*, October 2, 1948, 8.

14. "Mizzou, S.M.U. Tied, 7–7, in Third Period," *St. Louis Star and Times*, October 9, 1948, 13; "SMU Guns Rice 33–7," *Valley Morning Star* (Harlingen, TX), October 17, 1948, 11.

15. Jack Gallagher, "Sideline Slants," *Austin American-Statesman*, October 25, 1948, 13.

16. Harold V. Raliff, "69,000 to Watch Cotton Bowl Tilt," *Austin American-Statesman*, December 31, 1948, 2.

17. Harold V. Raliff, "'49 SWC Grid May Beat '48," *Austin American-Statesman*, January 6, 1949, 16; "Replacements Confront Bell—Gil Johnson Seen Big Loss to Team," *Longview News Journal*, September 21, 1949, 7; Ed Fite, "SMU's Second Half Spurt Downs Wake Forest 13–7—Doak Passes Mustangs to Narrow Win," *Valley Morning Star* (Harlingen, TX), September 25, 1949, 12.

18. "Art Weiner Selected Top Lineman," *El Paso Times*, October 6, 1949, 18.

19. "Arkansas Selects All-Opponent Southwest Conference Eleven," *Lubbock Avalanche-Journal*, November 20, 1949, 15; "Longhorns Pick All-Opponent Football Team," *Pampa Daily News*, November 30, 1949, 6.

20. "Eight SWC Grid Stars Playing in Senior Bowl," *Baytown Sun*, January 7, 1950, 8.

21. "Life Is Hard on Walker—He's Pro with No Pro Bid," *Galveston Daily News*, January 10, 1950, 9.

22. "Senior Bowl Costs Players of Southwest: SMU's Jack Halliday Goes $207 in Hole by Losing School Aid," *Arizona Republic*, January 9, 1950, 8.

23. "Life Is Hard on Walker—He's Pro with No Pro Bid," 9.

24. Bob Carroll, ed., *Total Football: The Official Encyclopedia of the National Football League* (New York: HarperCollins, 1997), 1492.

25. Interview with James Halliday, May 12, 2020; Interview with John Halliday, May 28, 2020.

26. "Rams Complete Training Roster," *Wilmington Daily Press Journal*, July 14, 1951, 8.

27. Frank Finch, "Veterans Two Deep: Sixty Players Go After Thirty-Three Ram Jobs" *Los Angeles Times*, July 16, 1951, IV-3; "Vets, Rookies Clash Today in Ram Scrimmage," *Los Angeles Times*, July 28, 1951, III-3.

28. Frank Finch, "Veterans Vanish: Rams Must Depend on Rookie Tackles," *Los Angeles Times*, July 26, 1951, IV-3.

29. Frank Finch, "Necessary Changes: Stydahar Plugs Holes in Rams' Line-up for Battle with Browns," *Los Angeles Times*, September 13, 1951, I-33; Finch, Frank, "Rookie Linemen Likely Starters Against 'Skins," *Los Angeles Times*, August 13, 1951, IV-1, 2.

30. Finch, Frank, "Rams Win Thriller from Giants, 23–21," *Los Angeles Times*, September 21, 1951, IV-1, 2.

31. Interview with James Halliday, May 12, 2020. The Halliday family still has the ball, one of the few keepsakes recovered after the family home was destroyed by Hurricane Camille in 1969.

32. Interview with James Halliday, May 12, 2020.

33. Frank Finch, "Redskins Blast Rams by 31–21," *Los Angeles Times*, November 26, 1951, IV-1, 2; Frank

Finch, "Sellout Looms—Rams Below Peak, Physically, for Important Bear Tilt Sunday," *Los Angeles Times*, November 29, 1951, I-29.

    34. "Browns Realize 'Fears,' Drop Pro Football Title to Rams," *Minneapolis Star*, December 24, 1951, 10; Interview with James Halliday, May 12, 2020.

    35. Interview with James Halliday, May 12, 2020.

    36. "L.A. Gives Dallas Eleven Players for Les Richter," *Odessa American*, June 13, 1952, 6.

    37. "Nine Grid Players Are Released by Dallas Grid Team," *Mexia Daily News*, September 24, 1952, 6.

    38. Interview with John Halliday, May 28, 2020.

    39. Jack Parker Halliday, *Ancestry.com*, https://www.ancestry.com/family-tree/person/tree/72849830/person/122006139611/facts.

    40. 1958 Ft. Worth, TX, City Directory, 458; Texas, Death Certificates, 1903–1982, for Jack Parker Halliday, *Ancestry.com*, https://www.ancestry.com; interview with James Halliday, May 12, 2020.

    41. Interview with James Halliday, May 12, 2020.

    42. "Jack Parker Halliday," *Findagrave.com*, www.findagrave.com/memorial/99746862.

    43. "Jack Parker Halliday"; Interview with James Halliday, May 12, 2020.

    44. Fernando Dominguez, "51 Rams Celebrate Their Title Season," *Los Angeles Times*, August 17, 1991, C1.

    45. City and Telephone Directory, *Archives.com*, https://www.archives.com; "Jack Parker Halliday"; Interview with James Halliday, May 12, 2020.

    46. "Jack Parker Halliday"; interview with James Halliday, May 12, 2020.

Norb Hecker

Greg D. Tranter

Norb Hecker was selected with the 10th pick in the sixth round of the 1951 NFL draft by The Los Angeles Rams. He was the 72nd overall pick in the draft held on January 18–19, 1951, at the Blackstone Hotel in Chicago. He was excited to be drafted into the NFL and to be going to a contending team like the Rams.

Playing as a rookie in the NFL championship game for the Rams on December 23, 1951, at the Los Angeles Memorial Coliseum, was a thrill for Hecker. Making the most pivotal play of the game, the highlight of his football career, to secure the Rams' first ever championship in Los Angeles, was beyond his fondest dreams.

With the Rams holding on to a precarious 24–17 lead, Cleveland quarterback Otto Graham moved the Browns to the Rams' 42-yard line facing a fourth down and one for a pivotal first down, with a little over two minutes remaining in the game. On the crucial fourth-down play, Graham pitched the ball to Dub Jones in the left flat—who earlier in the game had scored a key Browns touchdown—"Hecker came in like a shot and speared the Dubber for a 2-yard loss."[1] Hecker's play saved the day for the Rams, allowing them to almost completely run out the clock and secure the championship.

Norb Hecker later became the Atlanta Falcons' first head coach.

Norb Hecker was born in Berea, Ohio, on May 26, 1927, and grew up in Olmsted Falls, Ohio, a 19-mile drive to Cleveland. It is ironic that he made the crucial play to secure the championship game defeat of his hometown team.

Hecker served in Germany in World War II before matriculating at nearby Baldwin-Wallace College. He played four varsity sports while at the college, lettering in all four: baseball, basketball, football and track. He played at wide receiver in his senior year, catching 34 passes for 614 yards, helping the Yellow Jackets to a 5-2-1 record. He was named to the Little All-America team in football following the 1950 season. In 1966, Hecker was inducted into the school's athletics hall of fame.

During his rookie year with the Rams in 1951, Hecker played on both sides of the ball at safety and wide receiver, starting and playing in 10 games. He had three interceptions from his safety position, returning them for 74 yards. He also caught four passes for 35 yards. He scored his first career touchdown on a 20-yard pass from Bob Waterfield versus Detroit on October 14 in the team's 27–21 victory.

Following his rookie season in 1951, he played two more years with the Rams, helping the team tie for the National Conference championship with Detroit in 1952, only to lose in the playoff game to the Lions, 31–21. He co-led the team in interceptions with Woodley Lewis with seven in 1953, but the Rams finished third in their conference.

Hecker was traded to the Washington Redskins at the conclusion of the 1953 season. However, he decided to sign a contract with the CFL's Toronto Argonauts. He played pretty much everywhere for the 1954 Argonauts. He started at wide receiver, snatching 44 passes for 652 yards and scoring two touchdowns, and played defensive back grabbing one interception. He also was the team's primary placekicker booting 31 extra points in 33 tries, making two of three field goal attempts and securing one single. He led the 6–8 Argos in scoring with 48 points. He was released following the season and came back to the Redskins where he played for three more years from 1955 to 1957.

Hecker led the Redskins in interceptions in each of his three years with the team, snaring six, eight and three (shared with Don Shula who also had three), respectively, returning them for 52, 26 and 39 yards. In his first year with the team he played wide receiver and was the back-up placekicker in addition to playing safety. He scored a receiving touchdown and kicked two extra points. In 1956, he had a fumble return for a touchdown for his final professional touchdown. In his final two years with the club he was relegated to only playing safety, though he started 18 games.

Hecker—along with 11 other players—helped found the National Football League Players Association in 1956 and briefly was the Redskins' player representative.

Hecker was released by the Redskins near the end of training camp in 1958 as he struggled with knee problems. He joined on with the Hamilton Tiger-Cats of the CFL to give it one more try and to also begin his coaching career, becoming a player-coach. He played two games for the Tiger-Cats, catching one pass for nine yards and kicking five extra points. At the conclusion of the Tiger-Cats' season he retired as a player.

He began is full-fledged coaching career in 1959, joining the staff of new Green Bay Packers head coach Vince Lombardi on February 23, 1959. He served as an assistant to Lombardi for seven seasons, winning three NFL championships. With the Packers' incredible success aiding him, Atlanta Falcons owner Rankin Smith, Sr., hired the 38-year-old Hecker to become the Falcons' first head coach in franchise history.

He was named head coach on January 26, 1966. "The selection of the 38-year-old Hecker was a complete surprise to most"[2] was the way the media viewed the hire. However, team owner Rankin Smith, Sr., said, "We feel he will bring us a winner"[3] and he acknowledged that Vince Lombardi's recommendation had a lot to do with the decision.

The Falcons lost their first nine games in 1966, not securing their first victory in franchise history until November 20—with a 27–16 decision over the New York Giants. Their first home victory came on December 11, a 16–10 win over the St. Louis Cardinals. The team finished their inaugural campaign 3–11, tying the NFL record for most wins by an expansion team.

In Hecker's second season the team struggled to a 1–12–1 finish with their lone victory a 21–20 decision over the Minnesota Vikings in week seven. The Falcons started the

1968 season 0–3 and Falcons owner Rankin Smith, Sr., had seen enough, firing Hecker and replacing him with his former teammate—the fiery Norm Van Brocklin. Smith noted, "I have felt for some time that the club was not making the kind of progress I had anticipated in order for it to become competitive in the National Football League."[4] "Norb is a fine man...."[5] Hecker's head coaching record with the Falcons was a dismal 4–26–1.

Hecker joined the New York Giants' coaching staff in 1969 as defensive coordinator, serving in that capacity through the 1971 season. He left the NFL after being fired by the Giants and joined the coaching staff at Stanford University. During his first five years at Stanford he was a defensive assistant on Jack Christiansen's staff. Bill Walsh became Stanford head coach in 1977 and kept Hecker on his staff

When Walsh left Stanford to become head coach of the San Francisco 49ers in 1979 he brought Hecker along as an assistant defensive coach. Hecker served on Walsh's coaching staff through 1986 coaching linebackers and defensive backs and winning two Super Bowl rings. He moved into the 49ers' front office serving the franchise for five more years, adding another two Super Bowl rings and retiring in 1991.

Hecker spent most of his retirement years in Palm Desert, California. He gave football one last fling in 1995 as a coach/administrator with the Amsterdam Admirals of the World League of America Football. It lasted only a single season and he went back to retirement.

Hecker was part of eight NFL championships, one as a player with the Rams, three as an assistant coach for the Packers under Lombardi and four as an assistant/administrator in San Francisco. Not many NFL players/coaches can say they have been a part of eight NFL championships.

However, in retirement, when reflecting on his career, he called his seven seasons at Stanford the highlight. "He wanted to coach at the college level and mold some of the youngsters who were learning football," Mr. Hecker's son Jeffrey said. "Doing that at Stanford was a pinnacle career move for him, he felt."[6]

He married Barbara Anne Ritchie on May 4, 1952. They were married for 46 years before her death in 1998. They had five children: Doug, Jeffrey, Janie, Karen and Cheryl. Hecker died of cancer March 14, 2004, at his son's Los Altos home. He was 76.

Bill Walsh said about Hecker after his death, "He was a charismatic man, an astute judge of talent and an excellent teacher."[7]

Notes

1. Frank Finch, "Rams Whip Browns 24–17, Win Pro Title," *Los Angeles Times*, December 24, 1951, IV-2.
2. Jan Van Duser, "Packers Hecker to Coach Falcons," *Atlanta Constitution*, January 27, 1966, 1.
3. Van Duser, "Packers Hecker," 1.
4. Al Thomer, "I'm Glad It's Over—Hecker," *Atlanta Constitution*, October 2, 1968, 33.
5. Thomer, "I'm Glad It's Over," 33.
6. Simone Sebastian, "Norbert Hecker—Football Player, 49ers, Stanford Soach," *SFGate.com*, March 25, 2004, https://www.sfgate.com/bayarea/article/Norbert-Hecker/-football-49ers/-2776005.php.
7. "Norb Hecker, 76; Coached 49ers, Falcons," *Boston.com News*, March 19, 2004, http://archive.boston.com/news/globe/obituaries/articles/2004/03/19/norb_hecker_76_coached_49ers_falcons/.

Elroy Hirsch

Rick Schabowski

Elroy Hirsch was a multi-talented person. He was not only an outstanding football player, being inducted into both the Pro Football Hall of Fame in 1967 and the College Football Hall of Fame in 1974, but also an actor and a successful sports executive.

On June 17, 1923, Elroy Leon Hirsch was born in Wausau, Wisconsin. At an early age he was adopted by his foster parents, Otto Peter and Mayme Sabena (Magnuson) Hirsch. Otto worked for 45 years at the Wausau Iron Works.

The family lived two miles away from the school that Elroy attended, and he always ran to school. He found that he was great at catching footballs. He would go to a park near his house, run fast toward a tree, and dodge away from it at the last minute, which improved his route-running ability. Hirsch was 5'10" and weighed only 122 pounds in his sophomore season at Wausau High School. He averaged around four minutes of playing time that season, but things would change dramatically the following year.

As a junior, Hirsch gained 40 pounds, saw extensive playing time, and his coach, Win Brockmeyer, became a lifelong friend. He noted Brockmeyer's impact on his life years later. "Win was the single most important influence on my football career. He taught me early that football was an 11-man game. He taught me other things too, trust, the importance of cooperation, courtesy, and honesty."[1] The Hirschs named their son Win when Elroy became a father in 1949.

Another big event occurred while he was attending Wausau High School—he met his future wife. Ruth Stahmer happened to be the pretty daughter of a Methodist minister, who met Hirsch at a church party. Ruth commented, "He didn't know then, as king of the prom, he selected me to be his queen, I had selected him long before that."[2]

Elroy Hirsch, nicknamed "Crazylegs," was the NFL's leading receiver in 1951.

196   Part 3: The Team

Wausau's football team compiled a fantastic 1940 season, going undefeated while outscoring opponents 299–12. Hirsch served as the team captain and led the Wisconsin Valley Conference in scoring with 102 points.

Several universities recruited Hirsch after he graduated from high school, including Minnesota, Tulane, Notre Dame, and Wisconsin. Coach Brockmeyer was a Minnesota alumnus and would have liked to have Hirsch attend his alma mater, but Wisconsin won the right to Hirsch's services thanks to the efforts of *Wisconsin State Journal* columnist Joseph "Roundy" Coughlin.

Coughlin went with Hirsch to Madison, showed him around town, and took him out to eat. It didn't hurt matters that Hirsch would be close to his sweetheart, Ruth.

Wisconsin fans were excited about Hirsch, Coughlin informing them that "a lot of people asked me what kind of football player this new man Wisconsin has got this year Elroy Hirsch in the backfield will be. Don't ask me. All my advice is buy a ticket, and hold on to your seat. This baby can really step he would look good on a crutch [*sic*]."[3]

Freshmen were ineligible for varsity sports, so Wisconsin fans had to wait until the 1942 season. It was worth it, Hirsch produced a superb season, rushing for 767 yards on 141 carries, completing 18 passes for 226 yards, intercepting six passes, and returning 15 punts for 182 yards. He earned selection as a first-team halfback to the AP 1942 All-Big Ten Conference team. One of the highlights of the season was defeating top-ranked ranked Ohio State, 17–7, on Halloween. Hirsch threw a touchdown pass and accounted for over 200 total yards. The Badgers posted an 8-1-1 record, losing a controversial game at Iowa and tying Notre Dame. Wisconsin ranked third in the final AP poll.

Another highlight of the season was picking up his nickname, "Crazylegs." During a game against Great Lakes Naval Academy at Soldier Field on October 17, 1942, *Chicago Daily News* sports reporter Francis Porter wrote about Hirsch's 61-yard touchdown run. "Hirsch ran like a demented duck. His crazy legs were gyrating in six different directions at the same time."[4]

Unfortunately, because of World War II, Hirsch only played one season at Wisconsin. He enrolled in the Marine Corps V-12 unit, and as a result, was transferred to the University of Michigan. He made the most of the opportunity, lettering in football, basketball, baseball, and track during the 1943–1944 academic year, the only athlete in Michigan history to accomplish this feat.

The Wolverines had a great season in 1943, winning the Big Ten title, finishing the regular season ranked third in the nation, with their only loss to the eventual national champion, Notre Dame. Hirsch, along with nine other players, four of them starters who came over in the transfer from Wisconsin, played a major role in Michigan's success. These players were referred to as the "Lend-Lease Badgers."[5]

Another event stands out in Hirsch's collegiate career. On Saturday, May 13, 1944, Hirsch won the broad jump event with a 24-foot, 2¼-inch jump at a track meet in Ann Arbor. After competing in the track meet, he then traveled to Columbus, Ohio, and pitched a one-hit, 5–0 shutout over Ohio State.

Hirsch later made a confession about why he played one of the sports. "The only reason I went out for the baseball team was so I could make the spring trip back to Madison to see Ruth."[6]

After his stint at Michigan, Hirsch was transferred to Parris Island, South Carolina, for boot camp. He then reported to Camp Lejeune, North Carolina, for pre-officer training, and he completed his officer training at Quantico, Virginia. In May of 1945, Hirsch was commissioned as an officer, and he was honorably discharged as a Second Lieutenant in May of 1946.

Football played a role in Hirsch's stint with the Marines. While stationed at a Marine Base Air Station in El Toro, California, he played for the El Toro Marines, one of the top service football teams. Hirsch scored four touchdowns for the Marines against the Pacific Coast Professional Football League's Los Angeles Bulldogs.

Hirsch's amateur days ended at the College All-Star Game in front of 97,380 fans at Soldier Field in Chicago on August 21, 1946. He left his college days behind with a splash by scoring two touchdowns against his future team, the Los Angeles Rams in a 16–0 upset victory. His efforts landed him the game's Outstanding Player award.

Hirsch considered this the highlight of his athletic career. He recalled, "As they introduced each starter, they played the school song. I can still feel the chills up and down my spine as they called out my name and *On Wisconsin* started to play. It was a great, great moment."[7]

The Cleveland Rams had selected Hirsch in the first round (fifth overall) of the NFL draft on April 8, 1945. He was still in the military and turned down the Rams intending to return to Wisconsin to finish his education. The All-America Football Conference's Chicago Rockets were also interested in Hirsch. Furthermore, football was not the only sport seeking Hirsch's services. The Chicago Cubs also wanted him to pitch for their AA San Antonio Missions team. Hirsch signed with the Rockets because of his friendship with their coach, Dick Hanley, who had coached him at El Toro. The Rockets gave Hirsch $1,000 for signing and a contract for $6,000. Hirsch needed the money because he was now a husband. He and Ruth were married on June 27, 1946.

Hirsch had a solid 1946 season, despite the Rockets posting a mediocre 5–6–3 record. He compiled 1,289 all-purpose yards in 14 games, including 384 yards and a touchdown on kick returns, 347 receiving yards with three touchdowns, 235 yards and a touchdown on punt returns, 226 rushing yards with a touchdown, 156 yards passing with a touchdown, and 97 return yards on the six interceptions he pilfered. He also passed for 156 yards and a touchdown.

Things didn't go well for the Rockets or Hirsch in 1947. The Rockets finished with a 1–13 record, and Hirsch only appeared in five games due to various injuries. Hirsch did have one highlight—he set an AAFC record for the longest touchdown reception, a 76-yard touchdown reception from quarterback Sam Vacanti against the Buffalo Bills on September 19, 1947.

The Rockets duplicated their 1–13 performance in 1948, but things were worse for Hirsch. During a September 26 game against the Browns, he was kicked in the right side of his head and suffered a skull fracture. Hirsch's season was over, and Michael Reese Hospital in Chicago was his home for the next month.

Hirsch's long hospital stay was not pleasant. "On my back in the hospital day after day, I figured I was through as a player."[8] It was a difficult time for his wife Ruth. She commented that "it was terrible for him to see his career blowing up at age 23, but I wanted him to quit. I didn't want any more injuries. I wanted him to get on with his life anywhere but on the football field."[9]

The injury had also affected his coordination. Hirsch recalled his attempts at rehabilitation. "The first time I tried to exercise in the gym was another convincer. I tossed a basketball with another fellow but couldn't get my hands up to prevent it from hitting me in the face. I simply had no muscular reaction at all."[10] He was suffering headaches, but he was determined to continue his efforts to return to the playing field.

Realizing that his career could be over, and expecting a child, the family invested their life savings in a food brokerage firm located in Milwaukee to help achieve financial stability.

It took some time, but he was pronounced ready to resume his football career after regaining his coordination and other physical skills after three months of rehabilitation.

In June 1949, Hirsch claimed that the Hornets (the Rockets' nickname was changed to the Hornets) had breached their contract with him by not paying him a scheduled bonus payment. He wanted a release from his contract and wanted to play for his home state Green Bay Packers. There was one problem—the Rams still held Hirsch's rights due to the 1945 NFL draft. The issue was resolved when Hirsch signed a contract with the Rams in July. He was elated with the contract offer. "If that hadn't happened, I would have quit football, but I sure hated being small peanuts in the brokerage business."[11]

Hirsch knew the Rams were good, and he was concerned about even making the team, but he did. Coach Clark Shaughnessy played Hirsch primarily as a running back but also as a receiver. He produced immediate results in the Rams' opener against the Detroit Lions on September 23, 1949. Hirsch scored two touchdowns, one rushing and the other on a 19-yard touchdown pass from Norm Van Brocklin in a 27–24 win. Hirsch finished the season with 22 catches for 326 yards and four touchdowns, 287 rushing yards with one touchdown, and 2 interceptions for 55 return yards.

During the course of the 1949 season, Hirsch suffered a minor head injury, and coach Shaughnessy had an idea to help his young star. He helped design a helmet molded from an extra-strong light plastic that was being utilized in the construction of fuel tanks for fighter planes. Hirsch loved the helmet. "It was great. Extra padding around my right ear where the injury had been, weighed only 11 ounces—about a third as much as the leather one. It made me feel a whole lot safer right away."[12] Hirsch was one of the first NFL players to wear that type of helmet.

The Rams hired a new coach for the 1950 season, Joe Stydahar. He streamlined the a three-end offense and switched Hirsch from halfback to end. Stydahar's decision to revamp the offense was a huge success. Though the Rams lost the 1950 NFL championship game to the Browns, Hirsch developed into a premier receiver during the season, catching 42 passes for 687 yards and seven touchdowns.

The Rams had one clear mission in 1951—win the NFL championship. The season did not start well for Hirsch. In an exhibition game against the Chicago Cardinals on September 8, he suffered a broken left cheek bone in the third quarter. A hole had to be drilled through his cheek into the depressed bone. A screw was then inserted, and the bone was pulled back into place in a manner similar to using a corkscrew to pull a cork from a bottle. Rams trainer Dee Jay Archer estimated that it would take five to six weeks for a complete recovery.

The opening game was against the New York Yanks on September 28 and miraculously Hirsch was ready to play. They Rams won, 54–14. Van Brocklin passed for an NFL record 554 yards, with 173 of those yards and four touchdown receptions belonging to Hirsch.

Hirsch produced the best season of his career in 1951. He led the NFL in scoring (102 points), pass receptions (66), receiving yards (then an NFL record 1,495 yards), yards per reception (22.7) and receiving touchdowns (17—tying Don Hutson's record). He played in the Pro Bowl and was voted First Team All-Pro. In addition to all of these accomplishments on the playing field, Hirsch earned his bachelor's degree from Baldwin-Wallace College in Ohio.

One of the many big receptions by Hirsch took place against the San Francisco 49ers on November 4. The Rams trailed 16–13 with eight minutes and 30 seconds remaining, Bob Waterfield connected with Hirsch on a 76-yard touchdown pass, giving the Rams the lead. Coach Joe Stydahar said it was one of the best catches he ever saw, but Hirsch was very humble about it. "As far as I'm concerned it was just a routine catch. I ran fast, looked up over my shoulder, stuck up my hands, and Waterfield laid the ball right in place. They tell me there were a couple of 49ers around me, but I didn't see them."[13] Hirsch also had a three-touchdown game against the Green Bay Packers in a 42–14 victory on December 16. The Rams captured the 1951 NFL title, with a 24–17 victory over the Cleveland Browns on December 23.

Hirsch's personal success continued in both 1952 and 1953. He led the NFL with 23.6 yards per reception in 1952. One year later, Hirsch finished third in receptions with 61. He played in the Pro Bowl both seasons and was named first team All-Pro in 1953 by the AP.

Film producer Hall Bartlett was so impressed with Hirsch's rise to stardom that he produced a film about it titled *Crazylegs: All-American*, in which Hirsch played himself. To help meet production costs, Hirsch mortgaged a farm property he owned in Illinois. The film, which had its premiere in Wausau, Wisconsin, on November 15, 1953, was a big hit, and Hirsch became Bartlett's partner. (A review in *Time* said that he "looks like a dark-haired Kirk Douglas and meets every cinema crisis with the wooden impassivity of Alan Ladd.")[14]

Bob Hope was very impressed with Hirsch's acting. "He has warmth, earnestness and a typical All-American quality which he doesn't spoil with his acting tricks, because he doesn't know any. He has virility that's real."[15]

Hirsch acted in two other movies. In the 1955 film *Unchained*, he portrayed a man incarcerated in a minimum-security prison who was torn between serving his sentence and trying to escape. In *Zero Hour!* he played a pilot of an in-flight commercial airliner whose crew and passengers, and he himself, began to experience symptoms of food poisoning. *Zero Hour!* was the basis for the 1980 comedy film *Airplane!*

Hirsch retired in grand fashion at the conclusion of the 1954 season. He tore his uniform into pieces, which he threw to the fans. The Rams also gave him a pastel-tinted Oldsmobile. When training camp opened for the 1955 season, injuries had depleted the Rams' roster, and Hirsch was talked into coming back.

At the conclusion of the 1957 season, Hirsch retired for good. He finished his career with 387 receptions for 7,029 yards and 60 receiving touchdowns. Those accomplishments resulted in his inclusion on the Pro Football Hall of Fame's 1950s All-Decade Team and the NFL's 50th and 100th Anniversary All-Time Teams. Hirsch was enshrined in the Hall of Fame in 1968.

In 1974, Hirsch recalled the thrill of playing pro football. "We made only $10,000 or $12,000 a year, and we didn't have agents or lawyers, and we didn't drive fancy cars or own fancy homes," he said, "[but] we had fun and we looked forward to a game every Sunday."[16]

A former teammate of Hirsch in 1953–54, Harland Svare, who later served as head coach of the Rams, spoke highly of Hirsch. "Crazy Legs was not only a great Hall of Fame receiver, but also a Hall of Fame teammate. He was already Crazy Legs when he got here, but his style of catching passes was so unique. He used to swing underneath the pass and take it in over his head. It made it very difficult for anyone to defend him."[17]

Michael MacCambridge, author of *America's Game*, elaborated on Hirsch's special abilities on an NFL Films segment. "We talk today about yards after the catch, but he would get acres of yards after the catch because he was so elusive in the open field. When the ball was up in the air, he looked like Willie Mays in center field. He could adjust and wind up catching the ball over his shoulder in stride about as well as anyone. If you take a look at the offensive stats in pro football then, he was not just the best in the league, he was head and shoulders above his competitors."[18]

Hirsch later accepted a position with the Union Oil Company and served as a director of sports and special events. He helped produce a weekly, half-hour television show, *76 Sports Club*, and traveled, setting up sports clinics and speaking to local groups.

Hirsch returned to football in March 1960 when he became the general manager of the Rams. He signed a three-year contract to replace Pete Rozelle, who was hired as the NFL's commissioner. The Rams began rebuilding under Hirsch, with draft choices including Roman Gabriel, Deacon Jones, and Merlin Olsen. Hirsch later served as assistant to Rams president Dan Reeves.

In February of 1969, the University of Wisconsin–Madison needed a new athletic director. Hirsch was a leading candidate and accepted the job after talking with his family and Dan Reeves.

It would be a difficult assignment. Wisconsin hadn't recorded a winning season in football since 1963 and had a two-year, 20-game winless streak. When he arrived, Wisconsin football game attendance averaged 43,000. With hard work and fundraising, the team became competitive, and four years later it was averaging more than 70,000 per game.

In December 1986, Hirsch announced he was stepping away from his beloved university effective July 1, 1987. He had been a big factor in Wisconsin's resurgence.

Pat Richter, a two-time All-American end at Wisconsin who also served as athletic director, spoke highly of Hirsch. "There has never been a more loved and admired ambassador for Wisconsin sports than Elroy Hirsch. His charismatic and charming personality brought smiles to many Badger fans."[19]

In addition to the Pro Football Hall of Fame, Hirsch is in the College Football Hall of Fame, the Wisconsin Athletic Hall of Fame, and the University of Michigan Hall of Fame. The #40 he wore as a football player while attending Wisconsin is a retired number.

Hirsch passed away from natural causes on January 28, 2004, at an assisted-living facility in Madison. He was 80.

Notes

1. Jack Pearson, "Elroy Hirsch: The Man. The Athlete. The Legend," *Exclusively Yours*, December 1986, 50.
2. Ronnie Deane, *Crazylegs: A Man and His Career* (Madison, WI: Montzingo & Gustin Advertising, 1987), 6.
3. Deane, *Crazylegs*, 7.
4. Bill Hart, "Elroy Hirsch," *Marathoncountyhistory.org*, www.marathoncounty/history.org/PeopleDetails.php?PeopleId=360.
5. Terry Frei, *Third Down and a War to Go* (Madison: Wisconsin Historical Society Press, 2005), 141–142.
6. Pearson, "Elroy Hirsch," 50.
7. Pearson, "Elroy Hirsch," 52.
8. Edward Prell, "Hirsch, Who Took Beating as Rocket, Finds It's Fun to Ramble with Rams," *The Sporting News*, December 12, 1951, 2–5.
9. Deane, *Crazylegs*, 21.
10. Prell, "Hirsch," 2–5.
11. Deane, *Crazylegs*, 22.

12. Deane, *Crazylegs*, 25.
13. Cal Whorton, "Climax Catch Just Routine, Says Elroy," *Los Angeles Times*, November 5, 1951, IV-1.
14. Mark Bechtel, "Gams and the Man," *Sports Illustrated*, February 9, 2004, 24.
15. Gregg Hoffmann, *Immortalized in Bronze* (Milwaukee: M&T Communications, Milwaukee Brewers, Milwaukee Journal Co., 2010), 81
16. Bechtel, "Gams," 24.
17. Shay Olick, "Elroy 'Crazy Legs' Hirsch, 80; Football Hall of Famer Was an L.A. Rams Star," *Los Angeles Times*, January 29, 2004, B12.
18. *#87: Elroy "Crazy Legs" Hirsch: The Top 100 NFL's Greatest Players* (NFL Films, 2010).
19. Olick, "Elroy 'Crazy Legs' Hirsch," B12.

Dick Hoerner

Greg D. Tranter

Fullback Dick Hoerner, a 6-foot-4-inch, 220-pound "speedster and a murderous linebacker,"[1] played for the Los Angeles Rams from 1947 through 1951 and was the Rams' all-time leading rusher when he left the team in 1952.

Lester Junior "Dick" Hoerner was born on July 25, 1922, in Dubuque, Iowa. He attended Dubuque High School, winning letters in football, basketball and track. He led the Dubuque football team to the Mississippi Valley Conference High School championships in 1939 and 1940, simultaneously being honored as an All-State football player in both years. Hoerner was also an accomplished track star, winning several meets in the shot put, javelin, discus and hurdles. He was the state shot put champion in 1941 and also gained high point honors in the state track meet.

He matriculated at the University of Iowa in the fall of 1941. Hoerner played football as a sophomore in 1942 for the Hawkeyes, helping lead the team to a 6–4 record. He had an 88-yard kick-off return for a touchdown at Michigan in their 28–14 loss to the ninth-ranked Wolverines. For the season he gained 266 yards on 69 carries and scored 30 points.

On May 16, 1943, Hoerner was inducted into the U.S. Army at Camp Dodge, Iowa, interrupting his college football career. He served in the U.S. military for three years in France, Germany and Austria as a corporal during World War II.

Throughout his World War II service he also played football for the 71st Division Red Circlers. "On Thanksgiving Day 1945, the Red Circlers won the European championship."[2]

Hoerner was discharged from the Army in March 1946 and returned to the University of Iowa in the fall of that year.

Dick Hoerner led Iowa to a 5–4 record and a fourth-place finish in the Big Nine highlighted by victories over 15th-ranked Wisconsin 21–7 and 18th-ranked Indiana 13–0. Hoerner, the battering ram fullback, rushed for 335 yards on 72 carries scoring three touchdowns for the season. At the conclusion of the 1946 season, the national champion Notre Dame Fighting Irish named their most respected backfield. They named three players from second-ranked Army (Doc Blanchard, Glenn Davis and Arnold Tucker) and Hoerner. He was named First Team All-Big-Nine fullback and was also named to the All-America team.

Hoerner chose not to return to Iowa for the 1947 season, though he had a year of eligibility remaining. He had been selected by the Cleveland Rams in the 17th round of the 1945 NFL draft and was ready to pursue his professional career.

Hoerner joined the Rams for the 1947 season, with the team now having moved to Los Angeles.

He signed with the Rams while the *Los Angeles Times* touted his potential: "When you find a 6-foot, 4-inch, 220-pounder that can move you have something. But when you run across one who is downright fast, can handle himself like a 160-pounder and can kick and pass to boot, then you have Lester [Dick] Hoerner, The Los Angeles Rams' great fullback prospect."[3]

Hoerner played only four games in his rookie year rushing for 124 yards on 30 carries. He made his debut on September 29, 1947, at Forbes Field versus the Pittsburgh Steelers in a 48–7 Rams victory. Midway through the second quarter, he took a hand-off from Bob Waterfield, and blasted through the line for a three-yard touchdown run, giving the Rams a 13–0

Rams running back Dick Hoerner averaged a career best 6.1 yards per carry in 1951.

lead and scoring his first professional touchdown. Midway through the third quarter, Hoerner caught a screen pass from Bob Waterfield and toted it 20 yards to the Steelers nine-yard line, setting up a Kenny Washington touchdown on the next play. It was his first pass reception as a pro.

He scored his second career touchdown on a one-yard run against the Chicago Cardinals on October 19 in the Rams' 27–7 victory. However, his 1947 season was cut short with a broken foot during the game, first diagnosed as a bruised in-step.

Hoerner came back in 1948 with a vengeance, leading the team in rushing with 354 yards, averaging 4.7 yards per carry. He also played linebacker, snaring his only career interception.

The highlight of Hoerner's season, for the 6–5–1 Rams, was his three-touchdown game versus the New York Giants, tying a Rams franchise record. Hoerner scored on a nine-yard run, a four-yard run and a 12-yard pass reception from Bob Waterfield in the Rams 52–37 victory.

Coveted by several teams, Hoerner, resigned a contract with the Rams on June 11, 1949. He helped lead the Rams to the Western Division championship and their best season since moving to Los Angeles with an 8–2–2 record. The Rams lost the 1949 NFL championship game 14–0 to the Philadelphia Eagles.

Hoerner had his best rushing season in 1949 with 582 yards, sixth best in the NFL. He scored six touchdowns. He also played every game at linebacker and was a hard-hitting rangy defender. He was named second team All-Pro.

Hoerner was a member of the Rams' famed "Bull Elephant backfield." The backfield, which included Hoerner, Paul "Tank" Younger, and Dan "Deacon" Towler, was referred to by reporter Allen Wolfe as "the greatest ground attack since Rommel's Afrika Corps."[4]

"Everybody referred to me as the baby of the three," recalled Hoerner.[5]

"There was nothing sophisticated about it. I know they carried a lot of opposing linemen off the field on stretchers-and occasionally one of us."[6]

Fully recovered from nagging injuries in 1947 and 1948, Hoerner scored 11 touchdowns in 1950, tied for second in the NFL. On November 19 in a 43–35 win over the New York Yanks, Hoerner rushed for the most rushing yards in a game in his career with 129. The smash mouth fullback garnered second team All-Pro and Pro Bowl honors while rushing for 381 yards and catching 26 passes out of the backfield for 446 more yards. He continued his stalwart play at linebacker as well.

The Rams lost the 1950 NFL championship to the Cleveland Browns 30–28 in spite of Hoerner's brilliant performance. He rushed for 86 of the Rams' 106 rushing yards, scoring two touchdowns. He scored on a three-yard slashing run in the first quarter giving the Rams a 14–7 lead. In the third quarter Hoerner ran seven consecutive times beginning from the Browns' 17-yard line, finally scoring on fourth-and-goal from the one-yard line giving the Rams a 21–20 lead. Hoerner ran trap plays, delays, counters and even a Statue of Liberty play as he continually pounded the Browns at the line of scrimmage. The *Los Angeles Times* described his running in the game as "charging like a Bull."[7] He also played an active game at linebacker, but in the end, it was not enough as Browns kicker Lou Groza booted the game winning field goal in the last minute of play.

In 1951 Hoerner averaged a career best 6.1 yards per carry, garnering 569 rushing yards. The "Bull Elephant Backfield" was now in full bloom. The combination of Hoerner, Towler and Younger created a vaunted rushing attack. The Rams led the league with a 5.2 average yards per rush and finished third in total rushing yards. They were also second in the league with 22 rushing touchdowns with Hoerner contributing six of those.

Hoerner was a very unselfish player, willing to help his teammates and one such player was Tank Younger. Younger was struggling with the complex playbook of the Rams' offense and Hoerner offered to help him. "I used to go up to Dick's room every afternoon to study the offensive formation and the terminology. Dick helped me a great deal."[8] Hoerner wanted to win a championship and he knew helping Younger would enable them to achieve that goal.

The Rams captured that elusive championship in 1951 with a 24–17 victory over the vaunted Cleveland Browns with Hoerner scoring the first touchdown of the game staking the Rams to a 7–0 lead. Though he only rushed for five yards in the game on five carries he brought a physical presence to the game that helped set the tone for a hard-fought Rams victory.

Hoerner ended his Rams career in 1951 as the leading rusher in Rams history with 2,010 rushing yards.

Hoerner finished his pro football career in 1952 with the Dallas Texans. He was traded to the Texans on June 12, 1952. The Rams traded eleven players, including Hoerner, to the Texans for the rights to Les Richter. The trade was described as "unquestionably the biggest shift of pigskin personnel in National Football League history."[9]

He was upset about the trade to Dallas, hoping to payback the Rams. However, the trade did not work out well for Hoerner. The Texans were a disastrous 1-11 and Hoerner rushed for only 162 yards, averaging 2.9 yards per carry.

The Baltimore Colts joined the NFL and assumed the roster of the failing Texans. The Colts traded Hoerner to the Detroit Lions for rookie quarterback Tom Dublinski, but Hoerner never played for the Lions, announcing his retirement on July 14, 1953.

He moved to California following his retirement, at first working for American Aviation. He followed that with a job at Standard Coil and began managing a restaurant in 1954. After leaving the restaurant business, he spent the remainder of his career specializing in helping struggling businesses turn around their performance.

Hoerner still had football in his blood and formed a youth football program in southern California. He oversaw the development and growth of the program for many years as it spread throughout the state.

At age 88, Hoerner passed away on December 11, 2010, at St. Jude Medical Center, Fullerton, California, due to a stroke.

His wife Kathy survived him as well as daughters Cecilia Hoerner, Leslie Hoerner and Louise Hubbard. He is interred at Rose Hills Memorial Park, Whittier, California.

He was inducted into the Iowa High School Athletic Association Hall of Fame in 1980 and was elected to the Dubuque Senior High School Sports Hall of Fame with its inaugural class in 1992.

Notes

1. Frank Finch, "Dick Hoerner Repaired for Steeler Tilt," *Los Angeles Times*, December 10, 1948, IV-2.
2. "Lester J. 'Dick' Hoerner," *EncyclopediaDubuque.org*, www.encyclopediadubuque.org.
3. "Know Your Redskin and Ram Pro Gridders," *Los Angeles Times*, August 10, 1947, II-5.
4. Allen Wolfe, "Dick Hoerner Still Bowling Them Over," *Long Beach Independent*, November 17, 1970, C5.
5. Wolfe, "Dick Hoerner," C5.
6. Wolfe, "Dick Hoerner," C5.
7. Frank Finch, "Browns Edge Rams, 30–28, to Win Title," *Los Angeles Times*, December 25, 1950, IV-1, 4.
8. "The Black Athlete in The Golden Age of Sports," *Ebony*, September 1970, 118.
9. Frank Finch, "Rams Trade Hoerner, 10 Others For Les Richter," *Los Angeles* Times, June 13, 1952, IV-1.

Marvin Johnson

John Maxymuk

The short-lived highlight of Marv Johnson's pro football career was the rookie's interception in the Rams' victory over the Browns in the 1951 NFL championship game. Ten months later, he was an ex-Ram.

Marvin Leland Johnson was born on April 13, 1927, in San Francisco to Roy and Marie Adeline Johnson. He was one of six children, with brothers Gene, Norman and James and sisters Velma and Loretta, and grew up in California's Bay Area. Marv graduated from Fremont High School in Sunnyvale and enrolled at nearby San Jose State College.[1]

At San Jose State, Johnson lettered in both football (four years) and track (two years). On the track team, his specialty was the 220-yard dash, and his best time was 23.0 seconds for that event, although that was not among the top three times recorded at San Jose while he was there.[2] Marv was a more significant contributor on the gridiron, as the starting left halfback for a Spartans squad that featured future 49ers star end Billy Wilson and in 1948 listed former Chicago Bears back/end Hampton Pool as an assistant coach.

Despite battling injuries as a senior in 1949, Johnson averaged 5.4 yards per carry as a speedy, shifty runner.[3] His two touchdowns that season both came on spectacular plays. On November 18, San Jose upended the St. Mary's Gaels 40–13, with Marv running back the second half kickoff 99 yards for a touchdown.[4] He led the team that year with a kick return average of 36.2 yards.[5] On November 24, San Jose clinched the California Collegiate Association Conference title by whipping Fresno State 43–7, and Marv again struck in the third quarter, this time on defense, when he picked off a Fresno pass and raced 90 yards for the score.[6]

Johnson was not drafted by the NFL but did not give up on football in 1950. Instead, he joined the semi-pro powerhouse San Jose Packers along with several of his college teammates. The Packers began their season by beating their first two opponents by a combined 140–0 score. The team swept undefeated through its first 11 games, scoring 464 points and allowing just 65.[7] The Packers dropped their finale to Petaluma, but Johnson finished second in the Northern California

Marvin Johnson had a key interception in the 1951 NFL title game.

Athletic Conference in rushing average with a mark of 8.4 on 43 carries for 360 yards.[8] He ran for long touchdowns of 95, 81, 48 and 34 yards, while again playing both offense and defense.

Los Angeles, where Hampton Pool now served as an assistant coach, signed the speedster as a defensive halfback in June 1951, but then cut him in August, a month before the start of the NFL season.[9] Marv began the 1951 season with the semipro San Jose Brewers,[10] but on October 4 he was re-signed by the Rams after starting safety Herb Rich was injured in the final preseason game.[11] Johnson would not appear in a game until week four against Green Bay, but he stuck with the team for the remainder of the season, even after Rich returned at mid-season. Marv even started two games for the Rams in the regular season, and then started in the title game on December 23.

Marv had an excellent game as part of a solid team defensive effort. In the second quarter, he batted away a deep pass to Dub Jones at the Rams' five-yard line. At the outset of the fourth quarter with the Rams nursing a 14–10 lead, Browns quarterback Otto Graham lofted an errant pass from his own 23 that Johnson snagged at the Cleveland 36 and returned 35 yards to the one-yard line. Although the Browns turned stingy and would not allow a touchdown, the interception led to a 17-yard Bob Waterfield field goal and a 17–10 lead. The pick would be his only one in a Rams uniform, although he did catch two passes for 38 yards on offense as a rookie.

Johnson made the team again in 1952 but lost his starting slot early in the season. When halfback Paul Barry returned to the Rams from two years in the military at the end of October, Marv was waived to make room on the roster for the runner.[12] By that time, Rams coach Joe Stydahar had been replaced by Pool and was serving as an advisor to Packers coach Gene Ronzani. On Stydahar's recommendation, Green Bay claimed Johnson in November, and he was a Packer again—but this time in the NFL.[13] He had appeared in five games for Los Angeles and would appear in five for Green Bay in the second half of the 1952 season, intercepting two passes.

Marv returned to the Packers in 1953 and started the first six games of the season before going down to a shoulder injury. He intercepted four passes and returned one 36 yards against the Colts in the first half of the season. Inactive due to his injury for the next four weeks, Johnson returned to action against the 49ers on December 6, but did not last the game, going down to a severe shoulder separation.[14] He would never play in the league again.

Johnson reported to the Packers again in 1954 but was bothered by his recurrent shoulder problem and was traded to the Chicago Cardinals for rookie guard Don Coleman.[15] However, neither man survived the final cut for their new teams. Marv tried again in 1955, signing with the Detroit Lions. Once again, he had shoulder problems in the preseason and was cut in August, officially ending his football career.[16]

In retirement, Marv went into the soft-water business and remained in the Bay Area for the rest of his life.[17] He helped out with the football team at his alma mater for a few years in the 1960s and 1970s and joined Mike White's staff at the University of California in 1972.[18] He died in Palo Alto on February 8, 1981, at the age of 53.

Notes

1. "James A. (Jim) Johnson Sr. [Obituary],"*Legacy.com*, accessed November 14, 2018, https://www.legacy.com/obituaries/mercurynews/obituary.aspx?n=james-a-johnson-jim&pid=188191587.

2. Lawrence Fan, Director of Athletic Media Relations for San Jose State University, email correspondence with author, January 1, 2019.
3. "Reedley Tigers Tabbed Favorites in JC Tourney," *Santa Maria Times*, December 15, 1949, 2.
4. "Spartan '11' Routs Gaels," *Long Beach Independent*, November 19, 1949, 16.
5. "Russell, Menges Set Grid Records at San Jose State," *Oakland Tribune*, November 30, 1949, 40.
6. Ed Orman, "Spartans Crush Fresno 43–7 to Cop CCAA Title," *The Fresno Bee*, November 25, 1949, 2B–3B
7. "Scoring Records," *Press Democrat*, November 18, 1950, 7.
8. "NCAC Statistics," *Press Democrat*, December 5, 1950, 8.
9. "Rams Engage Fast Halfback," *Los Angeles Times*, June 5, 1951, IV-3.
10. "Hawks Prepare for Brewers," *Santa Cruz Sentinel*, September 21, 1951, 9.
11. Frank Finch, "Van Brocklin to Start Against Browns Sunday," *Los Angeles Times*, October 5, 1951, IV-4.
12. "Rams Halfback Out of Army, Joins Club," *Oakland Tribune*, October 30, 1952, 27.
13. Art Daley, "Ferguson and Johnson Seek Ram Revenge," *Green Bay Press Gazette*, October 9, 1953, 17.
14. Wally Willis, "Ronzani Cheers During Marches by Green Bay," *Oakland Tribune*, December 7, 1953, 40.
15. Art Daley, "Packers Rookies to Get 'Good Test' Saturday," *Green Bay Press-Gazette*, September 2, 1954, 21.
16. "Marv Johnson Off Detroit Lions List," *San Francisco Examiner*, August 17, 1955, 30.
17. "Rams of 1951 Settled in Various Activities," *Los Angeles Times*, December 9, 1976, III-12.
18. "Names in the News," *Los Angeles Times*, February 7, 1972, III-2.

Tommy Kalmanir

John Grasso

Jerome is a coal-mining town in southwestern Pennsylvania about 80 miles southeast of Pittsburgh. It was formerly a company town owned by the Hillman Coal & Coke Company. Jerome had a population of about 3,000 people in the 1920s. The coal mine closed on March 31, 1954,[1] and by the 21st century less than 800 people remained in Jerome.

Thomas John Kalmanir, Jr., was born into this hardscrabble town on March 30, 1926, to Czech immigrant parents, Thomas and Mary (Oravec) Kalmanir. Kalmanir was one of five children: brothers John and Andrew and sisters Mary and Helen. The family surname was pronounced "Cal Miner."

Tommy was the first in his family born in the United States and the first to attend high school.[2] He attended Conemaugh Township Area High School in Davidsville, Pennsylvania, in Somerset County, graduating in 1943. While in high school he played football (left halfback), basketball (forward) and was on the track team participating in sprints and the broad jump for the team known as the Indians. He was only five feet, seven inches tall, and 160 pounds, and his size and speed earned him the nickname "Cricket" which stuck with him for the rest of his life. In 1943 he ran the 100-yard dash in 10.2 seconds, setting a record for Pennsylvania District 5 Class A high schools which remained for more than 20 years.[3]

Kalmanir set out to follow in his coal mining father's footsteps at the coal mine near his home. "When I went down in the pit the first day, I took one look at the water seeping through the rock and quit right then and there," he told the Los Angeles Times in later years.[4] Instead he enrolled at the University of Pittsburgh as a 17-year-old. In

Tommy Kalmanir, nicknamed "Cricket," once appeared as a guest on the popular game show *What's My Line?*

1943, he played for the Pitt football team under Clark Shaughnessy. The team only won three of their eight games. Kalmanir scored his first points as a collegian when he rushed for a 25-yard touchdown in a 20–0 victory over West Virginia on October 9, 1943.[5] Two weeks later he scored two touchdowns in an 18–0 defeat of Bethany. That prompted Chester Smith, sports editor of the *Pittsburgh Press*, to describe Kalmanir as "Shaughnessy's find of the year, as slick an article as has been draped in a Pitt uniform in many a year."[6] Kalmanir scored his final touchdown for Pitt that season one week later on a 27-yard pass reception in a 45–6 rout of Carnegie Tech.[7] He finished the season as Pitt's leading rusher with 301 yards on 41 carries.

He began the 1944 season with Pittsburgh and scored two touchdowns in their opening 26–13 win against West Virginia.[8] Two weeks later in Pitt's third game of the season Kalmanir scored three touchdowns in a one-sided victory over Bethany, 50–13.[9] Kalmanir left school on October 12, 1944, to await a call from the Army Air Corps.[10] After Kalmanir left, Pitt only won two of its remaining six games and finished at 4–5 for the season. Despite his abbreviated season, Cricket was the Panthers' leading scorer for 1944 with five touchdowns for 30 points.

When Kalmanir was discharged from the service, he and some friends from Jerome were trying to decide where to go to school when University of Nevada coach Jim Aiken came to town and said to follow him to Reno. Aiken gave the group a few silver dollars and so they did.[11] Kalmanir took his good friend, and Pittsburgh and Conemaugh Township teammate, Dick Trachok with him to Reno.

The 1946 Nevada Wolf Pack football team played as an independent with Aiken as head coach in his eighth season. Kalmanir, wearing uniform #24, was the starting left halfback and led the nation in yards per catch with 27.5 yards on 17 catches, nine for touchdowns.[12]

In the Wolf Pack's 38–14 homecoming game victory over Montana State, Kalmanir returned a kickoff 105 yards for a touchdown. The return tied Marion Motley's 1941 team record and was described by one paper "as crossing both goal lines on the same play."[13]

The NFL held its annual draft of collegians for 1947 on December 16, 1946, and Kalmanir was selected by the Pittsburgh Steelers in the 25th round, 229th overall, even though he still had two years of college eligibility remaining. Kalmanir opted to stay at Nevada. Joe Sheeketski took over as Nevada head coach on March 6, 1947, replacing Jim Aiken, who had resigned in January to accept the head job at Oregon.[14]

The 1947 edition of the Wolf Pack compiled a record of 9–2 and was invited to the inaugural Salad Bowl on New Year's Day in Phoenix where they defeated North Texas State, 13–6. The *Nevada State Journal* on September 24, 1947, claimed that Kalmanir was the "most photogenic football player in the nation."[15]

For the season, he averaged 5.7 yards per carry on 84 rushing attempts and finished in second place nationally with a kick return average of 38.4 on eight returns.[16] On November 25, 1947, he received honorable mention on the Associated Press All-Pacific Coast team.[17]

Nevada had one of its best seasons in 1948, winning nine of their first 10 games, outscoring their opponents 473–106 and twice scoring more than 70 points in a game before losing to Villanova, 27–7 in the Harbor Bowl in San Diego on New Year's Day. Kalmanir received Honorable Mention on the United Press All-America team.[18]

The Pittsburgh Steelers, which had drafted Kalmanir two years previously, traded their draft rights to him to The Los Angeles Rams on March 26, 1949, for halfback Don Samuel of Oregon State. Samuel had been drafted in the 1946 NFL draft but had not played yet in the NFL and played only six games between 1949 and 1950.[19] After Kalmanir signed with the Rams, he became ineligible for the remainder of the NCAA track season and became the track coach for Bishop Manogue High School in Reno.[20]

At the Rams' preseason camp Kalmanir demonstrated his speed as he edged out 1948 Olympic broad jump champion Willie Steele for third place in a 50-yard dash that was won by V.T. (Vitamin) Smith.[21] Steele was cut during training camp and never played in an NFL game. Kalmanir made the team and wore jersey #24, his college number. He played in all 12 regular-season games, starting only two. Kalmanir was used primarily as a punt and kickoff returner and backup halfback. He rushed for 218 yards on 29 carries, fumbled once and caught two passes for 36 yards. He also returned 14 punts for 164 yards and 18 kickoffs for 403 yards. A highlight of the season for Kalmanir was his first professional touchdown, a 45-yard run in the fourth quarter to help defeat the Green Bay Packers, 48–7 on October 2, 1949.[22] He scored his second touchdown in a second game against the Packers on October 23, 1949. This score came on a first quarter 62-yard punt return in a 35–7 Rams victory.[23] Kalmanir's 57-yard kickoff return in the fourth quarter helped to set up the Rams' final score as they defeated the Chicago Bears 27–24 on October 30, 1949. The victory gave the Rams their sixth consecutive win to start the season.[24] On November 20, 1949, Kalmanir had a 51-yard run in the final seconds to set up a potential game-winning field goal from the 11-yard line, but the Chicago Cardinals blocked Bob Waterfield's attempt and the game ended in a 28–28 tie. Kalmanir ended the day with 82 yards rushing on five attempts.[25] Three weeks later Kalmanir rushed for 55 yards against the Redskins on nine carries.[26] The Rams finished the season with a record of 8–2–2 under head coach Clark Shaughnessy (Kalmanir's first college coach at Pittsburgh) and won the Western Division. The Rams lost the NFL championship game to the defending champion Philadelphia Eagles, 14–0, at the Los Angeles Memorial Coliseum. Kalmanir carried just twice for no gain but still earned the loser's share of $789.[27]

On February 17, 1950, Clark Shaughnessy was fired as Rams coach even though he had taken them to the NFL championship game. Assistant coach Joe Stydahar was promoted to become the Rams' coach.[28] The Rams signed Glenn Davis, the former Heisman Trophy winner from Army who had completed his service obligation. Davis played left halfback and Kalmanir was moved to right halfback. Cricket did not have a good year statistically, scoring only one touchdown. Ironically the touchdown came on an odd 41-yard pass from Glenn Davis in a 45–14 victory over the Packers on November 12, 1950. Under modern rules the play would not have happened. The Rams had the ball at their own 49-yard line. Davis carried the ball and was chased back to the 30 and knocked down by a defender. The play was not whistled dead, so Davis got to his feet and threw the ball downfield to the 10-yard line. Kalmanir caught it and ran it in for a touchdown.[29]

For the season Kalmanir only carried 20 times for 83 yards with a long run of 33, caught five passes for 58 with the 41-yarder being his high, returned 13 punts for 116 yards with a 23-yard play being his longest and returned 13 kickoffs for 358 yards with a long return of 44 yards. Kalmanir hurt his knee in the second game of the season against the New York Yanks on September 22, 1950. The injury forced him to miss the next two games.[30] He played in the next game but was replaced as a starter the following week. His season highlights included a game on October 22, 1950, when the Rams set the NFL regular-season single game scoring record with a 70–27 win over Colts. Kalmanir carried five times for 35 yards, including a 33-yard reverse, although he did not score any of the Rams' 10 touchdowns which were scored by eight other teammates.[31]

The Rams finished the regular season with a 9–3 record and were tied with the Chicago Bears for first place in the newly formed National Conference (formerly the Western Division). A playoff between the teams was held on December 17, 1950, in Los Angeles. The Rams won the playoff, 24–14. Kalmanir suffered a hip pointer in that game,[32] but was able to play in the NFL championship game, held one week later. The Cleveland Browns defeated the Rams for the title, 30–28.

In July 1951, it was reported that Kalmanir signed a contract to play with the Ottawa Rough Riders of the Canadian Football League (then known as the Big Four Football Union).[33] This was later denied by Kalmanir.[34] Cricket played the entire 1951 season with the Rams, playing for a championship team although his individual statistics were not especially great. He was back at left halfback as Glenn Davis was moved to right halfback. He had 16 rushing attempts for 61 yards and caught six passes for 91 yards. His only scores of the season came against Green Bay on October 21, 1951, a 38-yard pass reception in a 28–0 victory,[35] and the Chicago Cardinals on November 11, 1951, a 67-yard punt return in a 45–21 win.[36]

The Rams finished with a record of 8–4, but exacted revenge in the NFL championship game on December 23, 1951, defeating the Browns 24–17. Kalmanir's participation in the championship game was limited to two punt returns for no yards.[37]

At a time when salaries were relatively low, the winner's share of $2108 was a considerable amount of money for Kalmanir. In later years Kalmanir reflected that "the most I ever made was $10,000 a year."[38]

In February 1952, Kalmanir moved to Las Vegas and opened a stock brokerage firm with partner Harold Kline. He later appeared as a guest on the television game show *What's My Line?* on September 14, 1952. He was the first contestant whose occupation was guessed correctly (by Arlene Francis) during the initial free guess round.[39] Kalmanir was released less than one week later along with six rookies on September 19, 1952, after attending the Rams' preseason training camp and playing in their exhibition games.[40] At that point in his career he was primarily used as a returner, and he gained just nine yards on six punt returns in seven exhibition games leading to his dismissal. He was out of football for the entire 1952 season.

January 1953 found Kalmanir as Recreation Director of the Hotel Flamingo in Las Vegas.[41] He signed with the Baltimore Colts and returned to football on March 21, 1953.[42] The Colts compiled a record of 3–9 that season under coach Keith Molesworth, finishing in fifth place in the six-team Western Conference. Kalmanir played in nine games for the Colts, wearing #40. His final stat line shows 53 yards rushing on 16 carries, three pass receptions for 31 yards and one touchdown, two punt returns for 19 yards and three kickoff returns for 51 yards. He had his best rushing game of the season on November 22, 1953, when he picked up 35 yards on two carries as the Colts lost to the Rams 21–13 at home. He suffered a shoulder separation during the game that finished his season and his NFL career.[43] Kalmanir announced his retirement on March 31, 1954, to pursue a new career after purchasing a half-interest in a night club/restaurant in Minneapolis.[44]

His retirement didn't last long. Kalmanir signed with the Edmonton Eskimos of the Western Interprovincial Football Union, now known as the Canadian Football League, on March 16, 1955.[45] In one of his first efforts for Edmonton he suffered a broken rib in an intrasquad game on July 16, 1955.[46] He was cut six weeks later on August 30, 1955, after playing in just three games due to a league rule limiting roster spaces for only 12 non–Canadian players and the Eskimos had reached that total.[47]

In 1956 Kalmanir married Frances Louise Brown (Frankie) of Youngstown, Ohio. They met while she was working as a flight attendant.

Kalmanir signed on as assistant backfield coach for Hampton Pool and the Toronto Argonauts of the Canadian League on January 7, 1957.[48] He stayed with the Argos only one year, resigning in January 1958 for personal reasons and began working on a master's degree at UCLA.[49] Later that year he became an assistant coach at Glendale Junior College. On June 15, 1958, his first daughter, Karen Ann, was born. Karen Ann later became the assistant federal prosecuting attorney in Fresno. Another daughter, Kathryn, was born on May 8, 1961, and later became a teacher.

In 1959 he applied for the vacant University of Nevada head coaching position.[50] Alas, his good friend and former teammate, Dick Trachok, got the job.[51] On March 22, 1960, Kalmanir returned to football as the offensive backfield coach for the newly formed Oakland Raiders of the American Football League.[52] Kalmanir was promoted to assistant coach during the 1962 season, but the team only won one game that season. When Al Davis took over in 1963, Kalmanir was out of a full-time job in football.

After football Kalmanir sold real estate[53] and served as a sales representative for The Ivory System, a national company that reconditioned and manufactured sporting equipment.[54] He later became owner of a sporting goods store in suburban San Francisco, and that was his primary livelihood for the next 30 years. Tommy also occasionally worked as a commodities broker and as a scout for the San Francisco 49ers and Baltimore Colts.

In 1991 Kalmanir had triple bypass heart surgery and then had two strokes.[55] Doctors said he would never walk again, but in less than a year, with physical therapy three times a week, he was back on his feet walking albeit with a cane. By August 1998 he no longer needed the cane.[56] After his strokes he and his family relocated to Fresno, California.

In 2001 he was injured after twice falling and was unable to continue therapy.[57] He died on October 12, 2004, in Fresno after a bout with pneumonia.

Among the many honors in his career was induction into the Nevada Wolf Pack Hall of Fame inaugural class on October 27, 1973,[58] Cambria County Area Sports Hall of Fame in Johnstown, Pennsylvania, in 2002[59] and selection to the University of Nevada Team of the Century as a running back on June 4, 1998. At the Team of the Century awards ceremony he stated, "I've had a lot of great honors in my life but this is the greatest."[60]

In 1977, Kalmanir's former Los Angeles Rams teammate Tom Fears was a technical advisor on the film *Semi-Tough* starring Burt Reynolds. In talking about the film Fears said that as a football player Burt Reynolds reminded him of Cricket Kalmanir.[61]

Coach Joe Sheeketski said in 1967 when recalling Kalmanir, "he had a deceptive style of running that made him tough to cover. He was a smooth strider who could cut well on either leg. He also had a tremendous pair of hands for catching a football."[62]

Notes

1. "Mine Shuts Down Near Somerset," *Pittsburgh Post-Gazette*, March 31, 1954, 2.
2. Rollan Melton, "Kalmanir Needs Friends' Support to Tackle this Foe," *Reno Gazette-Journal*, September 26, 1991, 1E.
3. "Track, Baseball are in Spring Spotlight Here," *The Republic* (Meyersdale, PA), April 2, 1964, 4.
4. Shav Glick, "Tommy Kalmanir, 78; Halfback on L.A. Rams' '51 Championship Team," *Los Angeles Times*, October 15, 2004, B9.

214 Part 3: The Team

5. Chester L. Smith, "Pitt's 'T' Too Strong for Mountaineers Who Bow, 20–0," *Pittsburgh Press*, October 10, 1943, 3–12.
6. Chester L. Smith, "The Village Smithy," *Pittsburgh Press*, October 25, 1943, 18.
7. Carl Hughes, "Pitt Laces Tech, 45–6," *Pittsburgh Press*, October 31, 1943, 3–12.
8. Chester L. Smith, "Panthers Defeat Mountaineers, 26–13," *Pittsburgh Press*, September 24, 1944, 31.
9. Carl Hughes, "Bethany Scores Twice but Panthers Triumph, 50–13," *Pittsburgh Press*, October 8, 1944, 33.
10. "Eastern Football Notes," *The Morning Call* (Allentown, PA), October 13, 1944, 42.
11. Glick, "Tommy Kalmanir," B9.
12. "Nevada Passing Attack Tops National Mark," *Reno Gazette-Journal*, December 14, 1946, 14.
13. "Kalmanir's 105 Yard Run Hits Record Book," *Reno Gazette-Journal*, December 16, 1946, 18.
14. "New Football Coach Named for University of Nevada," *Reno Gazette-Journal*, March 7, 1947, 22.
15. Ty Cobb, "Inside Stuff," *Nevada State Journal*, September 25, 1947, 10.
16. "Off-Beat Statistics Department Show Surprising Facts About Nevada Pack," *Reno Gazette-Journal*, December 9, 1947, 13.
17. "Kalmanir, Beasley Get Coast Mention," *Reno Gazette-Journal*, November 25, 1947, 19.
18. "Heath Chosen on First String All-America," *Reno Gazette-Journal*, December 1, 1948, 17.
19. "Kalmanir Inks Ram Contract," *San Francisco Examiner*, March 27, 1949, 25.
20. "Nevada Sports—Kalmanir in the News," *Reno Gazette-Journal*, March 26, 1949, 9.
21. Frank Finch, "Rams Rookies Like Blue Darts," *Los Angeles Times*, August 3, 1949, IV-2.
22. Frank Finch, "Rams Humble Packers by 48–7 Margin," *Los Angeles Times*, October 3, 1949, IV-1.
23. Frank Finch, "Rams Humble Packers 35–7," *Los Angeles Times*, October 24, 1949, IV-1.
24. Frank Finch, "Rams Topple Bears, 27–24, Before 86, 080 Fans," *Los Angeles Times*, October 31, 1949, IV-1.
25. Frank Finch, "Rams Tie Cardinals, Barely Miss Victory," *Los Angeles Times*, November 21, 1949, IV-1.
26. Frank Finch, "Rams Capture Western Title," *Los Angeles Times*, December 12, 1949, IV-1.
27. Frank Finch, "Eagles Blank Rams, 14–0, Before 22,245," *Los Angeles Times*, December 19, 1949, IV-1.
28. "L.A. Rams Fire Coach Shaughnessy," *Nevada State Journal*, February 19, 1950, 14.
29. Frank Finch, "Rams Triumph, Bag Loop Lead," *Los Angeles Times*, November 13, 1950, IV-1.
30. Frank Finch, "Rams Bounce Back into Title Fight," *Los Angeles Times*, September 24, 1950, II-13.
31. Frank Finch, "Rams 'Coast' to 70–27 Win," *Los Angeles Times*, October 23, 1950, IV-1.
32. Cal Whorton, "'Rams Have Best Air Eleven' Says Halas," *Los Angeles Times*, December 18, 1950, IV-1.
33. "Tom Kalmanir Signs with Ottawa Club," *Los Angeles Times*, July 5, 1951, IV-3.
34. "Riders to Lose Kalmanir," *Ottawa Journal*, July 6, 1951, 1.
35. Frank Finch, "Rams Batter Packers, 28–0," *Los Angeles Times*, October 22, 1951, IV-1.
36. Frank Finch, "Rams Thump Cards, 45–21, to Tie for Lead," *Los Angeles Times*, November 12, 1951, IV-1.
37. Frank Finch, "Rams Whip Browns, 24–17; Win Pro Title," *Los Angeles Times*, December 24, 1951, IV-1.
38. Joe Santoro, "From the Pack to the Packers," *Reno Gazette-Journal*, January 25, 1997, 1D.
39. "Straight from the Notebook," *The Evening Standard* (Uniontown, PA), September 24, 1952, 4.
40. "Kalmanir, 6 Rooks Dropped by Rams," *Los Angeles Times*, September 20, 1952, III-4.
41. Ty Cobb, "Inside Stuff," *Nevada State Journal*, January 17, 1953, 7.
42. "Tom Kalmanir, Former Los Angeles Ram Back, Becomes Colt," *Baltimore Sun*, March 22, 1953, 3D.
43. James Ellis, "Taliaferro Masters 'T' with Surprising Ease," *Baltimore Sun*, November 23, 1953, 41.
44. Walter Taylor, "Pellington Becomes 35th to Sign Pact," *Baltimore Sun*, April 1, 1954, 42.
45. "Kalmanir Signs with Edmonton," *Reno Gazette-Journal*, March 17, 1955, 14.
46. "2,000 Football Fans Attend Esk Scrimmage," *Edmonton Journal*, July 18, 1955, 12.
47. "Few Surprises in WIFU 1955 Import Selections," *Edmonton Journal*, September 1, 1955, 14.
48. "Tommy Kalmanir Will Assist Pool," *Reno Gazette-Journal*, January 9, 1957, 13.
49. "Argonaut Coach Kalmanir Resigns," *Edmonton Journal*, January 9, 1958, 11.
50. "Nevada to Name Coach," *Arizona Republic* (Phoenix, AZ), April 7, 1959, 26.
51. "Dick Trachok Named Nevada Grid Coach, *Philadelphia Inquirer*, April 12, 1959, S5.
52. "Tom Kalmanir Joins Oakland Football Staff," *Oakland Tribune*, March 22, 1960, D33.
53. "Kalmanir is Selling Real Estate," *Oakland Tribune*, June 17, 1963, 33.
54. George Ross, "Flood of TV Gold," *Oakland Tribune*, January 29, 1964, E40.
55. Rollan Melton, "Two Nevada Athletes in Our Thoughts," *Reno Gazette-Journal*, October 14, 2001, 7B.
56. "UNR Alum Named to All-Century Squad," *Reno Gazette-Journal*, August 23, 1998, 10B.
57. Melton, "Two Nevada Athletes in Our Thoughts," 7B.
58. "Thirteen Selected to Wolf Pack Hall of Fame," *Reno Gazette-Journal*, September 24, 1973, 16.
59. Guy Clifton, "Another Honor for Pack Great," *Reno Gazette-Journal*, August 31, 2002, 1D.
60. Guy Clifton, "Team of Century Hailed," *Reno Gazette-Journal*, October 31, 1998, 1F.
61. John Hall, "Semi-Coach," *Los Angeles Times*, November 15, 1977, III-3.
62. Ed Leavitt, "More Ed Leavitt," *Oakland Tribune*, September 22, 1967, 55.

Tom Keane

John Grasso

Thomas Lawrence Keane (pronounced "Cane")[1] was born on September 7, 1926, in Bellaire, Ohio, a small town located across the Ohio River from Wheeling, West Virginia. Keane attended Linsly Military Institute in Wheeling and played basketball and football there. After graduating in 1944, he attended The Ohio State University where he played football as a freshman quarterback. The Buckeyes won all nine games they played under Carroll Widdoes, outscoring their opponents 287–79. The team was named national champions by the National Championship Foundation and the Sagarin Ratings. Keane joined the U.S. Navy after his freshman year and served for twenty months. Upon his discharge from the service he enrolled at West Virginia University upon the recommendation of his high school coach, Albert Glenn,[2] and played football (halfback, quarterback and punter) in 1946 and 1947. As a punter he was among the best in the nation.[3]

On December 19, 1947, the six-foot, one-inch, 192-pound Keane was the 18th overall pick in the 1948 NFL draft, going to the Los Angeles Rams in the third round. He was the first player selected by the Rams that year as they had traded their first-round draft choice to the Detroit Lions and the second round was only for the two teams (Lions and Giants) that had finished last in their divisions in 1947. Although Keane still had one more year of college eligibility remaining, he signed with the Rams on July 25, 1948.[4]

Keane played with the Rams from 1948 through 1951, although he was briefly with the Chicago Cardinals during the 1950 preseason. He then spent 1952 with the Dallas Texans, 1953–1954 with the Baltimore Colts and 1955 with the Chicago Cardinals. He played in 87 regular-season and four playoff games in the NFL at defensive halfback, safety, offensive end and once as an emergency quarterback.

Keane played in 11 games for the 1948 Rams, carrying the ball seven times for 16 yards and catching 11 passes for 195 yards and two touchdowns. Both touchdowns and most of his receiving yardage came

Tom Keane was an assistant coach on Don Shula's staff with the Miami Dolphins during Miami's 1972 and 1973 Super Bowl championships.

in a 34–27 victory over the Detroit Lions at Briggs Stadium on October 24. Keane's first touchdown was on a 16-yard pass in the third quarter and the second one was a 10-yard pass in the fourth quarter as backup quarterback Jim Hardy led the Rams back from a 21–0 halftime deficit after Bob Waterfield suffered a shoulder injury. Keane caught seven passes overall for 137 yards including one for 57 yards.[5]

In 1949, Keane played in 10 games, missing two games with bruised ribs.[6] Keane caught just four passes for 70 yards with a long gain of 44 yards. He also appeared in the Rams' NFL championship game loss to the Eagles as a defensive back.

During the All-America Football Conference dispersal draft on June 2, 1950, the Chicago Cardinals received tackle Bob Reinhard from the defunct Los Angeles Dons. The Cardinals then traded Reinhard to the Rams for Keane, end Bob Shaw and fullback Gerry Cowhig.[7] After playing in preseason games for the Cardinals, Keane was waived on September 11, 1950.[8] He was not unemployed for long. He was re-signed by the Rams later that month. New Rams head coach Joe Stydahar said, "I'm glad we re-signed Tom Keane as our 33rd player. When he was with the Cards he played the best defensive halfback game against us that I've seen all year."[9]

Keane played in only nine games for the 1950 Rams, primarily on defense, with just one reception for 19 yards. He intercepted six passes, returning them for a total of 50 yards and one touchdown. His touchdown came on a 25-yard interception return of a Frankie Albert pass in the third quarter in a November 5, 1950, game against the San Francisco 49ers at the Coliseum. Keane's pick six provided the margin in the Rams' 28–21 win.

During the Rams' 1951 championship season, Keane played in 10 of the 12 regular-season games as well as the NFL championship game although a shoulder separation sidelined him for a bit.[10] He was used both on offense and defense, catching 12 passes for 133 yards with a long gain of 21 and no touchdowns while also intercepting two passes. In the championship game he recovered a fumble. On September 28, 1951, in a 54–14 victory over the New York Yanks he even attempted a pass, but it was intercepted.

Keane was part of one of the most lopsided trades in professional sports on June 12, 1952. He was one of 11 Rams traded to the Dallas Texans for just one player—Les Richter.[11] Keane had a stellar season for the woeful 1–11 Texans, leading the team with 10 interceptions, the second most thefts in the NFL that year. He returned the interceptions for 93 total yards and recovered two fumbles. Keane also played a little offense at end, catching three passes for 73 yards, including one for 47 yards. He also returned one punt for eight yards. On October 26, 1952, Keane was used briefly as an emergency quarterback but did not attempt a pass nor run with the ball in a 48–21 loss to the San Francisco 49ers.

The Dallas Texans folded by the end of the 1952 season. Meanwhile, the city of Baltimore was promised an NFL franchise by Commissioner Bert Bell if the prospective owners could sell at least 15,000 season tickets by January 22, 1953.[12] As part of the agreement with the league they would also be given the rights to the former Texans' entire roster. They reached their goal, and the new Baltimore Colts (including Keane) replaced the Dallas Texans in the NFL for the 1953 season.[13]

It was reported in April that Keane was considering retiring from football.[14] Two months later, however, he signed with the Colts.[15] Under coach Keith Molesworth, Keane had his best statistical season for the struggling 3–9 Colts. He started all 12 games at safety, finishing second in the NFL with 11 interceptions. He returned those interceptions for 118 yards with a long gain of 35 yards and had four fumble recoveries. On offense,

Keane caught three passes for 61 yards with a long gain of 37. On special teams, Keane was the backup punter and averaged 41.8 yards per punt on 18 punts and even returned one punt for three yards. On November 15, 1953, Keane tied a Colts record set earlier in the season by Bert Rechichar by intercepting three passes in a 45–14 loss to the Eagles.[16] Keane tied the record the following season in a December 4, 1954, victory over the Rams. Amazingly, no Colt has surpassed it and as of 2021 the record still stands although it has since been tied by seven other Colts.[17] Keane was selected to the Pro Bowl and named to the All-Pro First Team by the Associated Press, the United Press and the *New York Daily News*.

Keane returned to Baltimore in 1954 and the team again had a dismal 3–9 record for new coach Weeb Ewbank. He started all 12 games at safety and recorded five interceptions, tying Don Shula for the team lead, and recovered one fumble.

Keane was traded to the Chicago Cardinals for rookie halfback-fullback Dick Young on June 27, 1955. Keane appeared in 11 of 12 games for the 4–7–1 Cardinals at safety. He intercepted six passes for 64 yards with a long return of 32.

On May 17, 1956, Keane signed with the Cardinals for his ninth pro season. After playing in most of the preseason games, he sustained an injury in a 69–21 preseason loss to the Rams on September 7, 1956. Keane spent the entire 1956 regular-season on the injured list. The injury was originally described as a "slight back sprain" and "not serious."[18] A few days later the injury was described as "a knee injury."[19]

On May 6, 1957, he was signed by the Cardinals as an assistant to head coach Ray Richards and began a second career as a football coach.[20] He spent most of the next 28 years in that capacity with the Chicago Cardinals, Pittsburgh Steelers and Miami Dolphins of the NFL, Calgary of the Canadian League, and the Wheeling Ironmen of the United Football League. He was primarily a defensive backs and special teams coach but was the head coach for the minor league Ironmen.

On May 8, 1962, he was named the head coach of the Ironmen in the newly expanded eight-team United Football League.[21] He led them to an 8–4 regular-season record and a 30–21 victory over the Grand Rapids Blazers in the league championship game. He was also named UFL Coach of the Year for his accomplishments.[22] Following the season he was named the team's general manager in addition to being its head coach. As a result he had to resign his position as deputy sheriff for Belmont County, Ohio.[23]

The Ironmen repeated as league champions in 1963, but they dropped to 7–7 in 1964 finishing in second place. Keane resigned to take a job as a defensive backfield coach with the Pittsburgh Steelers of the NFL. That job lasted just one year. Head coach Mike Nixon was fired along with all of his assistants after the Steelers finished an abysmal 2–12 in 1965. Keane was not without a job for long as he was hired as an assistant coach under George Wilson for the new Miami Dolphins team that would begin play in the 1966 AFL season. Keane remained with the Dolphins through thick and thin for the next 20 seasons working for Wilson and Don Shula. Surprisingly, Keane was fired after the 1985 season. Shula apparently had been unhappy with the Dolphins' defensive backs in 1984 and had switched Keane to special teams coach in 1985. Although Keane was anxious to get back into football, he was not hired by anyone.[24]

Among the highlights of his career was winning the NFL championship in 1951 with the Rams; being named as a First Team All-Pro by the Associated Press, the United Press and the *New York Daily News* and selected for the Pro Bowl in 1953; being a coach on the Miami Dolphins Super Bowl champions in 1972 and 1973; and being elected to the Ohio

Valley Athletic Conference Hall of Fame and West Virginia University Sports Hall of Fame.

Tom Keane died on June 19, 2001, in Baptist Hospital in Miami, Florida, after never recovering from open heart surgery in January 2001. "Tom was an important member of my original staff. He was an outstanding coach and friend," said Don Shula upon learning of Tom's passing. Tom was survived by his wife of 49 years, Mary; four children, Candice, Tom, Tim and Mary; and five grandchildren.[25]

NOTES

1. Frank Finch, "Scouting the Pros," *Los Angeles Times*, November 24, 1948, IV-2.
2. "Under Old Coach," *Des Moines Tribune*, September 5, 1946, 28.
3. "West Virginia to Miss Punts of Tom Keane," *Cumberland Evening Times* (Cumberland, MD), September 14, 1948, 16.
4. "Tom Keane of W.Va, Will Play with Rams," *Baltimore Sun*, July 27, 1948, 13.
5. Frank Finch, "Hardy Hero as Rams Rally to Top Lions," *Los Angeles Times*, October 25, 1948, IV-1.
6. Frank Finch, "Philly Makes Eagles Choice," *Los Angeles Times*, November 5, 1949, III-2.
7. "Bears Draft Dobbs, Trade Stickel," *Chicago Tribune*, June 3, 1950, 2–1.
8. Edward Prell, "Curly Lambeau Gives Cardinals Crew Haircut," *Chicago Tribune*, September 12, 1950, 3–4.
9. Frank Finch, "'Rams Can Lick 'Em All'—Jumbo Joe," *Los Angeles Times*, September 26, 1950, IV-3.
10. "Pack in Big One Sunday," *The Daily Tribune* (Wisconsin Rapids, WI), October 20, 1951, 6.
11. Frank Finch, "Rams Trade Hoerner, 10 Others for Les Richter," *Los Angeles Times*, June 13, 1952, IV-1.
12. "Colt Ticket Sale At 12,753," *Baltimore Sun*, January 1, 1953, 32.
13. Paul Menton, "Colts are Reborn After Struggle of Two Years," *Baltimore Sun*, January 12, 1953, 21.
14. "Keane May Quit Pro Grid," *Baltimore Sun*, April 16, 1953, 49.
15. Cameron C. Snyder, "Hilgenberg Fetes Colts," *Baltimore Sun*, June 28, 1953, 5D.
16. "Colt Records," *Baltimore Sun*, September 12, 1976, 38.
17. Matt Conti et al, 2018 *Indianapolis Colts Media Guide*, 540, http://static.nfl.com/static/content/public/static/pdf/media-guides/IND-Media-Guide.pdf.
18. "'Rams Jell,' Says Gillman of Rout," *Los Angeles Times*, September 8, 1956, II-6.
19. "Bears Face 1–2 Punch Next," *Chicago Tribune*, September 11, 1956. F2.
20. "Name Tom Keane Chi-Card Aide, " *Green-Bay Press Gazette*, May 7, 1957, 17.
21. "Keane to Coach Wheeling's Pro Football Team," *The Raleigh Register* (Beckley, WV), May 9, 1962, 13.
22. "Tom Keane Is Named UFL's Coach of the Year," *The Newark Advocate* (Newark, OH), December 13, 1962, 42.
23. "Keane Named GM of Wheeling Team," *The Tribune* (Coshocton, OH), January 17, 1963, 13.
24. Charlie Nobles, "Still Waiting for the Phone to Ring," *The Miami News*, August 14, 1986, 3B.
25. "Keane Dies, Original Dolphins Assistant," *South Florida Sun Sentinel* (Fort Lauderdale, FL), June 21, 2001, 2C.

Bill Lange

Richard C. Flowers II

Born on January 12, 1928, in Delphos, Ohio, William Henry Lange, known as Bill Lange in his playing days and "Billy" to his family, was born to play football.[1] He was a tough offensive guard, known for an aggressive style and his propensity to brawl at times.[2] He played his high school football for St. Rose High School in Lima, Ohio, graduating in 1946, earning a scholarship to the University of Dayton.[3]

Lange played for the Flyers from 1946 until 1950, when he was drafted by The Los Angeles Rams in the 30th round with the 389th overall selection of the 1950 NFL draft. A knee injury in the third exhibition game sidelined him for the 1950 season.[4]

During the 1951 championship season, his first full season of playing time, Lange started at right guard in 10 games. In the 1952 season, in a game on September 28, Lange had a memorable fight with Cleveland Browns Hall of Fame defensive end Len Ford which resulted in both men being ejected from the game in the fourth quarter. The irony of this act was that it was the only game Lange's mother was able to see her son play in as it was in their home state.[5]

Lange would go on to play in the inaugural season of the Baltimore Colts in 1953 before playing his last two seasons with the Chicago Cardinals in 1954 and 1955.[6] After the 1955 season, Lange became a member of the Rams' scouting department, helping to scout talent in his native Ohio.[7]

In 1976, Lange was enshrined in the University of Dayton's athletic Hall of Fame, along with former NBA first round pick Jim Paxson, whose sons Jim Jr. (Class of 1985) and John would not only also play in the NBA but would both become NBA general managers as well.[8]

Ohio native Bill Lange was selected by the Rams with the 389th overall pick of the 1950 NFL draft.

Lange left the game in very good health, with no lingering affects of his career in terms of significant injuries and no apparent head trauma. Aside from his love of cigars, he had no major vices either.[9]

Lange and his wife, Phyllis, had two daughters, Jeannie and Patti, who were born in 1955 after his playing career ended.[10]

After working for the Rams, Lange retired and bought a cottage in Ohio off Indian Lake with the proceeds of his playing career, including a $2,500.00 bonus he received for the 1951 NFL championship season. Lange died on April 7, 1955, in Bellefontaine, Ohio, of a sudden heart attack. The family kept the cottage for another 10 years after Lange's death.[11]

Notes

1. "Bill Lange," *Wikipedia.org*, https://en.wikipedia.org/wiki/Bill_Lange_(offensive guard).
2. Author phone interview with Jon Diedam, January 21, 2019.
3. "Bill Lange."
4. "Bill Lange"; Author phone interview with Jon Diedam, January 21, 2019.
5. Author phone interview with Jon Diedam, January 21, 2019.
6. Author phone interview with Jon Diedam, March 7, 2019.
7. Author phone interview with Jon Diedam, March 7, 2019.
8. "Bill Lange-Dayton Hall of Fame," *Daytonflyers.com*, https://daytonflyers.com/sports/2013/8/1/GEN_0801133555.aspx.
9. Author phone interview with Jon Diedam, January 21, 2019.
10. Author phone interview with Jon Diedam, November 30, 2019.
11. Author phone interview with Jon Diedam, January 21, 2019; Author phone interview with Jon Diedam, March 7, 2019.

Woodley Lewis

Mark Fellin

Woodley Carl Lewis, Jr., was born in 1925 in Los Angeles. He attended Manual Arts High School and played football at Los Angeles City College before moving on to the University of Oregon.[1]

As a junior in 1948, Lewis was a starting halfback with the Oregon Webfoots, playing alongside future Rams teammate, quarterback Norm Van Brocklin. Oregon tied California for the Pacific Coast Conference (pre–Pac 12) title, which earned the Webfoots a Cotton Bowl berth against SMU. In Oregon's 21–13 loss to the Mustangs, Lewis became the first black player to play in Cotton Bowl Stadium. In 1949, Lewis led the nation in kickoff returns, ranked seventh in interceptions with eight, and led the team in rushing with 473 yards and a 6.8-yard average.[2] In recognition of his standout senior season, Lewis received the university's Hoffman Award, bestowed upon the team's most outstanding player.[3]

Lewis finished his two-year career in Eugene as the school's record-holder in kickoff return average (34.1), single-season return average (43.2), career rushing yards per carry (5.6), longest punt return (92 yards against archrival Oregon State in 1949), and longest kickoff return (102 yards against Colorado in 1949). He was inducted into the University of Oregon Athletics Hall of Fame in 1999.[4]

The Rams selected Lewis in the eighth round of the 1950 NFL draft, the 103rd overall pick.[5] The 6-foot, 185-pound college star had an immediate impact, setting a Rams rookie record with 12 interceptions.[6] Lewis's dozen regular season picks tied him for second in the league with the Detroit Lions' Don Dell, one behind league-leader Spec Sanders of the New York Yanks.[7] The rookie high mark would be reset two years later by Lewis's Los Angeles teammate Dick "Night Train" Lane, who picked off 14 passes in 1952.[8] Lewis added a 13th interception in the Rams' 24–14 playoff win against the

Woodley Lewis intercepted 12 passes during his rookie campaign in 1950.

Bears.[9] He completed his spectacular rookie season with an appearance in the Pro Bowl, played on his home field at the Los Angeles Memorial Coliseum.[10]

Lewis started every game of his sophomore season in Los Angeles, including the 1951 NFL championship game victory over the Browns.[11] He displayed his skills early on, with preseason exploits that included a 22-yard interception return for a touchdown in a thrilling 23–21 win over the Giants[12] and a spectacular 102-yard interception and lateral against the Chicago Cardinals. On the play, Lewis ran the ball out of his own end zone to midfield before flipping the ball to Herb Rich, who sped the remaining 50 yards to pay dirt.[13]

Lewis continued making big plays once the real games started. In a key Week 3 battle with the up-and-coming Lions in Detroit, he intercepted a third quarter Bobby Layne pass near midfield. A few plays later Bob Waterfield tossed a touchdown pass, sealing the victory.[14] In a crucial Week 6 win against the 49ers, Lewis's kicking skills proved pivotal. He booted four kickoffs deep into the end zone, limiting the damage done by San Francisco's master returner Joe Arenas.[15] Lewis was an important contributor down the stretch, picking off passes in key wins over the Cardinals[16] and Yanks[17] as Los Angeles battled to secure the conference title. However, it wasn't all sunshine and lollipops for Lewis. In summarizing the Rams' 44–17 drubbing at San Francisco in Week 5, Frank Finch of the *Los Angeles Times* described how Lewis and Vitamin Smith "staged an Alphonse-and-Gaston routine on the 49ers' first kickoff," referring to the comic strip bumblers whose extreme politeness ("After you, my dear Alphonse") would routinely lead to disaster.[18]

Playing with the Rams from 1950 to 1955, Lewis recorded 23 interceptions and was a mainstay on special teams, returning 107 punts (7.6 yards per return and three touchdowns) and 108 kickoffs (23.8 yards per return and one touchdown).[19] His prowess was on particular display in a 1953 win over the Detroit Lions, when he gained 120 yards on punt returns, including a 78-yard touchdown return, and added 174 yards in kickoff returns.[20]

The Rams traded Lewis to the Chicago Cardinals in 1956,[21] where, in addition to patrolling the defensive backfield and returning kicks, he expanded his role as a receiver. Lewis caught 21 passes during his six years in Los Angeles. As an end with the Cards, he hauled in 101 passes for 1,648 yards and 12 touchdowns over three seasons. Lewis finished his NFL career with the expansion Dallas Cowboys in 1960.[22]

In addition to his Pro Bowl rookie season, Lewis earned Associated Press All-Pro honorable mention and United Press second team All-Pro honors in 1953. In 1958, *The Sporting News* selected Lewis as an All-Conference offensive end.[23]

While capable of delivering singular moments of electricity, Lewis also was a model of consistency. He did not miss a single game in the '50s, playing in all 120 of his teams' regular season contests from 1950 to 1959.[24] Furthermore, between 1950 and 1960, Lewis gained 1,026 yards on punt returns. Only Hall of Famer Emlen Tunnell had more punt return yardage during that time.[25]

Lewis died of kidney and heart problems in 2000. He was eulogized by several of his Rams teammates, with whom he had remained close. "Not only was he an excellent football player, he was an authentic human being and a great community leader once he left football," said former fullback Dan Towler. "He gave a lot of his time to youth organizations in South Central Los Angeles, and left his mark." Paul "Tank" Younger added, "He could really play."[26]

Notes

1. Jason Lewis, "Los Angeles' Long and Rich History of Black Professional Football Players," *Los Angeles Sentinel*, August 11, 2011, https://lasentinel.net/los-angeles-long-and-rich-history-of-black-professional-football-players.html.
2. "Woodley Lewis—Football," *Oregonsportshall.org*, November 19, 2018, http://oregonsportshall.org/timeline/woodley-lewis-football/.
3. Ron Bellamy, "Lewis Won't be Forgotten," *The Register-Guard* (Eugene, OR), January 1, 2011, 1C.
4. "Woodley Lewis—Football."
5. "Woodley Lewis," *Pro-football-reference.com*, https://www.pro-football-reference.com/players/L/LewiWo00.htm.
6. Lewis, "Los Angeles' Long and Rich History."
7. "1950 NFL Defense," *Pro-football-reference.com*, https://www.pro-football-reference.com/years/1950/defense.htm#defense::7.
8. Lewis, "Los Angeles' Long and Rich History."
9. "Divisional Round—Chicago Bears at Los Angeles Rams—December 17th, 1950," *Pro-football-reference.com*, https://www.pro-football-reference.com/boxscores/195012170ram.htm.
10. "Browns' Americans Win Pro Bowl Game, 28–27," *Pittsburgh Post-Gazette*, January 15, 1951, 19.
11. "Woodley Lewis."
12. Frank Finch, "Rams Win Thriller from Giants, 23–21," *Los Angeles Times*, September 20, 1951, IV-1.
13. Frank Finch, "Cards Lead Rams in Fourth, 22–14," *Los Angeles Times*, September 8, 1951, II-9.
14. Frank Finch, "Rams Capture 27–21 Thriller," *Los Angeles Times*, October 14, 1951, IV-1.
15. Frank Finch, "Waterfield & Co. Deal 23–16 Loss to 49ers," *Los Angeles Times*, November 5, 1951, IV-1.
16. Frank Finch, "Rams Thump Cards, 45–21, to Tie for Lead," *Los Angeles Times*, November 21, 1951, IV-1.
17. Frank Finch, "Rams Conquer Yanks, 48–21," *Los Angeles Times*, November 19, 1951, IV-1.
18. Frank Finch, "Zilly Breaks Arm; Rich Rejoins Rams," *Los Angeles Times*, October 30, 1951, IV-2.
19. "Woodley Lewis."
20. "1953 National Football League," *Profootballresearchers.com*, http://profootballresearchers.com/members-only/Linescores/1953Linescore.pdf (members-only access).
21. "Rams Trade Lewis," *The Pittsburgh Press*, September 26, 1956, 44.
22. "Woodley Lewis."
23. John Hogrogian, Paul Klatt, John Turney, *The Best of Each Season, All-Pro Football Teams: 1920-present* (Guilford, NY: Professional Football Researchers Association, 2011), 88, 100, 117, http://www.profootballresearchers.org/members-only/The%20Best%20of%20Each%20Season.pdf (members-only access).
24. "Woodley Lewis."
25. "Ex-Rams Player Woodley Lewis Dies," *Associated Press*, January 1, 2001, https://apnews.com/4c69516ceef384d48c37c785abba7551.
26. "Ex-Rams Player Woodley Lewis Dies."

Leon McLaughlin

John Maxymuk

Football historian T.J. Troup has noted that in the 1951 NFL championship game, the Rams did something that was never done before and has not been repeated since—their five starting offensive linemen were all rookies.[1] The fulcrum of that first-year cluster of fine blockers was center Leon McLaughlin, a man who would go on to spend 40 years as either a player or coach at all levels of the game. Leon Clifford McLaughlin was born in San Diego, California, on May 30, 1925. He was one of three sons of Mr. and Mrs. Claud McLaughlin.[2]

The family later moved up the coast to Santa Monica, and Leon excelled on the gridiron. Starring at Santa Monica High School under Coach Jim Sutherland, McLaughlin was named to the first team of the All-Southern California prep squad as both a junior in 1941 and senior in 1942.[3]

Upon graduation, McLaughlin enlisted in the Navy and spent three years as a Seabee, building airfields and such in the war effort. At the conclusion of the war, McLaughlin returned to civilian life and resumed his education and football career at UCLA. He was a freshman on one of the finest Bruin teams in history in 1946. That team featured several imminent pro players, including future Rams teammates Tom Fears and Don Paul and went undefeated before losing to Illinois in the Rose Bowl.[4]

1951 Rams center Leon McLaughlin was a Navy Seabee during World War II.

Paul was the starting center at UCLA in 1946 and 1947, but McLaughlin lettered both years as the sturdy second-string man. He fractured a bone in his right hand as a sophomore but did not let that deter him from playing.[5] Once Paul graduated, Leon assumed the starting center/linebacker position. As a junior in 1948, he led the team in minutes played with 447 in 10 games,[6] and then as a senior, he again was the club's ironman with 404 minutes played in nine games.[7] For the latter season, he was awarded the Jake Gimbel Award, given to a senior athlete based on scholarship, attitude and character.[8]

Due to his age, McLaughlin had been drafted with the 193rd selection of the 1947 NFL draft by the

Rams and also by the Los Angeles Dons (205th pick) of the All-America Football Conference in 1948. In 1950, though, his rights were owned by the Washington Redskins, but he eschewed the pro game to work as an assistant coach at his alma mater, Santa Monica High, under his old coach, Jim Sutherland.[9]

A year later, the Rams obtained Leon's rights from the Redskins for a reported $100 and signed him.[10] He moved into the starting lineup immediately and would start all 63 regular season and postseason games the Rams would play from 1951 to 1955. In fact, he played every minute on offense for the team in his first two seasons, including preseason games.[11] He was the Rams' iron man; a solid pro who was named to the Pro Bowl in 1954. On the rare occasion that he had to leave the lineup, his presence was missed.

In the 1953 finale against Green Bay, McLaughlin injured his knee and had to leave the game. Coach Hampton Pool later commented on the Rams lackluster 33–17 win over the two-win Packers, "We went gradually downhill after McLaughlin went out."[12] Two years later in the lead up to the 1955 title game against the Browns, Leon was reported as being doubtful for the game because he had come down with mumps.

McLaughlin, of course, played anyway, and sportswriter Jerry Izenberg later related a possibly apocryphal anecdote about that. "[Paul] Brown the staid disciplinarian, allowed himself the luxury of a last-second quip. The Rams' center, Leon McLaughlin, had come down with mumps the week of the title game, but had gallantly played most of the contest. 'How about that guy?' Brown demanded. 'None of our guys wanted to make contact with him. They were so scared they wanted me to come up with a new defensive formation for them.'"[13]

About to turn 31 in 1956, McLaughlin made a career transition in 1956. "'I had this offer to coach at Washington State,' he recalled. 'I decided to hit Sid [Gillman, head coach] for a raise, so I went in and told him about the offer' and he said, 'Congratulations. You'll make a great coach.'"[14]

Leon, indeed, was hired to be the line coach at Washington State, under Jim Sutherland again, but stayed just one year. In 1957, he again returned to Santa Monica High, but this time as the head coach. In two seasons there, he was very successful, leading SMHS to an 18–4–1 mark. In 1959, he moved up a level and became the line coach for Stanford under Jack Curtice. Even when Curtice was replaced by John Ralston in 1963, McLaughlin was retained. Leon optimistically applied for the head coach position at UCLA in 1965, but the Bruins hired Tommy Prothro instead. Prothro had been an assistant coach at UCLA during McLaughlin's senior year.

Leon again moved up a level in 1966 when he was hired by new Steelers head coach Bill Austin to be Pittsburgh's line coach. Austin had played against McLaughlin in college and said at the hiring, "McLaughlin has the knack of getting his words across and should make an excellent teacher. Leon is one of those dedicated fellows who puts everything into a job."[15] Austin was fired three years later and replaced by Chuck Noll, but McLaughlin took a step up by becoming head coach at San Fernando Valley State College, now known as California State, Northridge.

However, his results there were mediocre, as he posted a 4–5 record in 1969 and 4–6 in 1970. Offered a chance to return to pro football in 1971, Leon accepted the job of line coach on Tommy Prothro's Rams staff, although he would share the duties with longtime Prothro assistant Bobb McKittrick. McLaughlin would remain a pro assistant for the remainder of his career. In the 1970s, he was a well-traveled line coach: 1971–72 under Prothro in Los Angeles; 1973–74 under Don McCauley and Rick Forzano in Detroit;

1975–76 under Bart Starr in Green Bay; 1977 under Chuck Fairbanks in New England. However, the two best linemen he handled in that time, Gale Gillingham in Green Bay and John Hannah in New England, both had very negative things to say about him afterwards. Gillingham recalled, "I had no faith in what they were doing. I had no faith in the line coach. I had enough of that crap. I had enough of losing. I didn't believe in anything we were doing as far as the offensive line goes."[16] Hannah, speaking of McLaughlin and Rod Humenuik, grumbled, "I had two terrible line coaches when I was playing here," and then referred specifically to McLaughlin as, "One didn't know anything so he'd just draw up the defenses and we had to come up with the blocking schemes on our own."[17]

After leaving the Patriots, McLaughlin was hired by Bud Wilkinson of the Cardinals as a quality control coach who would scout the team's opponents, break down film and chart tendencies. He was also the "Turk" during training camp—the coach who would tell players to turn in their playbooks to the head coach. Leon worked for the Cardinals from 1978 to 1989 in both St. Louis and Arizona. In 1990, the 65-year-old McLaughlin retired.[18]

Leon once humbly commented about his position. "A lot of coaches don't know much about centers, either. The thing is that a lot of centers aren't necessarily good athletes. The quicker kids in high school, college or pro are usually guards and tackles and ends. I was a center because I wasn't fast or quick enough to play anything else."[19] McLaughlin was a talented, reliable force in the middle of the best offense in football and worked his entire life in the game. He died on October 27, 2014, in King County, Washington, and was survived by his wife and seven children.

Notes

1. T.J. Troup, "27-M-Sockem: The Champion Los Angeles Rams of 1951," *Pro Football Journal*, December 22, 2015, http://nflfootballjournal.blogspot.com/2015/12/27-m-sockemthe-champion-los-angeles.html.
2. "Leon McLaughlins Honeymooning at Beach and Desert," *Los Angeles Times*, December 31, 1949, I-7.
3. "Ted Bare, Chino High Champion, and Glenn Davis, Bonita Ace, Win All-Southern Cal Rating," *Chino Champion*, December 25, 1942, 5.
4. Bernie Milligan, "Bernie Milligan [column]," *Valley News*, January 10, 1971, 23.
5. "Center Ignores Fractured Hand," *Arizona Republic*, September 17, 1947, 19.
6. "Leon McLaughlin, UCLA," *Los Angeles Times*, September 2, 1949, IV-3.
7. " Leon McLaughlin to Receive Bruin Football Trophy," *Los Angeles Times*, December 14, 1949, IV-4.
8. "McLaughlin, Seelig Given UCLA Honors," *Long Beach Independent*, July 3, 1950, 10.
9. Jimmy Miller, "Steelers Add Offensive Line Coach to Staff," *Pittsburgh Post-Gazette*, February 3, 1966, 22.
10. Frank Finch, "Fuller Standout in Ram Scrimmage," *Los Angeles Times*, July 29, 1953, IV-3.
11. Finch, "Fuller Standout," IV-3.
12. Jack Geyer, "Hirsch Gives Shirt for Alma Rammy," *Los Angeles Times*, December 13, 1953, IV-10
13. Jerry Izenberg, *Championship: The Complete NFL Title Story* (New York: Four Winds Press, 1966), 87.
14. Charles Donaldson, "New VSC Grid Coach Expects No Race Woes," *Los Angeles Times*, February 3, 1969, II-8.
15. Miller, "Steelers Add Offensive Line Coach," 22.
16. Jerry Poling, "Effort, Enthusiasm: Gillingham Uses Both in His New Field," *Leader-Telegram*, October 31, 1990, 4C.
17. Ron Borges, "Hannah: Humenuik Coaching Leaves Line Defenseless," *Boston Globe*, December 10, 1992, 81.
18. Norm Frauenheim, "Cardinals Rely on McLaughlin to be Bearer of Bad News to Hopefuls," *Arizona Republic*, July 17, 1988, D5.
19. Mal Florence, "Center of Anonymity," *Los Angeles Times*, November 18, 1971, III-1.

Don Paul

Patrick Gallivan

Bobby Layne of the Detroit Lions made the cover of *Time* magazine near Thanksgiving of 1954. That was unusual because professional football did not get much recognition in the national media in the fifties. At the time, professional baseball and college football had many more fans. The cover story talked of the high caliber play. "The pros play better and more complex football than even the best college team," wrote the editors of *Time*. "They also play rougher."[1] The writers admitted Layne's Lions play rough football, but it also said most Lions agree about who earned the title as dirtiest player in the league.

"Most of them agree that Don Paul (6'1" and 228 lbs.), captain of The Los Angeles Rams and a rib-cracking linebacker of the old school, is the dirtiest player in the league," continued *Time*.[2] "But I got tagged as a dirty player and that's the way people thought of me," admitted Paul. "To be honest, I really didn't mind it that much."[3]

There was talk around Los Angeles that Paul's pride motivated him to carry a clipping of the *Time* article but his nephew, Ronnie Paul, called that untrue.[4] Maybe Don Paul took the comment as a compliment because football in the fifties definitely was a man's sport. He was proud that someone considered him the number one villain in the league. Paul credited Leon Hart of the Lions as the one behind the accusation. "I relished what Leon Hart said all my life," claimed Paul. "But I always felt there was a great deal of difference being dirty and being rough. For instance, in all my years in football, I never bit anybody. But I was bitten."[5]

Despite the talk of the *Time* article in his wallet, Paul was not sure he merited the title. He claimed only three ejections over his entire eight-year, 87-game career. "It isn't what you do," he said. "It is what they see you do."[6]

Was being bitten the worst thing to happen to him over his football career? No, he said. "Once I had my helmet ripped off and then was hit over the head with it. Can you imagine that? My own helmet."[7]

"I didn't hit with my fists," continued

The Rams' defensive leader, hard-hitting linebacker Don Paul.

Paul, "but when I hit a ball carrier and there is a split second between then and the time the whistle blows, I hit them again, hard."[8] Footage from the era confirms he played a physical brand of football.

Some claim Paul got more roughing the passer penalties than any other player of the era had. Statistics are not available to prove that assertion. Long after his playing career was over, a reporter asked him if he regretted the rough reputation. "Naw," he said with a grin. "Quarterbacks are like the rich little kids on the block. You have to teach them what life is all about. I was doing them a favor. I was making a man of them."[9]

"I always tried to discern the difference between a dirty and aggressive player," Paul told the *Los Angeles Times* in 1978, many years after he had retired. "I never thought of myself as a dirty player. To me, a dirty player is a cheap-shot artist—a biter, a kicker, that sort of thing.... But a rough guy usually plays it to the hilt and gives no quarter whatsoever. He can be called dirty, but people really mean that he's super aggressive."[10]

The game was a rough one in the fifties. Everyone on the field could dish out the damage, even those on the sidelines. "Whenever I made a tackle on the Chicago sideline, I always kept an eye on Halas," said Don Paul in an interview. "It was not uncommon for him to stick you with one of those ripple shoes."[11]

"Off the field, Paul is the gentlest young man in Los Angeles, and one of the cleanest," wrote Bob Oates, who covered the Rams for decades. "But in football games, he plays with unlimited enthusiasm."[12]

Paul played most of his football in southern California. He played collegiately at UCLA and then for the hometown Rams. He was a local kid who made good in the big city. Paul was born March 18, 1925, in Fresno, California, where his immigrant parents became successful farmers in Central Valley. The 12,000-acre family farm in Fresno and Madera counties grew peaches, plums and nectarines. As a young man, Paul helped haul produce to markets in Los Angeles. In addition to table grapes, the farm produced wine grapes sold to Ernest & Julio Gallo and other winemakers. Orson Welles, spokesman for Paul Masson Wines, appeared at the farm to sign autographs, according to nephew Ronnie Paul.[13]

After a successful prep career, he was offered a college scholarship at UCLA. Paul's collegiate career was interrupted by World War II in 1945, when he served in the Navy, but he made an immediate impact at UCLA. Paul was a four-year letterman, three-time team captain, and the first player elected captain of the UCLA varsity football team as a freshman. He was All Pacific Coast in 1946 and 1947.

He was selected by the Rams in the third round (21st overall) in the 1947 draft. During his eight seasons with the Rams (1948–1955), Paul played on four conference championship teams and in three Pro Bowl games. He was the defensive signal caller for seven years and team captain four seasons. In 1951, he led the defense for the title team that beat the Cleveland Browns in the big game. He also played center on offense.

When the Rams took the field on the final weekend of the 1951 regular season, they needed help to make the title game. The players were watching the scoreboard seeking updates on the other contests during their game. "It was hard to concentrate on the job at hand, but when the shock wore off our gang hit harder than ever," said Don Paul, who played both center and linebacker in the game.[14]

Things broke perfectly for the Rams, creating a rematch of the prior season's title game with the Browns. Prior to the game, football fans asked one question: Who could stop the Browns?

Don Paul's thoughts were of the 1950 championship game, and Lou Groza'a last minute game winning field goal. "Every time I think of that game, I have one visual image," said Paul. "[Linebacker] Fred Naumetz is in the end zone and a Graham pass is hitting him in the hands. This is right before they got the field goal. I can still see Naumetz's hands—the fingers are curved instead of open and the ball hits him on the knuckles. Oh, God, how it killed me to see that ball hit the ground."[15]

Captain Don Paul led the Rams' defense out against the high-powered Browns offense. A critical play during the 1951 championship game came with his interception of an Otto Graham pass. After the game, he ran into Graham. He complimented the Cleveland quarterback on his passing during the game.

"I sure threw a nice one to you," replied Graham.

"I'm too slow," said Paul. "I should have scored on that interception."[16]

The 1951 title game marked the first victory for the Rams over the Browns in four tries, including an exhibition game. "We've blown three games against these guys," said Paul. "I never felt we had them until that final gun."[17]

"He was the play-caller on defense," said his nephew Stephen with pride. "Don Paul was the only Ram player to be a defensive captain and play caller who won a championship at the L.A. Memorial Coliseum."[18]

In addition to helping the Rams to the 1951 title, Paul contributed to the legacy of the game. He came up with the nickname for the man who told players they would no longer be part of the team.[19] Over a long history, "The Turk" visited players to advise them the head coach wanted to see them with a reminder to bring their playbook. This meant they had been released from the squad. When Clark Shaughnessy was Rams coach, he asked someone in the organization to wake the player in the middle of the night thinking that player would be less angry because he was still trying to wake up. When the rest of the squad woke up, the released player was already gone. "The Turk strikes at night," said Paul coining the nickname.[20]

The Rams of the Don Paul era played for the love of the game. "I got $6,000 a year most of the time," he said. "I think I worked all the way up to $10,000. Of course, that didn't make me a limousine liberal."[21]

Paul was also a warrior. Coach Hamp Pool singled out Don Paul and Les Richter as two men who could endure extreme pain and still play in the game at a high level. Pool said broken bones did not slow them down. "I broke my jaw on the third play of a game at Philadelphia in 1951 and I stayed in," recalled Paul. "Then I felt blood coming out of my ear and I had to leave. The next week I played without a protector *because it wasn't ready yet!* I put a rubber bit in my mouth and clamped on it. We went into Detroit and I played the piano in front of that damned Leon Hart for four quarters. That was when we first used the birdcage, by the way, the protector they finally fixed to shield my jaw. That's what linemen and linebackers wear today."[22]

After retiring from playing, Paul went into coaching. First, he coached with the College All-Star team. He coached the defensive All-Stars in 1957 against the Giants and in 1958 when his crew defeated the Lions 35–19. The following three years, 1959 to 1961, he was a defensive assistant coach with the Rams.[23] "When Don played football he set the standard for his physical play," recalled nephew Stephen Paul. "He passed that attitude on to his players when he coached defense with the Rams."[24]

Later, Paul teamed with Gil Stratton on Rams telecasts for CBS. He also taped *The Don Paul Show*, a show that recapped the previous game action. Paul's television schedule provided him time to run his restaurants: The Rams' Horn and Seven Kitchens.[25] The highlight of Paul's restaurant career was catering the Super Bowls played in Los Angeles and Pasadena.

Paul continued to be a huge Rams fan in his retirement. The Rams' Horn continued to be a hangout for players and fans of the football franchise. When the league approved the Rams' move to St. Louis in 1994, Don Paul expressed his view by putting a dish on the menu called "Lack of Ram."[26]

After a long illness, Paul died of respiratory failure on November 8, 2014, in Woodland Hills, California, at the age of 89.

NOTES

1. "November 29, 1954: The NFL Makes the Grade," *Profootballdaly.com*, November 29, 2014, http://profootballdaly.com/nov-29-1954-the-nfl-makes-the-grade/.
2. "November 29, 1954."
3. Steve Bisheff, *Great Teams' Great Years, Los Angeles Rams* (New York: Macmillan Publishing Company, 1973), 117.
4. Author phone interview with Ronnie Paul, December 21, 2018.
5. Bisheff, *Los Angeles Rams*, 117.
6. Bob Oates, *The Los Angeles Rams* (Culver City, CA: Murray & Gee, 1955), 60.
7. Bisheff, *Los Angeles Rams*, 117.
8. "November 29, 1954."
9. Jim Murray, "The Man Who Didn't Bite Quarterbacks," *Los Angeles Times*, May 16, 1986, III-1, 13.
10. Mal Florence, "Don Paul: Rams' First 'Hit Man,'" *Los Angeles Times*, June 20, 1978, III-1.
11. Andy Furillo, *The Steamer: Bud Furillo and the Golden Age of L.A. Sports* (Solano Beach, CA: Santa Monica Press, 2016), 32.
12. Oates, *The Los Angeles Rams*, 60.
13. Author phone interview with Ronnie Paul.
14. Cal Whorton, "Rams Celebrate Two Victories after the Game," *Los Angeles Times*, December 17, 1951, IV-1.
15. Mickey Herskowitz, *The Golden Age of Pro Football: A Remembrance of Pro Football in the 1950s* (Dallas: Taylor Publishing Company, 1990), 55.
16. Paul Zimmerman, "Fears Calls Van Brocklin's Toss 'Best Thrown Pass I Ever Caught,'" *Los Angeles Rams*, December 24, 1951, IV-1.
17. "Lost by an Eye Lash, Says Brown After Defeat," *Pittsburgh Post-Gazette*, December 24, 1951, 12.
18. Author phone interview Stephen Paul, January 8, 2019.
19. Jon Kendle, "Coach Wants to See You. And, Bring Your Playbook!" *Profootballhof.com*, https://www.profootballhof.com/news/coach-wants-to-see-you-and-bring-your-playbook/.
20. Roger Mooney, "Beware the Turk at Cut-Down Time in NFL," *Tampa Bay Times*, September 3, 2006, https://www.tampabay.com/sports/football/bucs/beware-the-turk-at-cut-down-time-in-nfl/2292208/.
21. Murray, "The Man Who Didn't Bite Quarterbacks," III-1, 13.
22. Herskowitz, *The Golden Age of Pro Football*, 55–56.
23. "Don Paul dies at 89; Helped L.A. Rams to NFL Championship," *Los Angeles Times*, November 16, 2014, AA7.
24. Author phone interview with Stephen Paul.
25. Author phone interview with Ronnie Paul.
26. Michael MacCambridge, *America's Game: The Epic Story of How Pro Football Captured a Nation* (New York: Random House, 2004), 395.

Joe Reid

Joshua Milton Anderson

Put good people in the right position and let them do their job. This was a lesson Joseph Reid learned during his season with the Rams under head coach Joe Stydahar.¹ Reid put it into practice as president of a billion-dollar oil company and then passed it on by helping students at his beloved Louisiana State University.

Joseph Edmund Reid was born on March 18, 1929. His father, Ben, was a bridge foreman and his mother, Lattie, a housewife. They lived in Meridian, Mississippi, with his older sister and two younger siblings.²

In high school, Reid was a leader on his school's basketball and football teams, the Meridian Wildcats, and even threw the discuss on the track team.³ Standing six foot, three inches tall and weighing 195 pounds before he was 17, he was a significant athletic force. As the starting center he led the Meridian basketball team to the conference championship as a junior and was named to the All-Big Eight First Team both his junior and senior years.⁴ Come football season, Reid played linebacker and center on a Wildcats team that went 4–4–1 in 1946.⁵ He made the Third Team on the 1946 All-Big Eight Football Squad at center, and he was one of the centers named to the All-South Squad.⁶ Not only was he a star athlete, but he finished his high school academic career with a "straight 'A' average."⁷

LSU was one of several schools in the Southeast that recruited Reid, and he choose LSU once he was assured that he would receive his education regardless of whether he made the football team.⁸

In 1947, Reid played on the "B," or non-varsity team at LSU at center and was soon considered to be one of "several outstanding varsity prospects who are sure to be heard from."⁹ The highlight of his freshman season was a blocked punt that was

Joe Reid was the last surviving member of the 1951 Rams championship team when he passed away in 2020 (courtesy Kim Reid).

a key play in the B team's victory over Vanderbilt.[10] In 1948 he made the varsity team and was viewed as "a giant and still growing and "ticketed for stardom."[11] Reid was being recognized by the Associated Press on its weekly nominations for the All-Southeastern squad by the end of that season.[12] Not only did he do well on the field, but he continued his strong academic performance with an A- average through his first two years of college.[13]

As a junior in 1949, Joe Reid beat out five other centers to be chosen the varsity starter.[14] Reid also directed the Tigers' defensive formations while holding down the "non-ball-handling center spot."[15] At the end of the season he earned an Honorable Mention on the United Press All-Southeastern team, as chosen by conference coaches and sports writers.[16] His play and that of his fellow linemates was a major factor in LSU's surprising 8–2 record, which earned them a trip to the Sugar Bowl, where they lost to Bud Wilkinson's undefeated Oklahoma Sooners 35–0.

Though LSU's 1950 season was not nearly as impressive, with a 4–5–2 record, Reid was still nominated for top "offensive center" on the coaches' ballots for All-SEC.[17] His performance on the field did not distract him too much academically, as he maintained a solid 2.34 average on a 3.0 scale.[18] If academics and football were not enough, he was also in ROTC training and served as the LSU student body president.[19]

Reid was drafted in the 13th round of the 1951 NFL draft with the 156th pick by the Los Angeles Rams. While doing ROTC training, he had a diving accident that injured his ear and made it impossible for him to serve in the military.[20] The Rams were still interested in Reid, and they offered him a contract for $4500. Proving his intelligence extended beyond academics he was able to negotiate the team up to $5500 for the year.[21] Reid signed his contract, and since the Rams already had a strong center, he was moved to linebacker, a position he probably enjoyed playing more than center.[22]

While not consistently starting for the Rams, he regularly took the field during their 1951 championship season.[23] In the third week of the season, Reid was injured in the Rams' victory over the Lions and had to miss the Green Bay game the next week. However, he saw at least some action in all of the other games that year.[24] His key play of the season occurred in the Rams' 48-21 win over the Yanks in Week 8. The Rams had an early 27–7 lead, but the Yanks had come back to make the score 34–21. With the Yanks one yard away from making it a one-touchdown game, Reid recovered Yanks' quarterback George Ratterman's fumble in what was called the "turning point for that game."[25]

The next season (1952) Reid was one of 11 players traded by the Rams to the Dallas Texans in exchange for Les Richter.[26] Though traded in June, it was not clear if Reid would choose to play for the Texans. It was reported that Reid and Billy Baggett, a teammate also included in the trade, had "transferred from their alma mater, Louisiana State, to the SMU law college."[27] Ultimately, neither one decided to attend law school but instead continued playing football. It was noted when Reid signed with the Texans that although he spent much more time at linebacker while playing for the Rams, he was projected to be placed in his secondary position of center with the Texans.[28]

Reid was among the five players to make the team out of the 11 traded to the Texans.[29] He started the season as a backup on the defensive line and played on kickoff teams. In Week 4 against the Green Bay Packers, Reid took over at right linebacker when Pat Cannamela was removed from the lineup due to injury.[30] He generally played well, but the season was difficult as the team finished a woeful 1–11.[31]

In the next to last game of the season against the Eagles, Reid was seriously injured on a kickoff play in the second quarter and had to be carried off the field on a stretcher. At St. Mary's Hospital he was unconscious, but he partially regained consciousness a short time later. X-rays determined that he did not have a fractured skull.[32] Reid was unable to play in the Texans' final game as he was still recovering from the blow to his head.[33]

After the 1952 season ended, the Texans folded, and Reid was free to play for anyone. There were several teams interested and he briefly signed with the Baltimore Colts. For a few days, there were news reports, such as "Reid is motoring from Meridian, Miss." to the Colts' training camp, but he eventually decided to leave football. He devoted his time to learning the oil business while working in Baytown, Texas for Shell Oil.[34]

Always an excellent student, Reid enrolled in the Harvard Business School MBA program and married Bobby Ray in 1955.[35] He would go on to become a very successful oil executive and a respected community leader, eventually settling his family in Houston.[36]

Now secure financially, Reid passed his good fortune forward at his beloved alma mater, LSU, the school that had given him so much. "I hope I have a legacy. I like those words. When I was in school, there was an alumni from Shreveport in the oil business. He had a scholarship of sorts, and I'd get $25 a semester. I thought, 'How nice of him. If I get to that point, maybe I can do something to add a little joy to spending money,'" Reid remembered.[37] He established a scholarship at LSU to help student athletes and made endowments to the Colleges of Engineering and Science.[38]

Though long retired from football, Reid still followed the game.[39] He continued to reside in Houston with his second wife Kim (married March 14, 1992) and a few cats when not enjoying their second home in Maui.[40] He was the last surviving member of the 1951 Rams' championship team and passed away on March 5, 2020.

Notes

1. Author interview with Joseph Reid, February 8, 2019.
2. 1940 Federal Census, *Ancestry.com*, https://www.ancestry.com/interactive/2442/M-T0627-02040-00022?pid=119924642&backurl=https://search.ancestry.com/cgi-bin/sse.dll?indiv%3D1%26dbid%3D2442%26h%3D119924642%26tid%3D%26pid%3D%26usePUB%3Dtrue%26_phsrc%3Drjo94%26_phstart%3DsuccessSource&treeid=&personid=&hintid=&usePUB=true&_phsrc=rjo94&_phstart=successSource&usePUBJs=true&_ga=2.33568801.1874013112.1558302992-1750616143.1554934192-1940. Federal census.
3. "Tigers Poor Third in Triangular Meet," *Hattiesburg American*, April 20, 1946, 10.
4. "Six Placed on All-Big Eight Five," *Clarion-Ledger*, March 5, 1946, 8; "Big 8 Basketball Team Selected: Laurel Places Two Men on Stellar Squad," *The Greenwood Commonwealth*, March 3, 1947, 8.
5. "Standings," *Hattiesburg American*, November 29, 1946, 12.
6. Associated Press, "The 1946 All-Big Eight Squad," *The Greenwood Commonwealth*, December 14, 1946, 2; "62 'All-Southern' Prep School Gridders Picked by Writers and Coaches," *The Shreveport Times*, December 23, 1946, 27.
7. "A-Man," *The Bunkie Record*, June 20, 1947, 7.
8. "Number 52," *Cornerstone*, Summer and Fall 2017, 30–31.
9. "Vanderbilt and LSU Bees to Play in Power Bowl Football," *The Decatur Daily*, November 2, 1947, 13.
10. Glynn Halbrooks, "LSU Defeats Vanderbilt 12 To 0 In A Mud Battle Game," *The Decatur Daily*, November 16, 1947, 13.
11. Barney Ghio, "Barney's Corner," *The Shreveport Times*, September 5, 1948, 18.
12. Sterling Slappey, "All-Star Votes Go to Southeastern Centers," *The Atlanta Constitution*, November 17, 1948, 11.
13. Barney Ghio, "Barney's Corner," *The Shreveport Times*, March 17, 1949, 16.
14. Jack Gates, "LSU Builds for Grid Upsetter," *The Tampa Tribune*, September 8, 1949, 18.
15. "Mississippi Boys Will Play Big Parts For LSU," *Clarion-Ledger*, October 22, 1949, 5.
16. "UP All-Southeastern," *The Anniston Star*, November 29, 1949, 10.
17. Edwin Pope, "Vito Parilli Voted Brightest in SEC," *The Atlanta Constitution*, November 25, 1950, 6.

234   Part 3: The Team

18. "Boys with Brains Besides Brawn to Battle in Sugar," *Miami* (OK) *Daily News-Record*, December 21, 1949, 4.
19. Dan Hardesty, "Up-and-Down LSU Lacks '49 Drive," *The Atlanta Constitution*, October 10, 1950, 8.
20. Reid interview.
21. Reid interview.
22. Claude Anderson, "Sport Slants," *The San Bernardino County Sun*, June 28, 1951, 38; Reid interview.
23. "Joe Reid," *Pro-football-reference.com*, https://www.pro-football-reference.com/players/R/ReidJo20.htm.
24. Finch, Frank, "Knee Sprain Sidelines Fears for Important Packer Contest," *Los Angeles Times*, October 16, 1951, IV-1; "Rams Late Rally Hands Green Bay Packers 28–0 Loss; Coast Rookie Stars, " *The Capital Times*, October 22, 1951, 13.
25. "Rams Wallop Hapless Yanks for NFL Lead," *Hanford* (CA) *Morning Journal*, November 20, 1951, 6.
26. "Dallas Texans Acquire 11 Gridders From LA," *The Austin American*, June 13, 1952, A-20.
27. Arch Ward, "In the Wake of the News," *Chicago Tribune*, July 10, 1952, 6-1.
28. "Advance Guard of Texans Leave for Kerrville Today," *The Eagle*, July 27, 1952, 6; "Finnell, Reid Ink Texans Contracts," *The Baytown Sun*, July 28, 1952, 7.
29. Frank Finch, "Scouting the Pros," *Los Angeles Times*, October 9, 1952, IV-2.
30. Preston M'Graw, "Texans Seek First Pro Victory at Expense of Packers Tonight," *The Daily Times*, October 18, 1952, 7-A.
31. "'Forget Records,' Warns Bears's Halas," *The Akron Beacon Journal*, November 27, 1952, 77; "Joe Reid"; "1952 Dallas Texans," *Pro-football-reference.com*, https://www.pro-football-reference.com/teams/dtx/1952.htm.
32. "Texans' Joe Reid Carried Off Field," *Austin American-Statesman*, December 8, 1952, 18.
33. Latshaw, Bob, "Lions Face Texans in Title Bid," *Detroit Free Press*, December 13, 1952, 13.
34. Reid interview; "Former LSU Center Inks Baltimore Pact, " *El Paso Times*, May 27, 1953, 19; Ellis, James, "Fullback No Problem with Toth on Squad," *The Evening Sun*, July 27, 1953, 22; James Saggus, "Potpourri of Bi-State Sports," *Enterprise-Journal*, August 24, 1953, 3; "Joseph E. Reid," *Legacy.com*, https://www.legacy.com/obituaries/houstonchronicle/obituary.aspx?n=joseph-e-reid&pid=195626070&fhid=6290.
35. "Joseph E. Reid"; Reid interview.
36. "Joseph E. Reid."
37. "Number 52," 31.
38. "Number 52," 31.
39. Reid interview.
40. Reid interview; "Joseph E. Reid."

Herb Rich

Mark Fellin

Richard Herbert ("Herb") Rich was born in 1928 in Newark, New Jersey, and grew up in Miami Beach, earning all-state honors in football and basketball at Miami Beach High School. Following a distinguished collegiate career at Vanderbilt University, where he was a three-sport star, Rich spent seven years in the National Football League. He played for the Baltimore Colts, Los Angeles Rams, and New York Giants, winning two championships along the way.[1]

Rich wasted no time making a name for himself upon enrolling at Vanderbilt in 1946. He earned letters as a freshman in football, basketball, and baseball, and he did the same as a sophomore while serving as president of his class. As an upperclassman, Rich led the team in rushing with a combined 1,282 yards during the 1948–1949 seasons. He also averaged nearly 28 yards per kickoff return in 1948, helping the Commodores finish the season ranked No. 12 in the country.[2]

A two-time All-Southeastern Conference selection, Rich was named Best Offensive Back in the SEC as a senior and ranked fourth nationally in rushing attempts.[3] He played for Vanderbilt's legendary head coach Red Sanders his first three years and for Bill Edwards in his senior season as the Commodores compiled a 24–15–1 record.[4]

The Baltimore Colts chose the 5-foot-11, 181-pound collegiate star in the sixth round of the 1950 NFL draft, the 67th overall selection.[5] Rich played in every game as a rookie. He patrolled the backfield as a defensive halfback, picking off three passes and returning one for a score while also returning 12 punts for 276 yards and a touchdown and 17 kickoffs for 434 yards.[6] His 23-yard average per punt return set an NFL rookie record that stood for more than five decades.[7] However, Rich played primarily as a defensive back and was seldom utilized as a returner following his rookie season.[8]

Herb Rich played on two NFL championship teams during his career.

When the Colts folded after the 1950 season, Rich was drafted by the Rams and became a key contributor on the 1951 championship squad. As he'd done at Vanderbilt and in Baltimore, Rich hit the ground running in Los Angeles, intercepting passes in preseason contests against the Redskins,[9] Bears,[10] and Browns.[11] In a tune-up against the Cardinals played in Salt Lake City, Rich carried a lateral from fellow defensive back Woodley Lewis 50 yards for a score.[12] The former Colt was proving to be the kind of "polished back"[13] that the Rams were hoping could anchor an improved pass defense.[14]

Unfortunately, Rich suffered a hematoma—also known as a king-sized Charley horse—in the team's final preseason game, a 23–21 victory over the Giants on September 20 at the Polo Grounds, that would keep him on the sidelines for the Rams' first five games.[15]

Rich returned to the field on November 4, making his Rams regular season debut in a vital home rematch against the 49ers. A week earlier, San Francisco shredded Los Angeles 44–17 at Kezar Stadium. Both clubs came into the game at 3–2, looking to keep pace with the National Conference leading Chicago Bears. Rich's first "real" game as a Ram was auspicious. His "standout" performance "did wonders for the Rams' pass defense" in the 23–16 victory over the Niners. His contributions included a fumble recovery that led to the Rams' first touchdown in the tense showdown with their Golden State rivals.[16]

Rich played in the final seven regular season games, intercepting three passes and helping the Rams win the conference. In the title game against the defending champion Cleveland Browns, Rich took part in two crucial plays in the third quarter. First, he batted away Browns quarterback Otto Graham's long pass, which fellow back Jerry Williams intercepted. The turnover helped swing the battle for field position in the Rams' direction. Later in the period, Rich made a diving interception of a Graham pass on the Cleveland 30-yard line—except the officials didn't see it that way, judging that the ball had hit the ground.[17] It was an unpopular and seemingly incorrect call.[18] Regardless, the Browns' drive petered out and Los Angeles pulled out the 24–17 victory to win the 1951 NFL title.

Rich played in 18 games for the Rams during the 1952–1953 seasons, recording 11 interceptions and returning a pair for touchdowns.[19] Following the '52 season, he was named a first team All-Pro by the United Press and *New York Daily News*, and second team All-Pro by the Associated Press.[20]

In 1954, Rich was traded to the Giants. He intercepted 12 passes in 27 games during his three seasons in New York.[21] Rich served as a defensive captain on the Giants' 1956 championship squad.[22]

Rich retired from professional football after the '56 season. In his seven-year career, he played in 64 regular season games, nabbing 29 interceptions and two championships.[23]

His gridiron days behind him, Rich returned to Nashville to practice law. A 1954 graduate of Vanderbilt Law School, he was a member of the Nashville and Tennessee Bar associations for nearly five decades, and an active community leader.[24]

Rich was elected to the Tennessee Sports Hall of Fame in 1992 and was honored in 1996 by the Middle Tennessee Chapter of The National Football Foundation and College Hall of Fame for his contribution to amateur football. In 2000, he became Vanderbilt's seventh "SEC Football Legend." Herb Rich passed away in 2008.[25]

Upon Rich's death, Vanderbilt head football coach Bobby Johnson stated, "This is a terrible loss for the Vanderbilt community. Herb was an extremely kind person who always was supportive, not only of the Vanderbilt football team but of the entire athletic program. During his time at Vanderbilt, Herb was a fantastic athlete who enjoyed a great NFL career. Herb also distinguished himself off the field in the way he lived his life."[26]

Notes

1. "Herb Rich," *Tshf.net*, http://tshf.net/halloffame/rich-herb/.
2. "Former Athlete Herb Rich Passes Away," *Vucommodores.com*, March 28, 2008, https://vucommodores.com/news/2008/3/28/Former_athlete_Herb_Rich_passes_away.aspx.
3. "Herb Rich," *Tshf.net*.
4. "Former Athlete Herb Rich Passes Away."
5. Bob Carroll, et al., eds., *Total Football II* (New York: HarperCollins, 1999), 1213, 1454.
6. "Herb Rich," *Pro-football-reference.com*, https://www.pro-football-reference.com/players/R/RichHe20.htm.
7. "Former Athlete Herb Rich Passes Away."
8. Carroll, 1213.
9. Art Rogers, "Rich Haul (photo)," *Los Angeles Times*, August 16, 1951, IV-1.
10. Frank Finch, "Savage Rams Win, 42–14," *Los Angeles Times*, August 24, 1951, IV-1, 3.
11. Frank Finch, "Groza Again 'Kicks' Rams," *Los Angeles Times*, September 14, 1951, III-1, 3.
12. Frank Finch, "Cards Lead Rams in Fourth, 22–14," *Los Angeles Times*, September 8, 1951, II-9.
13. Frank Finch, "Rookie Linemen Likely Starters Against 'Skins," *Los Angeles Times*, September 14, 1951, IV-1, 2.
14. Paul Zimmerman, "Sportscripts," *Los Angeles Times*, August 27, 1951, IV-1.
15. "Ram Halfback Rich Out of Yank Game," *Los Angeles Times*, September 24, 1951, IV-1.
16. Frank Finch, "Waterfield & Co. Deal 23–16 Loss to 49ers," *Los Angeles Times*, November 5, 1951, IV-1.
17. Braven Dyer, "Old Age, Angelenos Finally Catch Browns," *Los Angeles Times*, December 24, 1951, IV-1, 2.
18. Frank Finch, "Rams Whip Browns, 24–17; Win Pro Title," *Los Angeles Times*, December 24, 1951, IV-1, 2.
19. Carroll, 1213.
20. Carroll, 401.
21. Carroll, 1213.
22. "Herb Rich," Tshf.net.
23. "Herb Rich," *Pro-football-reference.com*.
24. "Former Athlete Herb Rich Passes Away."
25. "Herb Rich," *Tshf.net*; "Former Athlete Herb Rich Passes Away."
26. "Former Athlete Herb Rich Passes Away."

Andy Robustelli

John M. Vorperian

Reflecting upon the famed New York Giants front four of Rosey Grier, Jim Katcavage, Dick Modzelewski, and Andy Robustelli, that he coached as Big Blue's defensive coordinator, Hall of Fame coaching great Tom Landry said of Robustelli, "He put more book time into his work than the others. He thought all the time. Not just on the field, but in his room, at the dining table."[1] Teammate and Hall of Famer Frank Gifford declared, "He was bright, smart. He was always like another coach on the field."[2] Giants head coach Allie Sherman once said of the 6'1", 230-pound lineman, "Watch him. You will be studying a real master. Speed of mind, hands and feet make him the best. But there's something else you can't even begin to measure. Without his burning desire, he would have been just an ordinary player."[3]

Andy Robustelli played 14 seasons in the NFL with the Los Angeles Rams and New York Giants. A seven-time Pro Bowl (1953; 1955–1957; 1959–1961) defensive end, Robustelli played in eight NFL championship games, two with the Rams and six with the Giants. A seven-time first team All-Pro and a four-time second team All-Pro selection, in 1962 Robustelli was honored with the Maxwell Football Club's Bert Bell Award as the NFL's most outstanding player. He was the first defensive position player to garner this prestigious accolade.

In 175 regular season games, the NFL pro from tiny Arnold College recovered 22 opponents' fumbles, nabbed two interceptions and scored five touchdowns. In 1971, Robustelli was elected to the Pro Football Hall of Fame. From 1974 to 1978 he served as director of operations for the New York Giants. When he retired from the NFL after the 1964 season, his business acumen led to the creation of a sports marketing company, initially titled National Professional Athletes. The brilliance and purposeful thinking he demonstrated on the field easily

Rams defensive stalwart Andy Robustelli later starred for the New York Giants.

translated into success in the world of commerce. Today, Robustelli Corporate Services Ltd remains a key establishment based in his hometown.

Andrew Richard Robustelli was born on December 6, 1925, in Stamford, Connecticut, to Lucien Robustelli and Katherine (nee Galasso). The couple had five other children: Lucien Jr., Angela, Susan, Anna and Edith. Lucien was a barber and Katherine a seamstress. Both parents worked full-time, but on Saturdays Kate would clean, without pay, Sacred Heart Roman Catholic Church in Stamford. Religion played an important role in Andy's upbringing. He was involved with a number of activities at Sacred Heart. Teammates would later report they never could think of an instance in which they ever heard Andy curse or swear.

The Robustelli family lived on Stamford's West Side, a low- to middle-income, racially mixed neighborhood. The section was predominantly Italian but with a number of black families. The Robustellis lived in a six-family tenement on Spruce Street. The building's five other tenants were African Americans. Andy felt no prejudices were ever present. Recalling those days, he said, "It was a great neighborhood to grow up in." "Hardly anyone ever got into any kind of trouble, and maybe it was because most of us were always playing baseball, football or basketball. Also we had very strict parents who kept us in line, along with older brothers in some cases, who made sure you stayed out of trouble."[4]

Andy's parents instilled a strong work ethic in him. At a young age, he learned the value of a dollar and how to look for business opportunities. Those fiscal values and principles were carried steadily into adulthood. The youngster bagged and delivered groceries and did other chores for Sclafani's grocery store. Andy's wages were contributed to the family budget. At Stamford High School, he was a three-sport athlete for the Black Knights, playing varsity basketball, catcher on the baseball team and two-way end, offense and defense, on the football squad. Andy also played for the church's sport teams and sometimes would forgo a school game for a Sacred Heart CYO contest.

Upon high school graduation in June 1943 Andy got a scholarship to LaSalle Military Academy (Oakdale, New York). The grant required he play three sports—baseball, football and basketball. Andy attended the academy in the hopes it would prep him for either Manhattan College or Fordham University. His friends were enlisting to fight the Axis Powers. He wanted to join the World War II war effort but was underage and his mother adamantly refused to sign the enlistment waiver. He was at LaSalle for four months and then turned 18. Andy went to the local draft board. He volunteered but told his mother he had been drafted.

Robustelli spent two and a half years in the Navy. His LaSalle stint was viewed as "military service" by the Navy. Accordingly, he was initially assigned as a drill instructor at a naval basic training school. Then Andy was placed as a water-tender and a 20 mm anti-aircraft gunner aboard a destroyer escort—the USS *William C. Cole* (DE-641). His tour of duty took him to the Pacific theater where he was part of the invasion of Okinawa. Honorably discharged, the war veteran returned home to Stamford in April 1946.

In the fall of 1947, Andy registered at Arnold College. The tiny New England school, founded in 1921, existed for just 32 years, absorbed into the University of Bridgeport in 1953. However, in its day, the Connecticut school on Long Island Sound had a reputation of having a strong athletics program. Although he longed to attend Fordham the fact was several of his high school buddies were already at Arnold. Robustelli decided to join them and pursue a physical education degree. His plan was to become a gym teacher and coach. After freshman year, in 1948, he married his high school sweetheart Jeanne Dora.

Football at Arnold had been dropped during World War II but post-war the sport was quickly reinstated. Even though he had not played football during his military service, Andy successfully tried out for Arnold's grid team. A two-way end, the Stamford denizen was a sure-handed pass-catcher, a ferocious tackler and swift pass rusher. He also had a talent for blocking punts, picking up the ball and running for touchdowns. He was named to the Associated Press 1948 Little All-America team and repeated on the squad in 1949 and 1950.

Lou DeFilippo, a Fordham line coach and Eastern region birddog for the Los Angeles Rams, sent glowing and resounding reports on Robustelli. The former New York Football Giants guard repeatedly told his NFL West Coast outfit, "He'd be good against anybody," "definitely worth a look."[5]

DeFilippo was one of roughly a hundred part-time scouts or "birddogs" on the Los Angeles franchise payroll scoping out talent at remote schools or small colleges. The novel idea for this innovative intelligence network belonged to Rams co-owner Dan Reeves and scouting chief Eddie Kotal.

Based on DeFilippo's accounts, the Rams dispatched ends coach Red Hickey to watch Robustelli. Hickey saw what would be Andy's last college game against St. Michael's in Winooski Park, Vermont. On that day in October 1950, Andy was a true road warrior. He had about a half dozen pass receptions, nearly a dozen tackles and blocked multiple punts. On the second to the last play of the contest he broke his leg and was carried off on a stretcher.

Nevertheless, the Rams selected the Arnold grid standout in the 19th round (228th player overall) of the 1951 NFL draft. All 18 players the Rams picked before Andy were from nationally known colleges.

Growing up Andy never followed professional football. His interests were high school football and listening to Notre Dame Football games on the radio on Saturday afternoons after helping his mom at Sacred Heart. During college, he did visit and talk with players of the New York Yankees of the All-America Football Conference (AAFC) at their training camp at Cheshire, Connecticut.

In June 1951 the New York baseball Giants offered Robustelli a tryout. Robustelli had been a star third baseman at Arnold batting nearly .400 and known for his tremendous tape measure homers. This was baseball's Golden Age. New York City was home to three major league clubs, the Dodgers, Giants and Yankees. The Connecticut native had grown up a zealous Giants fan. He often journeyed to the Polo Grounds to see his favorite baseball team. Two days before he was to leave for Rams training camp, the Giants extended a $400 per month contract to play in their farm system (it was also rumored that Robustelli would play pro football in Canada—see chapter on 1951 NFL draft). Additionally, Andy was offered a $2,400 position to teach physical education and coach football at a high school in Meriden, Connecticut.

Faced with this three-sided career dilemma, Andy sought advice from a person with connections into the world of sports, public relations executive and *Stamford Advocate* sports columnist J. Walter Kennedy. Kennedy would later become the city's mayor and NBA commissioner. Kennedy told Robustelli, "Stick to the teaching and coaching by all means. You've got a wife and a baby, so you can't afford to gamble on something chancy as professional football—certainly not with your small college background."[6]

Afterwards he talked with Lucien about his options, a man who, by Andy's own account, did not understand sports. His father said, "You've got to take a chance. If you don't, you'll spend the rest of your life wondering whether you could have made it. But then, you've got to make up your own mind."[7]

Make up his mind he did, taking a train west to California. The Rams offered him $4,250 for the season, if he made the club. Upon arrival at the University of Redlands, 20 miles from Palm Springs, it was made clear to the rookie end he had no chance at displacing famed Rams receivers Tom Fears and Elroy "Crazylegs" Hirsch or even Bob Boyd, who was in his second season with the club.

The first two weeks in camp Andy trained with the defense. Unsure of his chances, homesick, sleepless, and concerned about his family, Robustelli hadn't even unpacked his bags. The teaching job possibility preyed upon his mind.

Andy met with Rams head coach Joe Stydahar to inform him he was thinking of forgoing pro football and returning to Connecticut. Stydahar bellowed, "If you go home now, you'll be cheating yourself, and that Polish wife of yours will hit you over the head with a broomstick! And she should do that if you don't stick it out and give it a fair shot. You can't quit now, and I won't let you quit. Now get the hell out of here."[8]

Jeanne actually was of Slovak heritage, but the skipper's forceful monologue influenced Robustelli to remain. What Andy did not know was Stydahar and the Rams were fully impressed with DeFilippo's detailed comments about Robustelli's defensive prowess, in particular his ability to block punts. Later on, Robustelli was told by Eddie Kotal, "Well, when we get down to 18th or 19th pick ... we're drafting on speculation, and any guy who can block nine or ten punts like you did in one season has got to have something. That's why we drafted you."[9]

Andy's opportunity came when starting right end Jack Zilly broke his arm. The four-year pro from Notre Dame was out for the season. In his first full scrimmage at the position, Robustelli spun past the offensive left tackle several times, harassed and sacked the quarterbacks and racked up a number of tackles on the ball carriers.

His camp life steadied. Stydahar ran a tough, controlled and methodical operation. Robustelli thrived in that environment. Andy viewed himself as a disciplined individual and naturally his military experience further helped him to succeed. Veterans like Linebacker Don Paul and even Jack Zilly assisted the novice to improve his football techniques. Homesickness subsided as he struck up a rapport with Harry Thompson, a second-year guard from UCLA. Thompson had a relative who was married to Connecticut resident Jackie Robinson. The two Rams were able to converse about Connecticut, the Brooklyn Dodgers, and football. Andy's closest friends on the 1951 team were three other rookies: Leon McLaughlin, Herb Rich, and Don Simensen.

Robustelli recalled another aspect of camp life which brought amusement; particularly to the vehicle-less rookies. Stydahar demanded all players stay on campus until 5 p.m. Whenever the Rams' preseason games were home contests, veterans would look forward to sleeping one night in a Los Angeles hotel. They had cars and getting out first at five o'clock became a major challenge. About the phenomena Andy said, "[They] lined up their cars, engines revving, as if it were a Grand Prix race. The moment that clock hit five ... they all took off.... Waterfield had a Jaguar, Hirsch a Cadillac. It was a competitive thing to see who could get to town first. One time Don Paul even swerved up on an embankment to get out in front."[10]

Andy played well during his rookie campaign, appearing in 11 regular season games and starting eight times. Robustelli missed the final game of his inaugural NFL regular season with a knee injury—a 42–14 home victory over the Packers that clinched the National Conference crown for the Rams. It was the only game he would miss in his entire pro career.

The 1951 NFL championship pitted Paul Brown's Cleveland Browns in a title rematch against the Rams. Andy's impact play came early in the third quarter with the Rams trailing 10–7. Cleveland had the ball on their own 41-yard line. Legendary quarterback Otto Graham went back to throw, and Rams defensive end Larry Brink crashed through the line and blindsided the signal caller. Graham fumbled.

Robustelli picked up the ball and sprinted for the end zone. Browns running back Marion Motley tackled him at the two-yard line. Three running plays later Dan Towler scored a touchdown and Bob Waterfield converted the PAT and the Rams had a 14–10 lead. With the final score 24–17, the team with the horns was crowned league champions.

In the Los Angeles clubhouse, Andy told reporters how Motley caught him, "I never got a really good grip on the ball because I just grabbed it off-balance and began to run. I stumbled as soon as I started, and it seemed I kept stumbling all the way down the field, trying to keep the ball in my grasp."[11] Player shares for the Rams amounted to $2,108.44. Robustelli used his winnings to buy ownership in a Stamford sporting goods store.

Robustelli flourished with Los Angeles. He earned first team All-Pro honors in 1953 and 1955. The 29-year-old had a marvelous 1955 season with five fumble recoveries, one interception and two defensive touchdowns all which helped the Rams (8–3–1) return to the NFL title game, which they lost 38–14 to Cleveland. During his time there Los Angeles always had a winning record. Robustelli would later say while with the Rams he "was more of a spectacular player ... and played with a little bit of reckless abandon."[12]

The Rams were fully embraced by Hollywood's star citizens. It was common for the players to rub elbows with Rams part owner Bob Hope and Jane Russell, quarterback Bob Waterfield's wife, along with other Tinseltown celebrities like Dean Martin and Frank Sinatra.

Entering his sixth season on the eve of 1956 training camp, Andy phoned head coach Sid Gillman to explain he would need a few more days before leaving Stamford as Jeanne was about to give birth to their fourth child. Gillman was fiery and adamant that Robustelli report immediately. "I don't care if it's a couple of days or not. You get your ass out here. That's all I can tell you."[13] The next sound the $7,000 a year All-Pro heard was a dial tone.

Days later, with Jeanne and baby boy home from the hospital, while packing to leave, Andy got a phone call from Wellington Mara, New York Giants owner Tim Mara's youngest son. Wellington said the Giants and Rams were in trade talks and he wanted to know, "do you think you could play two or three more years? If so, we'd certainly love to have you...."[14]

Andy was initially dismayed by the call. He liked playing with the Rams. But as the conversation progressed, he realized how much the Giants wanted him to be part of their organization.

On July 27, 1956, the Giants shopped their 1957 first round draft pick to the Rams for Robustelli. (Los Angeles selected Baylor University wide receiver Del Shofner, who later became a Giants teammate of Andy's.) After the trade, Giants head coach Jim Lee Howell was quoted as saying that Robustelli became available because of his "increasing reluctance to leave his Stamford, Connecticut home and play on the West Coast."[15]

With his young family growing, Robustelli was indeed concerned about them, but he wanted to remain a Ram. However in time he came to view his alignment with the NFL's Big Apple outpost as a good fit.

Why did Gillman swap Robustelli? Some observers contend Gillman was an uncompromising individual with his own steadfast football operation concepts. One story was he wanted to shake up the Los Angeles defense. After Robustelli, Gillman traded defensive unit starters Big Daddy Lipscomb and Ed Hughes. No doubt there was a shake-up. In 1955 the Rams allowed 231 points; 4th out of the 12 NFL team defenses. The 1956 Rams (4–8) hemorrhaged 307 points which ranked them 10th out of 12.

Robustelli saw contrasts between the two organizations. Whereas the Rams catered to their pros, laying out their jerseys, socks, pads, etc., Giants players were not spoiled. New York pros were expected to go get their gear and ready themselves for hard nose football. In New York, the focus was not the glamour of the offense but the raw, battering, bruising power of the defense. During Robustelli's tenure with the Giants a newly heard chant of "Dee-fense, Dee-fense, Dee-fense" echoed through the Bronx on autumn Sundays.

Giants training camp was held in Vermont at St. Michael's College which brought to Andy memories of his collegiate athletic achievements. Ex-Marine Jim Lee Howell, like Stydahar, ran camp in a highly structured and organized manner. Howell delegated command of his offense and defense to his assistant coaches, Vince Lombardi and Tom Landry, respectively.

In his first season with New York, just as he had in Los Angeles, Robustelli was a member of an NFL championship team. On December 30, 1956, the Giants annihilated the Chicago Bears 47–7. It was the Giants' first title triumph since 1938. Andy brought down Bears quarterback George Blanda for a five-yard loss and had a fumble recovery in the win. Big Blue player shares amounted to $3,779.19 apiece.

Andy and his Giants teammates were welcomed guests in renowned Manhattan establishments like Toots Shor's, P.J. Clarke's and Mike Manuche's steak house. It was common for them to be regularly acknowledged by fellow patrons, like Jackie Gleason, Ernest Hemingway, Ed Sullivan, Joe DiMaggio, Frank Sinatra and other celebrities.

The proximity of his football club and his sporting goods business allowed him to oversee both ventures to success. Robustelli commuted from Stamford to Yankee Stadium. In 1957, Tom Landry rented a Stamford home from one of Andy's friends. The duo would carpool for three seasons. Occasionally, they would be joined by another Stamford resident, sports broadcaster Howard Cosell.

During those many rides, the two G-Men discussed defensive strategy. Andy remarked, "No one on the Giants knew Landry and his system better than I did."[16] Landry relied on middle linebacker Sam Huff and Andy to communicate to the other players his various schemes and designs. In 1960, Landry became the Dallas Cowboys' first head coach. From 1962 to 1964 Robustelli would act as a player-coach with the Giants.

In 1964, Andy was in his fourteenth season. After appearing in five NFL championship games from 1958 to 1963, the aging Giants (2–10–2) had finished last in the Eastern Conference. At season's end Robustelli retired from the game. After retiring, he bought a travel agency. Robustelli's travel agency and sporting goods business both prospered. He then opened National Professional Athletes (NPA). Pros like Merlin Olsen (Rams), Pete Retzlaff (Eagles), Nick Pietrosante (Lions), Gino Cappelletti (Patriots), Joe Morrison (Giants), Mike Ditka (Bears) and others affiliated with NPA.

A year later with all his business enterprises thriving, Robustelli returned to pro football. NBC television's Chet Simmons hired him as a color commentator covering the upstart American Football League games along with play-by-play announcer Charlie Jones. Andy was mindful not to be prejudiced but he clearly felt his loyalties were with the established NFL. He left after one season.

One of the most enjoyable football jobs Robustelli ever had was for half a year in 1966. He was the Brooklyn Dodgers' (Continental Football League) head coach. Jackie Robinson was general manager and the Dodgers' home field was not in Brooklyn, but Downing Stadium on Manhattan's Randall's Island. Though the Dodgers finished 5–9 under his tutelage, Robustelli felt the experience was in a personal sense successful, particularly when the Giants midway through the season signed Dodgers quarterback Tom Kennedy and made him their starter. The Dodgers were sold and moved to Akron (now the Vulcans) for the 1967 season, where they failed financially after only four games.

On July 31, 1971, Robustelli was inducted into the Pro Football Hall of Fame. A first ballot inductee, his presenter was his old friend (and now NBA commissioner) J. Walter Kennedy. Robustelli's Hall class included Jim Brown, Bill Hewitt, Frank (Bruiser) Kinard, Vince Lombardi, Y.A. Tittle and Norm Van Brocklin.

Robustelli's several businesses continued their ascendancy as he added real estate holdings in the Caribbean, an Italian restaurant and partial ownership of a railroad car company to his portfolio. But Andy could not keep away from football. In 1972, he began doing a weekly television program with former New York Jets offensive lineman Sam DeLuca.

On December 17, 1973, Andy was invited to Wellington Mara's home. New York had finished the season in last place in the NFC Eastern Division with a 2–11–1 record. They talked about the Giants and his rejoining the Big Blue family. He re-upped for another tour with New York as director of operations.

Robustelli was, in essence, the general manager handling scouting and team personnel. He attempted to rebuild the Giants, but they continued to underperform.

On December 18, 1978, Andy resigned. During his stint as director of operations, New York was 21–51.

Afterwards, he spent even more time tending to the continued success of NPA (now known as Robustelli Corporate Services Ltd.) as well as giving care to his family and civic devotion to the Stamford community.

On October 3, 2010, the Giants unveiled their Ring of Honor which included Robustelli along with 22 other players and eight executives.

On May 31, 2011, Andrew Richard Robustelli passed away at Stamford Hospital due to complications from surgery. He was 85 years old. Jeanne predeceased him on April 1, 2011. Andy was survived by his nine children and their spouses, 29 grandchildren and six great-grandchildren.

Robustelli once wrote, "Sports are a most excellent device with which to tell a man's character."[17] Clearly his athletic career speaks volumes to such.

Notes

1. Richard Goldstein, "Andy Robustelli, Giants' Hall of Fame Defensive End, Dies at 85," *New York Times*, May 31, 2011, https://www.nytimes.com/2011/06/01/sports/football/andy-robustelli-giants-hall-of-fame-defensive-end-dies-85.html.

2. Jerry Izenberg, "Izenberg: Andy Robustelli Almost Never Made It Here, But He Became the Perfect Giant," *NJ.com*, June 1, 2011, updated March 31, 2019, https://www.nj.com/ginats/indexssf/2011/06/Izenberg_andy_robustelli.html.

3. Izenberg, "Izenberg: Andy Robustelli."

4. Jack Cavanaugh, *Giants Among Men: How Robustelli, Huff, Gifford, and the Giants Made New York a Football Town and Changed the NFL* (New York: Random House, 2008), 78.

5. Cavanaugh, *Giants Among Men*, 6.

6. Cavanaugh, *Giants Among Men*, 7.

7. Cavanaugh, *Giants Among Men*, 7.

8. Cavanaugh, *Giants Among Men*, 9.

9. Stuart Leuthner, *Iron Men: Bucko, Crazylegs, and the Boys Recall the Golden Days of Professional Football* (New York: Doubleday 1988), 6–7.

10. Andy Robustelli with Jack Clary, *Once a Giant, Always: My Two Lives with the New York Giants* (Boston: Quinlan Press, 1987), 6.

11. "1951: Cleveland Browns @ Los Angeles Rams," *Golden Football Magazine*, http://goldenrankings.com/nflchampionshipgame1951.html.

12. Leuthner, Iron Men, 8.

13. Cavanaugh, *Giants Among Men*, 10.

14. Cavanaugh, *Giants Among Men*, 10.

15. Cavanaugh, *Giants Among Men*, 10–11.

16. Robustelli, *Once A Giant*, 29.

17. "Rare 1951 Arnold College Year Book, Wave, Milford Connecticut Andy Robustelli," *Ebay.com*, accessed September 10, 2018, https://www.ebay.co.uk/itm/Arnold College Year Book, Wave, Milford, Connecticut Andy Robustelli-/2612559510883.

Don Simensen

Mark L. Ford

"Son, I've had a headache for 20 years," Don Simensen told a high school player, two decades after being forced to retire from pro football.[1] His NFL career lasted only two seasons, but he was the starting offensive tackle in all but four of the 26 Rams games in 1951 and 1952. He sustained multiple concussions in his athletic career. At the time, none of them were considered serious enough to prevent him from returning to the field for the next Rams drive.

Almost 30 years after the fact, a *Los Angeles Times* reporter wrote that Simensen "played the entire second half of the 1951 championship game after a concussion, and to this day can't recall anything about the final 30 minutes."[2] The lifelong headache would come at the end of the 1952 season, during a tiebreaker playoff game in Detroit. Even then, he "regarded it at the time as just slightly more serious than a hangover."[3] It was a lot more serious than that. The headaches got worse and, less than two months after the Detroit game, he checked into a hospital. A few days later, he was undergoing emergency surgery for a cerebral hemorrhage. He survived, but what had been a promising NFL career was over after two seasons.

Donald Ray Simensen was born on September 11, 1926, in Minot, North Dakota. He grew up in Minnesota and was a year-round athlete at Central High School in St. Paul—football in the autumn, ice hockey in the winter and baseball in the spring. Known to his friends as "Si" rather than "Don," Simensen had a reputation for being tough. One college teammate recalled that "when Si hit you on the football field, you felt it for a couple of days."[4] Si was also known, however, for the impact that his skull was taking, and not just in football. "He was hit in

The 1951 Rams' offensive lineman Don Simensen's NFL career lasted only two seasons.

the head by a pitch four or five times playing semi-pro baseball," another friend told a reporter. "When he was asked why he was beaned so often, he would grin and say, 'You never know when the pitch is going to break.'"5

After a couple of years away from school, Simensen stayed in St. Paul and enrolled at the College of St. Thomas. While most people have never heard of them, the "Tommies" still have a Division III football team and have sent 24 players to the NFL, including Hall of Famer Walt Kiesling. Si was a star tackle in college, and the gridiron "Tommies" did well. In 1949, they even played on New Year's Day, getting invited to the short-lived Cigar Bowl postseason game in Tampa (for the record, St. Thomas and the Missouri Valley College Vikings played to a 13–13 tie on New Year's Day in 1949).6 Si was team captain for the 1950 season.

He wasn't picked in the 1951 NFL draft, but Si got word that the Rams had nobody playing tackle on either offense or defense. Bob Reinhard, Gil Bouley and Bill Smyth retired after the 1950 NFL championship game. Dick Huffman and Ed Champagne went north to play Canadian football. "If memory serves," Frank Finch wrote for the *Los Angeles Times*, "no National Football League team ever before went into training camp without at least one experienced tackle on deck."7

Of course, Simensen wasn't the only person who recognized the Rams' shortage of tackles. When camp opened, eleven rookies were trying out for the four available starting positions. At 220 pounds, Si was listed as a candidate for a guard position, but even as other players were being sent home, Si remained on an ever-decreasing roster. Coach Joe Stydahar was impressed enough to let him suit up for the first exhibition, in San Diego—and sit on the bench.

Two days before that first test, a Los Angeles area newspaper ran a large photo captioned "CHARLES TOOGOOD OF NEBRASKA 'Rams Best Rookie Tackle Prospect.'"8 Charlie Toogood had been the Rams' third round pick in the '51 draft. Stydahar started him at left tackle position for the San Diego exhibition (against Navy personnel), then used the same starting lineup for the preseason game against the Redskins. Simensen watched from the sideline as Toogood started one game after another. With only two weeks left before the regular season opener, the Rams went to Cleveland for a preseason rematch of the 1950 championship game—and Charlie Toogood twisted his knee. Fate had given Don Simensen the job as starting left tackle.

As you'll see in the chapter on Toogood, the Nebraska lineman would later be a Rams starter, but in '51 and '52, Don Simensen owned the spot on the front line, and got his first pro start in the preseason closer against the Giants in New York. The Rams' 23–21 win at the Polo Grounds was hard fought. Exhibition or not, 14 of the Rams required treatment for injuries after a game that Frank Finch wrote "must have set a new league record for casualties."9 Simensen was one of the lesser hurt in the "banged up" but would "probably be ready"10 for the 1951 season opener against the New York Yanks. He was ready.

"Don Simensen. I'll never forget his first game," Norm Van Brocklin recalled in a 1976 interview. "Came back to the huddle with his face all bloodied. I said, 'Hey, Si, any problems up there?' Ol' Si just blinked and said, 'Hell, no, I'll be all right, soon as I find that sonuvabitch with the hammer.'"11 Si's first game, in this case, just happened to have been the same one where Van Brocklin rewrote the NFL record book, passing for 554 yards in the 54–14 win over the Yanks.

Simensen was the starting left tackle in all but one of the regular season games.

Charlie Toogood, who had missed the first four games while recuperating from his preseason knee injury, was activated for the October 28 game at San Francisco, but Coach Stydahar brought Si back off the bench for the rematch at home the next week. As with any offensive lineman, Si's contribution during the 1951 Rams' season went unnoticed by most fans and unrecorded by the statisticians.

In football's first 150 years, there still hasn't been a stat for how much rushing yardage a blocker has cleared the way for; nor how many seconds have been bought by being the person between the defensive lineman and the quarterback. We tend to notice the offensive linemen only when they fail to do their jobs. While the front five are catching the brunt of the acceleration and mass of the behemoths charging toward the passer, we're all looking at who has the football.

The contribution of the all-rookie front five was evident from the Rams' stats on offense in 1951. On average yards gained per play, be it run or pass, the Rams had led in both 1950 and 1951. In 1950, their 6.0 average was about a foot better than the Yanks' 5.7. In 1951, though, every Rams attempt at a run or a throw was averaging well over a yard ahead of the next best team—6.7 each time, compared to 5.4 for the Lions. On passing, the Rams got two extra yards per attempt more than any of the other 11 teams—8.3 yards, with the Lions a distant second at 6.3 yards per attempt. The difference among the teams on rushing average in 1951 wasn't as dramatic (the Rams got 5.2 yards per carry, while the Lions, Bears, 49ers and Cardinals were the next best, at 4.5), but whereas the Rams had been seventh in a 13-team league in 1950, their 5.2 was the best in 1951.[12]

As the '51 season progressed, Frank Finch praised Simensen and the rookie linemen following the rematch in New York against the Yanks, a 48 to 21 "touchdown orgy" (Finch's words), adding, "Keep that running attack going, gang. The Bear game's less than two weeks away."[13] Following the Rams' win in Chicago over the Bears, "Si" got mention from *Times* sports columnist Paul Zimmerman. "Remember," Zimmerman noted of the Rams, "that here was a team that started the season off without a single veteran tackle. That's a situation without precedent in NFL annals."[14]

You know the rest of the story of 1951; the Rams backed into the championship name, their National Conference pennant coming down to their win and the Lions' loss. Simensen was the left tackle on offense for the entire game. On game day, he weighed 209 pounds,[15] and he lined up across from Cleveland's 251-pound tackle, John Sandusky, on every play. No matter. "Sheer size means less than nothing in the National League," Frank Finch wrote a few months later. "I could name you half a dozen blubber-bellies who got by for awhile on beef alone without contributing one iota to their teams' success. Tom Dahms and Don Simensen, a couple of Ram yearling tackles weighing well under 225, frequently knocked enemy human hippos for loops last year."[16]

A little more than six months later, training camp opened at Redlands for the 1952 season. Simensen had bulked up during the offseason, adding muscle to reach 230 pounds,[17] and his future looked bright. He didn't know that his second year in the NFL would be his last. While he had never left a game for a fracture or even a sprain, he was absorbing a lot of head shots without even being referred for an x-ray. "In fact," an investigative reporter wrote decades later, "when doctors finally did examine Simensen, they couldn't believe the number of bumps and scars on his skull."[18] Si commented in that interview, "The doctor said my head had run into everything that a head could run into."[19]

Sometimes, things ran into him. The hit that got notice came in a Wednesday night exhibition game against the visiting 49ers on September 3. Tempers flared up frequently, and there were 170 yards of penalties called between the two teams (120 of them on the visitors). Eight Rams were injured, some of them in plays that didn't draw a flag. For perhaps the first time in his pro career, Si was pulled because of a concussion, delivered by one of the most aggressive players in NFL history. "Tackle Don Simensen was severely shaken when racked up on a blind-side block by man-eating Hardy Brown,"[20] the L.A. paper noted the next day. Even 49ers fans thought it was a bit over the top. *San Francisco Examiner* columnist Eddie Muller commented, "Some of the 49ers are still talking about the 'knuckle block' linebacker Hardy Brown threw at the Rams' Don Simensen ... in the other night's brawl. Describing it as a 'beauty,' they say it all but uncoupled the Ram tackle. Perhaps they'd be wiser if they kept their enthusiasm under their hats. Brown is a tough cookie, but the 49ers will invite reprisals from the rest of the league if they brag too much about their ability to dish it out."[21]

After three games as a starter, Simensen was replaced for awhile by Len Teeuws. Coach Hamp Pool told the press that Si and fellow starting tackle Tom Dahms "simply weren't giving our passers adequate protection,"[22] Both players came back with new resolve, however, and Si had his best NFL game ever on November 30, getting awarded the game ball for his work in a 34–21 win at San Francisco,[23] drawing praise for punching through the 49er defensive line. One reporter noted that "a couple of sterling offensive tackles, Tom Dahms and Don Simensen, time and again opened huge gaps in the San Francisco line through which rugged Dan Towler stormed to lead the Rams on the ground. You could drive a 1953 Mack truck through those holes, to bring an old saying up to date."[24]

If the Rams hadn't gone on an eight-game winning streak to close out 1952, Simensen might well have gone on to bigger things in 1953. Their successful run, however, put them at 9–3–0, in a tie with the Lions at the top of the National Conference at the end of regular play, and occasioned a rare tiebreaker playoff. Somewhere during that December 21 game, Si got his last sports concussion and the headache that would never go away. "After the Detroit game," it would be said years later, "Simensen complained of nausea. He then developed 'a headache that I thought was going to blow the top of my head off.' A blood vessel had broken in Simensen's brain, and was hemorrhaging."[25]

Right after the playoff game, Simensen returned to Minnesota for the off-season. On February 19, 1953, he was ice-fishing with friends at Mille Lacs Lake, north of the Twin Cities, when he suddenly found that he couldn't move his legs. "His friends have always wondered whether the football hits or baseball beanings played a part," a friend said after Si's death. "Anyway, he was paralyzed from the waist down. He insisted on being driven to St. Paul."[26] Once home, instead of calling for an ambulance, he waited for his father to get a taxi so that he could be admitted. After a few days of testing, it was clear that Simensen needed immediate surgery, and he underwent a six-hour operation at Charles T. Miller Hospital.[27]

The team waited to see whether Si would survive before releasing the news. Rams fans were stunned to read on February 28: "Don Simensen, 26, starting left offensive tackle for The Los Angeles Rams for the past two seasons, has played his last game of football."

Coach Pool told the press, "Don is doing as well as can be expected but his recovery will take a long time. The Rams will miss Don's hard blocking and fiery spirit."[28]

Simensen's health was even worse than the public knew. "Sorry to report that the condition of Don Simensen yet is extremely serious," the *Times'* Frank Finch wrote two weeks after the operation. "Don is unconscious most of the time ... and has shown little, if any, improvement."[29] It wasn't until May 17 that Finch was finally able to say that Simensen was "making a splendid recovery"[30] and had been released. It was an exaggeration to say that "the wisecracking Ram tackle (he'll never play again) is up and about at his St. Paul home."[31] It had taken two months for Simensen to recover his eyesight, and he was wheelchair-bound and preparing to start rehabilitation in order to walk again.

Still, there was no longer a fear that Si was at death's door (indeed, Simensen would live another 40 years). A booster organization, the Rams Club, arranged one of the most star-studded touch football games in history as a fundraiser to pay Si's medical bills.[32] The 93,000-seat Coliseum opened its gates on July 19, 1953 (coincidentally, the day that the Korean War came to a halt), and folks who bought tickets got to come on to the field to get autographs and take photos with almost everyone from the 1952 Rams coming out on behalf of their teammate. Bob Waterfield, who had already announced his retirement, came back for the event,[33] and Glenn "Mr. Outside" Davis, who had announced a comeback attempt, was there as well.

With no helmets and no pads, wearing shorts and T-shirts that bore their jersey numbers, the players took turns on a seven-man squad. For the record, The Los Angeles Rams defeated the San Pedro Dolphins, 20 to 13.[34] Though only 4,000 people turned out, the *Times* noted that many of the people who bought a $1.20 ticket were just doing so for a good cause. In all, $9,511.28 was raised for Simensen's bills,[35] equivalent to $89,000 in today's dollars.[36] By October, Simensen's bills had been paid. By then, he was able to regain the use of his left leg, though he dragged his right foot for the rest of his life.[37] In November, when the Rams were in Chicago to face the Cardinals, he was well enough to come down from Minnesota to sit one last time on the bench with his teammates.[38]

The rest of the story is that Don Simensen, ineligible for a pension or disability compensation, went back to work when he was well again (when he had reached what insurers call "maximum medical improvement"). His alma mater, St. Thomas College, hired him as an assistant football coach[39] while he went back to get a degree in education,[40] and he became a history teacher and football coach in the St. Paul schools. When Van Brocklin came to the Twin Cities in 1961 to serve as the Vikings' first coach, Simensen was among the Dutchman's best friends. Working around tremors—"I can pour a cup of coffee, but if I pick it up, I get more on the floor than in the cup,"[41] he once said—and his decreased mobility, Simensen finished out his teaching career at Washington High School in St. Paul, retiring as head coach after the school closed in 1979.[42] He lived to be 67, dying at home from a sudden heart attack on April 22, 1994. Despite the bad hand that life had dealt him, Don Simensen was not known to be bitter, but he did have a warning for his fellow pro footballers, long before CTE became an issue in the game. "A helmet will never be invented," he said, "to protect the skull."[43]

Notes

1. Mike Augustin, "Simensen Remembered as Tower of Strength," *St. Paul* (MN) Pioneer Press, April 27, 1994, 2D.
2. Allen Greenberg, "The Old Rams Just Limp Away," *Los Angeles Times*, April 8, 1980, III-1, 8.
3. Greenberg, "The Old Rams," III-1, 8.
4. Augustin, "Simensen Remembered," 2D.
5. Augustin, "Simensen Remembered," 2D.
6. "Missouri Valley, St. Thomas Battle to 13–13 Tie," *St. Petersburg Times*, January 2, 1949, 28.

7. Frank Finch, "Rams Must Depend on Rookie Tackles," *Los Angeles Times*, July 26, 1951, IV-3.
8. "Charles Toogood of Nebraska (photo)," *Wilmington* (CA) *Press-Journal*, August 2, 1951, 6.
9. Frank Finch, "Groza Again 'Kicks' Rams," *Los Angeles Times*, September 15, 1951, III-1.
10. Frank Finch, "Waterfield, Four Other Rams Out of Loop Opener," *Los Angeles Times*, September 22, 1951, III-3.
11. Jack McKinney, "Word or No, Dutchman's Pigs Gotta Eat," *Philadelphia Daily News*, January 30, 1976, 70.
12. All 1950 and 1951 Rams statistics are from *pro-football-reference.com*.
13. Frank Finch, "Towler Takes Pro League Running Lead," *Los Angeles Times*, November 20, 1951, IV-3.
14. Paul Zimmerman, "Sportscripts," *Los Angeles Times*, December 6, 1951, IV-1.
15. Frank Finch, "Richter Called into Service, Lost to Rams," *Los Angeles Times*, July 23, 1952, IV-1, 3.
16. Frank Finch, "Scouting the Pros," *Los Angeles Times*, March 27, 1952, IV-3.
17. Finch, "Richter Called into Service," IV-1, 3.
18. Greenberg, "The Old Rams," III-1, 8.
19. Greenberg, "The Old Rams," III-1, 8.
20. Frank Finch, "Carey, Lewis May Miss Eagle Fracas," *Los Angeles Times*, September 5, 1952, IV-1, 3.
21. Eddie Muller, "Shadow Boxing," *San Francisco Examiner*, September 5, 1952, 30.
22. Frank Finch, "Dahms, Simensen Benched by Pool," *Los Angeles Times*, November 7, 1952, IV-3.
23. Frank Finch, "Buck Shaw Says Rams Now Better Than Ever," *Los Angeles Times*, December 1, 1952.
24. Art Knight, "Sports of the Times," *San Mateo Times*, December 1, 1952, 6.
25. Greenberg, "The Old Rams," III-1, 8.
26. Augustin, "Simensen Remembered," 2D.
27. "Rams' Simensen Fair After Brain Operation," *Philadelphia Inquirer*, February 28, 1953, 16.
28. "Rams' Simensen Undergoes 6-Hour Brain Operation," *Los Angeles Times*, February 28, 1953, II-2.
29. Frank Finch, "Scouting the Pros," *Los Angeles Times*, March 12, 1953, IV-3.
30. Frank Finch, "Scouting the Pros," *Los Angeles Times*, May 17, 1953, II-9.
31. Finch, "Scouting the Pros," May 17, 1953, II-9.
32. "New Rams Club to Sponsor Benefit Game," *Los Angeles Times*, May 22, 1953, I-31.
33. "Waterfield Plays Sunday in Benefit," *Los Angeles Times*, July 17, 1953, IV-2.
34. "Rams Defeat Dolphins in Touch Tilt, 20–13," *Los Angeles Times*, July 20, 1953, I-25.
35. Frank Finch, "Scouting the Pros," *Los Angeles Times*, September 29, 1953, IV-3.
36. Comparisons of dollar amounts from the past to their worth in "today's dollars" are based on the monthly Consumer Price Index, maintained by the Bureau of Labor Statistics of the U.S. Department of Labor. The "CPI Inflation Calculator" is a useful tool on the Bureau's website at https://data.bls.gov/cgi-bin/cpicalc.pl.
37. Augustin, "Simensen Remembered," 2D.
38. "Don Simensen Sits on Ram Bench," *Los Angeles Times*, November 16, 1953, IV-4.
39. Finch, September 29, 1953, IV-3.
40. "Don Simensen Sits on Ram Bench," IV-4.
41. Greenberg, "The Old Rams," III-1, 8.
42. Augustin, "Simensen Remembered," 2D.
43. Greenberg, "The Old Rams," III-1, 8.

Vitamin Smith

Randy Snow

Verda Thomas Smith, Jr., was known to professional football fans as Vitamin T. Smith. He was a small, speedy halfback who caught passes out of the backfield and returned kicks. He played five seasons in the NFL (1949–1953), all of them with the Los Angeles Rams.

Smith was born on October 30, 1923, in Sweetwater, Texas. His family lived in Goldendale, Washington, when he started to make a name for himself on the high school football field from 1939 to 1941. His father was a minister for the Church of Christ and was eventually transferred to Ventura, California. Verda Jr. played football at Ventura High School in 1942. While there, he was a backup to fullback Jack "Moose" Myers, who played college football at UCLA and was drafted by the Philadelphia Eagles in 1948. Smith and Myers became teammates years later, in 1952, when Myers left the Eagles and signed with the Rams.

After high school, Smith served in the U.S. Army during World War II. He was a supply sergeant with the 100th General Hospital during the D-Day invasion of Normandy in 1944.[1]

The Rams' fleet-footed return specialist, the colorful Vitamin Smith.

Smith enrolled at Abilene Christian University in Texas in 1946. His father had also attended college there. "I was pretty good in high school," Smith, Jr., once said, "but after three years in the Army nobody remembered me. I had my mind made up to go to school in Abilene so I was a walk-on with a GI Bill."[2]

He became a star on the Wildcats' football team and was also a standout in track and field as a sprinter and in the javelin throw. He won three Texas Conference titles in the javelin and one league championship in the 100-yard dash.

Smith never missed a game at Abilene Christian due to an injury despite breaking an arm in his sophomore season in a game against West Texas State. He did not tell his coaches and continued to play the rest of the game. He returned a punt for a touchdown later in the game and even made a defensive play that helped the Wildcats maintain the lead in the game. Smith played the next five games with a cast on his arm.[3]

He was known for his ability to return kicks and punts. He once ran three consecutive kickoffs back for touchdowns.

In 1948, Smith became the first football player from Abilene Christian to be named a Little All-American and was also named Texas Conference Player of the Year. When he graduated, he was the school's all-time record holder in rushing yards and total offense. He amassed 2,656 yards in total offense during his three seasons, from 1946 to 1948.[4]

When he signed as a rookie free agent with the Rams in 1949, he still had one year of college eligibility left. He joined a Rams team with two other rookies that year who all went on to have pretty good careers in the NFL: quarterback Norm Van Brocklin and fullback Paul "Tank" Younger.

Chicago Bears head coach George Halas wanted to draft Smith to play for the Bears, but he was under the impression that Smith would not be available to sign with an NFL team until 1950. Halas had a fit when he found out that the Rams had signed Smith and was quoted as saying, "Smith will become the best halfback in the National League."[5]

Soon after he joined the Rams, he received the nickname "Vitamin T" from *Los Angeles Times* sports reporter Frank Finch (the T in the nickname stood for Tomato)[6].

Smith, one of the smallest players on the team at just five feet, eight inches tall and 176 pounds, impressed the Rams' coaching staff from the very beginning with his football skills. In a Blue-Gold intra-squad game during his rookie training camp, he caught three touchdown passes for the Blue team from fellow rookie Norm Van Brocklin and he had a 94-yard kickoff return to set up another score.

During his rookie season, Smith led the NFL in punt returns, returning 27 kicks for 427 yards including a 51-yard touchdown against the Chicago Cardinals and an 85-yard return against Green Bay that was the longest of the season. He was producing on the field, but his running style and his feet always came under criticism from his coaches, in college and in the NFL.

His coach at Abilene Christian, Tonto Coleman, once said that Smith had "duck feet.... Awkwardest boy I nearly ever saw. Looked like he did everything backward."[7] This sentiment was also noticed and even praised a few years later by Rams coach Clark Shaughnessy who once made this observation of Smith's feet, "A boy that toes out markedly like that has good balance when he runs and can change direction quickly."[8]

Smith was not only a good player, but he also had a great sense of humor. An example of his wit was featured in the February 11, 1957, issue of *Sports Illustrated*. The story goes that the Rams traveled to Philadelphia for a game on October 7, 1950. One of the Rams' owners, Ed Pauley, Sr., was so certain that his team was going to defeat the Eagles that he brought several of his friends along with him on the train from California to attend the game. One of those friends was U.S. Army General Mark Clark.

The Rams found themselves down 28–0 to the Eagles at halftime. Pauley and General Clark visited the Rams locker room and Clark gave the team an inspirational speech before they came back out for the second half.

On the opening kickoff to begin the third quarter, Eagles kick returner Russ Craft returned the ball 103 yards for a touchdown. Smith, who was sitting on the sideline bench, turned to Rams coach Joe Stydahar and said, "Coach, ask the general what do we do now?" The Rams lost the game 56–20.[9]

Being from Texas, Smith spoke in a slow, southern drawl. However, he was anything but slow on the football field. *Los Angeles Times* reporter Frank Finch said that Smith "walks like a duck and runs like a deer."[10]

His Texas drawl and his sense of humor did not go unnoticed by the Los Angeles sports reporters and newspaper beat writers who covered the team. They enjoyed printing his remarks just the way he spoke them. An example of this came when he was tackled hard on a kick return. They quoted him as saying, "Ah was carrying the ball in my stomach and fell right on top of it with someone else right on top of me. When ah got up, you could see the print of the laces on the back of my jersey."[11]

Another came when he talked about fielding punts and kickoffs. "When the ball beats the defense down the field, you got some running room. Those high kicks give the ends time to git all set with their fists doubled up while you're waitin' for the ball to come down. Ah usually let [Tommy] Kalmanir have the high ones."[12]

Then there was the time he talked about the amount of running they had to do in practice. "Ah never got so tired of runnin' in mah life. Lookie yonder at that foot. Why, I got a blister under a blister under a callus on the bottom of it."[13]

Smith and the Rams advanced to the NFL championship game in 1950, only to lose on the road to the Cleveland Browns 30–28. In the title game, Smith carried the ball four times for 11 yards and caught three passes for 46 yards. On special teams, he returned three kickoffs for 59 yards. He did not score in the title game.

He did, however, lead the NFL in kickoff returns in 1950, fielding 22 kickoffs for 742 yards and averaged 33.7 yards per return. Three of his kickoff returns resulted in touchdowns. One of them went for 97 yards.[14]

The 1951 season began well for Smith. In a preseason game against the Chicago Bears, Smith scored two touchdowns, returning a punt 71 yards for one touchdown and later catching a 21-yard pass from Norm Van Brocklin for a second touchdown. He also rushed 10 times for 52 yards and caught three passes for 51 yards.[15]

But the season was not all roses for Smith. While playing defense in a regular season game against the San Francisco 49ers, he had his "worse day at safety" misplaying two dropped Frankie Albert passes in a 44–17 loss to the Niners.[16]

After week seven of the 1951 regular season, Smith was ranked sixth in the NFL in punt returns with a 12.6-yard average.[17]

During the 1951 regular season, Smith rushed 52 times for 143 yards and one touchdown. He also caught 16 passes for 278 yards and one touchdown. In the return category, Smith returned 12 punts for 139 yard and returned 15 kickoffs for 274 yards, but no touchdowns.

In the 1951 championship game, he ran nine times for 15 yards and caught one pass for 18 yards. He also returned two punts for zero yards.[18]

But it wasn't all work and no play for Smith during his time in L.A. He and many of his teammates appeared as themselves in the 1953 movie *Crazylegs*, based on the life and football exploits of their teammate, Elroy "Crazylegs" Hirsch.

In May of 1954, Smith announced he was retiring from pro football at the age of 30. He had considered calling it a career prior to the 1953 season but changed his mind and stayed for one more season.

After his playing career was over, Smith did what any good Texan did. He went to work in the oil industry. He took a job with an oil well company in Abilene, Texas.[19]

He worked in the oil business for 32 years and traveled to Alaska, Norway, Scotland, Columbia and Ecuador for his job. He retired in 1985 and settled back home in Texas.[20]

In his five seasons with the Rams, Vitamin T. Smith played in 59 regular season games and started 30. He only missed one game and that was during the 1953 season. He ran the ball 208 times for 669 yards and seven touchdowns. He also caught 59 passes for 1,025 yards and 12 touchdowns. On special teams, he returned 75 punts for 814 yards and one touchdown as well as returning 57 kickoffs for 1,453 yards and three touchdowns.

While his pro football career was somewhat short, just five seasons, Vitamin Smith was a very productive member of the Rams' team. His career is somewhat overshadowed, however, due to the fact that he played on the same team with so many famed teammates.

He was one of the most popular players on the team during his playing days, even with younger fans. He was the unofficial mascot of Beverly Hills Cub Scout Troop #77, which was his jersey number.[21]

Smith passed away on February 14, 2000, in Lake Dallas, Texas, of Alzheimer's disease at the age of 76.

Notes

1. Frank Finch, "Scouting the Pros," *Los Angeles Times*, August 23, 1949, IV-2.
2. Garner Roberts, "One for the Record," *1986 NCAA Division II National Championship Game Program*, December 13, 1986, 42–43.
3. Roberts, "One for the Record," 42–43.
4. "Like Father, Like Son: Vitamin T. Smith's Son Signs with ACC Wildcats," *Abilene Reporter-News*, January 9, 1966, 5-D.
5. Finch, "Scouting the Pros," IV-2.
6. Braven Dyer, "Sports Parade," *Los Angeles Times*, August 20, 1949, III-1.
7. Roberts, "One for the Record," 42–43.
8. Roberts, "One for the Record," 42–43.
9. "19th Hole: The Readers Take Over," *Sports Illustrated*, February 11, 1957, 71.
10. Frank Finch, "V.T. Smith Retires from Pro Football," *Los Angeles Times*, May 28, 1954, I-31.
11. Braven Dyer, "Sports Parade," *Los Angeles Times*, August 14, 1950, IV-1.
12. Dyer, "Sports Parade," August 14, 1950, IV-1.
13. Dyer, "Sports Parade," August 14, 1950, IV-1.
14. "Vitamin Smith Wins Kickoff Return Title," *Los Angeles Times*, February 27, 1951, IV-2.
15. Frank Finch, "Savage Rams Win, 42–14," *Los Angeles Times*, August 24, 1951, IV-1.
16. Frank Finch, "Zilly Breaks Arm; Rich Rejoins Rams," *Los Angeles Times*, October 30, 1951, IV-2.
17. "Rams Lead Player, Team Statistics," *Los Angeles Times*, November 15, 1951, I-33.
18. "Vitamin Smith," *Pro-football-reference.com*, https://www.pro-football-reference.com/players/S/SmitVi21.htm.
19. Finch, "V.T. Smith Retires," I-31.
20. Roberts, "One for the Record," 42–43.
21. "No.77 Makes Vitamin Smith Cub Scout Idol," *Los Angeles Times*, November 19, 1951, IV-1.

Harry Thompson

Nicholas Ritzmann

In early spring 1950, 24-year-old undrafted rookie Harry Thompson left his home in Los Angeles, traveled less than seven miles to the offices of the Rams in Beverly Hills, and signed a contract to play professional football. After turning down a $4500 salary from the New York Yanks, the lineman sought to join a formidable Rams team that had lost the NFL championship game less than 130 days before and ended the 1949 season with only one African American player (Paul Younger). Less than 130 days *after* signing that contract, Harry Thompson started at offensive right guard in the opening exhibition game against the Washington Redskins, stepping in immediately and becoming a key blocker for an offensive machine that in 1950 "set twenty-two scoring records that season, averaging 38.8 points per game,"[1] an NFL record that still stands. He began a five-year career with the Rams where he "played more positions than any Ram—defensive end, middle guard, tackle, and offensive guard."[2] The Rams never had a losing record with him on their team, made three postseason appearances from 1950 to 1952, and won twice as many regular season games as they lost.

In August 1980 former Rams coach Hamp Pool named Thompson as a starting offensive guard on a team of All-Time Rams during the Pool era (1950–54 and 1960–62), and five years later he received votes from readers of the *Los Angeles Times* for their All-Time Rams team. Noted Los Angeles–based football writer and longtime friend Bob Oates described Thompson as "one of those self-sacrificing players that every good team has on its roster.... Harry was always the next-to-last-cut in training camp, but he never got cut, because he was always too good."[3]

Harry Julius Thompson was born on January 8, 1926, in Memphis, Tennessee, one of six children born to Abe Thompson and Viola Wright Thompson. After the family relocated to California, Harry played football at Los Angeles High School for Coach Bert LaBrucherie in the fall of 1943, identified in October as a 210-pound tackle transfer on the second team, and by the end of the season listed as a starting offensive tackle on an unbeaten team.

Harry Thompson was a versatile utility lineman for the Rams.

After graduating he served in the Navy, then was enrolled at Los Angeles City College in 1946, and played for the Cubs that season.

On Labor Day 1947 Harry Thompson was one of fifteen junior college transfers at the opening football practice of Loyola University in Los Angeles (along with fellow future Rams teammate Bob Boyd). But when UCLA kicked off its season in the Los Angeles Coliseum against Iowa on September 26, he was again playing for Coach LaBrucherie, who had moved to UCLA in early 1945. Thompson was listed as a left tackle on the Bruins' roster. He suffered a hip injury in October against Stanford and did not earn a letter in 1947, but did meet Bruins line coach Ray Richards, who had played professional football and would go on to coach Thompson with the Rams and Chicago Cardinals.

Thompson improved in 1948 and earned his first letter at UCLA, playing 119 minutes in 10 games, shifting between guard and tackle.[4] He began the year on the second team, made his first start against Oregon on October 23, and was one of four players ejected for fighting in a victory over Nebraska one week later. However, UCLA only won three football games and Coach LaBrucherie resigned in December.

Coach Henry "Red" Sanders came west from Vanderbilt in January 1949 to take charge of the UCLA football program. Sanders installed Thompson at the left tackle spot (he also played on the defensive line) and it was noted "the former Los Angeles City College star, who weighs 225 pounds and stands 6 ft. 2 in. appears to be faster and stronger than in other years."[5] At the end of the season he was named as the third-team tackle on the AP All Pacific Coast Team, and honorable mention at tackle by the coaches in the Pacific Coast Conference (PCC). One writer noted, "if the UCLA publicity department had been on their toes they could have made Harry all-coast and he may have made some All-Americans."[6] But it was more telling that the PCC Champion California Bears voted him as a tackle on their all-opponent team and how one writer noted, "I have the idea the man the Bruins will miss most of all is Harry Thompson the big tackle. Those who got in his way say he was the roughest and toughest man around and about."[7]

Although Harry Thompson was not "on anyone's draft list," he did have a recommendation from Red Sanders, who "cornered [Rams head coach Joe] Stydahar one day and talked Joe into giving Thompson a trial."[8] As Sanders said, "I like the Rams. They wouldn't have Harry Thompson and Leon McLaughlin if it had not been for me."[9]

During training camp in 1950, the Los Angeles Times reported that Thompson could "play either guard or tackle, is one of the fastest linemen and he moves like a cat."[10] Wearing number 44, Thompson started the season opener against the Chicago Bears, and while he did not start every game for the Rams, he was part of a true offensive juggernaut. Linebacker Don Paul noted, "We spent most of our practices working on the home run offense. We were more dangerous inside *our* fifteen-yard line than inside theirs. The record that still amazes me from 1950 was the forty-one points we scored in one quarter against a Detroit team with Bobby Layne that was going to win two straight titles a couple of years later."[11]

Thompson did a hitch at defensive end during a 70–27 blowout victory over the Baltimore Colts in October, impressing Coach Stydahar, who noted "it was only the second time that Thompson had played end, but I think you'll be seeing more of him there from now on."[12]

On March 7, 1951, Ray Richards, Thompson's former line coach at UCLA, accepted the same job with the Rams. Thompson continued to play outstanding football at multiple positions during the 1951 championship season. After an injury forced Stan West out of the final exhibition game, *Los Angeles Times* reporter Frank Finch gushed that Thompson "was one of the outstanding Ram heroes. [He] took over West's middle guard spot and played sensationally. The [player] from UCLA had never played that spot before."[13] He backed up Bill Lange on the offensive line for much of the season but saw extensive action at defensive end. He was one of three Rams recognized by Coach Stydahar as "our only standouts on defense"[14] in a November loss to the Washington Redskins, and sacked Bears quarterback Bob Williams late in a big December victory in Chicago.

Because of an effort by the NFL in 1952 to standardize uniform numbers, Harry Thompson switched his from 44 to 66. But this change in number did not alter his playing style, as he made vital contributions to a Rams team that got off to a slow start but won their final eight regular season games to finish 9–3, tying them with the Detroit Lions for first in the National Conference. While the Lions prevailed in the playoff game in Detroit four days before Christmas, Thompson made impacts on both offense and defense. After Hamp Pool took over as head coach for Joe Stydahar after the opening game, he had Thompson replace Larry Brink at defensive end for the game in Milwaukee against the Green Bay Packers on October 12. The following week in Detroit he filled in for Andy Robustelli in a loss to the Lions, and in November replaced Bill Lange in the lineup to "utilize [his] greater speed."[15]

Harry Thompson was a valuable player who fixed problems for his coaches. One writer noted he "must be the most versatile man in modern day football … [he] plays offensive guard for the Rams, can go to the tackle post in an emergency, and plays defensive end and middle guard for the Rams. You'll notice every time the Rams want to make yardage on those long end sweeps or outside tackle, Thompson is sent into the game to lead the play, being probably the fastest lineman on the squad."[16]

Thompson was also one of the first African Americans to play in the NFL after the reintegration of the pro football. He suffered the racism of the time. "In Washington, D.C., … we stayed in this hotel and we could sleep in the hotel. But we couldn't eat in the hotel restaurant." The Rams' black players were only permitted to order room service.[17]

As training camp began for the 1953 season, Thompson was penciled in as the starting right offensive guard by Coach Pool, who noted he was "one of three men on the team who make the fewest offensive mistakes."[18] He injured a hand in the exhibition season and was ejected from an exhibition game against the Eagles in Little Rock, Arkansas. He started at offensive guard in the Rams' opening day victory over the Giants and saw his usual heavy duty at offensive guard during the season. He suffered an injured hamstring in a November tie with the Chicago Cardinals at Comiskey Park and missed several games as the Rams finished their season in third place with an 8–3–1 record.

In 1954, Thompson continued playing guard, but it was away from the football field, as he was cast in motion pictures as a guard in the film *The Egyptian* and a prison guard in *We're No Angels*. He then went right back to starting at offensive guard when training camp opened in July. He started 11 of the 12 regular season games; however, the Rams record fell to 6–5–1 and Coach Pool departed at the end of the season.

In 1955 new head coach Sid Gillman placed Thompson on waivers just before the Rams' first regular season game on September 25, but on October 1 he was signed by the Chicago Cardinals, who were coached by Ray Richards, and played in all 12 games for the Cards, starting two.

After signing a contract with the Cardinals in June 1956, Thompson notified the Cardinals of his retirement in July. He received his bachelor's degree from UCLA, then began life after professional football. He had a long career as a marketing executive with a series of spirits companies in Southern California and worked tirelessly to help his community. In recognition of his 10-year anniversary with Schenley Industries in 1965, the company established two $2,000 scholarships in the name of Harry Thompson. It was part of an effort by the company to recognize "an outstanding member of the (African American) community, whose name would be attached to the scholarship."[19] He was involved with the Special Olympics and Athletes for a Better America. In May 1984 he was one of eight charter inductees into a Hall of Fame founded by the Challengers Boys and Girls Club of Los Angeles. But he never forgot about football and worked for both the Rams and Los Angeles Express of the United States Football League in security. He worked with the Rams Alumni Association and "became an advocate for pension benefits, particularly for those who played professional football during its early years. He served one year as president of NFL Alumni Inc. and attended each year's Super Bowl."[20]

Harry Thompson passed away on November 26, 2003, and is buried at Holy Cross Cemetery in Culver City, California.

NOTES

1. Michael MacCambridge, *America's Game* (New York: Random House, 2004), 69.
2. "Greatest Present Day Negro Football Players Here Sunday," *Los Angeles Sentinel*, December 20, 1951, B5.
3. Lonnie White, "Harry Thompson, 78; Key Blocker for Rams in 1950's," *Los Angeles Times*, November 29, 2003, B25.
4. "Block and Tackle Boys, These Trojans, Bruins," *Los Angeles Times*, September 4, 1949, I-16.
5. Paul Zimmerman, "Bruins Loaded at Tackle Positions," *Los Angeles Times*, September 9, 1949, IV-2.
6. Halley Harding, "Sports Events of Past Year Tops in Surprise and Quality," *Los Angeles Sentinel*, December 29, 1949, A6.
7. Claude Newman "Claude Newman Says," *Valley Times*, December 20, 1949, 8.
8. Paul Zimmerman, "Sportscripts," *Los Angeles Times*, August 4, 1950, IV-1.
9. Paul Zimmerman, "Sportscripts," *Los Angeles Times*, October 3, 1953, III-1.
10. Frank Finch, "Ram Coach Says Tackles Stronger," *Los Angeles Times*, August 2, 1950, IV-1, 3.
11. Mickey Herskowitz, *The Golden Age of Pro Football: NFL Football in the 1950's* (Dallas: Taylor Publishing Company, 1990), 53.
12. Frank Finch, "Ram Defense Too Generous to Enemy," *Los Angeles Times*, October 24, 1950, IV-3.
13. Frank Finch, "Rams Win Thriller from Giants," *Los Angeles Times*, September 21, 1951, IV-1, 2.
14. Frank Finch, "Rams Below Peak, Physically, for Important Bear Tilt Sunday," *Los Angeles Times*, November 29, 1951. I-29.
15. Claude Newman, "Patched-Up Waterfield Set," *Valley Times*, 11.
16. Stanley G. Robertson, "From the Press Box," *Los Angeles Sentinel*, November 27, 1952, A12.
17. White, "Harry Thompson, 78; Key Blocker for Rams in 1950's," B25.
18. Stanley G. Robertson, "From The Press Box," *Los Angeles Sentinel*, November 12, 1953, A11.
19. "Robinson Sparks Old Charter Banquet," *Los Angeles Sentinel*, June 24, 1965, B12.
20. Lela Ward-Oliver, "Last of the Rams' Original Five, Dead at 78," *Los Angeles Sentinel*, December 11, 2003, A13.

Charlie Toogood

Bill Lambert

Charlie Toogood was born July 16, 1927, in North Platte Nebraska. Nebraska in the 1930s was a challenging place to grow up. Nebraska was in the thick of the Dust Bowl, which Ken Burn's documentary *The Dust Bowl*, called "the worst man-made ecological disaster in American history." During the Dust Bowl, a rainstorm hit that couldn't be absorbed and more than 100 people died in the flooding of the Republican River. 1936 brought a massive grasshopper infestation.[1]

North Platte, Nebraska, was a typical town, but during World War II, it became somewhat famous for the North Platte Canteen. It was a railroad town and from Christmas Day, 1941 until April 1, 1946, about 7 million military passengers passed through and were greeted with doughnuts, coffee, pies, and pheasant sandwiches. Nearly 55,000 Nebraskan women served these soldiers.

At its peak the North Platte station was handling 2,000 military personnel a day. World War II veterans wrote thank you notes for decades. One officer said the Canteen was the last good meal his soldiers had for two and a half years. Some soldiers had traveled for days without money and were hungry. Their bellies and hearts were filled in North Platte.[2]

Toogood began his football career in earnest at North Platte High School. He was a regular tackle on the 1943 team. As the only returning regular for the North Platte varsity, he was elected captain of the 1944 Bulldogs.[3] Toogood was a two-time all-state football player in 1943 and 1944 at tackle.

The 1945 Nebraska state track championships gave Charlie a chance to highlight his skills in another sport. He scored 10 points in the field event finals by capturing first place in the discus and shot-put.[4]

After graduating from North Platte, Toogood served in the Marine Corps as a PFC during World War II. When he completed his service, he attended the University of Nebraska. During Charlie's time at Nebraska the team was pedestrian, suffering losing records each year he was there except for his final

Charlie Toogood played college football at Nebraska.

season. In 1950, under Bill Glassford, the team went 6–2–1 and was ranked as high as 16th during the year, finishing up at 17.[5]

During the 1950 season Charlie Toogood blocked for Bobby Reynolds, who rushed for 1,342 yards as a sophomore that year. On November 11, Nebraska played Missouri in Lincoln. It was a back-and-forth game with Nebraska leading 33–27 in the fourth quarter with the ball at the Missouri 33-yard line. Reynolds got the ball and dropped back to pass before a wave of Tiger players converged on him. He eluded tacklers all the way back to the Nebraska 45-yard line, then reversed his field three times. During the run, Charlie Toogood knocked down a defender and laid on his man pinning him to the ground. The defender said, "Let me up, Reynolds went the other way." Toogood agreed, but continued to hold the fellow down, explaining, "He might be coming back this way again!"[6]

Charlie earned All-Big Seven selections in both 1949 and 1950. He was a team captain in 1950 and played in the East-West Shrine game. Charlie won the inaugural Tom Novak Trophy. This award was established by J. Gordon Roberts in 1950 and is presented to the senior who "best exemplifies courage and determination despite all odds in the manner of Nebraska All-American center Tom Novak"[7]

Toogood continued his participation in track while at the University of Nebraska. He lettered in 1950. He scored in several meets that year including a second place versus Iowa in an indoor meet when he threw the shot 45–11.[8]

Charlie was selected by the Rams in the third round of the 1951 NFL draft with the 35th pick overall.[9] Toogood had also been drafted in 1950. He was taken with 338th pick overall in the 26th round by the Cleveland Browns. This came as no surprise as when Paul Brown was asked after the Shrine game which player impressed him most he said, "That Nebraska tackle, Charley [sic] Toogood."[10]

As Toogood began his career with the Rams, he received high praise from scout Eddie Kotal, who said, "The Rams and the coaching staff are very pleased with Charlie's work. He has performed exceptionally well for a first-year man and he's full of energy and ambition." Kotal cited Charlie as a great competitor with a great love for the game and remarked, "We have been using him on offense and his downfield blocking has been a great factor in springing Glenn Davis and Dick Hoerner for many long runs."[11]

Toogood played in eight games for the 1951 Rams and started one. He recorded one interception which he returned for no gain. Charlie also played in the 1951 NFL championship game victory over the Browns, the first of three playoff games that he was involved with during his career.[12]

Charlie's 1952 Rams, under Joe Stydahar and Hampton Pool, finished 9–3, tied for first in National Conference. They lost the Conference playoff game to the eventual NFL champion Detroit Lions 31–21. Charlie played in 10 games that season and started two. He also played in the playoff game versus the Lions.[13]

In 1953, the Rams went 8–3–1 under Hampton Pool but failed to make the playoffs. Charlie started all 12 games at defensive tackle. He recorded one interception and recovered two fumbles returning them for 21 yards. The 21 yards in fumble returns was the fifth best in the NFL that season. He even returned a kickoff for 19 yards. Toogood earned Associated Press All-Pro Honorable Mention at the conclusion of the season.[14]

The 1954 Rams were once again coached by Pool. They finished at 6–5–1 in Pool's last year and once again missed the playoffs. Toogood spent 1954 at right tackle on offense, playing in 12 games and starting 10 times. He recovered one fumble during the season and returned it for three yards and once again returned a kickoff, this time for 11 yards.

Nineteen fifty-five brought a new coach for the Rams, Sid Gillman. This was the future Hall of Famer's first head coaching job in the NFL. Gillman led the 1955 team to a mark of 8–3–1, first place in the NFL Western Conference. Charlie was once again at right offensive tackle; he played in 12 games and started eight.

The 1955 NFL championship game pitted Gillman's Rams versus old nemesis, Paul Brown and his Browns. The Rams were never really in the game, falling behind 31–7 after three and eventually losing 38–14.[15]

In Charlie Toogood's final season with the Rams in 1956, they finished 4–8, once again under Gillman's direction. Charlie started six games at right tackle and played in seven.

Toogood finished his career with the 1957 Chicago Cardinals coached by Ray Richards. The Cards traded one of their 1958 draft picks for Toogood.[16] The team went 3–9 that season. Early in the year, Charlie attempted to play right defensive end and some left guard. He ended up playing in six games and starting three.[17]

Toogood ended up playing in 67 regular season games, while starting 42. He played both offense and defense during his career. Charlie was able to garner three interceptions and recover three fumbles during his time in the NFL. He also returned four kickoffs for 54 yards.

In 1980, Charlie was named to a pair of all-time Los Angeles Rams Era teams at offensive tackle by two of four coaches in a *Los Angeles Times* survey. He was chosen as a member of the Hamp Pool Era squad (1950–54, 60–62) and Sid Gillman era team (1955–59).[18]

Gillman called Toogood the best lineman for his size that played the game. Charlie rated Chicago Bears linebacker Bill George as his toughest challenge. In 1975, Charlie stated that he "really loved playing in the NFL. I enjoyed playing against the very best and the opportunity to travel. And best of all, I didn't take near the physical beating that I did in the college ranks." He recalled that the pros employ "almost no contact work except for the day of the game. In college we were beating each other almost every night."[19]

Charlie worked in insurance during the off season and started the El Taco restaurant chain. After retiring from the NFL, Charlie taught economics, U.S. history and continuing education at St. Helena High School in California. He was the head football coach for the Saints for a number of years. Under his leadership the Saints complied a record of 66–53–1, won five North Central League I championships and a CIF North Coast Section Class A title in 1977 with Charlie being awarded the NCS Class A Coach of the Year. They were also NCS Class A runners-ups in 1975, 1976, and 1978. In 2015, Toogood was posthumously inducted into the St. Helena High Athletic Hall of Fame.[20]

With a name like Toogood, it's not a big surprise to learn how many halls of fames Charlie has been inducted into. In addition to the St. Helena High Hall of Fame, he became a member of the Nebraska Football Hall of Fame in 1984 and the Nebraska High School Sports Hall of Fame in 2005.

Charlie even managed to find time to act, having a bit part in *Crazylegs* with teammate Elroy Hirsch in 1953. He passed away on February 24, 1997, at the age of 60. He was survived by his wife Virginia, three daughters and a son, and many grandchildren.[21]

Notes

1. Jim McKee, "Jim McKee: Nebraska Was on the Edge of the Dust Bowl," *Lincoln Journal Star*, December 16, 2012, https://journalstar.com/lifestyles/misc/jim-mckee-nebraska-was-on-the-edge-of-the-dust-bowl/article_a17b8de4-2bf9-5cc7-8316-7cd306de0981.html.

2. Matthew Spencer, "North Platte Canteen," *Nebraska Life Magazine*, September/October 2012, http://www.nebraskalife.com/North-Platte-Canteen/.

3. "Toogood Elected as Platter Captain," *Nebraska State Journal*, November 28, 1943, 5-B.

4. "New High Champ to Wear Crown," *The Lincoln Star*, May 12, 1945, 8.

5. "Nebraska Cornhuskers School History 1950," *Sports-reference.com*, https://www.sports-reference.com/cfb/schools/nebraska/index.html.

6. Walt Sehnert, "Bobby Reynolds-Mr. Touchdown," *McCook Gazette*, October 15, 2018, https://www.mccookgazette.com/story/2558971.html.

7. "Nebraska Football Special Awards," *2018–19 Nebraska All-Sports Record Book*, 56–57.

8. Norris Anderson, "NU Cinder Crew Hobbles Cyclones," *Nebraska State Journal*, January 29, 1950, 1-B.

9. "1951 NFL Draft," *Pro-football-reference.com*, www.pro-football-reference.com/years/1951/draft.htm.

10. Paul Zimmerman, "Sportscripts," *Los Angeles Times*, July 26, 1951, IV-1.

11. Don Bryant, "LA Ram Scout Praises Toogood, Ray Richards," *The Lincoln Star*, November 14, 1951, 17.

12. "Championship-Cleveland Browns at Los Angeles Rams December 23rd, 1951," *Pro-football-reference.com*, www.pro-football-reference.com/boxscores/195112230ram.htm.

13. "Charlie Toogood," *Pro-football-reference.com*, https://www.pro-football-reference.com/players/T/ToogCh20.htm.

14. "Charlie Toogood"; *Jim Hock, Hollywood's Team* (Los Angeles: Rare Bird Books, 2016), 110–118.

15. "Championship-Cleveland Browns at Los Angeles Rams December 26th, 1955," *Pro-football-reference.com*, www.pro-football-reference.com/boxscores/195512260ram.htm.

16. "Cards Get Toogood," *Chattanooga Daily Times*, September 14, 1957, 12.

17. "Charlie Toogood"; T.J. Troup, *The Birth of Football's Modern 4–3 Defense: The Seven Seasons That Changed the NFL* (Lanham, MD: Rowman & Littlefield, 2014), 194.

18. "All-Time Rams: '50–77," *Los Angeles Times*, August 26, 1980, III-6.

19. Tom Gilmore, "Toogood Is a Man with a Record," *The Napa Valley Register*, March 22, 1975, 16V.

20. Marty James, "Charley [sic] Toogood—a St. Helena Legend," *Napa News*, June 29, 2015, https://napavalleyregister.com/sports/charley-toogood-a-st-helena-legend/article_2c3dacb1-a310-5b6a-a57e-1128e0e32a52.html.

21. "Charles Toogood," *IMDb.com*, www.imdb.com/name/nm1387719/.

Deacon Dan Towler

RICHARD C. FLOWERS II

Daniel Lee Towler, known as "Deacon" Dan Towler, was born March 6, 1928, in Donora, Pennsylvania,[1] also the home of legendary baseball Hall of Famer Stan "the Man" Musial.

Towler was a four-sport standout at Donora High School and led the Dragons to undefeated seasons and WPIAL football championships in 1944 and 1945. He scored 24 touchdowns during his senior season.[2]

He attended college at Washington & Jefferson College in Washington, Pennsylvania, where he was a member of the school's "Four Gazelles" backfield, along with Jack Sourbeer (who was recruited by the Rams in 1951 but chose to attend medical school instead). He was a two time All-American who led the nation in scoring with 133 points in 1948. In 1999, he was selected to the Washington & Jefferson Hall of Fame.[3] A good student, Towler graduated cum laude from Washington & Jefferson.[4]

Towler was drafted by The Los Angeles Rams in 1950 in Round 25 with the 324th overall selection.[5] He would go on to have a brilliant but brief career for the Rams, leading the league in rushing yards (894) and touchdowns (10) in 1952 and in touchdowns (11) again in 1954. From 1951–54, Towler gained 3,226 yards and scored 34 rushing touchdowns. He was named to four consecutive Pro Bowls (1951–54) and was a four time All-Pro, being named first team in 1951, 1952, and 1953 and second team in 1954.[6] He was also selected as the MVP of the 1952 Pro Bowl, rushing for 78 of the winning National team's 145 yards. The Nationals beat the Americans 30–13, which gave winning coach Joe Stydahar the victory over American coach Paul Brown, whose team defeated Stydahar's the previous year 28–27.[7]

Known as a member of the storied "Bull Elephant" backfield, Towler was a big (6–2, 225)

Deacon Dan Towler was the Rams' leading rusher in 1951, gaining 854 yards on the ground.

fullback who ran with speed and power, as did his backfield mates Dick Hoerner (6–4, 220) and Paul "Tank" Younger (6–3, 225). Of the remarkable backfield which came into vogue during the Rams' 1951 season, Towler once said that the genesis "for the Bull Elephants came during the 1950 season. We were playing in a sea of mud and the coaches alternated backfields hoping to rest us. The coach then realized he had three fullbacks of equal running ability and saw what a powerful weapon he would have with two 200-pounders leading a third."[8]

Teammate Elroy "Crazylegs" Hirsch recalled the effectiveness of the Bulls. "I'll never forget the picture we created with the Bulls' plays—like one we called 27-M-Sockem. I took the defensive end outside, the tackle turned the defensive tackle in, and Hoerner and Younger, shoulder to shoulder, flew head-on at the linebacker, with Towler, shifty as a scatback, carrying the ball behind them. It was an awesome sight and good for 15 yards almost any time."[9]

Towler's 1951 season began with the Rams' 54–14 win at home over the New York Yanks. In this game, he would rush only three times for six yards and a touchdown while hauling in two receptions for 30 yards. The following week, in a 38–23 home loss to Cleveland, Towler would lead the Rams with 33 rushing yards on eight carries and add a reception for 46 more yards. Towler and the Rams would bounce back a week later with a 27–21 win over the Lions in Detroit. He would again lead the team with 58 rushing yards on seven carries and add a reception for two yards. The Rams would continue their winning ways the next week at the Wisconsin State Fair Park with an impressive 28–0 shutout win over the Green Bay Packers. Towler once again led the ground attack with 144 yards on 11 carries, and a touchdown the best rushing performance for the week in the NFL. Their modest win streak would come to an end the following week, as the Rams would suffer a 44–17 loss to the San Francisco 49ers. In this one, Towler had seven rushes for 43 yards and an eight-yard reception.[10]

The rematch would fare better for Towler and the Rams, as they would avenge their loss the next week with a 23–16 win at home over the 49ers. Towler's 54 rushing yards on 11 rushes led the ground game for the Rams and he also had 2 receptions for another 38 yards. The Chicago Cardinals would come to town the next week, and the Rams would emerge with a 45–21 victory. Towler had a team leading 109 rushing yards on 11 carries and a reception for another seven yards. His rushing totals also led the league that week. Next, the Rams would complete a season sweep of the Yanks with an impressive 48–21 win. Towler would be far more productive than the season opener, as he ran for a season high 155 yards on 13 carries and one touchdown and had a 26-yard reception.[11]

The following week would see the Rams meet defeat for the third time, as they would lose to the Washington Redskins 31–21 at Griffith Stadium. Towler was kept in check on the ground, with just 14 rushing yards on 11 carries. He did add 5 receptions for 56 yards. The Rams would rebound in Chicago a week later with a 42–17 win where Towler led the ground attack with 76 yards and two touchdowns on 14 rushes and two receptions for 44 yards. The next week saw the Lions get payback as they would defeat the Rams 24–22 in Los Angeles. Towler did have 60 rushing yards and a touchdown on 17 carries, yet it wasn't enough as Doak Walker threw a 22-yard scoring toss to Leon Hart for the win. The final week of the regular season was another impressive four-touchdown win over the Packers, this time by a 42–14 score. Towler once again led the way on the ground with 102 rushing yards on 13 carries.[12]

In the Rams' 1951 championship game victory over the Browns, Deacon Dan gained

36 hard fought yards on 16 carries and scored a touchdown from one yard out to put the Rams ahead 14–10 in the third quarter.[13] Stated Towler, "I feel the '51 Rams was one of the greatest teams ever."[14]

A man of true religious conviction, Towler was so into his studies that he had an agreement with coach Joe Stydahar which allowed him to lead a team prayer before each game. In an interview in 1991, Towler said, "I asked Coach [Joe] Stydahar if I could have the players pray, and he said: 'It sure wouldn't hurt anything, and who knows? It might help.'" "We were the first NFL team to pray before each game," Towler added. "Now, it's a common thing. I think it helped with the team's camaraderie and fellowship, bringing us together."[15]

Towler retired in 1955 after obtaining his master's degree in theology from the University of Southern California's graduate school of religion. He became pastor of the Lincoln Avenue Methodist Church in Pasadena. After obtaining his doctorate in education from USC, Towler was a chaplain at the California State University–Los Angeles and later was named president of the Los Angeles County Board of Education. He also founded the Dan Towler Foundation which provided students studying nursing, education, medicine, and religion with financial assistance.[16]

"I want to put something back in," Towler said of the Foundation. "I was blessed as an athlete and football put me through college at Washington and Jefferson and graduate school at USC. I consider myself a debtor. I hope I can make a difference, make things a little better."[17]

Towler recalled his career with the Rams as a blur, since his first priority was obtaining a master's degree in theology. "I was a full-time student, a part-time football player. I had an agreement with Dan Reeves [the late Rams owner] that I would play football for him if I didn't have to miss any classes," Towler said. "I used to go to class early on the first three days of the week, practice in the afternoon, then go back to class. I missed most of the team meetings, and anytime there was a conflict, I was excused by the Rams to attend class. On a road trip to the East, when the team stayed over a week to play in another city back there, I'd fly back to Los Angeles right after our game Sunday, get in at 6 in the morning and rush to my 8 o'clock class. Then I'd fly back to the East overnight on Wednesday and usually go from the airport straight to practice. I was really on the run."[18]

Reflecting back on a career that was brilliant yet brief, Towler wondered what could have been had he focused on football full time instead of dividing his time between football and the ministry. "I was always worn out," he once said. "It's always been a question to me how good I would have been if I'd had the time and energy to concentrate on football as the No. 1 thing, like the other guys. A lot of times, I didn't even know the plays."[19]

Even though he divided his energy between his passion for religion and his passion for football, Towler channeled his boundless energy into improving the community where he once starred. "My football career," he said, "helped in many ways." For one thing, it helped him establish rapport with students whom he counseled. For another, it taught him a priceless lesson. "I learned not to give up in a tough situation," Deacon Dan Towler said. "Often you need only to make a first down, not a touchdown."[20]

Deacon Dan Towler died in his sleep on August 1, 2001, at his home in Pasadena after attending a Los Angeles Dodgers game the evening before. He was survived by his wife Rosalind, who herself passed away in 2017, and his daughter Roslyn.[21]

Towler was an unstoppable force on the football field and in life. Hall of Famer Dick

LeBeau paid him the ultimate compliment. Towler "was a great, great running back. He was a man with size, speed, strength, and elusiveness. This gentleman belongs in the Pro Football Hall of Fame and should be recognized as one of the greatest running backs to ever play in the NFL."[22]

Notes

1. "Dan Towler," *Wikipedia.org*, https://en.wikipedia.org/wiki/Dan_Towler.
2. Bruce Wald, "Donora Names Alley in Honor of Football Star Towler, Triblive.com, September 6, 2014, https://archive.triblive.com/news/donora-names-alley-in-honor-of-football-star-towler/; Stanley Grosshandler and Bob Van Atta, "Dan Towler," *The Coffin Corner* 18, no. 1 (1996), 1.
3. "Deacon Dan Towler," *Gopresidents.com*, https://gopresidents.com/hof.aspx?hof=127&path=&kiosk=.
4. Grosshandler, "Dan Towler," 1.
5. "Dan Towler," *Wikipedia.org*.
6. "Dan Towler," *Pro-football-reference.com*, https://www.pro-football-reference.com/players/T/TowlDa00.htm.
7. "National Pros Whip Americans, 30–13, *Pittsburgh Press*, January 13, 1952, 37.
8. Richard Goldstein, "Dan Towler, 73, All-Pro Back Who Studied for the Ministry," *New York Times*, August 3, 2001, A-21.
9. Goldstein, "Dan Towler," A-21.
10. "Dan Towler," *Pro-football-reference.com*.
11. "Dan Towler," *Pro-football-reference.com*.
12. "Dan Towler," *Pro-football-reference.com*.
13. "Championship-Cleveland Browns at Los Angeles Rams-December 23rd, 1951," *Pro-football-reference.com*, https://www.pro-football-reference.com/boxscores/195112230ram.htm.
14. Grosshandler, "Dan Towler," 1.
15. Earl Gustkey, "'Deacon' Dan Towler, 73, Dies," *Washington Post*, August 4, 2001, https://www.washingtonpost.com/archive/local/2001/08/04/deacon-dan-towler-73-dies/a6094a40-d6a3-4f6b-878a-aa48d671c853/.
16. Goldstein, "Dan Towler," A-21.
17. Ken Peters, "Deacon Dan: A Man for All Seasons and Reasons," *Los Angeles Times*, August 5, 1986, https://www.latimes.com/archives/la-xpm-1986-08-12-sp-18717-story.html.
18. Peters, "Deacon Dan."
19. Goldstein, "Dan Towler," A-21.
20. Grosshandler, "Dan Towler," 1.
21. Goldstein, "Dan Towler," A-21.
22. "Testimonials-Deacon Dan Towler," *Deacondantowler.com*, http://www.deacondantowler.com/.

Norm Van Brocklin

Bryan Lutes

Q—On a four-year basis, when does your class graduate?
A—1950.
Q—When will you graduate?
A—1949 ma.

It was a routine questionnaire that The Los Angeles Rams sent out to collegiate football players at the end of the 1947 season, including an unheralded sophomore at the University of Oregon named Norman Van Brocklin. The future Hall of Famer followed a couple of his friends in enrolling at Oregon in 1946, after spending three years in the Navy during World War II. Van Brocklin joined the football team (he needed the $75 scholarship money) but was not an immediate success. Oregon used the single-wing offense, which did not mesh well with Van Brocklin's abilities. "He's only a fair runner and he can't block," then head coach Tex Oliver said.[1] As a fifth-string tailback, Van Brocklin totaled nine pass attempts, zero completions and three interceptions.

Rams quarterback Norm Van Brocklin threw the game-winning touchdown pass in the 1951 championship game.

The story could have ended there, but the university hired a new football coach from the Ohio high school ranks named Jim Aiken in 1947. Aiken won Ohio state championships at Findlay (1925) and Canton McKinley (1934), followed by successful collegiate tenures at Akron and Nevada. Aiken quickly shelved the old single-wing offense and installed the more modern T-formation. He needed someone who could throw the football for the quarterback position. Van Brocklin was a natural fit.

It took some time for the Oregon players to learn the new system, and they started the 1947 season with only one win in their first four games. Once everything clicked into place, Van Brocklin led the Webfoots to six straight victories to finish with a 7–3 mark, the school's first winning record since 1935. The following season was even better for both the quarterback and the program. Oregon went 9–1 with Van Brocklin running the offense, earning a berth in the Cotton Bowl against

Doak Walker and Southern Methodist University. A 21–13 loss to SMU followed, but Van Brocklin established himself as one of the best passers in all of college football, finishing sixth in the Heisman Trophy voting and earning an All-America selection.

This unexpected success did not go unnoticed by the Los Angeles Rams. Owner Dan Reeves and scouting chief Eddie Kotal remembered Van Brocklin's questionnaire, and correctly interpreted Van Brocklin's response of 1949 "ma" to mean "maybe."

Further inspection by the Rams revealed that Van Brocklin's girlfriend (and soon to be wife), Gloria Schiewe, was a graduate lab instructor at the university. "I fell in love with the big stiff because he was so helpless,"[2] Gloria said. With summer studies as well as Gloria's assistance, Van Brocklin completed his college credits in three years. This fact went unnoticed by every NFL team except Los Angeles. Reeves contacted Van Brocklin and asked if he would be interested in turning pro for the 1949 season. Van Brocklin needed the money and confirmed that he would be interested (much to the chagrin of Oregon coach Jim Aiken). The Los Angeles Rams drafted Norm Van Brocklin in the fourth round (37th overall) of the 1949 NFL draft. Several other teams immediately challenged Van Brocklin's selection, but the NFL by-laws allowed for college players to be drafted upon graduating early. The Rams' selection of Van Brocklin stood.

Heading into the 1949 season, The Los Angeles Rams had the peerless Bob Waterfield as the starting quarterback, and Jim Hardy had proven himself as a capable backup quarterback. The drafting of Norm Van Brocklin might not have made sense on the surface, but as assistant coach Hampton Pool explained, "quarterbacks came first, though. In other words, if we had owned five quarterbacks at the time, we'd have drafted a sixth if one as outstanding as Van Brocklin had been available. They just weren't that easy to come by. If you had a chance to get a great one, you grabbed him, no matter who you currently had playing the position."[3]

Clark Shaughnessy was the returning head coach. His innovative offensive schemes and use of the passing game was a perfect fit for the rookie quarterback. Shaughnessy taught Van Brocklin the professional game, as well as imparting a bit of wisdom. "He used to tell me that playing quarterback is like driving a team of 10 mules," Van Brocklin said. "You've got 10 reins to use, and you can pull and push or do anything you want with them."[4] Shaughnessy was known for his sharp tongue, and perhaps his vocabulary had an impact on the impressionable Van Brocklin. He later became a legend himself regarding his colorful use of language.

Van Brocklin was not cut from the normal athletic quarterback mold of Sammy Baugh, Otto Graham or Bob Waterfield. George Halas of the Chicago Bears once snidely remarked, "Van Brocklin can throw. Period. In the full sense of the word, he is not a professional football player."[5] In the context of the Los Angeles Rams offense, Van Brocklin's passing excellence was more than enough to warrant his spot on the playing field.

Shaughnessy found ways to utilize Van Brocklin's right arm during the 1949 season. Van Brocklin led a late touchdown drive at the end of a Week 8 game against the Pittsburgh Steelers to allow the Rams to escape with an important 7–7 tie. The pivotal regular season game for both the Rams and Van Brocklin was the last game of the year against the Washington Redskins. Los Angeles needed a victory to earn a spot in the NFL championship game, and they had only one win in their last five games.

Attempting to kick-start his team, Shaughnessy gave Van Brocklin his first taste of extensive playing time. Splitting time with starter Bob Waterfield, the rookie quarterback demonstrated an innate ability to dissect a defense with his downfield accuracy. In a wide-open contest that would see more passes thrown (88) than in any previous NFL game,[6] Van Brocklin completed six of 10 passes for 152 yards and four touchdowns. The 53–27 trouncing of the Redskins gave the Rams the Western Division title and a berth in the NFL championship game. Although the Rams would fall short of their championship goal, it was a fine season for the young Van Brocklin.

The Rams' hopes were high for the 1950 season, even with a new head coach in Joe Stydahar taking control. With his sparkling debut the previous year, Van Brocklin forced his way onto the field. Assistant coach Hamp Pool was impressed. "What Van Brocklin had going for him was, first of all, an exceptionally strong arm. He could throw the ball as far as you needed to throw it. Then, he had big hands. They enabled him to throw any kind of pass. He could hang it up in the air, he could drill it or he could give you that nice, soft touch on screens."[7] To fully utilize the skills of their two quarterbacks, the Rams game planned for Waterfield to play the first and third quarters, with Van Brocklin handling the second and fourth quarters. Neither player was completely happy with this arrangement, but it was hard to argue with the results. Van Brocklin, in particular, took a big step forward, winning the league passing championship for the 1950 season. Pool's reference to Van Brocklin's exceptionally strong arm was evident in a game against the Detroit Lions. In one quarter of action, the Rams overwhelmed the Lions by scoring 41 points. Van Brocklin contributed four touchdown passes of 30 yards or more to four different targets, including Elroy Hirsch, Glenn Davis, Tom Fears and Bob Boyd. Such exploits earned Van Brocklin a reputation of being the greatest deep passer of his generation.

Van Brocklin's storybook season came to a bittersweet ending. Los Angeles finished the regular season tied with the rival Chicago Bears in the National Conference, so a playoff game between the two teams had to be scheduled. The Rams eventually beat the tough Bears 24–14, but Van Brocklin suffered a broken rib during the game. Waterfield quarterbacked the rest of the way. Norm's injury was kept secret heading into the league championship game against the Cleveland Browns. He stood on the sidelines for nearly the entire game, while a late field goal by the Browns' Lou Groza gave Cleveland a 30–28 lead. After the ensuing kickoff, there was only time for one more play. Coach Stydahar summoned Van Brocklin onto the field, and the quarterback threw his trademark long bomb toward a streaking Glenn Davis. Unfortunately, the Browns' Warren Lahr intercepted the pass just outside the end zone. The Rams came up short in the title game once again.

Van Brocklin's mercurial personality began to assert itself as he became more entrenched in the Rams' organization. At times, he could be jovial, as shown by his "Laughing Boy" nickname. Elroy Hirsch bet five dollars that he could get Van Brocklin to giggle in five minutes by telling him jokes. Hirsch won the bet. Other times, Norm could wither even the biggest of men with a choice word or a stern glare. Rams offensive tackle Tom Dahms once missed a block which resulted in Van Brocklin getting sacked. On the sidelines after the play, Van Brocklin got a cup of water and threw it in Dahms' face. Players learned not to trifle with their young quarterback. Opponents were targets of Van Brocklin's wrath as well. When a defensive tackle had roughed him up, Norm challenged him to a meeting under the stands after the game. The tackle might have taken Norm up on his offer, but Van Brocklin didn't show. "I may have a hot head," he later explained, "but it's not empty."[8]

One of his special talents was the bestowing of nicknames. Van Brocklin himself had the rather unimaginative moniker of "The Dutchman," but he gave a great variety of names to others. He coined the name "Buttercups" for Glenn Davis; Bob Boyd became "Seabiscuit." Tom Fears was "Skinhead" due to his premature baldness. Legend has it that Van Brocklin gave Richard Lane his familiar "Night Train" name. Van Brocklin's nicknames sometimes came with a tinge of sarcasm. Running back Paul Younger already was known as "Tank," but he became "Bass Eyes" to Van Brocklin. The nickname was a reference to how Younger would often tip the defense by rolling his eyes in the direction a play would go. He called offensive lineman Bobby Cross "Look Out," because when he was beaten in pass protection, he would yell, "Look out, Dutch!"

Los Angeles had title aspirations for the 1951 season, and things began well for both the team and Van Brocklin. The opener pitted the Rams against an overmatched New York Yanks team. A Rams victory was expected, but the manner in which it was achieved ended up being historic. The stage was set when Bob Waterfield couldn't play due to injury, giving Van Brocklin the opportunity to quarterback the club for an entire game instead of the usual rotation system.

Van Brocklin started out hot, throwing long touchdown passes to Elroy Hirsch and Vitamin T. Smith in the first period. The aerial barrage continued as the game went on. "We didn't rush him at all," said Yanks player George Taliaferro. "We didn't have that kind of a defense, so he [Van Brocklin] could sit in the pocket and let it go. He didn't have to scramble. Once he got back in the pocket, they were talented enough to divert us around the pocket. He took the ball from center, put it up beside his right ear and when he saw that the receiver had the defender beaten, he let it go. It wasn't that he threw a 5-yard pass and then the runner ran 95 yards. He was throwing it 50 and 60 yards."[9]

The Rams won the game easily, 54–14, thanks to Van Brocklin's performance. He completed 27 of 41 passes for 554 yards and five touchdowns. The yardage total eclipsed the single game record by 86 yards.[10] Perhaps the most impressive aspect of Van Brocklin's performance is that his record has stood for 70 years.

The Dutchman spent the remainder of the 1951 season splitting time with Waterfield. Although Van Brocklin was friendly with Waterfield, he did not like Coach Stydahar's two-quarterback system. Van Brocklin's distaste for this setup came to a head in the final regular season game of 1951 against the Green Bay Packers. Stydahar sent in a running play; Van Brocklin thought a pass was a better option and ignored his coach's instructions. Stydahar responded by pulling Van Brocklin and letting Waterfield quarterback the team for the rest of the game. It ended up being one of Waterfield's finest performances. He tossed five touchdown passes in a 42–14 rout as the Rams clinched a third straight championship game appearance. However, the final outcome angered Van Brocklin. Not only did Stydahar bench Van Brocklin, but Waterfield's great game pushed him narrowly past his teammate for the league passing championship. Never one to hide his emotions, the Dutchman let his frustrations be known to Stydahar, and this minor statistical footnote later had major repercussions.

The 1951 NFL title game was a rematch of the previous season's classic between the Rams and Cleveland Browns. Bob Waterfield started the game at quarterback for Los Angeles, and the first period ended in a 0–0 standoff. As retaliation for Van Brocklin's outburst after the Packers game, Coach Stydahar left the Dutchman on the sidelines and kept Waterfield under center into the third quarter.[11] The game was a tense, back-and-forth affair, with both defenses giving ground grudgingly. Los Angeles held a slim 14–10 lead late in the third period when Stydahar finally let Van Brocklin out of his doghouse.

The Dutchman had spent nearly three-quarters of the game watching the Browns' defense, analyzing it for weakness. Although he was only in his third professional season, Van Brocklin had already earned a reputation for being a fine strategist. Speaking of this aspect, assistant coach Hamp Pool said, "Probably even greater than his pure physical equipment, though, was his ability to come off the field after one series of plays, practically, and tell you exactly what the opponent's defense amounted to. He had this uncanny knack of getting a mental picture of almost everyone in that secondary. That's the thing that made him so successful. He could tell you when a middle linebacker was overrunning, not getting over to a certain spot, and then he'd keep that information in mind until just the right time—until you really needed it. Then he'd exploit it. He could do that better than anyone I've ever seen."[12]

With the league title hanging in the balance, Van Brocklin wasted no time. His first play was a long pass to Elroy Hirsch on the right side of the field that barely missed connecting. His second play was a long pass to Tom Fears to the left side of the field that did connect. Fears' 48-yard gain gave the Rams a first down on Cleveland's one-yard line. A touchdown appeared imminent, but the Browns defense rose up to meet the challenge. They stuffed the Rams' running game for three straight plays, which resulted in a total loss of three yards. A fourth down fake field goal attempt was sniffed out by the alert Brown defenders, and the Rams wound up with zero points to show for their efforts.

Later in the fourth period the Rams kicked a field goal, only to have the Browns follow up that score with a long touchdown drive of their own to tie the game at 17–17. Los Angeles received the ensuing kickoff, and Van Brocklin soon found himself with a second down and three yards situation from his own 27-yard line. He decided to go for broke. The Dutchman took the snap, patiently waited for Fears to make his cut toward the sideline and threw a perfect spiral downfield. Cleveland defensive backs Tommy James and Cliff Lewis were seemingly both in position to make a play, but the pass avoided their reach. Fears caught the pass perfectly in stride and sprinted the rest of the way for a 73-yard touchdown. Writer Jack Clary eloquently summed up the play by saying, "the glory that the Browns' defense had earned throughout the season was forgotten in one Van Brocklin pass."[13]

The Rams now led 24–17, and when the Browns failed to respond on their last three possessions, Los Angeles had won the NFL championship. In the locker room after the game, Van Brocklin said, "Boy, I'm going to have a party tonight. Our guys were really playing football. And those Browns. They are not only good, but they're tough. They never could stop Fears, though."[14] Van Brocklin threw only six passes, but they totaled 128 yards and the winning touchdown. He was the catalyst for the victory.

Hamp Pool recounted, "It was typical Van Brocklin to wait until the fourth quarter to unload like that. The pass was perfect, just perfect. I can't remember ever seeing a better one under that kind of pressure. It was as clutch a situation as you'll ever see, and the ball was right there."[15]

The 1952 season opened with Stydahar's firing after an opening-game loss. The Rams replaced Stydahar with his assistant, Hamp Pool, who became the Rams' third head coach in four years. Nonetheless, the Rams' winning ways continued. Pool kept Stydahar's quarterback rotation system, as Van Brocklin split the passing duties with Waterfield. The Rams' offense once again led the league in scoring. After a slow start, the Rams won their final eight regular season games to force a playoff game with the Detroit Lions. The Dutchman was a key figure in the Rams' turnaround, tossing 12 touchdowns in limited playing time during the winning streak. Van Brocklin continued to perform at a high level in the playoff against Detroit. He completed 15 of 19 passes for 166 yards and one touchdown, but the Rams lost a 31–21 heartbreaker to the Lions.

The two-quarterback system came to an end with Bob Waterfield's offseason retirement in 1953. Van Brocklin finally had the starting job all to himself. "I don't mean that you can be without reserve strength," Van Brocklin observed, "but your quarterback has to be your leader out there on the field and if the players or coaches or the press or anybody starts choosing sides on which of your quarterbacks is better than the other, you can tear the guts right out of your ballclub."[16]

The Rams' offense maintained their proficiency in 1953 under Van Brocklin's guidance, and the quarterback earned his fourth consecutive Pro Bowl berth. Unfortunately, Van Brocklin's unshakable self-belief sometimes did not produce dividends. In a game against the rival San Francisco 49ers, the Rams were leading 20–0 and Van Brocklin, who also handled Los Angeles' punting duties, stood in punt formation on his own 13-yard line. He thought the Niners would not be expecting a fake from this area of the field, so he threw a pass to "Night Train" Lane. The pass was dropped. San Francisco immediately scored a touchdown from their favorable field position, a comeback was put in motion, and the Rams eventually lost to the 49ers, 31–30.[17] Perhaps remembering this moment, Hamp Pool later confided that his association with Van Brocklin shortened his life span by at least eight years.[18]

Los Angeles missed the postseason in both 1953 and 1954, due to a combination of their own leaky defense and the ascension of a very talented Detroit Lions squad. This development led to a new head coach for the 1955 season—Sid Gillman of the University of Cincinnati. Having never coached in professional football, Gillman was impressed with the array of offensive talent at his disposal. "We had Dutch Van Brocklin, godawmighty what a passer he was," Gillman said. "We had Fears and Bob Boyd, the sprinter, and Hirsch back out of retirement, and a great back, Ron Waller."[19]

Van Brocklin recorded another Pro Bowl year in 1955, although there were times when both the quarterback and the offense struggled to produce. "Every time Van Brocklin threw the ball," Gillman said, "you could hear a little 'zzt!' as it left his fingertips. We commented about it in practice. Zzt! Zzt! It was an oddity. Well, one week Van Brocklin hurt his hand and he could hardly throw in practice. You no longer heard that 'zzt!' And then one day, he started throwing better and better, and suddenly we could hear it again. Everybody started laughing and yelling 'The zzt is back.'"[20]

The Rams and their new coach surprised everyone by winning the Western Conference with an 8–3–1 record and earning a spot in the league title game against the Cleveland Browns. The matchup initially recalled the two previous title games between the Rams and Browns, but the wheels came off for Van Brocklin and the Rams in the second period. Van Brocklin threw six interceptions and the Browns won in a blowout, 38–14. "It was the worst game I ever played," Van Brocklin said. "It still haunts me."[21]

Sid Gillman had let Van Brocklin run the show in 1955, but the coach's confidence in his quarterback wavered after the loss to the Browns. The honeymoon of the previous season was over, the organization made changes in 1956. Gillman split the quarterback duties once again, this time between Van Brocklin and former first round draft choice Billy Wade. The result was a disappointing 4–8 record despite a roster loaded with talented players. Gillman tried to make amends the following season by reinserting Van Brocklin as the full-time starter at quarterback, but he insisted on sending in the plays from the sidelines. The Dutchman was not pleased. "You give the quarterback a 'ready' list and feed him information," he said, "but he's the only one who can get the actual feel of the play on the field. The quarterback has to be the leader."[22]

The 1957 Rams' 6–6 mark may have been slightly less disappointing than the previous year, but the contentiousness between coach and quarterback had gotten worse.

Van Brocklin publicly announced that he would be retiring from football at the end of the season. Behind the scenes, the Dutchman asked Rams general manager Pete Rozelle to trade him. Rozelle said he could make offers to teams in the East, so there would be less likelihood of Van Brocklin facing his old teammates. Van Brocklin said he would prefer Cleveland, who had returned to prosperity thanks in part to a fine rookie running back named Jim Brown, but who also did not have an established quarterback. Instead, Rozelle traded him to the lowly Philadelphia Eagles.

It can be argued that Van Brocklin's accomplishments with the Eagles are even more impressive than his time with the Rams. Van Brocklin made the Pro Bowl on a team that went 2–9–1 and finished in last place in his first season. Two years later, Philadelphia and Van Brocklin found themselves squaring off with Vince Lombardi's Green Bay Packers in the 1960 NFL title game. Despite being outmanned (and outgained 401 yards to 296 yards), the Dutchman led the Eagles to a 17–13 win. It would be Van Brocklin's last game. He retired as the 1960 NFL Player of the Year with consensus First Team All-Pro honors.

The Norm Van Brocklin story with the Eagles did not end with his retirement. Current head coach Buck Shaw was retiring, and Van Brocklin claimed he had been promised the Eagles head coaching job when he first came to the club in 1958. After the 1960 season, the Eagles, well aware how important Van Brocklin the quarterback was to the team's success, asked Van Brocklin to be a player-coach. He said no. The Eagles countered with a one-year head coaching offer, but without control over the selection of assistants. Van Brocklin again declined. The Eagles circled back and asked Van Brocklin if he would consider returning just to play quarterback in 1961, to which the Dutchman replied, "I wouldn't play for you [expletives] if I was starving to death."[23]

In the end, Van Brocklin landed the head coaching position with the expansion Minnesota Vikings. Their general manager was Bert Rose, a former Los Angeles Rams publicity man who was familiar with Van Brocklin. Rose thought the Dutchman's natural leadership qualities and understanding of football strategy would make him a fine head coach.

Van Brocklin's years as an NFL head coach, first with the Vikings and then with the Atlanta Falcons, were just as tumultuous as his playing career, but without the same level of success. Qualities that served him well as a player, most notably his insatiable desire to win, were perhaps his undoing as a coach. "I find it hard to walk up to a player and tell him he did a helluva good job," Van Brocklin once remarked about his new vocation.[24] He drove his players as hard as he drove himself, demanding all-out dedication, but the wins never came often enough for Van Brocklin. The Falcons fired Van Brocklin in his 13th year of head coaching, and he never returned to the NFL.

Van Brocklin retired to his pecan farm in Georgia and quickly distanced himself from football. In 1978, Norm underwent brain surgery to remove blood clots. After the procedure, Norm told reporters, "I had a brain transplant. The doctors gave me a sportswriter's brain, one that had never been used."[25] Ill health continued to beset the Dutchman, and in 1983 he suffered a fatal heart attack. He was only 57 years old.

Obituaries had a difficult time capturing the many sides of Norm Van Brocklin. "You can't compare Van Brocklin to the average guy," said Tommy McDonald, a favorite target of the quarterback while he was on the Eagles. "You just can't put him down on one page. You need two pages for Van."[26]

Jim Klobuchar of the *Minneapolis Star Tribune*, who got to know Van Brocklin well during the early days of the Minnesota Vikings, offered this insight: "Van Brocklin sometimes brought his workaday tempests home with him, but he also brought a familial love that was constant. His wife, Gloria, was his partner, confessor and champion. His daughters adored him, with reason. With them he was a generous and demonstrative man, as he was with two Asian youngsters he and his wife adopted in later years."[27]

One of the obituaries related this story:

> Mal Florence of the Los Angeles Times covered a Ram-Viking game in Minneapolis when Van Brocklin was the Vikings' coach. On his way back to the hotel after writing his story, Florence was involved in an automobile accident and hospitalized with multiple injuries. "The first person to phone was Van Brocklin," Florence said. "I was amazed. He was concerned. But he tried to cover it up by being gruff, saying something like he was going to put me on waivers and that all sports writers would be better off having their heads busted."[28]

Perhaps the best summation of Norm Van Brocklin the man is Klobuchar's personal description, who wrote, "He was often wrong-headed and too often unfair. But he was real; he left a mark on the game he played and on his times, and he was an original. I've always missed our good times."[29]

Notes

1. Noah Smith, "'The Dutchman' and the Original Vertical Passing Game," *FishDuck.com*, June 17, 2015, https://fishduck.com/2015/06/the-dutchman-and-the-original-vertical-passing-game/.
2. Murray Olderman, *The Pro Quarterback* (Englewood Cliffs, NJ: Prentice-Hall, 1966), 234.
3. Steve Bisheff, *Great Teams' Great Years: Los Angeles Rams* (New York: Macmillan, 1973), 69.
4. Bisheff, *Los Angeles Rams*, 21.
5. Olderman, *The Pro Quarterback*, 234.
6. T.J. Troup, "Clark Shaughnessy and the 1949 Los Angeles Rams," *The Coffin Corner* 32, no. 4 (2010), 7.
7. Bisheff, *Los Angeles Rams*, 69.
8. Olderman, *The Pro Quarterback*, 236.
9. Judy Battista, "Still the Biggest Passing Day," *New York Times*, September 27, 2011, https://www.nytimes.com/2011/09/28/sports/football/norm-van-brocklins-passing-record-stands-60-years-later.html.
10. Battista, "Still the Biggest."
11. Mickey Herskowitz, *The Golden Age of Pro Football* (New York: Macmillan, 1974), 46.
12. Bisheff, *Los Angeles Rams*, 69.
13. Jack Clary, *Great Teams' Great Years: Cleveland Browns* (New York: Macmillan, 1973), 37.
14. Bisheff, *Los Angeles Rams*, 75.
15. Bisheff, *Los Angeles Rams*, 70.
16. Bisheff, *Los Angeles Rams* 20.
17. Bisheff, *Los Angeles Rams*, 20.
18. Herskowitz, *The Golden Age of Pro Football*, 46.
19. Herskowitz, *The Golden Age of Pro Football*, 56.
20. Herskowitz, *The Golden Age of Pro Football*, 56.
21. Olderman, *The Pro Quarterback*, 237.
22. Olderman, *The Pro Quarterback*, 237.
23. Olderman, *The Pro Quarterback*, 240.
24. Olderman, *The Pro Quarterback*, 240.
25. Chuck Johnson, "There Was No One Like the Dutchman," *The Milwaukee Journal*, May 5, 1983, 3–3.
26. Jim Lassiter, "Obituary Can't Cover Van Brocklin," *The Oklahoman*, May 5, 1983, https://oklahoman.com/article/2023569/obituary-cant-cover-van-brocklin.
27. Jim Klobuchar, *Knights and Knaves of Autumn (40 Years of Pro Football and the Minnesota Vikings)* (Cambridge, MN: Adventure Publications, 2000), 62.
28. Johnson, "There Was No One Like the Dutchman," 3–3.
29. Klobuchar, *Knights and Knaves of Autumn*, 69.

Bob Waterfield

George Bozeka

The *Los Angeles Times* once stated that Bob Waterfield's life read "like a Marvel comic book. He was Captain America and the mighty Thor rolled into one, a real-life superhero who rewrote the record book, won the big game and got the girl—a movie star, no less."[1]

Waterfield could do it all on the football field—run, pass, punt, kick, and play defense. Vincent X. Flaherty of the *Los Angeles Examiner* wrote of Waterfield that "no other athlete ever embodied so many different football skills and qualities. Waterfield is the finest all-around football player of the generation and perhaps of all time."[2]

Waterfield was an exceedingly quiet and reticent warrior; his Hollywood starlet wife Jane Russell called him "Old Stone Face" and "The Silent One," with sarcastic affection.[3] Linebacker and fellow teammate Don Paul once stated, "You could spend 10 days with him on a fishing trip ... and count the words he said on the fingers of one hand."[4]

Robert Staton Waterfield was born in Elmira, New York, on July 26, 1920. When Bob was a young boy his parents, Frances and Staton (Jack) moved their small family to Van Nuys, California. Jack owned a local business, the Van Nuys Transfer and Storage Company, and was an accomplished local baseball player. In 1939, Jack died suddenly. Bob was nine years old. It was a difficult time for Bob and his mother. She went to work as a nurse, working long hours. Bob was a reclusive boy who often had to fend for himself. He enjoyed solitary activities like hunting and fishing and playing sports with other neighborhood boys, roaming the San Fernando Valley for games. During high school, Bob worked physical summer jobs to help his mother.[5]

At Van Nuys High School, Waterfield played at all sports, but he did not distinguish himself on the football field. He characterized his high school career, stating, "I was quite small, weighing under 150 pounds. I loved playing, but I was far too light

The Rams' stoic field general Bob Waterfield was also an excellent placekicker, leading the NFL with 13 field goals in 1951.

to do much. My final year at Van Nuys, I did make the varsity, played tailback on the single wing."[6]

Waterfield wanted to become a better football player, and he worked hard honing his skills in his spare time, but he felt his size and family situation were still against him. "Playing college football was far from my dreams—not only because of my size, but because my father had died ... and I figured I had to get a job."[7]

And get a job he did, working on the assembly line at Douglas Aircraft and working various jobs in the Hollywood film industry. During this time, Waterfield filled out and UCLA offered him a gymnastics scholarship. He was an accomplished gymnast, often working out with other gymnasts at Santa Monica Beach, which had become known as Muscle Beach.[8]

Someone else noticed Waterfield at Muscle Beach—a former classmate named Jane Russell. She remembered Waterfield as a skinny hall monitor who had tried to ask her out at Van Nuys High School. Much like the underweight nerds in the famous Charles Atlas print ads, Russell noticed that Waterfield was now "well stacked," and she was immensely attracted to him. Bob and Jane started dating immediately.[9]

Urged on by his mother, Waterfield enrolled at UCLA in 1940. He didn't play freshman football, but as a sophomore he made the varsity football team in 1941, playing quarterback in head coach Edwin "Babe" Horrell's new T-formation offense, and leading the Bruins to a 5–5–1 record.

In 1942, Waterfield guided the Bruins to a 7–4 record, including their first ever victory over rival USC, a Pacific Coast Conference championship and their first ever berth in the Rose Bowl. Waterfield also became the first Bruin to pass for over 1000 yards in a season, and he was named first team quarterback on the All-Pacific Coast football team.[10]

Meanwhile, Russell had signed a seven-year contract with movie and aviation mogul Howard Hughes in 1940. In November of 1940, her first movie went into production. Production was completed in 1941, but the movie wasn't released until January of 1943 with a world premiere in February because of censorship issues. *The Outlaw* became an immediate sensation because of its salacious subject matter and shooting style, making Russell a Hollywood sex symbol in the process.[11]

Despite having a tempestuous on-again, off-again relationship, Waterfield married Russell in Las Vegas on April 24, 1943, and soon thereafter he reported to Fort Benning, Georgia, for officer candidate school, where he graduated a second lieutenant. Russell eventually joined him at Fort Benning where he played for the 176th Infantry football and basketball teams. Waterfield injured his knee and was given an honorable discharge from the army for a physical disabilty.[12]

Rams quarterback Bob Waterfield with his glamorous movie star wife Jane Russell.

The 1944 NFL draft was held on April 19. The Cleveland Rams selected Waterfield in the fifth round with the 42nd pick overall. Waterfield, however, decided to forgo the NFL and return to UCLA to play his final year of college football.[13]

The 1944 Bruins finished with 4–5–1 record. Waterfield was named to the West squad for the annual East-West Shrine Game and had a fantastic performance, leading the West to a 13–7 victory at Kezar Stadium in San Francisco on January 1, 1945. Waterfield averaged 6.7 yards per carry on the ground including a 13-yard run for the winning touchdown. In the air he completed 11 passes including a 45-yarder to set up the West's other touchdown. To complete his day he punted five times for a 59.4-yard average.[14] For his outstanding efforts he was named the Most Valuable Player for the game.[15] Waterfield was also named the second team quarterback on the United Press All-Pacific Coast football team.[16]

The performance raised Waterfield's profile, and he cashed in, signing with the Rams for $7,500. Cleveland's fourth estate heavily criticized the move. *Cleveland Press* columnist Franklin Lewis stated that "it is a trifle shocking to discover that raw college recruits weighted down with clippings are being signed for that much money!"[17]

Waterfield quieted the naysayers during his rookie season in Cleveland. In fact, his prowess became apparent on the very first day of training camp in Bowling Green, Ohio, as he boomed a series of long punts, one traveling 84 yards.[18] He proceeded to lead the Rams to a 3–1 record in exhibition games to become the Rams' new starting quarterback. Waterfield led the Rams to a 9–1 regular season record, the first winning season in the history of the franchise, and the Western Division berth in the NFL championship game against Sammy Baugh and the Washington Redskins.

He had developed into one of the best all-around players in the game. Nicknamed "Buckets" by his teammates, Waterfield completed 89 of 171 passes for 1609 yards and a league leading 14 touchdowns. He also scored five touchdowns on the ground, intercepted six passes, averaged 40.6 yards as a punter, and kicked a field goal and a league-leading 31 extra points. Opposing coaches marveled at his ball handling skills. Waterfield was a master at the Sally Rand play—the naked bootleg. Giants coach Steve Owen stated that he had to rerun the film of a Waterfield touchdown run seven times to see the fake.[19]

In a late season game at Detroit on Thanksgiving Day to determine the Western Division crown, Buckets was at his courageous best. Playing with three crushed ribs that made it difficult for him to raise his throwing arm and sick to his stomach with severe shooting pain, Waterfield completed 12 of 21 passes for 329 yards and two touchdowns and ran for another touchdown in a 28–21 victory over the Lions.[20] After the game, a Cleveland newspaper headline read "Waterfield Best Cleveland Pitcher Since Bob Feller," and Rams assistant coach Bob Snyder gushed that "it was the greatest exhibition of guts I've ever seen."[21]

Nearly a month later on December 16, the Rams played the Redskins for the NFL championship in frigid Cleveland. With temperatures near zero, gusty winds, and icy field conditions, Waterfield had another great performance completing 14 of 27 passes for 192 yards and two touchdowns to lead the Rams to a tight 15–14 victory and their first NFL championship. After the game, Rams head coach Adam Walsh called Waterfield "the greatest T-formation quarterback in the country."[22] Even Feller watching from the stands was impressed. "And he didn't even warm up."[23]

For his 1945 efforts, Waterfield was awarded the Joe F. Carr Trophy as the NFL's Most Valuable Player and was also named first team All-Pro by the Associated Press and UP.

Rams owner Dan Reeves rewarded Waterfield with a new three-year contract for $20,000 a year.[24]

Despite winning the championship, the Rams were losing money in Cleveland. On January 12, 1946, at the annual league meetings in New York, the NFL owners approved Reeves' plan to move the Rams west to Los Angeles. Waterfield was thrilled by the move telling Steve Bisheff years later when asked if he was disappointed, "Are you kidding? I loved the idea. I was going home."[25]

Bisheff explained in the *Orange County Register*. "Waterfield was the superstar Reeves could build around in Los Angeles." Waterfield and Russell immediately "became Hollywood's hottest couple."[26]

But Bisheff added that "unfortunately, for those who made a living writing about sports, Waterfield, despite his celebrated marriage, was hardly a charismatic figure off the field." He was the anti–Joe Namath, a quiet, almost shy man who never felt comfortable talking to the media. Once he strapped on his pads and slipped on his helmet, though, everything changed. Waterfield was an unquestioned leader on the field and teammates swore by him. "Waterfield," wrote Bob Oates, then with the *Los Angeles Examiner*, "led the Rams with the surety of Churchill and the quiet dignity of Ed Murrow."[27]

The 1946 preseason got off to a terrible start for Waterfield and the defending champions as they loss to the Elroy Hirsch led College All-Stars 16–0. In addition, Jim Hardy, a star quarterback from USC, had joined the team. Drafted by the Redskins, Hardy had been traded to the Rams. A heated rivalry soon festered between the outgoing Hardy and quiet Waterfield, with the Los Angeles press seeming to the favor the former Trojan.

Despite this backdrop, Waterfield solidified his position as one of the best all-around players in the league in 1946. The Rams finished second in the West with a 6–4–1 record, but Buckets led the league in passing attempts (251), completions (127), touchdowns (17), points after touchdowns attempted and made (a perfect 37 for 37), and field goal percentage (66.7), plus averaging 44.7 yards per punt and intercepting five passes. He was named first team All-Pro by both the AP and UP.

The press grumblings about Hardy continued in 1947, as the Rams and Waterfield had off years with Bob completing only 43.4 percent of his passes for 1210 yards and eight touchdowns, and the Rams finishing fourth in the West under new coach Bob Snyder with a 6–6 record. Waterfield did, however, average 42.4 yards per punt, intercept five passes, and lead the league in field goal attempts (16), field goals made (seven), and long punt (86 yards).

The Rams had their third coach in three years—the legendary Clark Shaughnessy—in 1948. Los Angeles finished with a mediocre 6–5–1 record with Waterfield and Hardy alternating at quarterback. Waterfield completed under 50 percent of his passes for a second consecutive season for 1354 yards and 14 touchdowns, but he intercepted four passes and again had the season's longest punt at a booming 88 yards.

Waterfield had a breakout moment with Rams fans in an early season game against the Eagles. Bisheff recalled, "The incumbent world champs from Philadelphia were pouring it on the Rams, mounting a seemingly insurmountable 28–0 lead with a minute left in the third quarter. Suddenly, as if a switch had been turned on in a nearby Hollywood sound stage, Waterfield got hot. He threw four passes and four times Rams receivers raced under the football to catch balls for touchdowns. Final score: Eagles 28, Rams 28. And just like that, a star was born. Waterfield was the first legitimate sports superstar in

L.A., the first player adults rushed for autographs, the first one kids wanted to imitate on sandlots."[28]

After the 1948 season, Hardy was traded to the Cardinals. In 1949, the Rams drafted Oregon star quarterback Norm Van Brocklin to pair with Waterfield, and the Rams were again a force in the West. As Ron Fimrite wrote in *Sports Illustrated*, "Shaughnessy used Waterfield to test the defense, then inserted Van Brocklin for the big play.... Aside from their considerable ability, Buckets and the Dutchman had virtually nothing in common physically or temperamentally. Waterfield was an amazing all-around athlete and one of the last of football's true 'triple threat' players—a gifted runner, passer and kicker—as well as a superb defensive back. Van Brocklin could throw and kick, period. He was the classic strong-armed drop-back passer who probably couldn't outrun Waterfield's wife. Not that anyone back then would have been motivated to run away from Jane Russell...."[29]

A statistical analysis of the 1949 season backs Fimrite's prose. The Rams finished first in the Western Division with an 8–2–2 record. Waterfield had career highs in passing attempts (296), completions (154) and yards passing (2168), tied his career high in touchdowns passes (17), and led the league with nine field goals. He was again named first team All-Pro by the AP and UP after a two-year absence. Meanwhile Van Brocklin completed 32 passes for 601 yards and six touchdowns, and a league leading 10.36 yards per passing attempt.

The Rams lost to the Eagles in the NFL championship game 14–0 in a rain-soaked quagmire at the Los Angeles Memorial Coliseum, as both Waterfield and Van Brocklin were ineffective.

In 1950, the Rams again had a new coach-Joe Stydahar. Waterfield and Van Brocklin both had Pro Bowl seasons, as the Rams had one of the most prolific offenses in NFL history. Van Brocklin led the league in passing, but Waterfield had a great all-around season. Buckets completed 122 of 213 passes with 11 touchdowns for a league leading and career best completion percentage of 57.3 percent. He also led the league in points after touchdown attempted (58) and made (54), kicked seven field goals and averaged 40.1 yards per punt.

The Rams finished the season with a 9–3 record and tied for the top spot in the National Conference with George Halas' Chicago Bears. This set up a playoff game on Sunday, December 17, at the Coliseum to decide the Conference crown. In the days leading up to the game, Waterfield took ill. On game day he was running a fever of 102. Van Brocklin started the game with Waterfield on the bench. The Dutchman was ineffectual, throwing eight straight incompletions. Crazylegs Hirsch remembered, "Stydahar approached Waterfield, late in the first quarter. 'Do you feel well enough to go in?' the coach asked. 'Yes,' Waterfield lied. When the Rams got possession of the ball again there were three minutes left in the quarter. Neither team had scored. Waterfield entered the offensive huddle slowly, and then he threw up. Gathering himself, the 30-year-old quarterback began marching the Rams downfield."[30]

Waterfield turned in a magnificent performance accounting for all of Rams scoring, kicking a 43-yard field goal, completing 14 of 21 passes for 280 yards and three touchdowns, all to Tom Fears, and converting three extra points as the Rams defeated the Bears 24–14 for a second consecutive berth in the NFL championship game.

In the championship game against the Browns on Christmas Eve at Cleveland Municipal Stadium, the Rams lost a heartbreaker, 30–28, on a last-minute field goal by

Lou Groza. Waterfield completed 18 of 31 passes for 312 yards and a touchdown but also contributed four interceptions to the losing cause.

The fans and the press assumed that a quarterback controversy was brewing in La-La Land. Russell, Hirsch and Fears stated that this was not the case. Russell indicated, "Robert and Norm got along a whole lot better than the press would have you believe. Maybe it's because they both had a sense of humor." Hirsch added that "I never heard either him or Waterfield say anything bad about the other." Said Fears, "We played just as hard for one as the other. Why shouldn't we? They were the best there was."[31]

Despite the civility, both men were very competitive. Waterfield recalled, "We really had competition. Especially in practice. We would have a two-hour passing drill in the morning, and when someone would drop a pass or get overthrown, it was a big check mark against you.... I think the competition actually helped both of us. It made us work that much harder."[32]

Los Angeles entered the 1951 season seeking redemption. The Rams again fielded a superior offensive team three-peating as Conference champions with an 8–4 record. Waterfield supplanted Van Brocklin as the league's leading passer, completing 88 of 176 passes for 1566 yards and 13 touchdowns including the longest touchdown pass of the NFL season (a 91-yarder to Hirsch in a December 2 victory over the Bears). He led the league in field goal attempts (23) and field goals made (13). In a December 9, 24–22 loss to the Lions at the Coliseum, Waterfield kicked a then-record five field goals in one game.

On December 23, the Rams faced the Browns in the championship game for the second consecutive year. Playing in the friendly confines of the Coliseum, the Rams won the title 24–17. Waterfield passed for 125 yards and kicked three extra points and a field goal. Waterfield was again named to the Pro Bowl for his efforts in 1951.

Waterfield may have been a silent and methodical tactician, but his teammates revered his toughness. Hirsch elaborated, "He was the toughest guy ever to walk into a huddle. I remember the time one of our backs was reluctant to carry the ball and Bob hauled off and slugged him right there in the huddle. And I remember once when I asked him to call a certain play because I felt I could beat the defensive man with that pattern. The pass was intercepted and when I got back to the sidelines, Bob walked up beside me. 'Elroy,' he said, 'if you don't know what you're talking about, keep your damned mouth shut!'"[33]

That toughness was on full display during Waterfield's final season in 1952. Assistant coach Hamp Pool replaced Stydahar one game into the season. The Rams and Lions finished in a tie for first in the Western Conference, with the Lions winning the playoff for the conference crown. Waterfield had his worst statistical season completing only 46.8 percent of his passes for 655 yards and three touchdowns, but he led the league in field goal percentage (61.1%) and points after touchdown attempts (45) and points after made (44).

Buckets had one final transcendent performance on October 12, 1952. Down 28–6 after three quarters to the Packers at Marquette Stadium in Milwaukee, Waterfield led the Rams to 24 fourth-quarter points and a 30–28 victory. The winning drive covered 92 yards with two and a half minutes to go. After the game, Flaherty gushed in the *Examiner*, "Games such as the Rams and the Rifle [Waterfield] played Sunday are the kind that set pro football apart, give it that extra touch of quality which makes it the finest game in the land."[34]

Pool added, "Bob's the greatest player I've ever seen when this club is behind. I still don't know how he brought us back this afternoon."[35]

On December 1, 1952, Waterfield announced that he would retire at the end of the 1952 season. On December 14, 1952, during the Rams' final home game against the Steelers, Waterfield was honored with Bob Waterfield Day and his jersey number 7 was retired by the Rams.[36]

Waterfield finished his career with 11,849 yards passing, completing 814 of 1671 passes with 97 touchdowns and 128 interceptions. He also ran for 13 touchdowns, kicked 60 field goals and 315 extra points, punted for a 42.4-yard average and intercepted 20 passes.

In 1955, Russell and Waterfield formed their own film production company, Russ-Field Productions. They signed a deal with United Artists and produced a number of pictures, including *Gentlemen Marry Brunettes* with Russell and Jeanne Crain, *The King and Four Queens* with Clark Gable and Eleanor Parker, and *Run for the Sun* with Richard Widmark and Jane Greer.

Waterfield worked as a kicking coach for the Rams and assistant to Hamp Pool with the Toronto Argonauts, before agreeing to become the head coach of the Rams in 1960. Waterfield fashioned a disastrous record of 9–24–1 before resigning eight games into the 1962 season. Jim Murray characterized Waterfield's coaching years in the *Los Angeles Times*. "No one ever played the game of football better than Bob Waterfield. But no one ever coached it less.... An aloof man who probably didn't get on a first-name basis with his mother till well after he learned to talk, Bob was an athletic aristocrat but as a coach preferred to be a kind of bored chairman. He communicated with his team by vast silences. You had the feeling he would rather play the films than live players."[37]

In 1965, Bob was inducted into the Pro Football Hall of Fame.

Russell and Waterfield separated in 1967 and were divorced in 1968. Ron Fimrite reported in *Sports Illustrated* that "like Bogie, Buckets liked his cocktails.... Waterfield increasingly addicted to nightlife would bring about his own gradual deterioration.... Russell ... complained that he was out until two or three in the morning continually."[38]

In 1969, the Pro Football Hall of Fame named Waterfield to its NFL 1940s All-Decade Team.

On March 25, 1983, with his second wife Jan at his side, Waterfield died of respiratory failure after a long illness at the age of 62. Upon his death, Murray stated,

"With a football in his hands, Bob Waterfield could always handle third-and-long yardage. In life, third-and-long yardage was not such a sure thing. Life sacked him.... The music had stopped, and the pompoms were put away for the old quarterback. You could find Waterfield in recent years in a small bar on Ventura Boulevard. In the morning. He was among friends who knew what Bob Waterfield was, he didn't have to tell them. Bob hated to have to tell anybody about himself."[39]

Perhaps Waterfield summed up his life best. Asked to describe the happiest time of his life, he simply stated, "The days when I played football."[40]

Notes

1. Rob Fernas, "Complete Package," *Los Angeles Times*, December 25, 1999, www.latimes.com/archives/la-xpm-1999-dec-25-sp-47304-story.html.
2. Steve Bisheff, *Great Teams' Great Years: Los Angeles Rams* (New York: Macmillan, 1973), 133.
3. Arthur Daley, "Sports of the Times," *New York Times*, November 12, 1962, 39.
4. Ron Fimrite, "Mr. Hollywood and the Dutchman," *Sports Illustrated*, Fall, 1995, 28.
5. Jack Sher, "The Bob Waterfield Story," *Sport*, November 1951, 72.

6. Sher, "The Bob Waterfield Story," 72.
7. David Condon, "In the Wake of the News," *Chicago Tribune*, August 2, 1966, 3–1.
8. James C. Sulecki, *The Cleveland Rams* (Jefferson, NC: McFarland, 2016), 134.
9. Jane Russell, *My Path & My Detours* (New York: Franklin Watts, 1985), 45.
10. "2019 UCLA Football Information Guide," *Isuu.com*, 80, 90, 145, https://issuu.com/uclabruins/docs/2019_fb_guide_full; "Bob Waterfield Hall of Fame Enshrinee," Pro Football Hall of Fame Press Release.
11. "The Outlaw (1943)," Turner Classic Movies, *Tcm.com*, http://www.tcm.com/tcmdb/title/14214/The-Outlaw/; "Jane Russell," Turner Classic movies, *Tcm.com*, http://www.tcm.com/tcmdb/person/167425|79325/Jane-Russell/.
12. Sulecki, *The Cleveland Rams*, 138; Russell, *My Path & My Detours*, 74–76.
13. Bob Carroll, et al., eds., *Total Football II* (New York: HarperCollins, 1997), 1448.
14. Bisheff, *Los Angeles Rams*, 76.
15. "MVP Award Recipients-Most Outstanding Offensive Players (1945–2020)," *Shrinegame.com*, https://www.shrinegame.com/past-inductees-mvp.
16. "McClure on All-Coast Team; Sorenson Makes Second Team," *Nevada State Journal*, December 14, 1944, 12.
17. Bisheff, *Los Angeles Rams*, 76.
18. Sher, "The Bob Waterfield Story," 69.
19. Daley, "Sports of the Times, 39.
20. Murray Olderman, *The Pro Quarterback* (Englewood Cliffs, NJ: Prentice-Hall, 1966), 208.
21. Bisheff, *Los Angeles Rams*, 77.
22. Bisheff, *Los Angeles Rams*, 77–78.
23. Cameron Shipp, "Romance at the Waterfields," *Sport*, November 1946, 23.
24. Bisheff, *Los Angeles Rams*, 78.
25. Bisheff, *Los Angeles Rams*, 134.
26. Steve Bisheff, "NFL 2016: Rams' Roots in L.A. Started with Pioneer Team Owner Dan Reeves," *Orange County Register*, https://www.ocregister.com/2016/09/07/nfl-2016-rams-roots-in-la-started-with-pioneer-team-owner-dan-reeves/.
27. Bisheff, "NFL 2016."
28. Bisheff, "NFL 2016."
29. Fimrite, "Mr. Hollywood and the Dutchman," 27–28.
30. Rick Smith, "I Remember," *Pro!*, September 19, 1976, 106.
31. Fimrite, "Mr. Hollywood and the Dutchman," 29.
32. Bisheff, *Los Angeles Rams*, 134.
33. Bisheff, *Los Angeles Rams*, 76.
34. Bisheff, *Los Angeles Rams*, 83.
35. Bisheff, *Los Angeles Rams*, 83.
36. "Waterfield Plans to Retire," *San Mateo (CA) Times*, December 1, 1952, 1; Frank Finch, "Fans Honor Waterfield Today as Rams Steelers Tangle," *Los Angeles Times*, December 14, 1952, II-6.
37. Jim Murray, "Bob Turns in Ulcer," *Los Angeles Times*, November 8, 1962, III-1.
38. Fimrite, "Mr. Hollywood and the Dutchman," 29.
39. Fernas, "Complete Package."
40. Fernas, "Complete Package."

Stan West

Jay Zahn

Jovial giant Stan West saw many changes in a pro football career that spanned more than four decades, including the elimination of his primary position on the field of play.

Stanley Byron West was born on September 22, 1926, in Weatherford, Oklahoma. He was the son of a Baptist minister, and the youngest of seven children. He grew up in Enid, about 100 miles north of Weatherford, where he became an all-state end on the high school football team. After graduation, with World War II in progress, Stan headed to San Diego for enrollment in the Naval Training Center, then on to the South Pacific for service.[1]

After the war, Stan was recruited by University of Oklahoma football coach Jim Tatum in a massive and successful push to turn the Sooners into a football power. Stan gained experience, but he didn't blossom until his senior year of 1949, playing guard both ways on an undefeated Oklahoma squad, the school's first. By this time, Bud Wilkinson had taken over the program. Stan had only good things to say about Bud. "He taught me more technique than I ever thought about learning from the pros," Stan would later say.[2]

Despite being Oklahoma's biggest player as a senior, Stan played a soft, read-the-offense style of defense. "If you bust through, you might miss the guy," he said.[3] Iowa State center Rod Rust said after facing Stan, "After the game was over, I didn't have a bruise or a sore place on my body but he still made every tackle that came through. I couldn't block him enough to even bruise myself. He could play so soft and maneuver so well without getting involved in body contact."[4]

Rams middle guard Stan West played for legendary head coach Bud Wilkinson at Oklahoma.

Stan's efforts in 1949 earned him a second team slot on several All-America teams.[5] The Sooners capped their season with a 35–0 pounding of LSU in the Sugar Bowl in New Orleans. The Tigers made little headway against Stan and his mates, gaining only 38 yards rushing. Stan lingered in Dixie after the game, playing in the first Senior Bowl in Jacksonville and earning $343 for his services.[6]

The rising Oklahoma football program attracted the attention of the NFL. Stan was the first guard chosen in the 1950 draft, selected by the Rams in the first round with the 12th overall pick. Stan outweighed his line mates at Oklahoma by 30 pounds while remaining mobile, making him an attractive prospect to the NFL.[7] Stan signed a contract with the Rams in May of 1950.

Despite winning the Western Division in 1949, the Rams' guard positions were in a state of flux. On offense, Hal Dean had retired to the Texas oil fields. The most prominent middle guard on defense, Milan Lazetich, had battled ulcer problems that lingered into training camp.[8] The Rams were also looking to shore up their run game defense, as the champion Eagles shredded it for 274 yards rushing in the 1949 championship game and 264 yards in a regular season game.

Stan's work with the Rams would have to wait as he first reported to Chicago to face those same Eagles in the College All-Star game played on August 11. Stan pitched in with some second half defensive work, and the Stars scored a big 17–7 upset in front of 88,885 fans.[9]

The thrills were just beginning for Stan. As prominent and well attended as the College All-Star Game was at the time, the Rams would do better. The Rams' first preseason game was against the Redskins in an annual charity game, a series that would extend into the 1960s. This edition proved to be the most well-attended football game in the 1950 NFL season and in Rams history to that point. "How would you feel, being a little 'ol country boy from Enid, Okla., playing your first pro ball right out there in front of 95,000 people?" Stan would later say.[10]

Due to his College All-Star duties, Stan had been absent from Rams camp. In a preseason game against the Redskins, Stan took the field at middle guard in the second quarter and was quite impressive. "West was outstanding," said Rams head coach Joe Stydahar.[11] Stan started the next preseason game at middle guard. Except for one preseason start at offensive guard against the Giants, Stan had found his calling with the Rams. He'd start every game at middle guard in the 1950 regular season.

The defensive or middle guard position was the middle member of a five-man line in a 5-2-4 defense popularized by Eagles coach Greasy Neale. The middle guard faced off consistently against the offensive center, with one or occasionally both hands in the dirt. On running plays, he bore the traditional run-stuffing responsibilities. However, in passing situations, he was free to pull directly back or to either sideline to guard against screens and short passes or to abort a hard pass rush charge to do the same. In coaching lingo, the position was given the "Mike" moniker later applied to the middle linebacker in a 4-3-4 defensive alignment.

Sizewise, Stan played the pro game at anywhere from 219 to 262 pounds, placing him snugly in the middle between lithe, quick guards such as Cleveland's 213-pound Bill Willis and mountainous guards like Detroit's Les Bingaman, who likely topped 300 pounds for most of his career.

The Rams got off to a slow start in Stan's rookie year of 1950, including a 56–20 thrashing at the hands of the Eagles, before beginning a win streak in their fifth game. Stan (described by a local columnist as "more destructive than a hotel laundry")[12] and the rest of the Rams' defense helped start the streak by holding the Lions to 58 rushing yards in a 30–28 victory at Detroit. Five more wins followed, with Stan drawing praise from Coach Stydahar for his work in a home victory against the 49ers.[13]

The Rams pulled even with the Bears in the season's final week, setting up a National Conference playoff game. Having lost twice to Chicago in the regular season, the Rams turned the tables on the Bears, coming up with a 24–14 victory. The 14 points matched the fewest the Rams' defense gave up all year.

The ensuing NFL championship game brought not the Eagles, but the Cleveland Browns. A back-and-forth game was decided by a field goal by the Browns' Lou Groza. The Rams had come up short again. Stan missed much of the second half of the contest in favor of Milan Lazetich.

NFL sophomore Stan found himself an instant veteran with the 1951 Rams. End Larry Brink returned, but two new tackles would be added to the defensive line, as Dick Huffman jumped to the CFL and Bob Reinhard retired. Rookies Jack Halliday and Jim Winkler took their places. A third rookie was added when Jack Zilly broke his arm during the season and Andy Robustelli stepped in.

As in 1950, the Rams' offense put up league leading statistics, while the defense had its ups and downs. In an early season rematch of the 1950 title game against the Browns, Stan put good pressure on Browns quarterback Otto Graham and picked up a sack. But Cleveland gashed the Rams for 293 rushing yards and won 38–23. Stan also received good notices for his work against the 49ers in a mid-season Los Angeles Coliseum game; the Rams won that one, 23–16.[14]

The Rams prevailed over the Lions, 49ers and Bears in another tight race for the National Conference crown in 1951, pulling away for a 42–14 victory over the Packers on the final weekend of the regular season. Captain Bob Waterfield awarded Stan the game ball for his efforts against the Packers as the Rams held Green Bay to 45 yards rushing.[15]

The whole league was taking notice of Stan. Stan made the Pro Bowl in 1951 for the first time. The *New York Daily News* also chose Stan as one of their defensive guards on their All-Pro team with Bill Willis; even though five-man lines were the norm in the NFL at the time, the All-Pro teams featured six defensive linemen, including two defensive guards. But the Rams would need better defense this time to defeat Willis and the defending champion Browns, owners of an 11-game winning streak, in the championship game.

Stan had a fairly quiet championship game, but the Browns didn't run up the middle much after the early going. In fact, they didn't rush nearly as often as their early season matchup, or as effectively—18 carries for 49 yards for the running backs. Quarterback Otto Graham scrambled for 43 yards but was also sacked five times. Stan saved the hard charges for Brink and Robustelli. Down 10–7 in the third quarter, Brink floored Graham with a sack, and Graham fumbled. Robustelli picked up the ball and scampered to the Brown two-yard line. Running back Dan Towler scored three plays later. Later Marvin Johnson picked off a Graham pass, and he got down to the one-yard line with the help of a block from Stan. Waterfield kicked a chip shot field goal from there, and the Rams led 17–10. With the lead, Stan frequently dropped back into coverage.

Graham and the Browns came back to tie the game; then the Rams untied it when Norm Van Brocklin threw a long touchdown pass. Graham would get three more chances, but he couldn't get past the Rams' 40-yard line. The final was 24–17, and the Rams were champions!

Beyond the thrill of victory, and the winner's share—$2,108 per Ram—winning championships opened doors elsewhere. Teammate Crazylegs Hirsch started a film career and Stan tagged along. Stan would be typecast, playing a football player in the *Crazylegs* biopic and a guard—a prison guard—in the prison drama *Unchained*. Good natured, popular Stan—he'd picked up the nickname "Santa Claus" in college for his frequent laughter—would show a knack for getting job offers.[16]

The Rams got off to a rough start in their 1952 title defense, losing three of their first four games. Stan and the Rams defense stepped up mightily. The Rams clipped the Bears

31–7 in Week 5, with the Rams giving up only one yard rushing! The total was considerably aided by a fourth quarter play where the Bears' Wilford "Whizzer" White retreated 51 yards, continuing to circle backward trying to extend a third-down play, with the Rams in hot pursuit. Stan caught the errant Bear on his own two-yard line, where White coughed up a fumble and Stan's teammate Ken Casner scored a touchdown.[17]

A later pair of games with the conference leading 49ers proved another highlight for Stan and the defense. A 35–9 victory over San Francisco was the third game in five weeks the Rams held their opponents to fewer than 10 points, a feat they'd accomplished only once in the 1950 and 1951 seasons combined. A 34–21 victory in San Francisco knocked the 49ers out of first place, leaving the Rams tied with the Lions. Stan wreaked havoc on the 49ers' ground game and stars Joe Perry and Hugh McElhenny averaged 75 yards combined in the two games, more than 40 below their combined average for the season.[18]

The Lions and Rams both won out, setting up another National Conference playoff. Playing in Detroit, the Lions took a 24–7 lead into the fourth quarter when Stan and the Rams struck. Stan made his first NFL interception with a nifty shoetop grab of a Bobby Layne pass at the Lion 21 and rumbled eight yards to the 13-yard line. The Rams cut the deficit to 24–21, but that was as close as the Rams would get. The Lions prevailed 31–21.

The press again recognized Stan's fine work at middle guard, as he was named first team All-Pro in all three major polls. He would also get named to his second Pro Bowl. The 1952 stretch run proved to be Stan's finest hour as a Ram, as the defense gave up the fewest points and the fewest yards per rushing attempt during his years on the team.

Stan reported to Rams camp in 1953 at a svelte 219 pounds. The impetus was a $10 bet with scout Eddie Kotal, who wagered that Stan couldn't report at under 220.[19] Whatever mobility Stan hoped to gain was lost when he injured his leg early in camp. The injury lingered into the regular season, affecting Stan's play enough that he was benched for Bud McFadin. Stan got his job back when McFadin suffered his own hamstring injury.[20] Later in the season, the Rams, like many teams of the time, began experimenting with a 4–3–4 defense. Stan took a few steps back from his middle guard position to try middle linebacker.[21] As a team the Rams took their own step back finishing third in the Western Conference.

Slender Stan was gone for 1954, as Stan reported at a more robust 240 pounds. But Stan's leg injuries persisted, and he missed three regular season games, his first as a pro. The Rams continued their slow fade, falling to fourth place with a 6–5–1 record. The finish cost then-head coach Hamp Pool his job, which would wind up costing Stan his own.

The Rams' new coach was Sid Gillman. Gillman set his sights on improving the Rams' defense. Gillman felt he had the ideal middle guard on the team … in linebacker Don Paul.[22] In preseason, Stan swung over to offensive center for a time. He'd get a chance at middle guard later, but it wasn't enough. Gillman carried through with his stated preference of going with younger players if possible.[23] Rookie Jack Ellena was given Stan's roster spot, and Stan was through with the Rams. Stan still had market value in the league, though, and the Giants gave up a draft pick for his services. In fairness to Gillman, he did improve the Rams' defensive statistics from 1954 as well as the team's record. Stan would have the last laugh when he outlasted both Don Paul and Jack Ellena as NFL players.

Stan had a solid 1955 season for the Giants, playing middle guard or defensive tackle as the defensive alignment required. Big things would be in store for the 1956 Giants, but Stan wouldn't be around for that. Instead, he took a job offer from an old boss of his—Rams owner Dan Reeves. Reeves offered Stan a job as a stockbroker with his firm. Stan was seemingly through with playing football, when another of his old bosses offered him a job.

This old boss was Ray Richards, who had been Stan's line coach on the Rams and was now the head coach of the Chicago Cardinals. He convinced Stan to come out of retirement, and the Cardinals traded a seventh-round draft pick to the Giants for Stan's rights. Stan started every game, the Cardinals defense gave up only 182 points, and the team improved to a 7–5 record, the Cardinals' best finish since 1948. Going back to Oklahoma, it was Stan's eleventh straight season on a team with a winning record.

The Cardinals would not make it 12 straight seasons for Stan in 1957, but Stan never completed the season. After getting off to a 2–4 start, the penny-pinching franchise began looking for ways to shed payroll. Stan, by now one of the oldest players on the Cardinals' roster, fell victim.[24] He was released in early November, ending his career as a player.

In retirement, Stan returned to Oklahoma as president of a tank truck company. But NFL expansion would create new jobs, and Stan would again be recruited to fill one. New Vikings coach Norm Van Brocklin hired Stan on as a line coach. Norm was not only an old teammate and roommate, he and Stan shared the same number; Stan wore Norm's number 11 before the NFL forbade such things for linemen.

With the Vikings, Stan was also responsible for scouting the central state colleges. Stan signed free agent Nebraska center and future Hall of Famer Mick Tingelhoff for the Vikings. Stan would leave the Vikings in 1964 for a business partnership in an Oklahoma oil business. But again, football called him back. Stan picked up a job with the Cardinals, now in St. Louis, "babysitting" college players sought by both the Cardinals and AFL teams in bidding wars. That job turned into a full-time scouting gig with the Cardinals. Stan's most significant accomplishment as scout was convincing the team to draft Henderson State's Roy Green, a future All-Pro.[25] Stan stayed with the Cardinals until retiring in 1991. By that time the Cardinals had moved to Phoenix, giving Stan the distinction of working for the franchise in three different cities.

After retirement, Stan permanently settled in Norman, Oklahoma. He died there on January 19, 2005. He was preceded in death by his wife Mary and survived by his sons Ted and Tom.

A few years earlier, the *Daily Oklahoman* newspaper chose teams to honor the best 20th-century Oklahoma players who played professional football, and also the best Oklahoma high school players from the same period. Stan joined Lee Roy Selmon as the only player to make first team on both squads.[26] There were four defensive linemen chosen for the pro team; no middle guard was chosen, the position having been eliminated long ago. Instead, Stan was chosen as an offensive guard, a position he rarely played in the pros. At least they remembered.

Notes

1. Braven Dyer, "Sports Parade," *Los Angeles Times*, August 25, 1952, IV-1.
2. Harold Keith, *Forty-Seven Straight: The Wilkinson Era at Oklahoma* (Norman: University Of Oklahoma Press, 1984), 17.
3. Keith, *Forty-Seven Straight*, 7.
4. Keith, *Forty-Seven Straight*, 43–44.
5. "1949 College Football All-America Team," *American Football Database*, accessed October 29, 2019, https://americanfootballdatabase.fandom.com/wiki/1949_College_Football_All-America_Team.
6. "Senior Classic Success, Flub," *Miami News-Record*, January 9, 1950, 3.
7. "OK Line Light but Attack Is Swift, Brutal," *Miami Daily News-Record*, November 15, 1949, 4.

8. Claude Anderson, "42 L.A. Rams Arrive in Redlands," *San Bernardino Daily Sun*, July 18, 1950, 19.
9. "Ram All-Stars Return for Times Game," *Los Angeles Times*, August 13, 1950, II-8.
10. Paul Zimmerman, "Sportscripts," *Los Angeles Times*, August 15, 1955, IV-1.
11. Frank Finch, "Stydahar Optimistic as Rams Open Drills for Card Invasion," *Los Angeles Times*, August 19, 1950, III-1.
12. Frank Finch, "Scouting the Pros," *Los Angeles Times*, October 17, 1950, IV-3.
13. Don Snyder, "Big Stydahar Heaves Big Sigh of Relief," *Los Angeles Times*, November 6, 1950, IV-1.
14. Frank Finch, "Waterfield & Co. Deal 23–16 Loss to 49ers," *Los Angeles Times*, November 5, 1951, IV-1.
15. Cal Whorton, "Rams Celebrate Two Victories After Game," *Los Angeles Times*, December 17, 1951, IV-1.
16. John Cronley, "Once Over Lightly," *The Daily Oklahoman*, February 24, 1952, D-3.
17. Frank Finch, "Rams Win on Four Late TD's, 31 to 7," *Los Angeles Times*, October 27, 1952, IV-1.
18. Harry Borba, "L.A. Rams Tie Up Race With 35–9 Pro Victory," *San Francisco Examiner*, November 24, 1952, 43, 45.
19. Frank Finch, "Barker and 25 Ram Veterans Arrive at Camp," *Los Angeles Times*, July 21, 1953, IV-1.
20. "Fears Injured, Out of Lineup for Month," *Redlands Daily Facts*, October 20, 1953, 6.
21. T.J. Troup, *The Birth of Football's Modern 4–3 Defense: The Seven Seasons That Changed the NFL* (London: Rowman & Littlefield, 2014), 27.
22. Sid Gillman, "In This Corner with Dick Zehms," *Long Beach Independent Press-Telegram*, July 24, 1955, B-3.
23. Frank Finch, "West and Thompson Cut from Ram Roster," *Los Angeles Times*, September 20, 1955, IV-2.
24. Casey Cohlmia, "West Ends 8-Year Pro Term as Clubs Look to Youngsters," *Daily Oklahoman*, November 14, 1957, 24.
25. Volney Meece, "Scout Master: Ex-Sooner West Stays on the Road in Search of Talent for Cardinals," *The Daily Oklahoman*, August 3, 1988, 25.
26. "Oklahoma's All Century Professional Football Team," *The Daily Oklahoman*, June 20, 1999, B-10.

Jerry Williams

Gary A. Sarnoff

At 5'10", 175 pounds, Jerry Williams was one the smallest players on the Rams' roster. But according to the *Los Angeles Times* "he demonstrated that good things come in small packages." As a coach, Jerry Williams was called an innovator. "George Allen made a big deal out of running the nickel defense [five defensive backs], but it originated with Jerry Williams," said Irv Cross. "The run-and-shoot. He ran that offense in Canada and we ran it the first year I was in Philadelphia"[1]

Jerry Ralph Williams was born November 1, 1923, and grew up below Bonito Park, located in the South Hill neighborhood of Spokane, Washington. He excelled athletically during his childhood, and although small for his age, he was competitive and unafraid of competing with bigger and older boys. He hoped to follow his older brother's footsteps by playing football at Spokane's Lewis and Clark High School, but that changed when the school's varsity football coach told him he was too small. "Hah!" said Bob Carey, a friend who lived two doors from the Williams family. "My brother and I were twice as big as Jerry and his brother Bill when we used to play football in the neighborhood, but they tackled well as they did the rest of their careers."[2]

With Lewis and Clark High School uninterested, Carey spoke with North Central High School football coach Archie Buckley and told him about his friend. "Send him over," Buckley replied. "So I went to their house and told them to report to North Central," said Carey. "Bill was a year older and a sophomore, and he would lose a year of eligibility [if he transferred], so he stayed, but Jerry went to North Central."[3]

At North Central, Williams played three years on the varsity football and baseball teams. He also played two seasons of varsity basketball and ran track. In 1941, Williams' senior year, he was named to the all-city football team. According to his senior year high school yearbook, "No account of the 1941 grid season could be complete without mention of Jerry Williams, hard-driving fullback, who

Jerry Williams had a long coaching career after his playing career was over, including stints in the NFL and CFL.

consistently plunged through all types of defenses to become the city's deadliest scoring threat and the leading ground gainer and scorer of the season." Coach Buckley paid tribute by calling Williams "the finest football player I've ever coached."[4]

After high school, Williams followed his brother and enrolled at the University of Idaho, but they did not stay long. With the country at war, the Williams boys decided to join the Army Air Corps. Jerry Williams became a P-38 fighter pilot, flew missions in the South Pacific and earned his wings in World War II. Following the war, he went back to college, electing to transfer to Washington State University. He lettered three years at Washington State (1946–1948), as a halfback, defensive back and a return specialist. During his senior year, he totaled 1,500 all-purpose yards to earn all-conference honors and a spot in the East-West Shrine Game. The following summer, Williams was one of the starting halfbacks for the College All-Stars in the 16th Annual All-Star Game at Chicago.

In the 1949 NFL draft, Williams was selected in the seventh round by the Los Angeles Rams. He also received an offer from the New York Yankees of the All-America Football Conference. He elected to play in Los Angeles and had a good rookie season for a team that finished first in the Western Division. He spent most of that season playing in the Rams' defensive backfield, returned a couple of punts and scored three touchdowns as a backup running back. On defense he snagged five interceptions, returning one for a touchdown. According to the *Los Angeles Times*, Williams proved he could run with the ball during his minimal playing time on offense, but his pass defense proved most valuable in 1949, where he covered ground, showed good range, knocked down several passes, and was considered one of the surest tacklers in the league.

As valuable as Williams was on defense the Rams were not counting him out on offense in 1950. "I hope to use Jerry as a ball carrier more this year," said Rams head coach Joe Stydahar. "Of course, pass defense is the most important phase of football today, so I have to have a good replacement for him at safety."[5]

During a preseason game in San Antonio, Williams made a run for 85 yards against the Colts to prove that he could do the job. However, Stydahar either had a change of heart or could not find the replacement he wanted in the Rams' secondary. During the 1950 season, Williams carried the ball fewer times and caught fewer passes than the year before. On defense, he intercepted three passes.

In the summer of 1951, they were once again talking about converting Williams into a running back. *Los Angeles Times* sportswriter Frank Finch, who had boosted Williams for offense ever since the Rams drafted him, claimed he was told by Rams backfield coach Hampton Pool that Williams would be given a chance to win a job on offense. Finch noted that his teammates agree that he "is as fast, if not faster, and even trickier than any other ball carrier on the team."[6]

Once again, Williams occasionally carried the football, caught a few passes and displayed his best work on defense, where he intercepted three passes and returned one of the errant passes for a touchdown. Heading into the last week of the season, the Rams needed to win at Green Bay to finish first in the National Conference. In the third quarter, with the Rams ahead, 21–14, a 50-yard Packers field goal attempt fell short. "Williams fielded it on the one ... slithered upfield, cut toward the Ram sideline behind two key blocks, and went all the way."[7] Williams' field goal return was the longest in NFL history, a record that stood for twenty seasons. The Rams won the game, played in the NFL championship game for the third consecutive season, and beat the Cleveland Browns, 24–17.

In 1952, Williams' and the Rams' strong bid for another trip to the championship game fell short when they lost to the Lions in a playoff game to determine National Conference crown. The following spring the Rams, feeling they had a crowded defensive backfield, traded Williams to the Eagles for a future draft pick. Williams played two seasons in Philadelphia, where he performed on both sides of the ball, plus returned punts and kickoffs. Playing more on the offensive side of the line in 1953, Williams rushed for 345 yards, caught 31 passes for 438 yards and led the Eagles in all-purpose yards. One year later, he made 44 catches for 668 yards and again led the Eagles in all-purpose yards. After the 1954 season, Williams, now over 30, decided to retire and pursue a career in coaching. In 1955, he was hired as head coach at the University of Montana.

Williams' coaching career got off to a rocky start. Three seasons as head coach of the Montana Grizzlies produced only six wins and 23 losses. Things were about to improve. In 1958, the Eagles hired a new coaching staff headed by Buck Shaw, that included Williams as the team's secondary and linebacker coach. Two years later, in 1960, the Eagles were NFL Champions, defeating the Lombardi Packers, 17–13, in the NFL title game. Williams was credited for his ability to out-wit and confuse opposing offenses throughout the season. "We knew we were better than them at all but maybe two positions," Packers assistant coach Bill Austin said after the championship game, "but it took us too long to figure that out."[8]

Shaw retired after the championship season. Nick Skorich became head coach and retained Williams as an assistant. Following back-to-back 10-loss seasons, Skorich and his staff were dismissed following the 1963 season, and Williams accepted a job in the CFL, as an assistant coach with the Calgary Stampeders. One season later, he became Calgary's head coach. As head coach, Williams compiled a 42–26–1 record in four seasons. In 1967, he was named CFL Coach of the Year, and in 1968 he coached Calgary to its first Grey Cup game in 19 years.

Although happy, popular and successful in Calgary, Williams greatest desire was to return to the NFL, especially after Pete Retzlaff, a former tight end who played for Williams in Philadelphia, told Williams, "If he [Retzlaff] ever moved into a position where he [Retzlaff] could hire a [head]coach, I would be his first choice."[9]

In May 1969, Retzlaff was hired as the Eagles new general manager. When hearing the news, Williams immediately resigned as Calgary's head coach and phoned Retzlaff. After meeting with Retzlaff and signing a three-year contract, he was introduced to the press as the Eagles' new head coach.

"One of the many positive traits he has is the ability to produce winners under adverse conditions by supplementing offensive imagination and defensive strategy when outmanned by superior personnel," Retzlaff told the sportswriters. "I've been following the fate of the Calgary Stampeders for the last thee or four years. I just noticed a sharp improvement ... from the time Jerry took over."[10]

To Philadelphia football fans, Williams represented a new era of hope and optimism. In 1968, the Eagles had plunged to their lowest level. Under the direction of unpopular head coach Joe Kuharich, the team lost their first 11 games of the season, and to make matters worse, team owner Jerry Wolman went bankrupt. After the season, Leonard Tose purchased the franchise, fired Kuharich, and went to work on restoring the Eagles as a winner by hiring Pete Retzlaff, who hired Williams.

Under the direction of Williams, the 1969 Eagles showed improvement from the previous season. With an emphasis on developing young players and installing a new team attitude, Philadelphia won two more games than they had in 1968. Although they finished last in the Capitol Division, they had a new spirit and earned the respect of the hometown fans, who gave them a five-minute ovation after giving the undefeated Rams a good battle before losing, 23–17[11] in Week 9.

The 1970 season was a different story. When the team lost their first seven games, it was speculated that Williams would be out after the season. The fans, expecting the Eagles to improve on their 4–9–1 record in 1969, expressed their disappointment week after week by showering the team with a salvo of boos. The Eagles rebounded and finished with a 3–3–1 record during the second half of the season.

Before the 1971 season, the final of Williams three-year contract, the sportswriters were predicting the worst for the Eagles. "Jerry Williams might as well look for another job right now," opined Jack Zanger.[12] After losing their first three games of the season, Williams was fired. "I just think I owe it to the fans," said Leonard Tose.[13] The fans, however, were not in favor of the decision. "They never gave him a chance," said a disgruntled fan.[14] "It is a great injustice that one man must bear the brunt of an entire organization's shortcoming," said Eagles linebacker Ron Porter, reading from the Philadelphia team's joint statement. "We as players have failed coach Williams in our performance on the field and must take the responsibility for what has happened."[15]

Williams hoped he could at least coach one more game, the coming Sunday game against the Minnesota Vikings, but his request was denied. Hurt, upset and disappointed, Williams spoke out of anger. "Unfortunately, I was working for a man who is without courage and character," he told the press.[16] When hearing this, Tose said he was shocked. "I think it took a lot of courage and character to make this move," he responded.[17]

Williams didn't have to wait long for another job. He was hired as an assistant by the Browns to finish out the 1971 season. In 1972, he returned to the CFL as head coach of the Hamilton Tiger-Cats, and in his first year he coached the Tiger-Cats to the Grey Cup championship.

After the 1975 season, Williams retired from coaching and relocated to Arizona. In 1979, he was inducted into the Washington State University Hall of Fame. Two years later, he returned to coaching as an assistant for the Stampeders. Late in the season, he was promoted to head coach for the season's last four games. He never coached again but left his mark on the game and touched a lot of people. "He was just a first-class person, an excellent guy with players, and a tough, fair guy you could really play for," said former Tiger-Cat Bill Etter. "Jerry was extra bright and always two or three steps ahead of everyone," said Irv Cross, who played and coached under Williams long before becoming a commentator on *The NFL Today*. "I owe an awful lot of what I know about football today to him."[18]

Jerry Williams died on December 31, 1998.

Notes

1. Jim Price, "Williams, Pro Player, Coach, Dies," *Spokane Review*, January 1, 1999, C1, C6.
2. Price, "Williams," C1, C6.
3. Price, "Williams," C1, C6.
4. *Tomahawk 1942* (North Central High School yearbook).
5. "Jerry Williams Set with Rams for 1950," *Los Angeles Times*, June 16, 1950, IV-2
6. Frank Finch, "Jerry Williams to Get Chance on Offense," *Los Angeles Times*, June 10, 1951, II-14.
7. Bob Myers, "99-Yard Chase, 49'er Result Fire Coasters," *Green Bay Press-Gazette*, December 17, 1951, 17.

8. Sandy Padwe, "Eagles, Retzlaff, Get Their Man," *Philadelphia Inquirer*, May 10, 1969, 22, 25.
9. Padwe, "Eagles, Retzlaff," 22, 25.
10. George Forbes, "Eagles Sign Williams as Head Coach," *Philadelphia Inquirer*, May 10, 1969, 1, 22, 25.
11. Jack Zanger, *Pro Football 1970* (New York: Pocket Books, 1970), 93.
12. Jack Zanger, *Pro Football 1971* (New York: Pocket Books, 1971), 90.
13. Frank Dolson, "Team Needing Everything Comes Up with Scapegoat," *Philadelphia Inquirer*, October 7, 1971, 25, 27.
14. Dennis Kirkland, "Shocked Fans Reaction Unanimous," *Philadelphia Inquirer*, October 7, 1971, 27.
15. Chuck Newman, "Players, as a Unit, Take Blame," *Philadelphia Inquirer*, October 7, 1971, 25.
16. Dolson, "Team Needing Everything," 25, 27.
17. Dolson, "Team Needing Everything," 25, 27.
18. Price, "Williams," C1, C6.

Jim Winkler

GREG SELBER

It took him awhile to get there, but once Jim Winkler arrived in the NFL, he made a solid impression during a brief three-year career.

Jim was born on July 21, 1927, to Otto and Ella Winkler on a stock farm his grandfather established in The Grove, Texas, after emigrating from Germany before the Civil War. He attended nearby Temple High School, graduating in 1945, and Texas A&M.

For the Aggies, Winkler was the latest in a line of excellent offensive and defensive standouts up front, a list which included Joe Routt, a two-time All-American who died in combat at the Battle of the Bulge and future NFL players Ernie Pennell, Marin Ruby and Marshall Robnett, who was ninth in the Heisman Trophy balloting in 1940.

Following these great Aggies of the recent past, the 6–2, 250-pounder was All-SWC in 1947 and 1948, playing on the offensive and defensive lines for Coach Homer Norton and then Norton's 1948 replacement Harry Stiteler. Texas A&M, which had compiled a sterling record of 29–3 between 1939 and 1941—winning a national title in 1939—had fallen on hard times by the late 1940s.

During Winkler's senior season he was captain for a squad that plummeted to 0–9–1. But the tie was memorable on Thanksgiving Day as the Aggies stopped the Texas Longhorns inside the 20-yard line five times and came up with a dramatic 72-yard touchdown pass inside the final four minutes for the deadlock. It was the program's first non-loss against the hated rival since the title season of 1939. Despite the struggles of the team, Winkler was selected for the West squad for the East-West Shrine Game played January 1, 1949, at Kezar Stadium in San Francisco.

Winkler was drafted by the Rams in the third round of the 1949 NFL draft held on December 21, 1948, one of eight SWC players taken among the first 33 picks, and also by the San Francisco 49ers of the fledgling All-America

Rams defensive lineman Jim Winkler was named to the Pro Bowl in 1952.

Football Conference—in the second round of the AAFC secret draft held on July 8, 1948. The secret, two-round draft was held to give the AAFC a jump on the NFL for players who would be seniors during the 1948 collegiate season.

Winkler graduated from A&M with a degree in animal husbandry and a commission of second lieutenant. But instead of becoming a professional football player, Winkler chose to serve his country ending up with the 81st Airborne Division, earning discharge as a captain just as the Korean War was heating up.[1]

After his service to his country, Winkler joined the Rams for the 1951 season in time to be a contributor to the first major pro sports championship by a Los Angeles-area team, starting 12 games at left defensive tackle on the '51 title team.

While training with the Rams at the Redlands, Winkler met Rebecca Reiter. On August 24, 1951, the lovebirds eloped with the marriage taking place in Las Vegas.

The 1951 Rams' defense was serviceable, collecting 19 interceptions, and limited the Yanks to 166 total yards in its best outing on September 28. For the season the defense allowed 261 points but was solid in the trophy game, holding Cleveland to 17 points. The Rams clinched the crown on a 73-yard pass late in the game, somewhat mirroring the joy Winkler's college team had experienced in the tie against Texas back in '48. They forced four turnovers that day, including three interceptions off Browns quarterback Otto Graham.

The next season, Winkler was again a regular on the defensive front, earning selection to the Pro Bowl along with six other Rams teammates, including middle guard Stan West. The defensive pass rush had a big hand in the league-high 38 interceptions posted by the 1952 Rams, a team that finished 9–3 and out of the hunt after a loss to Detroit in the playoff to determine the National Conference champion.

After the '52 season, Winkler signed with the Baltimore Colts—a club that had taken over the roster of the defunct Dallas Texans of 1952—and went just 3–9 under Coach Keith Molesworth, the old Chicago Bears back. The defense ranked last in the league that year (29.2 ppg allowed) with Winkler in a back-up role.

Winkler also gained a reputation for quirkiness during his time in the league. Colts teammate Art Donovan, in his classic autobiography *Fatso: Football When Men Were Really Men*, writes that Winkler was the craziest football player he ever met, a guy "whom I hope I never meet again in my life."[2]

The Colts nicknamed Winkler "Perch" because of his supposed fish face.

Donovan tells a funny story about the time Winkler went berserk in practice after the trainer refused to give him stitches for a tiny scratch on his face.

The Hall of Fame tackle noted that the former Aggie was always punching himself in the face and compared him to later tough guys such as Howie Long of the Raiders and Joe Klecko of the Jets.[3]

Winkler quit the game after his third NFL season and went on to various pursuits including a stint as an actor in Hollywood, where he appeared in *Demetrius and the Gladiators*.[4]

When he died in 2001, he remained one of the few professional players who had managed a world championship ring and a Pro Bowl appearance in just three NFL campaigns.

NOTES

1. "Obituaries: James Carl Winkler," *The Gatesville Messenger*, March 3, 2001.
2. Arthur Donovan, Jr., and Bob Drury, *Fatso: Football When Men Really Were Men* (New York: Avon Books, 1987), 189–191.
3. Donovan, *Fatso*, 189–191.
4. "Obituaries: James Carl Winkler."

Tank Younger

Rich Shmelter

Grambling, Louisiana, is known for sweltering hot and humid summers, and it was there that Paul Younger was born on June 25, 1928. Younger's 1,700-mile journey from the "Pelican State" to the "City of Angels" was paved with blood and sweat. Countless individuals have imagined existing among the palm trees, beaches, sunshine and glamour synonymous with the American utopia known as Southern California. However, a plethora of dreams are the reality of a select few. The differences in each case are often the individuals that help get those gifted enough to reach the highest level of competition the opportunities to achieve that goal.

Ralph Waldo Emerson Jones, Sr., Eddie Robinson, Ed Kotal, Clark Shaughnessy, and Joe Stydahar all gave Younger the guidance and opportunity needed to become a professional athlete, executive, and trailblazer. Their work transformed Younger into a person who inspired people to follow him and prosper.

Tank Younger was a member of the Rams' famed "Bull Elephant" backfield.

As an adolescent, Paul Younger was big for his age. His frame filled out until it reached 6'3", 225 pounds. He combined speed and power, dishing out punishment to anyone wearing a different uniform. While Younger developed into an excellent athlete, his family relocated to Los Angeles in 1940, looking for factory work. The opportunities for a better financial future helped the Younger family, and the foresight also helped them make a decision for Paul that paid off in the long run.

Ralph Waldo Emerson Jones was a native of Louisiana who devoted his life to education. He came to Grambling State University in 1926 when it was called North Louisiana Agricultural and Industrial School.[1] It was there that Jones taught chemistry, physics and mathematics. In 1936, Jones became president of Grambling. He was also Paul Younger's godfather. After the Youngers moved to Los Angeles, Jones requested that Paul be educated at Grambling. The Youngers agreed, but during summer breaks, he returned to Los Angeles.[2]

Younger met the legendary coach Eddie Robinson while at Grambling High School. Robinson was at the beginning of what became a 55-season coaching career at Grambling State University. World War II raged across Europe and the South Pacific during this time. Many left school for the military, which left the talent pool for college and professional sports dry. Missing players, Grambling did what so many other programs were doing across the country. They shut down for the duration of the war. Without a team to coach on the collegiate level in 1943 and 1944, Robinson mentored scholastic talent at Grambling High School until World War II was over.[3] Younger then followed Robinson to Grambling University when the war ended in 1945, after learning from the coach at the high school level.

With Younger's size, Robinson envisioned him being the main building block the coach needed to construct a solid defense. In the fall of 1945, Younger entered the Grambling campus as a raw tackle. However, the freshman recruit had his own goals, and they were not the same as his coach's, regarding his position. During punt return drills, Younger delivered hard hits, but instead of returning to the side where his fellow defenders were, he went to the back of the line designated for returners. This was the simplest way that Younger could convey his determination to prove his worth as a running back.[4]

Younger's defiance infuriated Robinson. Robinson responded to the disobedience by shouting out to the other players to hit Younger hard and knock him down. Robinson believed that if Younger was hit hard enough, then he might just reconsider his future as a ball carrier. Eddie Robinson remains one of the most respected and successful college coaches in the game's history, but on this occasion, he assumed wrong. Younger withstood the brutal beating his body endured, inflicting punishment on anyone attempting to hit him. His power-running quickly impressed Robinson. The coach responded by placing plays into Grambling's game plan which gave Younger a chance to carry the ball occasionally. The experiment worked. Younger powered his way through opposing defenses to lead the nation with 25 touchdowns in 1945.[5]

Eventually, Younger was playing regularly in the offensive backfield and returning punts and kickoffs. As a junior, Younger rushed for 1,207 yards and 18 touchdowns.[6] As a senior in 1948, Younger earned the Black College Player of the Year award, as well as All-America honors from the *Pittsburgh Courier*. It was also during this time that Younger received the moniker of "Tank," when Grambling's sports information director, Collie Nicholson, claimed that he ran like a Sherman tank.[7] By the time his college career was complete, Younger set a Grambling record by rushing for 2,632 yards, and his 60 trips to an opponent's end zone set a collegiate record that stood for over 30 years. Not bad for a player that came into college as a raw tackle. Instead of letting his dream die, Younger left Grambling as one of the top running backs in the country.[8]

Younger's accomplishments should have made him a solid bet to play professional football. Unfortunately, certain challenges made his journey to the NFL tougher than it should have been. As he was undrafted by any NFL teams, Rams scout Eddie Kotal deserves credit for Younger's acceptance into the NFL. Word of Younger's incredible ground-pounding abilities reached all the way from Louisiana to Los Angeles. On January 1, 1948, Grambling played in the Vulcan Bowl in Birmingham, Alabama. This bowl game showcased the talent pool from historically black colleges from 1941 through 1949 and again in 1952. In the 1948 contest, Younger scored a pair of touchdowns and set up a third in Grambling's loss to Wilberforce (now Central State). Younger was introduced to Kotal in the locker room following the game. Kotal's meeting surprised Younger since pro scouts were not seen scouring the black colleges for prospects.[9]

Kotal visited with Younger for only a few minutes, but he told Younger that the Rams would contact him in the near future. Kotal sent Younger a questionnaire to fill out. Word of Younger's talents was not only limited to the Rams, as the NFL's Detroit Lions expressed interest, and the Brooklyn Dodgers of the All-America Football Conference selected Younger in the 17th round of the 1949 AAFC draft with the 127th overall pick (Brooklyn merged with the New York Yankees prior to the start of the 1949 AAFC season). However, Los Angeles was Younger's destination.

Settling on a contract became the next step in Younger's journey to the NFL. After his senior season, Younger, Ralph Waldo Emerson Jones and Eddie Robinson met with Kotal at a hotel in Grambling during a heavy rainstorm. After negotiations between Jones and Kotal were complete, the Grambling star accepted Kotal's offer of $6,000 for one season, making Younger the first player from an historically black college to play in the NFL.[10]

Younger worked out at Grambling for a few weeks after graduating in the summer of 1949 prior to heading to Los Angeles. Before leaving for his first NFL training camp, Eddie Robinson sent Younger to Los Angeles with a special message. He told his former star runner that the eyes of every athlete from black colleges were focused on him hoping that he did not fail in his quest to land a roster spot. The path for all future opportunities would be a lot easier if he succeeded. However, if he failed, there was no telling when another football player from a black college program would receive a chance at the pros. With Robinson's words firmly engrained in his mind, Younger was determined not to fail.

Younger brought along two pairs of cleats from his days of battering Grambling opponents upon joining the Rams as an undrafted free agent. He was one of only four African Americans in training camp, but claimed he never felt any racial tension from other members of the team. Younger was remembered for having a great sense of humor throughout his career, but he was quiet during his first training camp. Before the Rams' final exhibition game in Omaha, Nebraska, head coach Clark Shaughnessy approached Younger by calling him "Big Boy" due to his stature. Shaughnessy informed Younger that he was going to start the rookie hopeful at right halfback. In fact, that was the way Shaughnessy always addressed Younger, as "Big Boy," right up until the coach's death decades later. This was a huge opportunity to secure a roster spot and live up to the high expectations set for him.

Younger not only provided the coaching staff with a great game in which he emerged as the leading ground gainer, but he also played both running back and linebacker during the second half, all on a pair of battered feet. Younger was down to his final pairs of cleats, and they began to fall apart, but he refused to come out of the game. Instead, his determination to make the team caused his feet to get torn up and bleed by halftime. He forged on through the pain and secured his place on the roster.[11]

Head coach Clark Shaughnessy had a brilliant mind for offensive football. Under his leadership, the Rams were primed for incredible success. The Los Angeles offense became a juggernaut, and Younger was right in the heart of it all. Shaughnessy's use of fast and smaller "Pony Backs," coupled with the power game of Younger and Dick Hoerner, wore defenses down. Quarterbacks Bob Waterfield and Norm Van Brocklin led the passing attack, utilizing skilled receivers Tom Fears and Elroy "Crazylegs" Hirsch.

Younger started eight of twelve games at right halfback, gaining 191 yards on 52 carries in his rookie season. He started in every game for the Rams throughout the next three seasons, including their exciting 1951 championship run under head coach Joe Stydahar, who took over the helm after Clark Shaughnessy's firing following the 1949 season.

Younger came into his own as a professional during the 1951 season. Over the course of twelve regular season games, "Tank" wreaked havoc as both a powerful runner and devastating hitter from his linebacker position. Even a painful hip injury suffered late in the year could not keep him on the bench. There were many outstanding individual performances turned in by members of the Rams during that championship season. On December 2, it was Tank Younger that delivered a special performance of his own against the Bears. Playing himself into state of exhaustion, "Tank" ran for 71 yards on just seven carries, scored the team's final touchdown on a 20-yard jaunt, caught two passes for 75 yards, and punished the Chicago from his linebacker position. With Younger leading the assault, Los Angeles improved to 7–3 on the year, and took over first place in the conference. His team honored his performance with the game ball. The NFL also acknowledged Younger's effort by naming him as the National Conference Defensive Player of the Week.[12] For his championship season efforts, Younger earned first team All-Pro honors from the Associated Press as a linebacker and his first of four trips to the Pro Bowl.

Younger continued on for another six seasons in Los Angeles and one more with the Pittsburgh Steelers before retiring following the 1958 season. He was selected to the Pro Bowl three more times (1952, 1953, 1955), and earned Second Team All-Pro honors in 1952 and 1954. In 1955, he led the NFL with an 80.5 yards per game rushing average. In 10 NFL seasons Younger amassed 3,640 yards rushing for a 4.7 yards per carry average, and 34 touchdowns. He also caught 100 passes for 1,167 yards and one touchdown.

Football was the main staple in Younger's professional life, and that continued after he retired. He became a scout for the Rams and then became the NFL's first African American assistant general manager, a position he held with the San Diego Chargers from 1975 to 1987. In 1992, the Rams hired him as director of player relations, a position he held until retiring three years later.[13]

Awards and honors also played a part in Younger's life after his playing days were long over. He was inducted into the Louisiana Sports Hall of Fame (1973), the College Football Hall of Fame (2000), and when the Black College Hall of Fame inducted its first-ever class in 2010, Paul Younger was a member of that inaugural class.

Unfortunately, that last hall of fame honor came posthumously. On Saturday, September 15, 2001, the "Tank" drew his final breath in Inglewood, California, passing away at age 73 following a long illness. After his death, the Tank Younger Award was created to honor NFL executives committed to racial and gender diversity within the league. The "Tank" might have left this Earth after close to seven-and-a-half decades, but his legacy will never die. For it is in that legacy paved with blood and sweat, that many others gained incredible accolades, all thanks to a powerhouse trailblazer.[14]

Notes

1. Grambling was known as Louisiana Normal from 1928–1946. In 1946 it became Grambling College, and in 1974 Grambling State University.
2. "Paul 'Tank' Younger," *Lasportshall.com*, https://lasportshall.com/?inductees=paul-tank-younger.
3. "Paul 'Tank' Younger."
4. Jerry Izenberg, *Through My Eyes: A Sports Writer's 58-Year Journey* (Haworth, NJ: St. Johann Press, 2009), 48.

5. "College Football Hall of Fame-Paul 'Tank' Younger," *Footballfoundation.org*, https://footballfoundation.org/hof_search.aspx?hof=1723.
6. "College Football Hall of Fame-Paul 'Tank' Younger."
7. Sam Farmer, "Paul 'Tank' Younger; Legendary Running Back for Rams Was 73," *Los Angeles Times*, September 16, 2001, B-10.
8. "Paul 'Tank' Younger," *Lasportshall.com*; "College Football Hall of Fame-Paul 'Tank' Younger."
9. Steve Bisheff, *Great Teams' Great Years: Los Angeles Rams* (New York: Macmillan, 1973), 141.
10. Bisheff, *Los Angeles Rams*, 141.
11. Bisheff, *Los Angeles Rams*, 142.
12. Frank Finch, "Rams Take Loop Lead, Batter Bears, 42–17," *Los Angeles Times*, December 3, 1951, IV-1.
13. Tim Kawakami, "The Times, Job Changes, but He Stays the Same," *Los Angeles Times*, July 1, 1992, C-6.
14. Farmer, "Paul "Tank" Younger," B-10.

Jack Zilly

Joe Ziemba

While Jack Zilly was growing up in Waterbury, Connecticut, probably the last thing that he envisioned for his future was being a Hollywood film star. Perhaps Zilly saw himself as a basketball phenom, or maybe a football stalwart, but a movie star? Never!

Yet as Zilly eased through a sea of honors, accolades, and injuries during his football career, his stint with the Los Angeles Rams from 1947 to 1951 afforded the rugged football standout the opportunity to be seen on a bigger stage than the gridiron. Playing for a professional football team located in the same neighborhood as the cinema capital of the world, Zilly's physical stature, natural charm, and engaging good looks opened doors in Hollywood. But more on that later.

Zilly first garnered attention at Lewis (now Southington) High School in Southington, Connecticut. Zilly was a mainstay in football, basketball, and track during his three years at Lewis. Zilly led the Lewis track squad to the 1938 Connecticut "Class B" high school state championship and was elected as captain of the 1938 basketball team.[1] However, Zilly transferred over to Cheshire Academy (Cheshire, Connecticut) in the fall of 1938 and spent two more years in the athletic spotlight. While at Cheshire, Zilly was captain of the football squad, the captain and starting forward on the basketball club, and the mainstay on the track team. Although the football team struggled to a 1–5 mark during the 1939 season, Zilly was a powerful force on both sides of the ball. During the 1940 track season, Zilly demonstrated his exceptional abilities in a meet against Suffield, earning victories in the javelin, discuss, pole vault, and shot put.[2]

Therefore, it was certainly a "big" deal in Southington when the news swept through town that Zilly was heading to South Bend, Indiana, to begin his collegiate football career under new Coach Frank Leahy at the University of Notre Dame.

Jack Zilly played for legendary head coach Frank Leahy at Notre Dame.

Leahy, a 1931 Notre Dame graduate, was hired away from Boston College following a lofty 20–2 mark over two seasons (1939–1940). While the hiring of the young Leahy was not totally embraced by Irish fans at the time, he quickly converted any doubters by posting an undefeated 8-0-1 record in his inaugural 1941 campaign. *The Notre Dame Scholastic* offered the following summary from Leahy at the conclusion of the season: "If ever a group of boys deserved an undefeated season," Coach Leahy asserted, "these boys did. They fully deserved just what they got, and I'm very happy for their sake and for Notre Dame. The team spirit was wonderful all year. The boys worked very hard and they fought every inch of the way all season."[3]

Since freshmen were not eligible to participate on the varsity squad at that time, Zilly worked out with his fellow freshmen in preparation for the 1942 season. By the time training camp opened on the Notre Dame campus in the late summer of 1942, Zilly was both anxious—and ready—to battle for a starting end position on the Irish. The first test for the varsity was the annual "opening" game against the Notre Dame freshmen, this year paced by promising halfback/quarterback Johnny Lujack. Zilly started at right end for the varsity and scored a touchdown when he recovered a blocked punt in the end zone to help the varsity grab an easy 44–0 victory.[4] Coach Leahy had been reluctant to even hold the contest due to an ever-increasing number of injuries suffered by varsity players. Unfortunately, Zilly was soon to join that talented group on the sidelines when he dislocated his right elbow in practice on September 22 and was reported to be unavailable to Leahy for an indefinite period.[5] It turned out that Zilly was lost for the season, a tough blow for the emerging athlete who seemed poised to accomplish great things on the Irish gridiron.

Despite the lingering effects of his injury, Zilly managed to return for his junior season and earned valuable playing time as both offensive and defensive end. Notre Dame was loaded with talent in 1943. Heisman Trophy–winning quarterback Angelo Bertelli expertly ran the new Irish T-formation snaring Coach Leahy a 9–1 record and the national championship. The only blemish on the Irish season came in the finale against the Great Lakes Naval Training Center, a club stocked with outstanding college and professional players. Steve Lach, late of Duke and the Chicago Cardinals, tossed a 46-yard scoring pass with less than 30 seconds to play ensuring that Great Lakes would pull off the surprising 19–14 upset over the undefeated Irish.[6] Bertelli missed the final three games after being called to active duty. Despite this limited action, Bertelli still captured the coveted Heisman Trophy.

By this time, Zilly—like many of his fellow students—was preparing for a possible military experience by joining the Navy ROTC program at Notre Dame, which included a summer training stint in 1943 aboard the USS *Wilmette*.[7] He then spent the next two years in service to his country, primarily in the Pacific. Zilly saw action at both Iwo Jima and Okinawa, before returning to Notre Dame to continue his studies in 1946. The *South Bend Tribune* anxiously reported the good news to Irish fans when Zilly stopped on campus to visit Leahy in April of 1946. The article concluded: "Zilly, nearly six feet, three and weighing 200 pounds, developed rapidly in the fall of 1943 until he was rated one of the best ends in this part of the country."[8]

The 1946 season proved to be a memorable one for the Irish as Zilly and his compatriots fashioned an 8-0-1 mark to capture another national championship. Zilly caught eight passes for 152 yards during the season but was known more for his ferocious work at defensive end. In the most compelling contest of the campaign, Notre Dame battled top-ranked Army to a 0–0 tie before over 75,000 at Yankee Stadium in New York. The tie snapped

Army's 25-game winning streak in what was known at the time as the "Game of the Century." Army was paced by a pair of exquisite backs in Glenn Davis and Doc Blanchard, but both were stymied by the aggressive Irish defense led by Zilly. After the game, the *Chicago Tribune* lauded the play of Zilly for his role in plugging the rushing lanes against the talented Army ground attack: "And what would have happened if there had been ... no Jack Zilly to sift into the Cadets' back field to break up plays behind the scrimmage line?"[9]

Notre Dame continued undefeated through the remainder of the season to edge Army in the final championship polls. Meanwhile, Zilly, who graduated with a degree in journalism, was drafted by the San Francisco 49ers of the All-America Football Conference. Instead of signing with San Francisco, Zilly decided to align himself with the Cleveland Rams of the National Football League. The Rams had drafted Zilly in the fourth round of the 1945 NFL draft while he was still in the service. Before reporting to the Rams, Zilly gladly accepted the honor of participating in the 1947 College All-Star football game in Chicago.

On August 22, the All-Stars, led by Frank Leahy, met George Halas' defending NFL Champion Chicago Bears at Soldier Field. The underdog collegians struck first by pushing across two touchdowns in the first period before an enthusiastic crowd of 105,840. Zilly scored the second of those early tallies on a 46-yard strike from fellow Notre Dame grad George Ratterman. The *Des Moines Register* reported that "Ratterman drilled one down the field as his Notre Dame mate, Jack Zilly, galloped. Zilly grabbed the ball over his shoulder on the 12-yard line and steamed on over the goal."[10] The two quick scores pushed the All-Stars ahead 13–0 after the first period and the recent grads held on to secure a 16–0 victory.

Zilly then moved over to the Los Angeles Rams' training camp and was quick to impress new head coach, Bob Snyder, a former assistant at Notre Dame. Zilly started seven games during the 1947 campaign and played in all 12 contests as the Rams finished with a 6–6 record. For the year, Zilly caught seven passes for 75 yards, but was lauded for both his defense and blocking prowess. During the off-season, Zilly married the former Eulalia O'Toole on May 22, 1948, in Niles, Michigan.[11]

Aside from the Zilly marriage, the other exciting news received by the Rams prior to the 1948 season was the acquisition of Heisman Trophy winner Glenn Davis of Army. Zilly and Davis had battled fiercely during the "Game of the Century" between Army and Notre Dame in 1946. Now with the prospect that the former adversaries would be teammates in Los Angeles, Zilly recalled their previous meetings: "Glenn was a constant threat. You had that feeling when he was in the game that something was bound to happen any minute. We were lucky to hold him scoreless in those '43 and '46 games. Our whole defense was designed to stop him ... that's how dangerous we knew he was."[12]

But Davis, as a graduate of the United States Military Academy, was committed to the service following his career at West Point. A quiet attempt to release Davis from that obligation was initiated by Davis in an effort to begin his professional football career. However, that appeal was denied and his time on the Rams was limited to one exhibition game on September 2, 1948. Although Davis was held to just one-yard rushing in a 21–10 loss to the Redskins, the game attracted 77,622 fans to the Los Angeles Coliseum who were no doubt drawn by the "star" appeal of Davis. It was understood that this would be the only Rams appearance by Davis, and he embarked on his three-year commitment with the 6th Infantry just a week later. While still absorbing the potential revenue loss from the departure of Glenn Davis to Korea, team president Dan Reeves received more bad news when head coach Bob Snyder suddenly resigned on September 3, citing health issues. There was some debate as to whether Snyder had been asked to resign, but Reeves simply stated, "in fairness to Bob's health and in fairness to the team it seemed best to accept the resignation."[13] Reeves quickly appointed assistant Clark Shaughnessy as the new head coach and under Shaughnessy, Zilly enjoyed an improved offensive showing in 1948. Although the team struggled to finish with a 6–5–1 record, Zilly caught 13 passes for 169 yards and four touchdowns with six starting roles.

Zilly first dipped his toes into the Hollywood acting waters during the summer of 1949. While never threatening to obscure Gregory Peck or Cary Grant from the top billing on the marquee, Zilly and other Rams players did manage to secure some initial speaking roles, much to the amusement of the *Los Angeles Times*: "At the moment, the bobby soxers are not clamoring for rugged thespians such as Jack Zilly or Tom Fears to replace Victor Mature in kissing scenes. But the fact remains that the muscular emoters from the gridiron are in constant demand and their paydays at the flicker factories are frequent."[14]

Apparently, Zilly was more in demand by filmmakers than his teammates, even spending some time in Florida filming a movie according to local reports: "Zilly, the blond giant from Notre Dame, is the only Ram yet to attain the status of a bit player, and he has some pals pea-green with envy. His first speaking 'part' was in 'Twelve O'Clock High,' a war picture, but you could engrave his lines in that epic on the head of a pin with a pool cue. Jack's lines in 'War Bride' hardly rank with Hamlet's soliloquy, either in length or content, but he did get to speak 14 lines as a sailor. Zilly spent one whole night practicing how to say, 'Ship ahoy!' and he was letter perfect before the cameras the next day."[15]

Years later, Zilly's son, Pat Zilly, explained why his father took on the numerous roles in that series of motion pictures: "The reason he did that was because the pay [for football] was so low. He used the movies to supplement his income. There really wasn't a lot of money in football at the time."[16]

As a team, the Rams started quickly in 1949 under Shaughnessy, rolling off six straight victories to start the season. Although the team struggled a bit down the stretch to finish 8–2–2, it was enough for the Rams to capture the Western Division title of the NFL. Playing mostly defensive end during the season, Zilly collected just three receptions for 35 yards, but remained a force on the other side of the line. Although the Rams dropped a tough 14–0 loss to the Eagles in the 1949 NFL championship game, Zilly was singled out for his defensive performance by the *Los Angeles Times*: "None of the Eagles was tougher on defense than tackle Jay McDermott, the former Washington Huskie end. And for the Rams, it was right end Jack Zilly who probably turned in the outstanding defensive job of the gloomy afternoon."[17]

Yet the 8–2–2 mark and a trip to the NFL championship game was not enough to save Coach Shaughnessy's job. On February 17, 1950, Reeves informed Shaughnessy that his services were no longer needed. Between the lines, Reeves subtly hinted that the marriage between the former coach and his staff was beyond repair. Line coach Joe Stydahar was appointed as the head coach and promptly produced another superior season, driving the Rams to a 9–3 record and a repeat as the newly named National Conference champs. A return trip to the title clash ended once again in frustration as the Rams fell to Cleveland 30–28. Zilly did his best to spark his club in the third quarter when his jarring tackle separated the ball from Cleveland ball carrier Marion Motley. Motley's fumble was recovered by the Rams' Larry Brink and Brink easily scored on the return giving Los Angeles a 28–20 lead.[18] Zilly started all 12 regular season games at defensive right end but was not needed on offense as the high scoring Rams established numerous team and league scoring records. Prior to the game, the great Detroit Lions halfback Doak Walker was interviewed by Los Angeles columnist Dick Hyland, who reported that "Walker thinks that the Rams were the toughest defensive club he has faced as a pro, mainly because of the work of Bob Reinhard, Dick Huffman, Larry Brink, and Jack Zilly. He thinks the latter pair, coupled with the Bears' [Ed] Sprinkle and [Bill] Wightkin, are the meanest ends in pro ball. He is not alone in that opinion."[19]

After two straight frustrating attempts to claim the NFL championship, Stydahar finally climbed the mountain to snare the 1951 title. The only problem for Zilly was that he was not on the field to enjoy the 24–17 conquest of the Browns. The long-time mainstay on the defensive line suffered a broken arm on October 28 against San Francisco and was lost for the year after appearing in just four games. Prior to the injury, Zilly was up to his old tricks, especially in an early season loss to Cleveland in a home game played in Los Angeles. With the temperature on the field creeping up to 114 degrees, Zilly constantly pressured Browns quarterback Otto Graham: "Defensive play of both clubs bothered the passers throughout. Jack Zilly ... slashed through to harass Graham...."[20] But even while relegated to the sidelines, Zilly continued to receive accolades for his previous fierce play on the field. Although playing in just those four games, his respectful teammates still voted Zilly a full share of the playoff winnings, a tidy sum of $2,108.

On March 14, 1952, Zilly was traded to the Philadelphia Eagles. The deal itself stunned some as the reliable Zilly and reserve quarterback Bobby Thomason were sent to the Eagles for veteran fullback Jack "Moose" Myers and Philadelphia's top pick in the draft following the 1952 season. The local press proclaimed that "the champion Los Angeles Rams of the National Football League have traded one of the game's greatest defensive ends for the fellow they believe is football's greatest blocker."[21] Zilly, while surprised at the trade which had been brewing for a couple of months, was pragmatic in his view of the transaction: "I hate to leave the Rams, but it's all in the game," said Zilly, who added that he would report to the Eagles "if the terms are right."[22]

By now, Zilly was 30 years old with three children and firmly entrenched in the Los Angeles area with a solid off-season job in the insurance business. Still, he reported to Philadelphia and started 10 of the 12 games in which he played for the 7–5 Eagles. Ironically, both Zilly and Myers would be out of the league following the 1952 season. While Zilly was able to maintain his productivity in Philadelphia, Myers found his time limited in Los Angeles and departed after the season to become the head coach of the University of the Pacific in 1953. With his growing family and a secure job, Zilly left the game of football in early 1953 ... but not for long.

Zilly started a lengthy coaching career as an assistant at Montana State University in 1955. By the following winter, Zilly moved on as an assistant at Notre Dame under head Coach Terry Brennan for the 1956 campaign. Zilly was primarily responsible for coaching the ends and remained with the Irish until 1959, when he was hired at Brown University. Zilly spent four seasons at Brown before securing his first head coaching job at the University of Rhode Island in February of 1963. His hiring was greeted with great fanfare by the university which pointed to his playing experience at both Notre Dame and in the NFL as a welcome advantage for his players. In addition, several colleagues were interviewed by the local press in an effort to provide further insight into the thoughts and capabilities of the rookie head coach. Ed "Moose" Krause, the athletic director at Notre Dame, was lavish in his praise of Zilly, identifying Zilly as a person of "great personality, great recruiting powers and a very good handler of young men … he will do a great job and be a credit to Rhode Island."[23]

Zilly coached the Rams for seven seasons, resigning after the 1969 season with a final record of 21–41–2.[24] Zilly was quickly grabbed up as an assistant for the Philadelphia Eagles in 1970, serving as the coach for the running backs and special teams until 1972.[25] From there, Zilly headed north to assume the role of line coach for the Hamilton Tiger-Cats of the Canadian Football League from 1972 to 1975. In 1978, Zilly coached the American squad in the inaugural Can-Am Bowl. This event pitted teams of collegiate all-stars from both sides of the border against each other in a game played strictly under Canadian football rules. Zilly led his team to an impressive 22–7 victory and then eased away from the coaching aspect of the game to focus on his real estate business.[26]

As a defensive lineman, Jack Zilly was not one to find his name in the newspaper after each game, especially since the keeping of important statistics including tackles and sacks were elusive to identify during his exceptional professional football career. Yet his ferocious play and pleasing personality were memorable among his teammates, opponents, fans, and the media. Perhaps reporter Frank Finch described Zilly best when it was learned that Zilly had been traded to the Philadelphia Eagles in 1952: "To exhume the badly eroded cliché, Zilly is a football player's football player."[27] Zilly passed away on December 18, 2009, at the age of 88.

Notes

1. "Southington Hoopmen Elect Jack Zilly," *Hartford Courant*, June 24, 1938, 12.
2. "U.S., School Yearbooks, 1900–1990," *Ancestry.com*, https, ://www.ancestry.com.
3. Ray Donovan, "Coaches and Undefeated Irish Team Relax After a Hard, Successful Season," *Notre Dame Scholastic*, November 1941, 16.
4. Jim Costin, "Off Again, On Again Frosh Game Won by Varsity, 44–0," *South Bend Tribune*, September 19, 1942, 12.
5. "Southington Player Injured at Notre Dame," *Hartford Courant*, September 23, 1942, 13.
6. Charles Chamberlain, "Long Pass Spoils Unbeaten Record," *Decatur Herald*, November 28, 1943, 12.
7. "U.S. World War II Navy Muster Rolls, 1938–1949," *Ancestry.com*, https://www.ancestry.com.
8. Jim Costin, "Zilly, Former Star N.D. End, To Play Again," *South Bend Tribune*, April 17, 1946, 3-1.
9. Arch Ward, "Notre Dame Plays Army to Scoreless Tie," *Chicago Tribune*, November 10, 1946, 2-1, 2-4.
10. Bert McGrath, "All-Stars Humble Bears, 16–0," *Des Moines Register*, August 23, 1947, 7–8.
11. "Michigan Marriage Records, 1867–1952," *Ancestry.com* https://www.ancestry.com.
12. Frank Finch, "Rams' Zilly and Cowhig Team Up with Old Notre Dame Foe-Davis," *Los Angeles Times*, July 25, 1948, I-24.
13. "Action Explained," *Los Angeles Times*, September 4, 1948, III-2.
14. "Rams Turn Hams During Off Season," *Los Angeles Times*, July 3, 1949, I-14.
15. "Rams Turn Hams," I-14.
16. John Goralski, "Mister Hollywood," *Southington Observer*, September 3, 2010, http://files8.webydo.com/92/9246638/UploadedFiles/2CA72D3F-6A15-29F6-512E-029238A79A8B.pdf.
17. Frank Finch, "Eagles Power Over Rams in Mud" *Los Angeles Times,* December 19, 1949, IV-1-2.
18. Frank Finch, "Groza's Field Goal in Last 20s. Decides Exciting Grid Battle," *Los Angeles Times*, December 25, 1950, IV-1, 4.
19. Dick Hyland, "Highland Fling," *Los Angeles Times*, January 13, 1951, III-2.
20. "Cleveland Comes from Behind to Register Victory," *San Bernardino County Sun*, October 8, 1951, 15.
21. "LA Rams Trade Jack Zilly for Eagles' Moose Myers," *Santa Clara Sentinel*, March 16, 1952, 13.
22. Frank Finch, "Eagles Get Zilly in Deal with Rams," *Los Angeles Times*, March 15, 1952, III-1.
23. "Jack Zilly, Ex-Irish Ace, New Rhode Island Mentor," *Hartford Courant*, February 8, 1963, 17.
24. "Southington's Jack Zilly Resigns Rhody Grid Post," *Hartford Courant*, November 20, 1969, 60.
25. "Eagles Name Jack Zilly as Assistant," *Courier Post*, April 23, 1970, 49.
26. Jim Henderson, "Can-Am Coaches: A Canadian Look," *The Tampa Tribune*, December 9, 1977, 6-C.
27. Frank Finch, "Stydahar Will Settle for Carmichael Now," *Los Angeles Times*, March 16, 1952, II-14.

Racial Integration and the Rams

Ryan C. Christiansen

The 1951 season proved to the Los Angeles Rams' front office that any apprehension[1] or coercive pressure[2] they might have felt in 1946 to be the first NFL team in thirteen seasons to sign a black player[3] was worth the investment. And it proved to those somewhat reluctant black athletes[4]—who knew they would be representing the entire black community and not just themselves[5]—that they had accomplished what they had hoped for when they broke the color line.

With a "Bull Elephant Backfield" that included black running backs "Deacon" Dan Towler and Paul "Tank" Younger,[6] as well as Dick Hoerner[7] (who was not black), and a defense that included Younger at linebacker with black defensive backs Woodley Lewis and Bob Boyd (who also played offensive end)—and with black lineman Harry Thompson[8]—the Rams in 1951 ended the Cleveland Browns' five-year pro football championship run[9] by winning the NFL title for themselves[10] and for all teams with NFL pedigree[11] in a revenge game after losing to the Browns in the championship game the year before.[12]

The contributions of the black athletes on the field were both substantial and influential in the 1951 title game. For the Rams, Towler started at left halfback and Younger started at right halfback, while Lewis, Thompson, and Boyd all came into the championship game as substitutes.[13] A crowd of 59,475 was on hand at the Los Angeles Coliseum for the game,[14] and because, for the first time, fans on the East Coast could watch live television broadcasts of sporting events on the West Coast, millions of football fans throughout the nation together watched a black player, Towler—with no protective cage covering his face, and with huge, ebony hands sticking out from his long-sleeved jersey[15]—score a touchdown in an NFL championship game,[16] the first black player to do so.[17] The Browns, too, fielded black players in that game. Marion Motley started at fullback,[18] Bill Willis started at defensive middle guard, and Len Ford started at right defensive end,[19] while fullback Emerson Cole and end Horace Gillom played on substitution.[20]

The 1951 championship game capped off a season that saw black athletes contribute significantly to the Rams' success. Towler and Younger rushed for a combined 1,077 yards on the ground, and together with Boyd, the trio contributed a combined 457 yards in receiving[21] to help the Rams reach 5,506 total offensive yards.[22] During the regular season, Towler rushed for an average 6.8 yards per carry while Younger ran for 6.2 yards per carry,[23] and for their efforts, Younger was named to the Associated Press All-League Defensive Team for 1951 while Towler was named to the United Press All-League Offensive Team for the season.[24]

A backfield featuring a majority of black players wasn't in the original plan for the

1951 season. It wasn't until the sixth game of the regular season when Rams head coach Joe Stydahar decided to use his bull elephants: The Rams were playing San Francisco for the second week in a row, and to counter the 49ers' speedy but small pass defense, Stydahar installed Younger,[25] who primarily played defense in 1950[26] and in the early games of 1951.[27] As a result, Stydahar had three big fullbacks for pass blocking and power running,[28] with Younger at 6-foot-4 and 226 pounds, Towler at 6-foot-2 and 220 pounds, and Hoerner at 6-foot-4 and 220 pounds.[29] The change in tactics worked in the rematch with the 49ers, so Stydahar continued to employ his bull elephants for the remainder of the season.[30] As a result, fan attention focused on a backfield that featured two black athletes, and this was especially true during the 1951 championship game when the Rams ran the ball 43 times to keep the ball away from Cleveland's offense.[31]

Ultimately, reintegration proved profitable for the Rams. From 1941 to 1950, Rams owner Dan Reeves personally lost $510,000 on his investment in the Rams,[32] and his partners lost money, too, but the Rams turned the corner in 1951 when the team turned a $10,000 profit.[33]

But reintegrating black athletes into pro football proved fruitful for the Rams (and for the Browns) even before the 1951 season. Los Angeles scored 466 points in 12 games on 3,709 yards passing in 1950; they gained 278 first downs and scored 64 touchdowns, more than five per game.[34] Much of the Rams' success in 1950 could be attributed to the same set of black players who played through 1951.[35] The team roster read like an all-star team with Van Brocklin, Waterfield, Hoerner, Younger, Towler, Vitamin Smith, Glenn Davis, Fears, Hirsch, Boyd[36]—thirty percent of whom were black. Meanwhile, the former AAFC,[37] new-to-the-NFL Browns beat the defending NFL champions, the Philadelphia Eagles, in their first game of 1950,[38] and the 1950 championship game featured the Browns and Rams, two teams that together had more black players (five on each team, for a total of 10) than the rest of the teams in the league combined.[39] Sherman Howard, a running back for the New York Yanks, said, "The Browns and the Rams were the teams that had the most blacks and those were the only teams we had trouble with in 1950."[40]

NFL owners could no longer dismiss the idea they were ignoring black talent,[41] but many still did. Five years after signing Kenny Washington, which desegregated pro football, the Browns and Rams remained outliers when it came to fielding black players in the NFL. By the end of the 1951 season, only 17 black athletes played on NFL teams, down from 19 at the beginning of the season,[42] and the Redskins, Steelers, Eagles, Cardinals, Bears, and Lions did not have any black players on their rosters, which benefited the Rams and the Browns.[43] Racial prejudice against African Americans playing pro football was rampant in some cities. In Baltimore, after the team acquired its first black player, Art Fletcher, white fans largely boycotted Colts games there, which contributed to the franchise's dissolution, and Fletcher did not find a home playing elsewhere.[44] The reintegration of pro football took place years ahead of what many consider to be the beginning of the civil rights movement, which some peg to the Montgomery Bus Boycott in 1955.[45] And even though the Rams benefited from considering black talent, they didn't prioritize acquiring black players. Tex Schramm, Rams executive during the 1950s, said the team didn't feel an urgency to draft black athletes because they could wait until late in the draft or after the draft to sign them. Other teams simply weren't signing black players.[46]

Before segregation and before the NFL, from 1888 through 1920, more than 50 black players[47] played what the black press called "mixed football"[48] for white colleges and four black athletes played professional football.[49] During the NFL's first 14 seasons,[50] at least one black athlete played each year, in a newly formed league that competed with college football for attention. Early NFL rosters included the best athletes they could find, which included black players.[51] The count reached a high of six players during the 1923 season.

From 1920 to 1933, a total of 13 black men played in the NFL, including a few greats. They included Fritz Pollard, Rube Marshall, Paul Robeson, Inky Williams, John Shelburne, Duke Slater, Jim Turner, Sol Butler, Dick Hudson, Harold Bradley, Sr., Dave Myers, Joe Lillard, and Ray Kemp.[52] During these first few decades of professional football, black newspapers rarely covered the sport, and like white fans, black fans focused their attention on the college game. But when Lillard,[53] the "Midnight Express,"[54] led the Chicago Cardinals to success,[55] the black press focused on his accomplishments.[56]

The two black players who played during the 1933 season, Lillard and Kemp, were not asked to return in 1934, and then for 12 seasons, no black athletes played professional football in the United States, and during that drought, the NFL passed on signing outstanding black athletes, including Ozzie Simmons, Wilmeth Sidat-Singh, Mel Reid, Bobby Vandever, Brud Holland, Jackie Robinson, Kenny Washington, Marion Motley, Bill Willis, and Woody Strode.[57]

The NFL's segregated years represented resurgent prejudices of the time. Before black players were ever given the chance to compete alongside whites, the dominant white culture leveraged poor scientific research that said African Americans were physically inferior to whites. And then when black athletes began to triumph in sports, the dominant white culture declared that while blacks had natural athletic abilities, in contrast white athletes displayed hard work and determination.[58] And those in favor of segregation argued that having black and white players together would raise the issue of race and would sow divisions within a team and within the fan base, which would affect the team's ability to win and to attract ticket-buyers.[59] After the Civil War,[60] when baseball's major leagues began to segregate in 1867,[61] pro football's relative obscurity offered opportunity for African Americans.[62] And because teams didn't have consistent rosters, home teams had no control over who might show up in the opposing team's uniform.[63] As rivalries grew between the clubs, owners felt increased pressure to find "ringers" who could help win games, and sometimes these role players included African Americans like Charles W. Follis, Charles "Doc" Baker, Clarence "Smoke" Fraim, Henry McDonald, and Gideon Smith,[64] black pioneers who endured nicknames like "jig," "dinge," "burr-head," and, inevitably, "nigger."[65]

But as soon as pro football began to rise in popularity, black athletes were banned from that sport, too.[66] There may have been occasions from 1934 through 1939 when NFL teams did consider signing black players, but either the black players chose not to sign or the team that was interested in a player could not gain consent from the rest of the league.[67] And owners had excuses for not hiring black players: George Halas claimed there weren't any black players good enough to play in the NFL, and Art Rooney claimed it was too expensive to scout the places where black athletes played, in black colleges or on white or integrated semiprofessional teams, despite the fact there were several accomplished black athletes on white college teams during the 1930s.[68] In the years during and immediately following The Great Depression, some owners justified not hiring African Americans because it would give a job to a black man when so many white men were unemployed.[69] Only owner George Preston Marshall, who founded the Boston Braves and who later changed the team name to the Redskins, and eventually moved the team to Washington, D.C.,[70] remained honest by saying he simply didn't want to hire black athletes.[71] Marshall was a West Virginia native who aligned his team with the Jim Crow laws of his southern fan base,[72] and he swayed league policy. When Marshall moved his franchise to D.C., the move positioned the team as the only one below the Mason-Dixon Line, and Marshall marketed the team as "the team of the South." The team's fight song was set to the tune of "Dixie,"[73] the de facto anthem of the Confederacy.[74] And so from a pure business standpoint, Marshall did not see value in marketing the game, and his team in particular, to the black audience.[75] In 1933, Marshall negotiated a gentleman's agreement with NFL owners to ban black players from the league, a ban that no owner would admit to.[76]

During pro football's segregation, some black players signed with teams in independent professional leagues, which in some ways served as minor leagues for the NFL,[77] and during World War II, black players played on military service football teams.[78] And like in baseball, black players formed their own teams,[79] for example, the Brown Bombers, who were particularly successful on the field against white semipro teams, including some former NFL teams.[80] In some cases, black teams resorted to performance, to singing and dancing, to attract crowds.[81] All the while owners continued to maintain they lacked scouting resources to find black talent, even though some of the black teams played on the same fields as NFL franchises.[82] And so despite facing a shortage of players during World War II, and while still facing the need to field a quality product on the gridiron, NFL teams did not hire black athletes.[83]

Multiple forces ultimately led the Los Angeles Rams and pro football to reintegrate black players into the game. For the Rams, more than anything, the team's desire to play in the Los Angeles Memorial Coliseum led the team to sign African Americans. The Coliseum, with its 100,000-seat capacity and Roman architecture, made for an attractive venue.[84] When the Rams entered negotiations with the Coliseum commission to lease the venue, the Rams believed the main point of resistance would be the commission's desire to keep professional football out of the venue. The commission was composed of mostly graduates of USC and UCLA, and both schools were protective of college football's dominant stature along the West Coast. And so to burgeon the Rams' chance for success with the commission, Reeves arranged for the team to play an exhibition game in 1946 against the Redskins[85]—which would be a replay of the NFL championship of the previous year[86]—to benefit *Los Angeles Times* Charities.[87] During lease negotiations, Rams general manager Chile Walsh, a Los Angeles native who had played football at Hollywood High School,[88] promised that the first preseason game would always be against the Redskins and that they'd name it the *Times* Charities Game with profits going to charity. The Chandler family, which owned the *Times*, had helped to secure financing and public support for the Coliseum in the 1920s.[89]

And the Rams weren't the only professional football team represented at the meeting: Executives from the Los Angeles Dons, an AAFC franchise owned in part by Hollywood stars Don Ameche and Bing Crosby, also sought to lease the Coliseum.[90] The Rams and the Dons were among multiple football teams competing for playing fields in the Los Angeles area, including the Pacific Coast Professional Football League Los Angeles Bulldogs, Hollywood Bears, and San Diego Bombers.[91]

But Walsh played a good hand with the college football-leaning commission, and he'd just participated in two major victories with the Rams, the first a 15–14 NFL championship victory over the Redskins in Cleveland, the second in convincing the NFL to allow the champion Rams to move to Los Angeles.[92] But what Walsh didn't expect was resistance from the black community combined with pressure to field a black player: At the commission meeting, Walsh came face-to-face with black weekly *Los Angeles Tribune* sportswriter[93] William Claire "Halley" Harding, a civil rights activist with a background playing football, basketball, and baseball and who had also boxed and acted.[94] Harding recognized the Rams needed the Coliseum to accommodate a large, ticket-buying audience, but he also recognized how a team from a segregated professional sport was seeking to make money in a stadium paid for, in part, by Los Angeles' black taxpayers.[95] He reminded the commission that California athletics had long included African Americans, and that the NFL had at one time also included black athletes[96] like Pollard and Robeson who had contributed to the early success of the professional sport. He also reminded everyone that since Lillard and Kemp had been dropped from their team rosters before the 1934 season, no black player had even had a tryout with a professional football team,[97] despite the fact integrated college teams across the country featured black players, including in bowl games.[98] Black soldiers, sailors, and airmen had fought valiantly in World War II to defend the ideals of freedom and equality,[99] and Harding argued that because the Rams would be playing in a publicly owned facility, they were obligated not to discriminate against African Americans.[100]

There were no rules against hiring black athletes, Walsh countered, but Harding reminded Walsh that just because a rule is not written down doesn't mean it's not practiced,[101] and he reminded the commission how a black athlete, Kenny Washington, had helped raise UCLA football to prominence,[102] and how despite leading the nation in total yards during the 1939 college football season and despite being awarded the Douglas Fairbanks Trophy as the nation's most outstanding player,[103] the all-white NFL passed on drafting Washington.

When he was ignored, Washington said, "It's unfair. It's because I am a Negro that they don't want me to play." And despite efforts by black sportswriters to encourage their Associated Press colleagues to name Washington to the All-America Team, he did not make that list.[104] At the time, NBC broadcaster Sam Balter called out the press and the NFL for their racist bigotry.[105]

But professional football had ignored Washington,[106] and Harding suggested the Rams would never allow their local college hero to play in the Coliseum because he was African American.[107]

The crowd at the commission meeting applauded Harding's speech, and at Harding's insistence, the commission drafted and signed a resolution that no organization that discriminated against anyone because of their race, color, or creed would be allowed to use the venue.[108] When the meeting ended, the Rams still did not have their lease to the Coliseum.[109]

Harding wasn't the only black sportswriter at that meeting. He was accompanied by Herman Hill, the West Coast editor for the *Pittsburgh Courier* who had played basketball at USC, and Abie Robinson, sports editor for the *Los Angeles Sentinel*.[110]

A week later, Harding surprised Walsh by inviting him to meet at the Last Word jazz club[111] on South Central Avenue in the heart of a black Los Angeles neighborhood.[112] Walsh, accompanied by Rams public relations director Maxwell Stiles who was a former sportswriter for the *Los Angeles Examiner*, met up with Harding, Hill, and Robinson, as well as J.C. Fentress, another West Coast correspondent for the *Pittsburgh Courier*, Eddie Burbridge and Leon Hardwick of the *California Eagle*, and five or six more media men from other newspapers and radio stations.

Harding and his contingency pressed the Rams to hire Washington, who at the time was playing for the Hollywood Bears of the Pacific Coast Professional Football League. Walsh argued the Rams would need to honor the Bears' contract with Washington, but Harding claimed he'd already spoken to the Bears and they would be willing to release Washington from his contract.[113] Walsh succumbed to their pressure[114] and agreed to give Washington a tryout.[115]

On March 21, 1946, the Rams held a press conference at the Alexandria Hotel in downtown Los Angeles to announce they had signed Washington to the team,[116] and Washington became the first black athlete to reintegrate a major league professional sport, even before Jackie Robinson, who didn't play major league baseball until 1947. And on May 7, the Rams signed another black athlete, former UCLA football player Woody Strode.[117] Together with Robinson at UCLA they had formed what the Los Angeles media dubbed "The Sepia Trio"[118] and had played for the only college team that wouldn't honor the gentleman's agreement in intercollegiate sports that said coaches shouldn't field black athletes against all-white schools.[119]

About the occasion, Washington later said, "When those NFL people began thinking about all those seats [in the Coliseum] and the money they could make filling them up, they decided my kind wasn't so bad after all."[120] Rams backfield coach Bob Snyder later acknowledged the team had only signed Washington so they could get the lease to the Coliseum.[121]

Nevertheless, Reeves recognized he needed superstars to entice spectators to the games, especially for a team that was new to Los Angeles.[122] Having played for UCLA, Washington was a gate attraction[123] who added glamour[124] to a team near Hollywood, the seat of glamour. Reeves cultivated relationships with members of the press, which resulted in more publicity for the Rams, and more exposure for its black players.[125] And the public's familiarity with integrated pro football grew with the rise of television: In 1950, a network affiliate in Los Angeles purchased the rights to broadcast Rams home games and agreed to pay for empty seats in the Coliseum.[126] Across the United States, the presence of Washington and Strode on the pro gridiron engendered pride in the black community, because they had followed their accomplishments when they had played at UCLA.[127]

After the Rams did finally obtain their lease to the Coliseum, the black press pointed out how racial bias had played a part in the negotiations, but sportswriters outside the black community focused on other biases. Bob Oates, a longtime sportswriter for the *Los Angeles Times*, in his 1955 book *The Los Angeles Rams*, wrote that the Coliseum commission had been "wrestling with its prejudices against the pros" and that Walsh had "[won the] fight against the commission." Oates made no mention of the issue of race.[128] And even after the Rams won the NFL championship in 1951, in its "A Chronology of Professional Football," *The Official National Football League Football Encyclopedia* in 1952 made no mention of the fact that 1946 was the year when the Rams reintegrated black athletes into the league.[129]

But there were other forces at work besides needing the Coliseum that led the Rams and professional football to reintegrate black players into the game. Franchise owners reintegrated their teams in part because of competition between the NFL and the upstart All-America Football Conference.[130] Pro football was gaining in popularity, and existing NFL owners had attempted to corner the market by rejecting suitors for expansion. Franchise seekers instead attempted to start their own leagues, including the AAFC but also the Trans-American Football League, which never really came to fruition, and the United States Football League.[131]

Meanwhile, African Americans had benefited economically from wartime work in the North and in the West,[132] and black Americans held more political influence in the nation's urban areas. The upstart AAFC recognized they could win fans in these cities by signing black athletes, and even the unborn USFL had taken a stand on the issue when USFL president Red Grange proclaimed, "Our new league has set up no barriers. Any athlete, regardless of color, will be invited to try out for our teams.... The Negro boys are fighting for our country; they certainly are entitled to play in our professional leagues."[133]

In addition, servicemen returning from duty in the Pacific landed in the West and decided to stay, which led to a population boom in Los Angeles[134] and a stronger market in the West for professional football.

The AAFC, backed by millionaire sponsors willing to compete and pay for talent in pursuit of gaining major league status, organized in 1944 and then took the field in 1946 in multiple major U.S. cities, including three where the NFL also had franchises.[135] To compete, the NFL allowed Reeves to move the Rams to Los Angeles despite having publicly criticized the AAFC for fielding teams in far-away cities.[136] Meanwhile, because the USFL didn't have franchise owners with deep-enough pockets,[137] the enterprise folded.

The first year the AAFC and the NFL competed for audience and players, the leagues reintegrated black athletes into professional football.[138] When the Rams signed Washington in March 1946, white daily newspapers said the signing wouldn't set a precedent for hiring other African Americans,[139] but soon afterward Paul Brown of the Cleveland Browns in the AAFC called on two black players he had coached previously, lineman Bill Willis at Ohio State and halfback Marion Motley at the Great Lakes Naval Academy.[140] On August 2, Brown invited Willis to training camp, and on August 17, Motley arrived at camp.[141]

At heart, Brown's actions may have been more magnanimous than the Rams,' because Brown said it didn't matter if a player was black or white when he chose to keep or cut him, he just wanted to win football games, and he'd already planned to sign Willis and Motley, despite the fact other AAFC owners would take exception, but he waited until after the team had started training camp to approach the two men[142] to lessen the length of the attention; and because the Rams had already broken the color barrier, Brown's actions received a lower measure of scrutiny,[143] which he preferred. Brown insisted his black players should be treated as equals. For example, when rookies from the South reported to the Browns for training camp, they were required to introduce themselves and to shake hands with the black players.[144]

The black press saw the reintegration of pro football as one of the top news stories of 1946,[145] but because Brown didn't want signing black players to become a distraction, he hasn't received as much credit for doing so. But while the Browns may not have been the first team to reintegrate pro football, they were the first professional football team in the modern era to *draft* black athletes,[146] albeit in the AAFC draft, and while the Browns voluntarily added black players to their roster, the Rams only did so under pressure from the black press.[147]

Back in Los Angeles, the Dons had also agreed to pursue hiring black players to get their lease to the Coliseum, but the Dons did not hire black athletes until 1947, *after* the Cleveland Browns upheld AAFC commissioner James Crowley's promise that the league would be "All American in every respect."[148]

Attendance during the first year of reintegration in 1946 shot up to levels that were not matched again until the 1955 season.[149] The AAFC attracted as much as 80 percent of the NFL in total paid attendance in 1946,[150] and the largest crowds for both NFL and AAFC games were for the Rams and the Browns, the only teams with black players. In the AAFC, the Browns drew the most fans, and they also utilized their black players more than the Rams did.[151]

But fan interest in the Rams and Browns did not equate to less discrimination against black players. In Los Angeles, fans cheered for the integrated Rams on the field, but off the field, blacks and whites clashed, and even the Rams' black athletes would not have been welcome in white neighborhoods.[152]

On road games, black athletes often could not stay in the same hotel as the rest of the team's white players.[153] For example, in Chicago, Washington and Strode weren't allowed to stay at the Stevens Hotel, which is where the Rams regularly stayed in that city.[154] When the Rams played exhibition games in the South, Younger recalled having to stay with black families instead of with the rest of the team.[155] Thompson said when the team traveled to Washington, D.C., the black players on the team were allowed to stay in the team hotel, but they were not allowed in the hotel restaurant and had to order room service.[156]

Black athletes faced discrimination at game venues, too. Before an exhibition game in San Antonio, the guard wouldn't let Younger and Willie Steele, a black rookie from San Diego State, through the gate until assistant coach George Trafton stood up for them in outrage. At that same venue, black fans were forced to sit in end zone seating, and after Younger caused a fumble, the white crowd started taunting him, so Rams head coach Clark Shaughnessy pulled him from the game, but Younger told Shaughnessy he didn't care, so the coach put him back in.[157] Sportswriters suggested the Rams should have boycotted southern games,[158] but even in the North, there was discrimination. For example, in Green Bay, to taunt Younger, fans let a black cat loose onto the field.[159]

On the gridiron, black players were marked men and targeted for extra violence[160] or at the very least they were called out with racial slurs, which sometimes resulted in retaliation. When opponents used aspersions against Younger, his teammates would come to his defense, and sometimes the slanderous opponent would have to be carted off the field.[161] It was not lost on the Rams' most anonymous white players, the offensive linemen, that they were sacrificing their bodies to open holes for black men to score touchdowns and receive admiration,[162] but they were teammates, after all. In Cleveland, Brown warned his players against retaliating,[163] but as Motley later said, "The only thing was to stop and get right up in their face and say, 'Your mother...' It stopped. Stopped a lot of it."[164] Within a backdrop of violence, in football, black athletes were asked to behave incongruently serene.[165]

Even within the Rams' organization there was a certain amount of racism. Towler said the Rams organization made him feel welcome, and that he rarely saw signs of racial discrimination,[166] but Shaughnessy gave Younger the nickname "Big Boy"[167] at a time when "boy" was frequently used in racial animus toward African Americans.[168] "I don't think he ever really knew my name," Younger later said. "I saw him six months before he died and he still called me Big Boy."[169] Being one of only a handful of black players in the league at the time, Younger said it didn't bother him, because he believed in getting along with other people, and he said he was only aware of the racial situation "when the press mentioned it." Younger said, "As far as the players and the organization were concerned, they always treated me as just another member of the ballclub."[170] And he didn't realize how significant his accomplishments were in terms of being a black athlete until he read it in the newspapers.[171] Before the Rams had approached him to sign a contract, Younger had never even considered becoming a professional athlete.[172]

Reeves announced on February 18, 1950, that he had fired Shaughnessy due to "friction between Shaughnessy and his assistants, players and others associated with the Rams" and that line coach Stydahar would take his place.[173] By contrast, Stydahar was 38 years old,[174] 20 years younger than Shaughnessy,[175] and only four years removed from playing the game himself,[176] but despite being closer in age to his players, Stydahar referred to all of them as his "kids."[177] During his rookie season, Towler, who continued to pursue a master's degree in religion at the University of Southern California while playing for the Rams,[178] approached Stydahar about leading the team in a pregame prayer, and Towler said Stydahar responded, "It sure wouldn't hurt anything, and who knows? It might help."[179] The team prayer included white teammates and the act received media attention.[180]

Non-black, non-white players didn't face the same level of discrimination. Rams end Tom Fears, for example, was Mexican American, born in Guadalajara, Mexico, to an American father and Mexican mother, and he was one of the first of his background to reach star status in professional football, but he received little attention for his background. In 1949, Fears broke Don Hutson's record for most receptions in a season,[181] and he scored the winning touchdown in the 1951 championship game[182] on a 73-yard pass from Norm Van Brocklin.[183]

The forces to reintegrate pro football didn't always include the players themselves. When the Rams signed Washington and Strode, both players were already past their prime,[184] and Washington had already suffered multiple knee injuries and surgeries.[185] After signing his NFL contract, Washington had surgery again to remove torn cartilage and scar tissues from his left knee.[186] Strode, meanwhile, got his job with the Rams because the organization told Washington he needed a black roommate. When Washington insisted on Strode, the Rams were reluctant because of Strode's interracial marriage to a Polynesian woman.[187]

Besides, Washington and Strode were making more money playing semi-professional football[188] than they would for the Rams,[189] and they weren't actively pursuing roles in major league pro football.[190] In contrast, when the Browns signed Willis and Motley, both men achieved significant income boosts on a per-month basis.[191]

But for the black community, and for some future players, the Rams' actions and those of Washington and Strode were significant, and the fact the Rams played Marshall's Redskins in their very first exhibition game in Los Angeles only increased the significance of the moment.[192] "I was very aware of the black players who went into pro football in 1946," said George Taliaferro, a tailback who was drafted by the Chicago Bears and the Los Angeles Dons in 1949. "Yes, sir. That was the year I was in the Army. All of a sudden, my dream of playing for the Chicago Bears wasn't so far-fetched."[193]

Washington and Strode's on-field contributions for the Rams were small. During the Rams' first-ever preseason game, the College All-Star Game at Soldier Field in Chicago, in a third-string backup role Washington threw an interception and was sacked for a safety. Meanwhile, Strode only played a few snaps on defense.[194] In their first exhibition game in Los Angeles, Washington only threw one incomplete pass.[195] At the time, Vincent X. Flaherty of the *Los Angeles Examiner* opined that black players weren't good enough to compete in the NFL.[196]

After the 1946 season, the Rams cut Strode, and Washington told Strode he believed it was because Reeves didn't approve of Strode's "Hawaiian lifestyle."[197] Strode left professional football bitter. "If I have to integrate heaven, I don't want to go," he told *Sports Illustrated*.[198] After Strode was cut, the Calgary Stampeders of the CFL recruited him, and Strode helped to lead the Stampeders through some of their greatest seasons[199]: Strode played for the Stampeders in 1948[200] when the team finished 12–0 and won the CFL championship[201] and in 1949[202] when they went 13–1.[203]

Washington did improve with the Rams, but he couldn't always play. In the 1947 and 1948 seasons, he started a total of five games at halfback and carried the ball 117 times for 745 yards and 7 touchdowns.[204] During the 1948 season, Washington had hip, knee, and ankle troubles, and after a great performance against the New York Giants in November, he announced his plans to retire. After the announcement, *Los Angeles Times* writer Frank Finch despaired Washington had never been given the chance to play in the NFL during his prime,[205] and Bob Mann, an undrafted wide receiver who played for the Detroit Lions in 1948, said, "Washington was a tremendous athlete, [but] he really didn't get to play until an age where he wasn't performing at his best. I remember him signing with the Rams.... He had been playing for years [semi-professionally] before that—he'd taken a beating running the ball all the time. I mean, he was still a heck of a player, but I think he had better years before then."[206]

In 1949, the year after Washington retired, the Rams increased their interest in black players and signed Younger. Younger wore 13, the same number Washington had worn for the Rams[207] (the same number of years it took for pro football to reintegrate).[208] The Rams also added black players in 1950: Towler, Lewis, Boyd, and Thompson.[209] And although the Dons of the AAFC had avoided signing black players at first, by 1949 they had six,[210] including Taliaferro from Indiana, who was the first African American to be selected in the NFL draft, but Taliaferro signed with the Dons, instead, who had picked him in the AAFC draft held the same day. The Dons led the AAFC in drafting black players, which may have contributed to Taliaferro's choosing the Dons over the NFL's Bears.[211]

But in pro football, reintegration was tentative and provisional. As Gretchen Atwood notes in her book *Lost Champions*, "If coaches or owners weren't racist themselves, they were skittish of the attention signing a black player would bring and they feared backlash from white fans."[212] Therefore, "most black players in the late 1940s carried the weight of representing more than just themselves.... If they failed, that could mean fewer chances for other black players."[213] As a result, black athletes like Strode didn't argue for playing time but instead chose to prove themselves during practice.[214] In his book *The Golden Age of Pro Football*, Mickey Herskowitz notes, "[Reintegration] required patience and courage and the answers were never quick or simple.... The steps taken to erase the traces of the color line were small ones, and slow. But they also were the hardest and the most meaningful, because they were the first."[215]

The slow process of reintegration meant many talented black athletes were never encouraged to think about playing pro football. "I never thought about being a professional football player," said Eddie Macon, a running back and defensive back who was a second-round draft choice by the Bears in 1952, "not even after Jackie Robinson started playing with the Dodgers and blacks started playing in the NFL. I was happy the same way I think all black people were, it was just progress for all of us. None of my coaches encouraged me in that direction and I didn't get any national recognition."[216]

There were 594 players on 18 pro teams in 1946, and only four players were black.[217]

Following that initial year of reintegration led by the Rams and Browns, a handful of teams signed one or two black players.[218] In 1947, after the Rams cut Strode, Washington was the NFL's only black player, while four AAFC teams invited a total of 15 black players to their training camps, including seven who made a team.[219] That year, John Brown of North Carolina Central and Elmore Harris of Morgan State were the first players from black colleges to play professional football, signing with teams in the AAFC, Harris with the Brooklyn Dodgers and Brown with the Los Angeles Dons.[220] AAFC owners found themselves in a bidding war for the services of Buddy Young, a black halfback who played at the University of Illinois, and who signed with the league's New York Yankees.[221] That year, more than 70,000 fans, including more than 25,000 black fans, attended a game in Yankee Stadium to watch the duel between Motley and Young, two black running backs. The attendance surpassed the number that attended to watch Grange and the Bears play the New York Giants in 1925.[222] Twice that year, the desegregated Browns played the desegregated Yankees, and the contests attracted 150,000 fans, including 40,000 African Americans.[223] The two franchises dominated their league and played in the AAFC championship game.[224] Back in Los Angeles, with three black players on the team compared to zero in 1946, the Dons more than doubled their attendance.[225] Of the 664 players on eighteen pro teams in 1947, only 10 were black,[226] and at the time old Fritz Pollard recounted how he and others in pre-segregated pro football, before 1934, had been used as gate attractions, and he expressed concern that the new crop of black players were being used for the same purpose. He wondered: As soon as pro football found its financial footing, would black talent once again be ignored?[227]

Only one more AAFC team, the San Francisco 49ers, signed black players in 1948. Meanwhile, in the NFL, the Lions and Giants added black players.[228] There were 14 black players in pro football in 1948.[229]

By 1949, 19 black athletes competed across the ranks of professional football, including seven in the NFL and 12 in the AAFC, yet nine professional football teams across the NFL and AAFC had yet to integrate black athletes onto their rosters[230]—in part because teams preferred obtaining black athletes who had played for white college teams.[231] That year, the Rams signed Younger,[232] a fullback from Grambling, and also the NFL's first black player to come from a black college.[233] "At no time did I ever doubt my ability," said Younger. "In spite of the fact I knew the odds were long."[234] But Grambling coach Eddie Robinson mentored Younger about how to make the team: run out extra yards during drills. "The longer you have the ball under your arm, the longer the man is watching you," Younger recalled Robinson telling him.[235] The fullback put in extra time studying the playbook with his Rams teammates,[236] and after he made the team, at one point George Halas told Younger after a game, "Tank, you're the greatest, dirtiest, best football player in the league. I just wish we had you."[237]

The NFL didn't *draft* a player from a black college until the Giants drafted Bob "Stonewall" Jackson from North Carolina A&T in 1950.[238] Pro teams did not actively obtain black athletes from black colleges until the AFL started in 1960.[239]

By the end of the 1940s, only 26 black players had played professional football in the NFL or AAFC. Many had played for only one year and hadn't been utilized as much as their white counterparts. When the decade was up, the Eagles, Steelers, Redskins, New York Bulldogs, Bears, Cardinals, and Packers in the NFL still had not reintegrated at some point, and only three teams, the Rams, Lions, and Giants, still had black players on their rosters. In the AAFC, only two teams, the Buffalo Bills and Baltimore Colts, were *without* black players.[240]

The AAFC only lasted four years, but the league signed more black players than the NFL.[241] Besides the Rams, the Lions were the only other NFL team to have more than one black player before the 1950 season,[242] but even after their black receiver, Bob Mann, led the NFL in receiving in 1949, the Lions dealt him to the New York Yanks when he refused to take a pay cut.[243]

The only black player on the Rams roster in 1949 was Younger, but in 1950 they added Boyd, Towler, Thompson, and Lewis.[244] In 1950, there were 19 black players in pro football.[245] In 1951, there were 17.[246] But after back-to-back championship matchups between the two teams with the most black players, other NFL franchises began to finally pay attention to black talent and teams selected a total of thirteen black players in the 1953 NFL draft.[247]

And yet despite the NFL's acknowledgment that black talent should be considered, the league's newest franchise, the Dallas Texans, suffered because of it. In January 1952, the Texans announced they would indeed play their black players, Young and Taliaferro, and the team realized low fan attendance at the Cotton Bowl during the season. The owners reported to the NFL commissioner the reason was white Texans' racial prejudice, and the black press reported stadium officials had made it difficult for black fans to gain entrance to the stadium and they didn't allow them to purchase good seats. The Texans finished their only season 1–11.[248] But not everyone involved saw the Texas experiment as a failure. "The Texans knocked out Jim Crow," remarked Young. "I think that was a breakthrough."[249]

Not only was reintegration slow in terms of the pure number and percentage of black players in pro football, teams were slow to use black players at all positions. Coaches followed an unwritten rule that said black athletes should only be allowed to play running back, receiver, cornerback, and defensive lineman, and teams typically had an even number of black players on the roster so that white players would not have to have black players as roommates.[250]

The Bears did not hire a black player during their first 32 seasons. The Giants didn't sign a black player until 1948. After releasing Ray Kemp following the 1933 season, the Steelers were all-white until 1952. The Redskins did not sign a black player until 1962,[251] when Marshall succumbed to pressure from the Kennedy administration[252] and the team signed Bobby Mitchell[253] as well as Leroy Jackson, John Nisby, and Ron Hatcher.[254] Marshall's refusal to acknowledge and sign black talent led Washington to become one of the worst teams in the league in the 1950s and early 1960s.[255]

In 1970, during the Rams' Silver Anniversary, Reeves named Younger, Towler, and Lewis to his all-time Rams team, out of 24 players named.[256]

Notes

1. Charles K. Ross, 1999. *Outside the Lines: African Americans and the Integration of the National Football League* (New York: New York University Press, 1999), 106.

2. A.S. "Doc" Young, "The Black Athlete in the Golden Age of Sports: Part VIII Pro Football Discovers the Black College," *Ebony*, September 1970, 116.

3. Jim Hock, *Hollywood's Team: Grit, Glamour, and the 1950s Los Angeles Rams* (Los Angeles: Rare Bird Books, 2016), 102–103.

4. Ross, *Outside the Lines*, 67.

5. Gretchen Atwood, *Lost Champions: Four Men, Two Teams, and the Breaking of Pro Football's Color Line* (New York: Bloomsbury, 2016), 182.

6. Howard Roberts, *The Story of Pro Football* (New York: Rand McNally & Company, 1953), 119.

7. Ross, *Outside the Lines*, 168–170.
8. "1951 Los Angeles Rams Starters, Roster, & Players," *Pro-football-reference.com*, .https://www.pro-football-reference.com/teams/ram/1951_roster.htm.
9. "Cleveland Browns Franchise Encyclopedia," *Pro-football-reference.com*, https://www.pro-football-reference.com/teams/cle/index.htm.
10. "Cleveland/St. Louis/LA Rams Franchise Encyclopedia," *Pro-football-reference.com*, https://www.pro-football-reference.com/teams/ram/index.htm.
11. Shav Glick, "On Prayer and a Pass, a Title Came to Town," *Los Angeles Times*, August 30, 1991, C1.
12. "Championship—Los Angeles Rams at Cleveland Browns—December 24th, 1950," *Pro-football-reference.com*, https://www.pro-football-reference.com/boxscores/195012240cle.htm.
13. Ross, *Outside the Lines*, 167–168.
14. Roger Treat, *The Official National Football League Football Encyclopedia* (New York: A.S. Barnes, 1952), 246.
15. Harold Rosenthal, *The Big Play* (New York: Random House, 1965), 41, 44–45.
16. Treat, *The Official National Football League Football Encyclopedia*, 247.
17. Ross, *Outside the Lines*, 168.
18. Treat, *The Official National Football League Football Encyclopedia*, 246.
19. "1951 Cleveland Browns Starters, Roster, & Players," *Pro-football-reference.com*, https://www.pro-football-reference.com/teams/cle/1951_roster.htm.
20. Treat, *The Official National Football League Football Encyclopedia*, 246.
21. "1951 Los Angeles Rams Statistics & Players," *Pro-football-reference.com*, https://www.pro-football-reference.com/teams/ram/1951.htm.
22. Steve, Bisheff, *Great Teams' Great Years: Los Angeles Rams* (New York: Macmillan, 1973), 29.
23. Cliff Christl and Don Langenkamp, *Sleepers, Busts & Franchise-Makers: The behind-the-scenes story of the pro football draft (1936-present)* (Seattle: Preview Publishing, 1983), 50.
24. Treat, *The Official National Football League Football Encyclopedia*, 81.
25. Phil Berger, *Championship Teams of the NFL* (New York: Random House, 1968), 43–44.
26. Berger, *Championship Teams of the NFL*, 40.
27. Berger, *Championship Teams of the NFL*, 43–44.
28. Berger, *Championship Teams of the NFL*, 43–44.
29. Berger, *Championship Teams of the NFL*, 40.
30. Berger, *Championship Teams of the NFL*, 43–48.
31. "Championship—Cleveland Browns at Los Angeles Rams—December 23rd, 1951," *Pro-football-reference.com*, https://www.pro-football-reference.com/boxscores/195112230ram.htm.
32. Bob Oates, *The Los Angeles Rams* (Culver City: Murray & Gee, 1955), 19.
33. Oates, *The Los Angeles Rams*, 24.
34. Bisheff, *Los Angeles Rams*, 29.
35. Ross, *Outside the Lines*, 166–167.
36. Mickey Herskowitz, *The Golden Age of Pro Football: NFL Football in the 1950s* (Dallas: Taylor, 1990), 53.
37. Atwood, *Lost Champions*, 3.
38. Alan H. Levy, *Tackling Jim Crow: Racial Segregation in Professional Football* (Jefferson, NC: McFarland, 2003), 101.
39. Atwood, *Lost Champions*, 3–5.
40. Andy Piascik, *Gridiron Gauntlet: The Story of the Men Who Integrated Pro Football in Their Own Words* (Lanham: Taylor Trade, 2009), 82.
41. Levy, *Tackling Jim Crow*, 101.
42. Ross, *Outside the Lines*, 126.
43. Ross, *Outside the Lines*, 126–127.
44. Ross, *Outside the Lines*, 125–126.
45. Atwood, *Lost Champions*, 7.
46. Christl and Langenkamp, *Sleepers, Busts & Franchise-Makers*, 50.
47. Charles K Ross, "Sports: Football (U.S.)," in *Encyclopedia of Race and Racism*, Patrick L. Mason, ed. (2nd ed. Gale, 2013).
48. Michael Oriard, "Pigskin Pioneers," *Villagevoice.com*, October 10, 2000, https://www.villagevoice.com/2000/10/10/pigskin-pioneers/.
49. Ross, "Sports: Football (U.S.)."
50. Piascik, *Gridiron Gauntlet*, 6.
51. Ross, "Sports: Football (U.S.)."
52. Piascik, *Gridiron Gauntlet*, 6.
53. Ross, *Outside the Lines*, 37.
54. Ross, *Outside the Lines*, 38.
55. Ross, *Outside the Lines*, 41.

56. Ross, *Outside the Lines*, 45.
57. Piascik, *Gridiron Gauntlet*, 4.
58. Oriard, "Pigskin Pioneers."
59. Levy, *Tackling Jim Crow*, 4.
60. Civil War, *A&E Television Networks*, 2019, https://www.history.com/topics/american-civil-war/american-civil-war-history.
61. "Segregated Baseball: A Kaleidoscopic Review," *Mlb.com*, 2019, http://mlb.mlb.com/mlb/history/mlb_negro_leagues_story.jsp?story=kaleidoscopic.
62. Ross, *Outside the Lines*, 4–5.
63. Robert W. Peterson, *Pigskin: The Early Years of Pro Football* (New York: Oxford University Press, 1997), 172.
64. Levy, *Tackling Jim Crow*, 23–24.
65. Levy, *Tackling Jim Crow*, 26.
66. Ross, *Outside the Lines*, 4–5.
67. Ross, *Outside the Lines*, 50.
68. Ross, *Outside the Lines*, 51.
69. Atwood, *Lost Champions*, 6.
70. "A Ban on Black Players Cost the NFL Its Most Exciting Quarterback," *Deadspin.com*, February 19, 2014, https://deadspin.com/the-big-book-of-black-quarterbacks-1517763742/1526239170.
71. Piascik, *Gridiron Gauntlet*, 5.
72. Gordon J. Hylton, "Who Was the First Black Redskin?" *Law.marquette.com*, November 8, 2009, "https://law.marquette.edu/facultyblog/2009/11/08/who-was-the-first-black-redskin/.
73. Atwood, *Lost Champions*, 6.
74. Christian McWhirter, "The Birth of 'Dixie'," *Opinionator.blogs.nytimes.com*, March 31, 2012, https://opinionator.blogs.nytimes.com/2012/03/31/the-birth-of-dixie/.
75. Levy, *Tackling Jim Crow*, 56.
76. "A Ban on Black Players Cost The NFL Its Most Exciting Quarterback."
77. Ross, *Outside the Lines*, 61.
78. Ross, *Outside the Lines*, 71.
79. Ross, *Outside the Lines*, 51.
80. Ross, *Outside the Lines*, 55.
81. Ross, *Outside the Lines*, 54.
82. Levy, *Tackling Jim Crow*, 58–60.
83. Levy, *Tackling Jim Crow*, 58.
84. Hock, *Hollywood's Team*, 97–104
85. Michael MacCambridge, *America's Game: The Epic Story of How Pro Football Captured a Nation* (New York: Anchor Books, 2004), 17.
86. Hock, *Hollywood's Team*, 98.
87. MacCambridge, *America's Game*, 17.
88. Hock, *Hollywood's Team*, 96–97.
89. Hock, *Hollywood's Team*, 98.
90. Hock, *Hollywood's Team*, 100.
91. Joseph Hession, *Rams: Five Decades of Football* (San Francisco: Foghorn Press, 1987), 22.
92. Hock, *Hollywood's Team*, 96–97.
93. Gretchen Atwood, "Unsung Heroes of Rams Football- Integration," *LA Weekly*, June 10, 2009, https://www.laweekly.com/news/unsung-heroes-of-rams-football-integration-2160172.
94. Hock, *Hollywood's Team*, 99.
95. Atwood, *Lost Champions*, 15–16.
96. Hock, *Hollywood's Team*, 101.
97. Atwood, *Lost Champions*, 15–16.
98. MacCambridge, *America's Game*, 17.
99. Atwood, *Lost Champions*, 15–16.
100. Young, "The Black Athlete in the Golden Age of Sports," 116.
101. Hock, *Hollywood's Team*, 101.
102. Atwood, *Lost Champions*, 15–16.
103. Ross, *Outside the Lines*, 63.
104. Lane Demas, *Integrating the Gridiron* (New Brunswick: Rutgers University Press, 2010), 41.
105. MacCambridge, *America's Game*, 18.
106. Atwood, *Lost Champions*, 15–16.
107. Hock, *Hollywood's Team*, 102.
108. Atwood, *Lost Champions*, 15–16.
109. Hock, *Hollywood's Team*, 102.
110. Hock, *Hollywood's Team*, 99.

111. Atwood, "Unsung Heroes."
112. Hock, *Hollywood's Team*, 102.
113. Atwood, *Lost Champions*, 17–19.
114. Young, "The Black Athlete in the Golden Age of Sports," 116.
115. Atwood, "Unsung Heroes."
116. Atwood, *Lost Champions*, 19.
117. Young, "The Black Athlete in the Golden Age of Sports," 116.
118. Demas, *Integrating the Gridiron*, 29.
119. Demas, *Integrating the Gridiron*, 28.
120. Levy, *Tackling Jim Crow*, 93.
121. Ross, *Outside the Lines*, 82.
122. Bisheff, *Los Angeles Rams*, 19.
123. Hession, *Rams: Five Decades of Football*, 22.
124. Bisheff, *Los Angeles Rams*, 151.
125. Bisheff, *Los Angeles Rams*, 16.
126. Herskowitz, *The Golden Age of Pro Football*, 21.
127. Ross, *Outside the Lines*, 88–89.
128. Oates, *The Los Angeles Rams*, 22.
129. Treat, *The Official National Football League Football Encyclopedia*, 21.
130. Craig R. Coenen, *From Sandlots to the Super Bowl: The National Football League 1920–1967* (Knoxville: University of Tennessee Press, 2005), 123.
131. Coenen, *From Sandlots to the Super Bowl*, 115–120.
132. Coenen, *From Sandlots to the Super Bowl*, 123.
133. Coenen, *From Sandlots to the Super Bowl*, 123.
134. Hession, *Rams: Five Decades of Football*, 21.
135. Coenen, *From Sandlots to the Super Bowl*, 115–120.
136. Coenen, *From Sandlots to the Super Bowl*, 122.
137. Coenen, *From Sandlots to the Super Bowl*, 115–120.
138. Peterson, *Pigskin: The Early Years of Pro Football*, 169.
139. Atwood, *Lost Champions*, 19.
140. Coenen, *From Sandlots to the Super Bowl*, 123–124.
141. Ross, *Outside the Lines*, 84–85.
142. Ross, *Outside the Lines*, 85–86.
143. Levy, *Tackling Jim Crow*, 89–92.
144. Herskowitz, *The Golden Age of Pro Football*, 19.
145. Ross, *Outside the Lines*, 96.
146. Hock, *Hollywood's Team*, 216.
147. Ross, *Outside the Lines*, 96.
148. Ross, *Outside the Lines*, 108.
149. Ross, *Outside the Lines*, 90.
150. Ross, *Outside the Lines*, 91.
151. Ross, *Outside the Lines*, 91.
152. Hock, *Hollywood's Team*, 106.
153. Hock, *Hollywood's Team*, 106.
154. Atwood, *Lost Champions*, 40–41.
155. Young, "The Black Athlete in the Golden Age of Sports," 116.
156. Lonnie White, "Harry Thompson, 78; Key Blocker for Rams in 1950s," *Los Angeles Times*, November 29, 2003, B25.
157. Bisheff, *Los Angeles Rams*, 142.
158. Young, "The Black Athlete in the Golden Age of Sports," 116.
159. Bisheff, *Los Angeles Rams*, 141.
160. Peterson, *Pigskin: The Early Years of Pro Football*, 172.
161. Young, "The Black Athlete in the Golden Age of Sports," 116.
162. Hock, *Hollywood's Team*, 107.
163. Levy, *Tackling Jim Crow*, 100.
164. Levy, *Tackling Jim Crow*, 99.
165. Levy, *Tackling Jim Crow*, 29.
166. Hession, *Rams: Five Decades of Football*, 58.
167. Bisheff, *Los Angeles Rams*, 142.
168. Roland S. Martin, "Understanding Why You Don't Call a Black Man a Boy," *Cnn.com*, April 15, 2008, http://ac360.blogs.cnn.com/2008/04/15/understanding-why-you-dont-call-a-black-man-a-boy/.
169. Bisheff, *Los Angeles Rams*, 142.
170. Bisheff, *Los Angeles Rams*, 141.

324   Part 3: The Team

171. Bisheff, *Los Angeles Rams*, 142–143.
172. Young, "The Black Athlete in the Golden Age of Sports," 116.
173. "Unexpected Move Finds Shaughnessy Fired as Los Angeles Head Coach," *The Tribune* (Coshocton, OH), February 19, 1950, 15.
174. "Joe Stydahar," *NFL.com*, http://www.nfl.com/player/joestydahar/2526780/profile.
175. "Clark Daniel Shaughnessy," *Britannica.com*, https://www.britannica.com/biography/Clark-Daniel-Shaughnessy.
176. "Joe Stydahar," *Profootballhof.com*, https://www.profootballhof.com/players/joe-stydahar/.
177. "Browns Favored by Rams' Coach," *The Morning News* (Wilmington, de), December 22, 1950, 28.
178. Richard Goldstein, "Dan Towler, 73, All-Pro Back Who Studied for the Ministry," *New York Times*, August 3, 2001, A-21.
179. Earl Gustkey, "'Deacon' Dan Towler; Rams' Star Gave Up Football for Ministry," *Los Angeles Times*, August 2, 2001, B12
180. Paul Putz, "Football and the Political Act of Prayer," *Religionandpolitics.org*, August 28, 2018, https://religionandpolitics.org/2018/08/28/football-and-the-political-act-of-prayer/.
181. Atwood, *Lost Champions*, 185–186.
182. Treat, Roger, *The Official National Football League Football Encyclopedia*, 246–247.
183. Glick, "On Prayer and a Pass, a Title Came to Town."
184. Young, "The Black Athlete in the Golden Age of Sports," 116.
185. Hock, *Hollywood's Team*, 102–103.
186. Atwood, *Lost Champions*, 20–21.
187. Ross, *Outside the Lines*, 84.
188. Ross, *Outside the Lines*, 67.
189. Ross, *Outside the Lines*, 67.
190. Ross, *Outside the Lines*, 67.
191. Ross, *Outside the Lines*, 86.
192. Hock, *Hollywood's Team*, 102–103.
193. Piascik, *Gridiron Gauntlet*, 104.
194. Atwood, *Lost Champions*, 39–40.
195. Atwood, *Lost Champions*, 41–42.
196. Atwood, *Lost Champions*, 37.
197. Atwood, *Lost Champions*, 121.
198. Hock, *Hollywood's Team*, 102–103.
199. Atwood, *Lost Champions*, 122.
200. "1948 Calgary Stampeders Roster," *Statscrew.com*, https://www.statscrew.com/football/roster/t-CFLCGY/y-1948.
201. "1948 Canadian Football League," *Statscrew.com*, https://www.statscrew.com/football/l-CFL/y-1948.
202. "1949 Calgary Stampeders Roster," *Statscrew.com*, https://www.statscrew.com/football/roster/t-CFLCGY/y-1949.
203. "1949 Canadian Football League," *Statscrew.com*, https://www.statscrew.com/football/l-CFL/y-1949.
204. "Kenny Washington," *Pro-football-reference.com*, https://www.pro-football-reference.com/players/W/WashKe21.htm.
205. Atwood, *Lost Champions*, 167.
206. Piascik, *Gridiron Gauntlet*, 35.
207. Atwood, *Lost Champions*, 181.
208. Hock, *Hollywood's Team*, 102–103.
209. Atwood, *Lost Champions*, 181.
210. Atwood, *Lost Champions*, 181–182.
211. Atwood, *Lost Champions*, 182.
212. Atwood, *Lost Champions*, 182.
213. Atwood, *Lost Champions*, 182.
214. Ross, *Outside the Lines*, 90.
215. Herskowitz, *The Golden Age of Pro Football*, 19.
216. Piascik, *Gridiron Gauntlet*, 158.
217. Ross, *Outside the Lines*, 104.
218. Atwood, *Lost Champions*, 7.
219. Coenen, *From Sandlots to the Super Bowl*, 124.
220. Piascik, *Gridiron Gauntlet*, 13.
221. Coenen, *From Sandlots to the Super Bowl*, 124.
222. Ross, *Outside the Lines*, 99.
223. Coenen, *From Sandlots to the Super Bowl*, 124–125.
224. Ross, *Outside the Lines*, 111.
225. Ross, *Outside the Lines*, 110.

226. Ross, *Outside the Lines*, 104.
227. Ross, *Outside the Lines*, 99.
228. Ross, *Outside the Lines*, 111.
229. Ross, *Outside the Lines*, 112.
230. Coenen, *From Sandlots to the Super Bowl*, 124.
231. Ross, *Outside the Lines*, 114.
232. Christl and Langenkamp, *Sleepers, Busts & Franchise-Makers*, 50.
233. Cliff Christl, "Kotal, Vainisi Found Talent to Build Powerhouse Teams," *Packers.com*, April 28, 2016, https://www.packers.com/news/kotal-vainisi-found-talent-to-build-powerhouse-teams-17073993.
234. Bisheff, *Los Angeles Rams*, 141.
235. Herskowitz, *The Golden Age of Pro Football*, 54.
236. Young, "The Black Athlete in the Golden Age of Sports," 116.
237. Bisheff, *Los Angeles Rams*, 141.
238. Christl and Langenkamp, *Sleepers, Busts & Franchise-Makers*, 50.
239. Ross, *Outside the Lines*, 115.
240. Ross, *Outside the Lines*, 100.
241. Ross, *Outside the Lines*, 121.
242. Levy, *Tackling Jim Crow*, 97.
243. Ross, *Outside the Lines*, 123–124.
244. Ross, *Outside the Lines*, 121.
245. Ross, *Outside the Lines*, 121–123, 125–126.
246. Ross, *Outside the Lines*, 126.
247. Ross, *Outside the Lines*, 131.
248. Ross, *Outside the Lines*, 128–129.
249. Herskowitz, *The Golden Age of Pro Football*, 9.
250. Ross, "Sports: Football (U.S.)."
251. Piascik, *Gridiron Gauntlet*, 5.
252. Ross, "Sports: Football (U.S.)."
253. Coenen, *From Sandlots to the Super Bowl*, 124.
254. Ross, "Sports: Football (U.S.)."
255. Levy, *Tackling Jim Crow*, 101.
256. Bisheff, *Los Angeles Rams*, 45.

The NFL's Fashion Pioneers

JOHN M. VORPERIAN

Since their 1937 arrival onto the gridiron scene in Cleveland Ohio, style has been a strong thread within the Rams. The club's nickname was adopted in tribute to the college football powerhouse of the day-the Fordham University Rams. The sobriquet was also a newspaper sports editor's dream as it fit well into a headline. Owner Homer Marshman, an attorney and businessman along with general manager Damon "Buzz" Wetzel collectively promoted the team.

The Rams' initial uniform colors were red and black. In keeping with their moniker's collegiate origins the cardinal hue was actually more of a maroon. Clearly a shade that would seamlessly match with a Fordham football jersey. Nonetheless, by 1938, the Rams donned blue and gold uniforms. The precise reason for this switch has become a mystery in history. The most repeated speculation was too many other pro teams were using red and the Rams sought to separate themselves from the pack.

In 1946, the Rams left the Buckeye State and moved to Los Angeles, After the Rams experienced a mediocre .500 season (6–6) in 1947, halfback Fred Gehrke had a novel idea to bolster team spirit. Gehrke, a key part of the Rams' 1945 NFL championship squad (season avg. 6.3 rushing yds. per carry; 11.3 yds. per reception; eight TDs) went to head coach Bob Snyder with a vogue proposal.

"I told him we needed to put some kind of design on our helmets," recalled the University of Utah art major. "No other team had anything like that, and I thought it was time for a change."[1] Gehrke took one of the brown leather helmets painted it dark blue and embellished the head cover with the now familiar Rams horns. The duo presented the prototype to owner Dan Reeves.

Reeves loved the idea and green-lighted the design. Gehrke decorated 75 helmets by hand. He was paid a dollar for each paint job. Gehrke continued playing on both sides of the ball, returning punts and kickoffs and also took up the task of maintaining the horns on the helmets during the season. The pigskin-playing Picasso recalled, "for two years I touched up the bonnets after every game. I kept a can of blue paint and a can of gold paint in my locker, and even took them along on road trips."[2]

In 1949, Riddell unveiled plastic football helmets. Now the Rams' horns were manufactured into the new headwear. Gehrke's artistic repair duties ceased. But head coach Clark Shaughnessy splashed a new color scheme onto the Los Angeles club.

The University of Minnesota alum designated a change to red and gold. The first pro football team to feature a logo made an alteration to the original emblem. Ridges were now added to the horns. Giving the horns a fiercer guise. Why red and gold?

Some sports historians argue the "Father of the T-Formation" tinted the switch to honor his old school. Others contend a marketing ploy to seize upon the University of Southern California's look and entice that particular fan base to the Los Angeles pro grid contests. Gehrke is on record that paying tribute to the Golden Gophers or even capturing Trojan boosters may not have been Shaughnessy's primary colored reason.

In correspondence dated 1974 with a Pro Football Hall of Fame researcher, Gehrke, then with the Denver Broncos, first as a scout and then front office executive, wrote about a rumor that Clark Shaughnessy "had an interest in a sporting goods manufacturing company which made the reordering of a complete uniform necessary, due to the change in headgear design and in color."[3]

In 1950, the Rams changed the canvas again. Blue and yellow were back. Red was cut out.

Following the Rams down the football fashion walkway, in 1954, the Philadelphia Eagles added silver wings to their helmets. The Colts slapped white horseshoe logos onto the back of their blue helmets. Five seasons later, the Washington squad added a feather down the middle of its headgear.

Entering the 1959 season these four teams had decorated helmets. By 1962, with the NFL inking the first league wide national television contract with CBS, all pro franchises, with the exception of the Cleveland Browns, had helmets adorned with logos.

By the mid–1960s yellow and/or gold had been erased from the Rams' palette. The helmet donned by "The Fearsome Foursome" of Rosey Grier, Deacon Jones, Lamar Lundy and Merlin Olsen was blue with a white horn.

Because of his helmet logo design, Fred Gehrke was summoned to Canton, Ohio, in 1972. The Pro Football Hall of Fame honored him with the first Daniel F. Reeves Memorial Pioneer Award for his creative artwork and contribution to the sport.

In 1995 the Rams moved east and into St. Louis, Missouri. SoCal fans may have been paled at the prospect of having no professional team in town, but the Rams had returned to the gold. That is the team wiped away the white horn on their helmets and replaced them with gold horns as the logo.

The Rams returned to the West Coast in 2016. During this time and as of this writing the pigment of the franchise's helmet logo continues an ever-changing act. Perhaps Fred Gehrke had a true, solid feeling his team spirit idea would resound with players and coaches. As he once said, "I spent the better part of my life in football, and I'll be best remembered for some work I did with a paintbrush but that's O.K. I've been called the Da Vinci of football helmets, and that's not all bad."[4] Indeed it isn't, Fred; thanks.

Notes

1. "The Rams Return to L.A. Where They Made NFL Helmet History," *www.sportingnews.com*, January 14, 2016, https://www.sportingnews.com/us/nfl/news/rams-move-los-angeles-st-louis-la-coliseum-stan-kroenke-helmets-uniforms/819wgb51t6gp1qp0y7h5xl8r9
2. "The Rams Return to L.A."
3. "The Rams Return to L.A."
4. "The Rams Return to L.A."

PART 4

The Stadium

Memorial Coliseum

Massimo Foglio

Known as "The Greatest Stadium in the World," the Los Angeles Memorial Coliseum can arguably be called "America's Most Historic Sports Stadium."

Designed by British architects John and Donald Parkinson, who left their mark on other famous landmarks in Los Angeles such as City Hall, Union Station and the Bullocks' Wilshire Building, the Coliseum was built in just under a year and a half, between December 21, 1921, date of the official groundbreaking ceremony, and May 1, 1923. At the time of its official opening in June 1923, it was the largest stadium in Los Angeles with a capacity of 75,144.[1]

Conceived as a stadium but also as a celebratory monument (hence the name "Memorial") originally dedicated to Los Angeles veterans who served during World War I and rededicated in 1968 to all United States veterans who served in World War I, the Coliseum is characterized by the main peristyle façade located at the eastern entrance

Los Angeles Memorial Coliseum (courtesy Pro Football Hall of Fame).

gate, where a series of bronze plaques celebrate events and celebrities who have written the history of the Coliseum. Some of the noteworthy names honored in the "Memorial Court of Honor" are Knute Rockne, Pop Warner, John F. Kennedy, Amos Alonzo Stagg, Dan Reeves, Jesse Owens, Pope John Paul II, Jackie Robinson, Elroy "Crazylegs" Hirsch, Pete Rozelle, Frank Leahy, Vin Scully, Babe Didrikson, and Nelson Mandela.

The architecture of the stadium was very innovative for the times. Particularly interesting is the constructive affinity of the Memorial Coliseum with the Colosseum in Rome. The main entrance is flanked by two original stones of the Colosseum in Rome and the original Olympic Stadium in Athens (Altis Olympia).

Built at a cost of $ 954,000,[2] the Coliseum underwent its first renovation in 1930, in anticipation of the 1932 Olympics, which were awarded to Los Angeles in 1923. A third tier was built adding about 30,000 seats, and the capacity passed from the initial 75,144 to 101,574,[3] reaching the maximum effective capacity in its history. The most visible intervention, in addition to the additional stands, was the construction of the Olympic cauldron torch, installed at the center of the peristyle, which is still lit up during USC football games.[4]

Another important restructuring took place in 1964, when the wooden and metal benches were replaced by individual theater style seats that reduced the capacity to about 93,000 seats. In 1977–78, Los Angeles Rams owner Carroll Rosenbloom had an additional grandstand built behind the east end zone to bring the spectators who were sitting in the extremities next to the peristyle a little closer to the field but reducing the capacity to a little more than 71,500 seats. For the 1984 Olympics, the athletics track was completely redone and the east stand was dismantled, bringing back the capacity to around 90,000 seats. In 1993 the stadium underwent a further massive renovation. The field was lowered by about 11 feet, obtaining fourteen new rows of seats to replace the athletic track. Individual chairs replaced the last surviving bleachers and a substantial renovation of the locker rooms and common areas was also completed.

In 2013, USC obtained the master lease for the venue, and began planning a further phase of renewal including the construction of a new press box that also includes box suites, premium lounges and V.I.P. sections in addition to the total replacement of all seats, some of which will be made more comfortable by increasing the width.[5] The renovations were completed in 2019, and the current capacity of the Coliseum is 77,500.

On October 10, 1923, the first football game was played at the Coliseum between USC and Pomona College. The Trojans won 23–7 in front of 12,836[6] spectators who almost lost themselves in the immensity of the bleachers.

In the ninety-eight years of its history, the Coliseum has hosted two editions of the Summer Olympics (Xth Olympiad in 1932, XXIIIrd Olympiad in 1984) and will become the only stadium in the world to host three when, in 2028, it will host the XXXIV Olympiad.

The Coliseum has also hosted two editions of the Super Bowl, the first between the Green Bay Packers and Kansas City Chiefs in 1967 and the seventh between the undefeated Miami Dolphins and the Washington Redskins in 1973.

Before the establishment of the Super Bowl, the Coliseum hosted three NFL championship games. The first was played on December 18, 1949, and saw the Philadelphia Eagles overcome The Los Angeles Rams 14–0. The game was played during a heavy rainstorm that transformed the field into a mud pit. Philadelphia opted for a run-oriented game plan, feeding their runners 61 times, but it was one of their five pass completions that put the Eagles on the scoreboard in the second quarter, a 31-yarder from Tommy Thompson to Pete Pihos. In the third quarter, the Rams were forced to punt near their own end zone, the kick was blocked and the ball was returned for a touchdown by Philadelphia's defender Leo Skladany. The two scores proved to be enough against a Rams team that was unable to move the ball either on the ground (24 rushes for a total gain of 21 yards) nor by pass (Norm Van Brocklin and Bob Waterfield combined for less than 100 yards in the air).

Two years later the Rams conquered the NFL by defeating the Cleveland Browns 24-17 at the Coliseum on December 23, 1951, becoming the first NFL team to win a title in two different cities.

Four years later, on December 26, 1955, the Browns and the Rams again squared off for the NFL title at the Coliseum, with the Browns winning 38-14 in front of 85,693 spectators, a record for an NFL final in the pre–Super Bowl era.

Since its inauguration, the Coliseum has been the football home of the USC Trojans, but the Coliseum has hosted several professional and collegiate football teams, starting with the UCLA Bruins that shared the playing field with their USC rivals from 1928 to 1981, when they moved to the Rose Bowl in Pasadena. The Los Angeles Rams used the Coliseum as their home field when they moved to California from Cleveland in 1946 and played their home games there until they moved to Anaheim in 1980. After the twenty-year spell in St. Louis, they returned to Los Angeles and the Coliseum in 2016, while waiting for the construction of SoFi Stadium in Inglewood, which was completed for the 2020 season.

The Los Angeles Rams played their first home game at the Coliseum on September 29, 1946, losing 25-14 from the Philadelphia Eagles. Since then, Rams have hosted 257 regular season and 12 postseason games at the Coliseum, compiling a total record of 158-91-8 in the regular season and 6-6 in the postseason. A global record of .610 is not bad from a home field advantage standpoint, but during the 1970s, arguably the best decade in team history, playing at the Coliseum was difficult for any opponent. During the 10-year span from 1970 and 1979, the Rams collected two perfect seasons at home (1973 and 1977) and won 52 out of 72 games with two ties and only 18 losses.

On the other side, before being able to compile two perfect seasons at home, the Rams were blanked at home on two occasions in 1959 and 1962, and in that four-year span the Rams were able to win only 6 out of 26 home games.

In addition to the three NFL championship games, the Memorial Coliseum has hosted a number of memorable games for the Rams.

On September 28, 1951, the opening weekend of the 1951 season, The Los Angeles Rams hosted the New York Yanks. En route to the Rams victory with a 54-14 score, Los Angeles quarterback Norm Van Brocklin passed for 554 yards, a record that still stands in the NFL. Van Brocklin connected with Elroy "Crazylegs" Hirsch for four touchdowns, throwing the fifth of the day to Vitamin Smith. Three receivers had a 100-plus yards game (Hirsch 9-173, Fears 7-162 and Smith 2-103).

On November 19, 2018, The Los Angeles Rams and the Kansas City Chiefs played in a game that the NFL Network ranked #33 on their 100 Greatest Games list[7] and the second best regular season game ever. The game was originally scheduled to be played in Mexico City as part of the 2018 International Series, but disastrous field conditions forced the NFL to move the game back at its original location: the Los Angeles Memorial Coliseum.

Los Angeles and Kansas City were both 9-1 for the season and had in Jared Goff and Patrick Mahomes two quarterbacks playing at an MVP level. The game resulted in a 54–51 shootout with the Rams' Lamarcus Joyner intercepting Mahomes with 13 seconds to play to preserve the Rams victory after numerous lead changes during the game. Goff (413) and Mahomes (478) combined for 891 passing yards, while the combined total offense between the two teams surpassed the 1000-yrd mark (1001). The 105 combined points scored by the two teams was a new record for a Monday Night Football game.

The Coliseum was also used as the home field for the Los Angeles Raiders (1982–1994), the Los Angeles Chargers (1960 AFL inaugural season), the Los Angeles Dons of the AAFC (1946–1949), the Los Angeles Express of the USFL (1983–1985), the Los Angeles Dragons of the SFL (2000), the Los Angeles Xtreme of the XFL (2001) and the Los Angeles Temptations of the LFL (2009–2011).

The Coliseum grass has not only hosted football games. On April 18, 1958, the Los Angeles Dodgers made their debut in this stadium after their move west from Brooklyn. The Dodgers' opponent on that day was the San Francisco Giants, who had also just moved to California from New York. The Dodgers prevailed by a score of 6–5 in front of 78,672 spectators. The Coliseum was not really suitable for baseball, but for four years, until the completion of the new Dodgers Stadium in 1962, MLB found itself forced to play Dodgers home games on a field that had an abnormal left field (251 feet down the line, 320 to left-center). The Dodgers erected a screen over the left field wall to try to minimize the possibility of easy home runs. In these four years the Coliseum had time to add the 1959 World Series to its long list of notable events hosted. An exhibition game between the Dodgers and Yankees honoring Dodgers catcher Roy Campanella drew 93,103 to the Coliseum on May 7, 1958, the largest crowd to attend a MLB game up to that time. On March 29, 2008, the Dodgers and the Boston Red Sox set a Guinness World Record for the largest attendance ever at a baseball game with a crowd of 115,300 for an exhibition game celebrating the 50th anniversary of the Dodgers in Los Angeles.

A few soccer teams have called the Coliseum home since 1967, when the Los Angeles Toros of the National Professional Soccer League and the Los Angeles Wolves of the United Soccer Association played their seasons there. In 1977 and 1981 NASL's Los Angeles Aztecs played their home games at the Coliseum.

In addition to major sporting events, the name of the Coliseum is also linked to a myriad of famous historical figures who have held several events inside the stadium—from U.S. presidents Franklin D. Roosevelt, Dwight Eisenhower, John F. Kennedy, Lyndon Johnson, Richard Nixon, and Ronald Reagan to Pope John Paul II, Martin Luther King, Jr., the Dalai Lama and Nelson Mandela.

In 1963 evangelist Billy Graham conducted his Southern California crusade from August 15 to September 8, with a crowd of 134,254[8] attending the final night. This is still an all-time attendance record for an event held at the Coliseum.

Several big music concerts have been held at the Coliseum, including Bruce Springsteen's *Born in the U.S.A.* tour in 1985, the Rolling Stones' *Steel Wheels* tour in 1989, and the Roger Waters concert *The Wall Live*, held at the Coliseum on May 19, 2012.

The Coliseum has served as a stage for several TV episodes and movies including *Columbo, Hunter, CHiPs, 24, The Incredible Hulk, Adam-12, The Amazing Race, Two-Minute Warning*, Warren Beatty's *Heaven Can Wait* (where the Coliseum hosts a fictional Super Bowl between the Pittsburgh Steelers and Los Angeles Rams), *North Dallas Forty, Escape from L.A.,* and *Money Talks*.

Notes

1. "Los Angeles Memorial Coliseum: The Story of an LA Icon," *Discoverlosangeles.com*, October 10, 2019, https://www.discoverlosangeles.com/things-to-do/los-angeles-memorial-coliseum-the-story-of-an-la-icon.
2. Elizabeth B. Greene and Edward George Salo, *Buildings and Landmarks of 20th- and 21st-Century America: American Society Revealed* (Santa Barbara, CA: Greenwood, 2018), 13.
3. *Official Report of the 1932 Olympic Games* (Los Angeles: Wolfer Printing Company, 1933), 66, *La84.org*, https://digital.la84.org/digital/collection/p17103coll8/id/7200.
4. "25 Best USC Football Traditions," *Reignoftroy.com*, https://reignoftroy.com/2015/07/28/25-best-usc-football-traditions/8/.
5. "USC Unveils Proposed Preliminary Plans to Renovate Coliseum," *Usctrojans.com*, October 29, 2015, https://usctrojans.com/news/2015/10/29/USC_Unveils_Proposed_Preliminary_Plans_To_Renovate_Coliseum.aspx.
6. Chris Epting, *Los Angeles Memorial Coliseum* (Chicago: Arcadia, 2002), 7.
7. "Chiefs Rams Takes MNF By Storm," *NFL.com*, http://www.nfl.com/videos/nfl-100/0ap3000001059545/NFL-100-Greatest-Games-No-33-Chiefs-Rams-takes-MNF-by-storm-in-2018.
8. "Greatest Non-Sports Moments Los Angeles Coliseum History," *Discoverlosangeles.com*, https://www.discoverlosangeles.com/blog/greatest-non-sports-moments-los-angeles-coliseum-history.

PART 5
The Press

Bob Kelley

Joe Marren

On his 1978 *Stranger in Town* album Bob Seger sang about "a Midwestern boy" who was caught up in the glitz of Hollywood and who was "too far from home" after love fell apart for him out on the coast.

Segue to Robert "Bob" Kelley, who was born May 17, 1917, in Kalamazoo, Michigan, about as Midwestern as the nearby corn and soybean fields. Variously known as The Mall City for its large pedestrian mall; the Paper City for the forests that once supplied the area's paper mills; and the one-time home to Gibson guitars, Kalamazoo typifies the Midwest. But unlike the dude in the Seger song, Kelley didn't necessarily need or want to go back "home." He was doing just fine, thank you, as the "Voice of the Rams," from its days in Cleveland in 1937 until his health gave out in Los Angeles in 1964. See, Kelley was home in those Hollywood Hills that Seger simultaneously praised and damned.

As sure as the "waves tumble over the sand," Kelley made a name and a new life for himself at radio station KMPC (710 on the AM dial) calling Rams games and the minor and major league baseball Angels. Bud Furillo, who for almost 60 years knew more about SoCal sports than an encyclopedia, proclaimed Kelley the gen-u-ine thing: "Ol' Kell was the best football announcer I ever heard."[1]

In a town of big names and booming voices it was Kelley's nightly radio show that popped out bright bolts of energy like a strobe light on steroids as his rants on people and issues rode on metaphorically "miles and miles up those twisting turning roads" of his mind.

The late and great *Los Angeles Times* sportswriter Jim Murray wrote that Kelley's "dinner-hour sports show made as many people gnash their teeth as cheer. But they listened. His mail was sulfuric. But they wrote."[2]

In 1961 Murray wrote: "Kelley became a major figure in the L.A. sport scene, not

Bob Kelley.

necessarily a universally popular one because he dealt in controversy.... Bob was not so good a baseball announcer as football but he blew on the flames of enmity between the old Pacific Coast League Angels and Hollywood Stars so energetically that sellout crowds usually attended the city series and *Life Magazine* once made a lead story out of a brawl he had fanned."[3]

The Dodgers were still the Bums in Brooklyn in 1946 when Kelley and the Rams relocated to the West Coast. But a talented guy with pipes like his couldn't be denied a microphone so he became a Los Angeles Angels fan (owned by the Wrigley family in Chicago—as in, you know, the Cubs) of the Pacific Coast League and called play-by-play of home games on KMPC from 1948 to 1957. And, as other radio stations of the time did, he recreated road games with sound effects.

He was known for his enthusiastic rhetoric when exclaiming, "Well, wotta you know about that!" if an Angels player did something dramatic.[4]

When singing cowboy Gene Autry brought the "new" (as in American League and definitely not PCL) Angels to town in 1961, Kelley got the announcing job on KMPC with Don Wells and Steve Bailey. But there was a catch: Kelley had to promise there would be no controversy. And that was a shame, Murray said, because it was "like giving a sedative to a fast horse. That made Kelley as dull as the league."[5] The dreariness only lasted the inaugural season. Kelley got out of the saddle and only Wells and Bailey again shared the booth in 1962.

But, really, how divisive was the man's style? Was Kelley the forerunner of modern radio shock jocks? Well, yes and no. Jim Healy, who got a star on Hollywood's Walk of Fame in 1991 for his radio career, said, "For its day, Kelley's show was considered red-hot and controversial. It'd just put you to sleep today."[6]

Healy knew what he was talking about because he molded his career after Kelley's and adopted the somewhat formulaic and controversial lightning bolt role, akin to a Kelley 2.0. (Healy was derisively called Dr. Heckle and Mr. Snide.)[7] It may have come with the radio dial because Healy started out at KMPC when Kelley hired him as a writer in the early 1950s for $75 per week.

And yet for Kelley it all started so quietly and innocently. He graduated from high school in Elkhart, Indiana (what Midwesterners will tell folks is the "RV capital of the world"), just 15 miles east of South Bend. From there it was a 243-mile drive east to Cleveland and Western Reserve University (today's Case Western Reserve University). Kelley soon got a job calling play-by-play for Notre Dame football. People noticed and by 1942 he was working at WJR in Detroit calling University of Michigan Wolverines games on Saturdays and then driving back to his other job as sports director at WGAR in Cleveland to do Rams games on Sundays.

Kelley went along for the ride when the Rams left Cleveland for the scene of postwar Los Angeles in 1946. From that moment on his voice chronicled the gametime highs and lows of legends like ends Elroy "Crazylegs" Hirsch and Tom Fears, and quarterback Bob Waterfield, among many others. He would broadcast the so-so 6-win seasons from 1946 to 1948, the glory years of 1949–55, and the slide into mediocrity from 1956, to his heart attacks in 1964 and 1965 and his death in 1966.

In 1958 he was not only calling Rams home games on radio, he had also moved to cover road games on Channel 2 in Los Angeles. It isn't an easy thing to switch from radio mode to TV mode, but Kelley was versatile enough to pull it off and colleagues called him one of the best technical announcers in the business, despite the aura of controversial shows he hosted. In fact, he was twice named the *Los Angeles Times* Sportscaster of the Year.

One of his sons, Pat ("Paraquat") Kelley (more on the son and his unique nickname a little later) said that his dad not only broadcast games but also did some front office work for the Rams when the team was in Cleveland. That camaraderie continued in Los Angeles, according to Kelley Fils.

"Actress Jane Russell would be over at the house sitting by the pool with Bob Waterfield [Russell and Waterfield were married from 1943 to 1968] who was the great quarterback for the Rams, No. 7. And Hamp Pool, who was a great head coach. And these people could party. They're all dead now, and it's not because they lived a long, healthy life. They loved to party,"[8] said Paraquat, who went on to do afternoon drive news at KMET ("the Mighty Met").

OK, time for the story of the nickname: Pat Kelley in the late 1970s once read a news story over the air about the Drug Enforcement Agency warning people who smoked marijuana that it could be laced with the herbicide paraquat, which could cause lung cancer. The incredulity in Kelley's voice and the mock shock struck a nerve with listeners. What shocked the younger Kelley? Why that people who listened to his station would smoke dope! Anyway, the shtick became a hit and so he was nicknamed Paraquat.

"KLOS, our main competitor, couldn't even do a story about paraquat without mentioning my name. It was a big issue back then, you know," Kelley explained.[9]

Regardless of such shenanigans, the coziness between the Kelleys and the team continued in Los Angeles. Rams owner Dan Reeves, after all, was Pat's godfather and Paraquat and his brother, Bob, had jobs helping equipment manager Bill Granholm lug pads and helmets, footballs and tape, water and chalkboards, around as youngsters during training camps at the University of the Redlands. Pat remembered those times in an *Orange County Register* article from 2016:

> One time Ollie Matson caught me taking his dime out of a payphone after he made a collect call, and he chased me until he tackled me and eventually gave me the nickname "The Bandit," which stuck with me.
> More Kelley family photos exist of Pat in his backyard with neighborhood friend Mark Harmon, wearing the Rams' uniforms supplied by their dads. Harmon sports No. 98, made famous by his father, Tom Harmon, the 1940 Heisman Trophy winner from the University of Michigan and one-time Rams player (1946–47) who Bob Kelley helped launch his successful L.A. sportscasting career.[10]

The bonhomie that existed between the team and the Kelleys wouldn't be accepted today. Unprofessional, people would tsk-tsk. But maybe, just maybe, there'd be a certain wistfulness and nostalgia to go with the eye rolls of disproval. Because, after all, it did have a ring of fun to it as the players, the press, the hangers-on and anyone else who could buy a drink gathered at a bar called The Pump Room on Ventura Boulevard that Kelley co-owned with some players.

"My poor mom, she put up with all that craziness," Pat said.[11]

Yet it all certainly helped Healy, as Pat related:

> My dad would leave home to do his sports program at KMPC.... Next door was a bar called The Hucksters. My dad and all the characters from KNXT/Channel 2 … all used The Hucksters as a place to hang.
> These guys were getting blind and Jim Healy would come by and remind my dad that he had to go on in five minutes. 'Go ahead Jim, you go on for me.' That's how Healy got on the air, nine times out of ten. It was because my dad was in there having cocktails with the boys.[12]

Healy essentially verified the story in a *Sports Illustrated* piece from 1978 when he remembered that "I got my first chance when Kelley didn't show up one day. It was at KMPC, which carried the Rams and UCLA games and Pacific Coast League baseball. I just went on the air over those 50,000 watts and did the show."[13]

Given the Kelley-Healy tale maybe things seemed a little loose at good ol' KMPC, but if you got the idea that it was heavy on sports then you caught the hint. By the mid-1940s KMPC (call letters came from a former owner—McMillan Petroleum Company) billed itself as "Southern California's Sports Station." It went through owners (Angels owner Autry owned it for a while) and format changes until reverting to sports again in the late 1990s when it changed its call letters to KSPN, or ESPN Radio 710.

But as far as the Rams and the airwaves were concerned, Kelley was the star, the legend, the pro, the voice. Here's some proof: At the start of the 1951 championship game after the kickoff Kelley was able to announce the name of every player on the field before the first snap from scrimmage. It was fast, but it was coherent.

And since it was Hollywood it shouldn't be a surprise that the radio star also had brief appearances in a movie or two: playing himself in the biopic *Crazylegs* (1953), and typecast (typical, eh?) as a TV announcer alongside friend Jane Russell in *The Fuzzy Pink Nightgown* (1957).

The work and the carousing combined to silence the voice on January 12, 1964, during his play-by-play of the 1964 Pro Bowl in the Coliseum. He was taken away on a stretcher and was well enough to be released from the hospital 10 days later. Kelley recovered for a while but had another heart attack on August 10, 1966. He never regained consciousness and died on September 9. He was 49. A young Dick Enberg, Kelley's broadcast partner in the booth, called the Rams' game two days later.

Pat Kelley was 16 when his father died. Years later, a family priest passed on through a mutual friend a letter the elder Kelley wrote to his son that said: "Dear Pat, Love your family and your God and most of all, love your life. Love, Dad."[14]

Notes

1. "Where Are They Now—Bob Kelley," *Laradio.com*, http://www.laradio.com/wherek.htm.
2. "My Dam Rams," http://mydamrams.tripod.com/index-160.html.
3. Keith Thursby "Bob Kelley—The Voice of the Rams," *Los Angeles Times*, October 12, 2008, https://latimes.com/thedailymirror/2008/10/october-12-1958.html.
4. Abraham Hoffman, "Angels in the Field," *Los Angeles City Historical Society Newsletter*, Summer 2014, 1, 3.
5. Thursby, "Bob Kelley."
6. Larry Stewart. "Healy Star Not Talk of Town," *Los Angeles Times*, November 8, 1991, http://articles.latimes.com/1991-11-08/sports/sp-821_1_healy-star.
7. William Leggett, "Between the Clacks, the Facts," *Sports Illustrated*, June 12, 1978., 46.
8. "Paraquat's Blessed Life," *Laradio.com*, http://www.laradio.com/paraquat.html.
9. "Paraquat's Blessed Life."
10. "50 Years Later, Rams Will Have a Kelley Back in the 710 Radio Booth," *Orange County Register*, August 19, 2016, https://www.ocregister.com/2016/08/19/50-years-later-rams-will-have-a-kelley-back-in-the-710-radio-booth.
11. "50 Years Later, Rams Will Have a Kelley Back in the 710 Radio Booth."
12. "Paraquat's Blessed Life."
13. Leggett, "Between the Clacks, the Facts."
14. "50 Years Later, Rams Will Have a Kelley Back in the 710 Radio Booth."

Bud Furillo and Sid Ziff

Joe Marren

Stop me if you've heard this one. An editor and a reporter walk into a bar…

So what, you say? What's the hook you wanna know? Well, let's develop it a bit. OK, let's see, an editor and a reporter can actually walk into a bar and nothing will happen, right? Or something could happen and it will be hail-fellow-well-met camaraderie. Or something could happen and it will range from just a garden-variety melee up to something awful and bloody. In Hollywood it all depends on the script. For instance—and this is purely hypothetical, you understand—let's say a managing editor (I see Glenn Close in the role) is on the pay phone (remember them?) and an angry citizen (Jason Alexander could *own* this role) takes a shot at the columnist (can we get Randy Quaid?) but misses and hits the ME instead, who is bleeding and asks her city editor (Robert Duvall is a natch) why bullets are coming out of the wall. Can't you feel audiences flocking to the movie?

This is Hollywood, babe, and this "script" from a hypothetical project called—hmmm, I don't know, let's call it *The Paper* for now—is all about the dynamics of a zany day at a big (and I mean *big*) city newspaper. The editor here is the key.

So what kinda editor do we want? Many former newsroom peeps from paragraph factories will say there are two basic types: The coach who patiently teaches and leads by example, and the gruff iron-fist-in-an-iron-glove autocrat who yells and kicks things around while at work but actually has a heart o' gold. Both types inspire and lead and make reporters better. The first type would quietly remind the reporter to do a good job and get the facts straight because it's only the Constitution that's at stake. The second type would yell, "Great Caesar's Ghost, don't call me chief!" and have the reporter make a few dozen more calls to double-check little things like facts.

Hypothetical? The stuff of movies? Oh no, it is very real and the trope has already been adapted. Two prototypes prove it.

Number 1: Bud Furillo wrote and talked about sports in Southern California for 60 years. Besides editing the sports section he also was a columnist for 15 years at the *Los Angeles Herald-Examiner*. His column was called "The Steam Room," and he was aptly nicknamed "The Steamer." After the HerEx (SoCal lingo for the *Herald-Examiner*) gig ended he took his talents to sports radio.

But it's his editing days that are our concern: "He [Furillo] pushed us harder than a drill sergeant, but also loved and nurtured us like a father who we sought desperately to please with our stories," wrote Ed Kociela when Kociela was the city editor of the *Utah Spectrum*.[1]

Another view from another former colleague: "Furillo was famous for his moods and quick temper. But he also could be generous. When one *Herald-Examiner* staff member bought a new house, Furillo gave him a bedroom set. When another bought a house, he took care of all the arrangements and expenses for a house-warming party. Another got a Las Vegas honeymoon, courtesy of Furillo."[2]

Our other prototype and also another Number 1 because it wouldn't be fair or accurate to call him Number 2 or even 1-A was Sid Ziff, who was cast from the same mold. His obituary in *The Los Angeles Times* called him "one of the most controversial and opinionated sports writers in Los Angeles history."[3]

Sid Ziff.

The theme continued a little further down in the article when it mentioned Ziff's editing days: "He was often a tyrant around his staff, but he bore no grudges. Moments after chewing out one of his writers or deskmen, he would casually ask about his family, golf game or night life with a genuine interest. Once, when a particular story didn't come out the way he wanted it, he picked up a typewriter and threw it across the room."[4]

So there we go, two editors trying out for the same role. Only way to choose is to do a screen test. OK, then. Ziff, take 1. Roll 'em.

Ziff was the youngest sports editor of his time when he took over the desk at the now defunct *Los Angeles Express* when he was 19 years old in 1924. But he was already a veteran because he started working at the paper as a copyboy when he was 16. He kept the sports editor's job when the *Express* merged with the evening *Los Angeles Herald* in 1931.

He served in the Army during World War II and went to work as sports editor of the *Valley Green Sheet* in the San Fernando Valley (later *Valley Times*) after his discharge. In May 1950 he was named sports editor of the *Los Angeles Mirror*. When the *Mirror* consolidated with *The Times* in January 1962 Ziff landed on his feet as a sports columnist. He retired from *The Times* five years later, in 1967.

"I'm going to retire now [at age 62] because I don't like writing obituaries about friends who are dying," Ziff explained.[5]

But let's get back to those notorious columns that seemed to be his stock in trade: What were they like? How did they define the man?

First, it helps to know how he wrote them. His writing style, as his obit stated, was conversational because he wrote like he talked, only better. "Old-timers at the *Times-Mirror* recall Ziff walking through the corridors, reading his column [on newsprint before it was printed in the paper] and chuckling to himself. He never looked up, so fellow employees learned to give him a wide berth."

"The guys in the composing room will remember him.... He would write his column and then [instead of rewriting] he would go to the composing room and make corrections after it was set in type. The Linotype operators used to dread seeing him coming," said former *Times* sports editor Paul Zimmerman.[6]

OK, he was quirky. His friends and colleagues also insist that he wrote first and thought later. So where does the controversy come from? Here's an example from a piece

Ziff wrote in early July 1965 about the Dodgers' season (FYI: Just three months later the Dodgers would beat the Minnesota Twins in the World Series, four games to three):

> The natives are getting restless and you can hardly blame them. They're fed up with the banjo hitting of both our local ball clubs. [National League Dodgers and American League Angels.] A red hot Dodger fan says it gets under his skin to see those Dodger peashooters go up to the plate, strike out or hit a little harmless grounder to the infield.
>
> He figures that if the opposition gets one run, the chances of the Dodgers losing the game are 50–50. If the opposition gets two runs, the chances are 85% that the Dodgers will lose, and if they get three runs, nine times out of 10, the game is hopelessly lost.
>
> "Isn't it about time for [general manager] Buzzie Bavasi to get up off his royal highness and get us a hitter or two?" he demands.[7]

Wow. Chill. Time for a review here: The Dodgers had been in first place for two months when Ziff wrote that. To be fair, other sportswriters in Los Angeles were gnashing their teeth over the tight pennant race with the San Francisco Giants up the coast, but the Dodgers would wind up second in the league in fielding (.979) and had reliable Sandy Koufax on the mound. Koufax would lead the league in innings pitched (335.2), wins (26) and ERA (2.04). So things weren't all the doom and gloom that Ziff bemoaned.

Ziff is also reputedly the real wit behind one of the great literary putdowns (which has also been attributed to Dorothy Parker): "This is not a novel to be tossed aside lightly. It should be thrown with great force." Revisionists say Ziff really wrote it, though differently, in a newspaper piece that was picked up by *Reader's Digest* in the February 1960 edition: "It is not a book to be lightly thrown aside. It should be thrown with great force."[8]

That great wit and force didn't mean that Ziff was always a "hey kid, get off my lawn!" type of guy. He knew talent when he read it and he supported it. For example, he supported Jeane Hoffman who covered the Dodgers: "She spent 12 years in Philadelphia and New York at major newspapers there, covering all sports, before she came to *The Times*. She knows the baseball picture there and here thoroughly."[9]

After his retirement Ziff led a quiet life with friends. He died at age 86 of an acute blood infection in November 1991.

OK, time for the second screen test. Furillo, take 1. Annnnd ... action!

Furillo was one of four original Angels beat reporters. But The Steamer really wrote about the whole Los Angeles sports scene as teams invaded the area from Cleveland (the Rams), Brooklyn (the Dodgers), and Minneapolis (the Lakers). What also caught his attention was USC football, UCLA basketball, horse races and boxing, among others.

With so much to cover, as well as to edit when he put on his green eyeshade, and with competition from other L.A. dailies and broadcasters, the HerEx sports section had to be lively through eight daily editions. To guard against the grind a little irreverence is to be expected, especially from a young staff earning pauper's wages compared to the reporters and editors at *The Times*. Whatever the HerEx had in creative capability, it was Furillo who helped find the right niche. Supposedly then-mayor Tom Bradley complained that the good people of Los Angeles would pull the sports section out of the HerEx to read and dump the rest of the paper, clogging drains all across La-La Land.

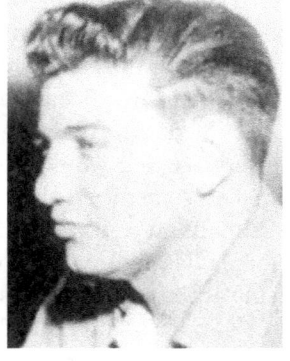

Bud Furillo.

Whether that's true or not, Furillo had fun with the aura and panache the section set for the paper. When he actually decided to take that rare vacation his "The Steam Room" column space would not be filled with a canned column from long ago, but instead it would say "Bud Furillo's Typewriter Is Broken. His Column Will Resume When It Is Fixed."

And that biting humor carried over to more personal dealings. Lakers owner Jack Kent Cooke moved the press box waaaay up to the rafters in the Forum and Furillo was, shall we say, less than pleased. So once, when Cooke was showing Furillo pix of his Santa Barbara ranch, Furillo pointed to a spot waaaay up on a mountain looking down on the ranch and said, "Look, Jack, there's the press box."[10]

That irreverence, that cheek, that impertinence was all part and parcel of being a newsperson, of not being afraid to check and to challenge.

"Bud taught us how to look beyond the box score for a story, how to write tightly, how to dig for a story, how to be a reporter. We knew we were in the shadow of greatness, we just didn't realize at the time how great," Kociela wrote.[11]

Former baseball manager and Hall of Famer Sparky Anderson grew up with Furillo and said of him: "He was honest. You could trust him. I never cared if Bud gave me a little tap. Because if he wrote it, it was true."[12]

But the honesty came with a price. Furillo was driven and although he had crazy mad skills and dedication to his craft, he also had an intricate personality.

"If he was something mechanical, he'd be an elevator. He [was] as complex as Chinese geometry," said a former KABC-AM colleague, Tommy Hawkins, the former Lakers player and Dodgers exec.[13] "He was totally dedicated to his craft. A hard-nosed journalist who wanted nothing to do with speculation, only facts. Yet he was on top of every story."[14]

Newspaper people generally agreed, but also knew what drove Furillo. Former protégée Steve Bisheff nailed it when quoted in this online piece written by Steve Dilbeck:

> Bud Furillo was an original. He worked hard, played hard, drank hard, lived hard.
>
> He was an absolute character. Equal parts moodiness and brilliance, old-school and innovator, teacher and celebrity, wild and serious.
>
> He was all sports journalist. Ink flowed in his veins, even years after he left as sports editor of the old *Herald-Examiner* to devote his full attention to sports radio.
>
> "I never met anybody who loved newspapering like he did," Bisheff told Dilbeck.[15]

Doug Krikorian, who cut his journalistic chops as a Furillo pupil, said the boss could write a column in 30 or so minutes and lay out an entire sports section in even less time. Maybe so, maybe not, but it's clear that the man was a force of nature in his own orbit and also kept pace with his celebrity friends du jour and of days gone by.

And did I mention celebrities? Simply put, he knew everyone. Walter Winchell would join him for drinks at Toots Shor's when Furillo was in New York City. Or he'd meander down Broadway to Jack Dempsey's restaurant to talk the fight game. Krikorian said it wouldn't be unusual for Elvis, or Brando, or Sinatra to call Furillo at the paper for a chat. Kociela would add Ali, Wilt the Stilt, Tommy Lasorda, Bear Bryant to the list. And Bisheff remembers the time that Furillo introduced him to jockey Eddie Arcaro, Arnold Palmer and columnist Jimmy Cannon. When Furillo was president of the Southern California Baseball Writers Association he got Sinatra, Dean Martin, and Sammy Davis, Jr., to sing at the organization's annual dinner.

So if Furillo had all these connections, what did he get out of it, besides a night of songs and jokes from some of the Rat Pack for his fellow newsfolks? Sing it with me now, R-E-S-P-E-C-T. Take care. TCB.

Here's the proof:

When John Robinson became USC's head football coach in 1972 he said Furillo's columns were must reading because Furillo was always there asking questions.

If you don't care for Robinson, how about former Dodgers manager Tommy Lasorda: "Bud Furillo was right in the middle of it.... You couldn't wait to read the *Herald-Examiner* to see what The Steamer was saying. He covered every sport and brought out things nobody else could ever do."[16]

All right, so you say you're not inclined to agree with a college football coach or a pro baseball manager. You say a college hoops star is more your cup of tea. Is that whom you'd like to hear from bunky? Then how about UCLA's own Bill Walton: "In 1972 I trusted Bud Furillo to tell my story. He got it better than perfect."[17]

Why did such a mix of people trust Furillo? Because he cared. He wanted to tell a story and get it right, it's what news people do. He was also a fan and cared about the teams he covered and the people who played the sports he loved. Objectivity? Nah. After all, readers want to care, too. Columnists and fans are allowed to bleed Dodgers and Rams blue.

Furillo was born in 1925 in Hubbard, Ohio, northeast of Youngstown and near the state line with Pennsylvania. The family moved to California in 1940. After graduating from high school in 1943 he served in the Merchant Marine until 1946. He briefly attended East Los Angeles College for a year while also working at the Bethlehem Steel plant in Los Angeles County.

All that was prelude for the start of his newspaper career in 1947 as a copy boy at the *Los Angeles Herald-Express*, which merged with the *Examiner* and became the *Herald-Examiner* in 1962. Furillo was sports editor from 1964 to 1974.

Besides editing, Furillo covered the NFL title game on December 23, 1951, in the Los Angeles Memorial Coliseum when the Rams beat the Cleveland Browns, 24–17.

Rams Coach Joe Stydahar had been alternating quarterbacks Bob Waterfield and Norm Van Brocklin all season. In the championship game, Stydahar put Van Brocklin in for the first time during the second half. It might not have been a genius move, but it worked. Late in the fourth quarter, with the score tied at 17 apiece, Van Brocklin connected with wide receiver Tom Fears for a 73-yard touchdown.

Van Brocklin later told Furillo that he noticed in the first half that Fears could get good separation on Browns defensive back Tommy James.

"So when I got in there I kept pitching to Tom [Fears] until we hit the jackpot," Van Brocklin told Furillo.[18]

It marked the end of five consecutive titles for the Browns (1946–49 in the AAFC and the 1950 NFL). So how did Paul Brown take it? In stride: "It was Joseph's [Stydahar] turn today," Brown told Furillo.[19]

Such stoicism wasn't always present in Furillo's own life. In 1974 Furillo started his sports talk show at KABC-AM. The HerEx essentially told him he had to pick one, either the paper or the radio; he couldn't keep both jobs. So Furillo chose radio, though not without some cost.

"He told me he cried the day he left the *Herald*," said former colleague Joe Jares.[20]

Furillo's voice also went over the airwaves at KIIS-FM, KFOX-FM, and KPSI-FM before he retired in 2000.

He wrote about sports and talked about sports as Los Angeles got its big league teams and its college teams shone in the spotlight. Furillo was in the middle of it all.

Hawkins put it best: "There was nobody bigger in this town that Bud Furillo as a sportswriter."[21]

Furillo died in July 2006. He was 80.

Notes

1. Ed Kociela "Chapter in Sports History Closes," *Utah Spectrum*, July 22, 2006, A6.
2. Larry Stewart, "Furillo Was a Different Type of Columnist," *Los Angeles Times*, July 20, 2006, D2.
3. Glick, Shav Glick, "Ziff, Former Columnist of The Times, Dies at 86," *Los Angeles Times*, November 5, 1991, C3.
4. Glick, "Ziff," C3.
5. Glick, "Ziff," C3.
6. Glick, "Ziff," C3.
7. Jan Weisman, "Remembering '65: Jim Murray and fellow critics scorn first-place Dodgers," *Dodgers. mlblogs.com*, https://dodgers.mlblogs.com/remembering-65-jim-murray-and-fellow-critics-scorn-first-place-dodgers-b1f0a175b86a.
8. "This Is Not a Novel To Be Tossed Aside Lightly. It Should Be Thrown with Great Force," *Quoteinvestigator.com*, https://quoteinvestigator.com/tag/sid-ziff.
9. Jean Hastings Ardell, *Sabr.org*, "Jeane Hoffman: California Girl Makes Good in Press Box," https://sabr.org/research/jeane-hoffman-california-girl-makes-good-press-box.
10. Steve Bisheff, "Bud Furillo 'Nailed It' as a Sports Journalist," *Orange County Register*, July 19, 2006, https://www.ocregister.com/2006/07/19/bud-furillo-nailed-it-as-a-sports-hournalist/.
11. Stewart, "Bud Furillo, 80: Covered Southland Sports," *Los Angeles Times*, July 19, 2006, B10.
12. Kociela, "Chapter in Sports History Closes," A6.
13. Steve Dilbeck, "'The Steamer' Was One of a Kind," *Thefreelibrary.com*, https://www.thefreelibrary.com.
14. Dilbeck, "'The Steamer."
15. Bisheff, "Bud Furillo 'Nailed It.'"
16. Mitch Chortkoff, "Bud Furillo, The Steamer; A Great Read for Sports Fans," *Culver City Observer*, July 14, 2016, https://www.culvercityobserver.com/story/2016/07/14/sports/bud-furillo-the-steamer-a-great-read-for-sports-fans.
17. Chortkoff, "Bud Furillo."
18. Andy Furillo, *The Steamer; Bud Furillo and the Golden Age of L.A. Sports* (Solana Beach, CA: Santa Monica Press, 2016), 33–34.
19. Furillo, *The Steamer; Bud Furillo and the Golden Age of L.A. Sports*, 33–34.
20. Dilbeck, "'The Steamer.'"
21. Dilbeck, "'The Steamer.'"

Bob Oates and Melvin Durslag

Joe Marren

Someone once said that the advantage to a long career is outliving the critics. Someone might actually think that's wryly funny. Ha, I guess.

Or one could take the opposite point of view and testify that a long career puts the shine to the trophy, pleases the critics and fans and wanna-be imitators as the world applauds. Such is the case of Bob Oates and Melvin Durslag, who each wrote about the Southern California sports scene for decades and decades (and decades and decades, almost—but not quite—ad infinitum. And I said "almost" because only plastic lasts forever).

Oates, the analytical Xs and Os guy, covered the Rams and so much more for the Hearst newspapers and then the *Los Angeles Times*. He was a sportswriter, either part- or full-time, for some 70 years (most of it in Los Angeles), and even wrote an online free-lance football column on *The Times*' website during retirement (along with a couple books) from 1995 to 2007. Finally—and emphasize that—retiring at age 91 in 2007.

People noticed. How could they not? In recognition of a distinguished career that was still in its metaphorical middle age at the time, Oates won the Dick McCann Memorial Award in 1974 from the Pro Football Writers of America.

The indefatigable Oates and *Green Bay Press-Gazette's* Art Daley were the last of the original 1962 Hall of Fame Selection Committee members for several years in the 21st century. Daley became the last surviving member when Oates died in April 2009. (Daley would die at age 94 just about two years later on February 19, 2011.)

Oates' long working streak included the first 39 Super Bowls. That streak only ended when he skipped Super Bowl XL (on February 5, 2006, in Ford Field, Detroit, when the Steelers beat the Seahawks, 21–10) at age 90. He took it off to care for his ailing wife, Marnie, who had fallen several months earlier. Marnie died later that month and Oates never worked another Super Bowl.

Moving on from Oates, Durslag wrote for Hearst corporation's *Los Angeles Examiner*, its later iteration as the *Herald-Examiner*, as well as a few years at the *Times* after the HerEx folded. He also free-lanced for a number of national publications.

His career spanned more than 50 years and included 10 Olympic Games, 35 Kentucky Derbys, 30 Masters Tournaments, 34 World Series, and championship bouts that included old(ish) school and even older boxers from Muhammad Ali, to Sugar Ray Robinson and even Rocky Marciano, among others. So with all that he had to have won some awards, right? Oh man, did he ever. Durslag won a National Headliners Award in 1960; was named California Sportswriter of the Year seven times; and was inducted into the

Bob Oates.

National Sportscasters and Sportswriters Association Hall of Fame on April 24, 1995.

Those weren't the only honors he received. Durslag was awarded a Bronze Star during service in the China-Burma-India Theater of Operations during World War II with the 20th Bomber Command. His experiences led him to write a short story that *Esquire* bought for $300, which his family thought would get him in the door as a screenwriter. Durslag, though, went back to the *Examiner*. Perhaps he was lured back by the princely salary of $75 per week? Umm, no, obviously there was more than mere money involved. Journalism suited Durslag because he also would later serve on the Board of Directors for the University of Southern California (he got his B.A. from there in 1943); was a member of Sigma Delta Chi; and was a voting member of the ESPY Awards Academy.

There it is, two sportswriters who had outstanding parallel careers in the same city. How lucky can one megalopolis be? To answer, let's look at both. Though Oates will be first.

He was born May 20, 1915, in Aberdeen, South Dakota. Writing teachers hate clichés, but if one were to use one then it could be said that Oates had ink in his veins: He published a weekly newspaper in high school and worked for a daily while a student at Yankton College (a small liberal arts college that was open from 1881 to 1984). On September 2, 1936, he traveled 544 miles almost directly east to cover the Chicago Charities College All-Star Game between the National Football League champion Detroit Lions and the college senior all stars for the *Yankton Press & Dakotan* newspaper. Maybe the game itself was so-so—it ended in a 7–7 tie—but it probably lit a fire in Oates because after graduation he and his wife moved to Los Angeles in 1937 so that Oates could write for a larger audience in what would soon enough become a major-league city.

Oates covered the USC and UCLA (where he earned a master's degree in journalism) football teams since 1939 for Hearst's *Examiner* newspaper, as well as the minor league Los Angeles Bulldogs (the team lasted from 1936 to 1948) and Hollywood Bears (with a shelf life from 1940 to 1948). When the NFL Rams moved from Cleveland to Los Angeles in 1946 Oates covered them, or other doings-around-the-league after the Rams moved to St. Louis in 1995.

Hearst merged the evening *Herald* and morning *Examiner* newspapers to create the *Herald-Examiner* (evenings and Sunday mornings) in 1962. Oates was part of the HerEx package until taking his talent and analytic skills to the *Los Angeles Times* in 1968. And make no mistake, his writing was very good, but it was his ability to analyze the details that made his stock soar.

"He loved the business, and he was the kind of writer who was fascinated by game strategy. He was part sportswriter and part coach," said one of his former editors at the *Times*, Bill Dwyre.[1]

Take this example that examines the play of offensive skill positions from a series of articles spanning decades. The insight alone is worth the price of admission and beats any time spent playing a video game named after a former NFL coach and broadcaster who hated to travel by plane. The study began with a September 3, 1991, article in the *Times* about rotating quarterbacks for strategic purposes:

> In the early 1950s after the Rams had drafted Norm Van Brocklin, they found themselves with two No. 1 quarterbacks on a team that Bob Waterfield led to the NFL championship in 1945.
> What to do?
> The coach, Joe Stydahar, had no hand in drafting either man and didn't welcome the problem but came up with a solution: He alternated Waterfield and Van Brocklin—not by the game, which would have been novel enough, but by the quarter.
> And in 1951, the Rams had another NFL championship ....

New York Giants president Wellington Mara, whose team was faced with the same unique choice between Phil Simms and Jeff Hostetler at the start of the 1991 season, toyed with those thoughts of rotating a QB.

"The Stydahar solution worked because (Ram owner) Danny Reeves had a sound ship. And I'm confident, in the same circumstances, it will work again," Oates wrote.[2]

For a little context, the Giants had beaten the Buffalo Bills, 20–19, in Super Bowl XXV on January 27, 1991, with Hostetler at quarterback filling in for an injured Simms. By contrast, the 25-year-old Van Brocklin and 31-year-old Waterfield were pretty evenly matched in 1951. In a 12-game regular season The Dutchman completed 100 passes for 1,725 yards and 13 touchdowns, and Waterfield connected on 88 passes for 1,566 yards and 13 touchdowns. Both went to the Pro Bowl.

But what about the role that coaches on the sidelines and receivers on the field play into how well a quarterback shines? In a series of blog posts by Oates from 2006 that the *Chicago Tribune* picked up from the *Times* the analyst nonpareil Oates puts it this way:

> The ever-increasing high quality of football is one of the NFL stories of the new century. Asked to explain what's going on, Philadelphia quarterback Donovan McNabb said, "Big-time players are making big plays in big games."
> It is, of course, the passers and their creatively designed offenses that are making the principal difference.
> It is a world of star quarterbacks that has arrived, not by chance but by design. Two forces make it inevitable.
> First, the NFL's club owners have been tinkering with the rules of football for years, steadily making a good game better.
> Second, within the context of all that, the coaching of football players and teams has for years steadily improved—on all three levels: pro, college and high school.
> NFL coaching staffs now often number 20 or 21 different experts who have devoted their lives to football.[3]

Break it all down and throwing is just one part of the passing game. A good quarterback needs good receivers to throw to. And coaches look for specific things in receivers, according to a 1991 Oates story:

> As for the ability to hustle, the minimum 40-yard speed is 4.6 seconds, for example, for wide receivers with a D body build.
> "D is an ideal body," analyst Duke Babb said at the national scouting combine office in Tulsa, Okla. "A is short and light, B short and heavy, C tall and light."
> In the NFL of two or three decades ago, nobody even asked about B builds, or even D. Although there probably was as much talent then, proportionally, as there is now, sports science was in its infancy.
> "In the '50s and '60s, we only had one full-time scout for the whole country," said Hall of Famer Sid Gillman. Gillman was a former coach of the Los Angeles Rams.[4]

OK, we've talked about quarterbacks and their receivers. So what's the role of the running game in all this? Just read and compare it to how the G.O.A.T., Tom Brady, uses it, as per Oates' observations:

> Part of his [Brady's] success over the years has been due to the nature of pass offense. Though it's difficult for any team to proceed on pass plays alone, it can occasionally be done by good passing teams. The opposite doesn't happen. A good running game isn't enough today without a pass-play threat.
>
> Indeed the reason to develop pass offense first, and running-play offense only subsequently, is that football teams can sometimes win on pass plays alone—if they pass smartly enough. By contrast, a good running team is no threat to beat a good passing team.[5]

Such is the analytical spirit Oates brought to his Los Angeles readers and, later, to the rest of the country.

"Coach" Oates died in late April 2009. He was 93.

A contemporary of Oates who shared newsrooms and pressboxes with him was Durslag, who was born on April 29, 1921, in Chicago. There's another connection with Oates: Both began their forays into journalism while in school. Durslag's family moved to Los Angeles when he was a child and he started working for the *Examiner* as a stringer getting paid 10 cents an inch when he was a senior at Los Angeles High School. He began working full-time at $15 a week in 1939 while a freshman at USC. He stayed at the *Examiner* (with time out for World War II), then later the HerEx, until it closed in 1989. Durslag spent the final two years of his career at the *Los Angeles Times*, from November of 1989 to May of 1991 when he retired.

But almost 50 years at one paper was not enough for a man with his talents. He also was a *Sporting News* columnist from 1950 to 1984, a columnist for *TV Guide* for 30 years, and contributed articles to the *Saturday Evening Post*, *Collier's*, *Sports Illustrated*, *Playboy* and *Esquire* magazines from 1947 to 1990.

It's obvious Durslag was in demand. He quite simply had a gift. The way he could paint a scene—his mise en scene, or artful way to tell a story—put readers in the locker room, on the field, in the coach's office, wherever there was action. An example comes from an article that ran in the *San Francisco Examiner* (like the *Los Angeles Examiner*, a Hearst newspaper) after the Cleveland Browns lost to the Rams in the 1951 title game (the scene, which reads like a movie script, is set outside Cleveland's locker room and shows Paul Brown reacting to the 24–17 loss):

Melvin Durslag.

> The pacing continued, the course narrowing now to small circles as football's miracle man twisted uneasily inside his jacket while dry washing his hands. Then stopping suddenly, he turned and snapped:
>
> "You saw the game didn't you? Well, draw your own conclusions. I haven't any kicks."
>
> He considered this a moment, then added, "Look, there was an interference penalty, a fumble with a guy running to our one-yard line, and an intercepted pass. Seventeen points, just like that. Okay? Well, okay. You saw the game...."

Turning to a player shuffling along the corridor, Brown called, "Hey, you, don't look so glum."

Brown sat down.[6]

Writing like that gets people reading and noticing, which means Durslag's beat wasn't always in sports. He was off the sports desk and writing a page 2 news column from 1953 to 1956, which is when he took over from lead sports columnist Vincent X. Flaherty. After that Durslag would write seven columns a week for about a decade and, in turn, those columns were syndicated by Hearst's King Features.

And because he worked in Los Angeles, there was also the entertainment biz close by. He wrote a 1950 episode of *You Asked for It*, which *IMDb* describes as a television show that "responded to requests from the viewer, e.g., [asking for] a look into the vaults at Fort Knox, showing $1 million in $1 bills, etc." And also a 1955 episode of *The Millionaire*, which *IMDb* says was a show in which "a millionaire indulges himself giving away one million dollars apiece to persons that he has never met."

Durslag never got any of the 1950s loot. It was fiction anyway. Nor did he get the job he tried out for in 1961. As the story goes, Jim Murray and Durslag were the final choices for a sports columnist gig at *The Times*. Murray got the job. Durslag's time at *The Times* would come along later, after the HerEx folded.

So let's review:

Durslag loses the loot in the fictional world of TV shows. Strike 1.

He doesn't get the job at *The Times*. Strike 2.

Ah, but unlike Casey he didn't strike out. In fact, Durslag hit a home run when measured in appreciation and praise for the causes he championed and from the friends and sources he made. (Newspaper columnists don't have foes ... right?)

For instance: In 1959 he was writing columns and articles supporting a referendum to give Los Angeles Dodgers owner Walter O'Malley (who had just moved his team from Brooklyn) property in Chavez Ravine to build a stadium. Dodger Stadium was completed in 1962.

In the early 1960s he criticized the Rose Bowl bosses for considering dropping the Big Ten in favor of schools that were segregated. They didn't.

And in the early 1980s he castigated the NFL and Commissioner Pete Rozelle in the legal battles to not allow Al Davis to move the Raiders to Los Angeles. They moved.

In short, Durslag saw that the game was changing. Sports owners, teams, leagues and administrators were making decisions based on business interests and not fan wishes. It was really always that way, but the sportswriters didn't wise up until people like Durslag wrote about the developments.

Three former colleagues appreciated his work and complimented him from different viewpoints, which is probably only natural for a man of Durslag's abilities.

Former HerEx sports reporter Bob Keisser wrote that Durslag "was a brilliant writer who was years ahead of the industry in focusing on the issues that have become standard in sports these days—franchise movement, over-reaching owners, the use of public money for facilities, performance-enhancing drugs."[7]

But it's the writing that matters, as former HerEx sports editor Rick Arthur noted: "The droll humour; the elegant turn of phrase; the mix of short, medium and long sentences; the engaging lede; the just-strong-enough-walk-off; the well-founded skewering of fools and villains—his writing provided lessons for us all."[8]

Former colleague Doug Krikorian wrote that Durslag was "the elder statesman of the Los Angeles sporting literati."⁹

The causes he cared about, the skills he brought to bear on everything he wrote made him, in the words of an appreciative Dodgers man, "the Rembrandt of sports columnists."

But even the great ones don't last forever. Durslag died after a brief illness in a Santa Monica hospital in July 2016. He was 95.

Notes

1. Claire Noland, "L.A. Sportswriter Covered 39 Straight Super Bowl Games," *Los Angeles Times*, April 29, 2009, A26.
2. Bob Oates, "'51 Rams Invested Their Quarters Wisely," *Los Angeles Times*, September 3, 1991, C5.
3. Bob Oates, "The Game Is Better Than Ever," *Chicago Tribune*, http://www.chicagotribune.com/la-sp-oates10oct10-story.html.
4. Bob Oates, "Unitas, Berry Wouldn't Measure Up Today," *The Baltimore Sun*, June 9, 1991, http://baltimoresun.com/news/bs-xpm-1991-06-09-1991160091-story.html.
5. Bob Oates, "False-Start Day," *Chicago Tribune*, December 26, 2006, http://www.chicagotribune.com/la-sp-oates26dec26-story.html.
6. Melvin Durslag, "Brown Laments 'Dinky Little Things'—Cites Breaks Leading to 17 LA Points," *San Francisco Examiner*, December 24, 1951, 17.
7. Kevin Roderick, "Melvin Durslag, 95, Longtime LA Sports Columnist," *Laobserved.com*, July 18, 2016, http://laobserved.com/archive/2016/07/melvin_durslag_95_longtim.php.
8. Roderick, "Melvin Durslag."
9. Jill Leovy, "Melvin Durslag, Longtime Los Angeles Sportswriter and Columnist, Dies at 95," *Los Angeles Times*, July 18, 2016, http://www.latimes.com/local/obituaries/la-me-melvin-durslag-20160718-snap-story.html.

Paul B. Zimmerman, Dick Hyland and Frank Finch

Joe Marren

Before you and I start this jaunt down memory lane there's something that needs to be cleared up right away, as in immediately, pronto, without delay. Ready? You sure? OK, here goes.

Paul Zimmerman of the *Los Angeles Times* was NOT the Paul Zimmerman of the *New York Post*, aka the celebrated Dr. Z from *Sports Illustrated*. They weren't even related. Sorta like "twin sons of different mothers," ya know.

Frank "Tricky Dick" Hyland was NOT the same "Tricky Dick" (Nixon) of presidential infamy, even if they did both live in Southern California at one time or another.

And Frank Finch was NOT even remotely connected to George Plimpton's Sidd Finch or Harper Lee's Atticus Finch. The first Finch was real, the second two were fictional Finchionals.

All right then, if we have the would-be confusion out of the way, the question becomes, "So who were they?" Well, clearly they have some connection to Los Angeles sports if they're in this book, more specifically to the media if they're in this section of the book. But to be precise, all three were at one time or another reporters, or columnists, and/or editors with the *Times* and other SoCal media outlets.

In particular:

Zimmerman was a sports editor at *The Times* from 1939 to 1968. It's believed (though records don't help with any degree of certainty) that he is the only sportswriter to have covered both the 1932 and 1984 Los Angeles Summer Olympics, as well as the 1960 Winter Olympics almost 500 miles north of Los Angeles in Squaw Valley, California. Actually, Zimmerman covered eight summer games, beginning in 1932 for the *Associated Press;* 1948–68 ('48, '52, '56, '60, '64 and '68) for the *Times;* and 1984 for the *Times* and a Japanese newspaper. Add on the 1960 winter games and he covered nine total Olympiads. (Although Zimmerman had retired by 1984, he still wrote some pieces for the *Times'* section that previewed the 1984 Olympics and did some work for the Japanese newspaper.)

Hyland was an Olympic rugby gold medal winner (Paris, 1924), who went back to football after the Olympics when he attended Stanford University. (He was an All-American halfback who played in the 1927 and 1928 Rose Bowl games; a sprinter on the track team; and he also played baseball for the college.) After college Hyland was a reporter and then columnist for the *Los Angeles Times*. For a while, starting in 1932, he simultaneously worked at KFWB radio in Los Angeles. In 1966 he moved about 120 miles east to Palm Desert, California, and became sports editor of the *Palm Desert Post*.

Finch covered the Pacific Coast League baseball teams in Los Angeles for the *Times* and then the major league Rams and Dodgers when the teams moved to the Los Angeles market. In all, he was a sportswriter for more than four decades.

Now that the introductions are done, let's get to know them a little better.

First, the un–Dr. Z: Covering college football was his forte, especially since the Rams didn't arrive in town until 1946. And speaking of shifting franchises, Zimmerman got a commendation from the City of Angels for his role in helping pave the way for Walter O'Malley to move his Dodgers there in 1958. We can imagine the Brooklyn fans had other thoughts about that.

In 1927, after graduation from the University of Nebraska, Zimmerman headed west to the coast. He eventually became sports editor back in the days when the editors were also known for their column inches expressing anything from outrage to sangfroid, or some-

Paul B. Zimmerman.

thing somewhere in-between. Zimmerman, however, was better known as an editor than a columnist. However, that didn't necessarily match his outlook.

"The writing was the part I liked," he said.[1]

But still, it was the editor in him that people admired.

"Zimmerman typified the old-time sportswriter and editor who emphasized the nuts and bolts of a sports section and was straightforward in his writing style," said Murray Olderman, the sports cartoonist and writer. (Don't get confused and think it's Keith Olbermann. The names just sound the same.) "There was still a lot of Nebraska in him in his approach to sports."[2]

Just about everyone respected him, including a future National Football League commissioner. Pete Rozelle (PR guy for the Rams 1952–1955, GM 1957–1960 and NFL commish 1960–1989) once said he "wanted to take his [Zimmerman's] job away someday." Rozelle knew all about Zimmerman because Rozelle worked weekends at the *Long Beach Press-Telegram* while in high school in Compton, California, and felt the fire of professional competition even then.[3]

Zimmerman wouldn't have surrendered his job to the young Rozelle, even though Zimmerman did have a touch of noblesse oblige. For instance, he was once director of *Times* Charities and director of the Helms Foundation Hall of Fame, which began in Los Angeles in 1936. He covered the *Times* charity game in Los Angeles for many years. As he pointed out about the significance of the game, "Los Angeles becomes the football capital of the world tonight…" and then he would insert whomever was playing that year.[4]

Also, Zimmerman was named to the National Football Foundation Honors Court in 1951; in 1968 he won the Jake Wade Award given to a media person who has made an outstanding contribution to intercollegiate athletics; and in 1976 he was presented with The Bert McGrane Award, given by the Football Writers Association of America to an FWAA member "who has performed great service to the organization and/or the writing profession." As if all that wasn't enough, in 1984 Zimmerman was named to the Orange County Sports Hall of Fame.

Such respect can even get you a seat in a restaurant regardless of the hour or circumstances. Oh, there are patrons in your private booth? Well, they'll just have to skedaddle.

"After putting the final edition to bed, the copy editors often repaired to the Redwood.... Paul Zimmerman, the old sports editor, maintained a booth there, and paying customers were expected to scram when he showed up. At the Redwood, there was a red telephone hanging from the wall. This editorial batphone ... had an extension on *The Times* switchboard," according to a nostalgic piece comparing the paper's old haunts around downtown Los Angeles to its new neighborhood in El Segundo, about 19 or so miles southwest from downtown.[5]

Zimmerman was just a phone call away from the paper's office. That's confidence. And he was equally confident about the '51 Rams because of the offensive talent. He believed that guys like quarterbacks Bob Waterfield and Norm Van Brocklin could light up the scoreboard with receivers Elroy "Crazylegs" Hirsch and Tom Fears. But it was the line play that worried Zimmerman in 1951:

> As everyone who follows [the] National Football League knows, [head coach Joe] Stydahar's Rams promptly won the Western Division title and had the lead in the title playoff with less than a minute to go when [Cleveland's] Otto Graham and clan nipped the greatest ambitions in the bud.
>
> This amazing turn of events only serves to indicate how absurd it is to count the Rams out this fall although their four veteran tackles are gone.
>
> What happened is history. Dick Huffman [offensive and defensive tackle], All-Pro tackle for four years, jumped to the Canadian League. Despite a Rams injunction, he hasn't returned. [And he wouldn't, 1950 was his last year in the NFL.] Bob Reinhard [defensive tackle] and Gil Bouley [OT and DT] retired. Ed Champagne [OT and DT] also moved north of the border.[6]

Still, Zimmerman wasn't ready to panic. He seemed relieved when he wrote a few days later "line coach Ray Richards has worked hard with rookies Charley [*sic*] Toogood [DT], Jim Winkler [DT], Howard Ruetz [DT who would play for the Green Bay Packers in 1951], Bobby Collier [OT, DT], and Tom Dahms [OT] to plug the gap."[7]

As it turns out, things worked out in the season and the championship game. That championship season of 1951 wasn't the only highlight in Zimmerman's career. The career was impressively bookended by Super Bowl games. Zimmerman covered the first Super Bowl (though it wasn't called that back then), on January 15, 1967, in the Los Angeles Memorial Coliseum when the Green Bay Packers beat the Kansas City Chiefs, 35–10. He died January 28, 1996, the day Dallas beat Pittsburgh, 27–17, in Super Bowl XXX. Zimmerman was 92.

Now on to "Tricky Dick" (real name Frank ... well, could be), the "famously immodest" Hyland. The star athlete-turned-sportswriter was also known as the "hottest typewriter" in the sports world, or so said Keith Monroe in *The Saturday Evening Post*'s November 13, 1948, edition.

Hyland might have been called "Tricky Dick," because it's tricky to nail down specifics in his bio. There are discrepancies about his real first name, how he got his nickname, and his vagabond lifestyle. The real answers are out there, but it depends on the sources one uses and how one weighs the facts to decide what sounds credible.

This much is known for sure: Hyland was born July 26, 1900. Maybe. Nah, just kidding, all research agrees on that. Things get murky from now on. He was christened

Francis William Hyland, Jr., but at various times and in various publications his name was also either Richard William Hyland, or Richard Francis Hyland; and several sources and some newspaper articles list him as Frank Hyland. Whoa.

To further complicate things, it's up for debate where Hyland got his moniker of "Tricky Dick." One source will say he earned it playing football on the playing fields of San Francisco's St. Ignatius Preparatory School.[8] Others will say he got it for his fast footwork playing football for Stanford before going off to the Olympics. Regardless of the case, he definitely had the nickname by 1924 when he was one of the stars of the U.S. Olympic Gold Medal rugby team. A 1989 story in *American Heritage* magazine mentioned that on the team was "the famously immodest ... ('Tricky Dick') Hyland, a Stanford football halfback."[9]

Dick Hyland.

Besides the conflicting claims about Hyland's name and background, there's also the very real knock against him being "famously immodest," which has been mentioned twice in two paragraphs. It has to do with a comparison a sportswriter once made between Hyland's athleticism and the equally impressive athletic prowess of Jim Thorpe. Hyland's ego couldn't let it go: "Hell, Thorpe never had my swerve!" he reportedly said.[10]

Thorpe also didn't have Hyland's personal life and his penchant for Hollywood starlet wives. And this will get vague again—sound familiar?—but some articles say all of the wives were connected with Hollywood. Some don't. *The Internet Movie Database* says that wife #1 (Adela Nora Rogers St. Johns) was a journalist, novelist and screenwriter though not an actor; wife #2 (Louise Matthews Lansburgh) had no connection with Hollywood as far as *IMDb* is concerned; but wives 3 (Ann Staunton) and 4 (Rochelle Elizabeth Hudson) really were starlets.

None of the marriages lasted more than a few years. For example, Hyland married his third wife during World War II when he was an officer in the Marine Corps attached to the 2nd Marine Aircraft Wing. They were divorced by 1946. But even here there is a discrepancy about his rank because one source said he was a captain and another said he was a lieutenant colonel.

Tired of the confusion? OK, let's get back to the professional life and not the personal. To be honest, though, confusion isn't the issue with the professional side of things. It's Hyland's ego that gets noticed. During the 1925 football season he was in the backfield for Stanford, coached by legendary Glenn Scobey "Pop" Warner. Their relationship could be rocky at times as Hyland didn't always follow instructions, so Warner would sometimes call Hyland another Frankie Merriwell (after the dime novel hero du jour).

When the Stanford football seasons were over Hyland was hired in 1927 as a technical expert for the silent movie *The Drop Kick* (one of John Wayne's first movies), which is where he met his first wife. It also led him into the Hollywood life.

By 1928 he was working for the *Times* and, in 1932, he was also simultaneously working for KFWB. That was the year he published his book, *The Diary of a Line Smasher*. He led an itinerant life between wives, living in SoCal and Hawaii and then joining the Marines during World War II. But after the war he was back at *The Times* until 1966.

Although writing a bio of Hyland can be a bit more like detective work sifting through facts and weighing possibilities rather than contextualizing his times and his work, there is a common thread that unites the themes and puts his life in focus: Hyland opposed segregation in sports. This came out in 1939 when he wrote several of his "Hyland Fling" columns in support of Jackie Robinson, then at UCLA.

In 1946, when the Cleveland Rams moved west, *Los Angeles Tribune* columnist Halley Harding pressed the nine-member public commission in charge of leasing the publicly owned Coliseum to make sure it would be open to all. In other words, not only would the stadium itself be free from segregation, but teams that leased the stadium would also have to be integrated.

In 1944, two years before the Rams' move, Harding wrote: "It seems very queer that a country fighting to uphold its belief in the quotation that 'every man is created equal, etc.' would allow two of its strongest publicity selling points, baseball and football, to contaminate our ideals with discrimination for all the world to see and note. Some day, some one has to see the light."[11]

The commission agreed. So did the Rams. In March and May of 1946 the team signed former UCLA players Kenny Washington and Woody Strode, who had played together in the 1939 Bruins backfield with Robinson. It was a gesture that Hyland wrote was too long in coming: "His [Washington's] break is coming five or six years too late. I believe he was the greatest college back I have ever seen ... [but now] he is beaten-up ballplayer who is neither so strong nor so quick in his reactions as he was before the war."[12] Washington retired after the 1948 season.

If the first Rams team in Los Angeles didn't excite Hyland, the 1951 version did because of its offensive firepower, as he wrote in the *Los Angeles Times*: "the old reliable, Bob Waterfield and Norm Van Brocklin. What a PAIR! [Emphasis is Hyland's.] Take one off the field and the replacement may be even better!"[13]

But what's a quarterback with a receiver? The Rams had a golden one in Elroy "Crazylegs" Hirsch and Hyland made sure people remembered that "there is no stopping that combination unless M. Hirsch is knocked flat on the line of scrimmage, a two-man job if ever there was one. Put two men on him and see what [Glenn] Davis and [Tom] Fears do. No defense, including the vaunted Eagle defense, is going to get anywhere with a Hirsch outrunning defensive backs. Not with Van Brocklin or Waterfield throwing."[14]

For his athletic abilities, and maybe also for his columns calling for a bit of justice for other athletes, Hyland was inducted into the Stanford Hall of Fame in 1961.

He died during the night on July 16, 1981, in the Wawona Hotel after playing in a pro-am celebrity golf tournament at the Wawona Yosemite National Park golf course. In 10 days he would have been 81.

And now the non–Finchional one, and there's another Hollywood connection here. Finch, born July 28, 1911, in Santa Monica, California, was the younger brother of actress Gloria Stuart (who played the older Rose in the 1997 movie *Titanic*).

He suffered from polio as a child and his right leg atrophied, which meant he had to wear a leg brace for the rest of his life. But it didn't slow him down as he covered the Rams and Dodgers after their respective moves to the Pacific coast. In all, he spent more than 40 years as a sportswriter for *The Times* and along the way got the nickname "Fearless."

Finch began by covering the Los Angeles Angels and the Hollywood Stars of the

Pacific Coast League. He also covered boxing and was sent to the big fights of Sugar Ray Robinson, Rocky Marciano and Jersey Joe Walcott in Los Angeles, Chicago and wherever the editors wanted him to go.

He covered the Rams after the 1946 move and, in 1958, asked editor Zimmerman to let him cover the Dodgers. Finch was the *Times*' first major league beat reporter. The experiences led him to write about it all in his book, *The First 20 Years of the L.A. Dodgers*.

Finch had a keen eye for detail as a reporter and was a little bit old school who gushed over athletes, as this excerpt from the 1951 championship game story shows:

Frank Finch.

> They beat the Browns!
> In their finest hour The Los Angeles Rams abruptly ended football's longest reign of terror by conquering mighty Cleveland, 24 to 17, to capture the National Football League championship yesterday [December 23, 1951].
> And it took a perfect play to do it—Norm Van Brocklin's 73-yard scoring shot to tall Tom Fears. Coming midway in the final quarter, the pay-off pitch shattered a 17–17 deadlock, which had threatened to send this tremendous battle of the giants into a "sudden-death" overtime period ....
> But the inspired Rams, spurred on by the highly partisan crowd of 59,475 Coliseum fans, simply would not admit defeat to the team which had beaten them three times in as many previous meetings....[15]

It isn't exactly a "show, don't' tell" style of journalistic writing, but it does paint a scene of joyous players jumping, yelling, whooping and shaking up foamy beverages in the locker room afterward to spray on anyone in sight. Journalism profs may disagree, but it sure beats "Rams beat Browns 24–17" because the reader knows why and how and what it feels like.

In fact, Finch's famous reply to others who deemed themselves experts about anything from rules and regs of journalism coverage to spectacular sports plays—"I'll be the judge of that!"—was legendary in the newsroom. And he was good at what he did, as this story relates:

> One night, [*Times* night sports editor Chuck] Garrity noticed Finch was slipping away to the back of the sports office, opening a floor-level drawer, taking a nip of bourbon, and then returning to his work. *I'll fix him* [original emphasis], Garrity thought. A figure from USC athletics had died that night, and Garrity assigned Finch to crash a deadline obituary. "He sat down, went to work on it, and turned out a great story in 15 minutes," Garrity said. There was a reason Finch was like Michelangelo.[16]

But even Michelangelo has to one day step aside. Finch retired at age 65 in 1976. He worked for another 14 years at a deposition firm. One thing that united his personality through both jobs was his penchant for solo travel around the country on planes, trains and automobiles. His last big trip, in May of 1991, just after he was diagnosed with leukemia, was a 2,500 trip by car to see the American West one last time.

He died August 11, 1992, in the Methodist Hospital in Arcadia, California. He was 81.

Notes

1. "Former *Times* Sports Editor Paul Zimmerman Dead at 92," *Los Angeles Times*, January 30, 1996, C2.
2. Gene Duffey, "Pillars of the FWAA: Paul Zimmerman (1903–96), Los Angeles Times," *The Fifth Down*, July 6, 2015, https://the5thdown.com/2015/07/06/pillars-of-the-fwaa-paul-zimmerman-1903-96-los-angeles-times/.
3. Duffey, "Pillars."
4. Paul Zimmerman, "Rams Favored to Whip Redskins in Coliseum Tonight," *Los Angeles Times*, August 15, 1951, IV-1.
5. Bryan Curtis, "Farewell to a Newspaper Office: The L.A. Times Sports Desk Bids Adieu," *Theringer.com*, July 16, 2018, https://www.theringer.com/2018/7/16/17575130/los-angeles-times-sports-desk.
6. Paul Zimmerman, "Sport Scripts," *Los Angeles Times*, August 11, 1951, III-1.
7. Zimmerman, "Rams Favored."
8. https://oztypewriter.blogspot.com/2015/10/the-hottest-typewriter-in-football-drop.html, retrieved March 20, 2019.
9. Mark Jenkins, "An American Coup in Paris," *American Heritage*, July/August 1989, https://www.americanheritage.com/american-coup-paris.
10. Jenkins, "An American Coup."
11. Nathan Fenno, "How the Media Helped Overturn the NFL's Unwritten Ban on Black Players," *Los Angeles Times*, January 28, 2017, https://latimes.com/sports/sportsnow/la-sp-kenny-washington-rams-20170128-story.
12. Fenno, "How the Media."
13. Dick Hyland, "The Hyland Fling," *Los Angeles Times*, August 14, 1951, IV-2.
14. Dick Hyland, "The Hyland Fling," *Los Angeles Times*, August 18, 1951, III-2.
15. Frank Finch, "Rams Whip Browns, 24–17, Win Pro Title," *Los Angeles Times*, December 24, 1951, IV-1.
16. Curtis, "Farewell to a Newspaper Office."

About the Contributors

Joshua Milton **Anderson** is a chess teacher, tournament director, and the president of the Chess Journalists of America. He has written articles for both *Chess Life* and the Professional Football Researchers Association's (PFRA's) *The Coffin Corner*.

George **Bozeka** is a retired attorney living in Akron. He edited *The 1966 Green Bay Packers: Profiles of Vince Lombardi's Super Bowl I Champions* and *The 1958 Baltimore Colts: Profiles of the NFL's First Sudden Death Champions*, the first two books in the PFRA's Great Teams in Pro Football History series published by McFarland.

Ryan C. **Christiansen** is a professor of English at North Dakota State University and a published technical writer, creative writer, and award-winning journalist.

Derek M. **Ciapala** teaches American history, pop culture, and sports history in Northeast Ohio. He is also the editor-in-chief at *Rams Talk*, which covers The Los Angeles Rams.

Denis M. **Crawford** of Lowellville, Ohio, is a Ph.D. candidate in American studies at Pennsylvania State University Harrisburg. He is the author or editor of several articles for the PFRA's *The Coffin Corner* and the author of three books.

Lee **Elder** is a member of the PFRA and has contributed several articles to *The Coffin Corner*. He is the author of *That Bloody Hill: Hilliard's Legion at Chickamauga* and contributed to *The 1958 Baltimore Colts: Profiles of the NFL's First Sudden Death Champions*.

Mark **Fellin** is a professional writer living in New York City. His fiction has appeared in a wide range of magazines and journals. He is a longtime member of the PFRA.

Ron **Fitch** is an e-learning and instructional technology professional at the University of Minnesota–Twin Cities. He has been a member of the PFRA since 2014.

Richard C. **Flowers** II is a social insurance specialist with the Social Security Administration living in Catonsville, Maryland. He has been a member of the PFRA since 2006.

Massimo **Foglio** is a lifelong Rams fan from Torino, Italy. He is the chief statistician with the Federazione Italiana Di American Football and in 2013 he published, with Mark L. Ford, *Touchdown in Europe,* the history of football in Europe.

Mark L. **Ford** is a lawyer and a radio station owner in Harlan, Kentucky, as well as an assistant editor for the PFRA's *The Coffin Corner*. He is the author of the two-volume book *A History of NFL Preseason and Exhibition Games*, covering the years 1969 to 2013.

Patrick **Gallivan** is a freelance writer living in San Antonio, Texas. He is a contributor to the PFRA's *The Coffin Corner* and Great Teams in Pro Football History series and the author of *Pro Football in the 1960s*.

Bert **Gambini** is a news content manager for the University at Buffalo. He worked for more than two decades in Buffalo radio, and is a frequent contributor to *The Coffin Corner* and among the contributors to the PFRA's book on the 1958 Baltimore Colts.

About the Contributors

Neal **Golden**, a teacher of mathematics and computer science since 1963, lives in New Orleans where he maintains his sports history website goldenrankings.com. He is the author of the book *LSU Bowl Games: A Complete History*.

John **Grasso** has written books on basketball, football, boxing, wrestling, tennis, bowling and the Olympic Games. He served as treasurer for the International Society of Olympic Historians (ISOH) from 2004 to 2016 and the PFRA from 2014 to 2019 and was the founder of the International Boxing Research Organization (IBRO) in 1982.

Ed **Gruver** is a longtime member of the PFRA and the author of seven books, including five on pro football. He and fellow NFL historian Jim Campbell co-authored the book *Hell with the Lid Off: Inside the Fierce Rivalry Between the 1970s Oakland Raiders and Pittsburgh Steelers*.

Matthew **Keddie** joined the PFRA in 2015, serving as an active member of the Hall of Very Good committee. His work includes contributions to the PFRA's book on the 1958 Baltimore Colts. An avid Steelers fan, he resides along the Gulf Coast, working in the petrochemicals industry as a quality control laboratory analyst.

Bill **Lambert** lives in the Detroit area and has been a member of the PFRA for more than 30 years. He is a fan of the Lions and Steelers and contributed to the 1958 Baltimore Colts book.

Bryan **Lutes** works in Chicago, Illinois, and is a longtime member of the PFRA. He enjoys spending time with his family and still laughs when watching *Son of Football Follies*. This is his first published work.

Joe **Marren** is a professor in the communication department at SUNY Buffalo State. Before entering academia, he was an award-winning newspaper reporter and editor in western New York. He is the author of numerous book chapters and journal articles on subjects ranging from sports to media theory

John **Maxymuk** of Cherry Hill, New Jersey, is a reference librarian at Rutgers University. He has written more than a dozen books on professional football history and four on libraries and computers. His latest work is *Pioneer Coaches of the NFL: Shaping the Game in the Days of Leather Helmets and 60-Minute Men*.

Rupert **Patrick** was a pro football historian and writer whose work appeared in the PFRA's *The Coffin Corner* and the *Wall Street Journal*. He was the posthumous recipient of PFRA's 2019 Ralph Hay Award.

Nicholas **Ritzmann** is a lifelong football fan with particular interests in the American Football League and the Dallas Cowboys during their Cotton Bowl era. He has been a member of the PFRA since 2009 and resides in northern New Jersey.

Gary A. **Sarnoff** of Alexandria, Virginia, has been an active PFRA member since 2014. He contributed three chapters, including one on Vince Lombardi, to the PFRA book *The 1966 Green Bay Packers*. He has also published two books on baseball, *The Wrecking Crew of '33* and *The First Yankees Dynasty*.

Rick **Schabowski** is president of the Wisconsin Old Time Ballplayers Association, president of the Ken Keltner Badger State Chapter of SABR, and a member of the Hoops Historians. He has contributed to a number of SABR book projects and to the PFRA's books on the Packers and Colts.

Greg **Selber** is a professor of journalism at the University of Texas–Rio Grande Valley and the author of books on high school football and college basketball. He has contributed to three PFRA books on the NFL.

Rich **Shmelter** is a writer and researcher specializing in sports history, American crime history, and Hollywood's Golden Age (1920–59). He is the author of several books, including team encyclopedias of the NFL's Raiders and USC Trojans football.

Randy **Snow** lives in Kalamazoo, Michigan, and has been a PFRA member since 2011. He has written more than 350 football-related articles for various newspapers and web sites. He has also maintained his own web site (www.theworldoffootball.com) since 2006.

Greg **D. Tranter** is a prominent Buffalo football historian, curator, and collector with a specialized expertise in Buffalo Bills history. He was the recipient of the PFRA's Bob Carroll Memorial Writing Award in 2019.

John **M. Vorperian** is host and executive producer of *Beyond the Game,* a nationally syndicated cable television program featuring sports and entertainment topics. He writes for www.boxscorenews.com covering baseball, soccer and football.

Jay **Zahn** has contributed to the PFRA's books on the 1966 Green Bay Packers and the 1958 Baltimore Colts, as well as *The Coffin Corner*. He resides in Madison, Wisconsin.

Joe **Ziemba** is the award-winning author of the books *When Football Was Football: The Chicago Cardinals and the Birth of the NFL* and *Cadets, Cannons, and Legends.* He has been a resource for articles or reports in *Sports Illustrated,* the *New York Times, Chicago Sun-Times, Chicago Tribune,* and *Daily Southtown,* among other publications.

Index

Abilene Christian 61, 252–253
Adamle, Tony 102–103, 142
Aiken Jim 210, 268–269
Albert, Frankie 36–37, 54, 111, 114, 116–117, 216, 254
All-America Football Conference (AAFC) 16–17, 22–23, 43, 59, 61, 70, 85, 91, 97, 99, 112, 116, 136–137, 174–176, 188, 197, 216, 225, 240, 291, 296, 300, 305, 310, 312, 314–316, 318–320, 334, 347
Allen, George 25–27, 30–31, 64, 290
Alley-Oop 35–36, 54
Ameche, Don 16, 23, 312
Army (West Point) 138, 173–177, 202, 211, 304–305, 308
Arnold College 41, 62, 68–69, 72, 78–79, 238–240, 245

Bacall, Lauren 6
Baldwin-Wallace College 41, 62, 71, 78, 192, 198
Baugh, Sammy 44, 81, 124–124, 137, 269, 278
Benton, Jim 137, 180
Black Dahlia 8
Blaik, Red 173, 175–176
Blanchard, Felix "Doc" 173–174, 202, 305
Blanda, George 126–128, 243
Bloody Christmas 8–9
Blyth, Ann 176
Bogart, Humphrey 6, 179
Bowron, Fletcher 7–9
Boyd, Bob 41, 45, 62–63, 78–80, 99, 105–106, 108, 110, 118, 121, 124–126, 148–149, 155–158, 241, 257, 270–271, 273, 309–310, 318, 320
Brando, Marlon 7, 346
Briggs Stadium 104–105, 137, 216
Brink, Larry 41, 61–63, 78, 111, 118, 127, 141, 143–144, 151, 159–161, 242, 258, 286, 306–307
Brown, Paul 22, 59, 65, 85, 102, 104, 137, 141–142, 145–146, 225, 230, 242, 261–262, 264, 315–316, 347, 352–354
Bull Elephant Backfield 40, 46, 60, 89–90, 92, 95, 115, 119–120, 122, 125, 128, 141, 143, 203–204, 264–265, 298, 309–310

Canadeo, Tony 108–111, 132–133
Canadian Football League (CFL) 69, 99, 122, 157, 180, 193, 212–213, 217, 247, 286, 290, 292–293, 308, 318, 324, 357
Canton McKinley High School 268
Carpenter, Ken 59, 101–104, 140–145
Carroon, Mary 20, 26
Celeri, Bob 98–100, 121, 123
Chicago Bears 10, 13, 22, 25, 27–33, 42–44, 46, 50, 52, 55, 58, 60, 68, 70–71, 81–83, 87–89, 100, 112–114, 117, 120, 124–128, 132, 135, 146, 150, 152, 161, 165–166, 170, 174–175, 180, 182, 189, 191, 206, 211–212, 214, 218, 222–223, 226, 234, 236, 243, 248, 253–254, 257–259, 262, 269–270, 280–281, 285–287, 293, 296, 301–302, 305, 307–308, 310, 312, 317–320, 346
Chicago Cardinals 12–13, 18, 22, 27, 31, 36, 42, 44, 48, 51–53, 68–71, 79, 82, 84, 87, 100–101, 117–120, 132, 146, 166, 168, 179–180, 189, 193, 198, 203, 207, 211–212, 214–219, 222, 226, 236, 248, 250, 253, 257–258, 262, 265, 280, 288–289, 304, 310–311, 319, 365
Chicago Rockets 61, 197–198
Chinatown 5
Christiansen, Jack 65, 104–107, 181, 194
Cigar Bowl 247
Cleveland Browns 2, 9, 16–17, 22, 29–30, 41–42, 45, 47, 49, 57, 59, 64–65, 68, 70, 72, 84–85, 88, 91–92, 94, 97, 100–104, 112–114, 117, 120, 124–125, 134, 136–146, 150, 152, 156, 159–160, 162, 166, 174–175, 180–182, 185, 189–192, 194, 197–199, 204–208, 212, 214, 219, 222–223, 225, 228–229, 236–237, 242, 245, 254, 261–263, 265, 267, 270–273, 275, 281, 286, 291, 293, 296, 307, 309–310, 315–317, 319, 321, 324, 327, 333, 347, 352, 360–361
Cleveland Municipal Stadium 6, 85, 136–138, 180, 281
Clift, Montgomery 7
College All-Star Game 28, 105, 174, 197, 229, 279, 285, 289, 291, 305, 308, 317, 350
Collier, Bobby 41, 50, 62–63, 77–78, 80, 125–126, 148, 162–163, 189, 357
Cooper, Gary 8
Corcoran, Jerry 14–15, 17
Cosell, Howard 243
Cotton Bowl 163, 187–188, 190, 221, 268, 320, 364
Crain, Jeanne 282
Crazylegs: All American 199, 254, 262, 286, 342
Crosby, Bing 16. 23, 312

Dahms, Tom 41, 50–51, 61, 63, 77, 79–80, 99, 163–168, 170, 248–249, 251, 270, 357
Daugherty, Dick 41, 61, 63, 69, 72, 77, 79–80, 94, 99, 123, 125, 132, 163, 169–172
Davis, Al 167–168, 213, 353
Davis, Glenn 1, 41, 45, 61–63, 78, 84, 92, 94–96, 99, 101–111, 113–116, 118, 121–122, 124, 129–130, 132, 138, 140–141, 143–145, 147–149, 156, 173–177, 202, 211–213, 226, 250, 261, 270–271, 305, 308, 310, 357
Davis, Sammy, Jr. 346
Dayton Flyers 61, 77–78, 219–220
Detroit Lions 12, 14, 29, 43, 47, 52, 62–63, 68, 70, 104–107, 113, 117, 120, 125, 127, 128–135, 137, 141, 143, 146, 151, 155–156, 166–168, 174, 176, 179–181, 193, 198, 204, 207–208, 215–216, 218, 221–222, 227, 229, 232, 234, 243, 248–249, 258, 261, 265, 270, 272–273, 278, 281, 283, 286–287, 292, 300, 307, 309–310, 318–320, 350, 364
Dibble, Dorne 104–106

367

DiMaggio, Joe 243
Donelli, Aldo "Buff" 21
Donovan, Art 34, 65, 165, 296
Doran, Jim 105, 107
Douglas, Helen Gahagan 7
Douglas, Kirk 199
Dudley, Bill 124–126
Durslag, Melvin 181, 349–354

11th US Naval District 79–80

Fears, Tom 1, 31, 41, 45, 59, 61–62, 78, 80–81, 83–84, 86, 88–89, 91, 94, 96–100, 102–107, 109, 115, 119, 126–134, 138, 140–141, 143–147, 149, 151, 161, 178–183, 191, 213, 224, 230, 234, 241, 270–273, 280–281, 289, 300, 306, 310, 317, 333, 340, 347, 357, 359–360
Finch, Frank 18, 30, 32–33, 46, 54, 58, 65, 72, 77, 79–88, 134–135, 146, 152, 158, 161, 165, 167–168, 170–171, 176–177, 183, 186, 189–191, 194, 205, 208, 214, 218, 222–223, 226, 234, 237, 247–251, 253–255, 258–259, 283, 289, 291, 293, 302, 308, 318, 355–361
Finlay, Jack 41, 62–63, 77, 102, 123, 170, 184–186
Fly T Offense 29, 89–97
Frankford Yellow Jackets 51
Furillo, Bud 25–26, 30, 33, 230, 339, 343–348

Gable, Clark 6, 8, 282
Gardner, Ava 6
Garland, Judy 6
Gehrke, Fred 326–327
Gillman, Sid 27, 30, 42, 54, 57, 97, 156–157, 166, 170–171, 218, 225, 242–243, 258, 262, 273, 287, 289, 351
Gillom, Horace 85, 101–102, 142–144, 309
Gilmer, Harry 81, 125
Gilmore Stadium 12–13, 16
Gleason, Jackie 243
Graham, Otto 59, 85, 99, 101–103, 114, 136–138, 140–146, 160, 192, 207, 229, 236, 242, 269, 286, 296, 307, 357
Grambling 40, 60, 62, 64, 298–302, 319
Grange, Red 10–11, 17–18, 315, 319
Grant, Cary 6, 8, 306
Green Bay Packers 2, 13, 22, 30–31, 37, 48, 53–58, 60, 64, 68–69, 77, 82, 86–87, 92–93, 97, 108–110, 113, 117, 124–125, 127, 131–135, 146, 166–168, 180–182, 188, 193–194, 198–199, 207–208, 211–212, 214, 218, 225–226, 232, 234, 242, 253, 258, 265, 271, 274, 281, 286, 291–293, 316, 319, 325, 332, 349, 357, 363–365
Greer, Jane 282
Griffith Stadium 124, 265
Groza, Lou 29, 85, 88, 101–104, 120, 136, 138–143, 145–146, 180, 204, 229, 237, 251, 270, 281, 286, 308

Halas, George 23, 25, 28, 30–33, 43, 60, 71, 82, 90, 128, 175, 214, 228, 234, 253, 269, 280, 305, 311, 319
Halliday, Jack 41, 50, 61, 63, 77, 79–80, 86, 185, 187–191, 286
Harder, Pat 105, 107, 129–131
Harding, Halley 23, 259, 313–314, 359
Hardy, Jim 117–119, 179, 216, 218, 269, 279–280
Harlow, Jean 8
Hart, Leon 105–107, 129–131, 227, 229, 265
Hawaiian Warriors 16–17
Hecker, Norb 41, 62–63, 69, 71, 78–79, 85, 99–100, 104–111, 116, 118, 120, 124, 143, 148–149, 192–194
Heisman Trophy 28, 61–62, 105, 127, 130, 163, 173, 176, 211, 269, 295, 304–305, 341
Hemingway, Ernest 21, 243
Hickey, Red 34–38, 54, 61, 180, 240

Hirsch, Elroy "Crazylegs" 1, 31, 43–46, 49, 61–62, 77–78, 80–84, 86, 88–89, 91, 94, 96–111, 113–114, 116–118, 120–121, 123–127, 129–134, 138, 141, 143, 147, 149–151, 157, 168, 195–201, 226, 241, 254, 262, 265, 270–273, 279–281, 286, 300, 310, 332–333, 340, 357, 359
Hoerner, Dick 1, 45–46, 60, 62, 64, 78, 80, 85–86, 88–89, 92, 95, 98–101, 104, 106, 108–111, 113–132, 134, 138, 140–141, 143–144, 147–150, 202–205, 218, 261, 265, 300, 309–310
Hoernschemeyer, Bob 43, 105–107, 129
Hollywood 1, 5, 6–8, 16, 23–24, 39, 55–57, 80, 136–138, 174, 176, 179, 182, 184–186, 199, 213, 242, 258, 263, 276–277, 279, 282–283, 286, 296, 303, 306, 308, 312, 314, 320, 322–324, 334, 339–343, 358–359, 364
Hollywood Bears 14–19, 22, 312, 314, 350
Hollywood blacklist 7
Hollywood Stars (football) 12–14, 18
Hope, Bob 16, 23–24, 133, 199, 242
HUAC 7
Hughes, Howard 277
Hutson, Don 55, 127, 133, 151, 180, 198, 317
Hyland, Dick 81, 87, 173, 177, 180, 307–308, 355–361

James, Tommy 136, 141, 143, 145, 272, 347
Johnson, Magic 1
Johnson, Marvin 62–63, 78, 82, 118, 120, 123, 125, 132–133, 141, 143–144, 148, 206–208, 286
Jones, Dub 101–104, 114, 140–141, 143–145. 192, 207

Kalmanir, Tommy 62–64, 78, 80–81, 83–84, 95, 98–99, 101, 103–104, 107–108, 110–111, 117, 120, 144, 147–149, 209–214, 254
Keane, Tom 62, 78, 80, 99, 102, 109, 114, 116, 118–119, 125, 132, 134, 143, 147–149, 215–218
Kelley, Bob 171, 339–342
Kezar Stadium 46, 111–112, 132, 166, 236, 278, 295
Kotal, Eddie 1, 37–42, 54–57, 60, 62, 72, 240–241, 261, 269, 287, 298–301, 325

Ladd, Alan 199
Lahr, Warren 101–103, 141–143, 270
Landry, Tom 35, 167, 238, 243
Lane, Dick "Night Train" 41, 47–48, 21, 271, 273
Lange, Bill 41, 61, 63, 77, 80, 99, 119, 123, 163, 165, 170, 219–220, 258
Lavelli, Dante 59, 101–104, 114, 138, 141–142, 144–145
Layne, Bobby 104–107, 129–131, 222, 227, 257, 287
Leahy, Frank 303–305, 332
Levy, Fred, Jr. 21, 24, 137
Lewis, Cliff 102, 142, 145, 272
Lewis, Woodley 41, 61, 63, 78, 84, 86, 102–103, 105–107, 116, 118–122, 142, 148–149, 193, 221–223, 236, 251, 309, 318, 320
Lillard, Joe 12, 311, 313
Lindheimer, Ben 16–17, 23
Lombardi, Vince 25, 48, 53, 69, 181, 193–194, 243–244, 274, 292, 363–364
Los Angeles Buccaneers 11, 18
Los Angeles Bulldogs 11–19, 22, 52–53, 185, 197, 312, 350
Los Angeles Dons 16–17, 19, 23–24, 26, 97, 99, 188, 216, 225, 312, 315, 317–319, 334
Los Angeles Wildcats (Wilson's Wildcats) 11–12, 18
Louisiana State University 62, 72, 77, 231–234, 284, 364
Lujack, Johnny 82, 100, 126–128, 304

Mann, Bob 108–110, 132, 134, 318, 320
Mara, Tim 10, 242

Mara, Wellington 23, 242, 244, 351
Marshall, George Preston 22, 81, 160, 311–312, 317, 320
Marshman, Homer 137–138, 326
Martin, Dean 6, 242, 346
Marx, Groucho 6
Massillon High School 137
Mayer, Louis B. 1, 16, 23
McBride, Mickey 22, 138
McLaglen, Victor 12
McLaughlin, Leon 41, 61–62, 77, 79–80, 99, 124, 163, 170, 224–226, 241, 257
Memorial Coliseum 5, 9–11, 16–17, 21–24, 26, 46, 49, 81–82, 98–99, 101, 113–115, 117, 119, 121–123, 129, 131–132, 134, 138, 140, 175, 178–180, 192, 211, 216, 222, 229, 250, 257, 280–281, 286, 305, 309, 312–315, 327, 331–333, 342, 347, 357, 359–361
Miami Seahawks 43
Modell, Art 138
Moore, Terry 1, 176
Motley, Marion 101–104, 138, 140–144, 146, 160, 210, 242, 306, 309, 311, 315–317, 319
Mulholland, William 5, 9

New York Brown Bombers 12, 18, 312
New York Giants 10, 31, 42, 45, 50, 54, 68–71, 85–86, 88, 99–100, 114, 117, 120, 124, 137, 146, 165–166, 168, 174–176, 189–190, 193–194, 203, 215, 222–223, 229, 235–236, 238, 240, 242–245, 247, 258–259, 278, 285, 287–288, 318–320, 351
New York Yanks 68, 71, 86, 98–102, 117, 121–124, 134–135, 146, 175, 185, 198, 204, 211, 216, 221–223, 232, 234, 247–248, 265, 271, 296, 310, 320, 333
Nicholson, Jack 5
1951 NFL draft 2, 62, 65–73, 105, 192, 232, 240, 247, 261, 263
Nixon, Richard 7, 9, 334, 355
Nomellini, Leo 111, 113

Oates, Bob 9, 26, 42, 56, 169–172, 228, 230, 256, 279, 314, 321, 323, 349–354
Ohio State 137, 196, 215, 315
The Outlaw 277, 283

Parker, Buddy 130–131
Parker, Eleanor 282
Parker, William 8
Paul, Don 1, 41, 43–44, 47–48, 61–62, 77–78, 109, 114, 116–117, 123, 141, 145, 149, 151, 224, 227–230, 241, 257, 276, 287
Pauley, Ed, Sr. 24, 253
PCPFL 11–12, 14–17, 19
Peck, Gregory 306
Perry, Joe 111, 114, 116, 160–161, 287
Phelan, Jimmy 99–100, 122
Philadelphia Eagles 12, 21, 27–30, 32, 36, 42–44, 68, 70, 72, 82–83, 88, 91, 112, 120, 146, 151, 166, 168, 175–176, 179–180, 182, 188–189, 203, 211, 214, 216–218, 232, 243, 252–253, 258, 274–275, 279–280, 285–286, 292–294, 306–308, 310, 319, 327, 332–333
Pittsburgh Steelers 12–13, 20–21, 36, 62–63, 68, 70, 72, 86, 101, 146, 160, 203, 210, 217, 225–226, 269, 282–283, 301, 310, 319–320, 334, 349, 364
Pollard, Fritz 12, 18, 311, 313, 319
Polo Grounds 85–86, 117, 120, 124, 236, 240, 247
Pool, Hamp 29–30, 38, 42–51, 58, 70, 79, 86–87, 89–95, 97, 156, 165–166, 170–171, 206–207, 213–214, 225, 229, 243, 249, 251, 256, 258, 261–262, 269–270, 272–273, 281–282, 287, 291, 341

Presley, Elvis 346
Pro Football Hall of Fame 1–2, 9, 25, 29, 31–34, 41–42, 47, 56–57, 60, 65, 68, 72, 77, 89, 94, 97, 101, 105, 116, 127, 137, 139, 142, 150, 165, 178, 182–183, 195, 199–201, 219, 222, 238, 241, 244, 247, 262, 266–267, 282–283, 288, 296, 327, 331, 349, 351
Pyle, C.C. 10

racial integration of NFL 1–2, 68, 258, 309–325
Raft, George 8
Ratterman, George 99, 121–123, 134, 232, 305
Rauch, John 99–100
Red Feather Bowl 156
Reeves, Daniel 1–2, 6, 9, 20–26, 29–30, 37–42, 47–49, 59–60, 62, 64–65, 81, 133, 137–138, 200, 240, 266, 269, 279, 283, 287, 305–306, 310, 312, 314–315, 317–318, 320, 326–327, 332, 341, 351
Reid, Joe 62–63, 69, 72, 77, 121, 123, 189, 231–234
Rich, Herb 62–63, 70–71, 77–78, 84, 99, 114–116, 121, 132, 144, 149, 207, 222–223, 235–237, 241, 255
Richards, Ray 38, 45, 49–54, 56, 58, 131, 166, 217, 257–258, 262–263, 288, 357
Richter, Les 42, 69, 189, 191, 204–205, 216, 218, 229, 232, 251
Riley, Pat 1
Robinson, Eddie 40, 60, 298–300, 319
Robinson, Jackie 15–16, 19, 23, 68, 116, 241, 244, 311, 314, 318, 332, 359
Robustelli, Andy 1, 41–42, 47, 62–63, 68–69, 72, 78–80, 87, 110, 115–116, 123, 128, 141, 143–144, 160, 238–245, 258, 286
Ronzani, Gene 30, 109, 133, 207–208
Rooney, Art 20, 311
Roosevelt, Franklin Delano 11, 21, 334
Rose Bowl 53, 179, 185, 224, 277, 333, 353, 355
Rote, Tobin 108–111, 131–133, 150
Rozelle, Pete 24–25, 200, 274, 332, 353, 356
Russell, Jane 1, 24, 137, 143, 242, 276–283, 341–342

Salad Bowl 210
San Francisco 49ers 16–17, 24, 34–37, 46, 49, 54, 62, 68, 70, 83, 92, 97, 104, 111–117, 128, 131–134, 141, 146, 156, 160, 166–169, 171, 174–175, 177, 180–181, 188, 194, 199, 206–207, 213, 216, 222–223, 236–237, 248–249, 254, 265, 273, 285–287, 289, 295, 305, 310, 319
Schissler, Paul 13–15
Schramm, Tex 22–24, 39, 42, 57, 310
Seley, Hal 24
Shaughnessy, Clark 29, 31, 37, 43–44, 46, 60, 90, 95, 159, 174, 179, 186, 198, 210–211, 214, 229, 253, 269, 275, 279–280, 298, 300–301, 306, 316–317, 324, 326–327
Shaw, Buck 46, 112–113, 251, 274, 292
Shaw, Frank L. 7
shotgun formation 34–35, 54
Shula, Don 65, 141, 167, 193, 215, 217–218
Siegel, Bugsy 8
Simensen, Don 41, 51, 61, 63, 77, 94, 99, 148, 163, 165, 170, 241, 246–251
Sinatra, Frank 6, 21, 242–243, 346
Smith, Vitamin 1, 41, 43, 45, 60, 63, 78, 81–82, 85, 89, 95–96, 98–105, 107–109, 111, 114–118, 121–124, 129–130, 140–141, 143, 147–149, 156, 211, 222, 252–255, 271, 310, 333
SMU 31, 61–62, 77, 162–162, 187–190, 221, 232, 269
Snyder, Bob 29, 60, 278–279, 305–306, 314, 326
Soltau, Gordie 111–114, 116
Speedie, Mac 101–102, 138, 141–145
Stewart, Jimmy 6

Strode, Woody 14, 23, 311, 314, 316–319, 359
Stydahar, Joe 27–33, 38, 42, 44–51, 58–60, 64–65, 77, 79–81, 83–90, 92, 94, 99–100, 104, 112–113, 115, 117–119, 122, 125–128, 130–133, 135, 138, 141–142, 144, 146, 165, 170–171, 180, 185, 189–190, 198–199, 207, 211, 216, 231, 241, 243, 247–248, 253, 257–258, 261, 264, 266, 270–272, 280–281, 285, 289, 291, 298, 301, 306–308, 310, 317, 324, 347, 351, 357
Sugar Bowl 232, 284
Summerall, Pat 27, 31–33
Svare, Harland 25, 42, 199
Taliaferro, George 98, 101, 121–123, 271, 317–318, 320
Tammany Hall 20
Taylor, Elizabeth 1, 176
Texas A&M University 61, 78, 188, 295
Thompson, Harry 41, 62–63, 77, 123, 241, 256–259, 289, 309, 316, 318, 320, 323
Tittle, Y.A. 35–36, 54, 65, 70, 111–114, 116, 244
Toogood, Charlie 41, 50, 56, 62–63, 69, 71, 78–80, 85, 99, 119, 149, 166, 185, 189, 247–248, 251, 260–263, 357
Toth, Zollie 98–99
Towler, Deacon Dan 1, 40–41, 45–46, 60, 63, 78–80, 82–83, 85, 89, 92, 94–96, 98–111, 114–130, 132, 135, 140–144, 147–151, 160, 203–204, 222, 242, 249, 251, 264–267, 286, 309–310, 316–318, 320, 324
Trippi, Charley 53, 118, 120
Turner, Lana 6

Unchained 199, 286
University of California–Los Angeles 6, 11, 14–15, 25, 49, 52–53, 61–62, 77, 116, 137, 178–179, 182–185, 23, 224–226, 228, 241, 252, 257–258, 277–278, 283, 312–314, 333, 342, 345, 347, 350, 359
University of Michigan 61, 71, 77, 196, 200, 202, 340–341
University of Nebraska 39, 51–52, 58, 62, 71, 78, 247, 251, 257, 260–263, 288, 356
University of Notre Dame 39, 112, 127, 130, 173, 196, 202, 240–241, 303–308, 340
University of Oklahoma 61, 72, 78, 232, 284, 288–290
University of Oregon 40, 61, 72, 77–78, 163, 169, 187–188, 210, 221, 223, 257, 268=269, 280
University of Pittsburgh 28, 174, 209–211, 214
University of Redlands 50, 77–79, 82, 84, 167, 241, 248, 289, 296, 341
University of Southern California 11, 21, 78, 185, 266, 277, 279, 312–313, 332–333, 335, 345, 347, 350, 352, 360, 364
University of Wisconsin 37, 176, 196–197, 200, 202

Van Brocklin, Norm 1, 27, 29, 31, 33, 40, 42–47, 50, 57, 61, 63–64, 77–78, 80–82, 84, 86, 89, 92, 94, 96, 98–115, 118–121, 123–130, 132, 134, 138, 140–141, 144–151, 156–157, 161, 175, 179–181, 183, 194, 198, 208, 221, 230, 244, 247, 250, 253–254, 268–275, 280–281, 286, 288, 300, 310, 317, 333, 347, 351, 357, 359–360

Vanderbilt University 62, 71, 232–233, 235–236, 257
Vulcan Bowl 40, 60, 299

Walker, Doak 104–107, 129–131, 163, 190, 265, 269, 307
Walsh, Adam 21, 29, 38, 137, 278
Walsh, Bill 194
Walsh, Chile 22–23, 312–314
Washington, Kenny 14–15, 18, 23, 40, 116, 203, 310–311, 313–319, 324, 359
Washington Redskins 14, 20, 22, 24, 28, 37, 43–44, 50, 53, 61, 67–68, 70, 72–73, 80–82, 87, 120, 124–128, 135, 146, 166, 174, 176, 179, 182, 189–190, 193, 211, 225, 236, 247, 256, 258, 265, 269–270, 278–279, 285, 305, 310–312, 317, 319–320, 332, 361
Waterfield, Bob 1, 21–22, 24–25, 27, 29, 31, 40–41, 44–47, 49–50, 60–62, 77–86, 88–89, 92, 96, 99–106, 108–121, 123–133, 135, 137–138, 140–151, 174, 179–180, 185, 193, 199, 203, 207, 211, 216, 222–223, 237, 241–242, 250–251, 259, 269–273, 276–283, 286, 289, 300, 310, 333, 340–341, 347, 351, 357, 359
Wayne, John 358
West, Stan 50, 61, 63, 77, 87, 123, 127, 151, 257, 284–289, 296
What's My Line? 209, 212
Widmark, Richard 282
Wilkinson, Bud 226, 232, 284, 288
Williams, Jerry 61, 63, 78–80, 82–83, 89, 98–99, 101, 103–104, 108, 110–111, 118, 121, 123–126, 128, 131–133, 141, 143–144, 147–149, 236, 290–294
Willis, Bill 102, 138–139, 142, 145, 285–286, 309, 311, 315, 317
Wilson, George "Wildcat" 10, 18
Winkler, Jim 41, 50, 61–63, 78–80, 82, 88, 107, 112, 115, 117, 286, 295–297, 357
Wisconsin State Fair Park 108–109, 265
World War II 6–9, 15, 43, 60, 66–67, 72, 113, 116, 137, 159, 164, 171, 173, 176, 178, 185, 192, 196–197, 202, 224, 228, 239–240, 252, 260, 268, 284, 291, 299, 304, 308, 312–313, 344, 350, 352, 358–359
Wrigley Field (Chicago) 46, 124, 126–127, 161

Yankee Stadium 10, 99, 243, 304, 319
Young, Buddy 23, 98–100, 121–123, 319
Younger, Tank 1, 40, 43, 45–46, 60–64, 78, 80–81, 89, 95, 102–104, 107–108, 111, 114–116, 118, 121–130, 132, 140–143, 147–149, 151, 203–204, 222, 253, 256, 265, 271, 287, 298–302, 309–310, 316–320

Zero Hour! 199
Ziff, Sid 47, 343–348
Zilly, Jack 62, 78, 115, 160–161, 223, 241, 255, 286, 303–308
Zimmerman, Paul 26, 41, 50, 56, 58, 82, 87, 134, 146, 161, 171, 176, 230, 237, 248, 251, 259, 263, 289, 344, 355–361
Zoot Suit Riots 8–9

www.ingramcontent.com/pod-product-compliance
Lightning Source LLC
Chambersburg PA
CBHW060334010526
44117CB00017B/2828